ILLUSTRATED SERIES™

ADVANCED

MICROSOFT® OFFICE 365® OFFICE 2019

DAVID W. BESKEEN
CAROL M. CRAM
LISA FRIEDRICHSEN
LYNN WERMERS

CENGAGE

Australia • Brazil • Mexico • Singapore • United Kingdom • United States

CENGAGE

Illustrated Series™ Microsoft® Office 365® & Office 2019 Advanced

David W. Beskeen, Carol M. Cram, Lisa Friedrichsen, Lynn Wermers

SVP, GM Skills & Global Product Management: Jonathan Lau

Product Director: Lauren Murphy

Product Assistant: Veronica Moreno-Nestojko

Executive Director, Content Design: Marah Bellegarde

Director, Learning Design: Leigh Hefferon

Associate Learning Designer: Courtney Cozzy

Vice President, Marketing-Science, Technology, and Math: Jason R. Sakos

Senior Marketing Director: Michele McTighe

Marketing Manager: Timothy J. Cali

Director, Content Delivery: Patty Stephan

Content Manager: Grant Davis

Digital Delivery Lead: Laura Ruschman

Designer: Lizz Anderson

Text Designer: Joseph Lee, Black Fish Design

Cover Template Designer: Lisa Kuhn, Curio Press, LLC www.curiopress.com

Mac Users: If you're working through this product using a Mac, some of the steps may vary. Additional information for Mac users is included with the Data files for this product.

Disclaimer: This text is intended for instructional purposes only; data is fictional and does not belong to any real persons or companies.

Disclaimer: The material in this text was written using Microsoft Windows 10 and Office 365 Professional Plus and was Quality Assurance tested before the publication date. As Microsoft continually updates the Windows 10 operating system and Office 365, your software experience may vary slightly from what is presented in the printed text.

Library of Congress Control Number: 2019939823

Student Edition ISBN: 978-0-357-36013-2
Looseleaf available as part of a digital bundle

Cengage
20 Channel Center Street
Boston, MA 02210
USA

Cengage is a leading provider of customized learning solutions with employees residing in nearly 40 different countries and sales in more than 125 countries around the world. Find your local representative at **www.cengage.com.**

Cengage products are represented in Canada by Nelson Education, Ltd.

To learn more about Cengage platforms and services, visit **www.cengage.com.**

Printed at CLDPC, USA, 06-19

Brief Contents

Contents

Getting to Know Microsoft Office Versions

Cengage is proud to bring you the next edition of Microsoft Office. This edition was designed to provide a robust learning experience that is not dependent upon a specific version of Office.

Microsoft supports several versions of Office:

- **Office 365:** A cloud-based subscription service that delivers Microsoft's most up-to-date, feature-rich, modern productivity tools direct to your device. There are variations of Office 365 for business, educational, and personal use. Office 365 offers extra online storage and cloud-connected features, as well as updates with the latest features, fixes, and security updates.
- **Office 2019:** Microsoft's "on-premises" version of the Office apps, available for both PCs and Macs, offered as a static, one-time purchase and outside of the subscription model.
- **Office Online:** A free, simplified version of Office web applications (Word, Excel, PowerPoint, and OneNote) that facilitates creating and editing files collaboratively.

Office 365 (the subscription model) and Office 2019 (the one-time purchase model) had only slight differences between them at the time this content was developed. Over time, Office 365's cloud interface will continuously update, offering new application features and functions, while Office 2019 will remain static. Therefore, your onscreen experience may differ from what you see in this product. For example, the more advanced features and functionalities covered in this product may not be available in Office Online or may have updated from what you see in Office 2019.

For more information on the differences between Office 365, Office 2019, and Office Online, please visit the Microsoft Support site.

Cengage is committed to providing high-quality learning solutions for you to gain the knowledge and skills that will empower you throughout your educational and professional careers.

Thank you for using our product, and we look forward to exploring the future of Microsoft Office with you!

Using SAM Projects and Textbook Projects

SAM and *MindTap* are interactive online platforms designed to transform students into Microsoft Office and Computer Concepts masters. Practice with simulated SAM Trainings and MindTap activities and actively apply the skills you learned live in Microsoft Word, Excel, PowerPoint, or Access. Become a more productive student and use these skills throughout your career.

If your instructor assigns SAM Projects:

1. Launch your SAM Project assignment from SAM or MindTap.
2. Click the links to download your **Instructions file**, **Start file**, and **Support files** (when available).
3. Open the Instructions file and follow the step-by-step instructions.
4. When you complete the project, upload your file to SAM or MindTap for immediate feedback.

To use SAM Textbook Projects:

1. Launch your SAM Project assignment from SAM or MindTap.
2. Click the links to download your **Start file** and **Support files** (when available).
3. Locate the module indicated in your book or eBook.
4. Read the module and complete the project.

sam ↓ Open the Start file you downloaded.

sam ↑ Save, close, and upload your completed project to receive immediate feedback.

IMPORTANT: To receive full credit for your Textbook Project, you must complete the activity using the Start file you downloaded from SAM or MindTap.

Integrating with Other Programs and Collaborating

CASE You've started working for Anthony Martinez, the VP of sales and marketing at the head office of JCL Talent, Inc., in Atlanta. Another colleague has developed content for a report marketing the company's website and has asked you to enhance the report with embedded objects from PowerPoint and Excel, and charts that you create in Word. You then use collaboration tools in Word to edit questions for an online survey aimed at job seekers who visit the JCL Talent website.

Module Objectives

After completing this module, you will be able to:

- Embed an Excel file
- Insert objects from other programs
- Link an Excel chart
- Link a PowerPoint slide
- Manage links
- Create charts
- Format and edit charts
- Track changes
- Work with tracked changes
- Manage reviewers
- Compare documents

Files You Will Need

IL_WD_8-1.docx
Support_WD_8-1.xlsx
Support_WD_8-2.xlsx
Support_WD_8-3.pptx
IL_WD_8-2.docx
IL_WD_8-3.docx
IL_WD_8-4.docx
IL_WD_8-5.docx
Support_WD_8-4.xlsx
Support _WD_8-5.xlsx
Support _WD_8-6.pptx
IL_WD_8-6.docx
IL_WD_8-7.docx
IL_WD_8-8.docx
IL_WD_8-9.docx
Support_WD_8-7.xlsx
Support_WD_8-8.pptx
Support_WD_8-9.xlsx
IL_WD_8-10.docx
IL_WD_8-11.docx
Support_WD_8-10.pptx
Support_WD_8-11.xlsx

Embed an Excel File

Learning Outcomes
- Embed an Excel file
- Edit an embedded Excel file

You embed an object, such as an Excel file, in Word when you want to be able to edit the file in Word. You edit the embedded object directly in Word using commands on the Ribbon associated with Excel, the source program. Because the objects are not connected or linked, the edits you make to an embedded object are not made to the object in the source file, and edits you make to the object in the source file are not made to the embedded object. CASE *The Marketing Report contains placeholder text to designate where you need to insert objects. You embed an Excel worksheet and then edit the embedded worksheet in Word using Excel tools.*

STEPS

1. **sam Start Word, open the file IL_WD_8-1.docx from the location where you store your Data Files, save it as IL_WD_8_MarketingReport, then click the Show/Hide button ¶ in the Paragraph group to turn on paragraph marks if they are not displayed**
2. **Delete the placeholder text EXCEL WORKSHEET after the "Access Methods" paragraph but not the paragraph mark so a blank line still appears above the page break**
3. **Click the Insert tab, then click the Object button in the Text group**
   The Object dialog box opens. You use the Object dialog box to create a new object using the commands of a program other than Word or to insert an object already created in another program.
4. **Click the Create from File tab, click the Browse button, navigate to the drive and folder where you store your Data Files, click Support_WD_8-1.xlsx, then click Insert**
   The path to the file Support_WD_8-1.xlsx is shown in the File name text box. Because you want to create an embedded object, you leave the Link to file check box blank as shown in FIGURE 8-1.
5. **Click OK, then double-click the embedded worksheet object**
   The embedded object opens in an Excel object window, and the Excel Ribbon opens in place of the Word Ribbon. The title bar at the top of the window contains the Word filename, indicating that you are still working within a Word file.

QUICK TIP
Double-click the Excel object when you want to make changes to the data.

6. **Click cell B3, type 250, press ENTER, click cell B8, then click the Bold button B in the Font group on the Excel ribbon**
   The total number of customers shown in cell B8 increases by 250, from 7955 to 8110. Because you did not select the link option when you embedded the Excel file into the Word document, the changes you make to the embedded file are *not* made in the original Excel source file.
7. **Click the Page Layout tab, click Themes in the Themes group, then select Basis**
   You formatted the embedded Excel file with the same theme (Basis) that has been applied to the Word document. The worksheet object appears in Word as shown in FIGURE 8-2.
8. **Click cell A1, then click to the right of the worksheet object to return to Word**
   The Excel Ribbon closes and the Word Ribbon opens. In Word, the embedded object is part of the paragraph and can be formatted as such.

QUICK TIP
Click the Excel object once to select the object and make changes to the object but not the data.

9. **Click the worksheet object to select it, click the Home tab, click the Center button in the Paragraph group, click anywhere in the Word document to deselect the worksheet object, then save the document**

FIGURE 8-1: Create from File tab in the Object dialog box

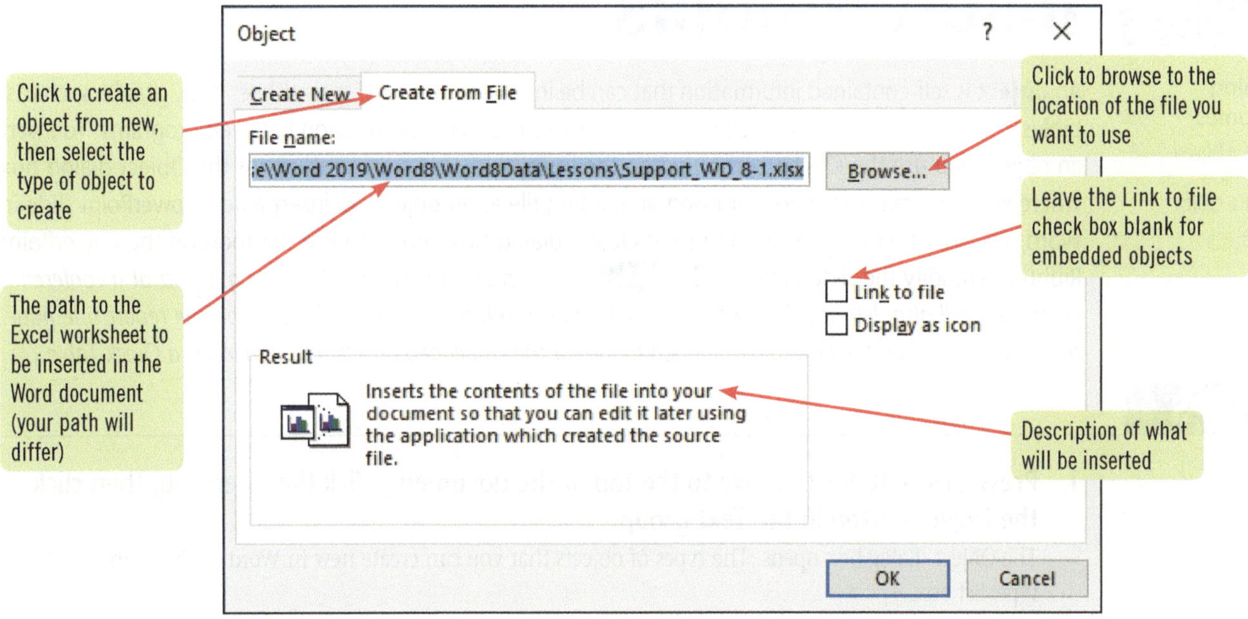

FIGURE 8-2: Excel worksheet embedded in Word document

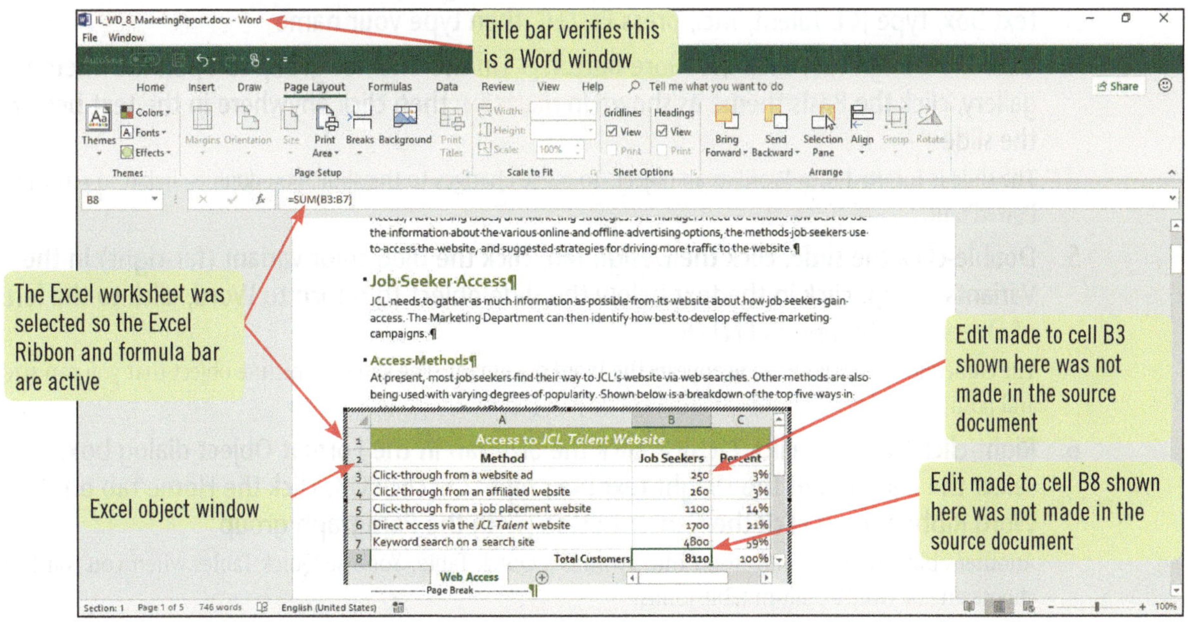

Understanding Object Linking and Embedding

The ability to share information with other programs is called **object linking and embedding (OLE).** Two programs are involved in the OLE process. The **source program** is the program in which information is originally created, and the **destination program** is the program the information is copied to. An embedded object uses the features of another program such as Excel, but it is stored as part of the Word document.

Insert Objects

Learning Outcomes
- Insert a PowerPoint slide
- Insert a Quick Table

An **object** is self-contained information that can be in the form of text, spreadsheet data, graphics, charts, tables, or even sound and video clips. Objects are used to share information between programs. To insert an object, you use the Object command on the Insert tab. This command opens the Object dialog box where you can create an object or insert an existing file as an object. To insert a new PowerPoint slide in Word, you use the Create New tab in the Object dialog box and then use the tools on the PowerPoint Ribbon to modify the slide in Word. CASE *You plan to distribute the Marketing Report at a conference where you will also deliver a PowerPoint presentation. You insert a PowerPoint slide on the report title page, then use the tools on the PowerPoint Ribbon to format the embedded object. You also insert a Quick Table.*

STEPS

1. **Press CTRL+HOME to move to the top of the document, click the Insert tab, then click the Object button in the Text group**
   The Object dialog box opens. The types of objects that you can create new in Word are listed in the Object type: list box.
2. **Scroll down, select Microsoft PowerPoint Slide in the Object type: list box as shown in FIGURE 8-3, then click OK**
   A blank PowerPoint slide appears along with the PowerPoint Ribbon.
3. **Click the Click to add title text box, type Marketing Report, click the Click to add subtitle text box, type JCL Talent, Inc., press ENTER, then type your name**
4. **Click the Design tab, click the More button in the Themes group to open the Themes gallery, click the Basis theme as shown in FIGURE 8-4, then click anywhere in the text below the slide**
   The slide is inserted into Word as an object. To make changes to the slide, you double-click it to return to PowerPoint.
5. **Double-click the slide, click the Design tab, click the blue color variant (far-right) in the Variants group, click in the text below the slide object to return to Word, click to the left of Overview, then press ENTER**
   The embedded PowerPoint slide appears the Word document. The slide is a picture object that you can size and position.
6. **Right-click the slide, click Picture, click the Size tab in the Format Object dialog box, select the contents of the Height text box, type 2.5, click OK, click the Home tab on the Word Ribbon, then click the Center button in the Paragraph group**
   Another object that you can insert into Word is a Quick Table. You use Quick Tables when you want to choose one of Word's built-in table forms.
7. **Press CTRL+END to move to the end of the document, press BACKSPACE to delete CALENDAR but not the paragraph mark, click Insert, click Table, point to Quick Tables to display the selection of built-in tables, then click Calendar 1**
   A table already formatted as a calendar is inserted into the document. You can modify the formatting of the calendar to make it easier to enter data.
8. **Drag the right edge of the table so it is even with the text at the right margin, click the table move handle in the top-left corner of the table to select the entire table, click the Table Tools Layout tab, then click Distribute Columns in the Cell Size group**
9. **Click after 5 in the box for December 5, press ENTER, type LAUNCH!, then save the document**
   The Calendar1 Quick Table appears as shown in FIGURE 8-5.

FIGURE 8-3: Create New tab in Object dialog box

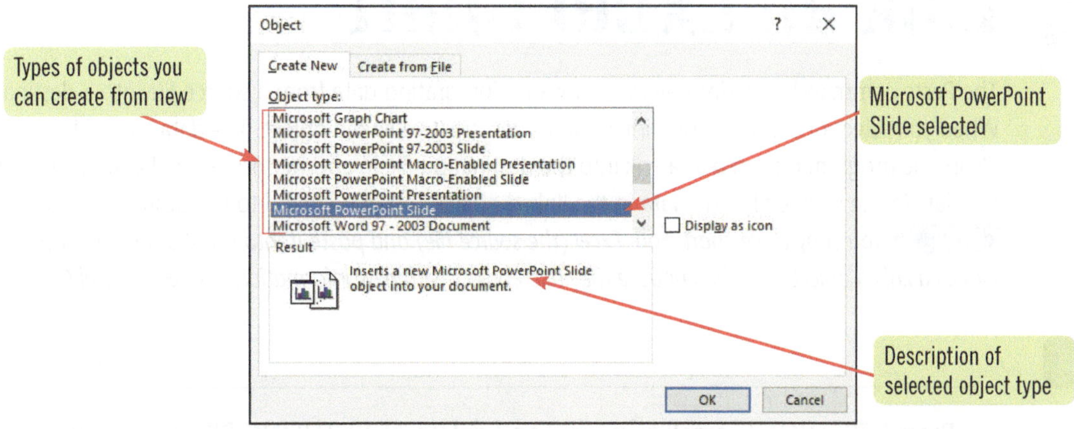

FIGURE 8-4: Basis theme selected

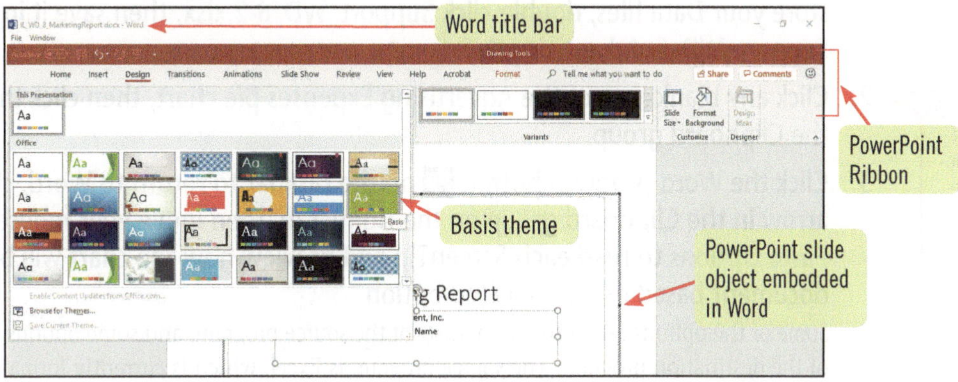

FIGURE 8-5: Calendar 1 Quick Table inserted and formatted

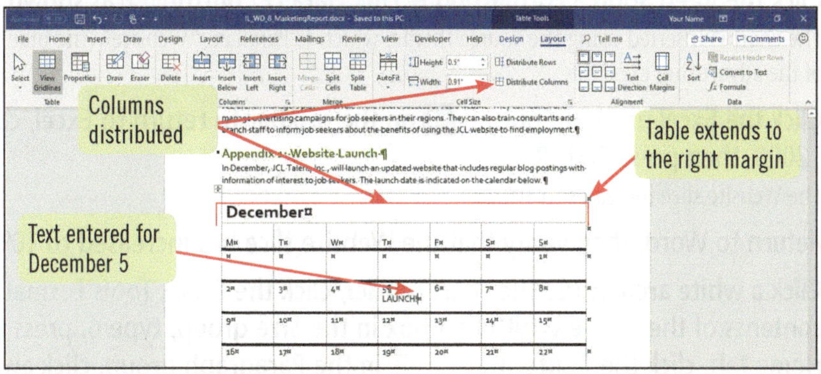

Word

Publishing a blog directly from Word

A blog, which is short for weblog, is an informal journal that is created by an individual or a group and available to the public on the Internet. A blog usually conveys the ideas, comments, and opinions of the blogger and is written using a strong personal voice. The person who creates and maintains a blog, the blogger, typically updates the blog regularly. If you have or want to start a blog, you can configure Word to link to your blog site so that you can write, format, and publish blog entries directly from Word.

To create a new blog post, click the File tab, click New, then double-click Blog post to open a predesigned blog post document that you can customize with your own text, formatting, and images. You can also publish an existing document as a blog post by opening the document, clicking the File tab, clicking Share, and then clicking Post to Blog. In either case, Word prompts you to log onto your personal blog account. To blog directly from Word, you must first obtain a blog account with a blog service provider. Resources, such as the Word Help system and online forums, provide detailed information on obtaining and registering your personal blog account with Word.

Link an Excel Chart

Learning Outcomes
- Copy an Excel chart to Word
- Update a linked chart in Word

The Paste command provides several options for integrating data from a source file into a destination file. When you select one of the paste link options, you create a linked object. The data copied from the source file in one program is pasted as a link into the destination file in another program. If you make a change to the data in the source file, the data in the linked object that you copied to the destination file is updated.

CASE *You copy a pie chart from Excel (the source file) and paste it into the Word report (the destination file) as a linked object. You then update the linked object with new information entered in Excel (the source file.)*

STEPS

1. **Press CTRL+HOME, scroll to page 2 and delete ADVERTISING PIE CHART, but not the paragraph mark, open File Explorer, navigate to the location where you store your Data files, double-click Support_WD_8-2.xlsx, then save it in Excel as Support_WD_8_AdvertisingData**
2. **Click any blank area of the Advertising Expenses pie chart, then click the Copy button in the Clipboard group**
3. **Click the Word program button on the taskbar to return to Word, click the Paste arrow in the Clipboard group on the Home tab, then move your mouse over each of the Paste Options to read each ScreenTip and preview how the chart will be pasted into the document based on the selected option**

   Some of the options retain the formatting of the source program, and some options adopt the formatting of the destination program. The source program is Excel, which is currently formatted with the Parallax theme. The destination program is Word, which is formatted with the Basis theme.
4. **Click the Keep Source Formatting & Link Data (F) button as shown in FIGURE 8-6**

   The chart is inserted using the source theme, which is Parallax. "Website" (the blue slice) accounts for 6% of the advertising expenses.
5. **Click the Excel program button on the taskbar to return to Excel, click cell B2, type 12000, then press ENTER**

   The Website slice increases to 10%.
6. **Return to Word, then verify that the Website slice has increased to 10%**
7. **Click a white area inside the chart border, click the Chart Tools Format tab, select the contents of the Shape Width text box in the Size group, type 6, press ENTER, click the Home tab, click the Center button in the Paragraph group, click away from the pie chart object to deselect it, then compare the pie chart object FIGURE 8-7**
8. **Click the Excel program button on the taskbar, save and close the workbook, then exit Excel**

   The IL_WD_8_MarketingReport.docx file in Word is again the active document.
9. **Save the document**

TROUBLE
Be sure a solid border with sizing handles surrounds the pie chart and all its related components. If only one component is selected, click outside the chart area, then repeat Step 3.

TROUBLE
If the pie chart did not update, click the chart, click the **Chart Tools Design tab**, then click **Refresh Data** in the Data group.

TROUBLE
If the Shape Width text box is dim and does not accept a value, click to the right of the chart and click the chart border again to be sure the entire chart object is selected.

FIGURE 8-6: Selecting a link paste option

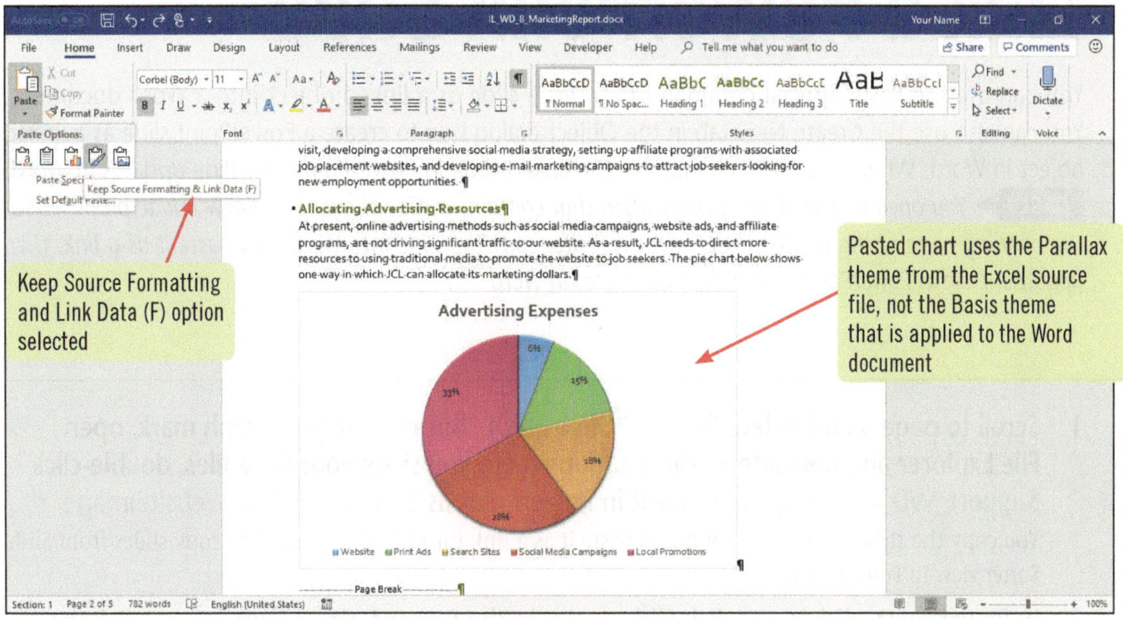

FIGURE 8-7: Linked pie chart updated in Word

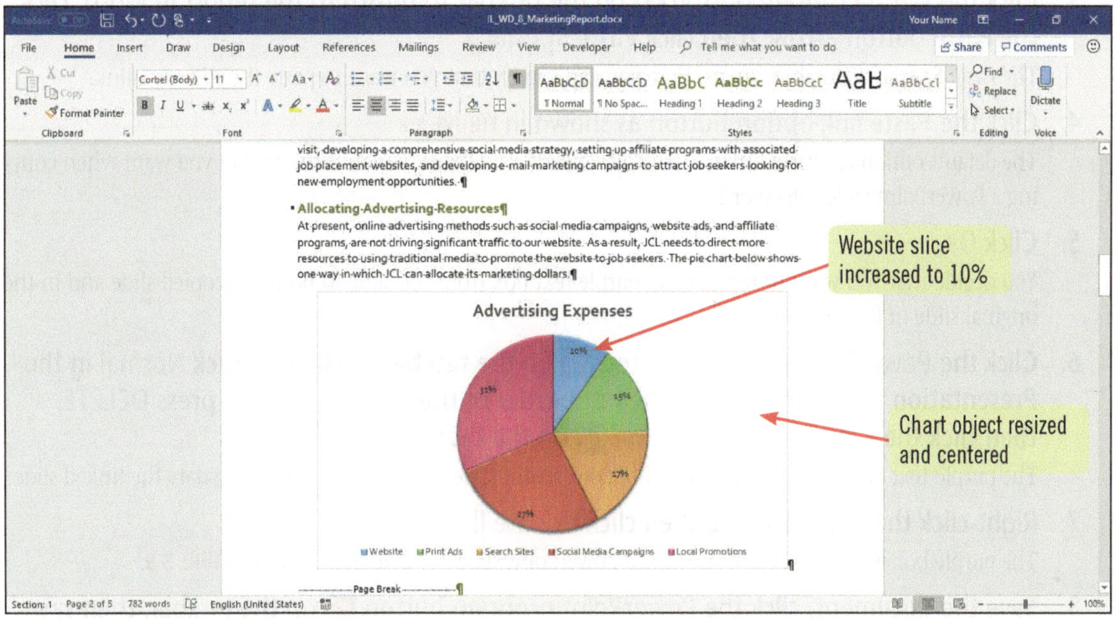

Using the Object dialog box to create a linked file

In addition to using the Paste options, you can create a linked object using the Object dialog box. You open the Object dialog box by clicking Object in the Text group on the Insert tab and then clicking the Create from File tab. You click the Browse button to navigate to and then select the file you want to link, click the Link to file check box to be sure that box is active (has a check mark), and then click OK. The file you select is inserted in the destination file as a linked object.

You create a linked object using one of the options available on the Paste menu when you want to copy only a portion of a file, such as selected cells or a chart in an Excel worksheet. You create a linked object using the Link to file check box in the Object dialog box when you want to insert the entire file, such as the entire worksheet in an Excel file.

Link a PowerPoint Slide

Learning Outcomes
- Link and update a PowerPoint Slide in Word

You can use the Paste Special command to insert a slide as a linked object into a Word document. You can also use the Create New tab in the Object dialog box to create a PowerPoint slide as a linked object in Word. When you make changes to the linked slide in PowerPoint, the slide updates in Word.

CASE *You open a PowerPoint presentation that contains a slide showing the new image proposed for the opening page of the updated JCL Talent website, copy the slide into Word and paste it as a link, then update the file in PowerPoint so that it also updates in Word.*

STEPS

1. **Scroll to page 3 and delete POWERPOINT SLIDE, but not the paragraph mark, open File Explorer and navigate to the location where you store your Data files, double-click Support_WD_8-3.pptx, then save it in PowerPoint as Support_WD_8_WebsiteImage**
   You copy the slide from PowerPoint and paste it as a link into Word. You need to copy slides from Slide Sorter view in PowerPoint.
2. **In PowerPoint, click View, click Slide Sorter in the Presentation Views group, click the Home tab, then click the Copy button in the Clipboard group**
3. **Click the Word Program button on the taskbar to return to the report in Word, click the Paste button arrow, then click Paste Special**
   The Paste Special dialog box opens. Here you can specify that you want to paste the slide as a link.
4. **Click the Paste link option button as shown in FIGURE 8-8**
   The default option for Paste link is Microsoft PowerPoint Object, which is the option you want when copying a PowerPoint slide into Word.
5. **Click OK**
   You decide that you want to remove the purple text box from the slide in both the copied slide and in the original slide in PowerPoint.
6. **Click the PowerPoint program button on the taskbar, click View, click Normal in the Presentation Views group, click the left border of the purple text box, press DELETE, then click the Word program button on the taskbar**
   The purple text box is still displayed on the PowerPoint slide in Word. You need to update the linked slide.
7. **Right-click the slide in Word, then click Update link**
   The purple box is removed from the linked PowerPoint slide in Word as shown in FIGURE 8-9.
8. **Save the document, click the PowerPoint program button on the taskbar, then save and close the PowerPoint presentation**
   You are returned to the document in Word.

FIGURE 8-8: Paste Special dialog box

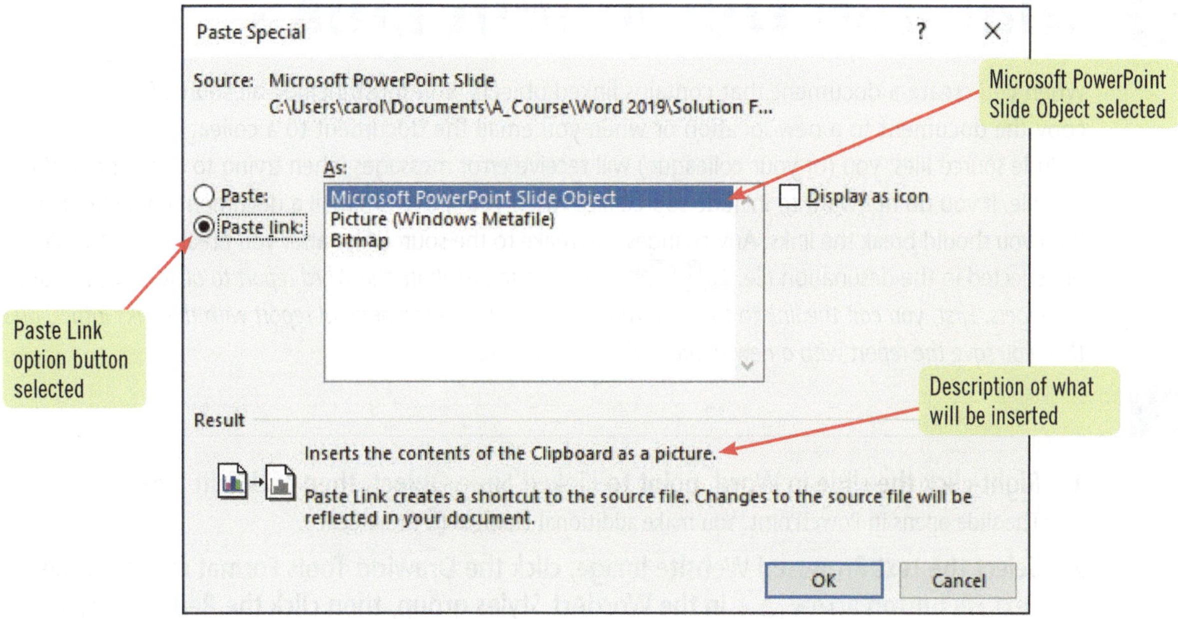

FIGURE 8-9: PowerPoint slide copied into Word as a link

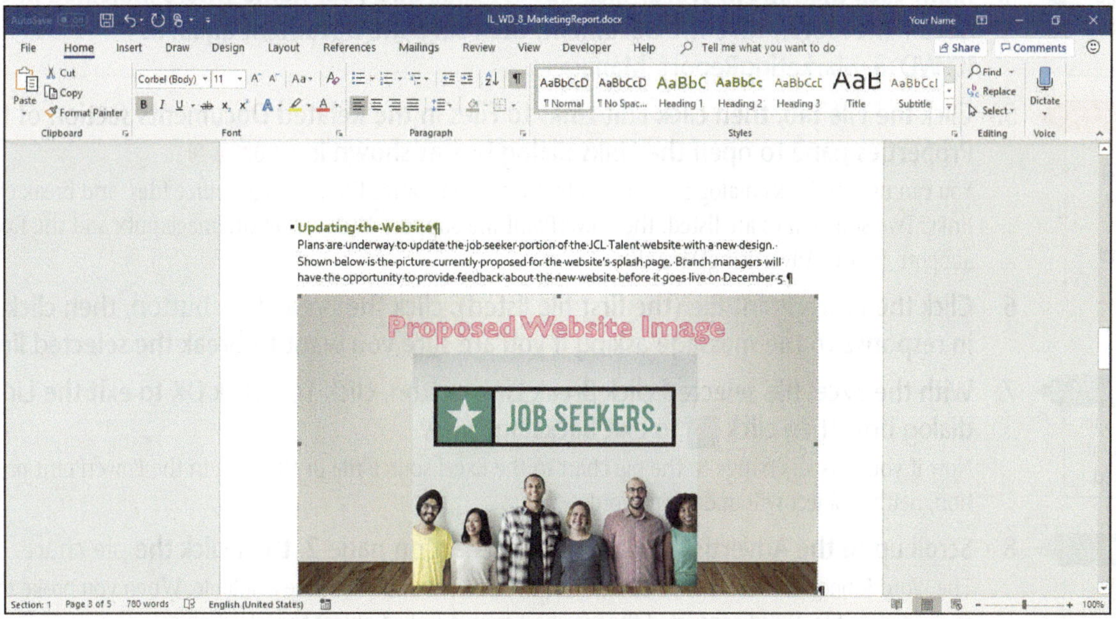

Rawpixel.com/Shutterstock.com

Creating a PowerPoint presentation from a Word outline

When you create a PowerPoint presentation from a Word outline, the Word document is the source file and the PowerPoint document is the destination file. Headings formatted with heading styles in the Word source file are converted to PowerPoint headings in the PowerPoint destination file. For example, each line of text formatted with the Heading 1 style becomes its own slide. To create a PowerPoint presentation from a Word outline, create and then save the outline in Word, close the document, then launch PowerPoint. In PowerPoint, click the New Slide list arrow, click Slides from Outline, navigate to the location where you stored the Word document, then double-click the filename. The Word outline is converted to a PowerPoint presentation, which you can modify in the same way you modify any PowerPoint presentation. Any changes you make to the presentation in PowerPoint are *not* reflected in the original Word document.

Manage Document Links

Learning Outcomes
- Edit a link to a file
- Break links

When you create a document that contains linked objects, you must include all source files when you copy the document to a new location or when you email the document to a colleague. If you do not include source files, you (or your colleague) will receive error messages when trying to open the destination file. If you do not want to include source files when you move or email a document containing links, then you should break the links. Any changes you make to the source files after you break the links will not be reflected in the destination file. **CASE** *You need to distribute the Word report to all JCL Talent branch managers. First, you edit the link to the PowerPoint slide and save the original report with the links intact, and then you save the report with a new name and break the links.*

STEPS

1. **Right-click the slide in Word, point to Linked Slide Object, then click Edit Link**
   The slide opens in PowerPoint. You make additional changes to the slide.
2. **Select the text Proposed Website Image, click the Drawing Tools Format tab, click the Text Fill button arrow in the WordArt Styles group, then click the Red, Accent 1 color box in the top row of the Color palette**
3. **Click away from the text, then save the presentation and exit PowerPoint**
4. **Right-click the slide in Word, click Update Link, add your name where indicated in the document footer, save the document, then save the document again as IL_WD_8_MarketingReport_Managers**
5. **Click the File tab, then click Edit Links to Files in the Related Documents section of the Properties pane to open the Links dialog box as shown in FIGURE 8-10**
   You can use the Links dialog box to update links, open source files, change source files, and break existing links. Two source files are listed: the PowerPoint file Support_WD_8_WebsiteImage.pptx and the Excel file Support_WD_8_AdvertisingData.xlsx.
6. **Click the PowerPoint file (the first file listed), click the Break Link button, then click Yes in response to the message asking if you are sure you want to break the selected link**
7. **With the Excel file selected click Break Link button, click Yes, click OK to exit the Links dialog box, then click to exit Backstage view**
   Now if you make a change to the pie chart in the Excel source file or the slide in the PowerPoint presentation, neither object will update in Word.
8. **Scroll up to the Advertising Expenses pie chart on page 2, then click the pie chart**
   The Word Ribbon is still active, and the Chart Tools contextual tabs are available. When you broke the link to the source file, Word converted the pie chart from a linked object to a chart object.
9. **Click the Chart Tools Design tab, click the More button in the Chart Styles group, click Style 11 (the second to the last selection), save the document, then compare it to FIGURE 8-11**
   The Style 11 chart style is applied to the chart and the theme updated to match the theme of the document (Basis.)

QUICK TIP
After you break links, the Update Links command cannot be used to update information in the destination file.

TROUBLE
You may need to scroll down to see the Edit Links to Files link in the lower-right corner of the screen.

QUICK TIP
An entry remains for the pie chart, but it is no longer linked.

QUICK TIP
You can use commands on the Chart Tools Design and Format tabs to modify the chart object, but you cannot change the content of the pie chart.

FIGURE 8-10: Links dialog box

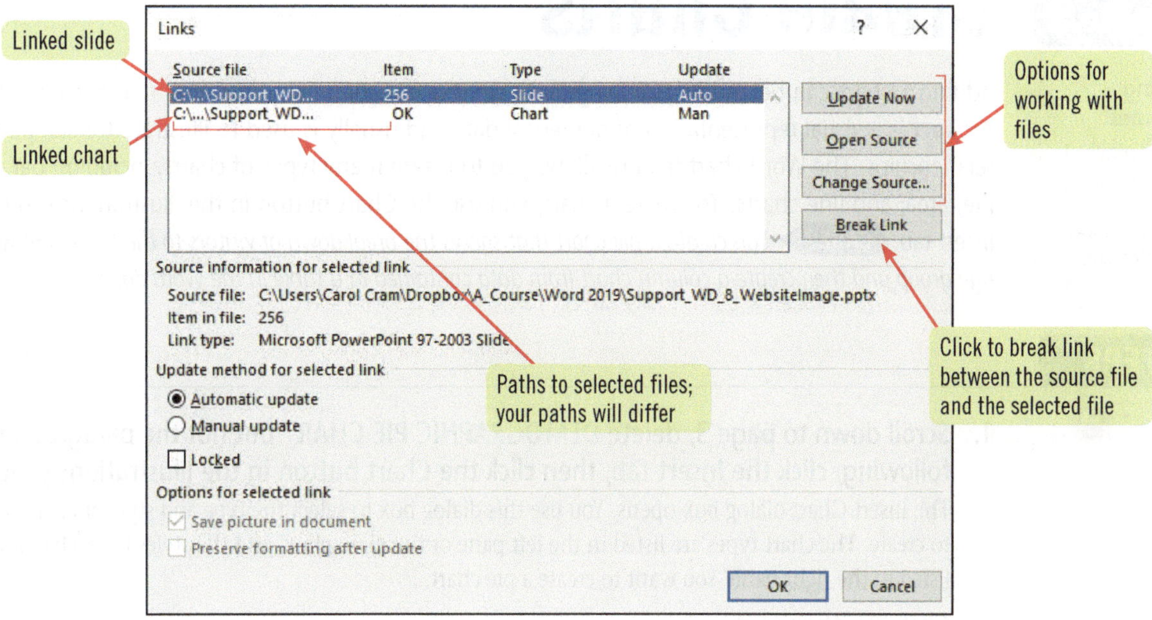

FIGURE 8-11: Formatted pie chart

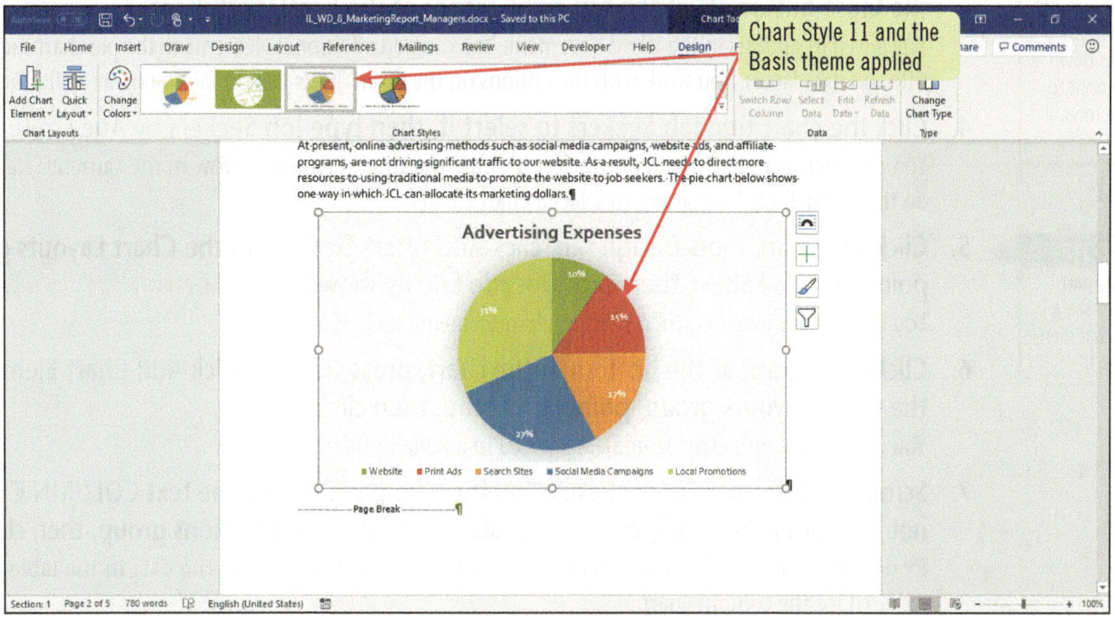

Create Charts

Learning Outcomes
- Insert a pie chart
- Insert a column chart
- Add and remove chart elements

Adding a chart can be an effective way to illustrate a document that includes numerical information. A **chart** is a visual representation of numerical data and usually is used to illustrate trends, patterns, or relationships. The Word chart feature allows you to create many types of charts, including bar, column, pie, area, and line charts. To create a chart, you use the Chart button in the Illustrations group on the Insert tab. **CASE** *You create a pie chart that shows the breakdown of visitors to the JCL Talent website by age group and then create a column chart from data contained in a table in the Word document.*

STEPS

1. **Scroll down to page 3, delete DEMOGRAPHIC PIE CHART but not the paragraph mark following, click the Insert tab, then click the Chart button in the Illustrations group**
   The Insert Chart dialog box opens. You use this dialog box to select the type and style of chart you intend to create. The chart types are listed in the left pane of the dialog box, and the styles for each chart type are listed in the right pane. You want to create a pie chart.
2. **Click Pie, then click OK**
   A worksheet opens in a Chart in Microsoft Word window, and a pie chart appears in the document. The worksheet and the chart contain placeholder data that you replace with your own data. The chart is based on the data in the worksheet. Any change you make to the data is made automatically to the chart.
3. **Click cell A1 in the worksheet, enter the labels and values shown in FIGURE 8-12, then click the Close button ☒ at the top right corner of the Excel worksheet**
   The pie chart appears in the Word document. You can add additional elements to the pie chart such as a chart title and data labels. You work with the options on the Chart Tools Design tab to further build the pie chart.
4. **Click the chart title Job Seekers to select it, then type Job Seekers by Age Group**
   You can click any chart element to select it or use the Chart Elements arrow in the Current Selection group on the Chart Tools Format tab to select a chart element.
5. **Click the Chart Tools Design tab, click Add Chart Element in the Chart Layouts group, point to Data Labels, then click Outside End as shown in FIGURE 8-13**
   You can also remove and then reinsert chart elements such as a legend.
6. **Click the legend at the bottom of the chart, press DELETE, click Add Chart Element in the Chart Layouts group, point to Legend, then click Right**
   You create a column chart from data entered in a table in the report.
7. **Scroll to "Customer Survey Results"on the next page, delete the text COLUMN CHART, but not the paragraph mark, click Insert, click Chart in the Illustrations group, then click OK**
   By default, a clustered column chart is inserted. You need to designate the data in the table as the data required for the column chart.
8. **Scroll up, click in the table, click the Table move handle ⊞ to select all the text in the table, press CTRL+X to cut the table from the Word document, click cell A1 in the Excel worksheet, then press CTRL+V to paste the chart data into the Excel worksheet**
9. **Close the Excel worksheet, click the chart title, type Educational Levels of Job Seekers, compare the chart to FIGURE 8-14, then save the document**
   In the next lesson, you will further enhance both charts you created in this lesson.

TROUBLE
Drag the lower-right corner of the worksheet object down and to the right to show more rows, if necessary.

QUICK TIP
Point to any part of a chart to see a ScreenTip that identifies the part.

FIGURE 8-12: Data for pie chart

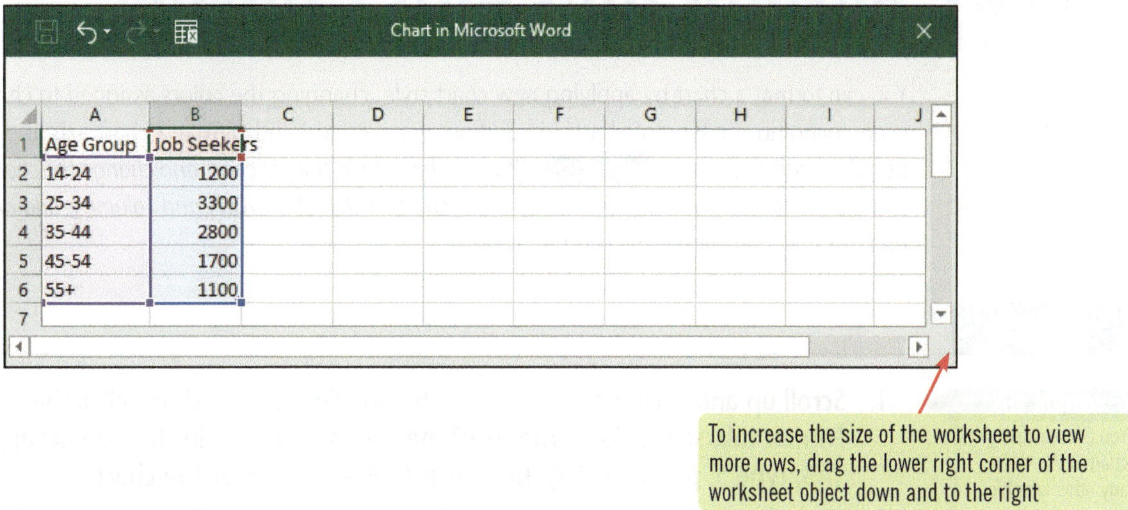

FIGURE 8-13: Adding data labels to a chart

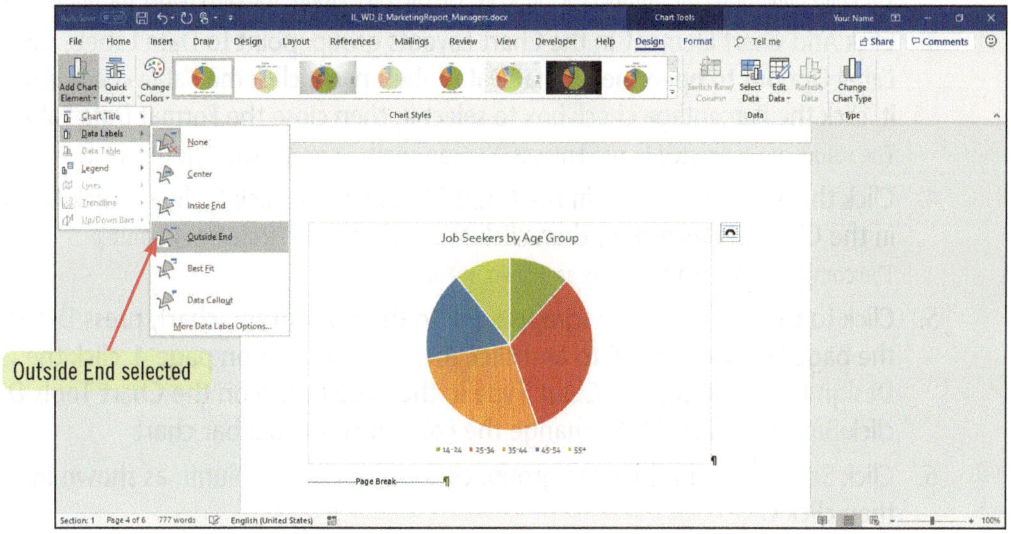

FIGURE 8-14: Column chart created in Word

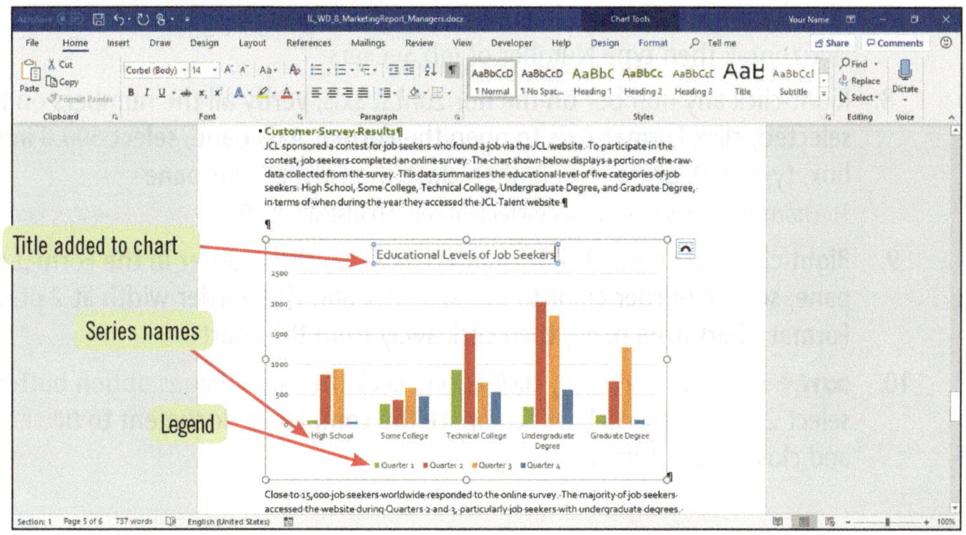

Format and Edit Charts

Learning Outcomes
- Edit chart data
- Format a chart and chart elements

You can format a chart by applying new chart style, changing the colors assigned to chart elements, and even changing the type of chart. In addition, you can add and format a chart axis and add a chart border, then edit chart data. **CASE** *You edit the data in the pie chart and change the chart colors, then you change the style of the column chart to a bar chart, switch chart rows and columns, add and format an axis and axis title, and enclose the chart in a border.*

STEPS

QUICK TIP
You can resize a chart in Word like any other graphic object.

1. **Scroll up and click the "Job Seekers by Age Group" pie chart, click the Chart Tools Format tab, select the contents of the Height text box in the Size group, type 3, press TAB, type 5, press ENTER, then press CTRL+E to center the chart**
2. **Click the Chart Tools Design tab, click Edit Data in the Data group, click cell B5, type 2200, press ENTER, then close the Excel worksheet**
   The chart data shows the numbers of job seekers in each age group. You can change the numbers to percentages.
3. **Click Add Chart Element in the Chart Layouts group, point to Data Labels, click More Data Label Options to open the Format Data Labels pane, click the Value check box to deselect it, click the Percentage check box to select it, then close the Format Data Labels pane**
   The values are converted to percentages. You can apply a preset chart style to format the chart.
4. **Click the More button in the Chart Styles group, click Style 12, click Change Colors in the Chart Styles group, then click Monochromatic Palette 4 (blue)**
   The completed pie chart appears as shown in FIGURE 8-15.
5. **Click to the left of the paragraph mark to the right of the chart, press DELETE to move the page break up, scroll to and click the column chart on page 4, click the Chart Tools Design tab, click Change Chart Type in the Type group on the Chart Tools Design tab, click Bar, then click OK to change the column chart to a bar chart**
6. **Click Select Data in the Data group, click Switch Row/Column as shown in FIGURE 8-16, then click OK**
   When you switch rows and columns, the series data is switched to become labels for the horizontal axis, and data on the horizontal axis is now the series data. In the bar chart, the chart displays "Quarter 1", "Quarter 2", etc. on the vertical axis and the number of job seekers on the horizontal axis.

QUICK TIP
To format any chart element, select it, then click the Format Selection button in the Current Selection group on the Chart Tools Design tab to open the Format pane for that chart element.

7. **Click Add Chart Element in the Chart Layouts group, point to Axis Titles, click Primary Horizontal, then type Number of Job Seekers**
8. **Right-click any number on the horizontal axis, verify all the numbers on the axis are selected, click Format Axis to open the Format Axis pane, select 500.0 in the Major text box, type 250, press ENTER, then close the Format Axis pane**
   The horizontal axis now shows increments of 250 instead of 500.
9. **Right-click the chart, click Format Chart Area, click Border in the Format Chart Area pane, set the border color to Black, Text 1 and the border width at 2 pt, close the Format Chart Area pane, then click away from the chart**
10. **sam Click the View tab, click Zoom, click the Many Pages option button, drag to select 2 x 3 pages, click OK, compare the completed document to FIGURE 8-17, then save and close the document**

FIGURE 8-15: Edited pie chart

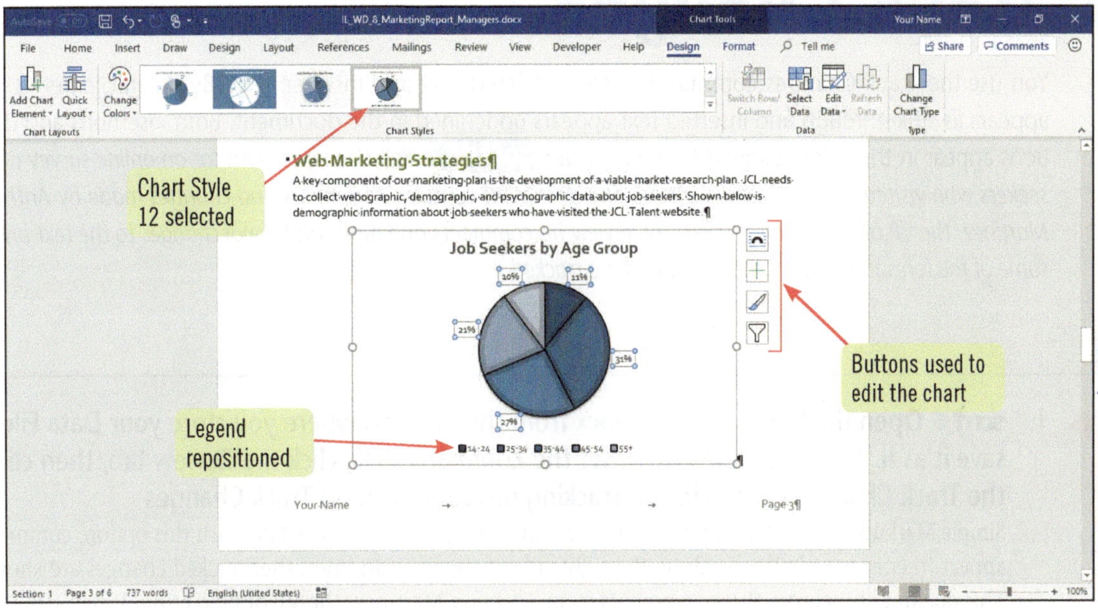

FIGURE 8-16: Select Data source dialog box

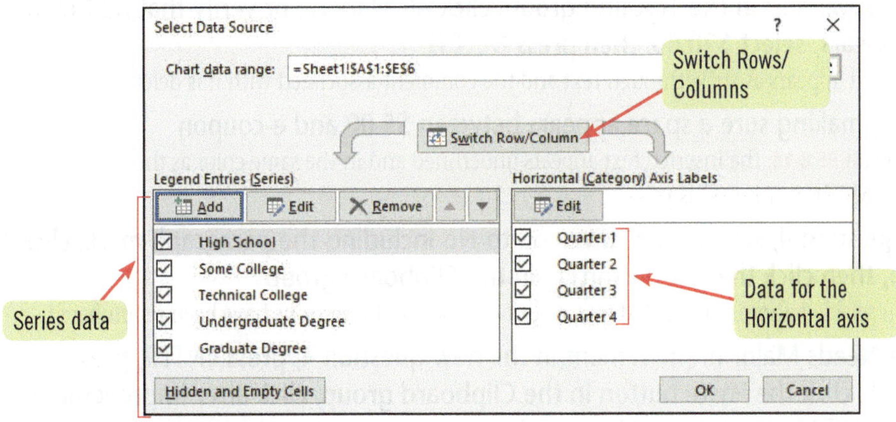

FIGURE 8-17: Completed report

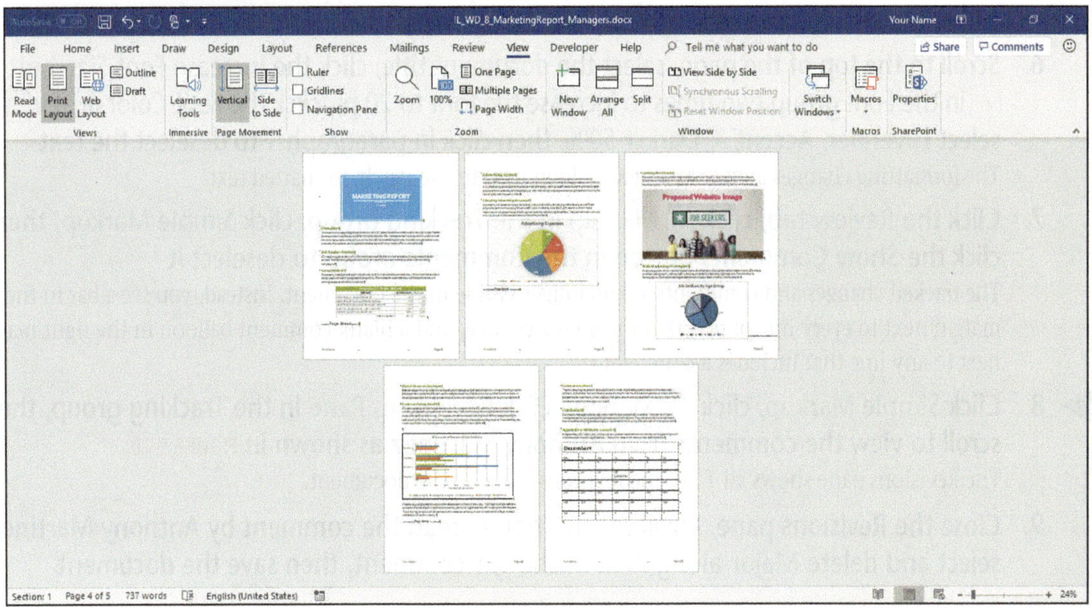

Rawpixel.com/Shutterstock.com

Word

Track Changes

Learning Outcomes
- Track insertions and deletions
- Track formatting changes

You use the Track Changes command to show deleted text and inserted text. By default, deleted text appears as ~~strikethrough~~ and inserted text appears underlined in the document. Both insertions and deletions appear in the color assigned to the reviewer. **CASE** *You open questions for an online survey of job seekers who visited the JCL Talent website. The document contains comments and changes made by Anthony Martinez, the VP of sales & marketing. You review his comments and make additional changes to the text and to some of the formatting. All of these changes are tracked.*

STEPS

TROUBLE
A different markup option may be selected if another user was working on the computer before you.

TROUBLE
Use your mouse to completely select "$10.00" so that when you press DELETE, the comment is also deleted.

QUICK TIP
You press BACKSPACE to remove a lettered line in a list and to leave a blank line.

QUICK TIP
The Revisions pane can also be displayed below the document window.

1. **sam Open the file IL_WD_8-2.docx from the location where you store your Data Files, save it as IL_WD_8_OnlineSurvey, set the Zoom at 120%, click the Review tab, then click the Track Changes button in the Tracking group to turn on Track Changes**
   Simple Markup is the default option in the Tracking group on the Review tab. With this option, comments appear in comment balloons along the right side of the page and no other tracked changes are shown. This document includes three comments from Anthony Martinez, the VP of marketing. When the Track Changes button is active, every change you make to the document will appear in colored text.
2. **Click Simple Markup in the Tracking group, click All Markup, or verify that All Markup already appears, select $10.00, then press DELETE**
   The deleted text appears as strikethrough text and the comment associated with it is deleted.
3. **Type $5.00, making sure a space appears between $5.00 and e-coupon**
   As shown in FIGURE 8-18, the inserted text appears underlined and in the same color as the color assigned to the reviewer, which in this case is you.
4. **Scroll to question 4, select from Have you to No including the paragraph mark, click the Home tab, then click the Cut button in the Clipboard group**
   The text you selected appears as deleted text, and the subsequent questions have been renumbered.
5. **Click after Needs Major Improvement in the new question 4, press ENTER, press BACKSPACE, click the Paste button in the Clipboard group, click after Improvement (4d.), press ENTER, then press BACKSPACE**
   As shown in FIGURE 8-19, both the cut text and the pasted text appear in a new color and are double-underlined. The new color and the double underlining indicate that the text has been moved.
6. **Scroll to the top of the page, select the document title, click the Increase Font Size button in the Font group two times to increase the font to 20 pt, click the Font Color arrow, select Lavender, Accent 3, Darker 50%, then click in paragraph 1 to deselect the text**
   The formatting changes appear in a new balloon next to the newly formatted text.
7. **Click the Review tab, click All Markup in the Tracking group, click Simple Markup, then click the Show Comments button in the Comments group to deselect it**
   The tracked changes and comments are no longer visible in the document. Instead, you see a bar in the left margin next to every line of text that includes a change, and a blank comment balloon in the right margin next to any line that includes a comment.
8. **Click Simple Markup, click All Markup, click Reviewing Pane in the Tracking group, then scroll to view the comments from Anthony Martinez as shown in FIGURE 8-20**
   The Revisions pane shows all 15 of the revisions made to the document.
9. **Close the Revisions pane, scroll to Question 4, read the comment by Anthony Martinez, select and delete Major along with Anthony's comment, then save the document**

FIGURE 8-18: Text inserted with Track Changes feature active

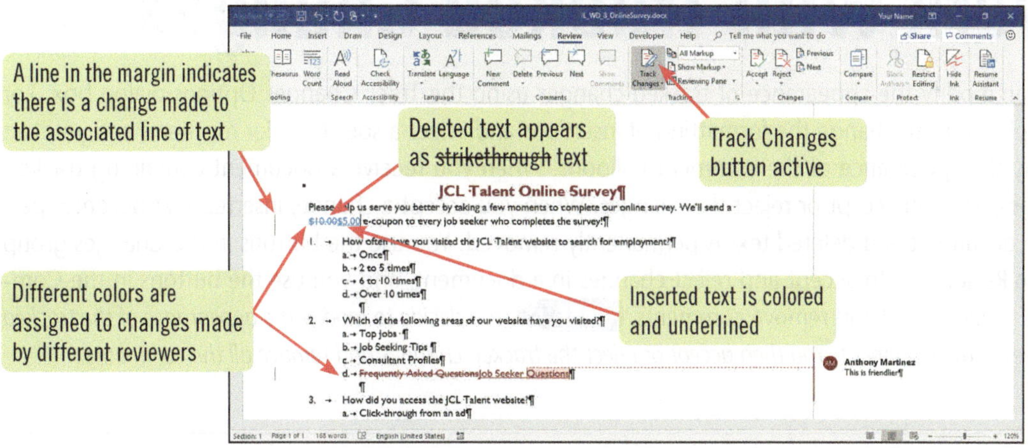

FIGURE 8-19: Tracked changes shows formatting for moved text

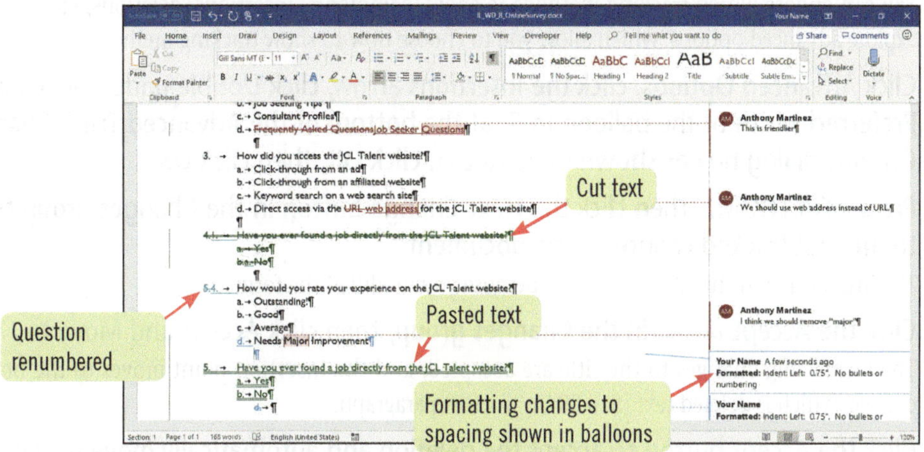

FIGURE 8-20: Document with Revisions pane open

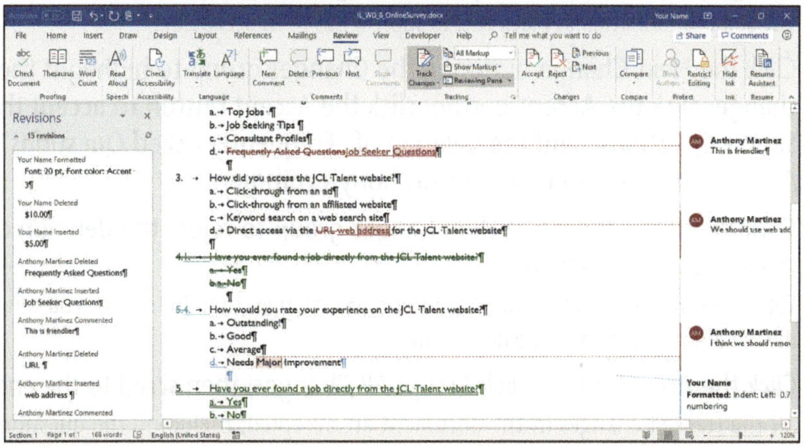

Using Paste and Paste All with tracked changes

If Track Changes is on when you are pasting items from the Clipboard, each item you paste is inserted in the document as a tracked change. If you cut an individual item and then paste it from the Clipboard into a new location, the item is inserted in a new color and with double underlining, which indicates that the item has been moved. If, however, you use the Paste All button on the Clipboard pane to paste all the items on the Clipboard at once, the items are pasted in the document as inserted text at the location of the insertion point. When you use the Paste All button, the items are pasted in the order in which you collected them, from the first item you collected (the item at the bottom of the Clipboard) to the most recent item you collected (the item at the top of the Clipboard).

Work with Tracked Changes

Learning Outcomes
- Change track changes options
- Accept and reject changes

You can modify the appearance of tracked changes using the Track Changes Options dialog box. For example, you can change the formatting of insertions and select a specific color for them, and you can modify the appearance of the comment balloons. When you receive a document containing tracked changes, you can accept or reject the changes. When you accept a change, inserted text becomes part of the document and deleted text is permanently removed. You use the buttons in the Changes group on the Review tab to accept and reject changes in a document, and you use the buttons in the Comments group to find and remove comments. **CASE** *You decide to modify the appearance of the tracked changes in the document. You then accept or reject the tracked changes and remove all the comments.*

STEPS

1. **Click the Launcher in the Tracking group to open the Track Changes Options dialog box**
   You can choose which tracking methods to show (comments, insertions, deletions, etc.), and you can explore advanced options, which allow you to choose how to show tracking methods.
2. **Click Advanced Options, click the Insertions arrow, click Double underline, change the Preferred width of the balloon to 2" at the bottom of the Advanced Track Changes Options dialog box as shown in FIGURE 8-21, click OK, then click OK**
3. **Press CTRL+HOME, then click the Next Change button in the Changes group to move to the first tracked change in the document**
   The insertion point highlights the title because you modified the formatting.
4. **Click the Accept arrow in the Changes group, then click Accept and Move to Next**
   The formatting changes to the title are accepted, and the insertion point moves to the next tracked change, which is deleted text ($10.00) in the first paragraph.
5. **Click the Accept button to accept the deletion and automatically move to the next change, then click the Accept button again to accept $5.00**
   The $5.00 is formatted as black text to show it has been accepted.
6. **Click the Next Change button in the Changes group to highlight the next tracked change, click the Accept button, click the Accept button to accept the insertion of "Job Seeker Questions" and the deletion of "Frequently Asked Questions", then click the Accept button again to accept Anthony's comment**
7. **Click the Reject button in the Changes group to reject the deletion of "URL", then click the Reject button again**
   You can continue to review and accept or reject changes individually, or you can choose to accept all of the remaining changes in the document.
8. **Click the Accept arrow, click Accept All Changes, then scroll to the end of the document**
   All the tracked changes in the document are accepted, including the question that was moved and renumbered.
9. **Click the Delete arrow in the Comments group, then click Delete All Comments in Document**
   Scroll through the document. Notice that all tracked changes and comments are removed from the document.
10. **sam Scroll to the bottom of the document, click the Track Changes button in the Tracking group to turn off Track Changes, type your name where indicated in the footer, close the footer, show the document in One Page view, compare it to FIGURE 8-22, then save and close the document, but do not exit Word**

QUICK TIP
You should always review all changes and comments before you use any of the Accept All Changes or Delete All Comments commands.

FIGURE 8-21: Advanced Track Changes dialog box

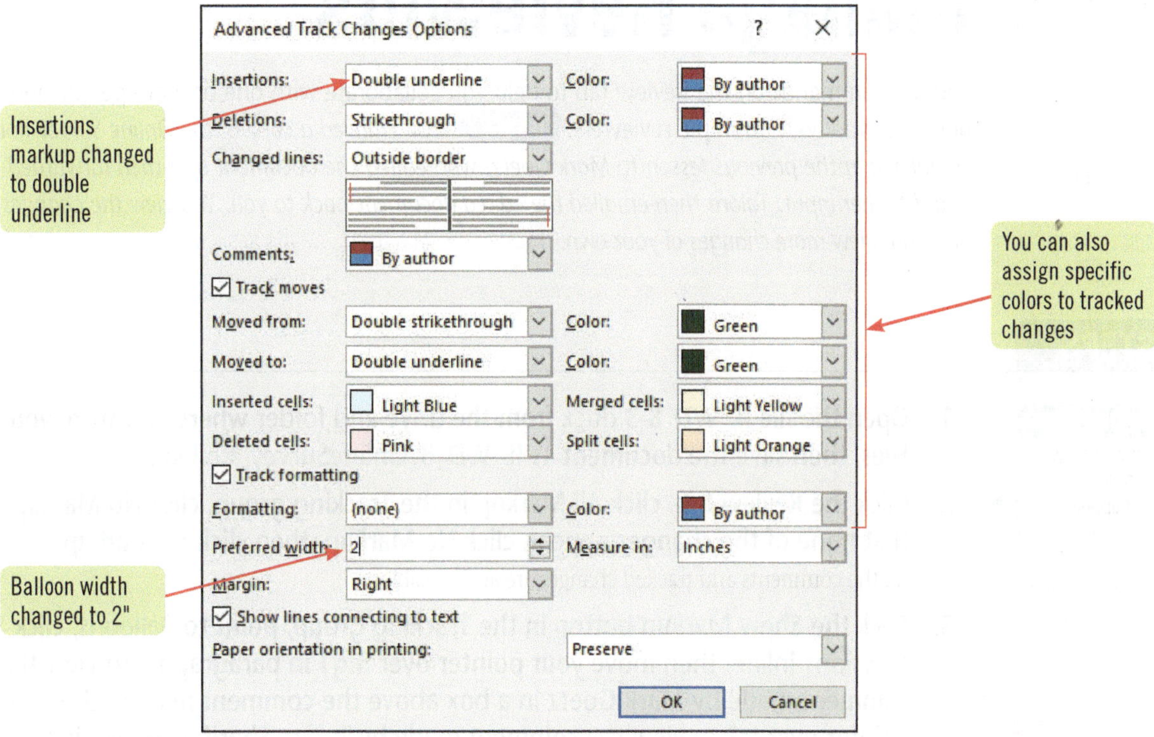

FIGURE 8-22: Completed document with tracked changes accepted and comments deleted

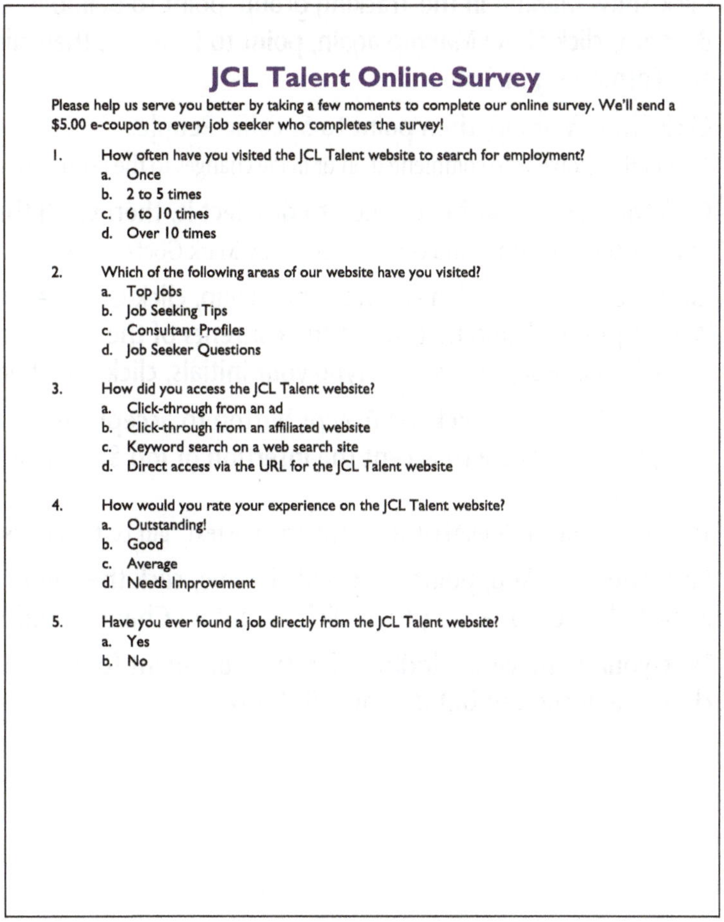

JCL Talent Online Survey

Please help us serve you better by taking a few moments to complete our online survey. We'll send a $5.00 e-coupon to every job seeker who completes the survey!

1. How often have you visited the JCL Talent website to search for employment?
   a. Once
   b. 2 to 5 times
   c. 6 to 10 times
   d. Over 10 times

2. Which of the following areas of our website have you visited?
   a. Top Jobs
   b. Job Seeking Tips
   c. Consultant Profiles
   d. Job Seeker Questions

3. How did you access the JCL Talent website?
   a. Click-through from an ad
   b. Click-through from an affiliated website
   c. Keyword search on a web search site
   d. Direct access via the URL for the JCL Talent website

4. How would you rate your experience on the JCL Talent website?
   a. Outstanding!
   b. Good
   c. Average
   d. Needs Improvement

5. Have you ever found a job directly from the JCL Talent website?
   a. Yes
   b. No

Manage Reviewers

Learning Outcomes
- View changes from multiple users

You use commands on the Review tab to help you collaborate with one or more people and to manage how you work with multiple reviewers. **CASE** *You emailed a copy of the Online Survey document you completed in the previous lesson to Mark Goetz, who edited the document and then forwarded it to Talora Sharif for her input. Talora then emailed the edited document back to you. You view the changes they made and add a few more changes of your own.*

STEPS

1. **Open the file IL_WD_8-3.docx from the drive and folder where you store your Data Files, then save the document as IL_WD_8_OnlineSurvey_Colleagues**
2. **Click the Review tab, click All Markup in the Tracking group, click No Markup, note that none of the changes appear, click No Markup, then click All Markup**
   All the comments and tracked changes are again visible.
3. **Click the Show Markup button in the Tracking group, point to Balloons, click Show All Revisions Inline, then move your pointer over mg1 in paragraph 1 to view the comment made by Mark Goetz in a box above the comment marker, then move your pointer over ts2 to view the comment made by Talora Sharif as shown in FIGURE 8-23**
   Instead of being contained in balloons, the comments are contained within the document.
4. **Click Show Markup in the Tracking group, point to Balloons, click Show Revisions in Balloons, click Show Markup again, point to Balloons, then click Show Only Comments and Formatting in Balloons**
5. **Click Show Markup, then point to Specific People**
   A list of the people who commented on or made changes to the document appears, as shown in FIGURE 8-24.
6. **Click the Talora Sharif check box to deselect it, then scroll through the document**
   Only the tracked change and comment made by Mark Goetz are visible.
7. **Click the Launcher in the Tracking group, click Change User Name to open the Word Options dialog box, select the contents of the User name text box, type your name if necessary, press TAB, type your initials, click OK, then click OK**
8. **Press CTRL+HOME, click the Accept button to accept the deletion in the title, click the Accept button twice to accept the insertion of Job Seeker, select e-coupon, then type gift certificate**
   The text "e-coupon" is marked as deleted, and the text "gift certificate" is marked as inserted.
9. **Click Show Markup, point to Specific People, click the Talora Sharif check box to select it, click the Accept arrow, then click Accept All Changes and Stop Tracking**
10. **Type your name where indicated in the document footer, save the document, then close the document but do not exit Word**

QUICK TIP
Additional changes in No Markup view will appear as tracked changes when you use All Markup view as long as the Track Changes button remains active.

TROUBLE
Increase the zoom as needed to see the initials in square brackets.

QUICK TIP
You can also change the username and initials by clicking the File tab, and then clicking Options to open the Word Options dialog box.

QUICK TIP
Your name appears as one of the reviewers and Mark's name is removed because you've accepted his change.

FIGURE 8-23: Manage Reviewers

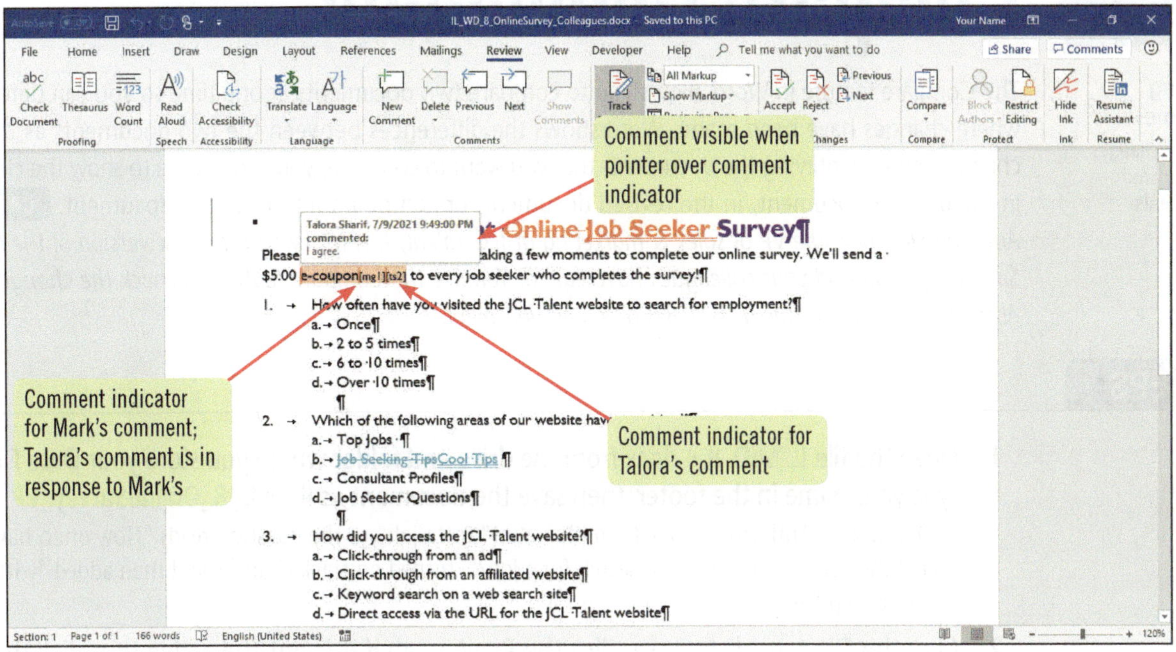

FIGURE 8-24: Showing reviewers

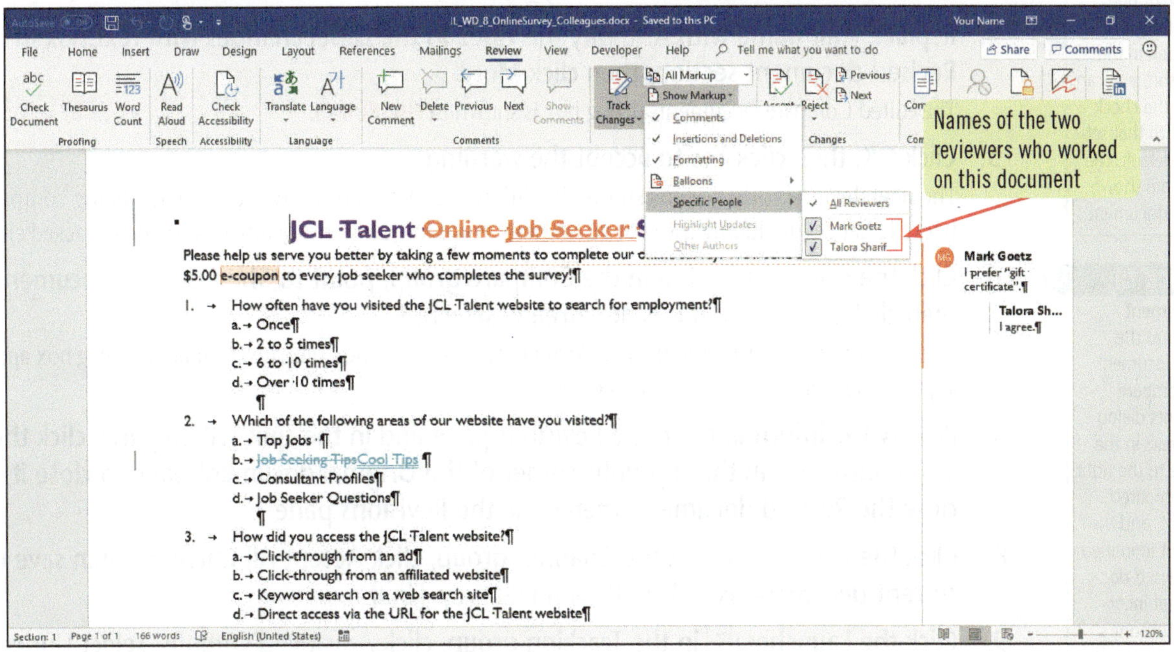

Compare Documents

Learning Outcomes
- Identify changes in compared documents

The Compare feature in Word allows you to compare two documents at one time so you can determine where changes have been made. Word shows the differences between the two documents as tracked changes. After identifying the documents that you want to compare, you can choose to show the changes in the original document, in the revised document, or combined into one new document. **CASE** *Anthony Martinez, the VP of sales & marketing at JLC Talent, has reviewed the latest version of the Online Survey that you and your colleagues have edited. You use the Compare feature to check the changes that Anthony made against the IL_WD_8_Colleagues document.*

STEPS

QUICK TIP
Check marks identify all the document settings that will be compared. If you do not want one of the settings to be included in the comparison, you can uncheck the check box next to that setting. By default, the changes are shown in a new document.

QUICK TIP
The document identified as the original document in the Compare Documents dialog box appears in the top pane to the right of the compared document, and the document identified as the revised document that incorporates Anthony's changes appears in the lower pane.

1. **Open the file IL_WD_8-4.docx from the drive and folder where you store your Data Files, type your name in the footer, then save the document as IL_WD_8_OnlineSurvey_VP**
   In Question 1, Anthony changed "employment" to "a job" so the question reads "How often have you visited the JCL Talent website to search for a job?", turned on track changes and then added "within 30 days of receipt" to paragraph one.
2. **Click the File tab, click Close, click the Review tab if it is not the active tab, click the Compare button in the Compare group, then click Compare**
   In the Compare Documents dialog box, you specify which two documents you want to compare.
3. **Click the Browse button in the Original document section, navigate to the location where you save the files for this module, double-click IL_WD_8_OnlineSurvey_Colleagues.docx, click the Browse button in the Revised document section, then double-click IL_WD_8_OnlineSurvey_VP.docx**
4. **Replace your name with Anthony Martinez in the Label changes with text box in the Revised document section, then click More**
   The edited Compare Documents dialog box is shown in FIGURE 8-25.
5. **Click OK, then click Yes to accept the warning**
   The new document that opens shows the differences between the two documents being compared as tracked changes, including the change Anthony made to Question 1 before he turned on tracked changes.
6. **Click the Compare button in the Compare group, point to Show Source Documents, then click Show Both if it is not already selected**
   The Revisions pane opens and the two documents selected in the Compare Documents dialog box appear in a split screen pane, as shown in FIGURE 8-26.
7. **Review the information in the Revisions pane and in the split screen pane, click the Close button in the top-right corner of the Original document pane to close it, close the Revised document, then close the Revisions pane**
8. **Click the Accept arrow in the Changes group, click Accept All Changes, then save the current document as IL_WD_8_OnlineSurvey_Final**
9. **Click the Launcher in the Tracking group, click Advanced Options, select Underline for insertions and 3.7" for the balloon width, click OK, click OK, submit all to your instructor, then close all open documents**

FIGURE 8-25: Compare Documents dialog box

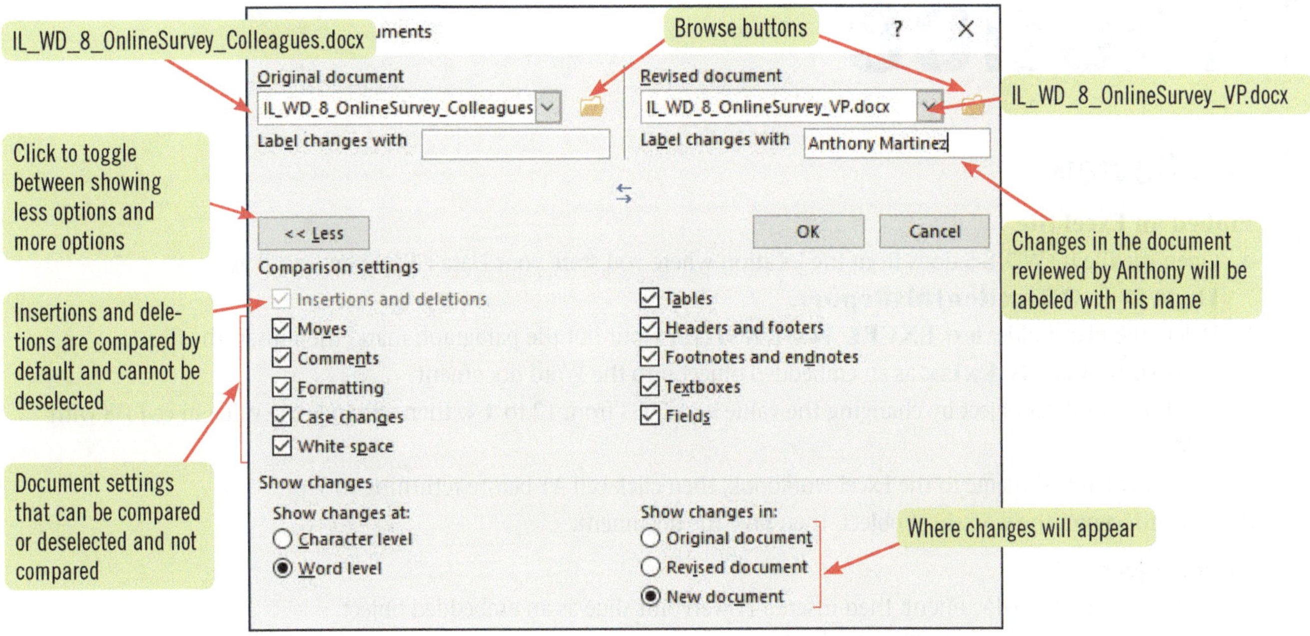

FIGURE 8-26: Comparing documents

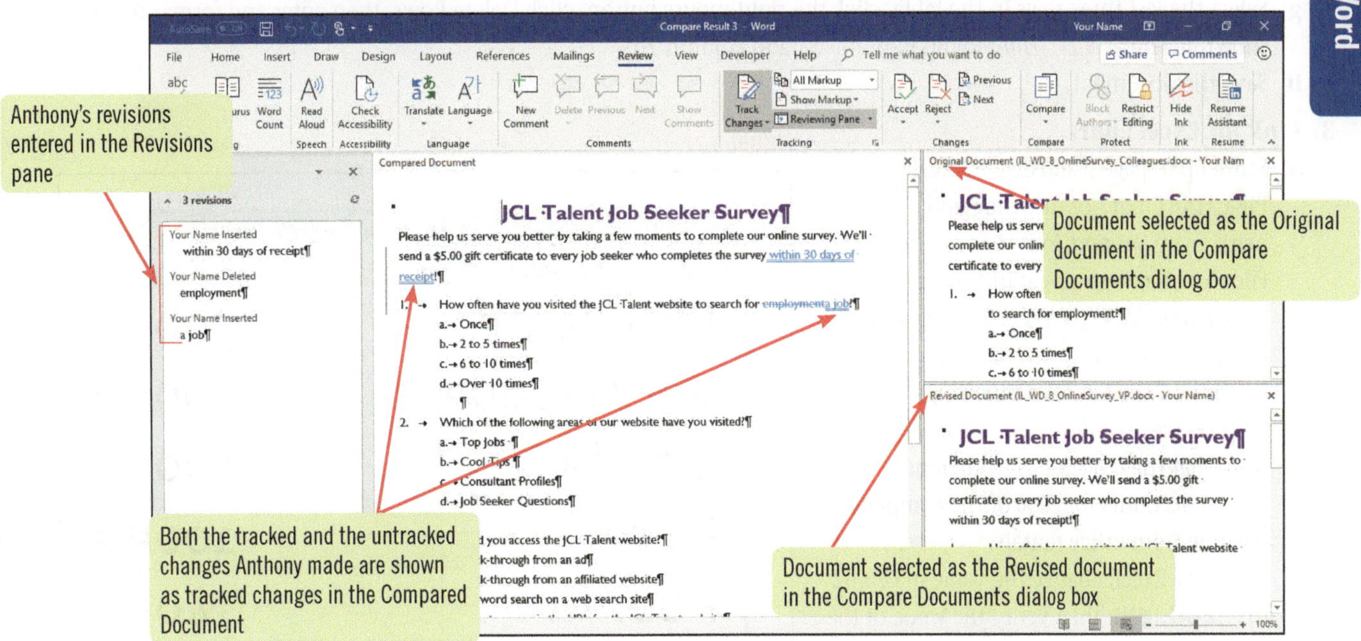

Practice

Skills Review

1. **Embed an Excel file**
   - **a.** Open the file IL_WD_8-5.docx from the location where you store your Data Files, then save it as **IL_WD_8_OfficeRentalsReport**.
   - **b.** Delete the placeholder text **EXCEL WORKSHEET** but not the paragraph mark, then insert the file **Support_WD_8-4.xlsx** as an embedded object into the Word document.
   - **c.** Edit the worksheet object by changing the value in cell C3 from 12 to **14**, then enhance the value in cell D8 with bold.
   - **d.** Apply the Banded theme to the Excel workbook, then click cell A1 before returning to Word.
   - **e.** In Word, center the worksheet object, then save the document.
2. **Insert objects**
   - **a.** Go to the top of the document, then insert a PowerPoint slide as an embedded object.
   - **b.** Enter the text **Gleeson Office Solutions** as the slide title, then enter your name as the subtitle.
   - **c.** In PowerPoint, apply the Banded theme to the slide object, then return to Word.
   - **d.** Double-click the slide object, apply the black, blue and green variant (far right), click in the text below the slide object to return to Word, then click to the left of "Overview" and press ENTER to add a line break.
   - **e.** Reduce the height of the slide object to **2.5**", then center the slide object.
   - **f.** Scroll to page 4, select and delete QUICK TABLE but not the paragraph mark, then insert the Tabular List Quick Table.
   - **g.** Select the last three rows in the table, click the right mouse button, click Delete Rows, then enter and format the data shown in FIGURE 8-27. (*Hint*: Right-align the data in column 2.)
   - **h.** Save the document.
3. **Link an Excel chart**
   - **a.** Scroll up to page 2 and delete EXCEL PIE CHART, but not the paragraph mark, open Support_WD_8-5.xlsx from File Explorer, then save it in Excel as **Support_WD_8_OfficeRevenue**.
   - **b.** Copy the pie chart, then paste it in Word using the Keep Source Formatting & Link Data (F) paste option.
   - **c.** Note that the red slice for Individual Offices accounts for 22% of the company revenue from office rentals.
   - **d.** Return to Excel, change the value in cell B2 to **2,200,000**, then verify the value of the Individual Offices slice (33%).
   - **e.** Return to Word and verify that the red slice is now 33%.
   - **f.** Switch to Excel, then save and close the workbook.
   - **g.** In Word, change the width of the pie chart to **5.5**", then center the pie chart and save the document.

FIGURE 8-27

Rating¤	Responses¤	¤
Excellent¤	3500¤	¤
Very·Good¤	1100¤	¤
Good¤	400¤	¤
Fair¤	100¤	¤
Poor¤	40¤	¤

¶

Skills Review (continued)

4. Link a PowerPoint slide

a. Scroll to the next page and delete POWERPOINT SLIDE but not the paragraph mark, open **Support_WD_8-6.pptx** from File Explorer, then save it in PowerPoint as **Support_WD_8_OfficeDesign**.

b. Go to Slide Sorter view in PowerPoint, copy the slide, then paste it in Word as a link.

c. Return to PowerPoint, view the slide in Normal view, then delete the blue text box.

d. Switch to Word and update the linked slide to reflect the change.

e. Save the document, go to PowerPoint, then save and close the PowerPoint presentation.

5. Manage document links

a. In Word, right-click the linked slide, then edit the link to open the slide in PowerPoint.

b. Select the text "Open Concept Office", then change the fill color of the text to Lime, Accent 2, Lighter 80%.

c. Save and close the PowerPoint presentation.

d. Update the link in Word, then save the document.

e. Save the document again as **IL_WD_8_OfficeRentalsReport_Distribution**.

f. Go to the Links dialog from the File tab, then break the link to the PowerPoint slide.

g. Break the link to the Excel pie chart.

h. Exit Backstage view, then scroll up and apply Chart Style 1 to the pie chart.

i. Save the document.

6. Create charts

a. Scroll to page 4, use CTRL+C to copy the Ratings Quick Table, then delete CUSTOMER PIE CHART but not the paragraph mark following.

b. Insert a pie chart.

c. Click cell A1 in the Worksheet window, then use CTRL+V to paste the table data into the Excel worksheet.

d. Change the chart title to **Customer Evaluations**.

e. Add data labels at the Outside End position.

f. Delete the legend, insert a legend to the right of the pie chart, then close the worksheet.

g. Scroll up to page 3 and select COLUMN CHART, but not the paragraph mark, then insert a Clustered Column Chart (the default chart type).

h. Select the table above the chart, use CTRL+X to cut the table, then use CTRL+V to paste the table into cell A1 of the Excel worksheet. Double-click between each column to widen the columns to view the data.

i. Close the Excel worksheet, enter **Annual Revenue by Location** as the chart title, then save the document.

7. Format and edit charts

a. Scroll down to the Customer Evaluations pie chart, change the width to **4**" and the height to **3**", then center the chart.

b. Edit the chart data by changing 100 to **200** in cell B5.

c. Format the data labels to show percentages instead of values.

d. Apply the Style 12 chart style to the pie chart, then change the colors to Monochromatic Palette 3.

e. Change 100 to **200** in the table so it matches the chart.

f. Scroll up to the column chart.

g. Change the chart type to Bar.

h. Switch the rows and columns so the city names appear on the Vertical axis. *Hint:* If the Switch Row/Column button is grayed out, click Select Data to open the Select Data Source dialog box, then click Switch Row/Column.

i. Add an Axis Title to the Primary Horizontal Axis with the text **Revenue**.

j. Format the Primary Horizontal Axis to show increments of $150,000 in the Major text box.

k. Format the chart area with a Dark Gray, Text 1 border with a weight of 3 points.

l. Reduce the height of the chart to **2.7**" and the width to **5**", then center it. The chart should fit on page 3. If not, remove the paragraph mark on the previous page, then remove any extra paragraph marks so the report fits on four pages.

Skills Review (continued)

m. View the report so that all four pages fit in the document window, compare the completed report to **FIGURE 8-28**, then save and close the document.

FIGURE 8-28

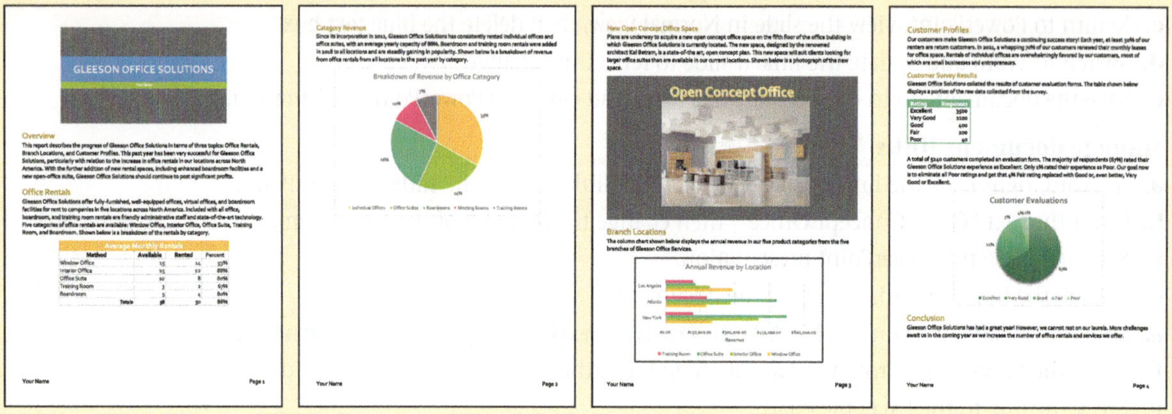

Zastolskiy Victor/Shutterstock.com

8. Track changes

a. Open the file IL_WD_8-6.docx from the location where you store your Data Files, save it as **IL_WD_8_CompanyDescription**, then turn on Track Changes from the Review tab.

b. Select All Markup if necessary, read the comment attached to "friendly" in the first paragraph, then select and delete friendly.

c. Type **welcoming**, adding a space after if necessary.

d. Scroll to the Company Background heading, cut the heading "Company Background" and the paragraph following, then paste it above the "Expansion Plans" heading.

e. Select the document title at the top of the document, decrease the font size to 28 pt, then change the font color to Aqua, Accent 1, Darker 50%.

f. Change the markup view to Simple Markup and show the comments.

g. Return to All Markup, then show the Revisions pane.

h. Close the Revisions pane, scroll to the Company Background paragraph, read the comment by Holly Stewart, delete "incorporated and" along with Holly's comment, then save the document.

9. Work with tracked changes

a. Open the Track Changes Options dialog box, show deletions as Double strikethrough, change the width of the balloon to 3", then exit the Track Changes Options dialog box.

b. Go to the beginning of the document, then use the buttons in the Changes group to go to the first change.

c. Accept the change to the title formatting, then accept the next three changes.

d. Reject the change from ten to fifteen so the number is again ten.

e. Accept all the remaining changes in the document, then delete all comments.

f. Save and close the document.

10. Manage reviewers

a. Open the file IL_WD_8-7.docx from the drive and folder where you store your Data Files, then save the document as **IL_WD_8_CompanyDescription_Colleagues**. This document includes changes made by Sara Ramos and Josef Lisowski to the document you just worked on.

b. Show No Markup in the Tracking group, then show All Markup.

c. Show all revisions inline, read the comment made by Sara in the first paragraph, then read the comment made by Josef.

d. Show revisions in balloons, then show only comments and formatting in balloons.

Skills Review (continued)

e. Show the list of people who worked on the document, then deselect the check box next to Josef Lisowski.
f. Change the user name to your name, if necessary.
g. Go to the beginning of the document, accept the formatting of the title, accept the insertion in the title, accept the deletion of the subtitle, then go to "modern" and change it to **up-to-date**.
h. Show the list of people who worked on the document again, select Josef Lisowski, then delete all the comments and accept all changes and stop tracking.
i. Type your name where indicated in the document footer, save the document, then close the document but do not exit Word.

11. Compare documents

a. Open the file IL_WD_8-8.docx from the drive and folder where you store your Data Files, type your name in the footer, then save the document as **IL_WD_8_CompanyDescription_Manager**.
b. In the last line of paragraph 1, Holly Stewart, the manager, changed "run" to "operate" before she turned on track changes. After she turned on track changes, she changed "facility" to "service" in the first line of the Company Background paragraph.
c. Close the document, then on the reviewing tab, click the Compare button to open the Compare Documents dialog box.
d. Open **IL_WD_8-CompanyDescription_Colleagues.docx** as the original document, then open **IL_WD_8_CompanyDescription_Manager.docx** as the revised document.
e. Type **Holly** in the Label changes with text box in the Revised document section if necessary.
f. Exit the Compare Documents dialog box, answering Yes when prompted, then show both source documents.
g. Review the information in the Revisions pane and in the split screen pane, close the Original document pane, close the Revised document pane, then close the Revisions pane.
h. Accept all the changes in the document, then save it as **IL_WD_8_CompanyDescription_Final**.
i. Return tracking options to the default settings: Underline for insertions and 3.7" for the balloon width.
j. The completed document with all changes incorporated appears as shown in FIGURE 8-29.
k. Submit all the documents you created in this Skills Review to your instructor, then close all open documents.

Word

FIGURE 8-29

Gleeson Office Solutions Company Description

Company Overview

Gleeson Office Solutions offers fully-furnished and well-equipped offices, meeting spaces, and training rooms for rent in five locations across North America: New York, Atlanta, Los Angeles, Chicago, and Toronto. Each location is conveniently located in the principal business district and provides welcoming administrative staff and up-to-date technology to help businesses operate smoothly and efficiently.

Company Background

Gleeson Office Solutions was launched in 2003 by Wendy Gleeson who saw a need for a service that provided local businesses with the opportunity to rent office space on a flexible schedule ranging from one hour to one year and beyond. Ms. Gleeson established her first office rentals in Los Angeles. In 2012, she expanded to New York and Chicago, and now manages five locations in the United States and one location in Canada. The company's focus on stellar customer service has won it a loyal clientele and several feature articles in prominent business magazines.

Expansion Plans

Ms. Gleeson is currently investigating opportunities to further expand Gleeson Office Solutions to ten more cities across North America. This plan will require a capital investment of $4.2 million to be repaid within two years.

Target Market

The company's principal competitors are Vista Offices with locations in twenty US cities and Offices For You with branches worldwide. Gleeson Office Solutions differentiates itself from its major competitors by its focus on superior customer service. No request is too small or too large and every office package is customized to each customer's unique needs. Gleeson Office Solutions will continue to build on its reputation for providing excellent personal service at competitive prices.

Independent Challenge 1

At Riverwalk Medical Clinic in Cambridge, Massachusetts, you've been asked to work on a summary of the clinic's charity work that includes results of a survey conducted of the clinic's many volunteers and a summary of the revenue generated through the clinic's charitable work. Almost all of the clinic's 340 volunteers (328 people) took the survey which was designed to collect data about volunteer ages, motivations, seasonal variations in volunteer hours, average hours worked, and the clinic programs in which they volunteered. You open the summary and complete it with objects inserted from Excel and PowerPoint, and charts you create in Word.

a. Start Word, open the file IL_WD_8-9.docx from the location where you store your Data Files, then save it as **IL_WD_8_GivingBackSummary**.

b. Insert an embedded PowerPoint slide above "Overview" at the top of the document that includes **Riverwalk Clinic Giving Back Summary** as the title and your name as the subtitle, then format the slide with the Savon theme and the green variant (third variant from the left).

c. Move "Overview" down one line.

d. Select and delete AGE PIE CHART but not the paragraph mark, then cut the table (contains Age Range and Number) and use the data to create a pie chart.

e. Edit the pie chart as follows: Enter **Age Range Distribution** as the chart title, apply the Style 5 chart style, change the colors to Monochromatic Palette 3, then add data labels that show percentages instead of values and with the labels in the Outside End position.

f. Change the position of the legend so it appears to the right of the pie chart, then enclose the pie chart in a black, 1 pt border.

g. Select and delete MOTIVATION TABLE but not the paragraph mark, then insert a Quick Table using the Tabular List format. Enter the data shown in FIGURE 8-30 into the table, change "Number of Volunteers" to **Volunteers**, right-align the data in column 2, then delete any unused rows.

h. Select and delete VOLUNTEER HOURS CHART but not the paragraph mark, open Support_WD_8-7.xlsx from File Explorer, then save it in Excel as **Support_WD_8_VolunteerHours**.

i. Copy the pie chart, then paste it in Word using the Keep Source Formatting & Link Data (F) paste option.

j. Note that the orange slice representing 21 to 30 Hours accounts for 37% of the volunteers who volunteer between 21 and 30 hours a month at the clinic. Return to Excel, change the value in cell B4 to **140**, then verify the value of the 21 to 30 hours slice (40%).

k. Return to Word and verify that the orange slice is now 40%. Change 37% to **40%** in the text above the chart.

l. Scroll to and select the table in the Seasonal Volunteering section, cut the table, then use the data to create a column chart.

m. Change the column chart to a bar chart, then switch the rows and columns.

n. Add **Number of Volunteers** as the horizontal axis title to the chart and change the chart title to **Volunteer Contributions by Season**.

o. Scroll to and delete POWERPOINT SLIDE, but not the paragraph mark, open Support_WD_8-8.pptx from File Explorer, then save it in PowerPoint as **Support_WD_8_Volunteer**.

p. Go to Slide Sorter view in PowerPoint, copy the slide, then paste it in Word as a link.

FIGURE 8-30

Reason	Number of Volunteers
To build skills & experience	102
To meet people	38
To have something to do	19
To contribute to the community	169

Independent Challenge 1 (continued)

q. In PowerPoint, delete the orange text box, then switch to Word and update the linked slide to reflect the change.

r. Delete the placeholder text CHARITIES WORKSHEET but not the paragraph mark, then insert the file **Support_WD_8-9.xlsx** as an embedded object into the Word document.

s. Edit the worksheet object by changing the value in cell C4 from 42 to **52**, apply the Savon theme to the Excel workbook, then click cell A1 before returning to Word.

t. Save the document.

u. Save the document again as **IL_WD_8_GivingBackSummary_Distribution**.

v. Open the Links dialog box, then break the link to the PowerPoint slide and the chart.

w. Scroll through the document, add a page break to the left of "Volunteer Hours" to move it to a new page, reduce the height of the "Volunteers" pie chart and the "Volunteer Contributions by Season" bar chart to 3.2", then move "Charity Work" to a new page.

x. View the five pages of the document in Multiple Pages view, compare it to FIGURE 8-31, then save the document, submit all files to your instructor, close the document, then exit Word.

FIGURE 8-31

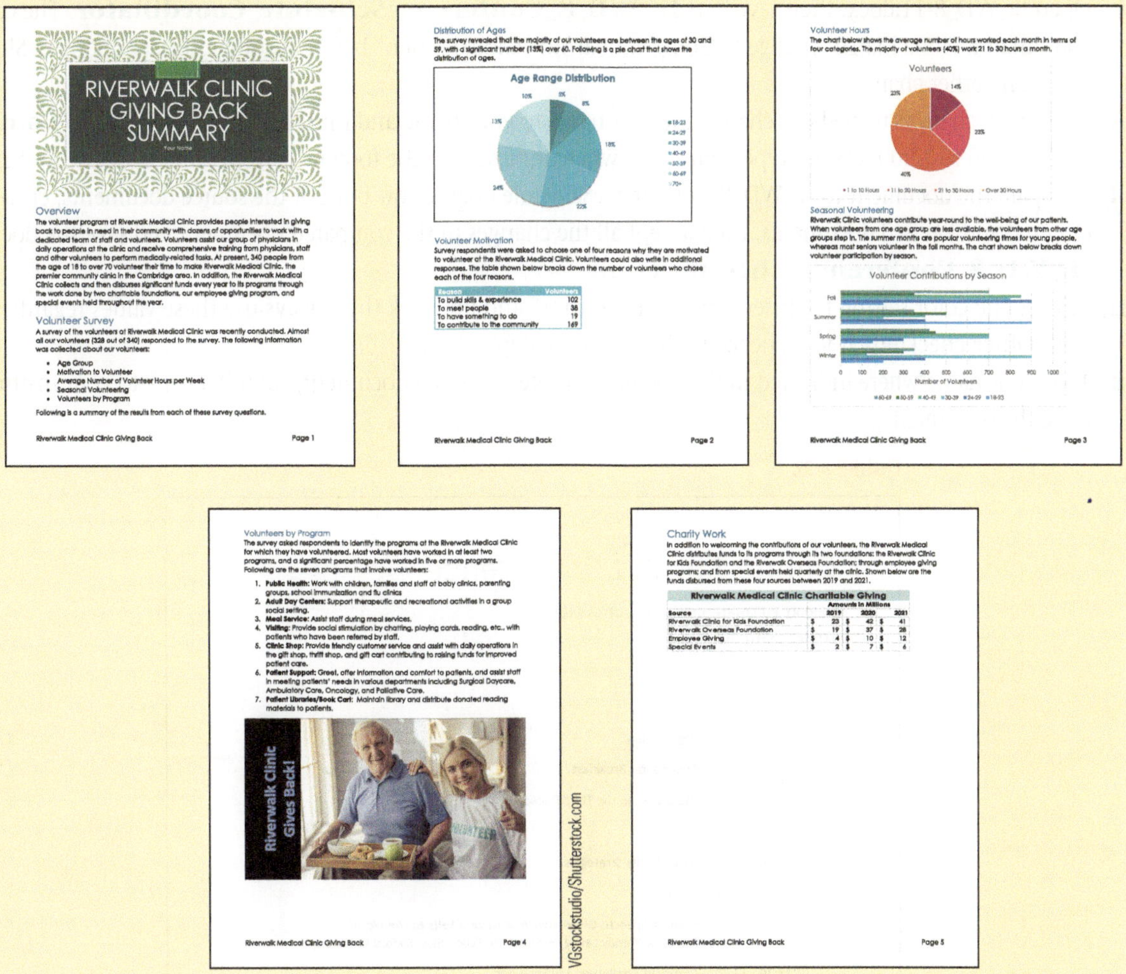

Word

Independent Challenge 2

You work for Online Solutions, a large application service provider based in Sydney, Australia. The company is sponsoring a conference called Online Results for local businesses and entrepreneurs interested in enhancing their online presence. Two of your coworkers have been working on a preliminary schedule for the conference. They ask for your input.

- **a.** Start Word, open the file IL_WD_8-10.docx from the drive and folder where you store your Data Files, then save it as **IL_WD_8_ConferenceSchedule**.
- **b.** Scroll through the document to read the comments and view the changes made by Mitzi Borland and Jake Haraki.
- **c.** Change the user name to your name and initials if necessary. (*Hint*: Add a check mark to the Always use these values regardless of sign in to Office check box if you checked this box when you completed the lessons.)
- **d.** Modify tracking options by changing the color of inserted text to Blue.
- **e.** In the 9:00 to 10:00 entry, select "E-Payment Systems: Trends to Watch", then insert a comment with the text **I suggest we change the name of this session to Micro-Cash in the Second Decade.**
- **f.** Be sure the Track Changes feature is active, then apply Bold to the two instances of "Break."
- **g.** Starting with the first comment, make all the suggested changes, including the change you suggested in your comment. Be sure to capitalize "continental" in Continental Breakfast.
- **h.** Accept all the changes, then delete all the comments in the document.
- **i.** Type your name where indicated in the footer, then save and close the document.
- **j.** Open IL_WD_8-11.docx, then save it as **IL_WD_8_ConferenceSchedule_Coordinator**. The conference coordinator, Fiona Marsh, changed "Going Global" to "Global Reach" before turning on track changes. She also made one other change.
- **k.** With track changes turned on, change the user name to your name and initials, change Someone to **Somebody** in the 16:00 to 17:00 session, type your name where indicated in the footer, then save and close the document.
- **l.** Compare the document to IL_WD_8-ConferenceSchedule.docx. Show both of the source documents, close the Original and Revised documents, then accept all the changes in the compared document and save the document as **IL_WD_8_ConferenceSchedule_Final**.
- **m.** Restore the color setting for Insertions to "By author" and uncheck the Always use these values regardless of sign in to Office check box if you checked it in an earlier step.
- **n.** Type your name where indicated in the document footer, save the document, submit a copy to your instructor, then close the document.

FIGURE 8-32

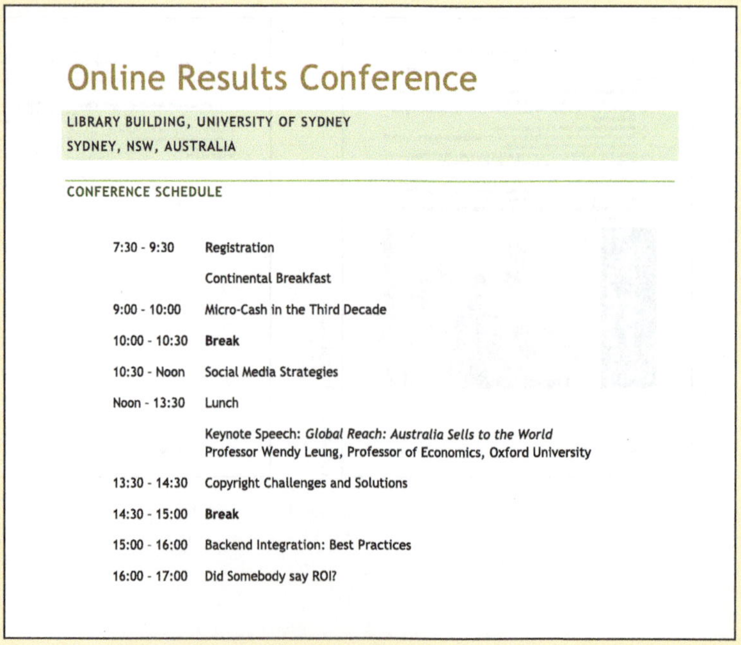

Online Results Conference

LIBRARY BUILDING, UNIVERSITY OF SYDNEY
SYDNEY, NSW, AUSTRALIA

CONFERENCE SCHEDULE

7:30 - 9:30	Registration
	Continental Breakfast
9:00 - 10:00	Micro-Cash in the Third Decade
10:00 - 10:30	**Break**
10:30 - Noon	Social Media Strategies
Noon - 13:30	Lunch
	Keynote Speech: *Global Reach: Australia Sells to the World* Professor Wendy Leung, Professor of Economics, Oxford University
13:30 - 14:30	Copyright Challenges and Solutions
14:30 - 15:00	**Break**
15:00 - 16:00	Backend Integration: Best Practices
16:00 - 17:00	Did Somebody say ROI?

Visual Workshop

Start a new document in Word, select the Celestial theme (or a different theme if the Celestial theme is not available), open the PowerPoint slide Support_WD_8-10.pptx, copy the slide, paste the slide as a Microsoft PowerPoint Object into Word (but *not* as a link), then edit the slide from Word to add your name to the subtitle. Below the slide in Word, add the text **The worksheet and pie chart shown below breaks down hours billed from September 1 to October 31 by our consulting engineers**. Embed the Excel worksheet from **Support_WD_8-11.xlsx**, then change the hours for Jorge Rosas to **82** and apply the Celestial theme (or the same theme you applied to the Word document). Below the worksheet object, create the pie chart using data from the worksheet. As shown in FIGURE 8-33, show the values as percentages with data labels positioned Outside End, then format the chart as shown. You'll need to modify the title, move the legend to the left, and apply Chart Style 12 and the Colorful Palette 2 color scheme. Change the hours for Carol Hughes to **90**. Add a 3 pt border with the color Blue, Accent 2, Darker 25%. Change the height of the chart to 3.2" and the width of the chart to 5.5". Save the document as **IL_WD_8_AtlantisAerospaceConsultants**, submit the file to your instructor, close the document, close the presentation in PowerPoint and the workbook in Excel, then exit all programs.

FIGURE 8-33

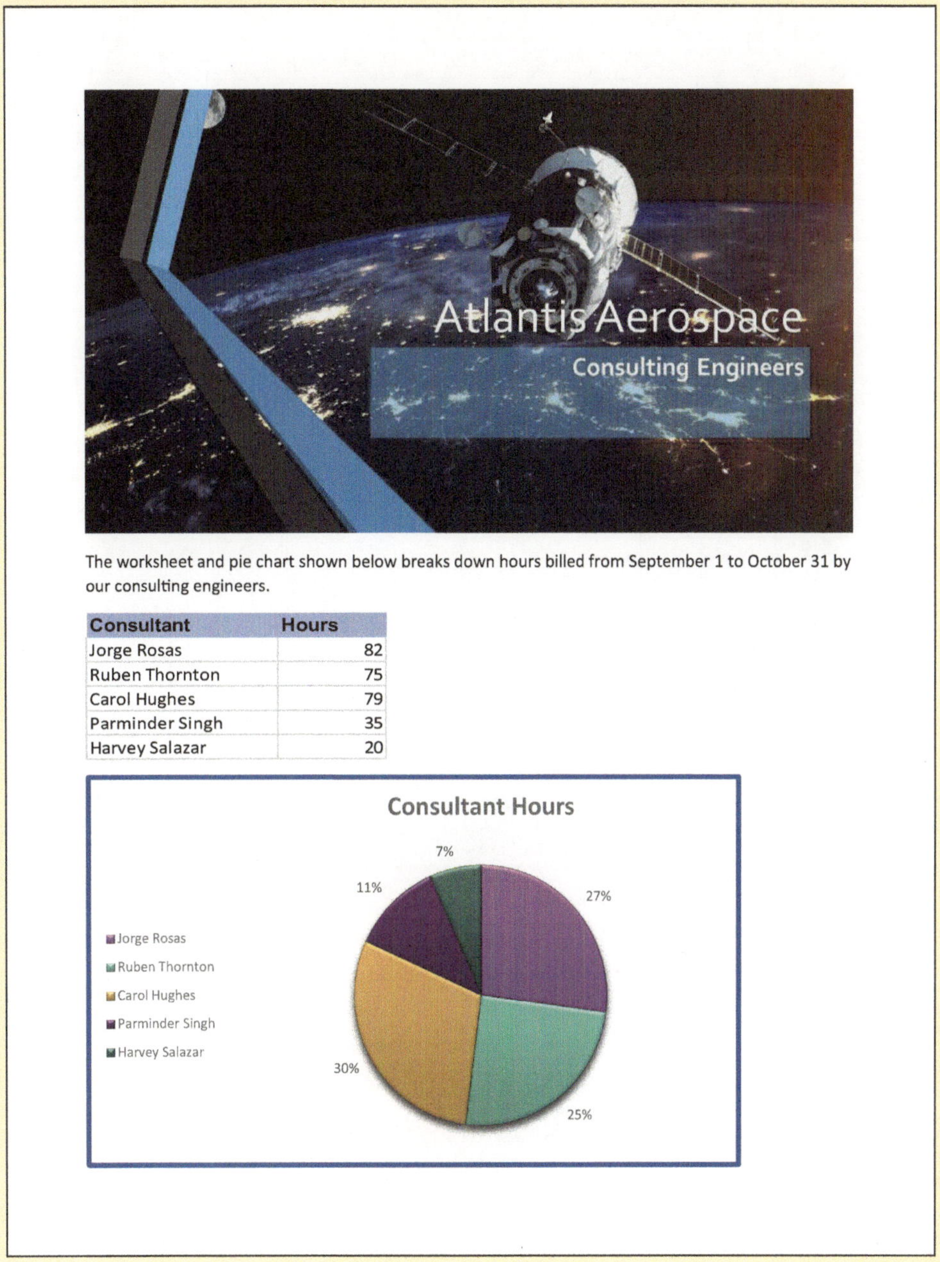

Word

Developing Multi-page Documents

CASE As an assistant to Anthony Martinez, the VP of sales & marketing at JCL Talent, Inc., you have been asked to edit and format a set of guidelines to help branch managers sponsor workshops for job seekers. You start by working in Outline view to revise the structure for the guidelines, and then you use several advanced Word features to format the document for publication.

Module Objectives

After completing this module, you will be able to:

- Build a document in Outline view
- Work in Outline view
- Navigate a document
- Create and modify screenshots
- Use advanced find and replace options
- Add and modify captions
- Insert a table of contents
- Mark text for an index
- Generate an index
- Insert footers in multiple sections
- Insert headers in multiple sections
- Finalize a multi-page document
- Work with equations
- Create Master documents and subdocuments

Files You Will Need

IL_WD_9-1.docx
Support_WD_9_WorkshopImages.docx
IL_WD_9-2.docx
Support_WD_9_InfoSessions.docx
IL_WD_9-3.docx
IL_WD_9-4.docx
Support_WD_9_CompanyImages.docx
IL_WD_9-5.docx
Support_WD_9_TopTalkPresenters.docx
IL_WD_9-6.docx
IL_WD_9-7.docx
Support_WD_9_MedicalInfoSessions.docx
IL_WD_9-8.docx
Support_WD_9_BusinessProgram.docx
Support_WD_9_CampusLife.docx
Support_WD_9_TheaterProgram.docx
IL_WD_9-9.docx
Support_WD_9_Banking.docx

Word
Module 9

Learning Outcomes
- Open Outline view
- Demote and promote headings

Build a Document in Outline View

You work in Outline view to organize the headings and subheadings that identify topics and subtopics in multi-page documents. In Outline view, each heading is assigned a level from 1 to 9, with Level 1 being the highest level and Level 9 being the lowest level. In addition, you can assign the Body Text level to each paragraph of text that appears below a document heading. Each level is formatted with one of Word's predefined styles. For example, Level 1 is formatted with the Heading 1 style, and the Body Text level is formatted with the Normal style. **CASE** *You work in Outline view to develop the structure of the workshop guidelines.*

STEPS

TROUBLE
If the headings do not appear blue and bold, click the Show Text Formatting check box in the Outline Tools group to select it.

QUICK TIP
Press TAB to move from a higher level to a lower level, and press SHIFT+TAB to move from a lower level to a higher level.

1. **Start Word, create a new blank document, click the Show/Hide button ¶ in the Paragraph group to show paragraph marks if necessary, click the View tab, then click the Outline button in the Views group**

   In Outline view, the Outlining tab is active. TABLE 9-1 describes the buttons on the Outlining tab.

2. **Type Workshops for Job Seekers**

   FIGURE 9-1 shows the text in Outline view. By default, the text appears at the left margin, is designated as Level 1 and is formatted with the Heading 1 style.

3. **Press ENTER, click the Demote button → in the Outline Tools group to move to Level 2, then type Workshop Requirements**

   The text is indented, designated as Level 2, and formatted with the Heading 2 style.

4. **Press ENTER, then click the Demote to Body Text button ⇒ in the Outline Tools group**

5. **Type the following text: Three activities relate to the organization of a job seeker workshop: gather personnel, advertise the event, and arrange the physical space.**

   The text is indented, designated as Body Text level, and formatted with the Normal style. Notice that both the Level 1 and Level 2 text are preceded by a plus symbol +. This symbol indicates that the heading includes subtext, which could be another subheading or a paragraph of body text.

6. **Press ENTER, then click the Promote to Heading 1 button « in the Outline Tools group**

   The insertion point returns to the left margin and the Level 1 position.

7. **Type Personnel, press ENTER, then save the document as IL_WD_9_JobSeekerWorkshopsOutline where you store your Data Files**

   When you create a long document, you often enter all the headings and subheadings first to establish the overall structure of your document.

8. **Use the Promote ←, Demote →, and Promote to Heading 1 « buttons to complete the outline shown in FIGURE 9-2**

9. **Place the insertion point after Workshops for Job Seekers at the top of the page, press ENTER, click ⇒, then type Prepared by followed by your name**

   In addition to Outline view, you can view a document in Draft view.

10. **Click the Close Outline View button in the Close group, click the View tab, click Draft view, then save and close the document**

FIGURE 9-1: Text in Outline view

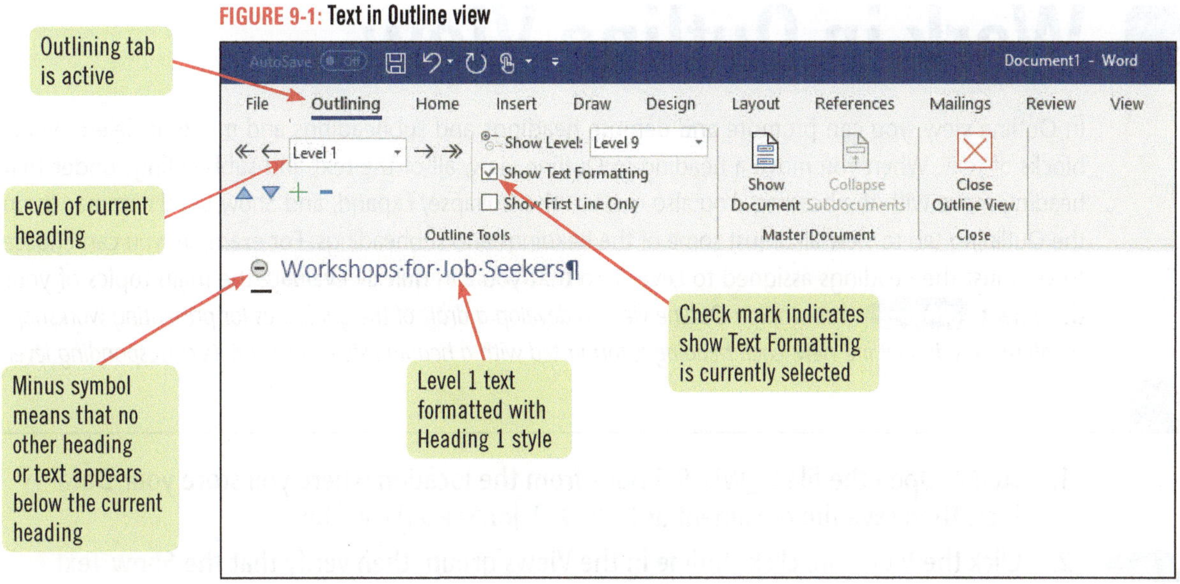

FIGURE 9-2: Completed outline

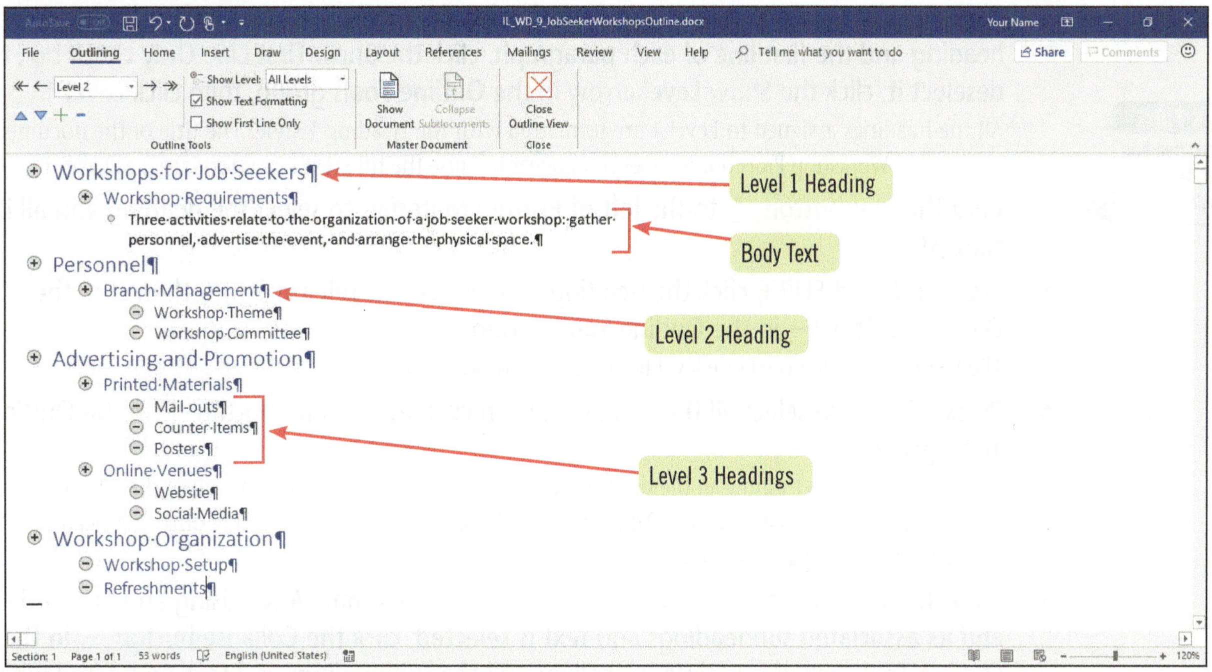

TABLE 9-1: Frequently used buttons in the Outline Tools group on the Outlining tab

button	use to	button	use to
↞	Promote text to Heading 1	▲	Move a heading and its text up one line
←	Promote text one level	▼	Move a heading and its text down one line
→	Demote text one level	+	Expand text
↠	Demote to body text	−	Collapse text

Word Module 9

Work in Outline View

Learning Outcomes
- Collapse/expand headings in Outline view
- Move headings and show levels

In Outline view, you can promote and demote headings and subheadings and move or delete whole blocks of text. When you move a heading in Outline view, all of the text and subheadings under that heading move with the heading. You also can use the Collapse, Expand, and Show Level commands on the Outlining tab to view all or just some of the headings and subheadings. For example, you can choose to view just the headings assigned to Level 1 so that you can quickly evaluate the main topics of your document. CASE *You work in Outline view to develop a draft of the guidelines for presenting workshops to job seekers. In Outline view, each heading is formatted with a heading style based on its corresponding level.*

STEPS

1. **sam Open the file IL_WD_9-1.docx from the location where you store your Data Files, then save the document as IL_WD_9_JobSeekerWorkshops**
2. **Click the View tab, click Outline in the Views group, then verify that the Show Text Formatting text box is selected**
   The document changes to Outline view, and the Outlining tab opens.
3. **Click the Show First Line Only text box to select it, scroll to view every heading and subheading and the first line of each paragraph, click the Show First Line Only check box to deselect it, click the Show Level arrow in the Outline Tools group, then click Level 1**
   All the headings assigned to Level 1 are formatted with the Heading 1 style. The title of the document "Job Seeker Workshop Procedures" does not appear because the title text is not formatted as Level 1.
4. **Click the Plus button ⊕ to the left of Printed Materials to select the heading and all its subtext**
5. **Press and hold SHIFT, click the heading Online Venues, release SHIFT, then click the Demote button → in the Outline Tools group**
   The headings are demoted one level to Level 2, as shown in FIGURE 9-3.
6. **Press CTRL+A to select all the headings, then click the Expand button + in the Outline Tools group**
   The outline expands to show all the subheadings and body text associated with each of the selected headings along with the document title. You can expand a single heading by selecting only that heading and then clicking the Expand button.
7. **Click the Advertising and Promotion plus button ⊕ so only Advertising and Promotion and its associated subheadings and text is selected, click the Collapse button − in the Outline Tools group two times to collapse all the subheadings and text associated with each subheading, click the Personnel ⊕, then click the Collapse button −**
8. **Click the Move Up button ▲ in the Outline Tools group once, then click the Personnel ⊕ three times**
   When you move a heading in Outline view, all subheadings and their associated text also move.
9. **Click the Show Level arrow, select Level 3, double-click the Printed Materials ⊕, click the Counter Items ⊕, press DELETE, then compare the revised outline to FIGURE 9-4**
10. **Click the Close Outline View button in the Close group, then save the document**

QUICK TIP
The pictures and the pie chart are not visible in Outline view.

QUICK TIP
The selected heading will be gray to indicate it is selected.

QUICK TIP
A horizontal line appears when you drag the mouse pointer up or down to a new location in the outline.

FIGURE 9-3: Headings demoted to Level 2

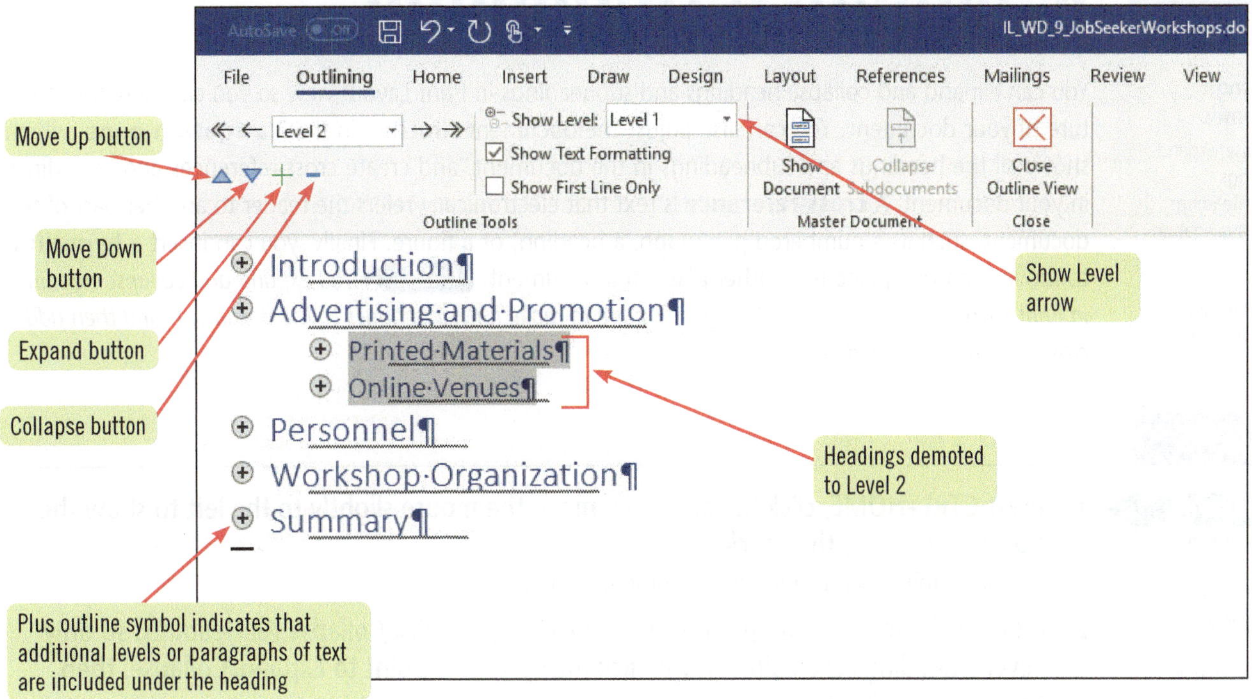

FIGURE 9-4: Revised outline

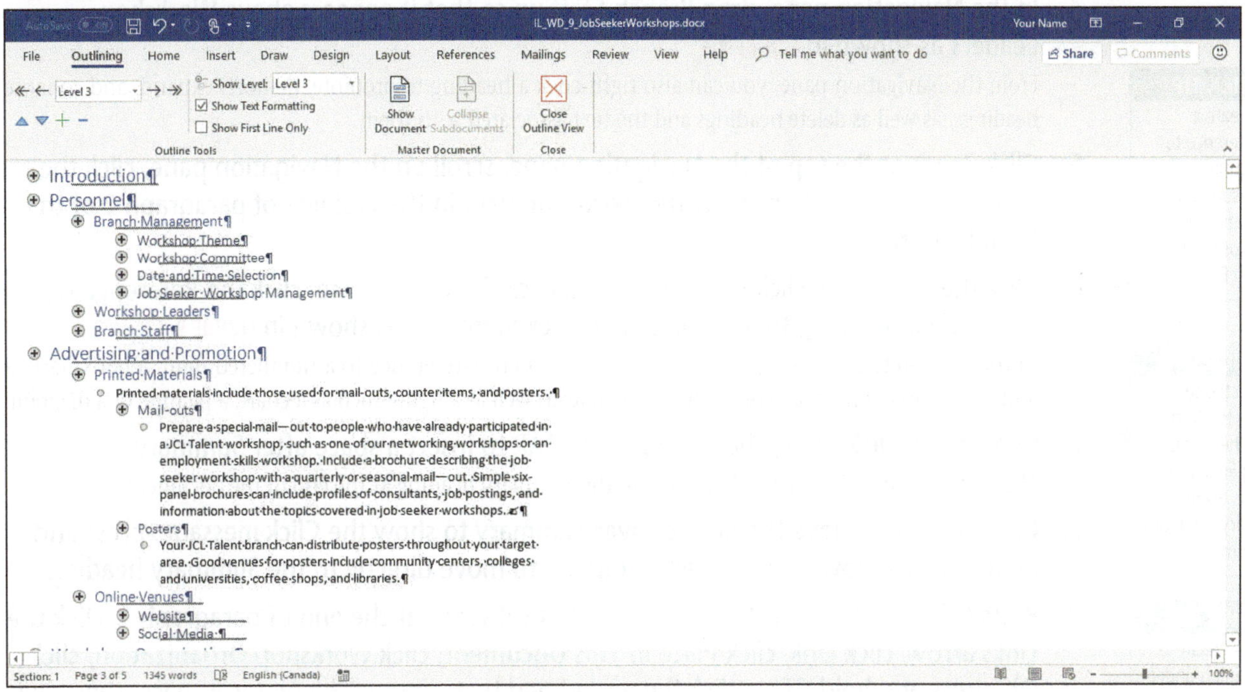

Word

Navigate a Document

Learning Outcomes
- Collapse/expand headings
- Move headings in the Navigation pane
- Create a hyperlink and cross-reference

You can expand and collapse headings and subheadings in Print Layout view so you can view the structure of your document. You can also adjust the document structure in the **Navigation pane**, which shows all the headings and subheadings in the document, and create cross-references and hyperlinks in your document. A **cross-reference** is text that electronically refers the reader to another part of the document, such as a numbered paragraph, a heading, or a figure. Finally, you can insert a **hyperlink** to move from one place to another place in a document. CASE *You expand and collapse headings in Print Layout view, work in the Navigation pane to make further changes to the document, and then add a cross-reference to a heading.*

STEPS

QUICK TIP
You can click the Expand arrow ▷ to expand the heading again so you can read the text associated with that heading.

1. **Press CTRL+HOME, click Introduction, move the mouse slightly to the left to show the Collapse icon ◢, then click ◢**
   The paragraph under the Introduction heading is hidden.
2. **Right-click Introduction, point to Expand/Collapse, click Collapse All Headings so only Level 1 headings are visible, right-click Introduction, point to Expand/Collapse, then click Expand All Headings**
   All headings and their associated text are visible again.
3. **Click the View tab, click the Navigation Pane check box in the Show group, click Headings at the top of the Navigation pane if it is not already selected, then click Branch Staff in the Navigation pane**
   The Branch Staff subheading is selected in the Navigation pane, and the insertion point moves to the Branch Staff subheading in the document.
4. **In the Navigation pane, drag Branch Staff up so that it appears above Workshop Leaders as shown in FIGURE 9-5**
   From the Navigation pane, you can also right-click a heading to promote, demote, expand, and collapse headings, as well as delete headings and the text associated with them.

QUICK TIP
If you create a cross-reference to an equation, you must ensure that the equation was created using the Equation Editor.

5. **Click Pages at the top of the Navigation pane, scroll up the Navigation pane, click the page 1 thumbnail, then select the word summary in the first line of paragraph 2 of the Introduction**
6. **Click the Insert tab, click the Links arrow, click Cross-reference, click the Reference type arrow, click Heading, then scroll to and click Summary as shown in FIGURE 9-6**
   In the Cross-reference dialog box, you can create a cross-reference to a numbered item, a bookmark, a footnote or an endnote, an equation, and a table, as well as a figure such as a chart, a picture, or a diagram.

QUICK TIP
The selected text takes on the formatting of the text it is being linked to, so in this example "summary" changes to "Summary".

7. **Click Insert, click Close, then press SPACEBAR to insert a space after Summary**
   The word "Summary" is now a hyperlink to the Summary heading at the end of the document.
8. **Click Summary, move the pointer over Summary to show the Click message, press and hold CTRL to show 👆, then click Summary to move directly to the Summary heading**

QUICK TIP
Text you specify as a hyperlink is underlined and shown in a different color.

9. **Press CTRL+HOME, select arrange the physical space at the end of paragraph 1, click the Links arrow, click Link, click Place in This Document, click Workshop Organization, click OK, press and hold CTRL, click the underlined text arrange the physical space, then save the document**
   The insertion point goes directly to the "Workshop Organization" heading in the document.

FIGURE 9-5: Changing the order of a subheading in the Navigation pane

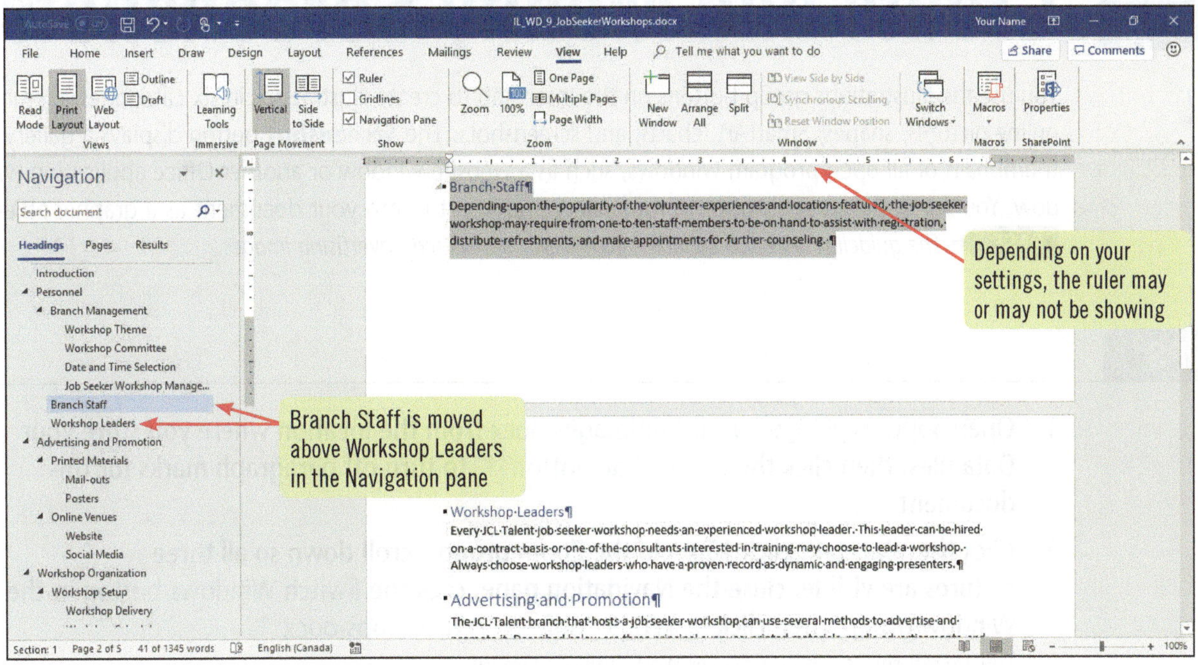

FIGURE 9-6: Cross-reference dialog box

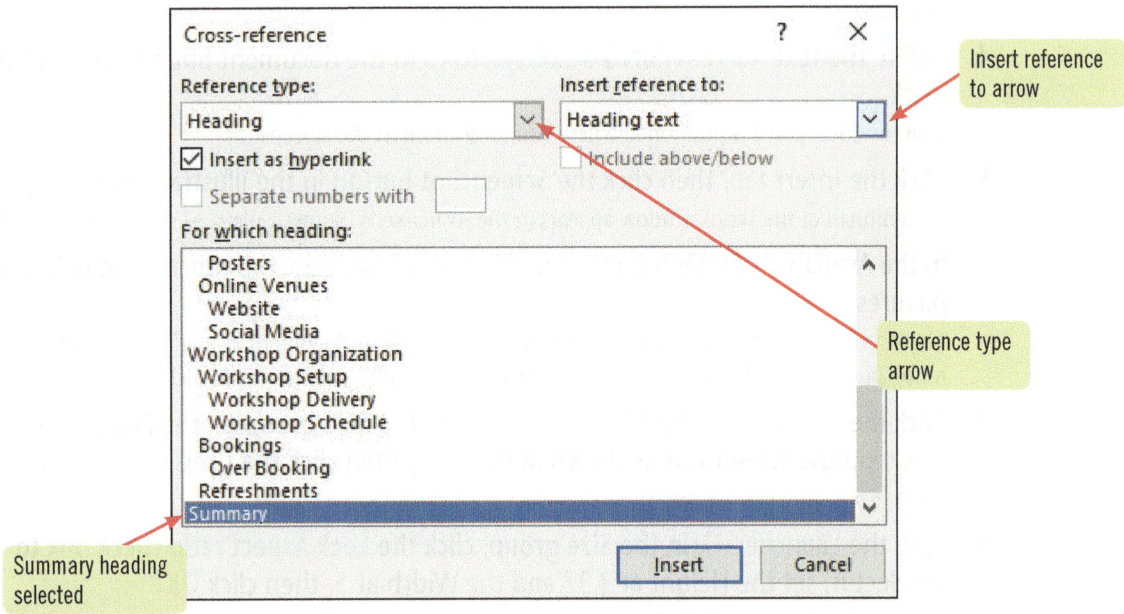

Using bookmarks

A **bookmark** identifies a location or a selection of text in a document. To create a bookmark, you first move the insertion point to the location in the text that you want to reference. This location can be a word, the beginning of a paragraph, or a heading. Click the Insert tab, then click Bookmark in the Links group to open the Bookmark dialog box. In this dialog box, you type a name (which cannot contain spaces) for the bookmark, then click Add. To find a bookmark, press CTRL+G to open the Find and Replace dialog box with the Go To tab active, click Bookmark in the Go to what list box, click the Enter bookmark name arrow to see the list of bookmarks in the document, select the bookmark you want to go to, click Go To, then close the Find and Replace dialog box. To delete a bookmark you no longer need, click Bookmark in the Links group, click the bookmark you want to remove, then click Delete in the Bookmark dialog box. You can also create a hyperlink to a bookmark. Click the Insert tab, click Link, click Place in This Document, click Bookmarks, click the bookmark you want the hyperlink to go to, then click OK.

Word
Module 9

Create and Modify Screenshots

Learning Outcome
• Insert a screenshot

You use the Illustrations group buttons on the Insert tab to create illustrations in six categories: pictures, online pictures, shapes, SmartArt, charts, and screenshots. The **Screenshot** button displays a gallery of thumbnails of all open program windows, such as a website window or another Office application window. You select the screenshot from the gallery and insert it into your document as a graphic object. CASE *The guidelines need to include a screenshot of selected advertising images.*

STEPS

1. **Open Support_WD_9_WorkshopImages.docx from the location where you store your Data files, then click the Show/Hide button ¶ to turn off paragraph marks for this document**
2. **Click the View tab, click 100% in the Zoom group, scroll down so all three pictures are visible, close the Navigation pane, click the Switch Windows button in the Window group, then click IL_WD_9_JobSeekerWorkshops.docx**
   You are returned to the Job Seeker Workshops document.
3. **Click Headings in the Navigation pane, then click the Advertising and Promotion heading**
4. **Delete the text ADVERTISING SCREENSHOTS in the document but not the paragraph mark**
   Your insertion point is positioned where you want to insert the screenshot.
5. **Click the Insert tab, then click the Screenshot button in the Illustrations group**
   A thumbnail of the Word window appears in the Available Windows gallery, as shown in FIGURE 9-7.
6. **In the Available Windows gallery, click the Word window thumbnail containing the pictures**
   The screenshot of the Word window is inserted in the Word document as a graphic object. You can crop, resize, position, and format the object just as you would any graphic object, such as a picture or a chart.
7. **Click the screenshot, click the Crop button in the Size group on the Picture Tools Format tab, crop the screenshot as shown in FIGURE 9-8, then click the Crop button to set the crop**
8. **Click the Launcher in the Size group, click the Lock Aspect ratio check box to deselect it, set the Height at 3.37 and the Width at 5, then click OK**
9. **Click the Picture Border button in the Picture Styles group, click the Black, Text 1 color box, click the Home tab, click the Center button in the Paragraph group, click away from the screenshot to deselect it, then continue to the next lesson to add a screen clipping**

FIGURE 9-7: Thumbnail of a window available for screenshot

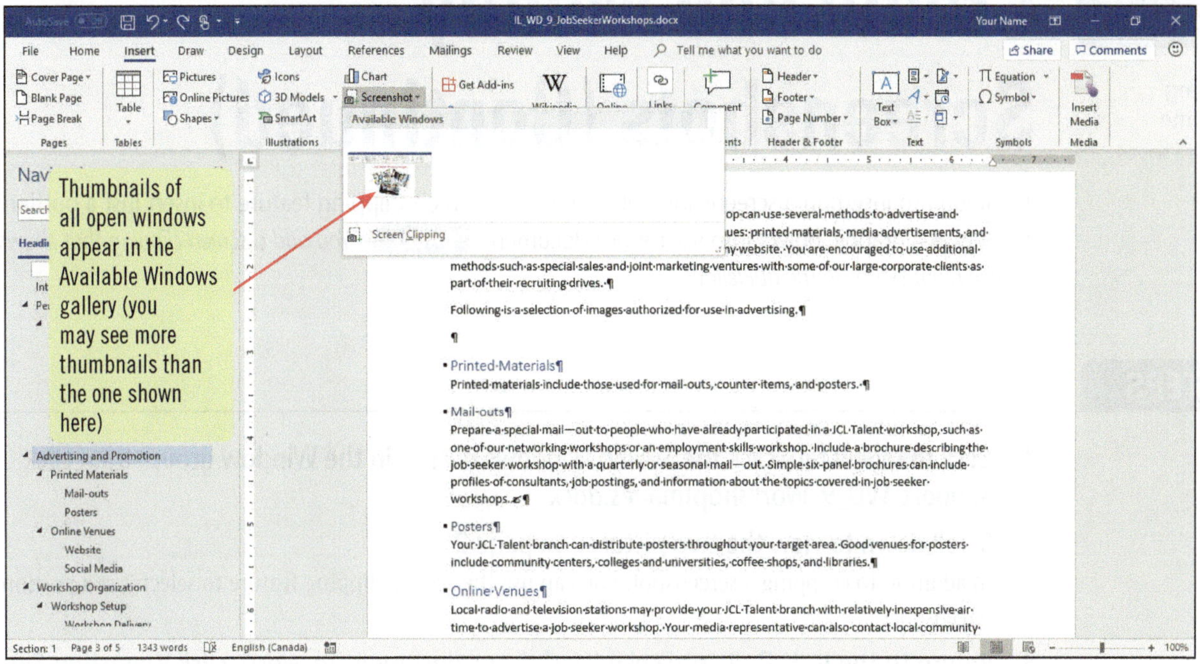

FIGURE 9-8: Screenshot cropped

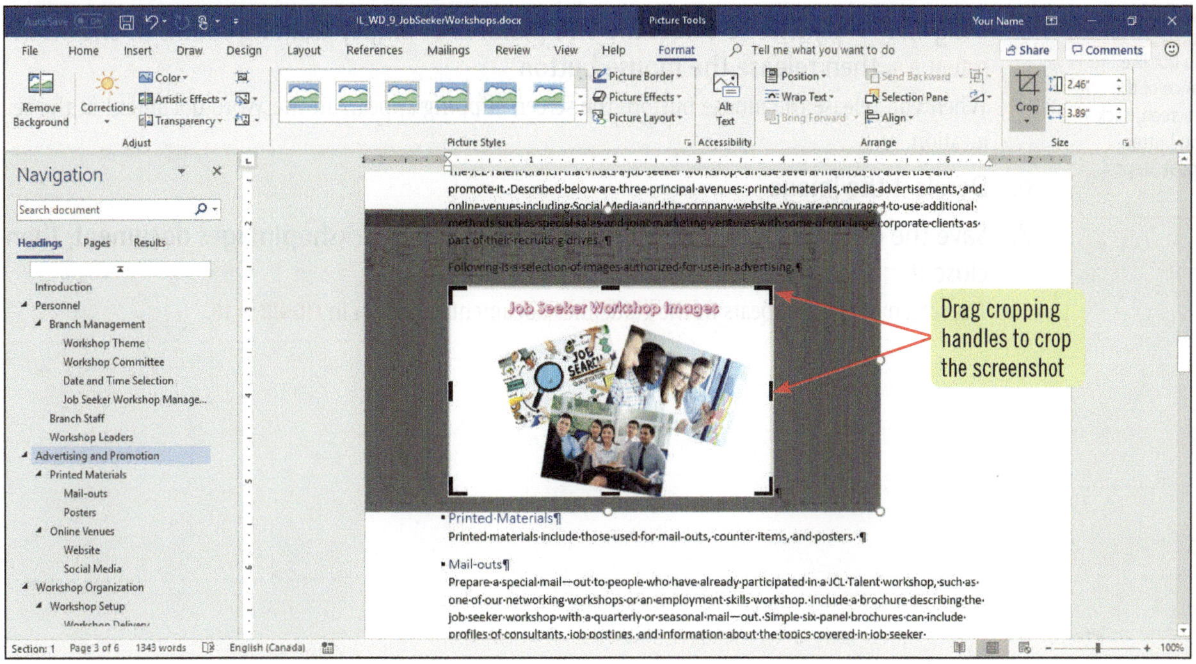

Word

tsyhun/Shutterstock.com; Rawpixel.com/Shutterstock.com; Dragon Images/Shutterstock.com

(Continued)

Word
Module 9

Learning Outcome
• Create a screen clipping

Create and Modify Screenshots (Continued)

In addition to inserting a screenshot, you can use the Screen Clipping feature to insert just a portion of a window as a graphic object into your Word document. **CASE** *You add a screen clipping that shows two sample room setups to the guidelines.*

STEPS

1. **Click the View tab, click the Switch Windows button in the Window group, then click Support_WD_9_WorkshopImages.docx**
2. **Scroll down to view the two pictures on page 2**
   In addition to cropping a screenshot, you can use the screen clipping feature to select just a portion of a screenshot.
3. **Return to the IL_WD_9_JobSeekerWorkshops document in Word, click Workshop Setup in the Navigation pane, then delete SETUP SCREENSHOT but not the paragraph mark**
4. **Click the Insert tab, click Screenshot in the Illustrations group, then click Screen Clipping**
   The Support_WD_9_WorkshopImages Word window fills the screen and is dimmed as shown in FIGURE 9-9.
5. **Drag the + pointer to select the two pictures of empty training rooms as shown in FIGURE 9-9, then release the mouse button**
   When you release the mouse button, the screen clipping appears in the Word document at the selected location.
6. **Deselect the image**
7. **Save the document, switch to the Support_WD_9_WorkshopImages document, then close it**
   The screen clipping appears in the guidelines document as shown in FIGURE 9-10.

TROUBLE
If you do not like the appearance of the clipped screen, click the Undo button, then repeat Steps 4 and 5.

FIGURE 9-9: **Selecting a screen clipping**

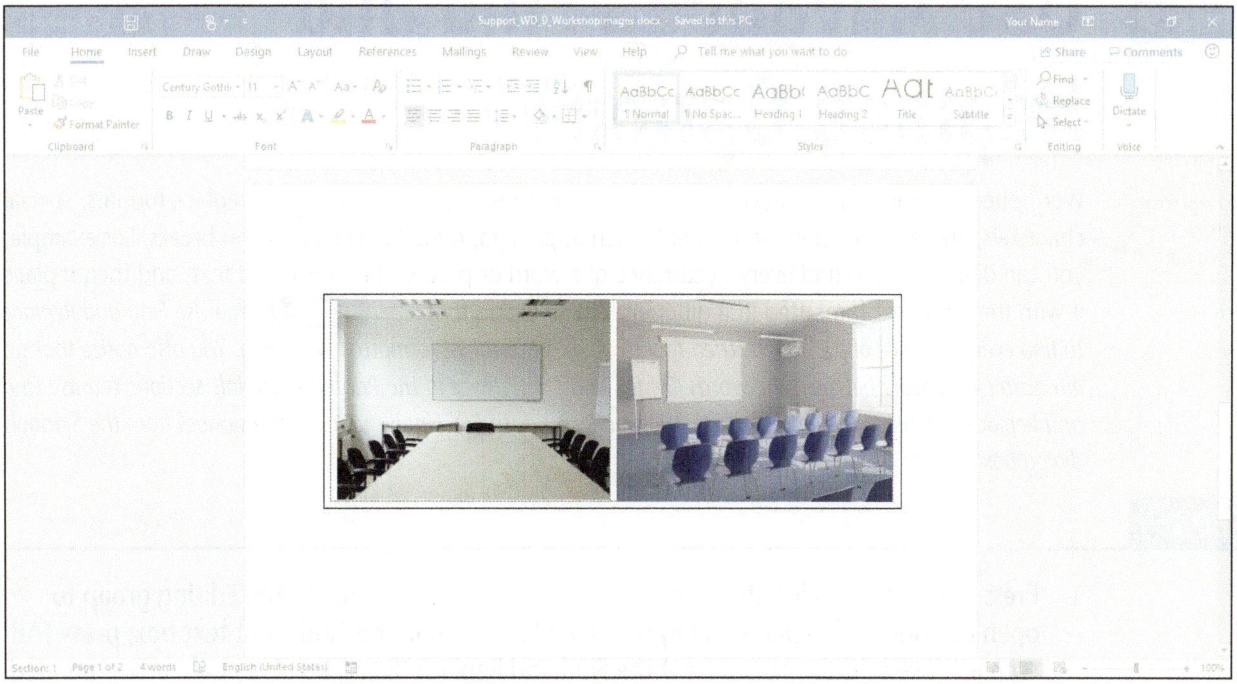

Robert Kneschke/Shutterstock.com

FIGURE 9-10: **Screen clipping inserted in the document**

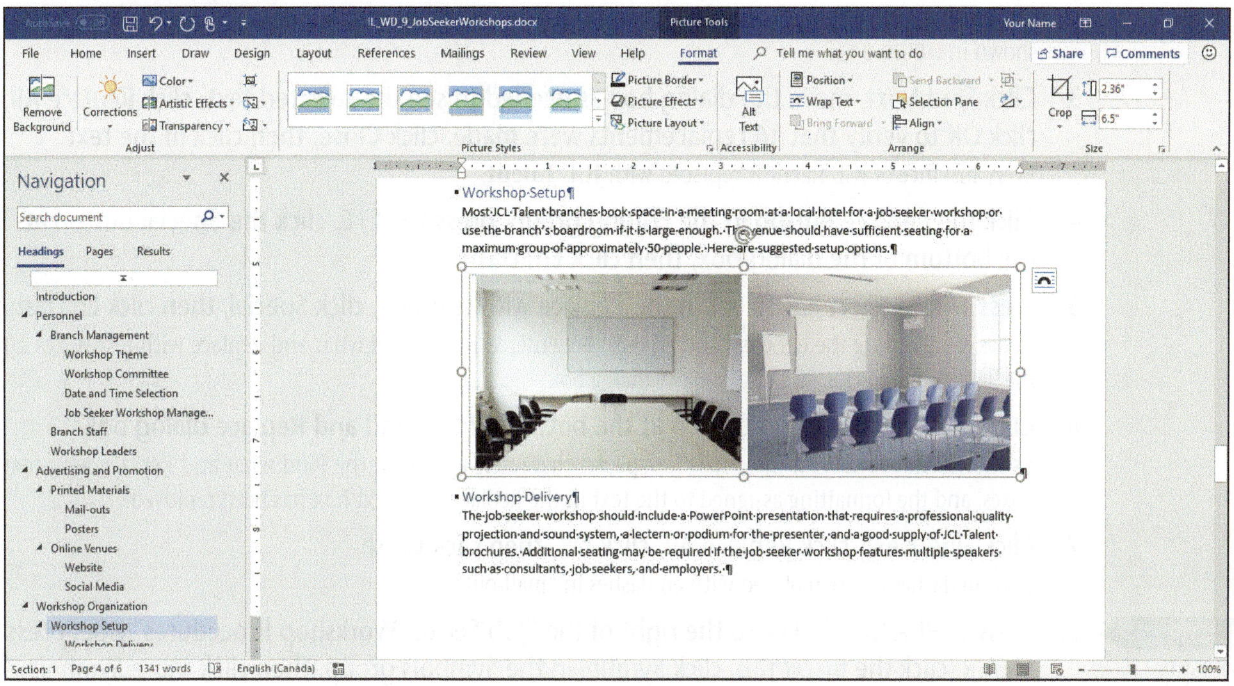

Robert Kneschke/Shutterstock.com

Word

Use Advanced Find and Replace Options

Learning Outcomes
- Find and replace formatting
- Find and replace special characters
- Insert a symbol

Word offers advanced find and replace options that allow you to search for and replace formats, special characters, and even nonprinting elements such as paragraph marks (¶) and section breaks. For example, you can direct Word to find every occurrence of a word or phrase of unformatted text, and then replace it with the same text formatted in a different font style and font size. **CASE** *You use Find and Replace to find every instance of JCL Talent, then replace it with JCL Talent formatted with bold. You also notice that an em dash (–) appears between the words "Mail" and "out" twice in the Printed Materials section. You use Find and Replace to replace the em dash with the smaller en dash (–). Finally, you insert a symbol from the Symbols dialog box into the document.*

STEPS

1. **Press CTRL+HOME, click the Home tab, click the Replace button in the Editing group to open the Find and Replace dialog box, type JCL Talent in the Find what text box, press TAB, type JCL Talent, then click More if the Find and Replace dialog box is not already expanded**
   The Find and Replace dialog box expands, and a selection of Search Options appears.
2. **Click the Format button at the bottom of the Find and Replace dialog box, click Font to open the Replace Font dialog box, click Bold in the Font style list, then click OK**
   The format settings for the replacement text "JCL Talent" appear in the Find and Replace dialog box, as shown in FIGURE 9-11.
3. **Click Find Next, move the dialog box as needed to see the selected text, click Replace All, click OK to verify that 16 replacements were made, click Close, then click in the text**
   Every instance of JCL Talent is replaced with **JCL Talent**.
4. **Click the Replace button in the Editing group, press DELETE, click the Special button at the bottom of the dialog box, then click Em Dash**
5. **Press TAB to select JCL Talent in the Replace with text box, click Special, then click En Dash**
   Codes representing the em dash and en dash are entered in the Find what and Replace with text boxes on the Replace tab in the Find and Replace dialog box.
6. **Click the No Formatting button at the bottom of the Find and Replace dialog box**
   As shown in FIGURE 9-12, the codes for special characters appear in the Find what and Replace with text boxes, and the formatting assigned to the text in the Replace with text box has been removed.
7. **Click Find Next, click Replace All, click OK, then click Close**
   Two em dashes (–) are replaced with en dashes in "mail-out".
8. **Press CTRL+HOME, click to the right of the "Job Seeker Workshop Procedures" title, press ENTER, click the Insert tab, click Symbol in the Symbols group, then click More Symbols**
   In the Symbols dialog box, you can select from hundreds of symbols in numerous fonts. Some of the symbols are like small pictures.
9. **Click the Font arrow, scroll the alphabetical list of fonts to Wingdings, click Wingdings, click the happy face symbol shown in FIGURE 9-13, click Insert, click Insert two more times, click Close, then save the document**
   Three happy face symbols are inserted below the document title.

QUICK TIP
Special characters are called symbols.

FIGURE 9-11: Find and Replace dialog box

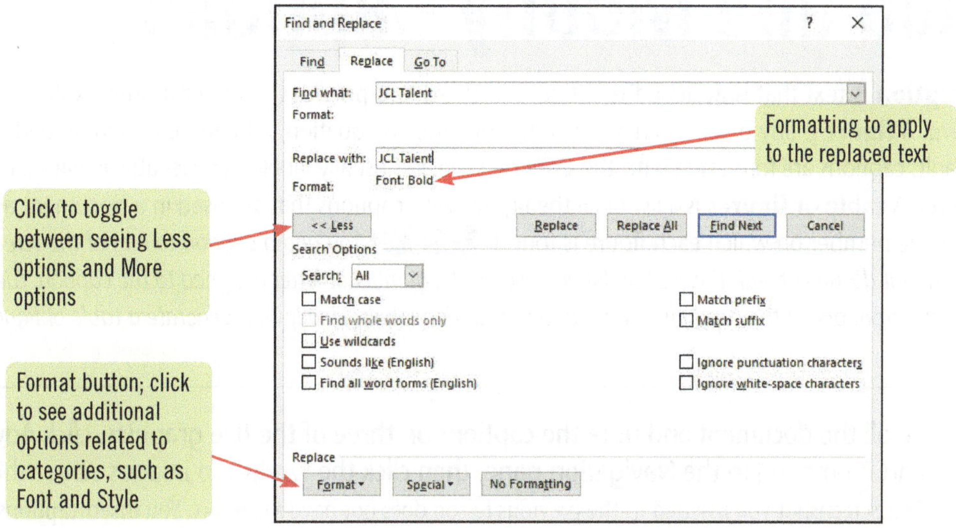

FIGURE 9-12: Find and Replace dialog box

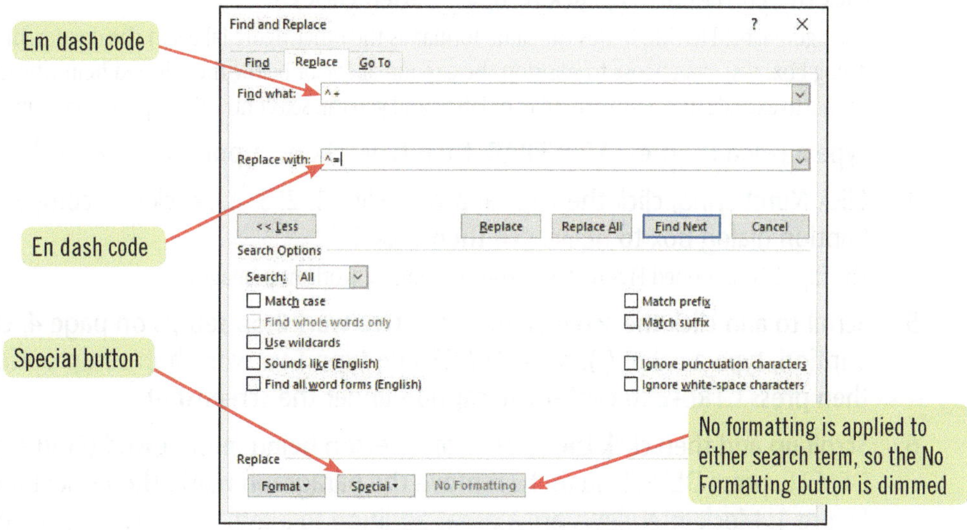

FIGURE 9-13: Symbol selected in the Symbol dialog box

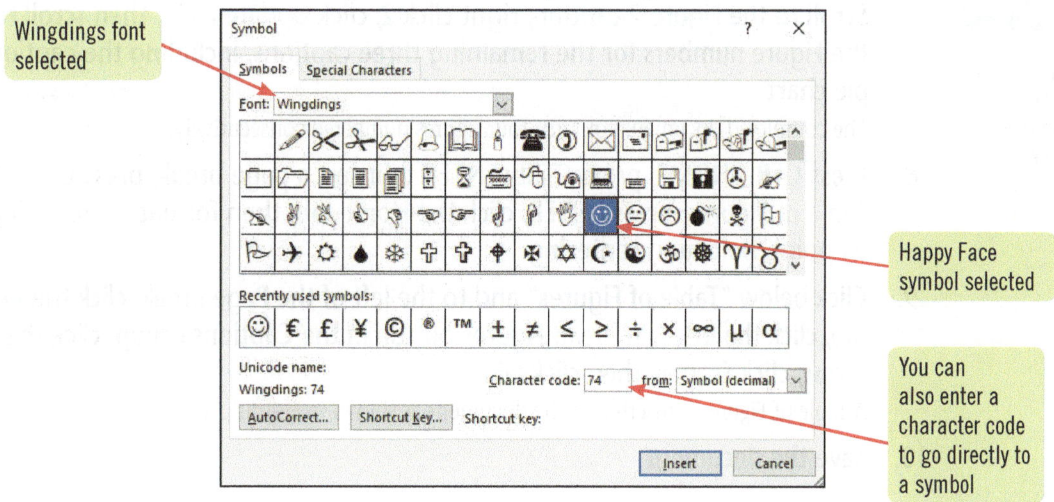

Add and Modify Captions

Learning Outcomes
- Insert and update captions
- Insert a table of figures

A **caption** is text that is attached to a figure in Word and provides a title or a brief explanation of the figure. A **figure** is any object such as a chart, a picture, an equation, a table, or an embedded object. By default, captions are formatted with the Caption style and usually labeled consecutively with a number or a letter. A **table of figures** is a list of all the figures with captions that are used in a document along with the page number on which each figure is found. **CASE** *You add a caption to one of the screenshots in the current document, edit the caption label, which is the number or letter assigned to the caption, then remove the label from one of the captions and update the caption labels. Finally, you generate a table of figures.*

STEPS

QUICK TIP
The figures are labeled using letters, FIGURE A, FIGURE B, and so on.

1. **Scroll the document and note the captions on three of the five graphics, click Advertising and Promotion in the Navigation pane, then click the workshop images screenshot**
   This screenshot you inserted in the previous lesson does not have a caption. You insert captions from the References tab.
2. **Click the References tab, click Insert Caption in the Captions group, click Numbering, click the Format arrow, click A, B, C,..., then click OK**
   The figure label FIGURE B uses the same format as the other figure labels in the document. In the Caption dialog box, you can choose to position the caption above or below the selected item (the default). You can choose to exclude the caption number or letter, and you can select how the captions are numbered or lettered.
3. **Type a colon (:), press SPACEBAR, then type Choose appropriate workshop images**
4. **Click Numbering, click the Format arrow, click 1, 2, 3, ... , click OK, compare the Caption dialog box to FIGURE 9-14, then click OK**
   The figure is captioned Figure 2: Choose appropriate workshop images.
5. **Scroll to and click the screenshot of the two workshop setups on page 4, click Insert Caption, type a colon (:), press SPACEBAR, type Two workshop setup options, click OK, then press CTRL+E to center the caption under the screenshot**
6. **Scroll up and then click the picture of a person being interviewed (Figure 1), press DELETE, press DELETE again to remove the paragraph mark, then select and delete Figure 1: Mock interviews are a great addition to a Job Seeker workshop and the extra blank line between the paragraphs**
   After you delete a caption, you need to update the numbering of the remaining captions.

QUICK TIP
Press F9 to update selected caption labels if your keyboard supports the F9 function key.

7. **Scroll to the Figure 2 caption, right click 2, click Update Field, then scroll to and update the Figure numbers for the remaining three captions, including the caption under the pie chart**
   The completed document contains four figures numbered consecutively.
8. **Press CTRL+HOME, press CTRL+ENTER to insert a page break, press CTRL+HOME, type Table of Figures, press ENTER, click the Home tab, then format Table of Figures using 24 point, bold, and centering**
9. **Click below "Table of Figures" and to the left of the Page Break, click the References tab, click the Insert Table of Figures button in the Captions group, click the Formats arrow, click Formal, then click OK**
   A Table of Figures is inserted in the document as shown in FIGURE 9-15.
10. **Save the document**

FIGURE 9-14: Caption dialog box

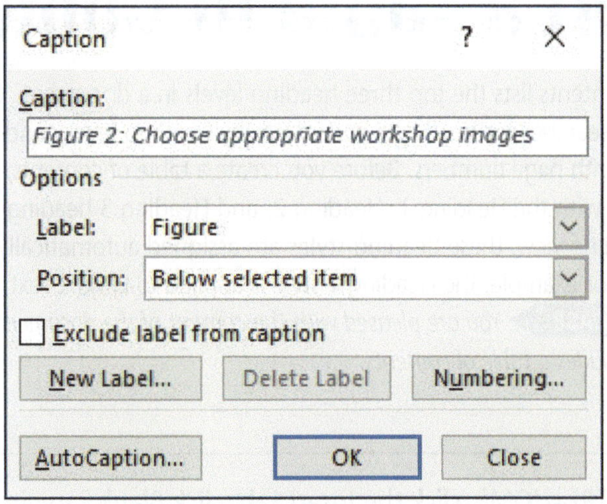

FIGURE 9-15: Table of figures

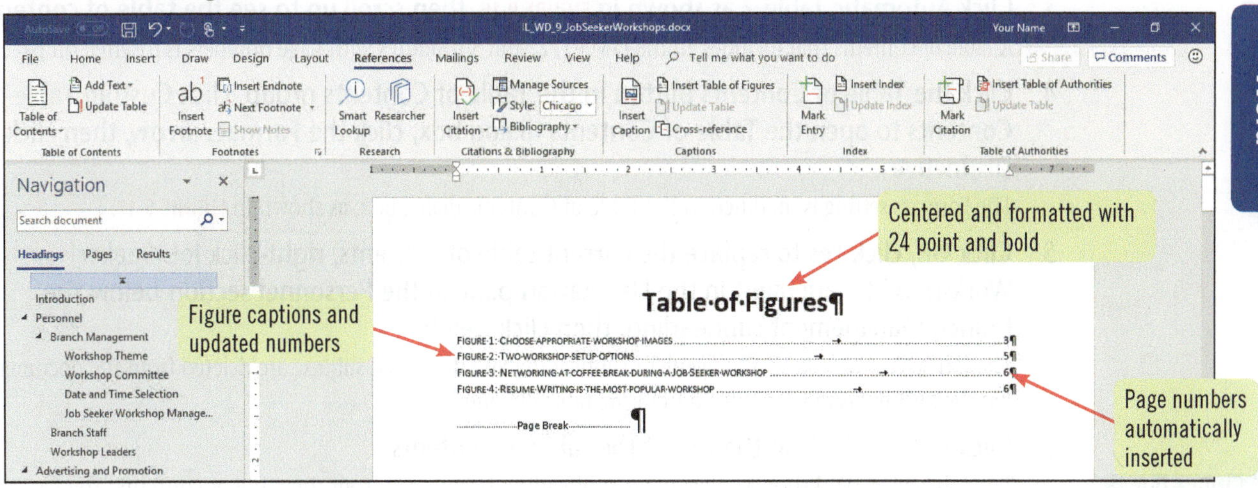

Table of Authorities

A table of authorities lists all the cases, statutes, rules, and other legal references included in a legal document, along with the page on which each reference appears. To create a table of authorities, click the References tab, go to the first reference (called a citation) that you wish to include in the table of authorities, then click the Mark Citation button in the Table of Authorities group. After you have marked all the citations in the document, click the Insert Table of Authorities button in the Table of Authorities group to build the table of authorities. Word organizes and then displays each citation you marked by category.

Insert a Table of Contents

Learning Outcomes
- Insert a table of contents
- Update a table of contents

A table of contents lists the top three heading levels in a document. When you generate a table of contents, Word searches for headings, sorts them by heading levels, and then displays the completed table of contents with page numbers. Before you create a table of contents, you must format the headings and subheadings with the Heading 1, Heading 2, and Heading 3 heading styles. When you organize a document in Outline view, these heading styles are assigned automatically to text based on the outline level of the text. For example, the Heading 1 style is applied to Level 1 text, the Heading 2 style to level 2 text, and so on. **CASE** *You are pleased with the content of the document and are now ready to create a new page that includes a table of contents.*

STEPS

1. **Press CTRL+HOME, click the Insert tab, click Blank Page in the Pages group, press CTRL+HOME, click the Home tab, then click the Clear All Formatting button in the Font group**
   The insertion point is positioned at the left margin where the table of contents will begin.
2. **Click the References tab, then click the Table of Contents button in the Table of Contents group**
   A gallery of predefined styles for a table of contents opens.
3. **Click Automatic Table 2 as shown in FIGURE 9-16, then scroll up to see the table of contents**
   A table of contents that includes all the Level 1, 2, and 3 headings with page numbers is inserted on page 1.
4. **Click the Table of Contents button in the Table of Contents group, click Custom Table of Contents to open the Table of Contents dialog box, click the Formats arrow, then click Distinctive**
   The Formats setting is modified in the Table of Contents dialog box, as shown in FIGURE 9-17.
5. **Click OK, click Yes to replace the current table of contents, right-click Job Seeker Workshop Management in the Navigation pane in the Personnel section below the Branch Management subheading, then click Delete**
   The Job Seeker Workshop Management subheading and its related subtext are deleted from the document, but the heading is not yet deleted from the table of contents.
6. **Click Update Table at the top of the table of contents**
   The Job Seeker Workshop Management subheading is removed from the table of contents. You can also change the appearance of the table of contents.
7. **Click the Table of Contents button in the Table of Contents group, click Custom Table of Contents, click the Tab leader arrow, click the dotted line tab leader style (top selection), click OK, click Yes, then scroll up to view "Table of Contents"**
   The Table of Contents is updated as shown in FIGURE 9-18.
8. **Move the pointer over the heading Online Venues in the Table of Contents, press and hold CTRL, then click Online Venues**
   The insertion point moves to the Online Venues heading in the document.
9. **Save the document**

QUICK TIP
To remove a table of contents, click the **table of contents** in the document, click the **References tab**, click the **Table of Contents button** in the Table of Contents group, then click **Remove Table of Contents**.

FIGURE 9-16: Inserting an automatic table of contents

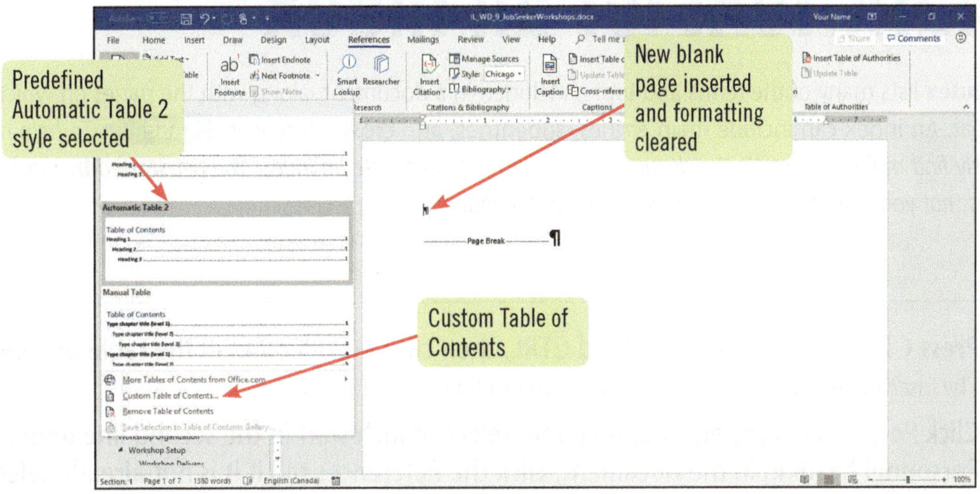

FIGURE 9-17: Table of Contents dialog box

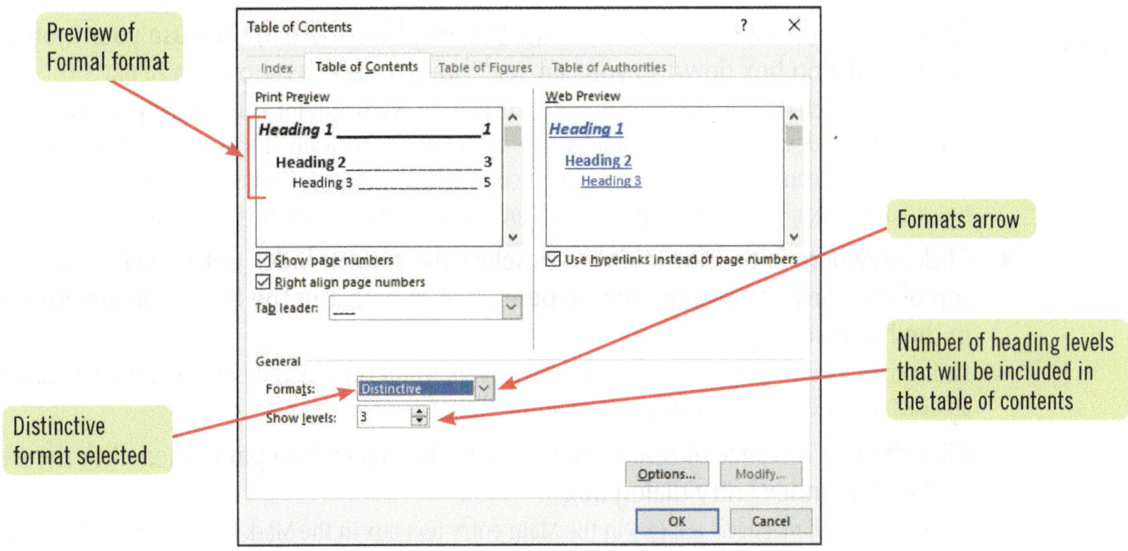

FIGURE 9-18: Formatted and updated table of contents

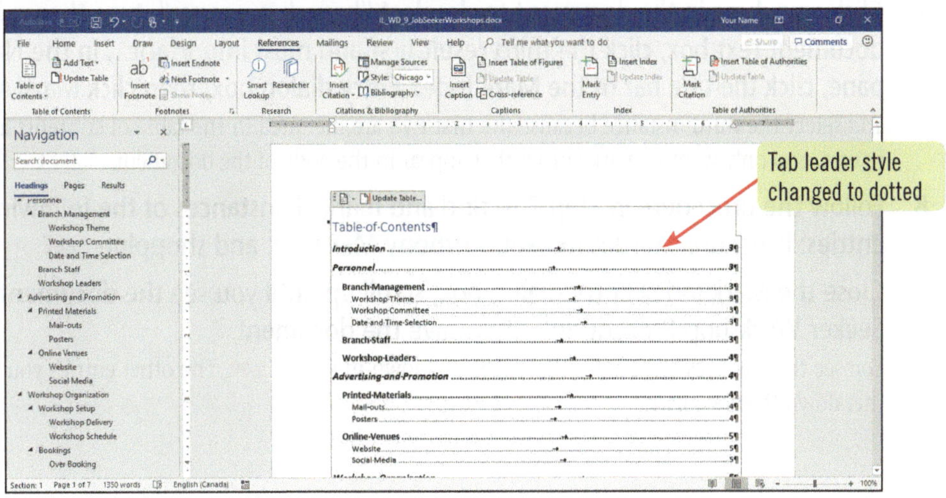

Mark Text for an Index

Learning Outcomes
- Mark index entries
- Search for text to index

An **index** lists many of the terms and topics included in a document, along with the pages on which they appear. An index can include main entries, subentries, and cross-references. **CASE** *To help readers quickly find main concepts in the document, you decide to generate an index. You get started by marking the terms that you want to include as main entries in the index.*

STEPS

1. **Press CTRL+HOME, press and hold CTRL, then click Introduction in the table of contents**
   The insertion point moves to the Introduction heading in the document.
2. **Click Personnel in the Navigation pane, select branch staff in the second line under the Personnel heading in the document, click the References tab if it is not already selected, then click the Mark Entry button in the Index group**
   The Mark Index Entry dialog box opens. By default, the selected text is entered in the Main entry text box and is treated as a main entry in the index.
3. **Click Mark All, click the Mark Index Entry dialog box title bar, then use your mouse to drag the dialog box down so you can see "branch staff" as shown in FIGURE 9-19**
   The term "branch staff" is marked with the XE field code. **XE** stands for **Index Entry**. When you mark an entry for the index, the paragraph marks are turned on automatically if they were not already on so that you can see hidden codes such as paragraph marks, field codes, page breaks, and section breaks. The Mark Index Entry dialog box remains open so that you can continue to mark text for inclusion in the index.

   QUICK TIP
   Hidden codes do not appear in the printed document.
4. **Click anywhere in the document to deselect the current index entry, click Results at the top of the Navigation pane, then type branch manager in the Search document text box in the Navigation pane**
   Each occurrence of the term "branch manager" is shown in context and in bold in the Navigation pane, and each occurrence is highlighted in the document.
5. **Click the first instance of branch manager in the Navigation pane, then click the title bar of the Mark Index Entry dialog box**
   The text "branch manager" appears in the Main entry text box in the Mark Index Entry dialog box.
6. **Click Mark All**
   All instances of "branch manager" in the document are marked for inclusion in the index.
7. **Click anywhere in the document to deselect "branch manager", type theme in the Search document text box, click the third result first and most important... in the Navigation pane, click the title bar of the Mark Index Entry dialog box, then click Mark All**
   You select the third instance because the first two are included in the table of contents and the table of figures. You only want to mark entries that appear in the body of the document.
8. **Follow the procedure in Step 7 to find and mark all instances of the following main entries: brochures, target market, Anthony Martinez, and shopping cart**

   QUICK TIP
   Make sure you click in the document to deselect the currently selected text before you enter another search term.
9. **Close the Mark Index Entry dialog box, scroll up until you see the document title "Job Seeker Workshop Procedures", then save the document**
   You see three entries marked for the index, as shown in FIGURE 9-20. The other entries you marked are further down the document.

FIGURE 9-19: Selected text in the Mark Index Entry dialog box

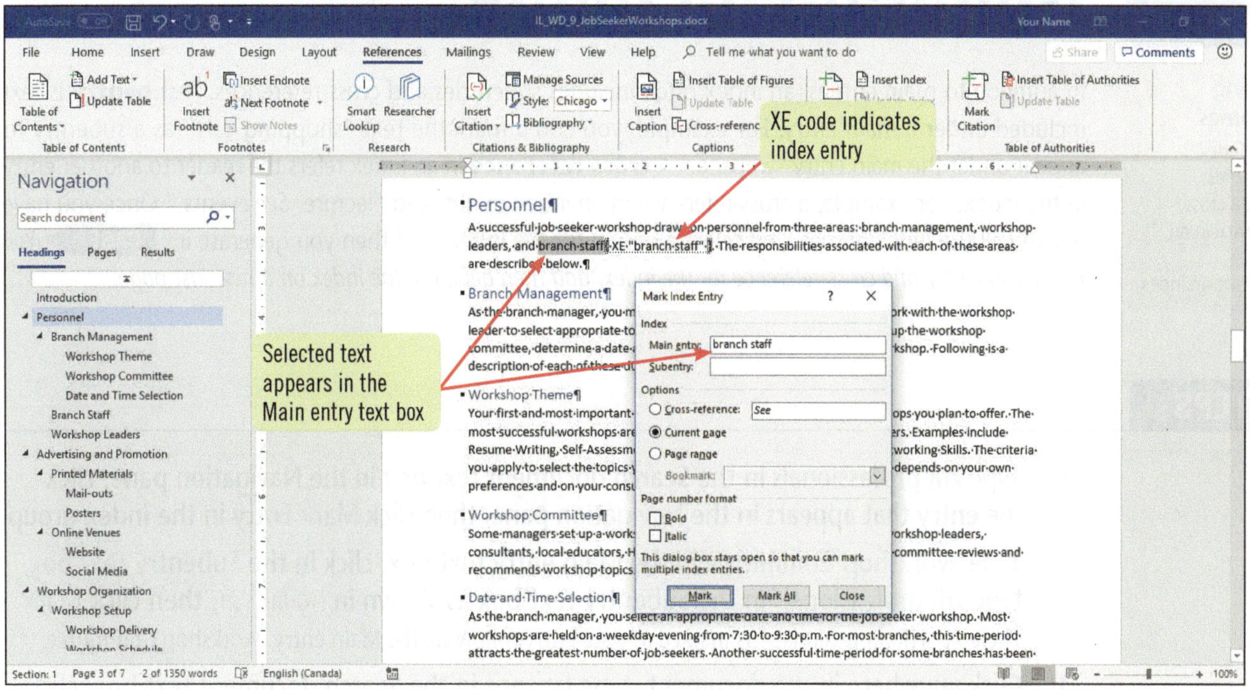

FIGURE 9-20: Index entries on the first page of the document

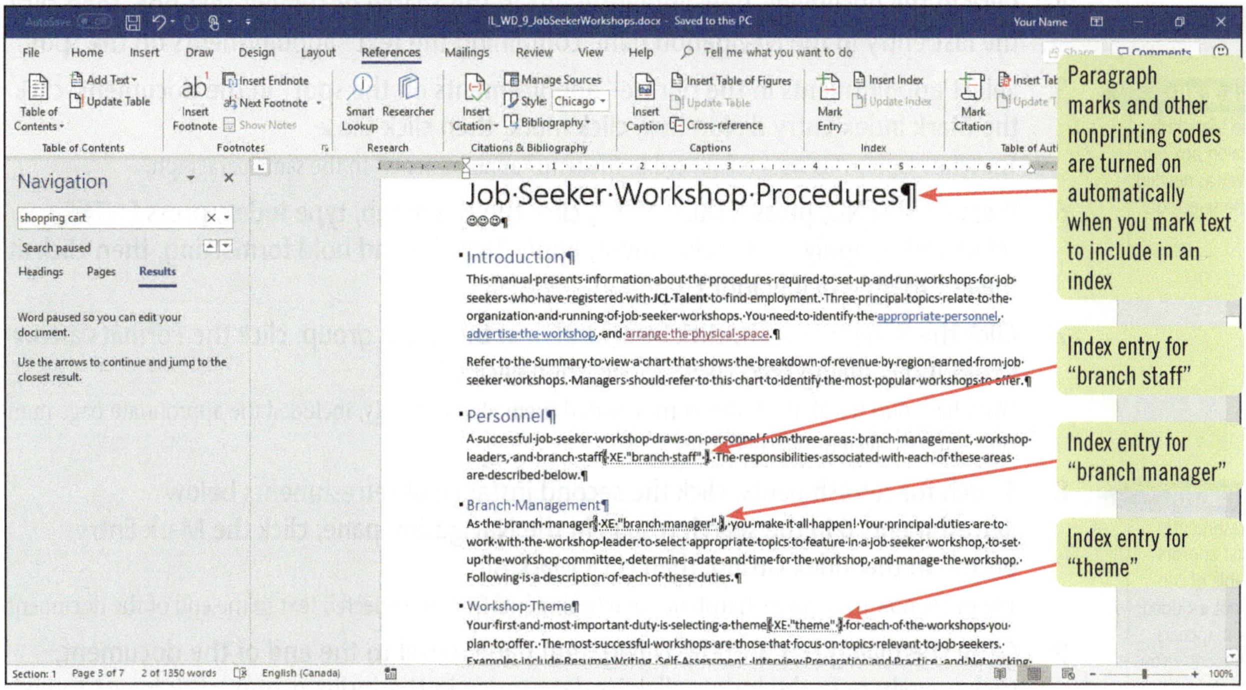

Word

Generate an Index

Learning Outcomes
- Mark index subentries
- Insert a cross-reference in an index
- Generate an index

In addition to main entries, an index often includes subentries and cross-references. A **subentry** is text included under a main entry. For example, you could mark the text "shopping cart" as a subentry to appear under the main entry "website." A **cross-reference** in an index refers the reader to another entry in the index. For example, a cross-reference in an index might read "lecture. *See* events." Once you have marked all the index entries, you select a design for the index, and then you generate it. CASE *You mark a subentry and cross-reference for the index, and then generate the index on a new last page.*

STEPS

1. **Type HR professionals in the Search document text box in the Navigation pane, click the entry that appears in the Navigation pane, then click Mark Entry in the Index group**
2. **Type Workshop Committee in the Main entry text box, click in the Subentry text box, type HR professionals in the Subentry text box as shown in FIGURE 9-21, then click Mark**
   The text "HR professionals" is marked as a subentry following the Main entry, Workshop Committee.
3. **Click anywhere in the document, type laptops in the Search document text box, click the Cross-reference option button in the Mark Index Entry dialog box, click after See, type appointments as shown in FIGURE 9-22, then click Mark**
   You also need to mark "appointments" so the Index lists the page number for "appointments."
4. **Click in the document, type appointments in the Search document text box, then click the last entry in the Navigation pane containing the text "appointments on the spot"**
5. **Select appointments in the phrase "appointments on the spot" in the document, click the Mark Index Entry dialog box, click Mark, then click Close**
   The term "laptops" is cross-referenced to the term "appointments" in the same paragraph.
6. **Press CTRL+END, press CTRL+ENTER, click the Home tab, type Index, press ENTER, select Index, apply center alignment, apply 18 point and bold formatting, then click at the left margin below Index**
7. **Click the References tab, click Insert Index in the Index group, click the Formats arrow in the Index dialog box, click Classic, then click OK**
   Word has collected all the index entries, sorted them alphabetically, included the appropriate page numbers, and removed duplicate entries.
8. **Search for refreshments, click the second instance of refreshments below Refreshments 6 in the search results in the Navigation pane, click the Mark Entry button in the Index Group, then click Mark All**
   The index now includes each instance of refreshments from the selected text to the end of the document.
9. **Close the dialog box and the Navigation pane, scroll to the end of the document, click anywhere in the index, click Update Index in the Index group, click Insert Index in the Index group, click the Formats arrow, scroll to and click Formal, click OK, click OK to replace the index, then compare the index to FIGURE 9-23**
10. **sam Save and close the document**

QUICK TIP
Drag the Mark Index Entry dialog box out of the way as needed to see the selected phrase.

QUICK TIP
The refreshments entry that appears in the table of contents is not included because it appears before the entry you selected.

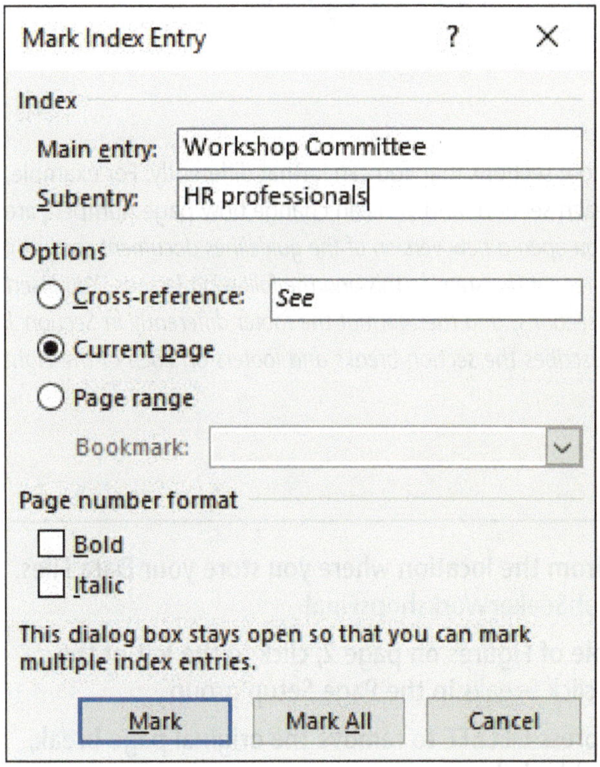

FIGURE 9-21: Subentry in the Mark Index entry dialog box

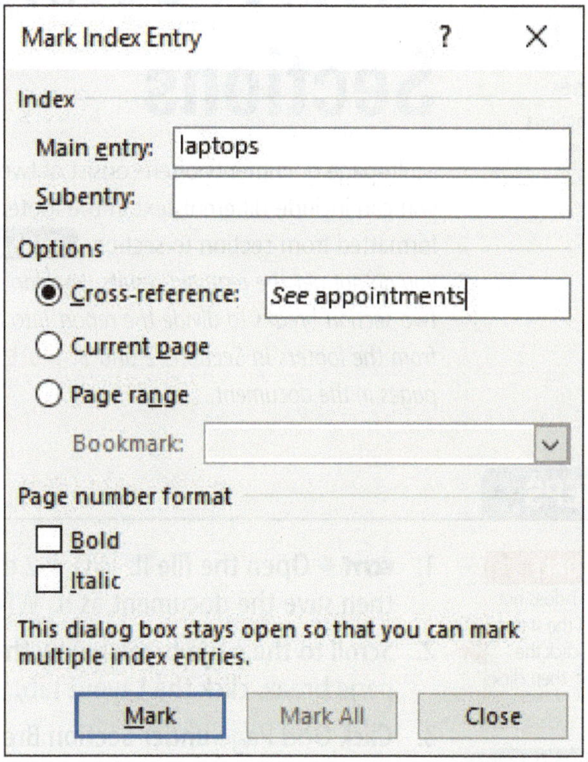

FIGURE 9-22: Cross-reference in the Mark Index entry dialog box

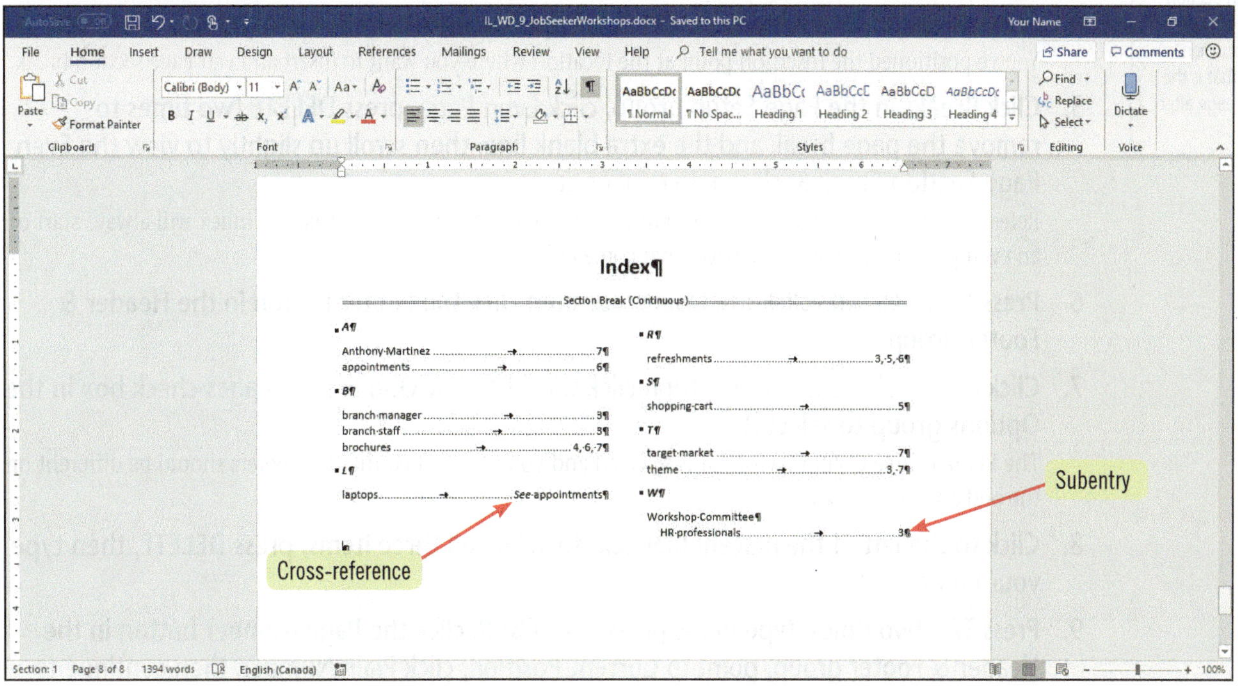

FIGURE 9-23: Completed index

Word

Word
Module 9

Learning Outcomes
- Insert sections
- Insert footers in sections

Insert Footers in Multiple Sections

Multi-page documents often consist of two or more sections that you can format differently. For example, you can include different text in the footer for each section, and you can change how page numbers are formatted from section to section. **CASE** *You open a new version of the guidelines document so that if you do not get the required results, you can easily repeat the steps in this and the following lessons. You insert two section breaks to divide the report into three sections, and then format the footer differently in Section 1 from the footers in Sections 2 and 3. **TABLE 9-2** describes the section breaks and footers on each of the eight pages in the document.*

STEPS

TROUBLE

If Section 1 does not appear on the status bar, right-click the **status bar**, then click **Section**.

QUICK TIP

If Section 1 contained 3 pages, Word would insert a blank page and start the Introduction in Section 2 on the fifth page of the document because that is the first odd page after Section 1.

1. **sam Open the file IL_WD_9-2.docx from the location where you store your Data Files, then save the document as IL_WD_9_JobSeekerWorkshopsFinal**
2. **Scroll to the page break below the Table of Figures on page 2, click to the left of the page break, click the Layout tab, then click Breaks in the Page Setup group**
3. **Click Odd Page under Section Breaks, press DELETE to remove the original page break, then press DELETE to remove the extra blank line**

   By inserting an Odd Page section break, you guarantee that page 1 of the document always starts on an odd number, regardless of what page comes before it. Section 1 contains the Table of Contents and the Table of Figures and Section 2 contains the body of the document and the index.
4. **Scroll to page 7, click to the left of the page break on page 7, then press ENTER once**

   You've positioned the insertion point at the location where you want to insert an Even Page section break.
5. **Click Breaks in the Page Setup group, click Even Page, press DELETE two times to remove the page break and the extra blank line, then scroll up slightly to view the Even Page Section Break as shown in FIGURE 9-24**

   Refer again to TABLE 9-2 so you understand where to insert footers. Note that the index will always start on an even page, regardless of the pages that come before it.
6. **Press CTRL+HOME, click the Insert tab, then click the Footer button in the Header & Footer group**
7. **Click Blank (Three Columns), then click the Different Odd & Even Pages check box in the Options group to select it**

   The Blank (Three Columns) format is selected and you've specified that the footers should be different on the odd and even pages.
8. **Click to the left of the placeholder text to select all three items, press DELETE, then type your name**
9. **Press TAB two times, type Page, press SPACEBAR, click the Page Number button in the Header & Footer group, point to Current Position, click Plain Number, then continue to the next lesson to finish inserting footers**

   The Odd Page Footer for the entire document contains your name at the left margin and the page number at the right margin.

FIGURE 9-24: Even page section break on page 7

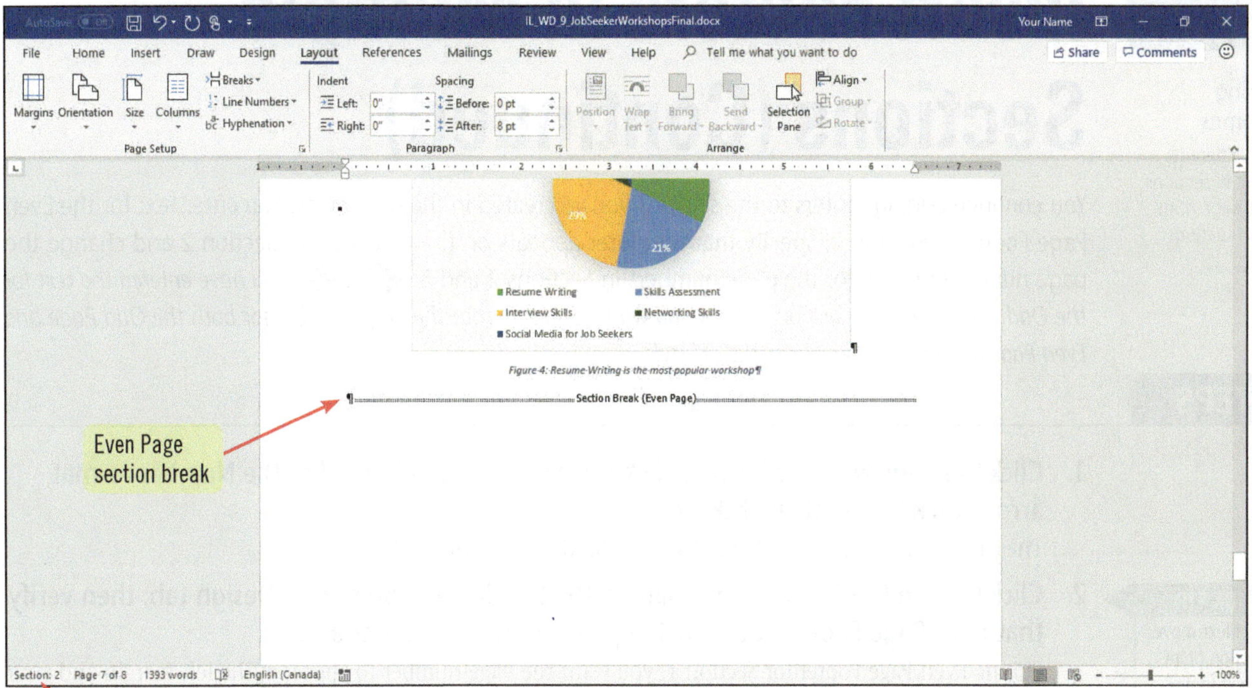

TABLE 9-2: Description of document sections and footers

Section	Page	Footer
Section 1	Table of Contents – page i	Odd page footer with Your Name at the left margin and the "i" style page number at the right margin
Section 1	Table of Figures – Page ii	Even page footer with the "i" style page number at the left margin and Your Name at the right margin
Section 2 – Must start on an Odd Page	First page of the document ("Introduction")	No footer: specified that the first page footer for Section 2 is different from the other footers.
Section 2	Second page of the document	Even page footer with the "1" style page number at the left margin and Your Name at the right margin
Section 2	Third page of the document	Odd page footer with Your Name at the left margin and the "1" style page number at the right margin
Section 2	Fourth page of the document	Even page footer
Section 2	Fifth page of the document	Odd page footer
Section 3 – Must start on an even page	Sixth page of the document	Even page footer

(Continued)

Word
Module 9

Learning Outcomes
- Insert different footers in sections
- Insert page numbers in sections

Insert Footers in Multiple Sections (Continued)

You continue adding footers to the sections you've created in the document. You enter text for the Even Page Footer in Section 2, specify that no footer appears on the first page of Section 2 and change the page numbering style for the page numbers in Sections 2 and 3. **CASE** *You have entered the text for the Odd Page Footer for Section 1. Now you want to specify that the page number for both the Odd Page and Even Page footers in Section 1 use the "i" style.*

STEPS

1. **Click the Page Number button, click Format Page Numbers, click the Number format arrow, click i, ii, iii, then click OK**
   The page number for the Odd Page Footer in Section 1 is formatted as i.

QUICK TIP
Clicking Next moves the insertion point to the next footer, which in this case is the even page footer for Section 1 as indicated by the section number in the status bar and on the Footer tab.

2. **Click Next in the Navigation group on the Header & Footer Tools Design tab, then verify that Even Page Footer - Section 1 appears above the footer area**
   On the Even Page Footer for Section 1, you want the page number to appear at the left margin and your name to appear at the right margin.
3. **Type Page, press SPACEBAR, click the Page Number button in the Header & Footer group, point to Current Position, click Plain Number, press TAB two times, then type your name**
4. **Click Next in the Navigation group to go to the Odd Page Footer for Section 2, then click the Different First Page check box in the Options group to select it**
5. **Click the Link to Previous button in the Navigation group to deselect it**
   The Link to Previous button is deselected when it is no longer shaded gray. Deselecting the Link to Previous button is a crucial step when you want to make sure that the contents of the current footer (in this case, no text) is different from the contents in the previous footer, which includes your name and a page number.
6. **Click the Page Number button in the Header & Footer group, click Format Page Numbers, click the Start At option button, verify that 1 appears, then click OK**
7. **Click Next in the Navigation group, verify that Page 2 appears at the left margin and your name at the right margin as shown in FIGURE 9-25, click Next, verify that your name appears at the left margin and Page 3 appears at the right margin, then click Next to go to Section 3, which is Page 6 (the Index page)**
   You do not need to deselect Link to Previous for the Even Page Footer for Section 3 because you want it to display the page number and your name the same way as for the other pages of the document.
8. **Click the Close Header and Footer button, verify you are returned to page i, the Table of Contents page, then save the document**

FIGURE 9-25: Even Page footer in Section 2

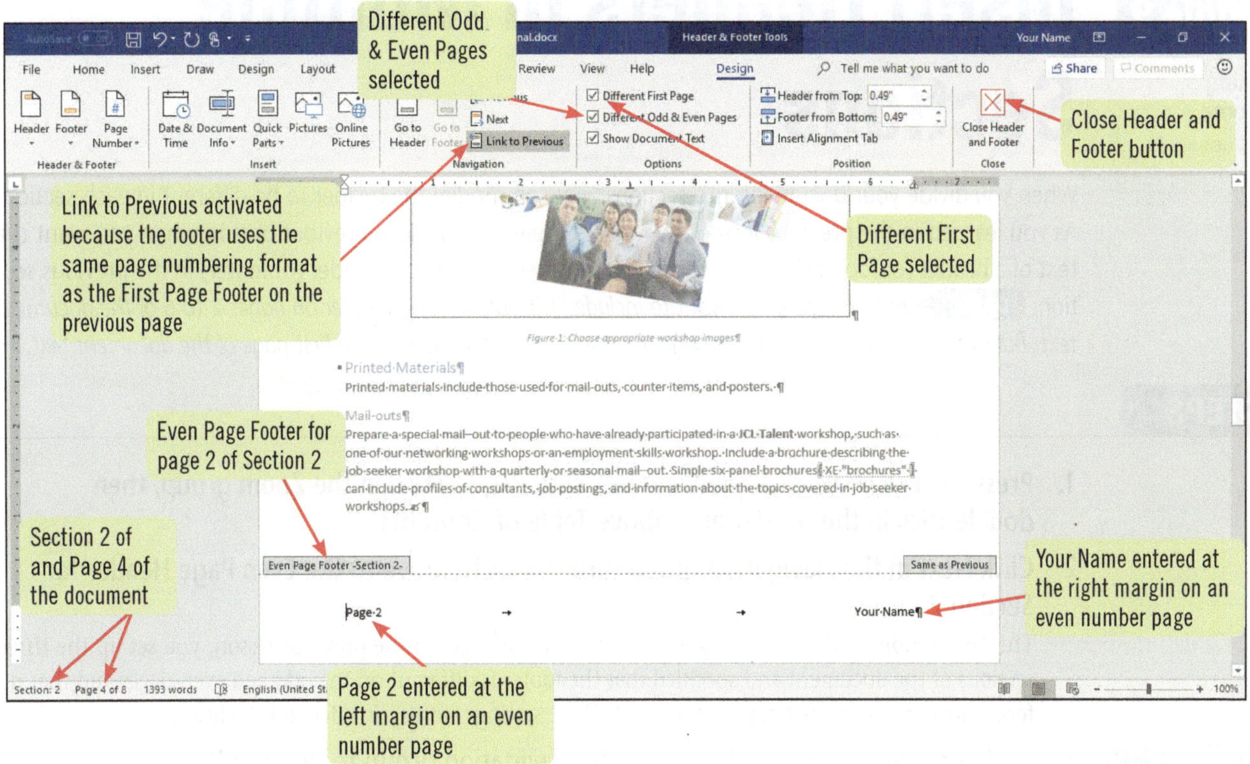

Rawpixel.com/Shutterstock.com; tsyhun/Shutterstock.com; Dragon Images/Shutterstock.com

Using text flow options

You adjust text flow options to control how text in a multi-page document breaks across pages. To change text flow options, you use the Paragraph dialog box. To open the Paragraph dialog box, click the launcher in the Paragraph group on the Home tab, and then select the Line and Page Breaks tab. In the Pagination section, you can choose to select or deselect four text flow options. For example, you select the Widow/Orphan control option to prevent the last line of a paragraph from printing at the top of a page (a widow) or the first line of a paragraph from printing at the bottom of a page (an orphan). By default, Widow/Orphan control is active. You can also select the Keep lines together check box to keep a paragraph from breaking across two pages.

Word

Word
Module 9

Insert Headers in Multiple Sections

Learning Outcome
- Insert headers in sections

When you divide your document into sections, you can modify the header to be different in each section. As you learned in the previous lesson, you must deselect the Link to Previous button when you want the text of a header (or footer) in a new section to be different from the header (or footer) in the previous section. **CASE** *In this lesson, you want to include "JCL Talent" as a header on pages 2 to 6 of the document text, but* not *on the table of contents page, the table of figures page, or the first page of the document text.*

STEPS

1. **Press CTRL+HOME, click the View tab, click Page Width in the Zoom group, then double-click in the header area above Table of Contents**
2. **Click Next in the Navigation group three times to move to the Even Page Header for Section 2**
   The "Workshop Leaders" heading is at the top of the page. In the previous lesson, you set up the three sections of the document and specified that the footer is different on the odd and even pages and that no footer appears on the first page of Section 2. These settings are also in effect for the header.
3. **Click the Link to Previous button in the Navigation group to deselect it**
   You deselect the Link to Previous button because you don't want the header text to appear on the even page header in Section 1 of the document.
4. **Type JCL Talent, select the text JCL Talent including the paragraph mark, click the Home tab, increase the font size to 14 point, apply bold, then center the text as shown in FIGURE 9-26**
5. **Click the Copy button in the Clipboard group**
6. **Click the Header & Footer Tools Design tab, then click Next in the Navigation group**
   The insertion point moves to the left margin of the Odd Page Header – Section 2.
7. **Click the Link to Previous button to deselect it so the header doesn't appear on page i of Section 1 (the Table of Contents page), press CTRL+V to paste the text, click the Close Header and Footer button in the Close group, press CTRL+HOME, then scroll through the document to verify the headers and footers are inserted correctly**
   No header text appears on the Table of Contents and Table of Figures pages in Section 1. No header and no footer appear on the first page of Section 2 (the first page of the document text). The text ("JCL Talent") appears in both the odd and even headers for Sections 2 and 3. The status bar displays the total number of pages in the document. The page numbers reflect the pagination you specified in the footers.
8. **Press CTRL+HOME, change the Zoom to 100%, update the table of contents, compare the updated table of contents to FIGURE 9-27, save the document, then continue to the next lesson to adjust the page layout**

QUICK TIP
You *must* click the Link to Previous button *before* you add text to a header when you don't want the text to appear in the header in the previous section.

TROUBLE
If the headers and footers do not appear as described, close the document, then return to the lesson "Inserting Footers in Multiple Sections" and repeat the steps.

FIGURE 9-26: Header text entered on the Even Page Header for Section 2

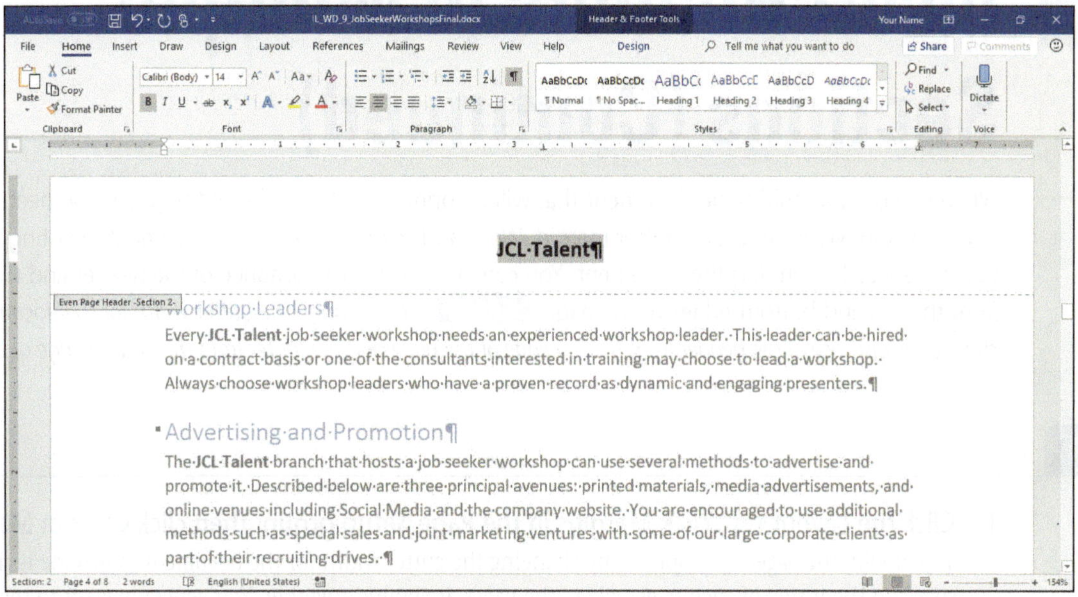

FIGURE 9-27: Updated table of contents

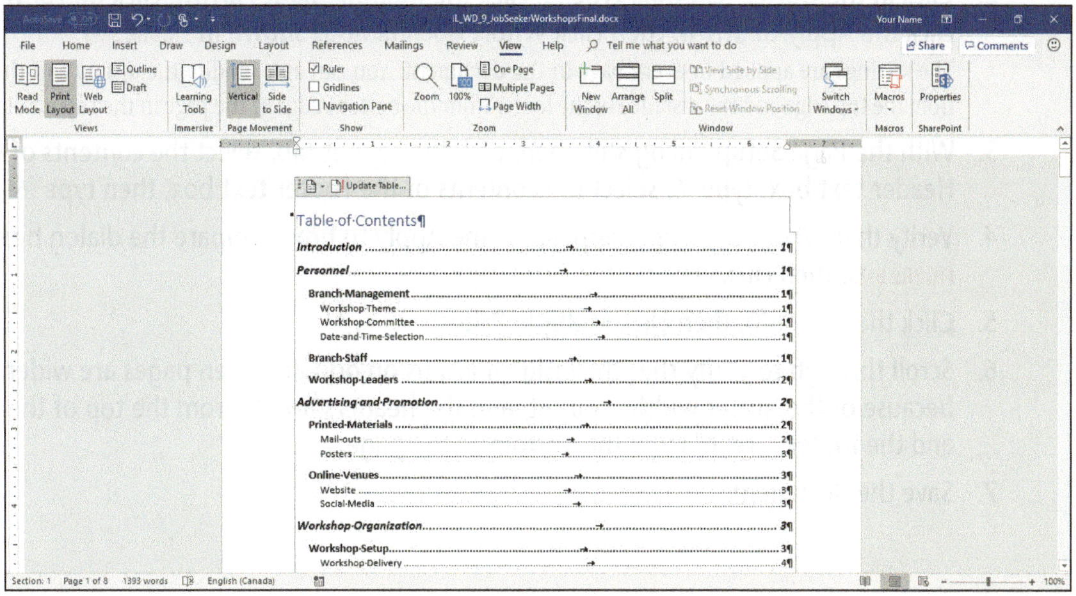

Understanding headers, footers, and sections

One reason you divide a document into sections is so that you can modify the page layout and the headers and footers differently in different sections. You can even modify the header and footer within a section because each section consists of two parts. The first part of a section is the first page, and the second part of the section is the remaining pages in the section. This section structure allows you to omit the header and footer on the first page of Section 2, and then include the header and footer on all subsequent pages in Section 2. To do this, place the insertion point in the section you want to modify, then click the Different First Page check box in the Options group to specify that you wish to include a different header and/or footer (or no header and footer at all) on the first page of a section. In addition, you can also choose to format odd and even pages in a document in different ways by clicking the Different Odd & Even Pages check box in the Options group. For example, you can choose to right-align the document title on odd-numbered pages and left-align the chapter indicator on even-numbered pages.

(Continued)

Word
Module 9

Learning Outcome
• Set a gutter margin

Insert Headers in Multiple Sections (Continued)

When you print a multi-page document that will be printed on two sides of the page, you need to set a gutter margin. When you set a gutter margin, Word adds extra space to the document's existing margins to allow space for binding the document. You can also modify the distance of the header and the footer from the top and bottom edges of the page. CASE *You change the gutter width for the document and change the distance of the header from the top edge of the page and the footer from the bottom edge of the page.*

STEPS

1. **Click the Layout tab, click Margins in the Page Setup group, then click Custom Margins**
   You modify the page setup options by changing the gutter width for the document. A **gutter** is the blank space on the inside of each page, where the pages are bound together. You generally want to set a gutter width that adds to the inside margin and is wider than the outside margin to allow room for binding.
2. **Click in the Gutter text box, type .5, click the Multiple pages arrow, click Mirror margins, click the Apply to arrow, then click Whole document as shown in FIGURE 9-28**
   The settings are applied to every page in the document. You can also modify the distance of the header from the top edge and the distance of the footer from the bottom edge of the page in the Layout dialog box.
3. **With the Page Setup dialog still open, click the Layout tab, select the contents of the Header text box, type .6, select the contents of the Footer text box, then type .6**
4. **Verify that Whole document appears in the Apply to box, compare the dialog box to FIGURE 9-29, then click OK**
5. **Click the View tab, then click Multiple Pages**
6. **Scroll through to verify that the inside margins on odd and even pages are wider because of the gutter widths you set, and the headers are .6" from the top of the page and the footers are .6" from the bottom of the page.**
7. **Save the document**

FIGURE 9-28: Setting the gutter width in the Page Setup dialog box

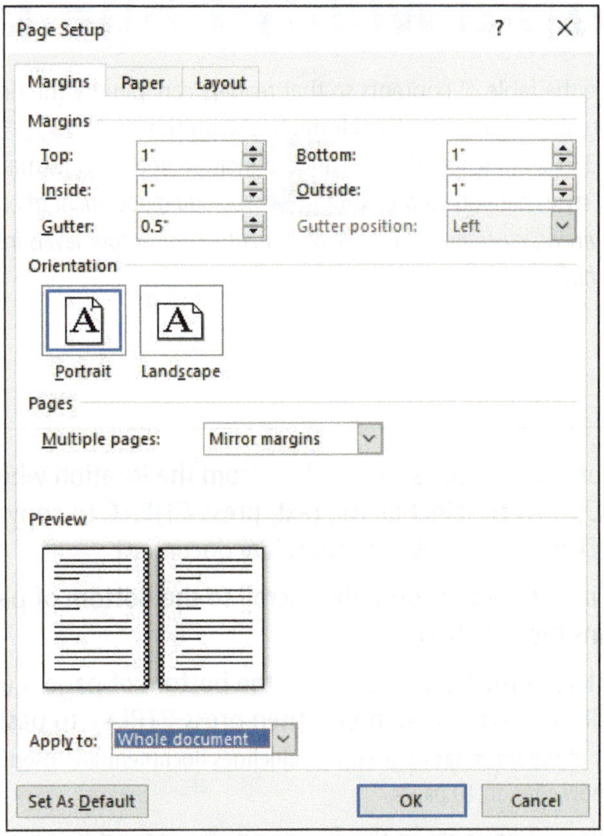

FIGURE 9-29: Setting the header and footer margin

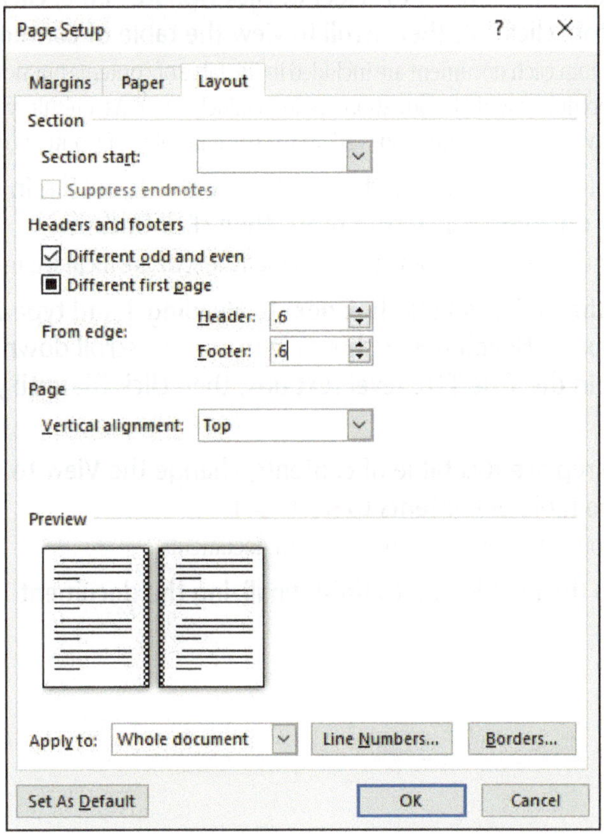

Word
Module 9

Finalize a Multi-Page Document

Learning Outcome
- Customize a table of contents

You can customize the table of contents so that readers can identify the document structure. By default, a table of contents shows only headings formatted with the Heading 1, Heading 2, or Heading 3 styles (Levels 1, 2, and 3 in Outline view). You can also include headings formatted with other styles, such as the Title style or a style that you create. **CASE** *You add a document about planning information sessions to the current document, customize the table of contents to show four levels instead of three, then change the spacing between entries.*

STEPS

1. **Open Support_WD_9_InfoSessions.docx from the location where you store your data files, press CTRL+A to select all the text, press CTRL+C to copy all the text, then switch to the IL_WD_9_JobSeekerWorkshopsFinal document**
2. **Click 100% in the Zoom group, then scroll to the bottom of page 5 of the document text (contains the pie chart)**
3. **Click to the left of the Section Break at the bottom of page 5 (below the chart), press CTRL+ENTER to insert a page break, then press CTRL+V to paste the copied text**
   The two pages of the Information Session Guidelines document are inserted into Section 2 and the document should now contain 10 pages.
4. **Verify that Page 7 appears in the footer on the second page of the Information Sessions Guidelines, then scroll up to the table of contents page**
5. **Click the Table of Contents to select it, click Update Table, click the Update entire table option button, click OK, then scroll to view the table of contents**
   The headings from each document are included in the table of contents but not the document titles ("Job Seeker Workshop Procedures" and "Information Session Guidelines."). As a result, you cannot easily see which headings belong to which documents. You work in the Custom Table of Contents dialog box to fix this problem.
6. **Click the References tab, click the Table of Contents button in the Table of Contents group, click Custom Table of Contents, then click Options**
   Specify that the two headings formatted with the Title style are included in the table of contents.
7. **Select 1 in the TOC level text box next to Heading 1 and type 2, type 3 next to Heading 2, type 4 next to Heading 3 as shown in FIGURE 9-30, scroll down to Title TOC level text box, type 1 in the Title TOC level text box, then click OK until you are returned to the document**
8. **Click Yes to replace this table of contents, change the View to One Page, scroll up, then compare the table of contents to FIGURE 9-31**
   The table of contents includes the titles of both documents.
9. **Continue to the next lesson to finish finalizing the document**

FIGURE 9-30: Table of Contents Options dialog box

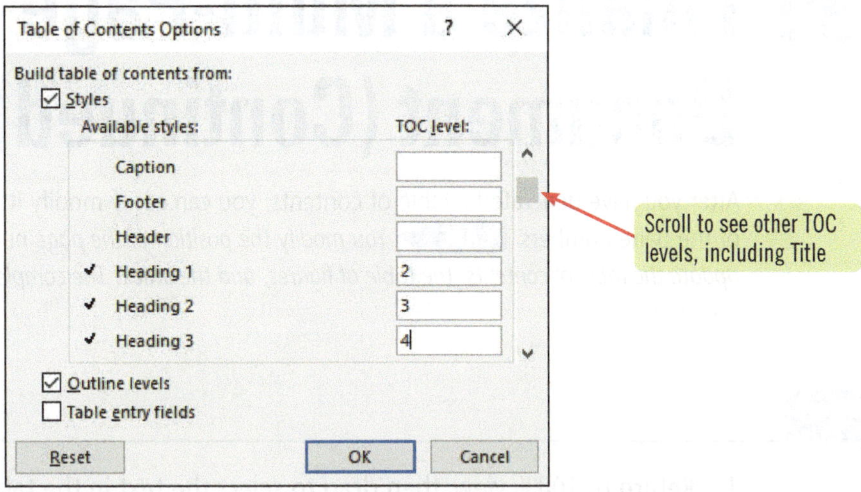

FIGURE 9-31: Revised table of contents

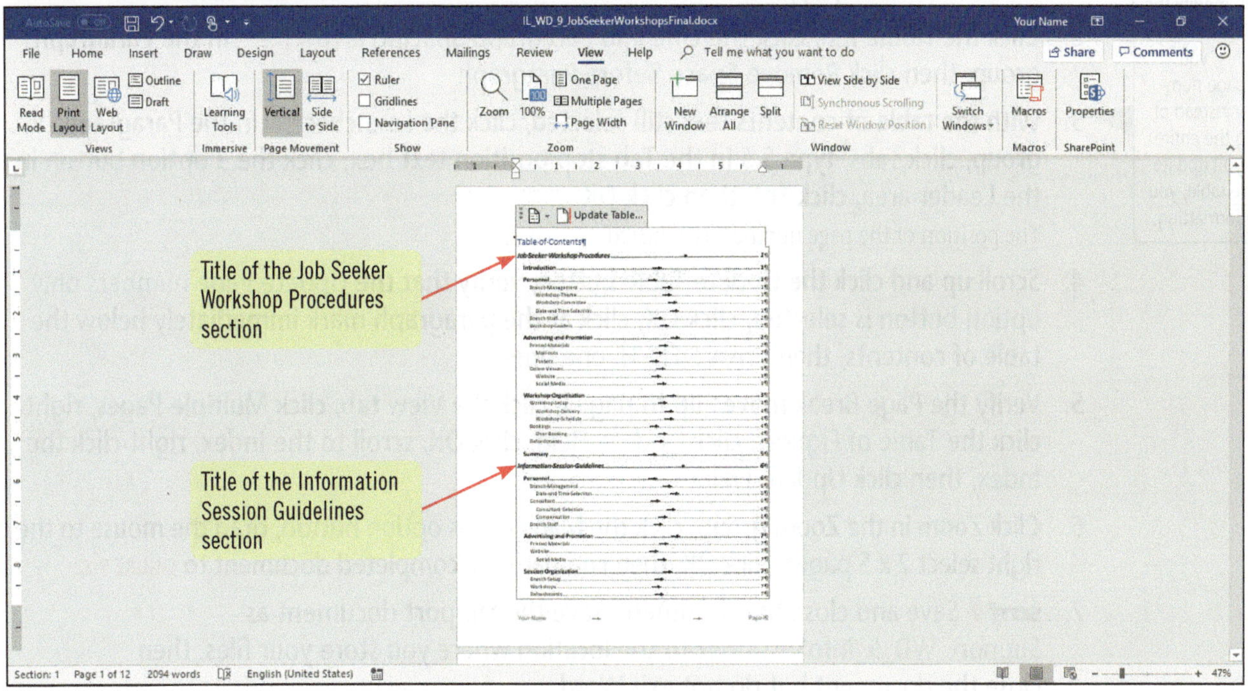

(Continued)

Learning Outcome
- Modify table of contents page numbers

Finalize a Multi-Page Document (Continued)

After you have generated a table of contents, you can easily modify its format and change the position of the page numbers. CASE *You modify the position of the page number in the table of contents, then update the table of contents, the table of figures, and the index. The completed document consists of a total of 10 pages.*

STEPS

QUICK TIP
After you modify the formatting of a table of contents, you update page numbers only instead of updating the entire table. If you update the entire table, you lose the formatting.

1. **Return to 100% view, then drag to select the text in the table of contents from Job Seeker Workshop Procedures to the page number following Summary (the text is shaded a darker gray)**
2. **Click the Home tab, click the Line and Paragraph Spacing arrow in the Paragraph group, then click Remove Space Before Paragraph**
3. **With the table of contents text still selected, click the Launcher in the Paragraph group, click Tabs, type 5.5 in the Tab stop position text box, click the 3 option button in the Leader area, click Set, then click OK**
   The position of the page numbers is adjusted.
4. **Scroll up and click the Update Table button, verify that the Update Page numbers only option button is selected, click OK, click at the paragraph mark immediately below the table of contents, then press DELETE one time**
5. **Verify the Page Break moves up to page i, click the View tab, click Multiple Pages, right-click the Table of Figures, click Update Field, click OK, scroll to the Index, right-click the Index, then click Update Field**
6. **Click Zoom in the Zoom group, click the Many Pages option button, drag the mouse to the right select 2 x 5 pages, click OK, then compare the completed document to FIGURE 9-32**
7. **sam Save and close the document, save the Support document as Support_WD_9_InfoSessions2 to the location where you store your files, then close the document but do not exit Word**

FIGURE 9-32: The 10 pages of the completed document

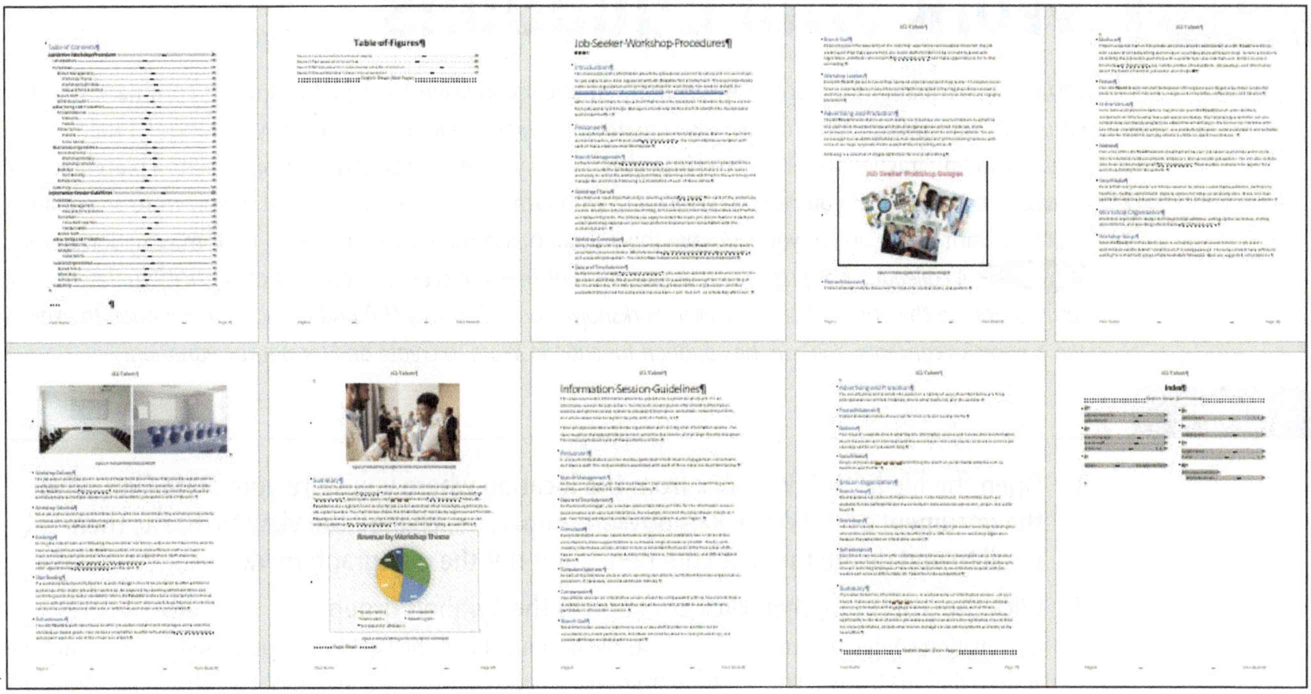

Syda Productions/Shutterstock.com; Robert Kneschke/Shutterstock.com

Rawpixel.com/Shutterstock.com; tsyhun/Shutterstock.com; Dragon Images/Shutterstock.com

Using Advanced Print Options

With Word 2019, you can scale a document to fit a different paper size, and you can choose to print pages from specific sections or a series of sections, even when the page numbering restarts in each section. To scale a document, click the File tab, click Print, click the 1 Page Per Sheet arrow, then click Scale to Paper Size and view the list of paper sizes available. You can also choose to print a multiple-page document on fewer sheets; for example, you can print the document on two pages per sheet up to 16 pages per sheet. In the Print dialog box, you can also specify how to print the pages of a multiple-section document that uses different page numbering in each section. You need to enter both the page number and the section number for the range of pages you wish to print. The syntax required is: PageNumberSectionNumber-PageNumberSectionNumber which is shortened to p#s#-p#s#. For example, if you want to print from page 1 of Section 1 to page 4 of Section 3, you enter p1s1-p4s3 in the Pages text box in the Settings area, and then click Print.

Word

Word
Module 9

Work with Equations

Learning Outcomes
- Create an equation
- Format an equation

You use the Equations feature to insert mathematical and scientific equations using commands on the Equation Tools Design tab. You can also create your own equations that use a wide range of math structures, including fractions, radicals, and integrals. When you select a structure, Word inserts a placeholder, a **content control**, that you can then populate with symbols, values, or even text. If you write an equation that you want to use again, you can save the equation and then access it from a custom equation gallery.

CASE *A colleague has prepared a document that uses the economic concept of elasticity to describe the result of raising the price of the Job Seeker workshops from $200 to $300 and includes an equation to express the economics concepts. You use the equation function in Word to create and format the equation.*

STEPS

1. **Open the file IL_WD_9-3.docx from the location where you store your Data Files, save the document as IL_WD_9_RaisingWorkshopPrices, change the view to 100%, then scroll to and delete the text Equation 1, but not the paragraph mark**
2. **Click the Insert tab, then click Equation in the Symbols group**
   An equation content control is inserted in the document and the Equation Tools Design tab becomes the active tab. This tab is divided into four groups: Tools, Conversions, Symbols, and Structures. TABLE 9-3 describes the content of each group.
3. **Click the Fraction button in the Structures group to show a selection of fraction structures, click the first fraction structure in the top row, then increase the zoom to 180%**
   Increasing the zoom helps you see the components of the equation.
4. **Click in the top half of the fraction (the numerator)**
   The box is shaded to indicate it is selected.
5. **Click the More button in the Symbols group to expand the Symbols gallery, click the Basic Math arrow on the title bar, click Greek Letters, then click the Delta symbol (Δ) as shown in FIGURE 9-33**
   You can select commonly used math symbols from eight galleries as follows: Basic Math, Greek Letters, Letter-Like Symbols, Operators, Arrows, Negated Relations, Scripts, and Geometry.
6. **Type Q, press DOWN ARROW to move to the bottom half of the fraction (the denominator), type Q, press RIGHT ARROW, type an equal sign (=), then complete the equation as shown in FIGURE 9-34, making sure to insert fraction structures as needed**
7. **Click the selection handle (a portion of the equation is shaded), click the Home tab, change the Font size to 14 point, click the Shading arrow in the Paragraph group, click the Green, Accent 6, Lighter 80% color box, then click away from the equation**
8. **Save and close the document, but do not exit Word**

TROUBLE
Follow Step 3 to insert the fraction structure each time; use the keyboard arrow keys to move to different parts of the equation. If your insertion point moves outside the equation, click in the equation again.

More equation options

From the Equation Tools Design tab, you can click the Ink Equation button to write an equation using a digital pen or other pointing device. Word converts the written symbols into typed symbols.

From the Shapes menu on the Insert tab, you can select one of the six equation shapes shown in FIGURE 9-35. You modify these shapes in the same way you modify any drawing shape.

FIGURE 9-35:

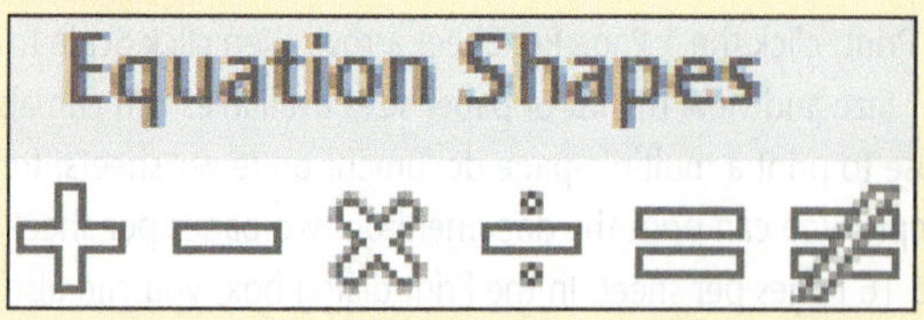

FIGURE 9-33: **Selecting a symbol**

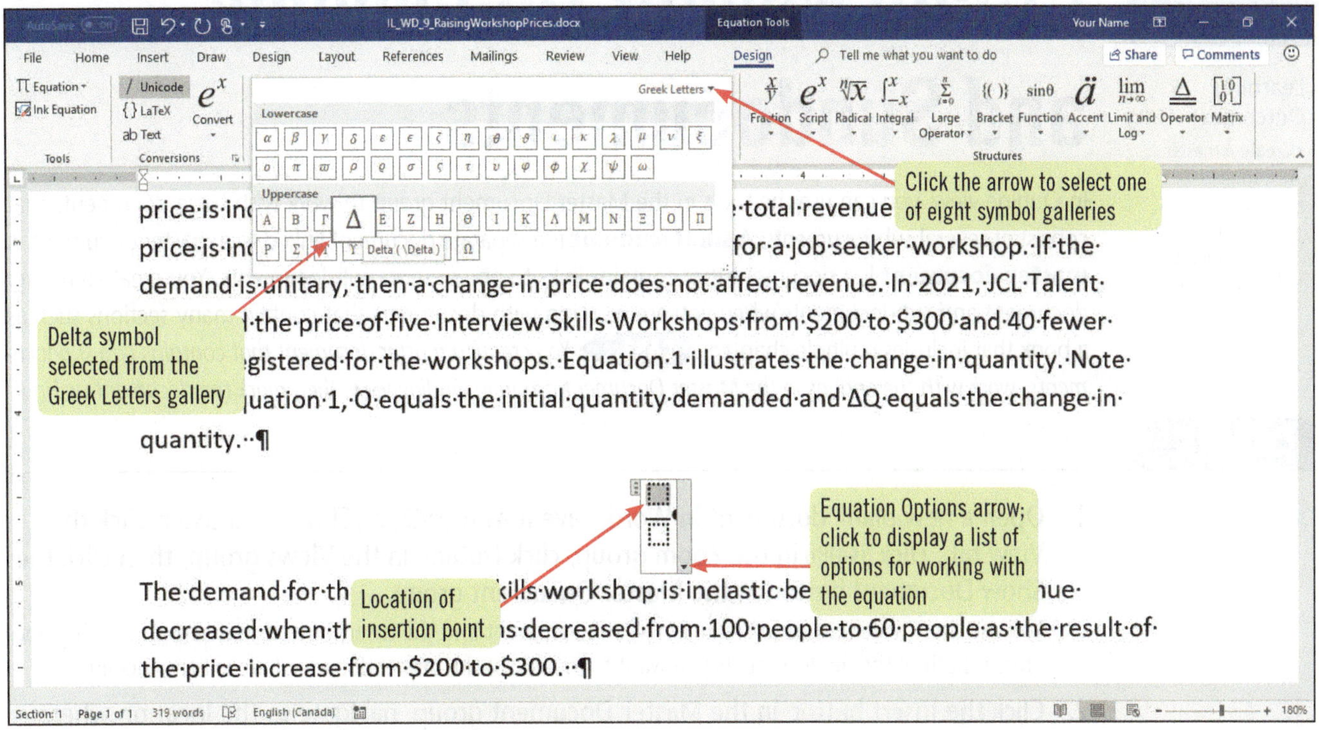

FIGURE 9-34: **Completed Equation 1**

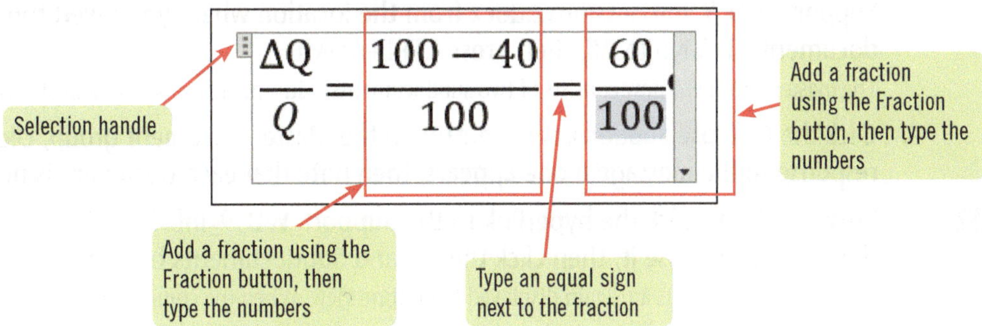

TABLE 9-3: **Contents of the Equation Tools Design tab**

Tools	• Use the Equation button to select a built-in equation • Select the equation style: Professional, Linear, or Normal Text • Click the Launcher to access the Equation Options dialog box where you can specify equation settings and access the Math AutoCorrect list of symbols
Conversions	• Convert equations to various formats; for example, you can convert an existing equation to a linear format
Symbols	• Select commonly used mathematical symbols such as (±) and (∞) • Click the More button to show a gallery of symbols • Click the arrow in the gallery to select the group for which you would like to see symbols
Structures	• Select common math structures, such as fractions and radicals • Click a structure button (such as the Fraction button) to select a specific format to insert in the equation for that structure

Word
Module 9

Create Master Documents and Subdocuments

Learning Outcomes
- Create a master document
- Add and work with subdocuments
- Mark a document as final

In Outline view, you can use the tools in the Master Document group to work with large documents that consist of several subdocuments. A **subdocument** is a separate document linked to a master document. A **master document** is a document that contains links to one or more subdocuments. You create a master document and subdocuments when you are working with documents that contain many sections such as a book that includes multiple chapters. CASE *You create a master document that contains two subdocuments, work with the options in the Master Document group in Outline view, then mark the document as Final.*

STEPS

1. **Open a new blank document in Word, save it as IL_WD_9_JCLTalent_Master, click the View tab, click 100% in the Zoom group, click Outline in the Views group, then click the Show Document button in the Master Document group.**
   You use the Create button to create a new subdocument and the Insert button to insert an existing document. Both of the subdocuments you want to include in the master document are existing documents.
2. **Click the Insert button in the Master Document group, navigate to the location where you saved the document IL_WD_9_RaisingWorkshopPrices, double-click IL_WD_9_RaisingWorkshopPrices, then click No to All**
3. **Click the Insert button in the Master Document group, insert Support_WD_9_InfoSessions2.docx from the location where you saved the document, click No to All, then press CTRL+HOME**
   The master document now consists of two subdocuments, with the first subdocument shown in FIGURE 9-36.
4. **Click the Collapse Subdocuments button in the Master Document group, click OK in response to the message if one appears, then note that each document is now a hyperlink**
5. **Press CTRL and click the hyperlink to the Support_WD_9_InfoSessions2 document, view the document, close it, then click the Expand Subdocuments button**
   The two subdocuments are again displayed in Outline view. When the combined files are not large, you can choose to unlink the subdocuments so they become part of the master document.

QUICK TIP
You keep subdocuments as links to a master document when you want to reduce the file size of a master document.

6. **Scroll to the Information Sessions document and click the Selection button to the left of the document, as shown in FIGURE 9-37 to select the entire subdocument, then click Unlink button in the Master Document group**
   The Information Sessions Guidelines document is no longer a subdocument and cannot be collapsed to a link.
7. **Scroll up and click the Increasing Workshop Prices document Selection icon, click the Lock Document button in the Master Document group, double click any word in the document, then try to type text**
   The subdocument is locked; you cannot make any changes. You can also protect the entire document from changes.
8. **Click the File tab, click Protect Document in the Info pane, view the protection options available, click Mark as Final, click OK, then click OK**
   When you open a document that has been marked as Final, a message appears telling you that the document was marked as final to discourage editing. If you wish to edit the document, click Edit Anyway.
9. **Click , close the document, submit the files to your instructor, then exit Word**

FIGURE 9-36: Subdocuments inserted in Outline view

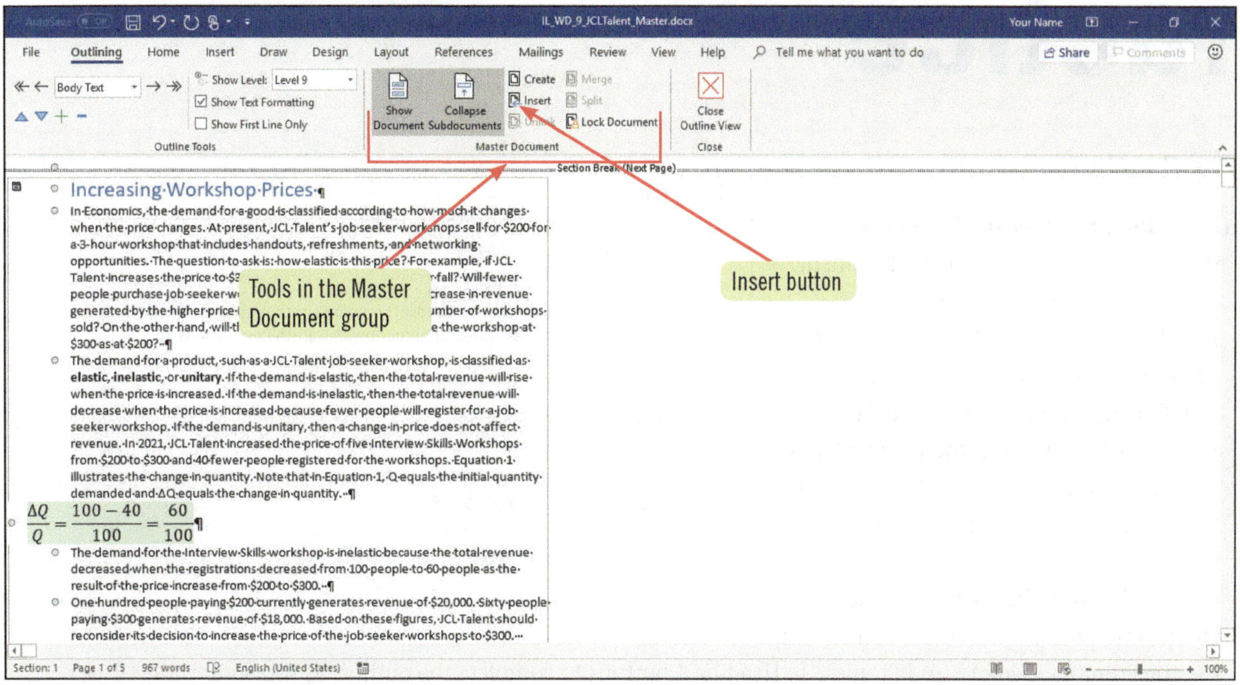

FIGURE 9-37: Subdocument selected in Outline view

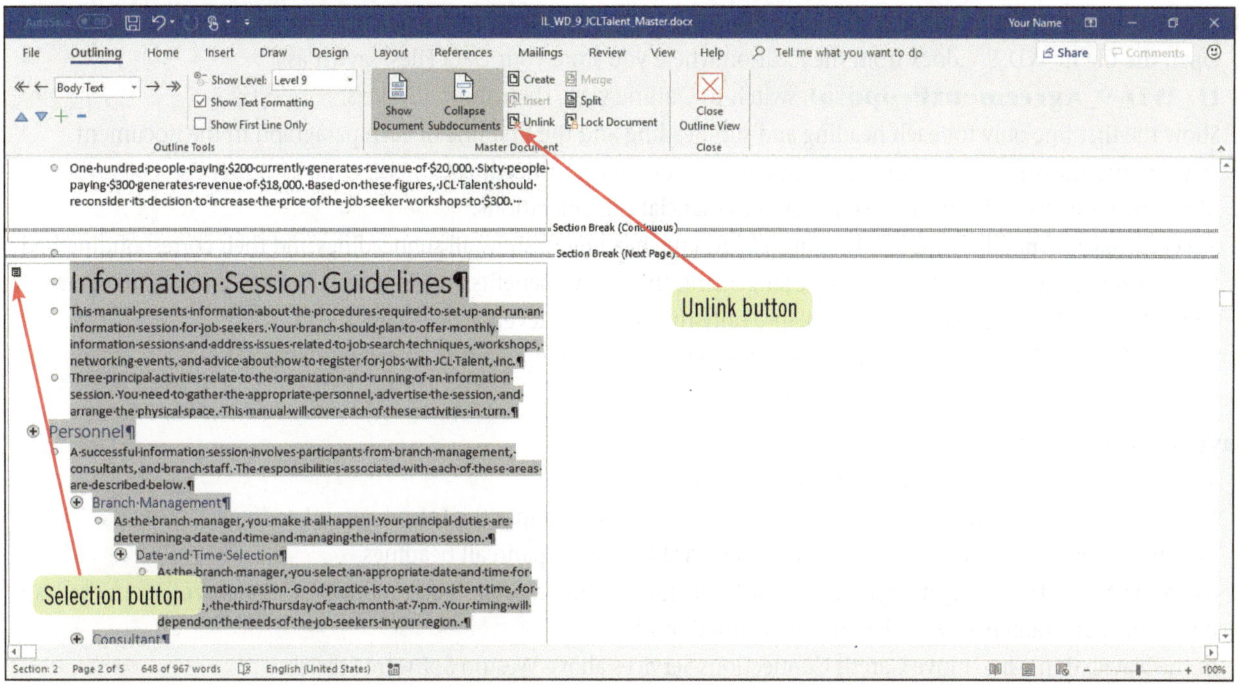

Inserting endnotes

Click the Insert Endnote button in the Footnotes group on the References tab to insert a note reference mark for an endnote. When you click the Insert Endnote button, the insertion point moves to the end of your document so that you can enter text for the endnote in the same way you enter text for a footnote. You click above the endnote separator to return to the text of your document. You work in the Footnote and Endnote dialog box to modify options for endnotes.

Practice

Skills Review

FIGURE 9-38

1. Build a document in Outline view.

- **a.** Start Word, create a new blank document, then switch to Outline view.
- **b.** Type **Introduction** followed by your name as a Level 1 heading, press ENTER, type **Background Information** as another Level 1 heading, then press ENTER.
- **c.** Type the text shown in FIGURE 9-38 as body text under the Background Information heading.
- **d.** Press ENTER after the body text, type **Benefits**, promote it to Level 1, then demote the heading to Level 2.
- **e.** Use the Promote, Demote, and Promote to Heading 1 buttons to complete the outline, as shown in FIGURE 9-38.
- **f.** Save the document as **IL_WD_9_AgreementOutline** to the location where you store your Data Files, then close the document.

2. Work in Outline view.

- **a.** Open the file IL_WD_9-4.docx from the location where you store your Data Files, save it as **IL_WD_9_AgreementProposal**, switch to Outline view, then show all levels.
- **b.** Show the first line only for each heading and sub-heading and the first line of each paragraph in the document.
- **c.** Deselect the Show First Line Only option, then show only Level 1 headings.
- **d.** Move the Products and Services heading above Financial Considerations.
- **e.** Select the Background Information heading, expand the heading to show all subheadings and their corresponding body text, collapse Benefits, collapse Business Arrangement, then move Benefits and its subtext below Business Arrangement.
- **f.** Expand all levels of the outline, then collapse only the Projected Revenues heading.
- **g.** Show only Level 3 headings, then select and delete the Package Opportunities heading.
- **h.** Close Outline view, then save the document.

3. Navigate a document.

- **a.** Show paragraph marks if they are not already visible.
- **b.** Move to the top of the document and then Print Layout view, collapse the Introduction heading.
- **c.** Collapse all headings so only Level 1 headings are visible, then expand all headings.
- **d.** Open the Navigation pane, navigate to Financing Required, then change "eight months" to **two years** in the last line of the paragraph below the Financing Required heading.
- **e.** In the Navigation pane, move Gareth Connections Services above Weston Software Services.
- **f.** View the thumbnails of the document pages in the Navigation pane, click the first page, scroll to the Benefits heading on page 2 of the document, then select the text "Projected Revenues" at the end of the paragraph.
- **g.** Create a cross-reference from the text "Projected Revenues" to the "Projected Revenues heading.
- **h.** Test the cross-reference.
- **i.** Go to the top of the document, create a hyperlink from the text "Products and Services" in the list of factors (the other two factors are already hyperlinks) in the middle of paragraph 1 under "Introduction," to the Products and Services heading, then test the hyperlink.
- **j.** Save the document and keep the Navigation pane open.

Skills Review (continued)

4. Create and modify screenshots.

a. Open **Support_WD_9_CompanyImages.docx** from the location where you save your Data files, turn off paragraph marks, then ensure the View is 100%.

b. Switch to the IL_WD_9_AgreementProposal document.

c. Scroll to and delete the text SEATTLE SCREENSHOT in the Background Information section on page 1, but not the paragraph mark.

d. Insert a screenshot of the Word window containing the support document showing the two pictures of Seattle.

e. Crop the screenshot to the edges of the document containing the "Awesome Seattle" heading and the two pictures.

f. Change the width of the cropped screenshot to 5", apply a picture border using the Black, Text 1 color, then center the screenshot.

g. Switch back to the Support_WD_9_CompanyImages document, then scroll to view the three pictures on page 2 of the document.

h. Return to the main document in Word, navigate to the Gareth Connections Services heading, delete SERVICES PICTURES but not the paragraph mark, then create a screen clipping that includes only the three pictures and the heading on page 2 of the Support document.

i. Change the width of the screen clipping to 5", apply a picture border using the Black, Text 1 color, then center the screenshot.

j. Save the document, switch to the Support document, then close it.

5. Use advanced find and replace options.

a. Go to the top of the document, then use Advanced Find and Replace to find every instance of **Gareth Connections** and replace it with **Gareth Connections** formatted in bold.

b. In the Find and Replace dialog box, delete the text in the Find what and Replace what text boxes and remove the formatting.

c. Use the list of Special characters from the Replace dialog box to find every instance of an Em Dash and replace it with an En Dash. You will make two replacements.

d. Search for **SQL skills**, then click after the period.

e. Insert three computer symbols (Character Code 58) from the Wingdings font.

f. Save the document.

6. Add and modify captions.

a. Scroll through the document and note the captions on three of the five graphics, then navigate to the Background Information heading and click the screenshot of the Seattle images.

b. Insert a caption on the picture using the A, B, C, numbering style.

c. Type a colon (:), press SPACEBAR then type **Most clients are based in Seattle** as the caption text.

d. Change the numbering style to 1, 2, 3, ..., then exit the Captions dialog box.

e. Scroll to and click the screenshot of the three services images, then insert a caption with that includes a colon (:) and the text **Gareth Connections uses these images to promote its services**.

f. Scroll up and then delete the picture and the caption of the people clapping.

g. Update the numbering for all the remaining captions in the document.

h. Go to the top of the document, insert a manual page break, press CTRL+HOME, then enter the text **Table of Figures** followed by a hard return at the top of the new blank page.

i. Center the text and format it with 24 point and bold.

j. Click after "Figures," press ENTER, then clear the formatting (*Hint*: Clear the Clear All Formatting button in the Font group on the Home tab).

k. Generate a table of figures using the Distinctive format.

l. Save the document.

Skills Review (continued)

7. **Insert a table of contents.**
   a. Go to the top of the document.
   b. Insert a page break, then return to the top of the document and clear all the formatting.
   c. Insert a table of contents using the Automatic Table 2 predefined style.
   d. Replace the table of contents with a custom table of contents using the Distinctive format.
   e. Use CTRL+click from the table of contents to navigate to Business Arrangement in the document, view the document headings in the Navigation pane, then right-click and delete the Eastways Communications heading from the Navigation pane.
   f. Update the table of contents, then save the document.
8. **Mark text for an index.**
   a. Show the Results section of the Navigation pane, find the words **computer labs**, then mark all occurrences for inclusion in the index.
   b. Find and mark only the first instance of each of the following main entries: **website design**, **networking**, **software training**, and **PowerPoint**. (*Hint*: Click Mark instead of Mark All.)
   c. Save the document.
9. **Generate an index.**
   a. Find **social media**, click in the Mark Index Entry dialog box, select social media in the Main entry text box, type **Gareth Connections Services** as the Main entry and **social media** as the Subentry, then click Mark All.
   b. Repeat the process to insert **business writing seminars** as a subentry of Gareth Connections Services.
   c. Find the first instance of the text **courses** after the table of contents, then create a cross-reference in the Mark Index Entry dialog box to **software training**. Note that you already have an index entry for software training.
   d. Close the Mark Index Entry dialog box and the Navigation pane.
   e. Insert a new page at the end of the document, type **Index** at the top of the page, center the text and format it with bold and 24 point.
   f. Double-click below the index, clear any formatting and press BACKSPACE so the insertion point appears at the left margin, then insert an index using the Modern format.
   g. Find the text **Seattle**, click the second entry in the Navigation pane, open the Mark Index Entry dialog box and click Mark All, then close the Mark Index Entry dialog box and the Navigation panes
   h. Scroll to the index page, update the index so it includes the new entry, then save and close the document.
10. **Insert footers in multiple sections.**
    a. Open the file IL_WD_9-5.docx from the location where you store your Data Files, then save it as **IL_WD_9_AgreementProposalFinal**.
    b. At the top of the document, check that Section 1 appears on the status bar and that the document contains 7 pages.
    c. Scroll to the page break below the Table of Figures on page 2, click to the left of the page break, then insert an Odd Page section break.
    d. Press DELETE to remove the original page break, then press DELETE again to remove the extra blank line.
    e. Scroll to the Index page, scroll up and click to the left of the page break on page 6, insert an Even Page section break, then delete the original page break and the extra blank line.
    f. On the table of contents page, insert a footer using the Blank (Three Columns) format.
    g. Select the Different Odd & Even Pages check box.
    h. Click to the left of the placeholder text to select all three items, press DELETE, type your name, press TAB two times, type **Page**, press SPACEBAR, then insert a page number at the current position of the insertion point using the Plain Number page number.
    i. Format the page numbers with the i, ii, iii style.
    j. Press Next in the Navigation group to go to the Even Page Footer for Section 1, type **Page**, press SPACEBAR, insert a Plain Number page number at the current position of the insertion point, press TAB two times, then type your name.

Skills Review (continued)

k. Click Next in the Navigation group, select the Different First Page check box, then click the Link to Previous button to deselect it (the button is no longer gray).

l. Change the format of the page numbers to start a 1.

m. Click Next to go to the next footer (Even Page Footer – Section 2), verify that Page 2 appears at the left margin and your name at the right margin, click Next, verify that your name appears at the left margin and Page 3 at the right margin, then click Next to go to Section 3, which is Page 6 (the Index page) and the Even Page Footer for Section 3. Note that Page 8 of 8 appears in the status bar because the entire document, including the table of contents and table of figures pages (Section 1) contains 8 pages.

n. Exit the footer area, then scroll through the document to verify that the footers appear correctly. Note that your name and Page i appears on the Table of Contents page, Page ii and your name appears on the Table of Figures page, no footer appears on the first page of the document text, Page 2 and your name appears on page 2 of the document text and your name and Page 3 appears on page 3 of the document text and so on to the end of the document.

o. Save the document.

11. Insert headers in multiple sections.

a. Press CTRL+HOME to go to the top of the document, change the View to Page Width, insert a header using the blank format, then move to the Even Page Header for Section 2. Verify that the Even Page Header – Section 2 appears *not* the First Page Header.

b. Deselect the Link to Previous button, then enter **Business Arrangement** as the header text.

c. Format the header text with a font size to 14 point, apply bold, center the text, then copy the header text, including the paragraph mark.

d. Move to the Odd Page Header – Section 2, deselect the Link to Previous button, then paste the "Business Arrangement" header text.

e. Exit the header area, then return to the top of the document.

f. Scroll through the document to verify that no header text appears on the first three pages of the document. The header text appears only on pages 2 to 8 of the document text.

g. In the Page Setup dialog box, set the Gutter width for the whole document to .5, then mirror the margins.

h. Set the distance of the Header and Footer from the top and bottom of the page to .3 for the whole document.

i. View the entire document in Multiple Pages view, verify the headers and footers are correct, then save the document.

12. Finalize a multi-page document.

a. Open **Support_WD_9_TopTalkPresenters.docx** from the location where you store your data files, select and copy all the text.

b. Switch to the IL_WD_9_AgreementProposal document, return to Page Width, scroll to the bottom of page 4 (contains the Conclusion), click to the left of the section break, then insert a page break.

c. Paste the copied text.

d. Update the entire table of contents.

e. Modify the table of contents options so that Heading 1 corresponds to TOC level 2 text, Heading 2 corresponds to TOC level 3 text, Heading 3 corresponds to TOC level 4 text, and Title text corresponds to TOC level 1 text.

f. Verify that the updated table of contents includes the titles of the two documents, select all the text in the table of contents, then remove the Before Paragraph spacing.

g. Open the Tabs dialog from the Paragraph dialog box, then set a tab of 5.5 with the 2 Leader style.

h. Update the Table of Figures, then update the Index.

i. View 2 x 5 pages in the Zoom dialog box, then compare the completed document to FIGURE 9-39.

j. Save and close the document, close the Support document, but do not exit Word.

Skills Review (continued)

FIGURE 9-39

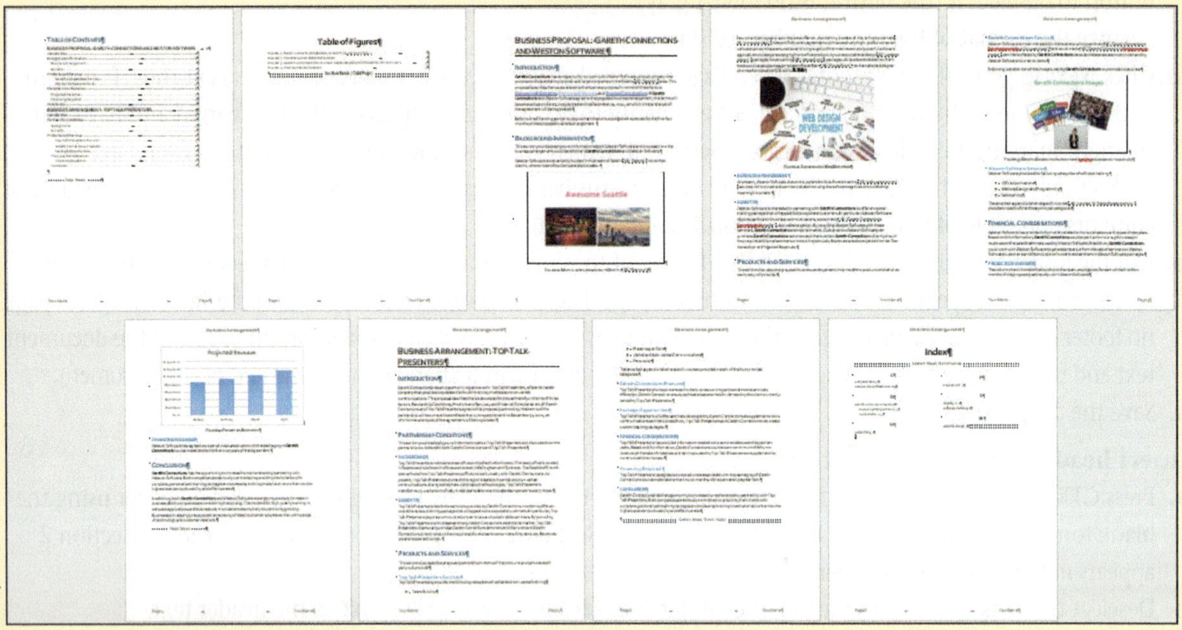

13. Work with equations

a. Open the file IL_WD_9-6.docx from the location where you store your Data Files, then save the document as **IL_WD_9_SeminarPrice**.

b. Go to the [Equation1] placeholder, then replace it with an equation content control.

c. Increase the zoom to 180%, then create the equation shown in FIGURE 9-40.

d. Format the new equation by increasing its font size to 16 point, then shade it with Blue, Accent 5, Lighter 80%. (*Hint*: Remember to select the equation content control before applying the shading).

e. Save and close the document. but do not exit Word.

FIGURE 9-40

$$\frac{\Delta Q}{Q} = \frac{100 - 30}{100} = \frac{70}{100}$$

14. Create master documents and subdocuments.

a. Open a new blank document in Word, save the document as **IL_WD_9_GarethConnections_Master**, then switch to Outline view.

b. Insert the document **IL_WD_9_SeminarPrice.docx** you saved in the previous activity, clicking No to All if prompted.

c. Insert **Support_WD_9_TopTalkPresenters.docx** from the location where you store your Data Files for this book, answering No to All if prompted.

d. Collapse the subdocuments, answering OK when prompted, click the hyperlink to the Support_WD_9_TopTalkPresenters.docx file, view the document, then close it.

e. Expand the subdocuments.

f. Select and then unlink the IL_WD_9_SeminarPrice.docx subdocument.

g. Collapse the Support_WD_9_TopTalkPresenters.docx subdocument, then use the Lock Document button to lock it.

h. Exit Outline view, then mark entire document as final.

i. Close the document, submit all the files you have created in this Skills Review to your instructor, then exit Word.

Independent Challenge 1

Tony Sanchez, RN, the office manager at Riverwalk Medical Clinic, asks you to help him develop guidelines related to office management, filing procedures, and receptionist duties at the clinic. Tony plans to use these documents as the basis for a Procedures Manual for the clinic.

a. Start Word, open the file IL_WD_9-7.docx from the drive and folder where you store your Data Files, save it as **IL_WD_9_MedicalOfficeGuidelines**, then switch to Outline view.

b. Show only Level 1 headings, select the Applications and Manual Content headings, then demote them to Level 2.

c. Select and expand all the headings, collapse both the Creating a Procedures Manual and the Designating Staff Positions headings, then move the Designating Staff Positions heading above the Creating a Procedures Manual heading.

d. Show only Level 3 headings, select and delete the heading Managing Suppliers and its associated subtext, then close Outline view.

e. Move to the top of the document, collapse the Introduction heading, collapse all headings, expand all headings, show the headings in the Navigation Pane, then drag the Administrative Meetings heading up so it appears above Staff Meetings.

f. View the thumbnails in the Navigation pane, scroll to and click the page 1 thumbnail, position the insertion point after "summary" in the last sentence in the paragraph below the Office Manager heading (fourth line), insert a cross-reference to the chart (Figure 1), then select Above/Below in the Insert reference to list.

g. Ensure a space appears before and after "below", then test that the cross-reference goes to the figure caption for the chart.

h. Move to the top of the document, insert a blank page, move to the top of the document again, press ENTER, press the Up arrow, then insert a table of contents using the Automatic Table 2 option, then replace the table of contents with a custom table of contents using the Formal format.

i. Use the Navigation pane to navigate to the Manual Format subheading, delete the subheading and its associated text, then update the table of contents.

j. Show Results in the Navigation pane, search for **Office Manager**, click the second instance in the Navigation pane, open the Mark Entry dialog box, then mark all instances of "Office Manager" for inclusion in the index.

k. Find and mark all instances of the following main entries: **Medical Office Assistant**, **equipment**, **orientation**, **budget**, **inventory**, **medications**, and **biologics**.

l. Search for **stock control**, then enter inventory in the Main entry text box and stock control in the Subentry text box. Mark the one instance.

m. Search for **office supplies**, then create a cross-reference for office supplies to inventory.

n. Go to the end of the document, insert an index using the Formal format, search for **support staff**, mark it for inclusion in the index, then update the index.

o. Move to the top of the document, scroll to the page break below the table of contents, replace the page break with an Odd Page section break, then remove the page break and the extra hard return.

p. Move to the page break above the index, replace the page with an Even Page section break, then remove the page break and the extra hard return.

q. On page 1 of the document (Section 1), insert a footer using the Blank (Three Columns) format, then select Different Odd and Even pages.

r. Delete the placeholder text, type **Page** at the left margin followed by a space and a plain page number, press TAB two times, type your name at the right margin, then change the page number format to i,ii,iii.

s. Go to Odd Page Footer-Section 2, then click the Link to Previous button to deselect it. Format the page numbers to start at 1.

Independent Challenge 1 (continued)

t. Go to the Even Page Footer-Section 2, Section 2—Even Page Footer, enter your name at the left margin press TAB twice to move to the right margin, type **Page** followed by the plain page number, then verify the page number format is 1, 2, 3.

u. Exit the footer area, save the document, then scroll to the chart, click after areas at the end of the caption for the chart, then add a page break to the left of the current Even Page section break.

FIGURE 9-41

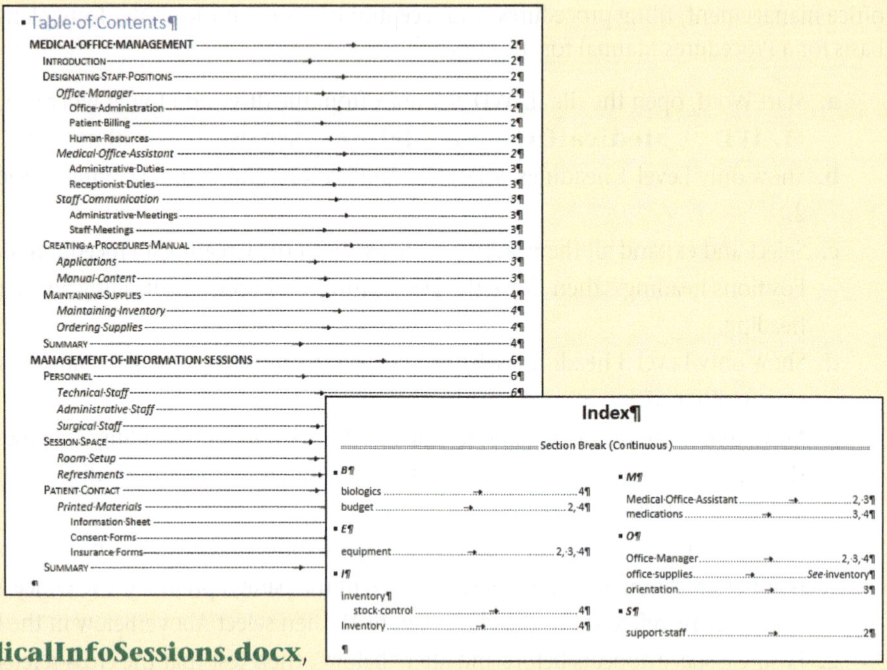

v. Open **Support_IL_9_MedicalInfoSessions.docx**, select and then copy all the text, switch to the document IL_WD_9_MedicalOfficeGuidlines, then paste the copied text.

w. Scroll up to the table of contents, update the table of contents, open the Custom Table of Contents dialog box, then designate heading levels as follows: Heading 1: 2, Heading 2: 3, Heading 3: 4 and Title: 1.

x. Select all the text in the table of contents, change the Before and After Spacing to 0, set the right tab at 5.5", then select the 3 tab leader style.

y. Scroll to and update the index, then compare the revised table of contents and updated index to FIGURE 9-41.

z. Save the document, submit the file to your instructor, then close all documents.

Independent Challenge 2

As the program assistant at Hansen College in Denver, Colorado, you are responsible for creating and formatting reports about programs at the college. You modify an existing report, then make the report a master document and insert two sub-documents that each contain information about a different college program.

a. Open IL_WD_9-8.docx, save it as **IL_WD_9_HansenCollegePrograms**, open **Support_WD_9_CampusLife.docx**, then turn off paragraph marks if they are showing. Set the view at 100%, then switch back to IL_WD_9_HansenCollegePrograms.

b. Select and delete STUDYING SCREEN CLIPPING but leave a blank line, then insert a screen clipping of the picture of students studying.

c. Clip the picture so only the oval picture is selected. Change the width of the screen clipping to 4", then center it.

d. In the Support_WD_9_CampusLife file, scroll to the second page, return to the main document, select and delete CAMPUS FUN SCREENSHOT, then insert a screenshot of the Word window containing the pictures of the students on campus.

e. Crop the screenshot in the main document so that only the pictures and heading are visible. Enclose the screen shot in a black border, center it, then change its width to 3.5".

f. Go to the top of the document, then use Advanced Find and Replace to find a section break and replace it with a manual page break.

g. Scroll to the page break, then if necessary delete any extra blank lines so the "Elementary Education" heading starts on page 3.

Independent Challenge 2 (continued)

h. Go to the top of the document, then use Advanced Find and Replace to find every instance of **Hansen College** and replace it with **Hansen College** formatted in bold and italics.

i. On the blank line below the document title "Hansen College", insert three symbols of a hand writing from Wingdings (symbol 63). Increase the font size of the three symbols to 18 point, then center them below the title.

j. Insert a caption on the oval picture with the text: **Students enjoy studying at Hansen College** using the a, b, c, style, then change the numbering style to the 1, 2, 3 style.

k. Insert a caption on the picture of the students on campus with the text: **The campus at Hansen College is a welcoming place.**

l. Scroll to the picture of the girl reading on page 2, update the caption number, then scroll to the next picture of children and update the caption number. (*Hint*: If a caption is not updated, select the entire caption, click the Insert Caption button, then click OK.)

m. Scroll up slightly, then delete EQUATION 1 but not the paragraph mark.

n. Insert the equation shown in FIGURE 9-42.

o. Format the equation by changing the font size to 16 point and applying the Purple, Accent 1, Lighter 80% shading.

p. Go to the top of the page, insert a Next Page section break, then return to the top of the page, type **Table of Figures**, clear the formatting, format it with 16 point and bold, center it, then add a blank line following the title.

q. Insert a table of figures using the Formal format.

r. Insert a header in Section 1 using the Blank (Three Columns) format, delete the placeholder text, go to Section 2, deselect the Link to Previous button, type the text **Hansen College Programs** at the left margin, press TAB two times to move to the right margin, enter your name at the right margin, then exit the header area.

s. Go to the end of the document, switch to Outline view, then click the Show Document button in the Master Document group.

t. Open the file Support_WD_9_BusinessProgram.docx from the location where you store your Data Files, save it as **Support_WD_9_BusinessProgram2**, close it, then insert it as a subdocument, answering No to All if prompted.

u. Open the file Support_WD_9_TheaterProgram.docx from the location where you store your Data Files, save it as **Support_WD_9_TheaterProgram2**, close it, then insert it as a subdocument, answering No to All if prompted.

v. Collapse the subdocuments, click OK in response to any message, scroll down as needed to verify that the two subdocuments are now hyperlinks, press and hold CTRL and click the hyperlink to the Support_WD_9_TheaterProgram2.docx file, view the document, then close it.

w. Expand all the Subdocuments, close Outline view, navigate to the picture of the young woman in the Theater Program document, verify that the figure is updated to Figure 5 or update it if necessary.

x. In the Master document, set the gutter width at .5" for the whole document and select Mirror Margins.

y. Update the table of figures, then compare it to FIGURE 9-43.

z. Save the document, close it, then submit your files to your instructor.

FIGURE 9-42

$$\frac{1}{2}X\frac{1}{2}=\frac{1}{4}$$

FIGURE 9-43

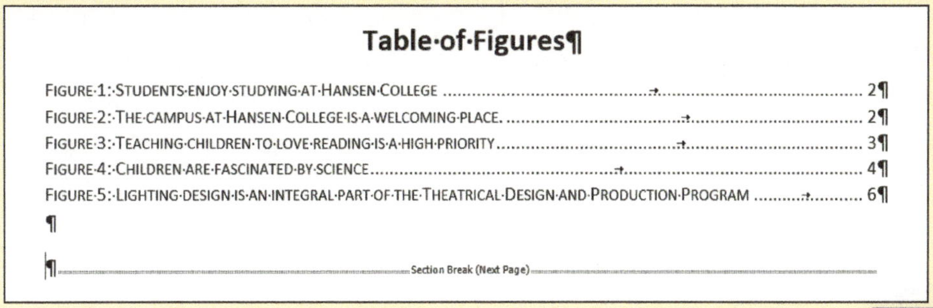

Table·of·Figures¶

¶

¶ .... Section Break (Next Page) ....

Word

Visual Workshop

Open the file IL_WD_9-9.docx from the drive and folder where you store your Data Files, then save it as **IL_WD_9_SeaviewBankMarketingPlan**. Switch to Outline view, then modify the outline so that it appears as shown in FIGURE 9-44. You need to change the order of two sections and demote two subheadings. Exit Outline view, add a Next Page section break at the beginning of the document, then on the new blank page generate a custom table of contents using the Fancy format with four levels showing. (*Hint*: Click the Show levels arrow in the Table of Contents dialog box, then click 4.) Insert a page break before Promotion in the text, then create a footer in Section 2 remember to deselect Link to Previous *before* you type text) with your name at the left margin and a page number that starts with 1 at the right margin. Make sure no text appears in the footer in section 1. In Print Layout view, insert and crop the screen clipping included in the file Support_WD_9_Banking.docx to the left of the page break. Refer to FIGURE 9-45. Change the width to 2.5", then add the caption **Online Banking: The Future is Here**. Update the table of contents. Save and close the document, then submit the file to your instructor.

FIGURE 9-44

FIGURE 9-45

Sinisa Botas/Shutterstock.com

Building Forms

CASE You work with Anthony Martinez, the VP of sales & marketing at JCL Talent, Inc., to create a form to survey branch managers about their experiences delivering workshops for job seekers. You start by creating the form template, then you add content controls, format and protect the form, and fill it in as a user.

Module Objectives

After completing this module, you will be able to:

- Convert tables and text
- Construct a form template
- Add Text content controls
- Add Date Picker and Picture content controls
- Add Repeating Section and Check Box content controls
- Add Building Block content controls
- Add Drop-Down content controls
- Insert Legacy Tools controls
- Format and Protect a form
- Edit a form
- Fill in a form as a user

Files You Will Need

IL_WD_10-1.docx
Support_WD_10_Trainer1.jpg
Support_WD_10_Trainer2.jpg
IL_WD_10-2.docx
Support_WD_10_Instructor.jpg
IL_WD_10-3.docx
Support_WD_10_Peru.jpg
IL_WD_10-4.docx
Support_WD_10_SolarEnergy.jpg

Word Module 10

Convert Tables and Text

Learning Outcomes
- Change the paper size
- Convert text to a table
- Convert a table to text

You can convert text that is separated by a tab, a comma, or another separator character, into a table. For example, to create a two-column table of last and first names, you could type the names as a list with a comma separating the last and first name in each line, and then convert the text to a table. The separator character—a comma in this example—indicates where you want to divide the table into columns, and a paragraph mark indicates where you want to begin a new row. Conversely, you can convert a table to text that is separated by tabs, commas, or some other character. **CASE** *You open a document containing much of the text needed for your form and convert a table containing the company's contact information into text and then convert the text required for the form into a table. You start by changing the page size.*

STEPS

1. **sam Start Word, open the file IL_WD_10-1.docx from the location where you store your Data Files, save the document as IL_WD_10_WorkshopSurveySetup, then click the Show/Hide button ¶ in the Paragraph group to show paragraph marks, if necessary**
2. **Click the Layout tab, then click the Size button in the Page Setup group**
   A selection of page sizes appears. The Executive page size is currently selected.
3. **Click Letter**
4. **Click anywhere in the table under JCL Talent, Inc., then click the table move handle**
   You select the table so that you can then convert the table into a line of text.
5. **Click the Table Tools Layout tab, then click Convert to Text in the Data group**
   When you convert a table into text, you can choose various ways in which you want to separate the text contained in each table cell. For this table, you want the text separated with the | symbol.
6. **As shown in FIGURE 10-1, click the Other option button, type |, then click OK**
   The company contact information appears as a line of text with the sections separated by the | symbol.
7. **Select the text from Name to Top Workshops**
   Notice the TAB characters between the text. You want each TAB character to convert into a table cell.
8. **Click the Insert tab, click the Table button in the Tables group, then click Convert Text to Table**
   The Convert Text to Table dialog box opens. In this dialog box, 4 is entered as the number of columns based on the number of TAB characters in the selected text, as shown in FIGURE 10-2.
9. **Click OK, click below the table to deselect it, then save the document**
   Word converts the TAB characters and text into a table containing four columns. The Word document appears as shown in FIGURE 10-3.

QUICK TIP
To enter the | symbol, press **SHIFT** and then the forward slash (\) key.

FIGURE 10-1: Convert Table to Text dialog box

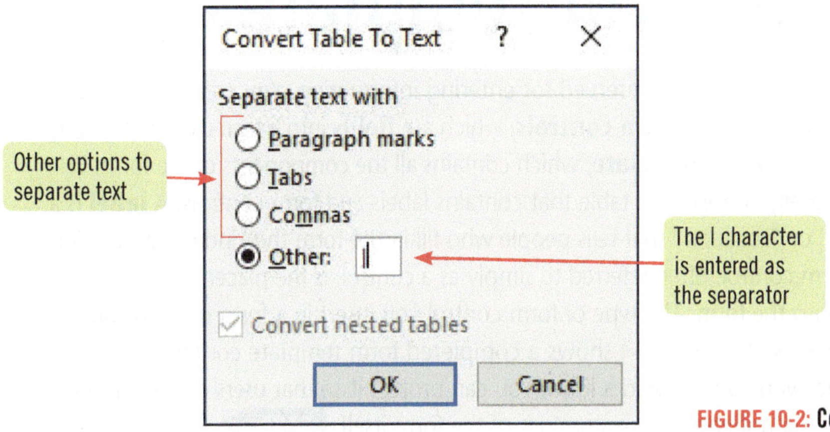

FIGURE 10-2: Convert Text to Table dialog box

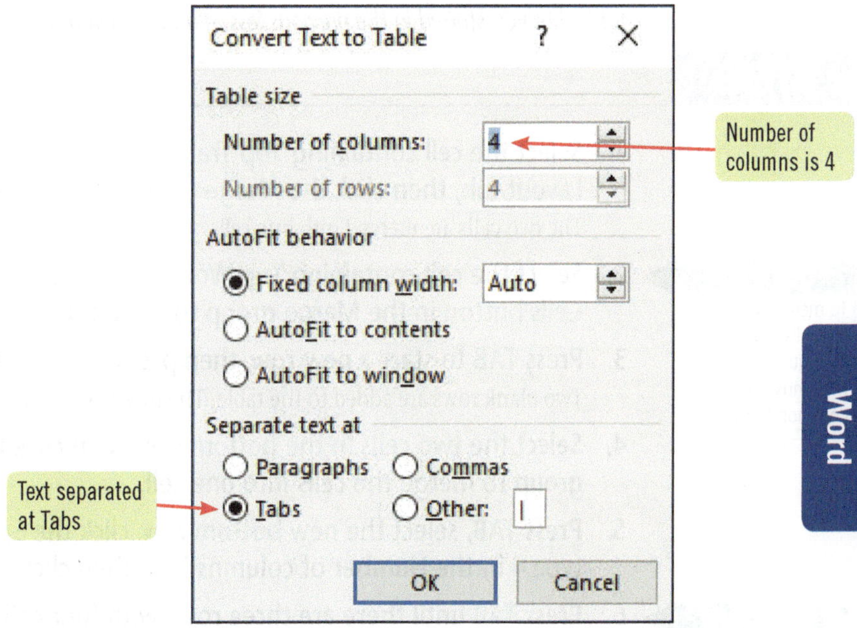

FIGURE 10-3: Table for the form

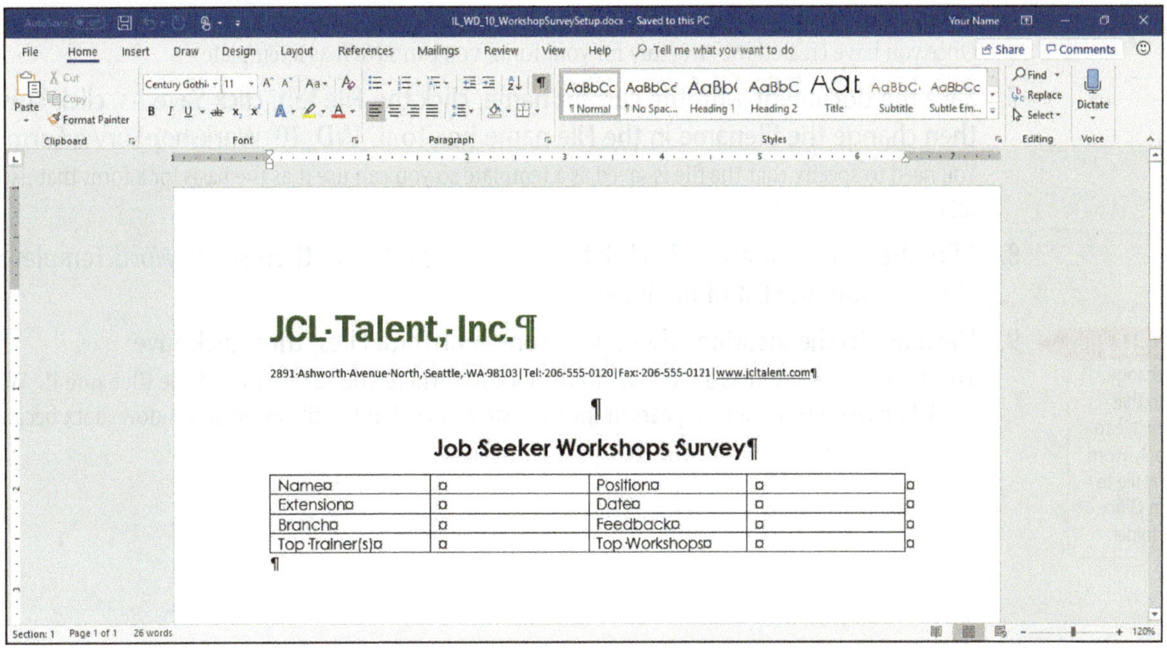

Word

Word
Module 10

Construct a Form Template

Learning Outcome
- Save a form as a template

A **form** is a structured document with spaces reserved for entering information. You create a form as a template that includes labeled spaces, called **form controls**, which are **fields** into which users type information. A Word form is created as a **form template**, which contains all the components of the form. The structure of a form template usually consists of a table that contains labels and form controls. A **label** is a word or phrase such as "Date" or "Location" that tells people who fill in the form the kind of information required for a given field. A form control, often referred to simply as a control, is the placeholder that you, as the form developer, insert into the form. The type of form control you insert in a form depends on the type of data you want users to insert. FIGURE 10-4 shows a completed form template containing several different types of controls. Once you have created a form, you can protect it so that users can enter information into the form, but they cannot change the structure of the form itself. CASE *You build on the table that you started in the previous lesson and then you save the document as a template.*

STEPS

1. **Select the cell containing Top Trainer(s) and the cell to the right, click the Table Tools Layout tab, then click the Merge Cells button in the Merge group**
   The two cells are merged into one cell.

QUICK TIP
To merge cells, the cells must be contiguous, that is, they must share a common border.

2. **Select the cell containing Top Workshops and the cell to its right, then click the Merge Cells button in the Merge group to merge the two cells into one cell**
3. **Press TAB to start a new row, then press TAB two more times**
   Two blank rows are added to the table. The insertion point is in the first cell of the bottom row.
4. **Select the two cells in the bottom row, then click the Merge Cells button in the Merge group to merge the cells into one cell.**
5. **Press TAB, select the new bottom row, click the Split Cells button in the Merge group, type 4 in the Number of columns box, then click OK**

QUICK TIP
Press TAB to move from cell to cell when entering text in a table.

6. **Press TAB until there are three rows with four cells in each row at the bottom of the table, merge the last three cells in the last row, then enter text in the table as shown in FIGURE 10-5**
   Once you have created the structure for your form, you can save it as a template.
7. **Save the document with the current name, click the File tab, click Save As, click This PC, then change the filename in the File name box to IL_WD_10_WorkshopSurveyForm**
   You need to specify that the file is saved as a template so you can use it as the basis for a form that users will fill out.
8. **Click the More options link, click the Save as type arrow, then select Word Template (*.dotx) from the list of file types**

TROUBLE
You *must* change the location that you save the file to. If you do not, Word will save the file to the Custom Office Templates folder.

9. **Navigate to the location where you store your Data Files, then click Save**
   The document is saved as a template to the location where you save files and the filename IL_WD_10_WorkshopSurveyForm.dotx appears in the title bar. Notice that the file extension is now .dotx because the file is a template.

FIGURE 10-4: Form construction

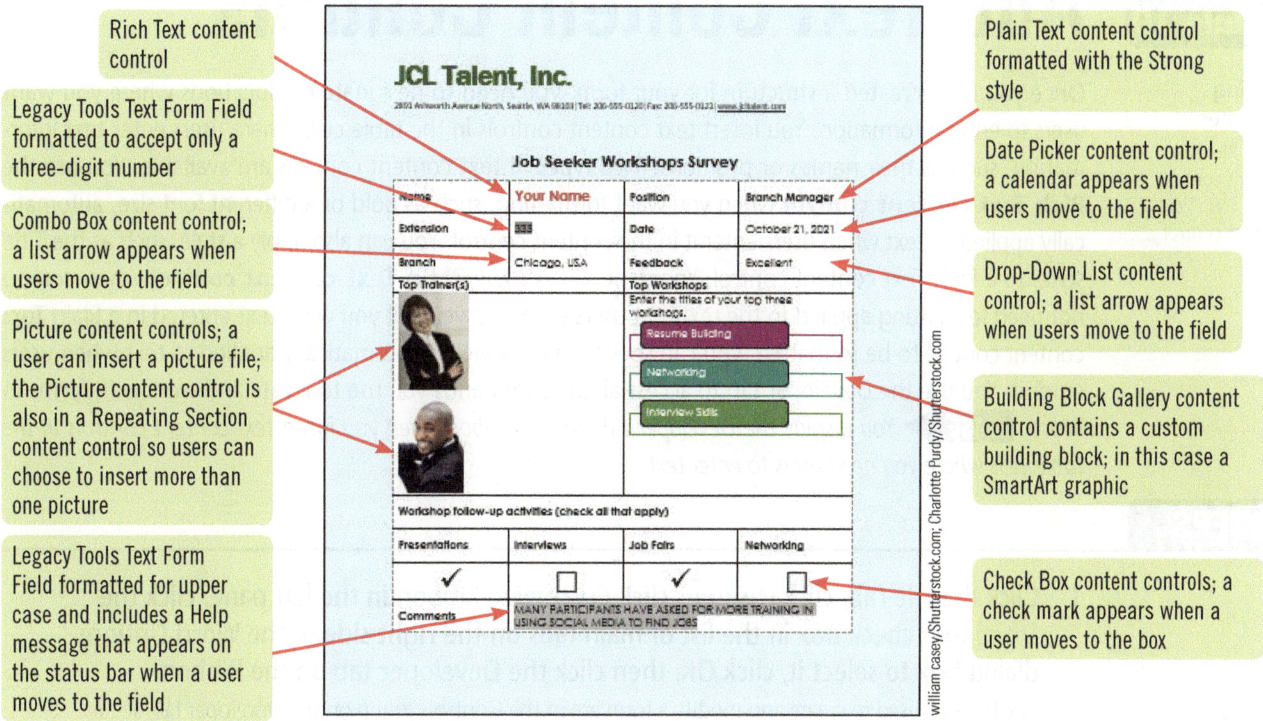

FIGURE 10-5: Table form with labels and merged cells

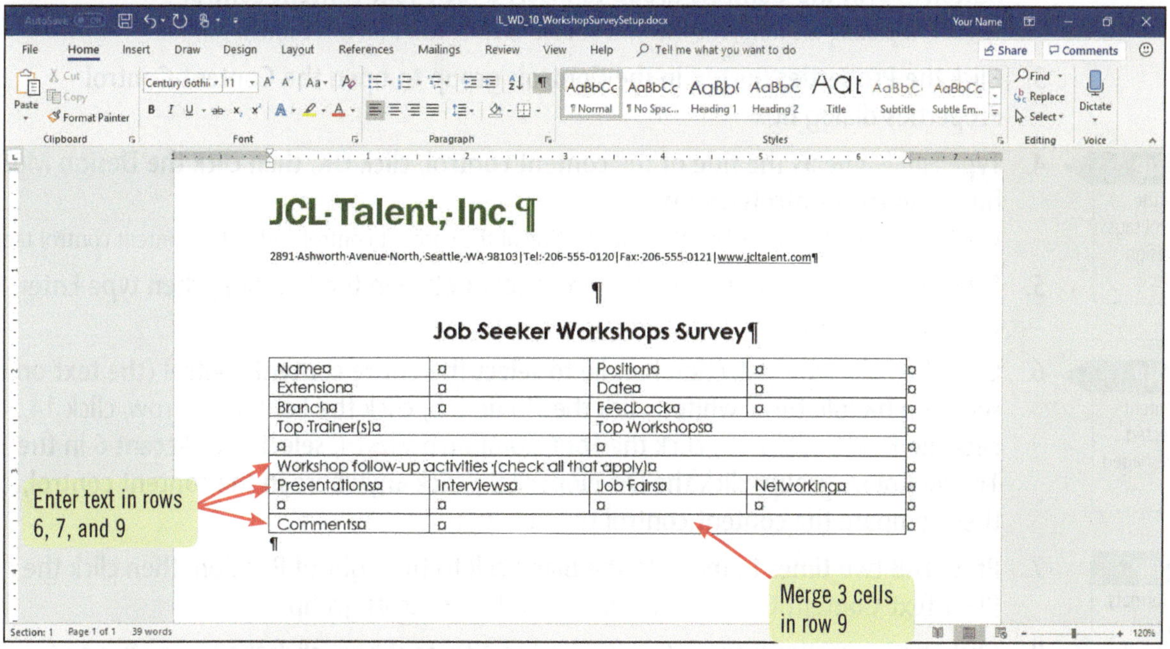

Editing a Template

A template is not the same as a document. You need to use a specific set of steps to open a template when you want to edit it. If you choose not to complete all the lessons in this module at one sitting, you will need to use the following procedure to open the template file so you can continue working. Click the File tab, click Open, click Browse, navigate to the location where you store your files for this book, click IL_WD_10_WorkshopSurveyForm.dotx, then click Open. If you double-click the file, a new document opens. Close this document and use the procedure described to open the template file so that you can continue working with it.

Word

Word
Module 10

Add Text Content Controls

Learning Outcomes
- Add a Rich Text content control
- Add a Plain Text content control

Once you have created a structure for your form, you need to designate the locations where you want users to enter information. You insert text content controls in the table cells where users enter text information, such as their names or positions. Two types of text content controls are available. You use the **Rich Text content control** when you want formatting, such as bold or a different font size, automatically applied to text when users enter it in the content control. You can also apply a style, such as the Title style, to a Rich Text content control. You generally use the **Plain Text content control** when you do not need formatting applied to the text that users enter. However, if you want text entered in a Plain Text content control to be formatted, you can specify that a style be automatically applied to text when users enter it. You use the Developer tab to access all the commands you use to create and work with forms in Word. **CASE** *You display the Developer tab on the Ribbon, then you insert text content controls in the table cells where you need users to enter text.*

STEPS

1. **Click the File tab, click Options, click Customize Ribbon in the left pane, click the Developer check box in the list of main tabs on the right side of the Word Options dialog box to select it, click OK, then click the Developer tab on the Ribbon**
   The buttons used to create and modify a form are in the Controls group on the Developer tab; see TABLE 10-1.
2. **Click in the blank cell to the right of Name, then click the Rich Text Content Control button Aa in the Controls group to insert a Rich Text content control**
   When completing the form, the user will be able to enter text into this content control.
3. **Click the Properties button in the Controls group to open the Content Control Properties dialog box**
4. **Type Full Name as the title of the content control, click OK, then click the Design Mode button in the Controls group**
   Word automatically assigns Full Name to the title of the content control and to the content control tags.
5. **Select the text Click or tap here to enter text between the two tags, then type Enter your full name here.**
6. **Click the Full Name selection handle to select the entire content control (the text on the selection handle turns white), click the Home tab, click the Font Size arrow, click 14, click the Bold button B, click the Font Color arrow A, select Red, Accent 6 in the Theme Colors group, click the Developer tab, click anywhere in the content control, then compare the content control to FIGURE 10-6**
7. **Press TAB two times to move to the blank cell to the right of Position, then click the Plain Text Content Control button Aa in the Controls group**
8. **Click the Properties button, type Job in the Title text box, click the Use a style to format text typed into the empty control check box, click the Style arrow, select Strong as shown in FIGURE 10-7, then click OK**
   If you want text entered in a Plain Text content control to appear formatted when the user fills in the form, you must apply a paragraph style. The Strong paragraph style that you applied to the Plain Text content control will show when you fill in the form as a user.
9. **Select the Click or tap here to enter text. text between the two Job tags, type Enter your job title here., click outside the table, then click the Save button on the Quick Access toolbar to save the template**

QUICK TIP
You can view the content control tags only when Design Mode is active.

QUICK TIP
When the content control is selected, the control is shaded gray.

QUICK TIP
If you apply formats, such as bold and font size, to the Plain Text content control, the formatting will be lost when the form is opened and filled in by a user. You can format both Rich Text and Plain Text content controls with a paragraph style.

FIGURE 10-6: Rich Text content control

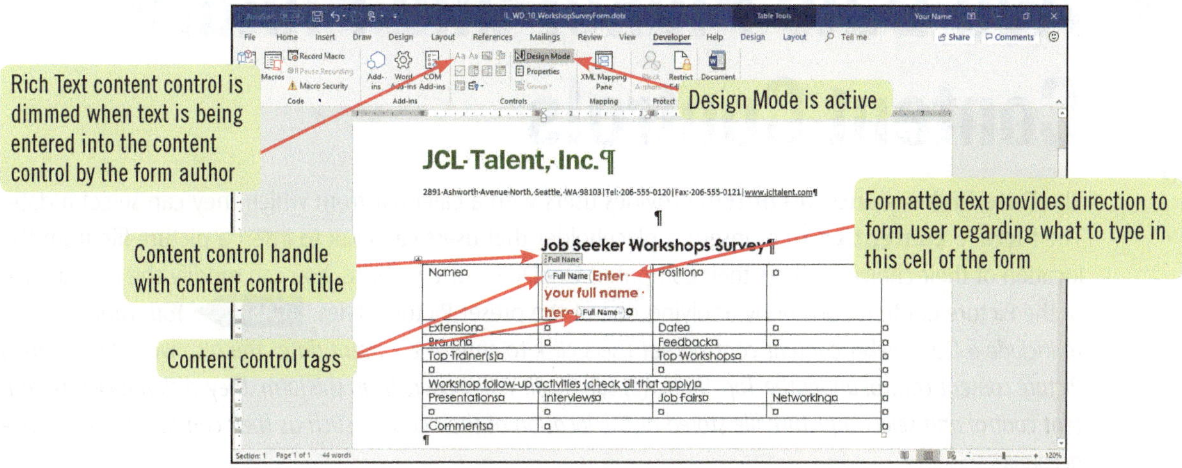

FIGURE 10-7: Content Control Properties dialog box

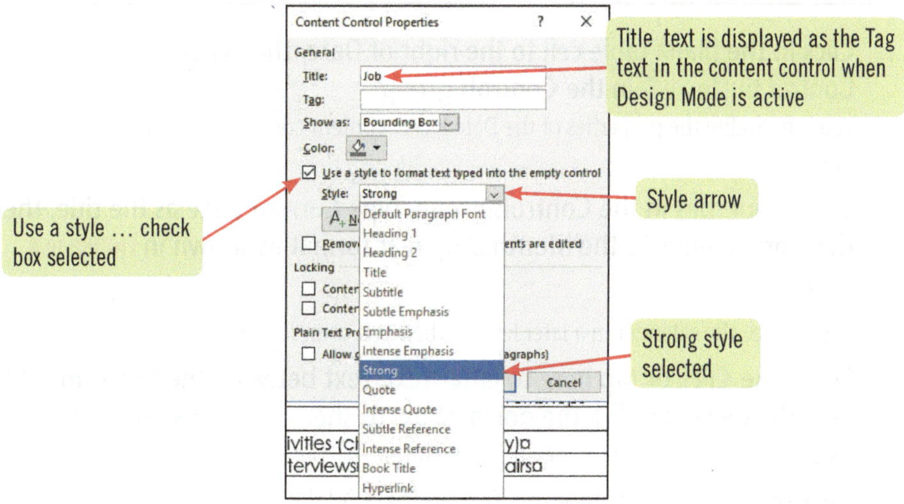

TABLE 10-1: Buttons in the Controls group

button	use to insert a
Aa	Rich Text content control when you want to apply formatting, such as bold, to text users type
Aa	Plain Text content control when you want the text that users type to display as plain, unformatted text
	Picture content control when you want users to be able to insert a picture file
	Building Block Gallery content control when you want to insert a custom building block, such as a cover page
	Check Box content control when you want to insert a check box that users can click to indicate a selection
	Combo Box content control when you want users to select from a list or be able to add a new item
	Drop-Down List content control when you want to provide users with a list of restricted choices
	Date Picker content control when you want to include a calendar control that users can use to select a specific date
	Repeating Section content control when you want to repeat content, including other content controls
	Controls from the Legacy Tools options when you want additional control over the content that can be entered into a control; if you have programming experience, you can insert ActiveX Controls into forms using the Legacy Tools button

Word
Module 10

Learning Outcomes
- Add a Date Picker content control
- Add a Picture content control

Add Date Picker and Picture Content Controls

The **Date Picker content control** provides users with a calendar from which they can select a date. The **Picture content control** inserts a placeholder that users can click to insert a picture file from the location of their choice, such as their computer, OneDrive, or a website. You can modify the appearance of the Picture content control by applying one of the preset Picture styles. **CASE** *You want the form to include a Date Picker content control that users click to enter the current date. You also want to include a Picture content control under the Top Trainer(s) table cell. When users fill in the form, they click the Picture content control and select a picture file stored at the location of their choice, such as their computer or OneDrive account.*

STEPS

1. **Click in the blank table cell to the right of Date, then click the Date Picker Content Control button in the Controls group**
   You can modify the properties of the Date Picker content control so the date users enter appears in a specific format.
2. **Click Properties in the Controls group, type Current Date as the title, then click the date that corresponds to the Month Day, Year format as shown in FIGURE 10-8**
3. **Click OK**
   You will see the calendar in a later lesson when you complete the form as a user.
4. **Select the Click or tap here to enter text. text between the two Current Date tags, then type the message Click the down arrow to show a calendar and select the current date.**
   Users see this message when they fill in the form.
5. **Click the blank cell below the Top Trainer(s) label**
6. **Click the Picture Content Control button in the Controls group**
   A Picture content control is inserted in the table cell. When users fill in the form, they click the picture icon to insert a picture file from a location of their choice, such as their computer's hard drive, their OneDrive account, or a website.
7. **Click Properties, type Insert up to three pictures as the title, then click OK**
   The title text advises users that they will be able to insert more than one picture.
8. **Click the Design Mode button in the Controls group to toggle out of Design mode, compare the table form to FIGURE 10-9, then save the template**
   You need to toggle out of Design mode so you can work with the Repeating Section content control in the next lesson.

FIGURE 10-8: Selecting a date format

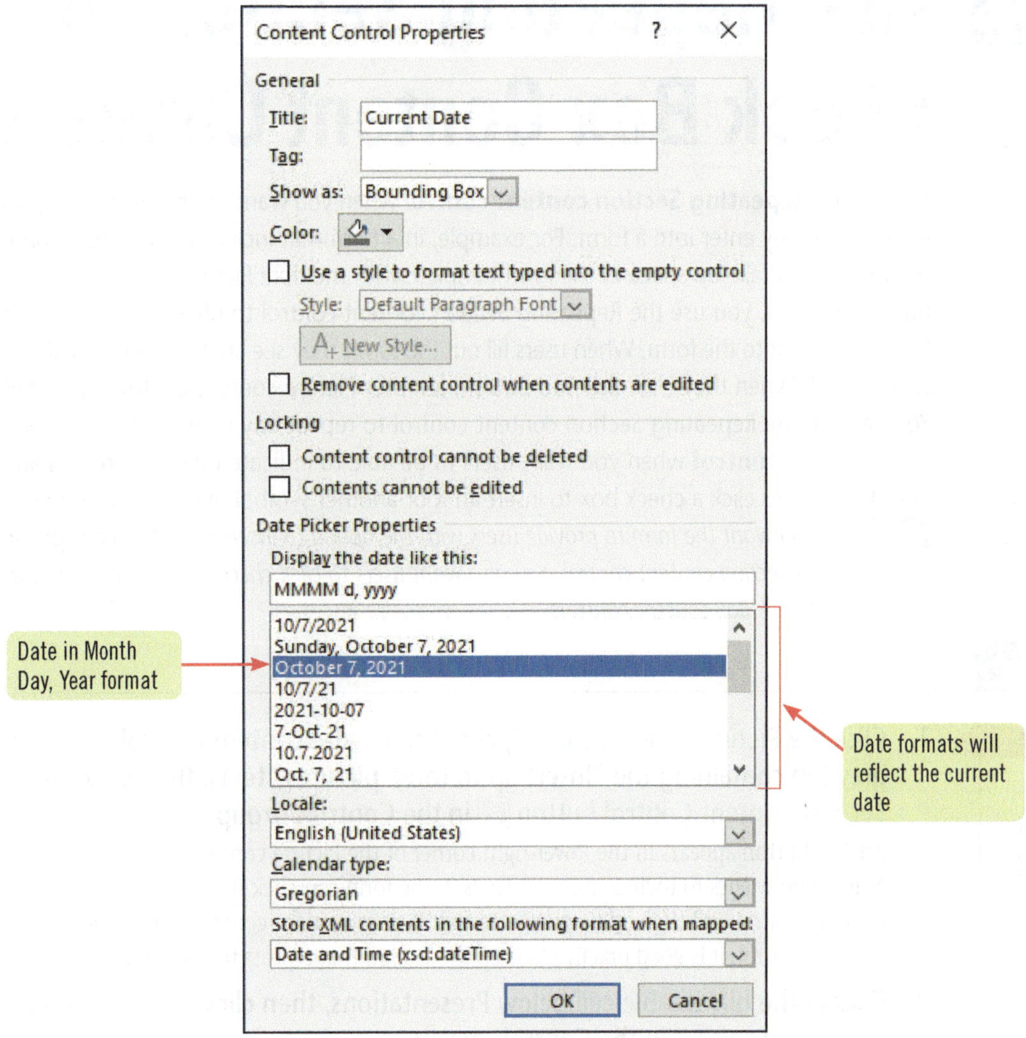

FIGURE 10-9: Picture content control

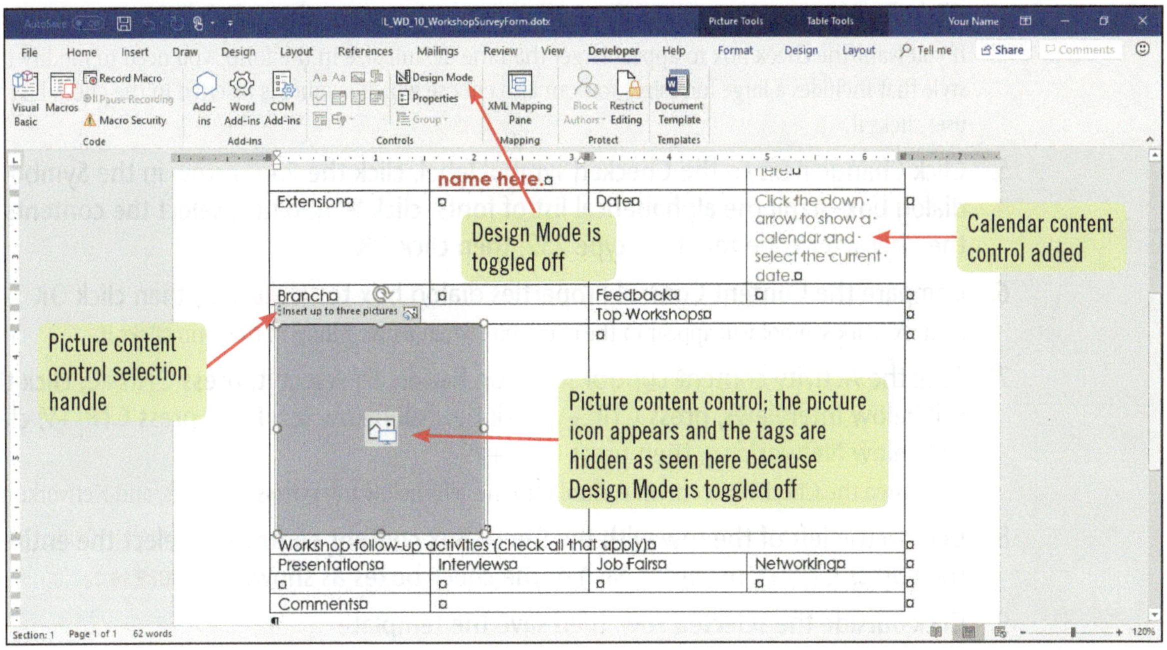

Word

Add Repeating Section and Check Box Content Controls

Learning Outcomes
- Use the Repeating Section content control
- Add Check Box content controls

You insert a **Repeating Section content control** when you want to give users the option to add to the information they enter into a form. For example, in a form that includes one Picture content control, you do not want to take up space in the form template with multiple Picture content controls that users may not use. Instead, you use the Repeating Section content control to give users the option to insert additional pictures into the form. When users fill out the form, they see an Add button next to the Picture content control. When they click the Add button, another Picture content control is inserted into the form. You can use the Repeating Section content control to repeat any content control. You insert a **Check Box content control** when you want users to be able to indicate their preferences among a selection of options. Users click a check box to insert an X or another symbol of your choice such as a check mark.

CASE *You want the form to provide users with the option to insert more than one picture so you include the Repeating Section content control. You also want users to click check boxes to indicate their preferences so you include Check Box content controls.*

STEPS

TROUBLE
If the Repeating Section Content Control button is dimmed, click the Design Mode button to toggle it off.

1. **Click the Picture content control, click the Picture content control selection handle (the grey tab containing the "Insert up to three pictures" text), then click the Repeating Section Content Control button in the Controls group**

   An Add button appears in the lower-right corner of the Picture content control, as shown in FIGURE 10-10. A user who wishes to include more pictures in the form can click the Add button to insert another Picture content control and then add a picture to that Picture content control. When adding a Repeating Section content control, it is good practice to keep the section that repeats to one table row.

2. **Click in the blank table cell below Presentations, then click the Check Box Content Control button in the Controls group**
3. **Click Properties, then type Activity**
4. **Click the Use a style ... check box, click the Style arrow, then click Title**

   If you want the check box to appear larger than the default size in the form, you need to modify it with a style that includes a large font size. You can also choose which symbol is inserted in the check box when a user clicks it.

5. **Click Change next to the Checked symbol label, click the Font arrow in the Symbol dialog box, scroll the alphabetical list of fonts, click Wingdings, select the contents of the Character code text box, type 252, then click OK**
6. **Compare the Content Control Properties dialog box to FIGURE 10-11, then click OK**

   A check mark symbol will appear in the check box when a user filling in the form clicks it.

7. **Click the Activity content control selection handle to select it, press CTRL+C, click the cell below Interviews, press CTRL+V, click the cell below Job Fairs, press CTRL+V, click the cell below Networking, then press CTRL+V**

   You pasted the Check Box content control into the cells below Interviews, Job Fairs, and Networking.

8. **Click to the left of the row with the Check Box content controls to select the entire row, then press CTRL+E to center each of the check boxes as shown in FIGURE 10-12**
9. **Click outside the selected row, then save the template**

FIGURE 10-10: Add button for the Repeating Section content control

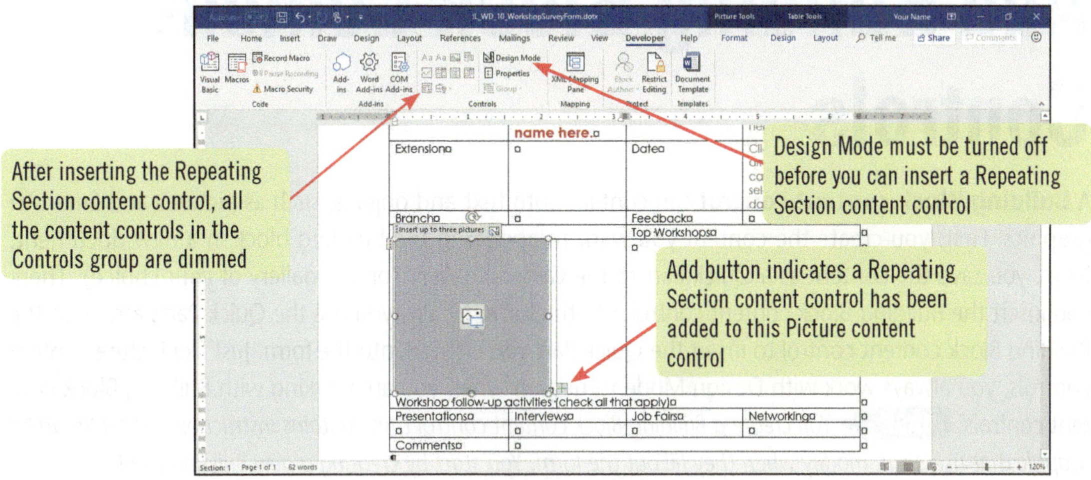

FIGURE 10-11: Check Box content control properties

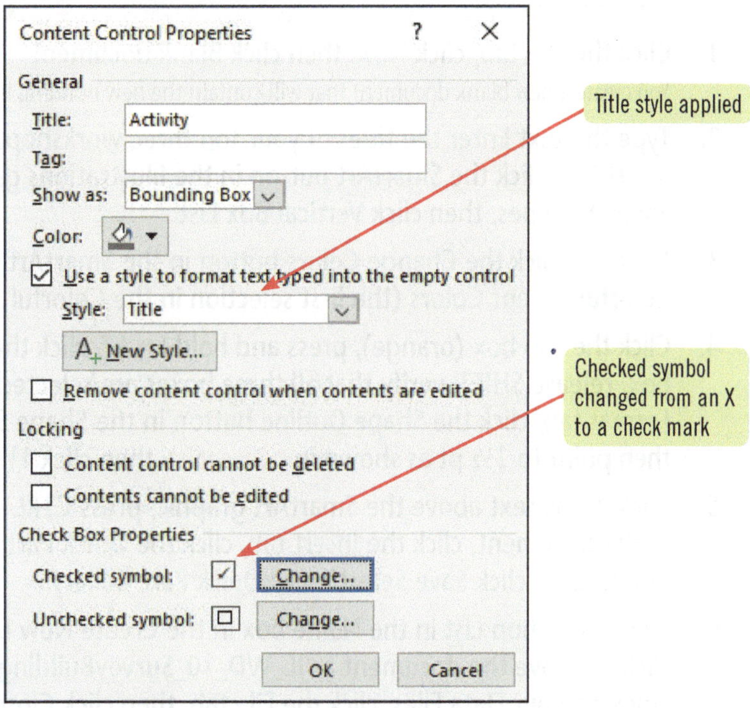

FIGURE 10-12: Table form with the Check Box content controls added

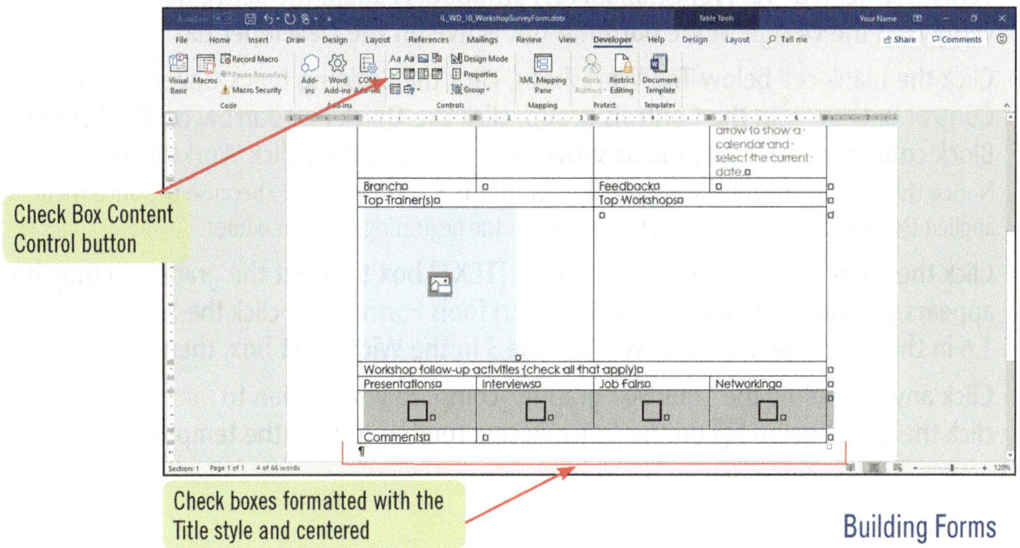

Word

Word
Module 10

Add Building Block Content Controls

Learning Outcomes
- Create a Quick Part
- Add a Building Block Content Control

A **Building Block content control** can contain both text and objects, such as pictures and SmartArt graphics. First, you create the content you want to appear in the building block in a new document. Next, you save the content as a Quick Part to the General gallery (or any gallery of your choice). Then, you insert the Building Block content control into the form. Finally, you use the Quick Parts arrow on the Building Block content control to insert the Quick Part you created into the form. Just like Picture content controls, you always work with Design Mode turned off when you are working with Building Block content controls. CASE *You create a Building Block content control that contains instructions and a SmartArt graphic that users can modify when they fill out the form. You start by creating a new Building Block.*

STEPS

1. **Click the File tab, click New, then click Blank document**
   You create a new blank document that will contain the new building block you want to appear in the form.
2. **Type the text Enter the titles of your top three workshops., press ENTER, click the Insert tab, click the SmartArt button in the Illustrations group, click List in the list of SmartArt types, then click Vertical Box List**
3. **Click OK, click the Change Colors button in the SmartArt Styles group, then click Colorful-Accent Colors (the first selection in the Colorful section)**
4. **Click the top box (orange), press and hold SHIFT, click the gray box, click the yellow box, release SHIFT, verify that all three boxes are selected, click the SmartArt Tools Format tab, click the Shape Outline button in the Shape Styles group, click Weight, then point to 1½ pt as shown in FIGURE 10-13, then click 1½ pt**
5. **Click in the text above the SmartArt graphic, press CTRL+A to select the contents of the document, click the Insert tab, click the Quick Parts button arrow in the Text group, then click Save Selection to Quick Part Gallery**
6. **Type Workshop List in the Name box in the Create New Building Block dialog box, click OK, save the document as IL_WD_10_SurveyBuildingBlock to the location where you save your Data Files, click the File tab, then click Close**
7. **Verify that IL_WD_10_WorkshopSurveyForm.dotx is again the active document, then verify that the Design Mode button is not active on the Developer tab**
8. **Click the blank cell below Top Workshops, click the Building Block Gallery Content Control button in the Controls group, click the Quick Parts arrow on the Building Block content control title tab as shown in FIGURE 10-14, then click Workshop List**
   Notice that a different color scheme is applied to the SmartArt graphic because the Slice theme was applied to the Word document that you opened at the beginning of this module.
9. **Click the white area to the left of the pink [TEXT] box to select the graphic, a gray box appears around the graphic, click the SmartTools Format tab, click the Size button, type 1.6 in the Height text box, press TAB, type 3 in the Width text box, then press ENTER**
10. **Click any cell below the SmartArt graphic, compare your screen to FIGURE 10-15, then click the Save button on the Quick Access toolbar to save the template**

QUICK TIP
The default Office theme was applied when you created the SmartArt graphic in a new document.

FIGURE 10-13: Shape Outline weight selected

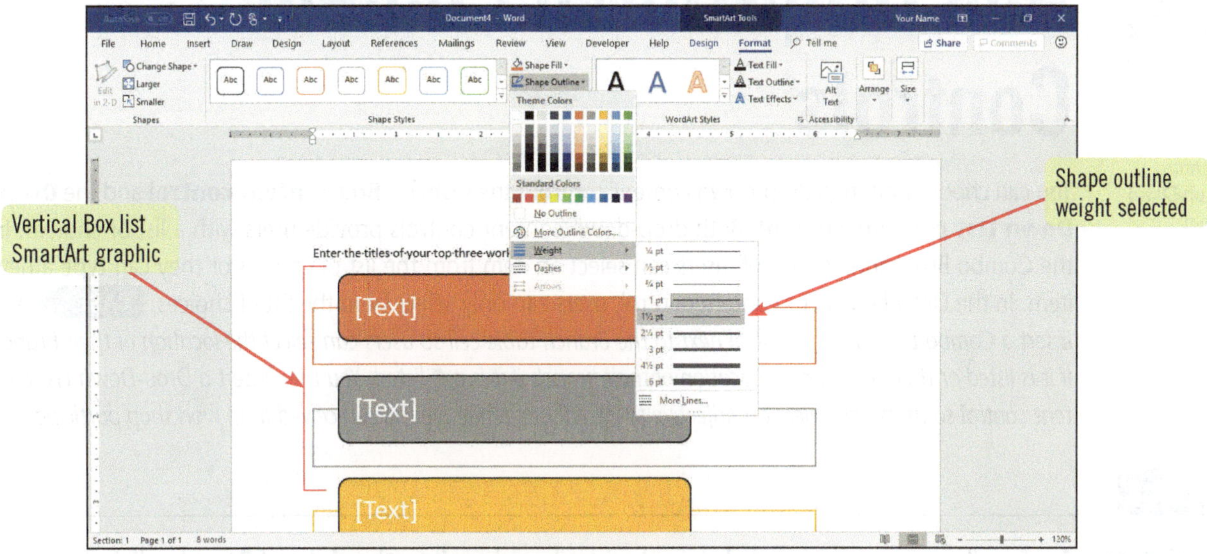

FIGURE 10-14: Inserting a Building Block content control

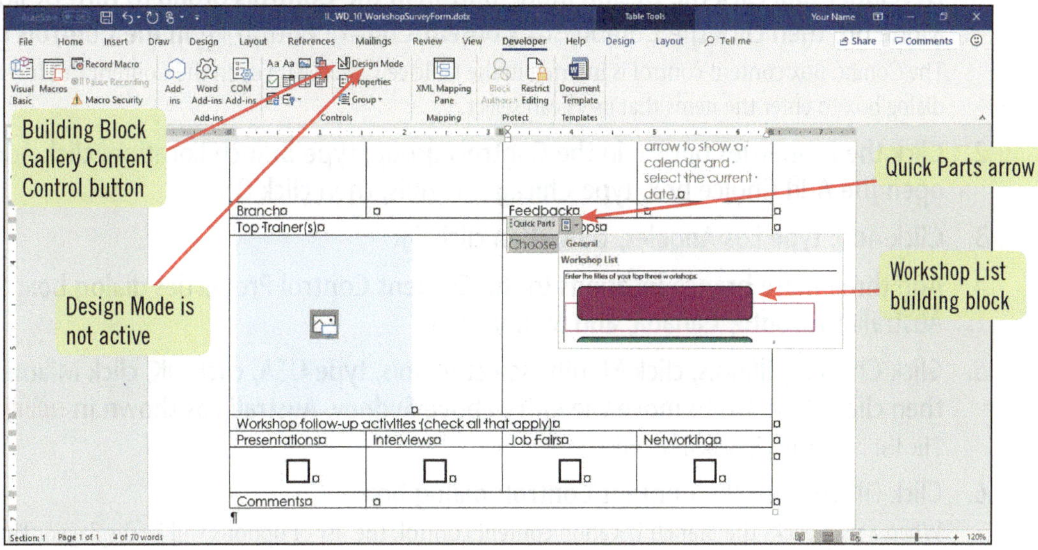

FIGURE 10-15: Completed Building Block content control

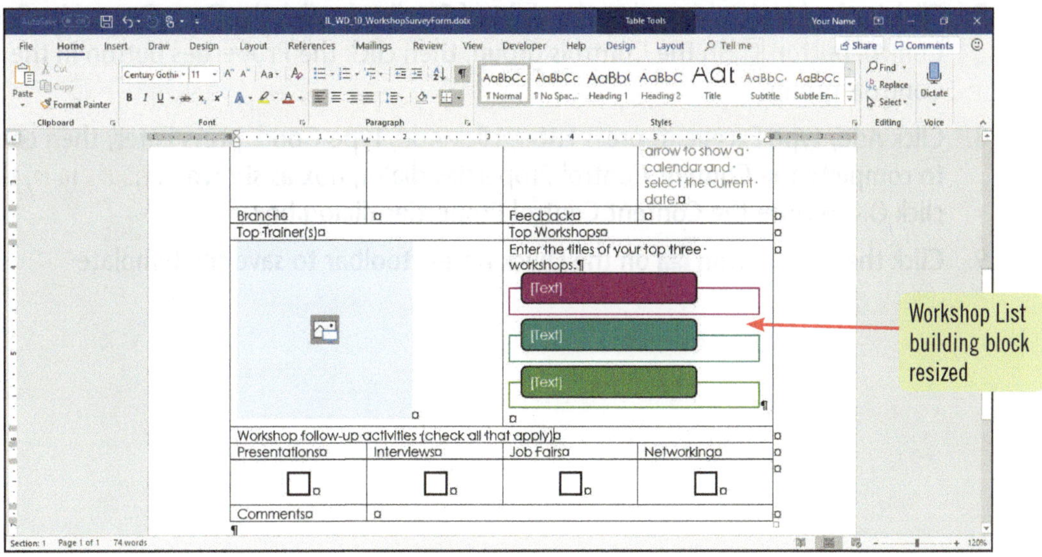

Word

Add Drop-Down Content Controls

Learning Outcomes
- Add a Combo Box content control
- Add a Drop-Down List content control

You can choose from two drop-down content controls: the **Combo Box content control** and the **Drop-Down List content control**. Both drop-down content controls provide users with a list of choices. In the Combo Box content control, users can select an item from the list of choices or they can type a new item. In the Drop-Down List content control, users can only select from the list of choices. **CASE** *You insert a Combo Box content control next to the Branch table cell so users can select the location of their branch if it is listed or they can type the location of their branch if it is not listed. You then insert a Drop-Down List content control so users can select an adjective to describe average feedback received from workshop participants.*

STEPS

QUICK TIP
With Design Mode on, you can see the tags associated with each content control.

1. **Scroll up as needed and click in the blank table cell to the right of Branch, click the Developer tab, click the Design Mode button in the Controls group to turn Design Mode on, then click the Combo Box Content Control button in the Controls group**
   The Combo Box content control is inserted in the table cell. Next, you open the Content Control Properties dialog box to enter the items that users can select.
2. **Click the Properties button in the Controls group, type Branch Location, click Add to open the Add Choice box, type Chicago, Illinois, then click OK**
3. **Click Add, type Los Angeles, USA, then click OK**
4. **Add three more branch locations to the Content Control Properties dialog box: Sydney, Australia; Toronto, Canada; and Miami, USA**
5. **Click Chicago, Illinois, click Modify, select Illinois, type USA, click OK, click Miami, USA, then click Move Up to move the entry above Sydney, Australia as shown in FIGURE 10-16**
   The list is now in alphabetical order.
6. **Click OK to close the Content Controls dialog box**
   When a user clicks the Branch Location content control, the list of options will be displayed. The user can select one of the options or type a branch location in the text box.
7. **Click in the blank table cell to the right of Feedback, click the Drop-Down List Content Control button in the Controls group, then click the Properties button in the Controls group**
8. **Click Add, type Excellent, press Enter, click Add, type Good, press Enter, then continue to complete the Content Control Properties dialog box as shown in FIGURE 10-17, then click OK to close the Content Control Properties dialog box**
9. **Click the Save button on the Quick Access toolbar to save the template**

FIGURE 10-16: Entries for the Combo Box content control

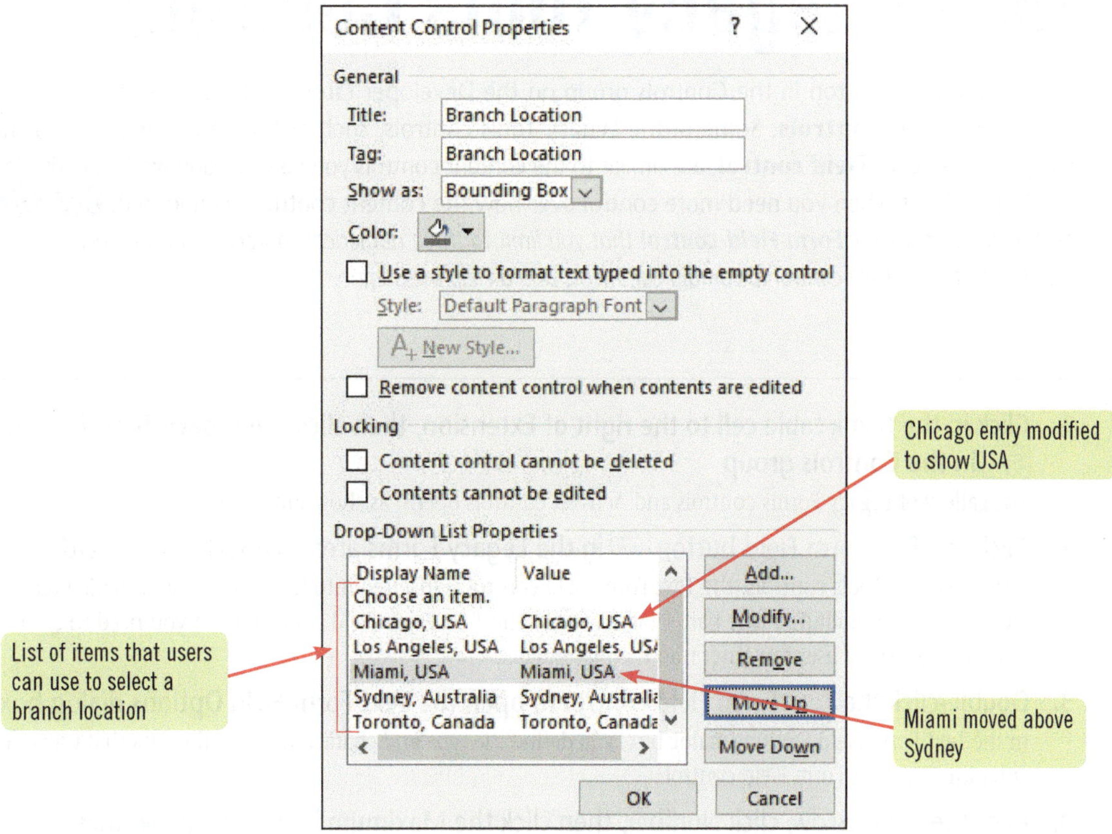

FIGURE 10-17: Entries for the Drop-Down List content control

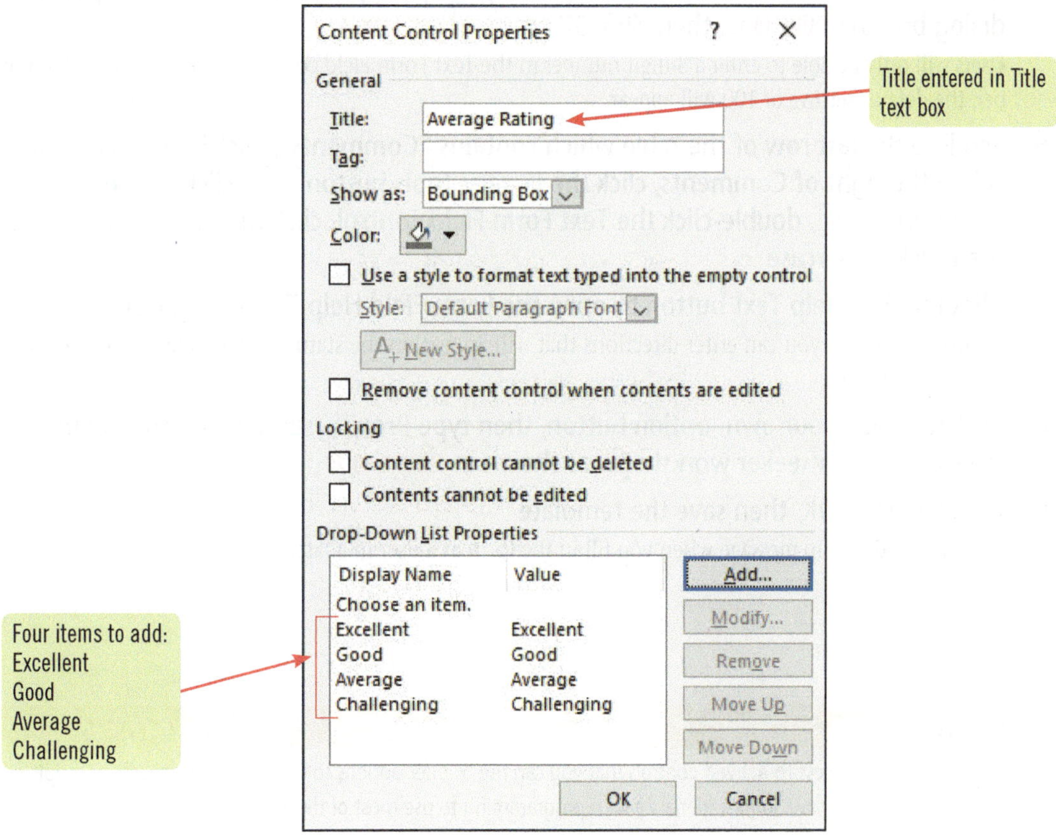

Word
Module 10

Insert Legacy Tools Controls

Learning Outcomes
- Insert a Text Form Field
- Add Help Text

The Legacy Tools button in the Controls group on the Developer tab provides access to a selection of **Legacy Tools controls**. Some of the Legacy Tools controls, such as the **Text control** and the **Drop-Down Form Field control**, are similar to the content controls you have already worked with. You use Legacy Tools when you need more control over how the content control is configured. CASE *First, you insert a* ***Text Form Field control*** *that you limit to three numerical characters, and then you insert another Text Form Field control to contain comments and a Help message.*

STEPS

1. **Click in the blank table cell to the right of Extension, then click the Legacy Tools button in the Controls group**
   The gallery of Legacy Forms controls and ActiveX controls opens, as shown in FIGURE 10-18.
2. **Click the Text Form Field button in the Legacy Forms area to insert a form field**
   Like all Legacy Tools controls, the Text Form Field control is inserted into the table cell as a shaded rectangle and does not include a title bar or tags. You use the Text Form Field control when you need to control exactly what data a user can enter into the placeholder.
3. **Double-click the Text Form Field control to open the Text Form Field Options dialog box**
   In the Text Form Field Options dialog box, you define the type and characteristics of the data that users can enter into the Text Form Field control.
4. **Click the Type arrow, click Number, then click the Maximum length up arrow three times to set the maximum length of the entry at 3**
5. **Click the Default number text box, type 100, compare your Text Form Field Options dialog box to FIGURE 10-19, then click OK**
   Users will only be able to enter a 3-digit number in the Text Form Field control. If users do not enter a number, the default setting of 100 will appear.
6. **Scroll to the last row of the table which contains "Comments", click in the blank table cell to the right of Comments, click the Legacy Tools button, click the Text Form Field button, double-click the Text Form Field control, click the Text format arrow, then click Uppercase**
7. **Click the Add Help Text button to open the Form Field Help Text dialog box**
   In this dialog box, you can enter directions that will appear on the status bar when users click in the Text Form Field control.
8. **Click the Type your own: option button, then type Provide suggestions to help us improve our job seeker workshops. as shown in FIGURE 10-20**
9. **Click OK, click OK, then save the template**
   You will see the Help message when you fill in the form as a user in a later lesson.

Using ActiveX controls

The Legacy Tools button also provides access to ActiveX controls that you can use to offer options to users or to run macros or scripts that automate specific tasks. You need to have some experience with programming to use most of the ActiveX controls.

FIGURE 10-18: Inserting a Text Form Field control

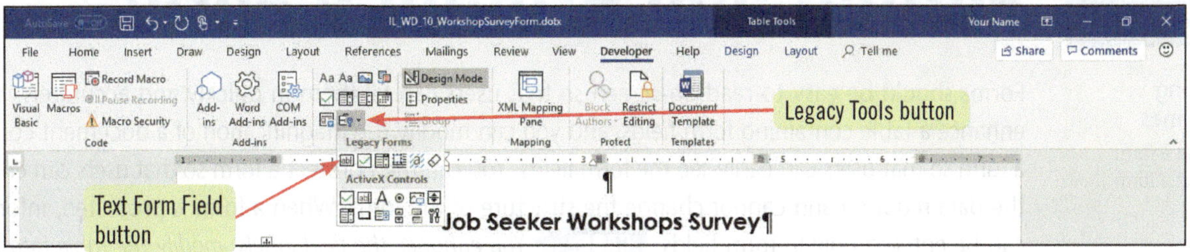

FIGURE 10-19: Text Form Field Options dialog box

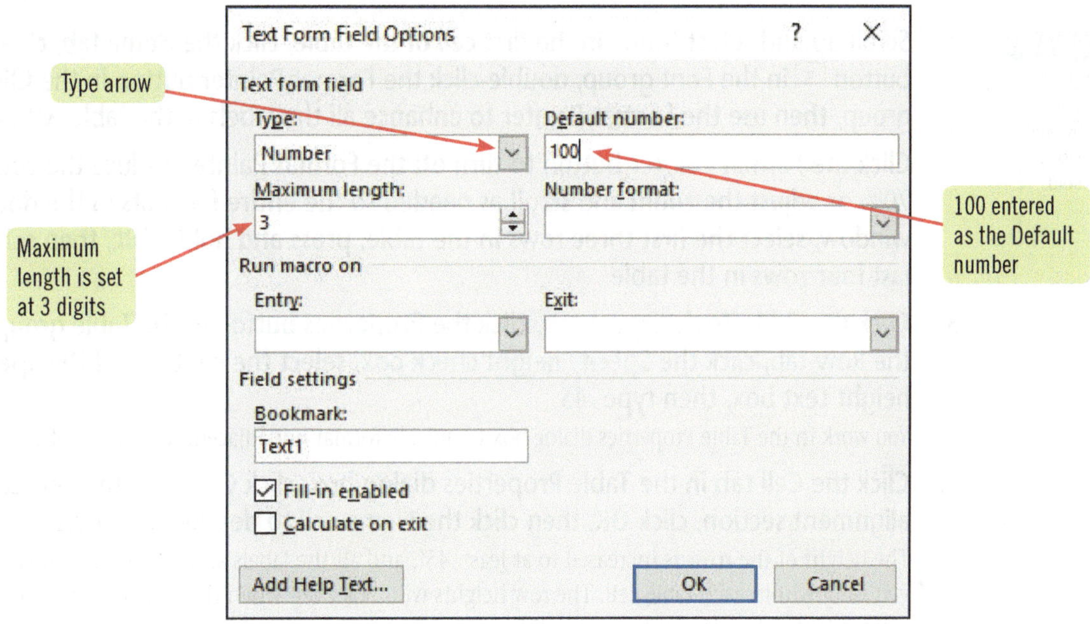

FIGURE 10-20: Adding Help text

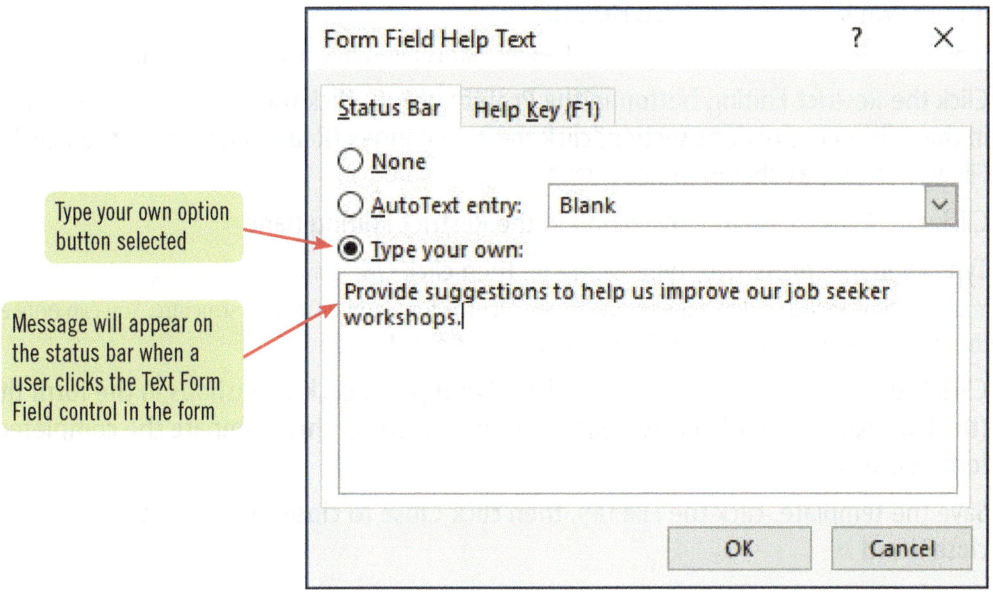

Word

Word
Module 10

Format and Protect a Form

Learning Outcomes
- Format a form
- Protect a form

Forms should be easy to read on-screen so that users can fill them in quickly and accurately. You can enhance a table containing form fields, and you can modify the magnification of a document containing a form so that users can easily see the form fields. You can then protect a form so that users can enter only the data required and cannot change the structure of the form. When a form is protected, information can be entered only in form fields. **CASE** *You enhance the field labels, modify the table form, specify that the Name content control cannot be deleted, and then protect and save the template.*

STEPS

QUICK TIP
Instead of using the Format Painter, you can use the CTRL key to select each label, then click the Bold button.

1. **Scroll up and select Name in the first cell of the table, click the Home tab, click the Bold button B in the Font group, double-click the Format Painter button in the Clipboard group, then use the Format Painter to enhance all the labels in the table with bold**
2. **Click the Format Painter button to turn off the Format Painter, reduce the zoom to 70% or adjust the zoom and scroll as needed so the entire form fits in the document window, select the first three rows in the table, press and hold CTRL, then select the last four rows in the table**
3. **Click the Table Tools Layout tab, click the Properties button in the Table group, click the Row tab, click the Specify height check box, select the contents of the Specify height text box, then type .45**
   You work in the Table Properties dialog box to quickly format nonadjacent rows in a table.
4. **Click the Cell tab in the Table Properties dialog box, click Center in the Vertical alignment section, click OK, then click the Name cell to deselect the rows**
   The height of the rows is increased to at least .45", and all the labels and content controls are centered vertically within each table cell. The row heights will look even when the content control directions are removed after the user enters information.

QUICK TIP
Before you protect a document, you must be sure Design Mode is turned off.

5. **Click the Developer tab, verify that Design Mode is not active, click the Position content control in the top row, rightmost cell of the form, click the Properties button in the Controls group, click the Content Control cannot be deleted check box to select it as shown in FIGURE 10-21, then click OK**
   You specify that a control cannot be deleted before restricting editing of the entire form.
6. **Click the Restrict Editing button in the Protect group, click the Allow only...check box in the Editing restrictions section, click the No changes (Read only) arrow, then click Filling in forms as shown in FIGURE 10-22**
7. **Click Yes, Start Enforcing Protection in the Restrict Editing pane**
8. **Type cengage, press TAB, type cengage, then click OK**
   You enter a password so that a user cannot unprotect the form and change its structure. You can only edit the form if you enter the "cengage" password when prompted.

TROUBLE
If the passwords don't match, you will be prompted to reenter the password.

9. **Click the Close button ✕ in the Restrict Editing pane, click Workshops in the form title (the Full Name content control appears to be selected), then compare the completed form template to FIGURE 10-23**
10. **Save the template, click the File tab, then click Close to close the template, but do not close Word**

FIGURE 10-21: Locking a content control

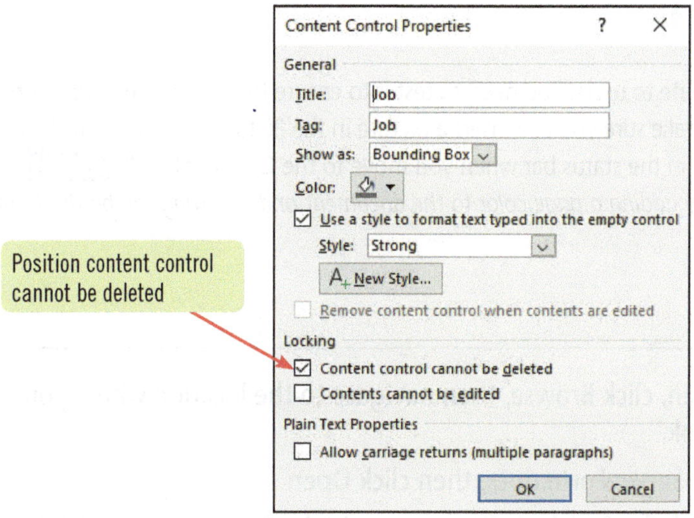

FIGURE 10-22: Protecting a form

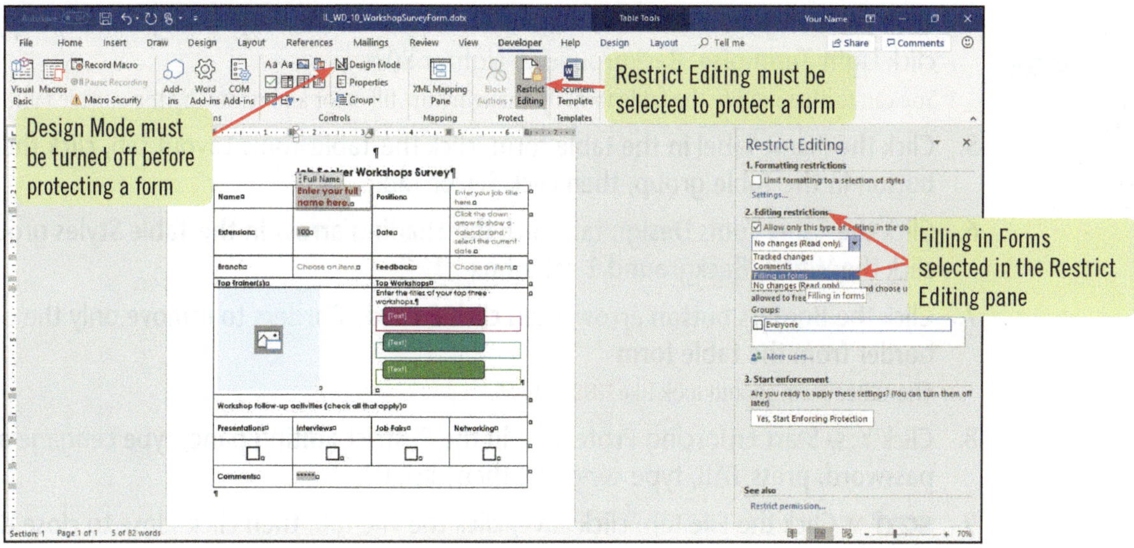

FIGURE 10-23: Completed form template

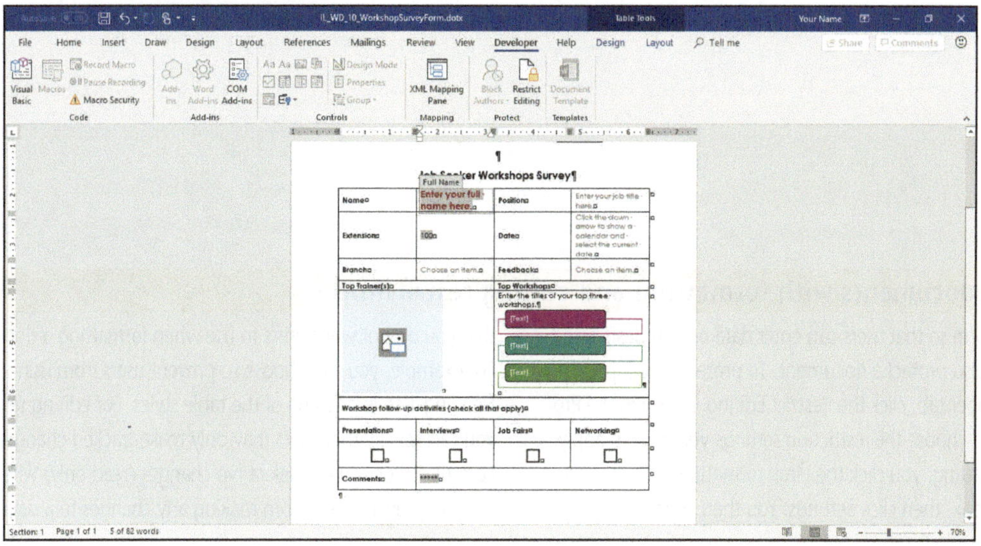

Edit a Form

Learning Outcomes
- Change the Page Color
- Edit a Form

Before you distribute a form template to users, you need to test it to ensure that all the elements work correctly. For example, you want to make sure you can insert a picture in the Picture content control and that the Help text you entered appears in the status bar when you move to the Comments cell. **CASE** *You open and edit the form template by adding a page color to the document and removing the border from the table form.*

STEPS

TROUBLE
Do *not* double-click the filename to open it. You must use the File, Open method to open the template file so that you can make changes to it.

QUICK TIP
Before you can edit any part of the template, you need to stop protection.

1. **Click the File tab, click Open, click Browse, then navigate to the location where you store your files for this book**
2. **Click IL_WD_10_WorkshopSurveyForm.dotx, then click Open**
3. **Click the Developer tab, click the Restrict Editing button in the Protect group, click Stop Protection in the Restrict Editing pane, type cengage as shown in FIGURE 10-24, then click OK**
4. **Click the Design tab, click the Page Color button in the Page Background group, then click Light Turquoise, Background 2, Lighter 80%**
   You can further modify the table form by changing the fill color and removing the outside table border.
5. **Click the Name label in the table form, click the Table Tools Layout tab, click the Select button in the Table group, then click Select Table**
6. **Click the Table Tools Design tab, click the Shading arrow in the Table Styles group, then click the White, Background 1 color box**
7. **Click the Borders button arrow, then click Outside Borders to remove only the outside border from the table form**
   The edited form should look like FIGURE 10-25.
8. **Click Yes, Start Enforcing Protection in the Restrict Editing pane, type cengage as the password, press TAB, type cengage, then click OK**
9. **sam Click the File tab, click Save, click the File tab, then click Close to close the template but do not close Word**
   You saved and closed the template but did not exit Word.

Protecting documents with formatting and editing restrictions

You protect a form so that users can enter data only in designated areas. You can also protect a document. To protect a document, click the Developer tab, click the Restrict Editing button in the Protect group, then choose the restriction settings you wish to apply. To restrict formatting, you click the Limit formatting to a selection of styles check box, then click Settings. You then choose the styles that you do not want users to use when formatting a document. For example, you can choose to prevent users from using the Heading 1 style or some of the table styles. For editing restrictions, you can specify that users may only make tracked changes or insert comments, or you can select No changes (read only) when you want to prevent users from making any changes to a document.

FIGURE 10-24: Unprotecting the form

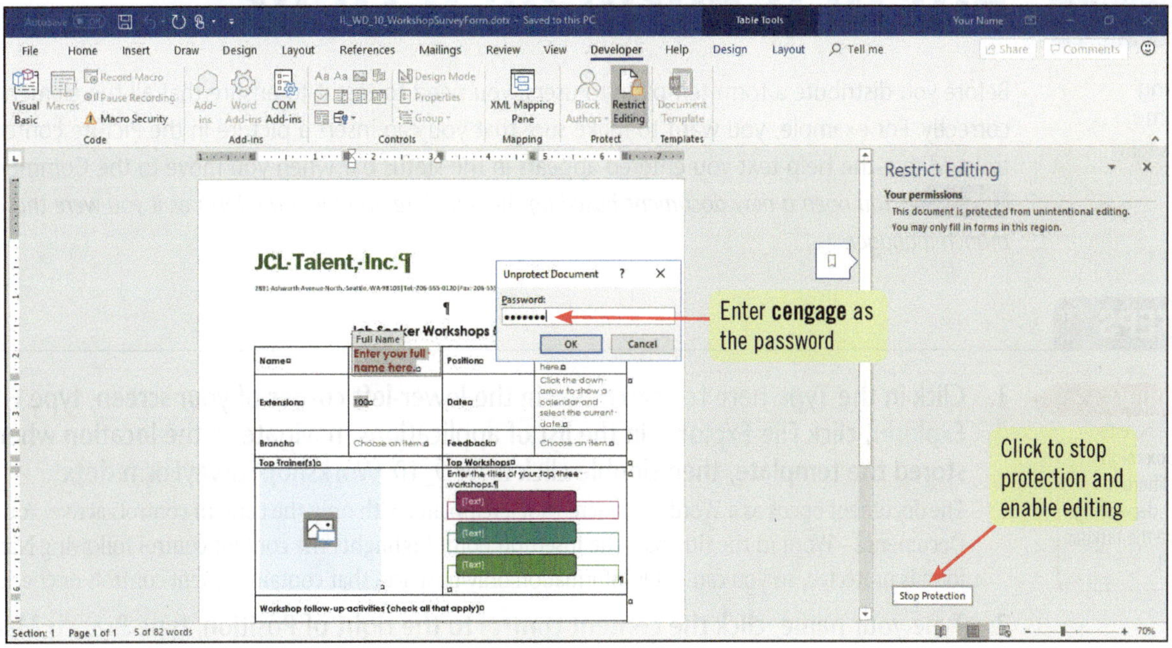

FIGURE 10-25: Formatted form

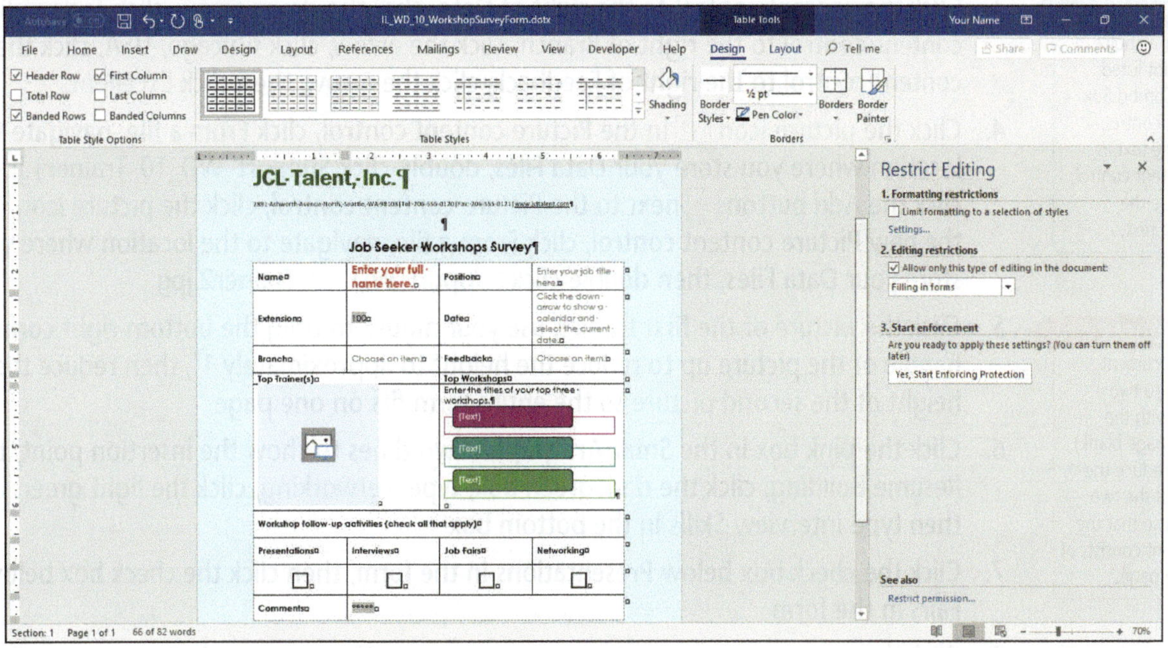

Word

Fill in a Form as a User

Learning Outcome
- Fill in a form

Before you distribute a form template to users, you need to test it to ensure that all the elements work correctly. For example, you want to make sure that you can insert a picture in the Picture content control and that the Help text you entered appears in the status bar when you move to the Comments cell. CASE *You open a new document based on the template and fill in the form as if you were the Chicago branch manager.*

STEPS

TROUBLE
The Type here to search box might be in a different location, depending on where the taskbar is docked.

QUICK TIP
To enter a choice that is not listed in the Combo Box content control, select the text in the content control, then type the required text.

TROUBLE
If the document extends to two pages (with the second page blank), further reduce the height of the two pictures so that the document consists of just one page.

TROUBLE
A form template that you open and fill as a user and then save as a Word document will open in Read Mode. To fill in the form with additional information or to edit it, click View on the Ribbon, then click Edit Document.

1. **Click in the Type here to search box in the lower-left corner of your screen, type File Explorer, click File Explorer in the list of applications, navigate to the location where you stored the template, then double-click IL_WD_10_WorkshopSurveyForm.dotx**
   The document opens as a Word document (not a template) with only the content controls active. You will see Document2 - Word in the title bar. The insertion point highlights the content control following Name. The form is protected, so you can enter information only in spaces that contain content controls or check boxes.
2. **Type your name, click the content control to the right of Position, type Branch Manager, double-click 100 next to Extension, then type 335**
   Notice how Branch Manager appears bold because you applied the Strong style when you inserted the Plain Text content control.
3. **Click the content control to the right of Date, click the down arrow, click Today, click the content control to the right of Branch, click the arrow, click Chicago, USA, click the content control to the right of Feedback, click the arrow, then click Excellent**
4. **Click the picture icon in the Picture content control, click From a file, navigate to the location where you store your Data Files, double-click Support_WD_10_Trainer1.jpg, click the Add button next to the Picture content control, click the picture icon in the new Picture content control, click From a file, navigate to the location where you store your Data Files, then double-click Support_WD_10_Trainer2.jpg**
5. **Click the picture of the first trainer, use your mouse to drag the bottom-right corner handle of the picture up to reduce the height to approximately 1", then reduce the height of the second picture so the entire form fits on one page**
6. **Click the pink box in the SmartArt graphic two times to show the insertion point, type Resume Building, click the dark green box, type Networking, click the light green box, then type Interview Skills in the bottom box**
7. **Click the check box below Presentations in the form, then click the check box below Job Fairs in the form**
8. **Click the content control next to Comments, note the message that appears on the status bar, then type the comment text shown in FIGURE 10-26, noting that it will appear in lower case as you type**
9. **Press TAB, scroll down, note that the text appears in uppercase, change the zoom so the form fills the screen, compare the completed form to FIGURE 10-27, save the document as a Word document with the name IL_WD_10_WorkshopSurvey_Completed to the location where you store your Data Files, submit all files to your instructor, then close the document and exit Word**

FIGURE 10-26: Comment entry

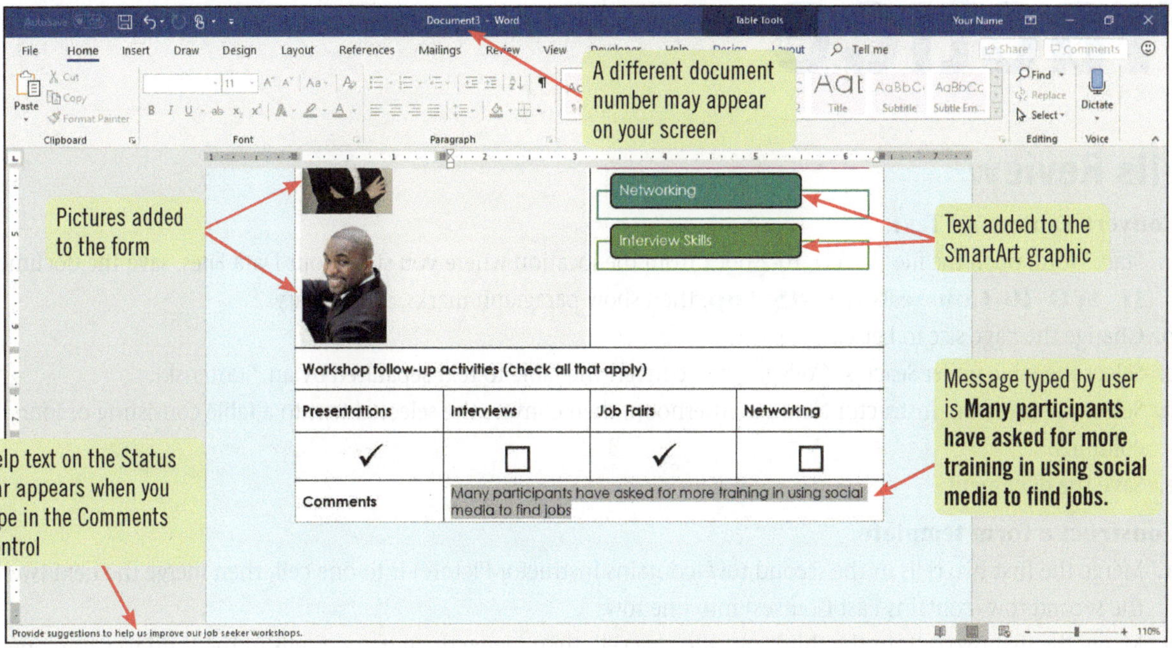

william casey/Shutterstock.com; Charlotte Purdy/Shutterstock.com

FIGURE 10-27: Completed form

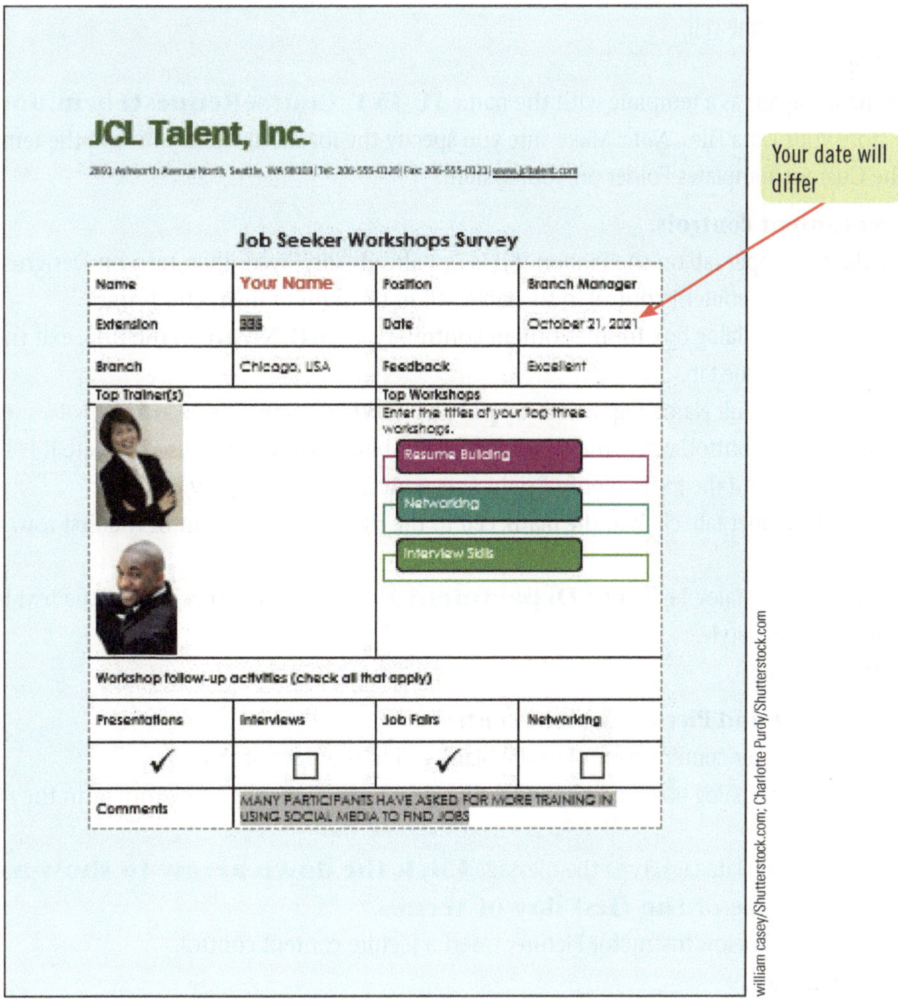

william casey/Shutterstock.com; Charlotte Purdy/Shutterstock.com

Practice

Skills Review

1. Convert Tables and Text.

a. Start Word, open the file IL_WD_10-2.docx from the location where you store your Data Files, save the document as **IL_WD_10_CourseRequestSetup**, then show paragraph marks, if necessary.

b. Change the page size to Letter.

c. Select the table under Seacrest College, then convert the table to text separated by an * (asterisk).

d. Select the text from Instructor Name to Afternoon, then convert the selected text to a table consisting of four columns.

e. Save the document.

2. Construct a form template.

a. Merge the first two cells in the second row (contains Instructor Picture) into one cell, then merge the next two cells in the second row (contains Past Courses) into one row.

b. Merge the first two cells in the third row into one cell, then merge the next two cells in the third row into one row so row 3 matches row 2.

c. Press TAB from the cell containing Afternoon to start a new row, press TAB another four times to start another new row, type **Comments** in the first cell of the last row, press TAB, then merge the three cells to the right of Comments into one cell.

d. Save the file.

e. Save the file again as a template with the name **IL_INT_CourseRequestForm.dotx** to the location where you store your Data Files. *Note:* Make sure you specify the location where you save the template so that it is not saved to the Custom Templates Folder on your system.

3. Add Text content controls.

a. Show the Developer tab on the Ribbon if it is not already displayed, then turn on Design Mode.

b. Insert a Rich Text content control in the table cell to the right of Instructor Name.

c. In the Properties dialog box for the content control, type **Full Name** as the title, exit the Properties dialog box, then click the Home tab.

d. Between the two Full Name tags, enter **Type the instructor's full name**.

e. Select the entire control, verify the control handle is blue with white text to indicate it is selected, change the font size to 14 point and the font color to Bright Green, Accent 5, then apply bold.

f. Click the Developer tab, click in the blank cell to the right of Department in the first row, then insert a Plain Text content control.

g. In the Properties dialog box, enter **Department** as the title, then specify that the text be formatted with the Intense Emphasis style.

h. Save the template.

4. Add Date Picker and Picture content controls.

a. Insert a Date Picker content control in the blank cell to the right of Date.

b. In the Properties dialog box, enter **Date** as the title, then change the date format to the format that corresponds to Month, Day, Year.

c. Between the two Date tags, type the message **Click the down arrow to show a calendar, then select the date of the first day of term**.

d. In the blank cell below Instructor Picture, insert a Picture content control.

e. Save the template.

Skills Review (continued)

5. Add Repeating Section and Check Box content controls.

a. Select the blank row below the Course Name, Course Number, Morning, and Afternoon labels, insert a Repeating Section content control, then turn off Design Mode to view the Add button. You will add controls to this row in a later step.

b. Turn on Design Mode, then insert a Check Box content control in the cell below Morning.

c. In the Content Control Properties dialog box, apply the Heading 2 style to the Check Box content control, then change the Checked symbol to Character code **251** (a stylized x) from the Wingdings font.

d. Select the Check Box content control, copy it, then paste it in the cell below Afternoon.

e. Save the template.

6. Add Building Blocks Content Controls

a. Start a new blank document, then type the text **Enter up to three of your most recent courses**.

b. Press ENTER, then insert a SmartArt graphic using the Basic Block List type in the List category.

c. Click the border of the left box in the row of two boxes to select it, press DELETE, then delete another box so only three boxes are included in the SmartArt graphic.

d. Apply Colorful Range-Accent Colors 4-5 to the SmartArt graphic, change the weight of the shape outline of all the boxes to 2¼ pt, then click away from the graphic to deselect it.

e. Press CTRL+A to select the contents of the document, then save the selection to the Quick Part Gallery using the name **Course List** as the building block name.

f. Save the document as **IL_WD_10_CourseRequestBuildingBlock** to the location where you store your Data Files, then close the document.

g. Verify that IL_WD_10_CourseRequestForm.dotx is again the active document, then verify that the Design Mode button on the Developer tab is not active.

h. Click the blank cell below Past Courses, then insert the Course List building block content control.

i. Select the graphic, then change the height to **1.3**" and the width to **3**".

j. Save the template.

7. Add Drop-Down content controls.

a. Click in the cell below Course Name, then insert a Combo Box content control.

b. In the Content Control Properties dialog box, enter **Course Name** as the title.

c. Add the following entries: **Blogging for Business**, **Networking**, **Social Media Marketing**, and **Planning**.

d. Change Planning to **Event Planning**, then move Event Planning up so it appears immediately after Blogging for Business.

e. Click in the cell below Course Number, then insert a Drop-Down List content control.

f. In the Content Control Properties dialog box, enter **Course Number** as the title, then add the following entries: **100**, **150**, **200**, **220**, **300**.

g. Save the template.

8. Insert Legacy Tools controls.

a. Insert a Text Form Field control from the Legacy Tools gallery in the blank cell to the right of Office Local.

b. Double-click the control to open the Text Form Field Options dialog box, change the Type to Number, change the Maximum length to **4**, then enter **1234** as the default.

c. Insert a Text Form Field control from the Legacy Tools gallery in the blank cell to the right of Comments.

d. Specify that the text format should be uppercase, add the help text: **Provide additional details if necessary**, then save the template.

Word

Skills Review (continued)

9. **Format and protect a form.**
   a. Turn off Design Mode, then apply bold to all the labels in the form template.
   b. Change the view to 90%, select the table, then change the row height to at least **.3**".
   c. Vertically center align the text in all the cells. (*Hint*: Use the Cell tab in the Table Properties dialog box.)
   d. Protect the document for users filling in forms using the password **skills**, then save and close the template but do not exit Word. (*Note*: If you turned Design Mode on, it must be turned off to protect the document.)

10. **Edit a form.**
    a. From Word, open the template IL_WD_CourseRequestForm.dotx (remember *not* to double-click it to open it), then stop protection using the **skills** password.
    b. Change the page color to Gold, Accent 3, Lighter 80%.
    c. Fill the table form with the White, Background 1 shading color.
    d. Remove only the outside border form the table form.
    e. Click below the table, press ENTER, then type your name.
    f. Protect the form again using the **skills** password.
    g. Save and close the template but do not exit Word.

FIGURE 10-28

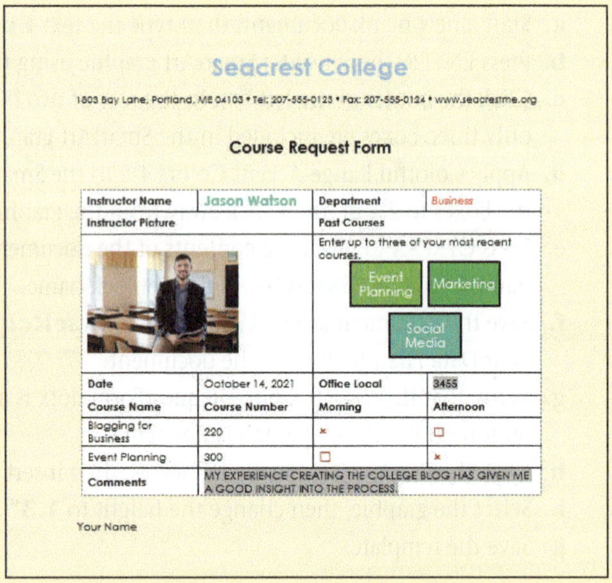

Africa Studio/Shutterstock.com

11. **Fill in a form as a user.**
    a. Open File Explorer, navigate to the Course Request template, then double-click it to start a new document.
    b. Refer to FIGURE 10-28 to complete the form. Insert Support_WD_10_Instructor.jpg in the Picture content control and **3455** for the Office Local.
    c. Select the current date, select the information for the first course (Blogging for Business), then click the Repeating Section content control and enter the information for the second course (Event Planning). The comment text is: **My experience creating the college blog has given me a good insight into the process**.
    d. Save the document as **IL_WD_10_CourseRequestForm_Completed** to the location where you store your Data Files, submit the file to your instructor, then close the document and exit Word.

Independent Challenge 1

You work in the Administration Department at Riverwalk Medical Clinic in Cambridge, MA. Several clinic administrators and senior medical staff take trips to hospitals and medical facilities around the world to investigate innovative programs in a variety of medical areas. Your supervisor asks you to create an itinerary form that staff can complete online to help them keep track of their travel details.

a. Start Word and open the file IL_WD_10-3.docx from the drive and folder where you store your Data Files. Save it as **IL_WD_10_ItineraryFormSetup**.
b. Turn on paragraph marks, if necessary, then convert the table containing the contact information for Riverwalk Medical Clinic into text separated by the | character. Center the line of text.
c. Select the text from Name to the paragraph mark following Picture of Location, then convert the selected text into a table consisting of four rows.
d. Merge the three cells to the right of Purpose of Travel into one cell, then merge the three cells to the right of Picture of Location into one cell.
e. Add two new rows. In the first new row, enter the following four labels: **Date**, **Location**, **Category**, **Details**.

Independent Challenge 1 (continued)

f. From the Developer tab, make the Design Mode active, then insert a Rich Text content control in the blank cell to the right of the Name label. Enter **Full Name** as the title, then format the control with 14 pt and bold.

g. Insert a Date Picker control in the blank cell to the right of Report Date. Enter **Date** as the title, then select the date format that corresponds with 17-Dec-21.

h. Insert a Drop-Down List content control in the blank cell to the right of Department. Enter **Department** as the title, then add **Surgical**, **Research**, and **Human Resources**, and put the entries in alphabetical order.

i. Insert a Text Form Field control from the Legacy Tools gallery in the blank cell to the right of Extension. Specify the type as Number, a Maximum length of **3**, and **200** as the Default number.

j. Insert a Plain Text content control in the cell to the right of Purpose of Travel. Enter **Travel Purpose** for the title, then apply the Emphasis style.

k. Copy the Date Picker content control you inserted next to Report Date, then paste it in the cell below Date.

l. Insert a Combo Box content control in the cell below Location. Enter **Location** as the title, then add three selections: **Hong Kong**, **London**, **New York**. Enter the text **Select a location or type your own**. between the two tags.

m. Insert a List Box content control in the cell below Category. Enter **Category** as the title, then add three selections: **Transportation**, **Accommodation**, and **Meeting** and put them in alphabetical order.

n. Insert a Rich Text content control in the cell below Details. Enter the text **Click the Add button for more rows**. between the tags, then open the Content Control Properties dialog box, enter **Details** as the title, and select the Orange color for the control.

o. Select the last row in the form (contains four content controls), then click the Repeating Section Content Control button. If the plus sign is not visible, turn off Design Mode. When users fill in the form, they can click the plus sign to add more rows to supply more itinerary details.

p. Insert a Picture content control in the blank cell to the right of Picture of Location. Click the Picture content control, then drag the middle-right sizing handle to the right to increase the width of the control so it almost fills the table cell.

q. Apply bold to all the form labels.

r. Save the document.

s. Save the document again as a template with the name **IL_WD_10_ItineraryForm.dotx** to the location where you store your Data Files.

t. Protect the form using the Filing in forms selection, enter **ic1** as the password, then save and close the template but do not exit Word.

u. Start a new document by double-clicking the IL_WD_10_ItineraryForm.dotx template file in File Explorer (verify that Document1 or another number appears in the title bar), enter your name and the current date in row 1, then enter **Research** as the Department, **239** as the Extension, and **To attend a conference for medical researchers in Peru.** as the Purpose of Travel.

v. Insert Support_WD_10_Peru.jpg in the Picture content control.

w. Enter itinerary information as shown in TABLE 10-2, clicking the Add button after you've entered data for each row for a total of four rows. Note that you will need to type the Location information ("Peru" and "Machu Picchu") in the Combo box control.

TABLE 10-2

date	location	category	details
5-Apr-21	Lima	Transportation	AA Flight 240 to Lima
6-Apr-21	Lima	Accommodation	Lima Ritz
7-Apr-21	Machu Picchu	Meeting	Day Trip to Clinic
8-Apr-21	Lima	Meeting	Presentation

x. Save the completed form as **IL_WD_10_Itinerary_Peru**, submit a copy to your instructor, then close the document and exit Word.

Independent Challenge 2

You work for a government agency that provides business skills workshops to the employees of companies and organizations in the San Diego area. Clients complete a feedback form after they participate in a workshop. You create a Word form to email clients.

a. Start Word and open the file IL_WD_10-4.docx from the location where your Data Files are located. Save it as a template with the name **IL_WD_10_EvaluationForm** to the location where you store your Data Files.

b. Change the page size to Executive.

c. From the Developer tab, switch to Design Mode, then insert and format controls as described in **TABLE 10-3**:

TABLE 10-3

location	content Control	title	properties
Name	Rich Text content control	**Full Name**	Format with Heading 1
Workshop Date	Date Picker content control	**Date**	Format with the 10.10.2021 date format.
Instructor	Drop-Down List content control	**Instructor**	Add the names of four instructors: **Oliver Greer, Tamsin Quinn, Kat Martin & Jasjit Singh** and put in alphabetical order by first name.
Subject	Combo Box content control	**Subject**	Add entries for three subjects in alphabetical order: **Social Media, Negotiating Skills,** and **Leadership Development**; type the text **Select a subject or enter a new subject.** between the form tags as a direction to users.
Workshop Element	Text Form Field control from Legacy Tools		Enter the Help text **Click the Add button to insert up to four more elements.**
Rankings	Check Box content control in each of the 4 blank cells for the ranking of a course element	**Rank**	Format with the Wingdings **254** check mark character (*Hint:* Insert and modify the first check box content control, then copy and paste it to the remaining table cells.)

d. Select the row containing the Text Form Field and Check Box content controls and make the row a Repeating Section. Turn off Design Mode and verify that the Add button appears to the right of the last cell in the row.

e. Save the template, then create a new blank document.

f. Turn on bold, then type the text: **Type three words that summarize your experience at the workshop you attended**.

g. Press ENTER, then insert the Converging Radial SmartArt graphic from the Relationship category.

h. Type **Feedback** in the circle shape, then apply the Color Range – Accent Colors 5 to 6 color scheme.

i. Select all the text and the SmartArt graphic, then save it as a building block with the name **Feedback** in the Quick Parts gallery.

j. Save the document as **IL_WD_10_FeedbackBuildingBlock** to the location where you store your Data Files, then close it.

k. In the form template, turn off Design Mode, then insert the Feedback building block into the last row of the table. Resize the size of the graphic to 2" high and 4" wide so the entire form fits on one page.

l. Click away from the table, then change the page color for the document to Light Green, Accent 2, Lighter 80%.

m. Protect the form for filling in forms, click OK to bypass password protection when prompted, then save and close the template but do not exit Word.

n. Open the template IL_WD_10_EvaluationForm.dotx and unprotect it, then remove Kat Martin from the list of the instructors in the Drop-Down List content control so the list includes only three instructors.

o. Protect the form again, then save and close the template but do not exit Word.

Independent Challenge 2 (continued)

p. Start a new document by double-clicking IL_WD_10_EvaluationForm.dotx in File Explorer, enter your name in the Name cell and the current date in the Workshop Date cell, select Jasjit Singh as the instructor, then type **Finance** in the Combo Box content control to the right of Subject.
q. In the content control below Workshop Element, type **Workshop Materials**, then click the 2 check box.
r. Use the Add button to add another row. (*Note:* Workshop Materials is entered, but you can type over it.) Enter **Instructor** as the course element and 4 as the rank, then add another row and enter **Location** as the course element and 3 as the rank.
s. Type these three words in the three boxes of the SmartArt graphic: **Informative**, **Helpful**, **Fun**.
t. Save the document as **IL_WD_10_Evaluation Form_Completed** to the location where you store the files for this book, submit it to your instructor, then close the document and exit Word.

Word

Visual Workshop

You work for Exhibitor Assist, a company that provides event planning, conference organization, and related business services to companies in the Vancouver area. You are organizing a Green Technology conference and need to create a form for exhibitors to complete in Word. Work in Design Mode to create and enhance the form template shown in FIGURE 10-29. The Organic theme is applied to the document, the Title heading is applied to "Green Technology Conference," and the Heading 1 style is applied to "Exhibitor Form." You do not need to include titles and tags on the controls for this exercise. Use the Rich Text content control for Company Name formatted with Bold and 14 pt; use the Plain Text content controls for Mailing Address and Email Address; use these entries for a Combo Box content control for Category: **Fuel Products**, **Building Materials**, **Engineering**, **Renewable Energy** and put them in alphabetical order. Use the Wingdings 171 symbol for the two check boxes and format the Check Box content control with Heading 1 and symbol 252. Resize the Picture content control so it is **1.7"** in height (the width will adjust automatically). Save the template as **IL_WD_10_ConferenceForm.dotx** to the location where you store your Data Files. Protect the form, but do not password protect it, close the template, then open a new document based on the template. Complete the form as shown in FIGURE 10-30, using the picture file IL_WD_10_SolarEnergy.jpg. Save the completed form as **IL_WD_10_ConferenceForm_Completed** to the location where you store your Data Files, submit a copy to your instructor, then close the document.

FIGURE 10-29

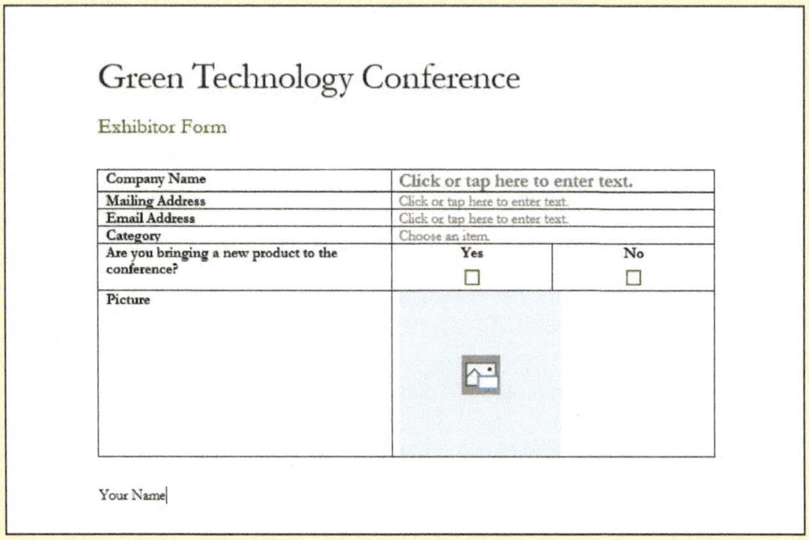

Green Technology Conference

Exhibitor Form

Company Name	Click or tap here to enter text.	
Mailing Address	Click or tap here to enter text.	
Email Address	Click or tap here to enter text.	
Category	Choose an item.	
Are you bringing a new product to the conference?	**Yes** ☐	**No** ☐
Picture		

Your Name

FIGURE 10-30

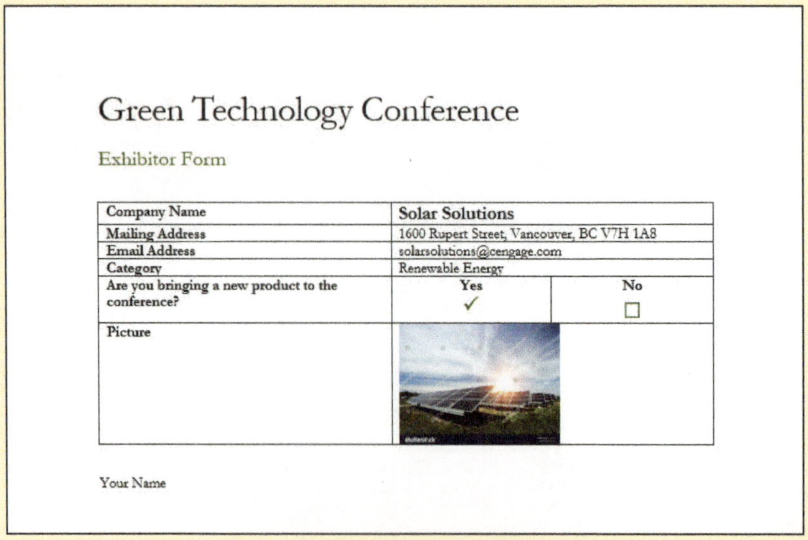

Green Technology Conference

Exhibitor Form

Company Name	**Solar Solutions**	
Mailing Address	1600 Rupert Street, Vancouver, BC V7H 1A8	
Email Address	solarsolutions@cengage.com	
Category	Renewable Energy	
Are you bringing a new product to the conference?	**Yes** ✓	**No** ☐
Picture		

Your Name

Diyana Dimitrova/Shutterstock.com

Word **Module 11**

Automating and Customizing Word

CASE As part of your duties in the sales and marketing department at JCL Talent, Inc., you have been asked to produce profiles of two of JCL Talent's top trainers who deliver workshops for job seekers. You also need to format a series of excerpts from employment journals created by successful job seekers. You start by formatting paragraphs and graphics and creating styles for a profile for top trainer Shaleen Dixon. You then create a macro to automate formatting tasks for the journal excerpts and you customize Word options. To finish up, you add a digital signature to the document.

Module Objectives

After completing this module, you will be able to:

- Manage pages
- Edit pictures
- Use layering options
- Arrange and compress graphics
- Create character styles
- Manage styles
- Plan a macro
- Record macro steps
- Run a macro
- Edit a macro in Visual Basic
- Customize Word
- Sign a document digitally

Files You Will Need:

IL_WD_11-1.docx
Support_WD_11_Shaleen.jpg
IL_WD_11-2.docx
IL_WD_11-3.docx
IL_WD_11-4.docx
IL_WD_11-5.docx
Support_WD_11_Solar.jpg
IL_WD_11-6.docx
IL_WD_11-7.docx
IL_WD_11-8.docx
IL_WD_11-9.docx
Support_WD_11_Clinic.jpg
Support_WD_11_SpringBulletin.docx
IL_WD_11-10.docx
IL_WD_11-11.docx
IL_WD_11-12.docx

Word
Module 11

Manage Pages

Learning Outcomes
- Set paragraph pagination options
- Format text as hidden

You apply pagination settings to control the flow of text between pages or between columns in a document. These settings specify where Word positions automatic page breaks. Choose the Keep with next option when you want a paragraph to appear together with the next paragraph on the same page. Choose the Keep lines together option to keep all the lines in a selected paragraph together on a page. To add an automatic page break before a specific paragraph, choose the Page break before option. You can set Widow/Orphan control options to control the number of lines appearing at the top or bottom of a page. Turned on by default, **Widow/Orphan control** ensures that at least two lines of a paragraph appear at the top and bottom of every page or column. You can also designate selected text in a document as hidden text. **CASE** *You open a document containing text needed for a two-page description of top trainer Shaleen Dixon, modify how the paragraphs break across pages, then designate selected text as hidden.*

STEPS

TROUBLE
Click the **Show/Hide button** ¶ in the Paragraph group to show paragraph marks, if necessary.

1. **sam Start Word, open the file IL_WD_11-1.docx from the location where you store your Data Files, verify paragraph marks are showing, then save the document as IL_WD_11_ShaleenDixonProfile**
2. **Scroll down and click in the Research the Employer heading, click the Launcher in the Paragraph group, then click the Line and Page Breaks tab**
   The Line and Page Breaks tab in the Paragraph dialog box opens as shown in FIGURE 11-1. By default, the Heading 1 style applied to the heading includes three settings: Widow/Orphan control, Keep with next, and Keep lines together.
3. **Click OK, click in the line that starts with Knowledge is power, click the Launcher in the Paragraph group, click the Keep Lines Together check box, then click OK**
   The three lines of the paragraph along with the heading move to the top of page 2.
4. **Scroll back up to page 1, click in the heading Top Tips for Job Interview Success, click the Launcher in the Paragraph group, click Page break before, then click OK**
5. **Scroll to the top of page 3**
   The last word in the paragraph appears alone at the top of the page. This line is a widow. A **widow** is the last line of a paragraph appearing along at the top of a page. An **orphan** is the first line of a paragraph appearing alone at the bottom of a page.
6. **Scroll back up to page 2, click in the paragraph under the Send a Thank-You Note or Email, click the Launcher in the Paragraph group, click the Widow/Orphan control check box, then click OK**
   The last two lines of the paragraph move to the top of page 3.

TROUBLE
If you select the paragraph mark and then hide the text, the blank line between the two paragraphs will be removed when the document is printed.

7. **Press CTRL+HOME, then select the sentence that begins From a very young age, but *not* the paragraph mark in the Early Life paragraph, as shown in FIGURE 11-2**
8. **Click the Launcher in the Font group, click the Hidden check box as shown in FIGURE 11-3, click OK, then click away from the selected text**
   A dotted line appears under the text. This text will not appear in the printed document.
9. **Click the File tab, click Print, note that the sentence does not appear in the Early Life section in the Print Preview screen, click the Back button to return to the document, then save the document**

FIGURE 11-1: Paragraph dialog box

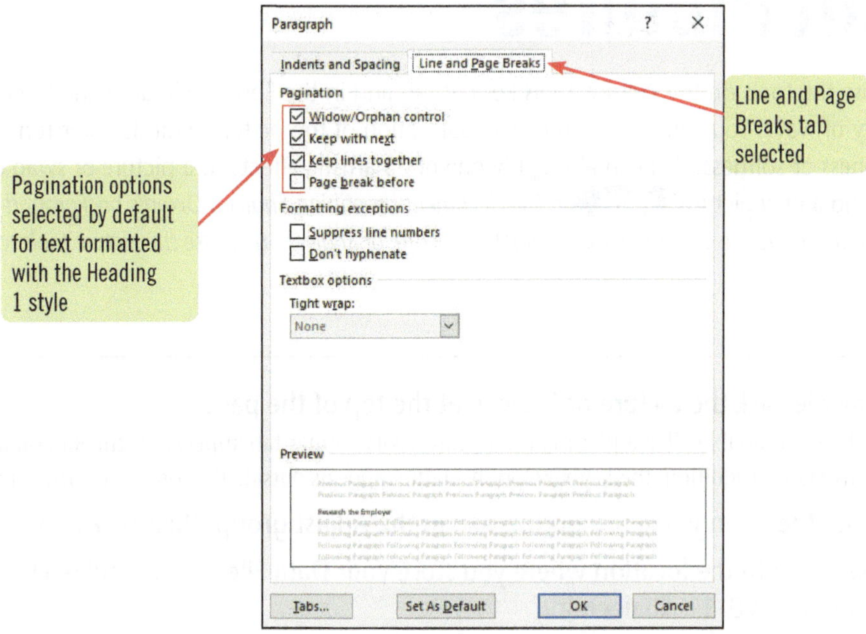

FIGURE 11-2: Text selected to make hidden

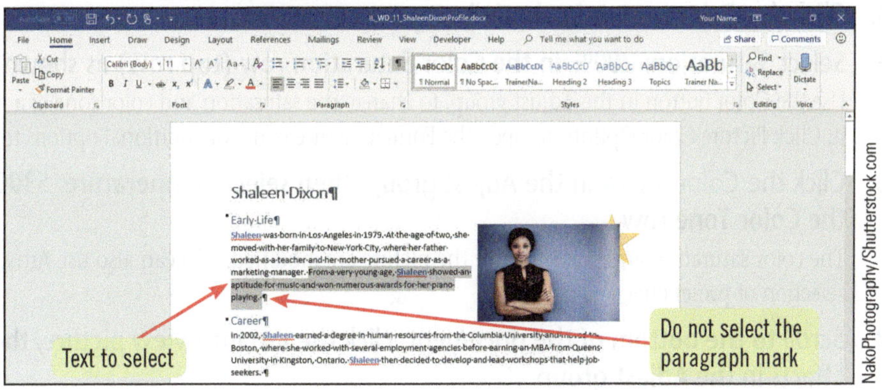

FIGURE 11-3: Hidden effect selected

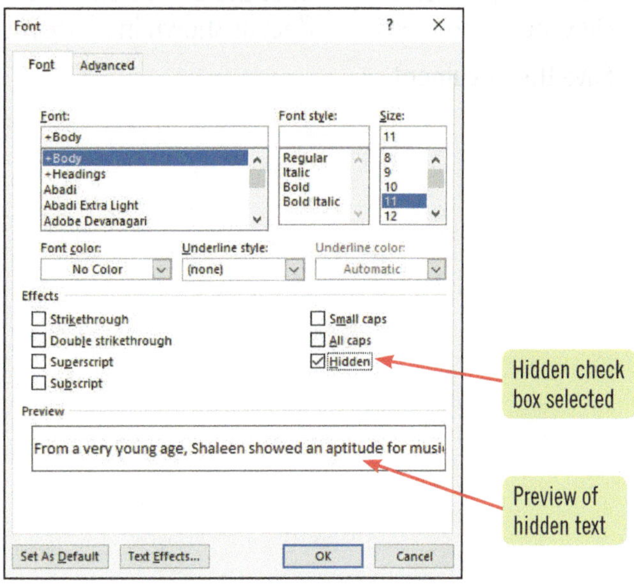

Word
Module 11

Edit Pictures

Learning Outcome
- Apply artistic and picture effects

You use the tools on the Picture Tools Format tab and in the Format Picture pane to edit a picture in a variety of ways. You can change the color saturation of the picture, edit its color tone, and modify its sharpness or softness. You can also apply one of 23 artistic effects to a picture or swap out a picture by selecting a new picture. **CASE** *The document describing Shaleen Dixon's background includes her picture. You change the current picture to another picture of Shaleen, then use the picture tools to edit the picture.*

STEPS

1. **Double-click the picture of Shaleen at the top of the page**
   When you double-click a picture, the Picture Tools Format tab appears on the Ribbon and becomes the active tab. In addition, the Layout Options button appears outside the top-right corner of the picture.
2. **Click the Change Picture button in the Adjust group, then click From a File**
3. **Navigate to the location where you store your Data Files, then double-click Support_WD_11_Shaleen.jpg**
   A different picture of Shaleen is inserted. You also make adjustments to the appearance of the picture using the Adjust group on the Picture Tools Format tab.
4. **Click the Color button in the Adjust group**
5. **Select Saturation: 200% in the Color Saturation row (top row) as shown in FIGURE 11-4**
   Use the Color button in the Adjust group, to change the saturation and color tone of a picture, or to recolor it. Click Picture Color Options to open the Format Picture pane for additional options to modify the picture.
6. **Click the Color arrow in the Adjust group, then select Temperature: 5300 K color tone in the Color Tone row**
   The color saturation and color tone of the picture are modified. You can also use Artistic Effects to apply a selection of preset effects to a picture.
7. **Scroll to the bottom of the document, click the Job Interview picture, then click Artistic Effects in the Adjust group**
   The selection of artistic effects opens.
8. **Move the pointer over each of the artistic effects to view how the picture changes, then click the Cement artistic effect as shown in FIGURE 11-5**
9. **Save the document**

QUICK TIP
Screen Tips appear to help you select the correct saturation or color tone effects.

QUICK TIP
To change the sharpness and contrast of a picture, click the Corrections button in the Adjust group.

FIGURE 11-4: Selecting color saturation

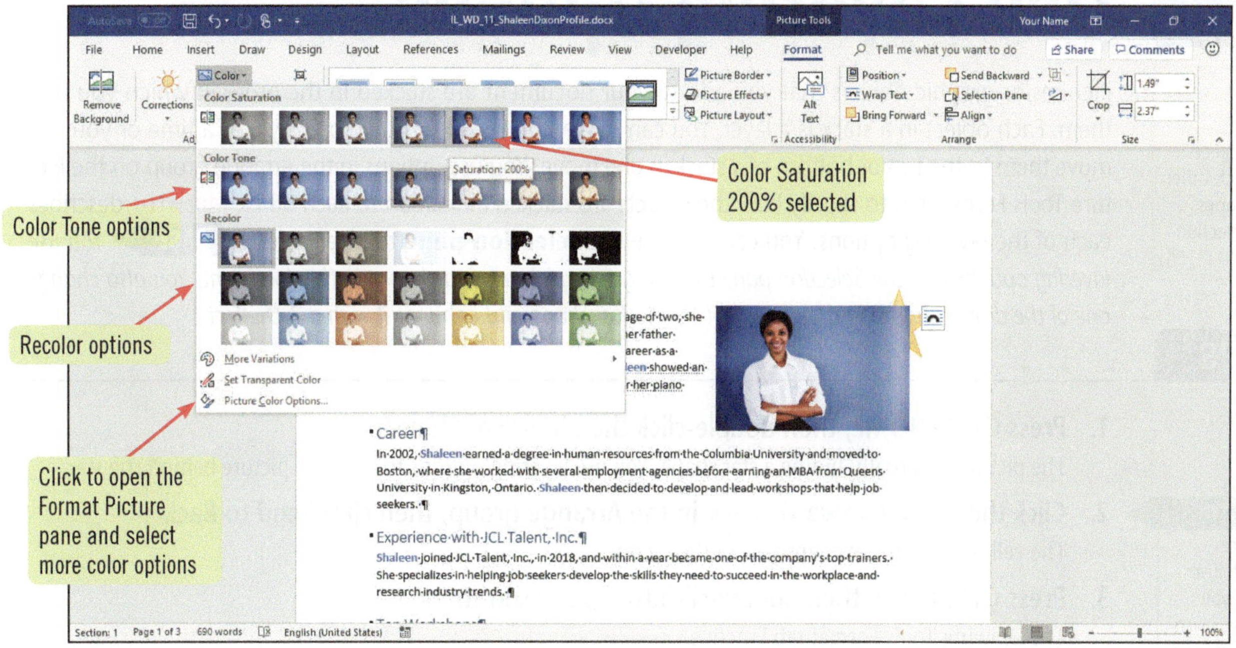

NakoPhotography/Shutterstock.com

FIGURE 11-5: Applying an artistic effect to a picture

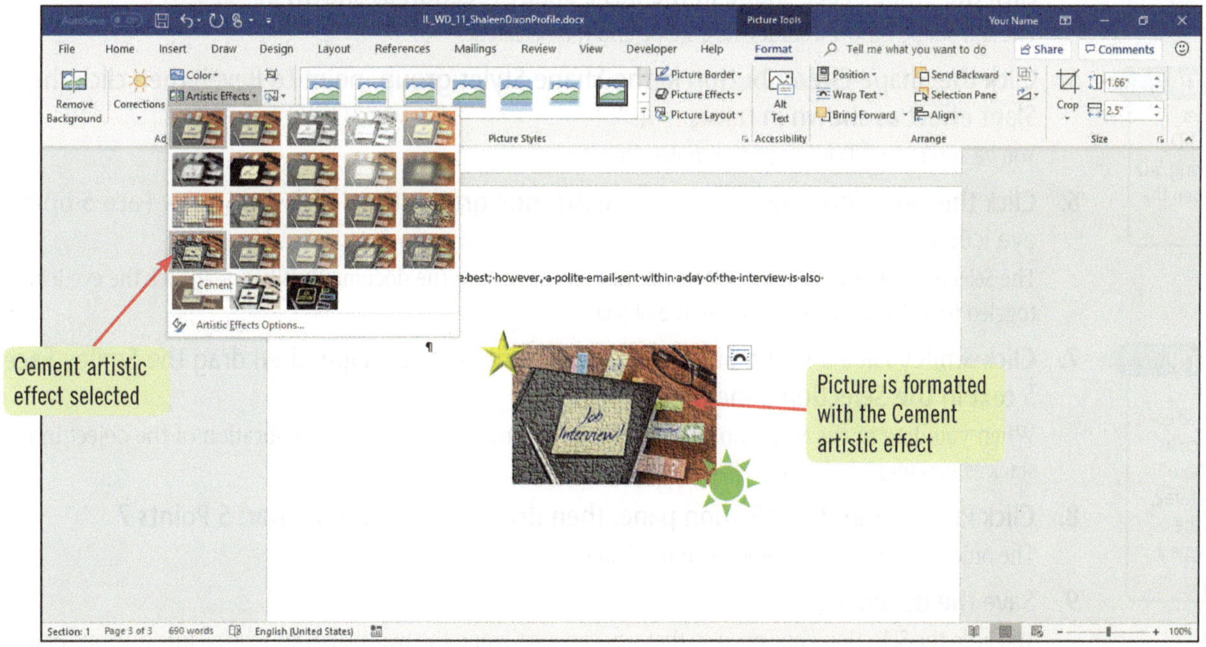

Zerbor/Shutterstock.com

Applying 3-D and 3-D Rotation effects to a picture

You can enhance a picture with a variety of picture effects including reflection, shadow, glow, soft edges, and bevel. The bevel picture effect applies a 3-D effect to the selected picture. To add a 3-D bevel effect, click the Picture Effects button on the Picture Tools Format tab, point to Bevel, then select a preset bevel effect. To further modify a bevel effect, click 3-D Options below the selection of bevel effects to open the 3-D Format section of the Format Picture pane. Here, you can specify the width and height of the top and bottom bevels, and specify a color, depth, contour, material, and lighting for the 3-D effect. You can achieve a wide variety of interesting 3-D effects by selecting different options in the Format Picture pane. Another 3-D effect you can apply to a picture is a 3-D Rotation effect. Click Picture Effects in the Picture Styles group, click 3-D Rotation, then select a 3-D rotation effect from one of three categories: Parallel, Perspective, and Oblique.

Word
Module 11

Use Layering Options

Learning Outcomes
- Arrange objects around each other
- Format shapes
- Use the Selection pane

Pictures or graphic objects that you add to your document are stacked in the order in which you add them. Each object in a stack is a layer. You can move objects up or down one layer at a time or you can move them to the top or bottom of a stack in one move. You use options in the Arrange group on the Picture Tools Format tab to specify how the objects are stacked in relation to each other. TABLE 11-1 describes each of the layering options. You can also use the **Selection pane** to layer objects. CASE *You use layering options and the Selection pane to arrange the pictures and shapes in the document. You also change one of the drawn shapes in the document to another shape and enhance it with a 3-D effect.*

STEPS

QUICK TIP
When you are working with just two objects, you have only two layers so you can also click Send Backward to move one object behind the other.

QUICK TIP
You can further enhance the 3-D effect by clicking 3-D Options to open the Format pane.

QUICK TIP
To rename an object in the Selection pane, such as "Interview Photo" instead of Picture2, double-click the name, then type a new name.

1. **Press CTRL+HOME, then double-click the picture of Shaleen**
   The picture is partially hiding a star shape. You use layering options to send the picture behind the star.
2. **Click the Send Backward arrow in the Arrange group, then click Send to Back**
   The yellow star now overlaps part of the picture.
3. **Press CTRL+END, then double-click the green sun shape**
   The Drawing Tools Format tab is active.
4. **Click the Edit Shape button in the Insert Shapes group, point to Change Shape, then click the Smiley Face shape in the Basic Shapes section as shown in FIGURE 11-6**
   The sun shape is now a smiley face shape and it is selected.
5. **Click the Shape Effects button in the Shape Styles group, point to Bevel, then click the Slant effect as shown in FIGURE 11-7.**
   You've applied a 3-D effect to the smiley face shape.
6. **Click the Selection Pane button in the Arrange group, then click the Smiley Face 5 open eye icon**
   The Selection pane shows the objects on the current page of the document. When you click the eye icon it toggled to a closed eye and you hid the object.
7. **Click Smiley Face 5 in the Selection pane to unhide the shape, then drag the Smiley Face 5 text in the Selection pane below Picture 2**
   When you drag in the Selection pane, a blue horizontal bar shows you the location of the object in the stack as you move it. Refer to FIGURE 11-8.
8. **Click Picture 2 in the Selection pane, then drag Picture 2 above Star: 5 Points 7**
   The order is now Picture 2, Star: 5 Points 7, and then Smiley Face 5.
9. **Save the document**
   You keep the Selection pane open so that you can next group the two shapes and the picture into one object.

TABLE 11-1: Layering Options

layering option	to move an object	layering option	to move an object
Bring Forward	up one layer	Send Backward	down one layer
Bring in Front	to the top of a stack of objects	Send to Back	to the bottom of a stack of objects
Bring in Front of Text	in front of text	Send Behind Text	behind text

FIGURE 11-6: Changing a shape to another shape

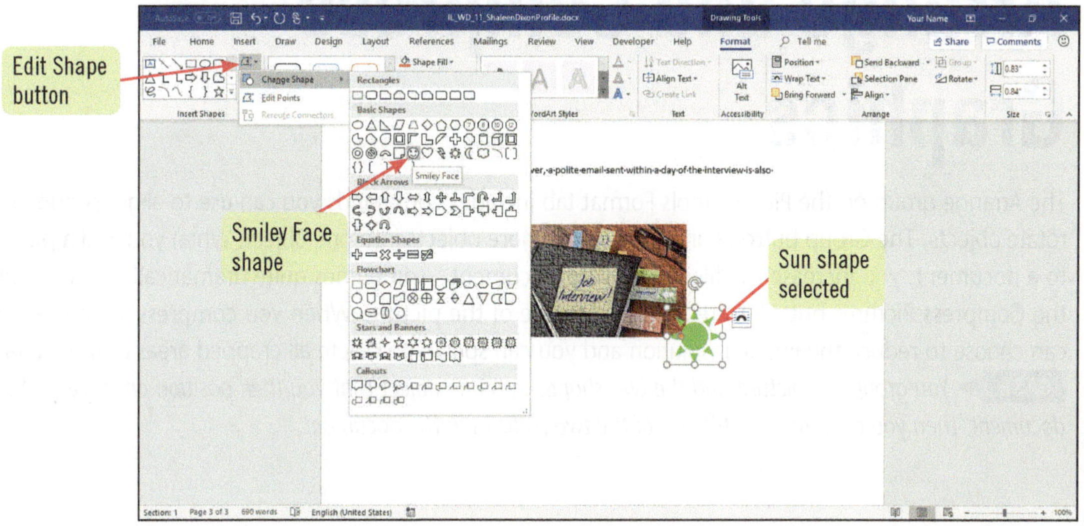

Zerbor/Shutterstock.com

FIGURE 11-7: Applying a Bevel 3-D effect

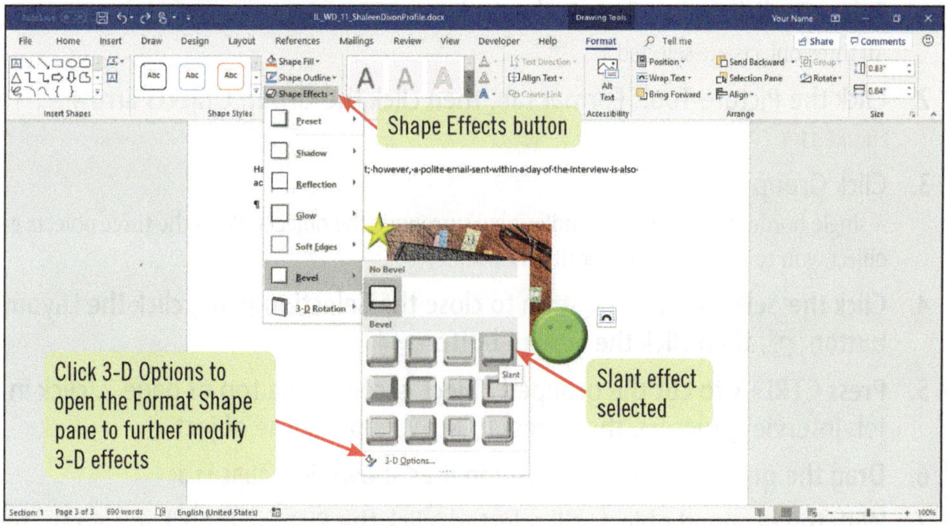

Zerbor/Shutterstock.com

FIGURE 11-8: Moving an object in the Selection pane

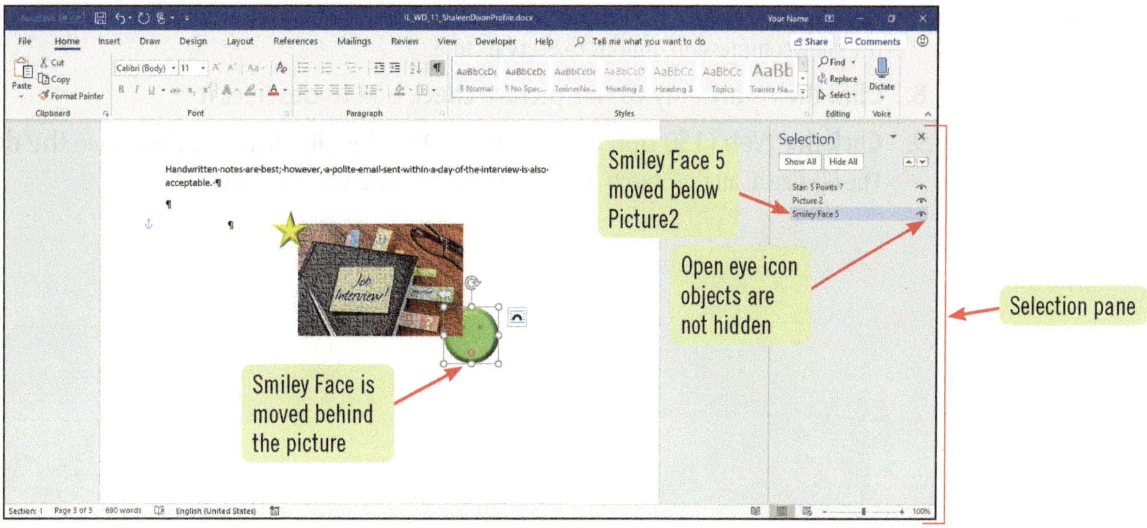

Zerbor/Shutterstock.com

Word

Word
Module 11

Learning Outcomes
- Group objects
- Compress pictures

Arrange and Compress Graphics

The Arrange group on the Picture Tools Format tab includes commands you can use to align, group, and rotate objects. The Group button combines two or more objects into one object. When you add a picture to a document, you increase the file size of your document—sometimes quite dramatically. You can use the Compress Pictures button to reduce the file size of the picture. When you compress a picture, you can choose to reduce the image resolution and you can specify to delete all cropped areas of the picture. **CASE** *You group the picture and the two shapes into one object that you then position on page 2 of the document, then you compress the file size of the two pictures in the document.*

STEPS

QUICK TIP In the Selection pane, the three objects are listed under Group to show they are all included in one group.

QUICK TIP To ungroup the object, click the Group Objects button, then click Ungroup.

QUICK TIP Choose 220 ppi (pixels per inch) for pictures that you want to print and 96 ppi for pictures that you want to send via email.

1. **In the Selection pane, verify that Picture 2 is selected, press and hold CTRL, click Star: 5 Points 7, click Smiley Face 5, then release CTRL**
   All three objects are selected.
2. **Click the Picture Tools Format tab, then click the Group Objects arrow as shown in FIGURE 11-9**
3. **Click Group**
   A single border with resizing handles now surrounds the objects. With the three objects grouped into one object, you can more easily reposition it.
4. **Click the Selection pane button to close the Selection pane, click the Layout Options button, then click the Square button**
5. **Press CTRL+X to cut the grouped object, scroll to the top of page 2, click in Top Tips for Job Interview Success, then press CTRL+V to paste the object**
6. **Drag the grouped object to position it as shown in FIGURE 11-10**
7. **With the grouped object still selected, click the Picture Tools Format tab, then click the Compress Pictures button in the Adjust group**
   The Compress Pictures dialog box opens as shown in FIGURE 11-11. Here, you can specify the resolution that you want to use. If you have more than one picture in a document, you can specify that you wish to apply the same compression options to every picture.
8. **Click the Apply only to this picture check box to deselect it**
9. **Click the Web (150 ppi) option button to select it, click OK, then save the document**
   The file size of all the objects and pictures in the document is reduced.

FIGURE 11-9: Grouping objects

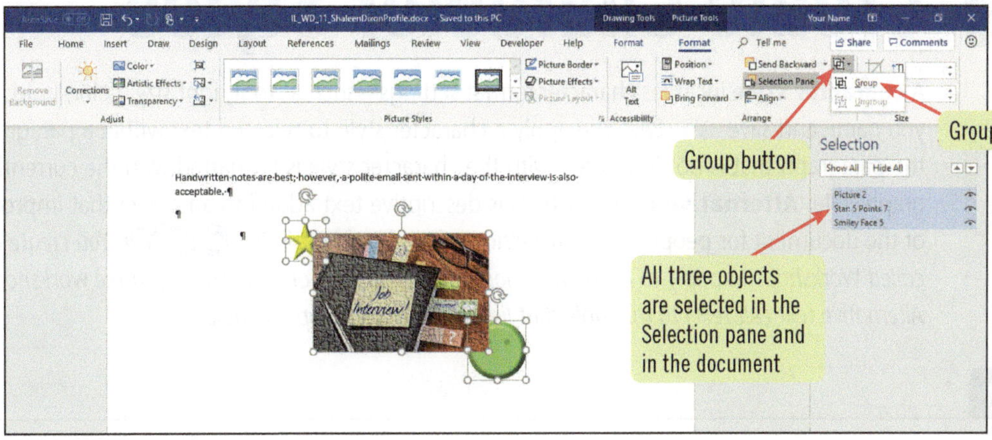

Zerbor/Shutterstock.com

FIGURE 11-10: Positioning the grouped object

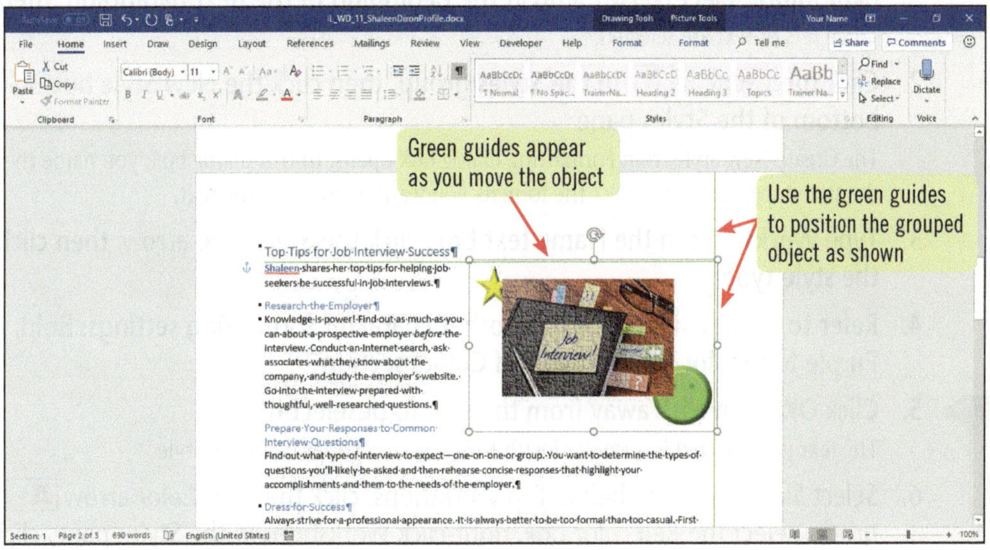

Zerbor/Shutterstock.com

FIGURE 11-11: Compress Pictures dialog box

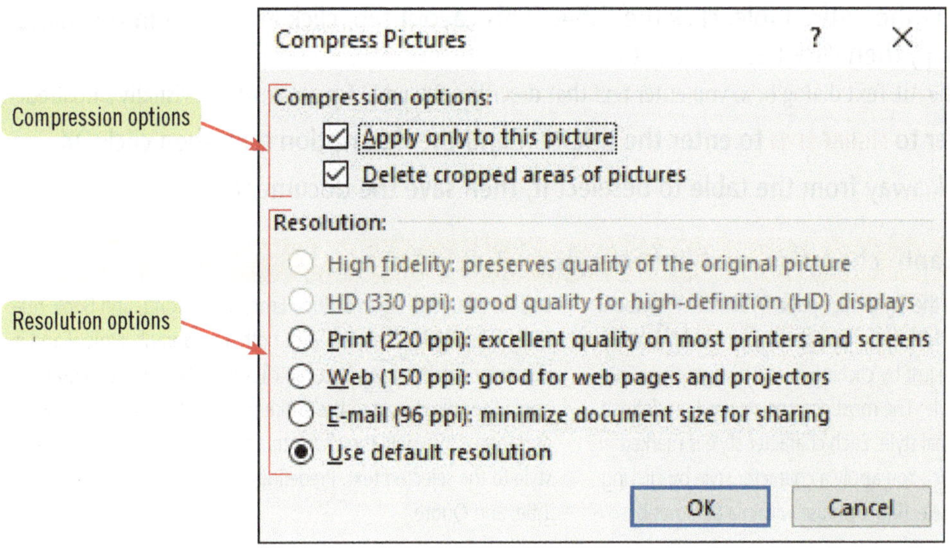

Create Character Styles

Learning Outcomes
- Create a character style
- Add Alt text to a table

A **character style** includes character format settings—such as font, font size, color, bold, and italic—that you name and save as a style. You apply a character style to selected text within a paragraph. Any text in the paragraph that is not formatted with the character style is formatted with the currently applied paragraph style. **Alternative text** (Alt text) is descriptive text added to an object that improves accessibility of the document for people who have vision or reading disabilities. **CASE** *You create a character style called Workshops to apply to each Workshop name in the list of Shaleen's top three workshops. You also add Alternative text (Alt text) to the table that lists the Fall workshop schedule.*

STEPS

QUICK TIP
You use CTRL to select all the non-contiguous text you wish to format with a new style.

1. **Scroll up to page 1, select Skills Inventory in the first line below the Top Workshops heading, press and hold CTRL, select Industry Research at the beginning of the next paragraph, select Networking at the beginning of the next paragraph, then release CTRL**
   Three sets of text are selected.
2. **Click the Launcher in the Styles group, then click the New Style button at the bottom of the Styles pane**
   The Create New Style from Formatting dialog box opens. In this dialog box, you name the new style, select the style type, and then select the formats you want to enhance the text.
3. **Type Workshops in the Name text box, click the Style type arrow, then click Character as the style type**
4. **Refer to FIGURE 11-12 to select the other character formatting settings: Bold, Italic, and the Purple font color in the Standard Colors section**

QUICK TIP
You can modify an existing character style.

5. **Click OK, then click away from the text to deselect it**
   The text you selected is formatted with the new Workshops character style.
6. **Select Skills Inventory below Top Workshops, click the Font Color arrow in the Font group, select the Red color box, right-click Workshops in the Styles pane, click Update Workshops to Match Selection as shown in FIGURE 11-13, then close the Styles task pane**
   The three phrases formatted with the Workshops character style are updated with the red font color.
7. **Click anywhere in the Fall Workshop Schedule table, click the table select icon to select the entire table, click the Table Tools Layout tab, click Properties in the Table group, then click the Alt Text tab**
   In the Alt Text dialog box, you enter text that describes the table for a user who is visually impaired.
8. **Refer to FIGURE 11-14 to enter the title text and the description text, then click OK**
9. **Click away from the table to deselect it, then save the document**

Identifying paragraph, character, and linked styles

Style types are identified in the Styles task pane by different symbols. Each paragraph style is marked with a paragraph symbol: ¶. You can apply a paragraph style just by clicking in any paragraph or line of text and selecting the style. The most commonly used predefined paragraph style is the Normal style. Each character style is marked with a character symbol: a. You apply a character style by clicking anywhere in a word or by selecting a phrase within a paragraph. Built-in character styles include Emphasis, Strong, and Book Title. Each linked style is marked with both a paragraph symbol and a character symbol: ¶a. You can click anywhere in a paragraph to apply the linked style to the entire paragraph, or you can select text and then apply only the character formats associated with the linked style to the selected text. Predefined linked styles include Heading 1, Title, and Quote.

FIGURE 11-12: Create New Style From Formatting dialog box

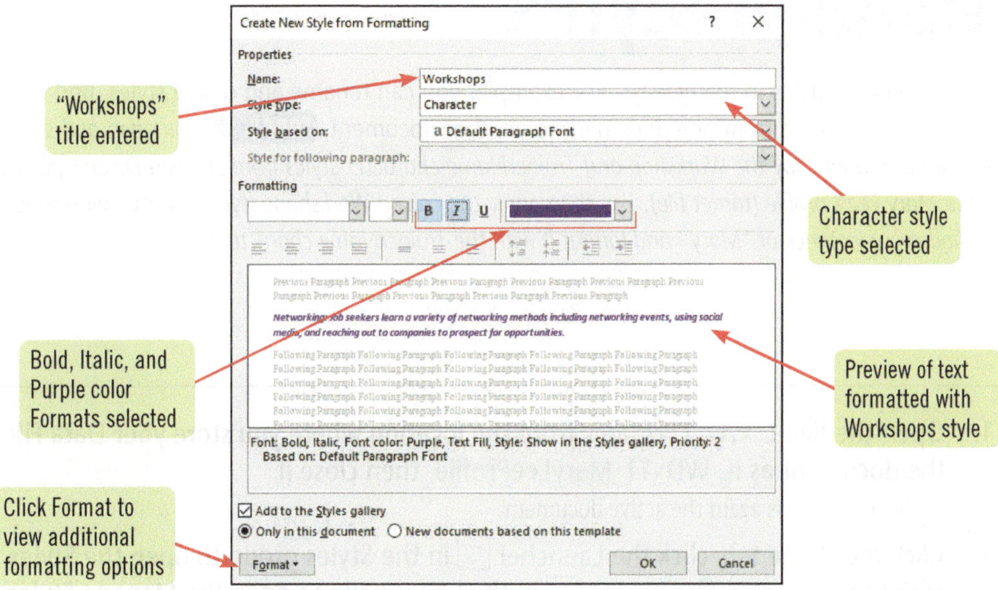

FIGURE 11-13: Updating the Workshop character style

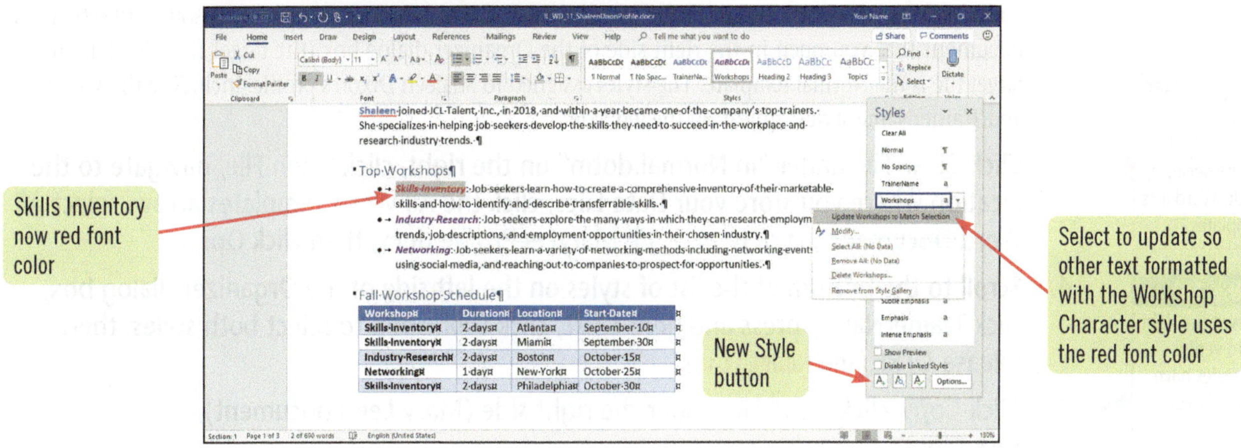

FIGURE 11-14: Adding Alt Text

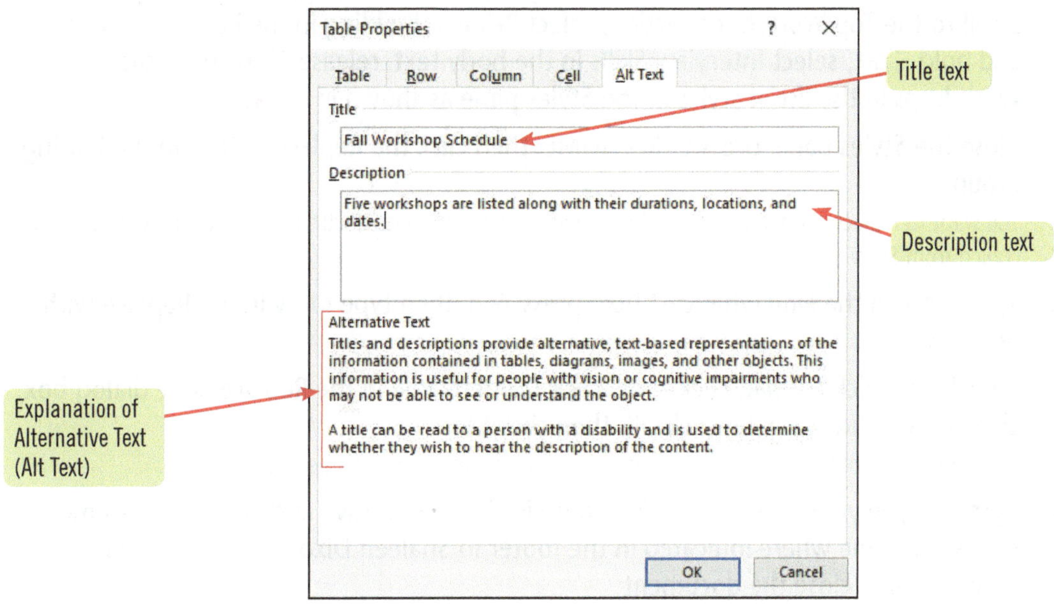

Word
Module 11

Manage Styles

Learning Outcomes
- Copy styles between documents
- Find and replace styles

You can manage styles in many ways. For example, you can rename and delete styles, find and replace styles, and copy styles from one document to another document. **CASE** *You open and save a profile for Mary Lee, then copy the Workshop and TrainerName character styles from Shaleen Dixon's profile (source file) to Mary Lee's profile (target file). You then apply the copied Workshops style to Mary's workshops. Finally, you find every instance of "Mary" and format it with the TrainerName character style.*

STEPS

1. **Open the file IL_WD_11-2.docx from the location where you store your Data Files, save the document as IL_WD_11_MaryLeeProfile, then close it**
   Shaleen's profile is again the active document.
2. **Click the Home tab, click the Launcher in the Styles group to open the Styles pane, click the Manage Styles button in the Styles pane to open the Manage Styles dialog box, then click Import/Export**
   You copy styles from the document in the left side of the Organizer dialog box (the source file) to a new document that you open in the right side of the Organizer dialog box (the target file). By default, the target file is the Normal template. The styles assigned to Shaleen Dixon's profile, including the Workshop and TrainerName styles, appear on the left side.
3. **Click Close File under "in Normal.dotm" on the right, click Open File, navigate to the location where you store your Data Files, click the All Word Templates arrow, select All Word Documents, click IL_WD_11_MaryLeeProfile.docx, then click Open**
4. **Scroll to the bottom of the list of styles on the left side of the Organizer dialog box, click TrainerName, press and hold CTRL, click Workshop to select both styles, then release CTRL (see FIGURE 11-15)**
5. **Click Copy, click Close File under the right side (Mary Lee's document), click Save, then click Close**
6. **Click File, click Open, click IL_WD_11_MaryLeeProfile.docx, open the Styles pane again, scroll to the Top Workshops section, select Resume Building in the body text, press and hold CTRL, select Interview Skills in the body text, release CTRL, then click Workshops in the list of styles in the Styles pane as shown in FIGURE 11-16**
7. **Close the Styles pane, press CTRL+HOME, then click the Replace button in the Editing group**
   You want to replace every instance of "Mary" with "Mary" formatted with the TrainerName style you just copied from Shaleen's profile.
8. **Type Mary in the Find what text box, press TAB, then type Mary in the Replace with text box**
9. **Click More, click Format, click Style, click TrainerName in the Replace Style dialog box, click OK, click Replace All, click OK, then click Close**
   All six instances of Mary's name are now formatted with the TrainerName character style.
10. **sam Type your name where indicated in the footer, save and close the document, type your name where indicated in the footer in Shaleen Dixon's profile document, then save and close the document**

TROUBLE
At first you do not see any Word documents because, by default, Word lists only templates.

QUICK TIP
Scroll down the right list box to verify that the styles have been copied over to that file.

TROUBLE
Do not select the text in the table.

FIGURE 11-15: Managing styles using the Organizer dialog box

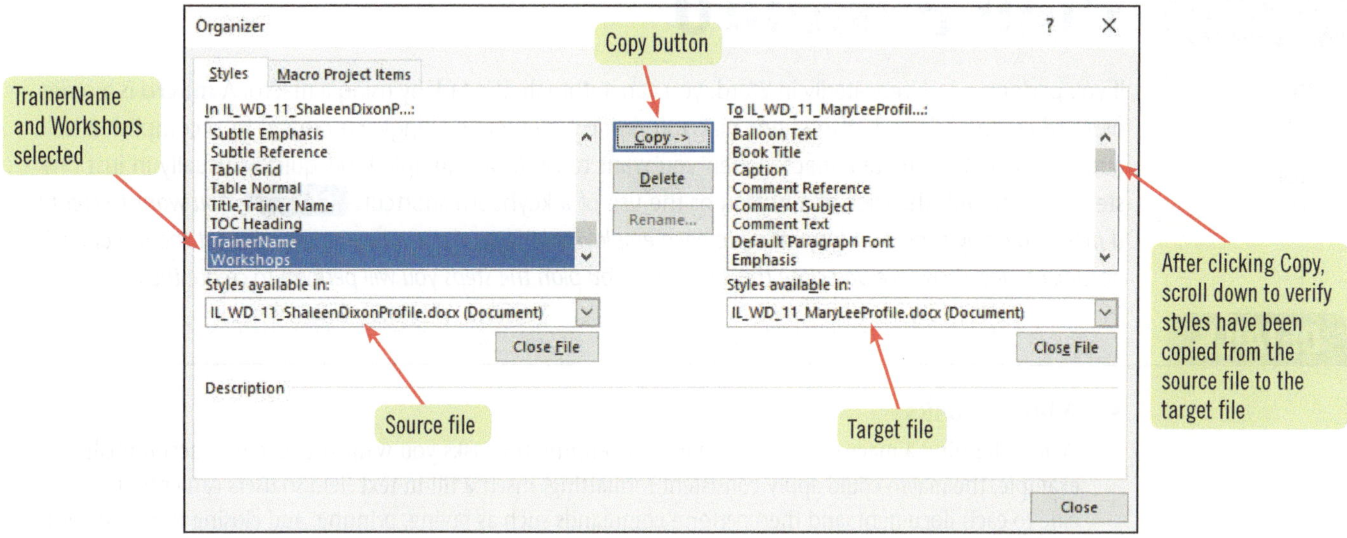

FIGURE 11-16: Applying the Workshop style

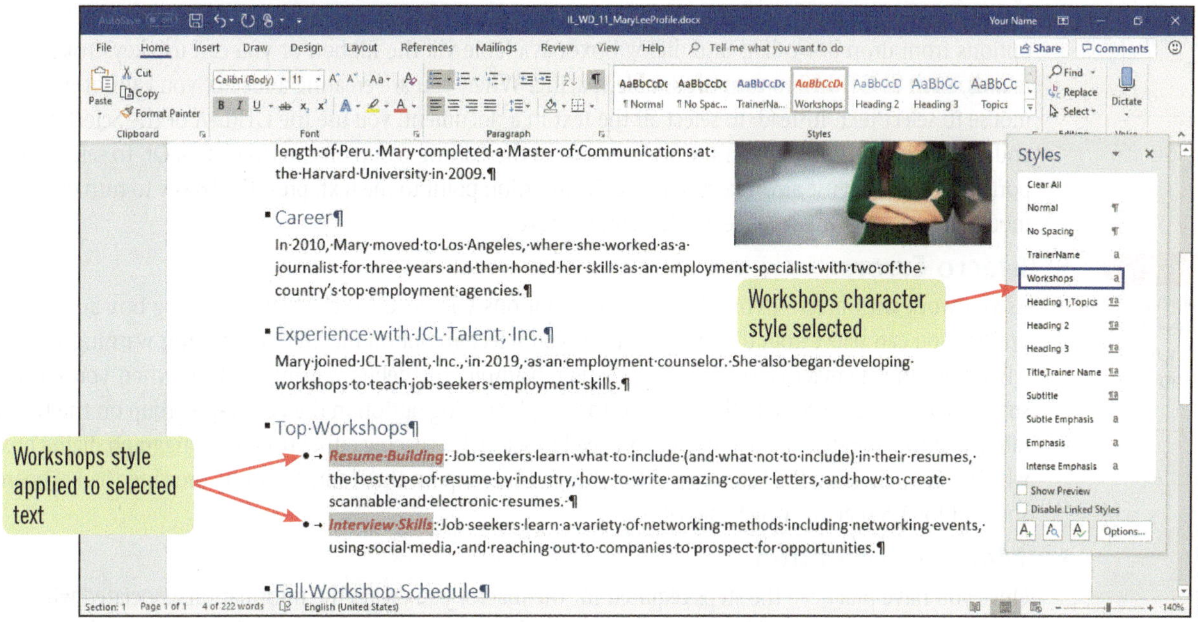

El Nariz/Shutterstock.com

Word

More ways to manage styles

To rename a style, right-click it in the Styles task pane, click Modify, type a new name, then press ENTER. To delete a style, right-click the style, then click Delete [Style name]. The style is deleted from the Styles task pane, but it is not deleted from your computer. Click the Manage Styles button at the bottom of the Styles task pane, select the style to delete, click DELETE, then click OK to close the Manage Styles dialog box.

Word
Module 11

Plan a Macro

Learning Outcomes
- Define macros
- Identify macro steps

If you perform a task repeatedly in Word, you can automate the task by using a macro. A **macro** is a series of Word commands and instructions that you group together as a single command to accomplish a task automatically. You create a macro when you want to perform multiple tasks quickly, usually in just one step, such as with the click of a button or the use of a keyboard shortcut. CASE *You want to create a macro to apply consistent formatting to each employment journal document, enter a title at the top of each document, and then save and close the document. You plan the steps you will perform to create the macro.*

DETAILS

- **Macro tasks**

  When planning a macro, the first step is to determine the tasks you want the macro to accomplish. For example, the macro could apply consistent formatting, insert a fill-in text field so users can enter text specific to each document, and then perform commands such as saving, printing, and closing the document. TABLE 11-2 lists all the tasks that you want your macro to perform.

QUICK TIP
You plan and practice the macro steps before you create a macro so you can perform the steps without error when you create the macro.

- **Macro steps**

  TABLE 11-2 also lists all the steps required to accomplish each task in the macro. If you make an error while recording the steps in the macro, you usually need to stop recording and start over because the recorded macro will include not only the correct steps but also the errors. By rehearsing the steps required before recording the macro, you ensure accuracy. While recording a macro, you can use the mouse to select options from drop-down lists and dialog boxes available via the Ribbon or you can use keystroke commands, such as CTRL+2 to turn on double spacing. When you are creating a macro, you cannot use your mouse to select text. Instead, to select all the text in a document, you use the CTRL+A or the Select button and the Select All command on the Select menu in the Editing group on the Home tab. Or, to select just a portion of text, you use arrow keys to move the insertion point to the text, press the F8 key to turn on select mode, then use arrow keys to select the required text.

TROUBLE
If a debug warning appears, you need to click End and then record the macro steps again.

- **Macro Errors**

  As you work with macros, you discover which options you need to select from a dialog box and which options you can select from the Ribbon. When you select an option incorrectly, a **debug** warning appears when you run the macro (see FIGURE 11-17). For example, the debug warning appears when you set line spacing by selecting 1.5 using the Line and Paragraph Spacing button in the Paragraph group on the Home tab. To set the line spacing in a macro, you need to select 1.5 spacing either from the Paragraph dialog box, which you open using the Launcher in the Paragraph group on the Home tab or by pressing the keyboard shortcut for 1.5 spacing, which is CTRL+5.

- **Macro information**

  Once you have practiced the steps required for the macro, you create the information associated with the macro. You open the Record Macro dialog box and then you name the macro and enter a short description of the macro. This description is usually a summary of the tasks the macro will perform. You also use this dialog box to assign the location where the macro should be stored. The default location is in the Normal template so that the macro is accessible in all documents that use the Normal template.

- **Record macro procedure**

  When you click OK after completing the Record Macro dialog box, the Macro Reorder pointer is the active pointer, indicating that you are ready to start recording the macro. In addition, the Stop Recording button and the Pause Recording button appear in the Code group on the Developer tab as shown in FIGURE 11-18. These buttons are toggle buttons. You click the Pause Recording button if, for example, you want to pause recording to perform steps not included in the macro. For example, you may need to pause to check information in another document or even attend to an email. You click the Stop Recording button when you have completed all the steps required for the macro, or when you have made a mistake and want to start over.

FIGURE 11-17: "Debug" warning that appears when the macro does not recognize a step

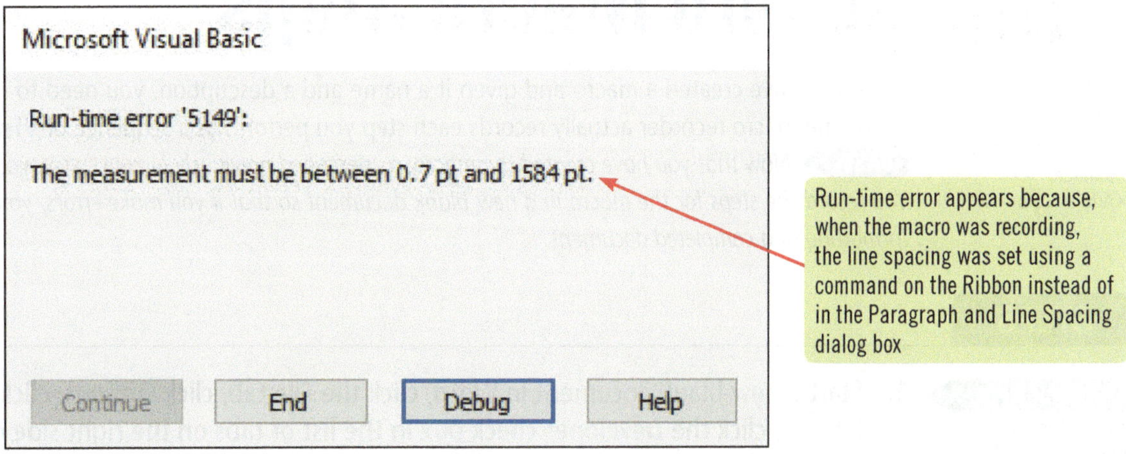

FIGURE 11-18: Recording a macro

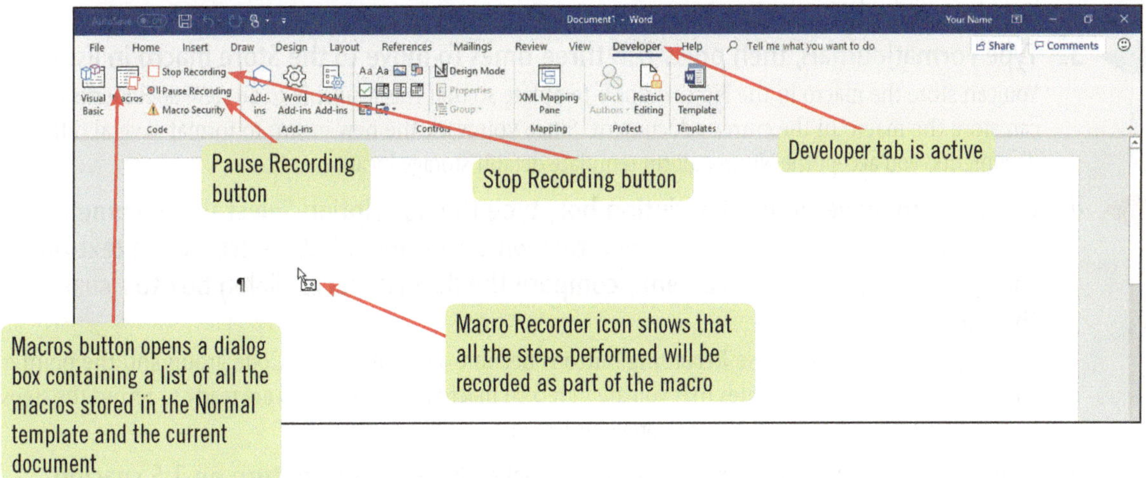

TABLE 11-2: Macro tasks and steps to complete the tasks

task to complete	steps to create macro
Select all the text	Press **CTRL+A**
Change the line spacing to 1.5	Press **CTRL+5**
Select the Arial font	Click the **Font arrow** in the Font group, then click **Arial**
Select 14 pt	Click the **Font Size arrow**, then click **14**
Insert a fill-in field text box	Press [↑] once to deselect the text and move to the top of the document, click the **Insert tab**, click the **Quick Parts button**, click **Field**, scroll down the list of Field names, click **Fill-in**, click **OK**, then click **OK**
Add a blank line	Press **ENTER**
Save the document	Click the **Save button** on the Quick Access toolbar
Close the document	Click the **File tab**, then click **Close**

Record Macro Steps

Learning Outcomes
- Create and record a macro
- Add a custom field

Once you have created a macro and given it a name and a description, you need to record the macro steps. The macro recorder actually records each step you perform as a sequence of **Visual Basic** codes.

CASE *Now that you have created the macro, as described previously in TABLE 11-2, you record the steps. You record the steps for the macro in a new blank document so that if you make errors, you do not affect the formatting of a completed document.*

STEPS

> **QUICK TIP**
> The Code group on the Developer tab contains the buttons you use to create and modify a macro.

1. **Start a new blank document in Word, click the File tab, click Options, click Customize Ribbon, click the Developer check box in the list of tabs on the right side of the Word Options dialog box if the box is not checked, click OK, then click the Developer tab**

2. **Save the blank document as IL_WD_11_JournalsMacroSetup to the location where you store your Data Files, press ENTER three times, then click the Record Macro button in the Code group**

   The Record Macro dialog box opens where you enter the macro name, the location where you want to store the macro, and a description.

> **QUICK TIP**
> A macro name cannot contain any spaces.

3. **Type FormatJournals, then press TAB three times to move to the Store macro in list box**

   You can store the macro in the Normal.dotm template so that it is available to all new documents or you can store the macro in the current document. Since you want the new macro to format several different documents, you accept the Normal.dotm template default storage location.

> **TROUBLE**
> DO NOT press any keys or click any other options except those specified in the steps. If you make a mistake, stop recording the macro and create the macro again, answering Yes to replace it.

4. **Press TAB to move to the Description box, type the description Select the document, change the line spacing to 1.5, format text with Arial and 14 pt, insert a fill-in text box, then save and close the document., compare the Record Macro dialog box to FIGURE 11-19, then click OK**

   The Stop Recording and Pause Recording buttons become available in the Code group and the pointer changes to [icon]. This icon indicates that you are in record macro mode. Now you are ready to record the steps in the macro that you identified in the previous lesson.

5. **Press CTRL+A to select all the paragraph marks, press CTRL+5 to turn on 1.5 spacing, click the Home tab, click the Font arrow in the Font group, scroll to and click Arial, click the Font Size arrow in the Font group, then click 14**

> **QUICK TIP**
> When you are recording a macro, you must use keystrokes to move around a document. You cannot use the mouse to position the insertion point.

6. **Press UP ARROW once to move to the top of the document, click the Insert tab, click the Explore Quick Parts button [icon] in the Text group, click Field, scroll down and click Fill-in from the list of Field names as shown in FIGURE 11-20, then click OK**

   When you run the macro, you will enter text in the fill-in field text box as shown in FIGURE 11-21.

7. **Click OK, press ENTER, click the Save button [icon] on the Quick Access toolbar, click the File tab, then click Close**

8. **Click the Developer tab, then click the Stop Recording button in the Code group**

   The file is saved and closed. The macro steps are completed, the Stop Recording button no longer appears in the Code group, and the Pause Recording button is dimmed.

9. **Click File, click Open, click IL_WD_11_JournalsMacroSetup to open this file, type your name on the first line, then save and close the document**

FIGURE 11-19: Record Macro dialog box

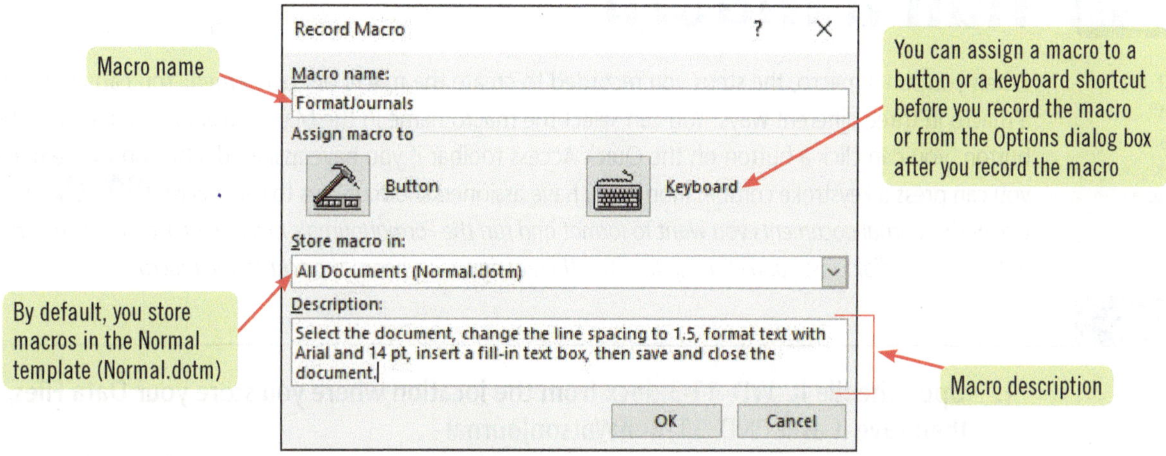

FIGURE 11-20: Field dialog box

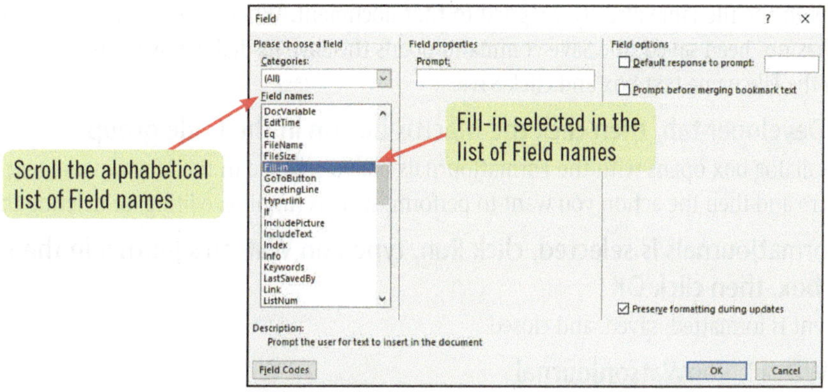

FIGURE 11-21: Inserting the Fill-in text box

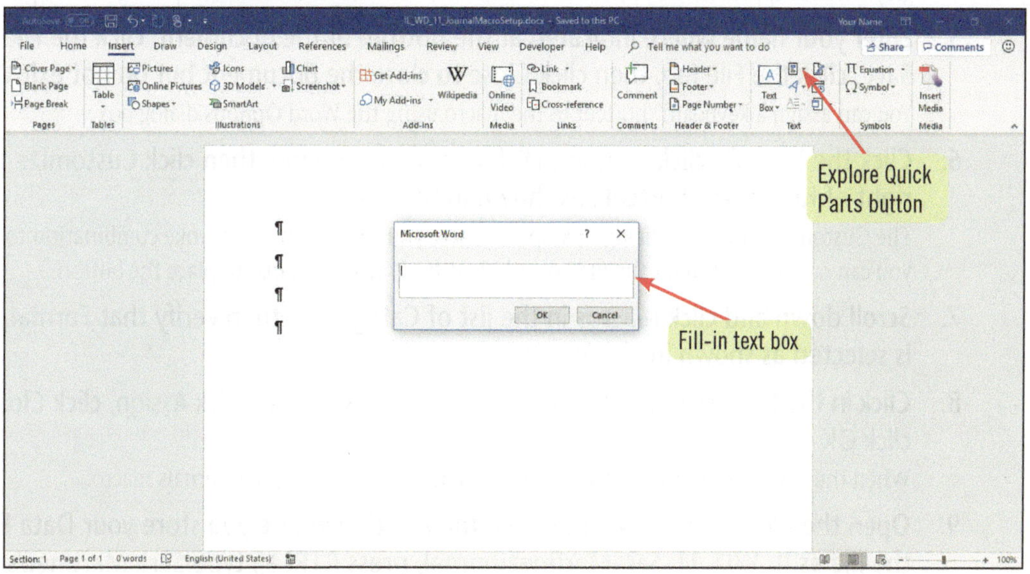

Pausing when recording a macro

If you need to interrupt the macro recording to perform other work such as checking an email or working on a different Word document, you can pause the recording. Click the Pause button on the Stop Recording toolbar. When you want to resume recording the macro steps, press the Pause button again.

Word

Run a Macro

Learning Outcomes
- Run a macro
- Assign a keyboard shortcut to a macro

When you run a macro, the steps you recorded to create the macro are performed. You can choose to run a macro in three different ways. You can select the macro name in the Macros dialog box and click the Run button, you can click a button on the Quick Access toolbar if you have assigned a button to the macro, or you can press a keystroke combination if you have assigned shortcut keys to the macro. **CASE** *You open one of the journal documents you want to format and run the FormatJournals macro by selecting the macro name in the Macros dialog box and clicking Run. You then assign a keyboard shortcut to the macro.*

STEPS

1. **Open the file IL_WD_11-3.docx from the location where you store your Data Files, then save it as IL_WD_11_RonWatsonJournal**

   The file contains a journal entry made by Ron Watson after he participated in three of the JCL Talent, Inc., workshops. When you run the macro on a document that you open, the Save command saves the document with the filename already assigned to that document. When you run the macro on a document that has not been saved, the Save command opens the Save As dialog box so that you can enter a filename in the File name text box and click Save.

2. **Click the Developer tab, then click the Macros button in the Code group**

   The Macros dialog box opens with the FormatJournals macro selected in the Macro name text box. You select a macro and then the action you want to perform, such as running, editing, or deleting the macro.

TROUBLE
If a run-time error appears when you run the macro, delete the macro, and repeat the previous lesson to record the macro again.

3. **Be sure FormatJournals is selected, click Run, type Ron Watson's Journal in the fill-in field text box, then click OK**

   The document is formatted, saved, and closed.

4. **Open IL_WD_11_RonWatsonJournal**

   The text you entered in the fill-in field text box appears at the top of the page highlighted in gray. The gray will not appear in the printed document. The document text uses 1.5 spacing and 14 pt, Arial text.

5. **Enter your name where indicated at the bottom of the document, click the File tab, click Save, click the File tab, then click Close to close the document but do not exit Word**

   You can assign a keyboard shortcut to the macro using the Word Options dialog box.

6. **Click the File tab, click Options, click Customize Ribbon, then click Customize to the right of Keyboard shortcuts as shown in FIGURE 11-22**

   The Customize Keyboard dialog box opens where you can assign a keystroke combination to a macro or you can create a button for the macro and identify on which toolbar to place the button.

7. **Scroll down and click Macros in the list of Categories, then verify that FormatJournals is selected as shown in FIGURE 11-23**

8. **Click in the Press new shortcut key text box, press CTRL+J, click Assign, click Close, then click OK**

   When the keyboard shortcut CTRL+J is pressed, it will run the FormatJournals macro.

9. **Open the file IL_WD_11-4.docx from the location where you store your Data Files, save the file as IL_WD_11_SaraMartinezJournal, press CTRL+J, type Sara Martinez's Journal in the fill-in field text box, then click OK**

   The macro formats, saves, and closes the document.

10. **Open the file IL_WD_11_SaraRamirezJournal.docx to verify that the macro has been applied, then close the file but do not exit Word**

FIGURE 11-22: Word Options dialog box

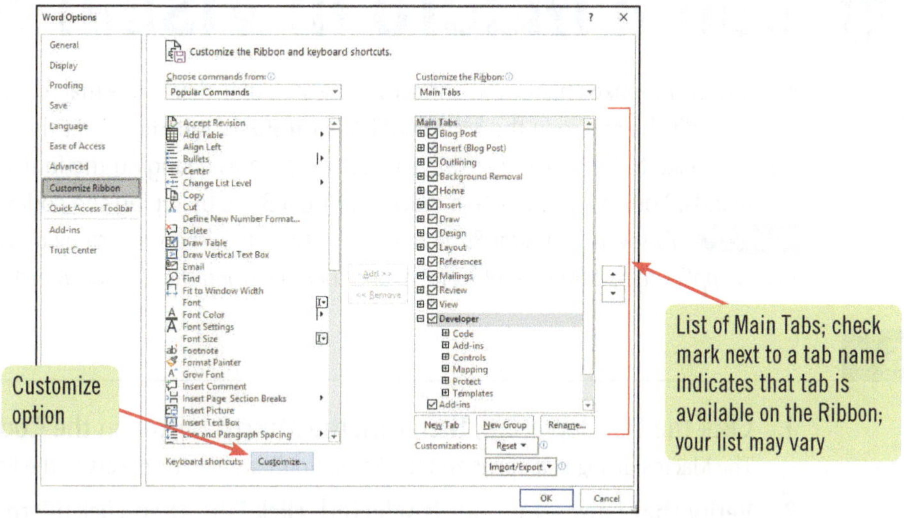

FIGURE 11-23: Customize Keyboard dialog box

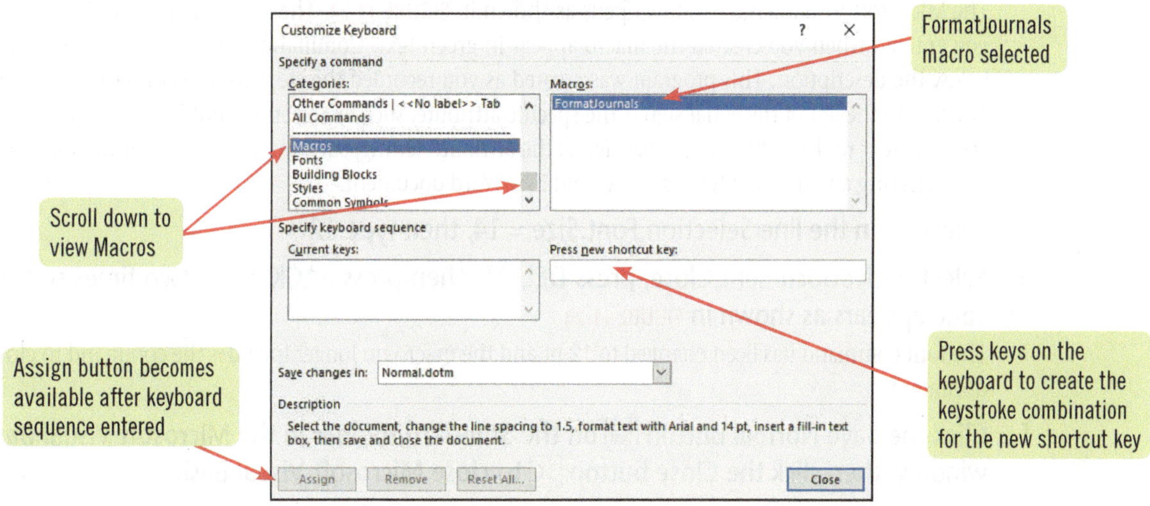

Finding keyboard shortcuts

Word includes hundreds of keyboard shortcuts that you can use to streamline document formatting tasks and to help you work efficiently in Word. You access the list of Word's keyboard shortcuts from Help. Click in the "Tell me what you want to do box" to the right of the tabs on the Ribbon, type "keyboard shortcuts", then click "Get Help on Keyboard shortcuts" in the menu that opens. In the Help window that opens, click links to articles to read more about keyboard shortcuts. You can also create your own keyboard shortcuts for procedures you use frequently. TABLE 11-3 shows some common keyboard shortcuts.

TABLE 11-3: Some common keyboard shortcuts

function	keyboard shortcut	function	keyboard shortcut
Bold text	CTRL+B	Print a document	CTRL+P
Center text	CTRL+E	Redo or repeat an action	CTRL+Y
Copy text	CTRL+C	Save a document	CTRL+S
Cut text	CTRL+X	Select all text	CTRL+A
Open a document	CTRL+O	Turn on double spacing	CTRL+2
Paste text	CTRL+V	Undo an action	CTRL+Z

Word Module 11

Edit a Macro in Visual Basic

Learning Outcome
- Edit a macro in Visual Basic

If you want to make changes to a macro you can either delete the macro and record the steps again, or you can edit the macro in the **Microsoft Visual Basic window**. Edit the macro when the change you want to make to the macro is relatively minor—such as changing the font style or removing one of the commands. You can also create a macro in Visual Basic by typing the codes in the Visual Basic window.

CASE *You work in Visual Basic to edit the FormatJournals macro by decreasing the font size that the macro applies to text from 14 pt to 12 pt and then removing the close document command.*

STEPS

1. **Click the Developer tab, then click the Macros button in the Code group**
   The Macros dialog box opens and the FormatJournals macro appears in the list of available macros.
2. **Verify that FormatJournals is selected, click Edit, then click ☐ to maximize the Microsoft Visual Basic window, if necessary**
   The Microsoft Visual Basic window opens as shown in FIGURE 11-24. The macro name and the description you entered when you created the macro appear in green text. Command codes, a basic program, appear below the description. This program was created as you recorded the steps for the FormatJournals macro. The text to the left of the equal sign is the specific attribute, such as Selection.Font.Name or Selection.Font.Size. The text to the right of the equal sign is the attribute setting, such as Arial or 14. You work in this window selecting and deleting text as you would in a Word document.
3. **Select 14 in the line Selection.Font.Size = 14, then type 12**
4. **Select ActiveDocument.Close, press DELETE, then press BACKSPACE two times so the code appears as shown in FIGURE 11-25**
   The font command has been changed to 12 pt and the macro no longer includes the command to close the document.
5. **Click the Save Normal button on the Standard toolbar in the Microsoft Visual Basic window, then click the Close button ☒ to close Microsoft Visual Basic**
6. **Open the file IL_WD_11_SaraMartinezJournal.docx from the location where you store your Data Files, press CTRL+J to run the macro, then click Cancel to close the fill-in field text box**
   The second time you run the macro you don't need to enter a title in the fill-in field text box. The font size of the document is reduced to 12 pt and the document is saved but not closed.
7. **Type your name where indicated at the bottom of the document, then save the document**
8. **Click the Developer tab, click the Visual Basic button in the Code group, press CTRL+A to select all the FormatJournals macro code in the Visual Basic window, press CTRL+C to copy the code to the Clipboard, then close the Microsoft Visual Basic window**
9. **Press CTRL+N to open a new blank Word document, press CTRL+V, press ENTER, type Created by followed by your name, save the document as IL_WD_11_MacroCodes, then close the document**
   The journal for Sara Martinez is again the active document.

QUICK TIP
You save a copy of your macro code so you have a reference to verify the macro steps you performed.

FIGURE 11-24: Visual Basic window

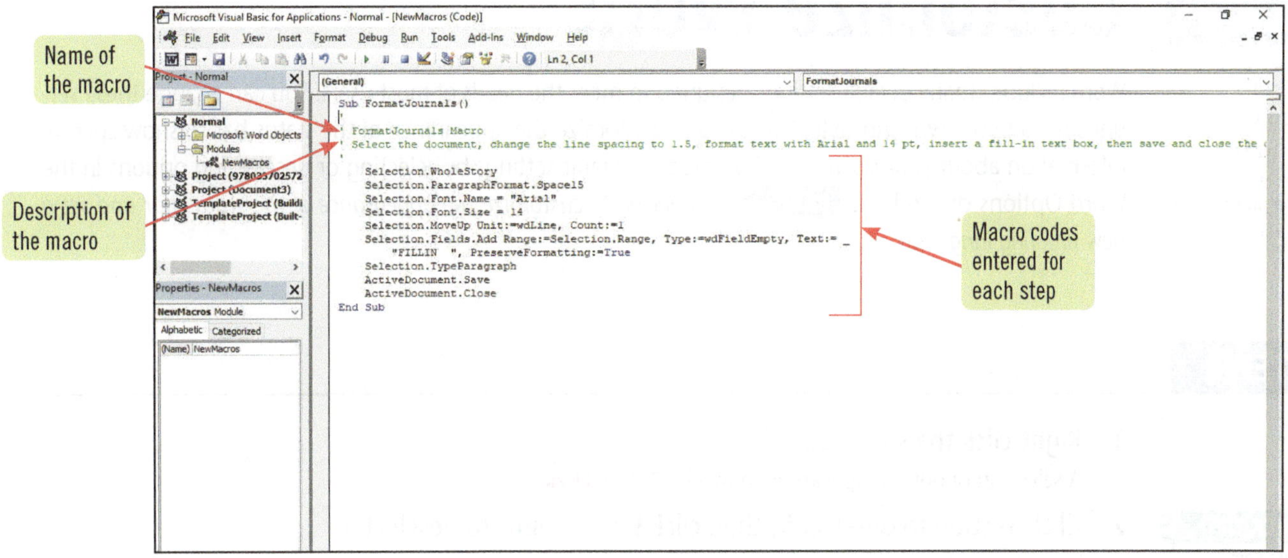

FIGURE 11-25: Edited macro

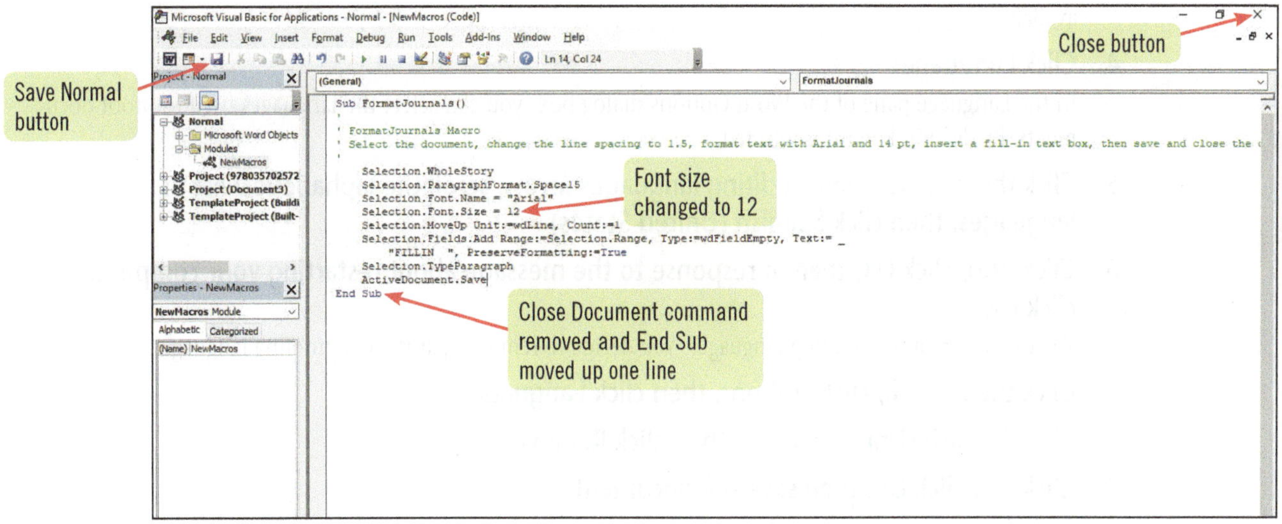

Creating a Macro in Visual Basic

You can create a macro by entering codes into Visual Basic. From the Developer tab, click Macros in the Code group, type a macro name, select the template or document in which to store the macro, then click Create to open the Visual Basic Editor. You can paste code from an existing or you can enter codes for the macro. To find a list of codes and information about working with Visual Basic, press F1 to open the Microsoft Visual Basic Help menu or click Help on the menu bar, then click Microsoft Visual Basic for Applications Help.

Word
Module 11

Customize Word

Learning Outcomes
- Customize the status bar
- Set the proofing language

Word includes many default settings designed to meet the needs of most users. You can change these settings to suit your working style. You can also customize the appearance of the status bar to show specific information about your document. You modify default settings by selecting or deselecting options in the Word Options dialog box. **CASE** *You decide to customize the appearance of the status bar and set a new proofing language.*

STEPS

1. **Right-click the status bar**

   A selection of options appears as shown in FIGURE 11-26

2. **Click Section to deselect it, then click Word Count to deselect it**

   These two options are now removed from the status bar.

QUICK TIP
To restore items, right-click the status bar, then click the items again.

3. **Click the File tab, scroll down, then click Options**

   From the Word Options dialog box you can customize the Ribbon and the Quick Access toolbar. You can also access nine other categories that you can modify to meet your needs. TABLE 11-4 lists the categories available.

4. **Click Language**

   In the Language pane of the Word Options dialog box, you can select the languages used to proof documents. By default, English is selected.

5. **Click the Add additional editing languages arrow, scroll the alphabetical list of languages, then click Spanish (United States)**

6. **Click Add, click OK, then in response to the message about restarting your computer, click OK**

   You can also remove proofing languages. You decide to remove Spanish as a proofing language.

7. **Click the File tab, click Options, then click Language**

8. **Click Spanish (United States), then click Remove**

9. **Click OK, click OK, then save the document**

Copying a Macro to Another Document

You can copy a macro that you saved in a document instead of in the Normal template to another document. You use the same procedure to copy a macro from one document to another document as you used to copy a style or selection of styles from one document to another document. Click the Launcher in the Styles group on the Home tab, click the Manage Styles button at the bottom of the Styles pane, then click Import/Export. In the Organizer dialog box, click the Macro Projects Items tab, open the file containing the macro you want to copy (the source file), open the file you want to copy the macro to (the destination file), select the macro in the source file, then click Copy.

FIGURE 11-26: Customize the status bar options

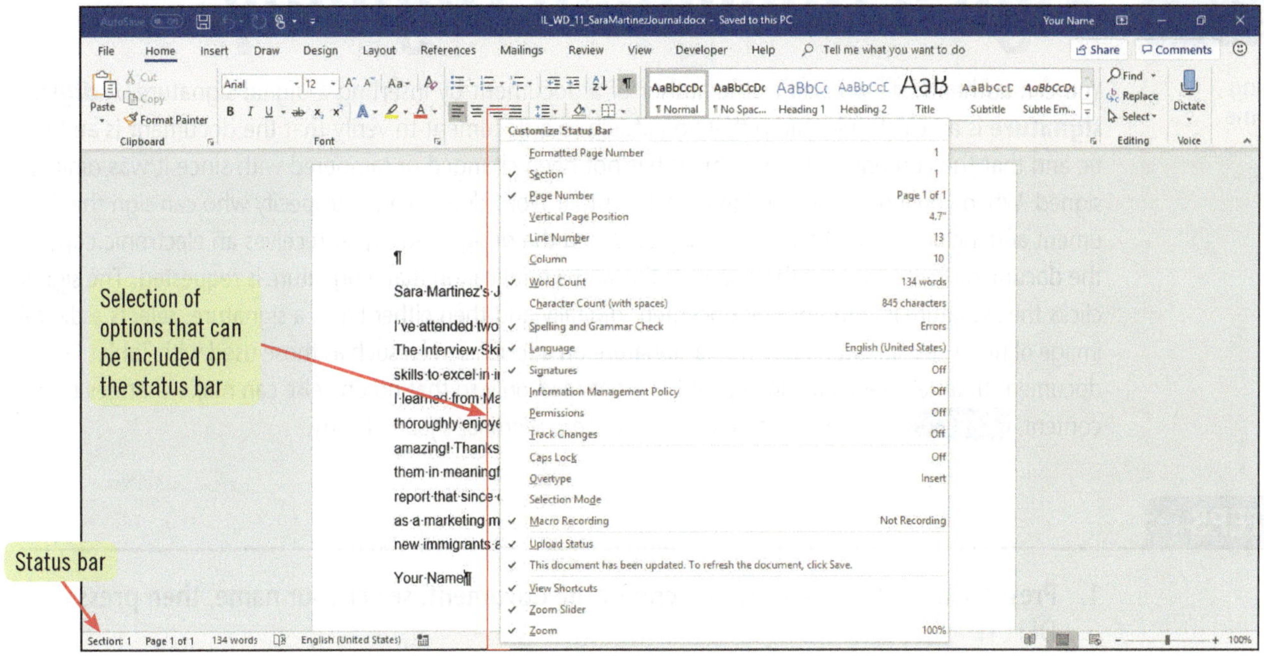

TABLE 11-4: Categories in the Word Options dialog box

category	description
General	Options include those used to modify the user interface, personalize Office, and modify Collaboration options
Display	Change the page display, formatting options and printing options
Proofing	Modify AutoCorrect and spelling and grammar options and exceptions
Save	Modify options related to saving documents and editing them offline
Language	Select editing, display and Help languages
Ease of Access	Select feedback options, application and document display options, and automatic Alt Text
Advanced	Modify options related to editing, images, document display, saving, and printing, layout, and document compatibility
Add-ins	Includes the list of programs included with or added to Word
Trust Center	Access security options and the Microsoft Word Trust Center

Word
Module 11

Sign a Document Digitally

Learning Outcome
- Add a digital signature

You can authenticate yourself as the author of a document by inserting a digital signature. A **digital signature** is an electronic stamp that you attach to a document to verify that the document is authentic and that the content of the document has not been changed or tampered with since it was digitally signed. When you insert a digital signature line into a Word document, you specify who can sign the document and include instructions for the signer. When the designated signer receives an electronic copy of the document, he or she sees the signature line and a notification that a signature is requested. The signer clicks the signature line to sign the document digitally and then either types a signature, selects a digital image of his or her signature, or writes a signature on a touch screen such as those used with Tablet PCs. A document that has been digitally signed becomes read-only so that no one else can make changes to the content. CASE *You add a digital signature to Sara Martinez's journal entry.*

STEPS

1. **Press CTRL+END to move to the end of the document, select your name, then press DELETE**
2. **Press ENTER to position the insertion point where want to add the signature line**
3. **Click the Insert tab, then click the Add a Signature Line button in the Text group**
   The Signature Setup dialog box opens. You enter information about the person who can sign the document in this dialog box.
4. **Type your name in the Suggested signer text box in the Signature Setup dialog box as shown in FIGURE 11-27**
5. **Click OK**
   A space for your signature, with an X and your name below a horizontal line appears in the footer at the position of the insertion point.
6. **Double-click the signature line, read the message that appears, then click No**
   If you click in the line and then click Yes, you are taken to a page on the Microsoft website that lists Microsoft partners that supply digital IDs. Once you have obtained a Digital ID, you can enter it in the signature line. However, you will not be obtaining a Digital ID, so the signature line will remain blank.
7. **Click in the document, then save the document**
8. **Submit a copy of all the files you created in this module to your instructor, click the File tab, then click Exit to exit Word**

FIGURE 11-27: Signature Setup dialog box

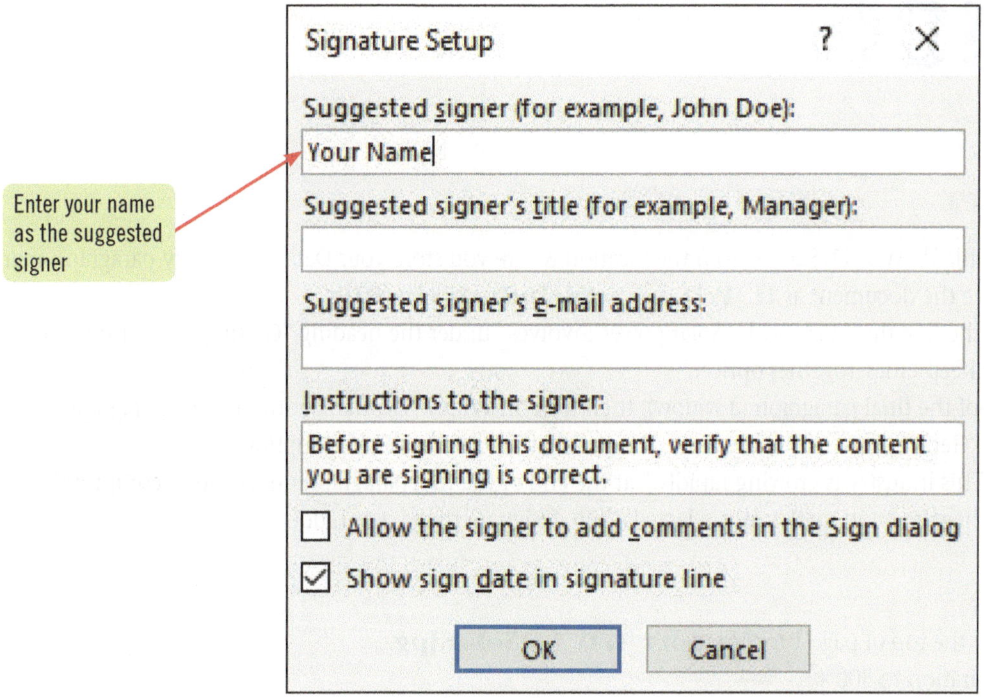

Word

Customizing the Quick Access toolbar

To customize the Quick Access toolbar, click the File tab, click Options, then click Quick Access Toolbar. The buttons included by default on the Quick Access toolbar appear in the list box on the right. These buttons are AutoSave, Save, Undo, and Redo. To add a new command to the Quick Access toolbar, select the command from the list box on the left, then click Add. To remove a button from the Quick Access toolbar, select the command in the list box, then click Remove.

Acquiring a Digital ID

You acquire a **digital ID** by purchasing one from a Microsoft partner. When you click Yes to acquire a digital ID, you are taken to a page with links to Microsoft partners. You can click on one of the links and purchase a digital ID. Other people can use the digital ID to verify that your digital signature is authentic. The Microsoft partner that issues the digital ID ensures the authenticity of the person or organization that acquires the digital ID.

Practice

Skills Review

1. Manage pages.

a. Start Word, open the file IL_WD_11-5.docx from the location where you store your Data Files, verify paragraph marks are showing, then save the document as **IL_WD_11_SolarIndustryProfile**.

b. Scroll down, click in the line that starts with "Solar power involves" under the heading "Getting Power from the Sun", then apply the Keep Lines Together option.

c. Scroll to the last line of the final paragraph (a widow), then turn on Widow/Orphan control for the paragraph.

d. Click in the heading "Getting Power from the Sun", then apply the Page break before option.

e. Select the sentence "This industry is growing rapidly." at the end of the first paragraph under the "Description" heading, verify that the paragraph mark is not selected, then designate the text as hidden text.

f. Save the document.

2. Edit pictures.

a. Change the picture at the top of page 1 to **Support_WD_11_Solar.jpg**.

b. Change the color saturation to 300%.

c. Change the color tone to Temperature: 8800 K.

d. Scroll to the bottom of the document, click the picture, then apply the Glow Diffused artistic effect.

e. Save the document.

3. Use layering options.

a. Go to the top of page 1, then send the picture of the solar panels behind the lightning bolt shape.

b. Go to the end of the document, then change the yellow cloud shape to a sun shape.

c. Apply the Round Convex 3-D bevel effect to the sun shape.

d. Open the Selection pane, hide the picture of the sun shape, then show the picture again.

e. Drag the picture of the sun shape below Picture 2.

f. Drag Picture 2 above Star: 10 Points 7 in the Selection pane.

g. Save the document.

4. Arrange and compress graphics.

a. In the Selection pane, verify that Picture 2 is selected, then use CTRL to select the other two objects so all three objects in the Selection pane are selected.

b. Group the three objects into one object.

c. Change the wrapping of the grouped object to Square.

d. Cut the grouped object, paste it at the top of page 2, then position it to the right of the "Getting Power from the Sun" heading as shown in the completed document in FIGURE 11-28.

e. Compress all the pictures in the document using the Web (150 ppi) option.

f. Save the document.

5. Create character styles.

a. On page 1, select the text "PV Power" in the first line below the Technologies heading, then use CTRL to select "CS Power" so both phrases are selected.

b. Create a new style called **Technology**, then designate it as a Character style.

c. Select these character formatting settings: a font size of 14 pt, Bold, and the Dark Red font color (first selection in the Standard Colors section).

d. Deselect the text.

Skills Review (continued)

- **e.** Select just "PV Power", change the font color to Green in the Standard Colors section, then update the Technology character style to match the selection.
- **f.** Close the Styles pane.
- **g.** Select the table below the "Geographic Segmentation" heading, then add the following Alt text: Title: **Locations of Solar Industry** and the Description: **Four geographic areas are listed along with their percent share of the solar power industry**.
- **h.** Save the document.

6. Manage styles.

- **a.** Open the file **IL_WD_11-6.docx** from the location where you store your Data Files, save the document as **IL_WD_11_WindIndustryProfile**, then close it.
- **b.** Open the Organizer dialog box from the Styles pane.
- **c.** Verify that the source file is IL_WD_11_SolarIndustryProfile.docx.
- **d.** Open IL_WD_11_WindIndustryProfile.docx as the destination file. Remember to select All Documents to view the Word document.
- **e.** Copy the styles **Energy** and **Technology** from the source file to the destination file.
- **f.** Close and save the destination file, then close the Organizer dialog box.
- **g.** Open IL_WD_11_WindIndustryProfile.docx, use CTRL to select the two configurations "Horizontal axis turbine" and "Vertical axis turbine", then apply the Technology character style.
- **h.** Go to the top of the document, then use the Replace feature to find every instance of **wind** and replace it with "wind" formatted with the Energy character style you just copied from the Solar Energy document.
- **i.** Type your name where indicated in the footer, save and close the document, type your name where indicated in the footer in the Solar Energy document, then save and close the document. The completed Solar Energy document appears as shown in **FIGURE 11-28**.

FIGURE 11-28

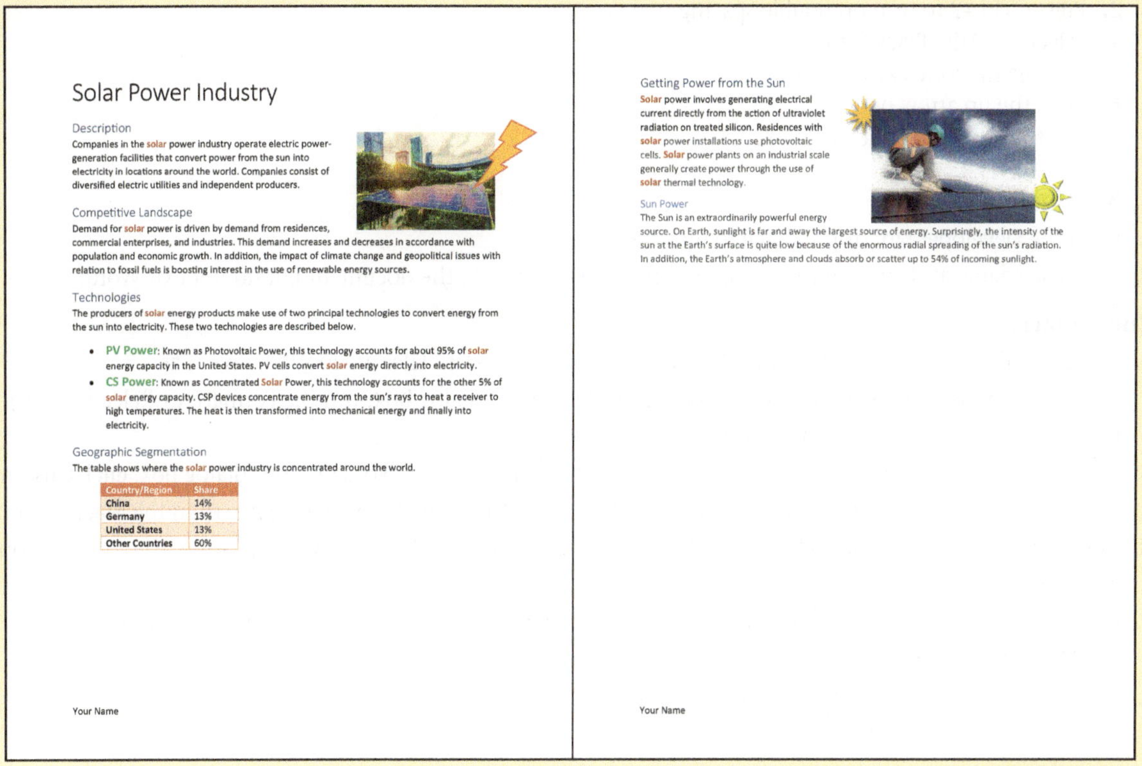

Solar Power Industry

Description

Companies in the solar power industry operate electric power-generation facilities that convert power from the sun into electricity in locations around the world. Companies consist of diversified electric utilities and independent producers.

Competitive Landscape

Demand for solar power is driven by demand from residences, commercial enterprises, and industries. This demand increases and decreases in accordance with population and economic growth. In addition, the impact of climate change and geopolitical issues with relation to fossil fuels is boosting interest in the use of renewable energy sources.

Technologies

The producers of solar energy products make use of two principal technologies to convert energy from the sun into electricity. These two technologies are described below.

- PV Power: Known as Photovoltaic Power, this technology accounts for about 95% of solar energy capacity in the United States. PV cells convert solar energy directly into electricity.
- CS Power: Known as Concentrated Solar Power, this technology accounts for the other 5% of solar energy capacity. CSP devices concentrate energy from the sun's rays to heat a receiver to high temperatures. The heat is then transformed into mechanical energy and finally into electricity.

Geographic Segmentation

The table shows where the solar power industry is concentrated around the world.

Country/Region	Share
China	14%
Germany	13%
United States	13%
Other Countries	60%

Your Name

Getting Power from the Sun

Solar power involves generating electrical current directly from the action of ultraviolet radiation on treated silicon. Residences with solar power installations use photovoltaic cells. Solar power plants on an industrial scale generally create power through the use of solar thermal technology.

Sun Power

The Sun is an extraordinarily powerful energy source. On Earth, sunlight is far and away the largest source of energy. Surprisingly, the intensity of the sun at the Earth's surface is quite low because of the enormous radial spreading of the sun's radiation. In addition, the Earth's atmosphere and clouds absorb or scatter up to 54% of incoming sunlight.

Your Name

asharkyu/Shutterstock.com

Federico Rostagno/Shutterstock.com

Skills Review (continued)

7. Plan a macro.

a. Refer to TABLE 11-5 to review the steps required for the macro you will create in the next step:

TABLE 11-5: Macro tasks plan

Macro tasks	steps to complete the tasks
Select all the text	Press **CTRL+A**
Change the line spacing to double	Press **CTRL+2**
Select the Arial Black font	Click the **Font arrow** in the Font group, then click **Arial Black**
Select 18 pt	Click the **Font Size arrow**, then click **18**
Insert a fill-in field text box	Press the up arrow once to deselect the text and move to the top of the document, click the **Insert tab**, click the **Quick Parts button**, click **Field**, scroll down the list of Field names, click **Fill-in**, click **OK**, then click **OK**
Add a blank line	Press **ENTER**
Save the document	Click the **Save button** on the Quick Access toolbar

8. Record macro steps.

a. Start a new blank document, then show the Developer tab if it is not already displayed on the Ribbon.

b. Press ENTER three times, then save the blank document as **IL_WD_11_PressReleaseMacroSetup**.

c. Make the Developer tab the active tab, open the Record Macro dialog box, then type **FormatPressRelease** as the macro name.

d. Enter the following description in the Description text box: **Select all the text, change the line spacing to double, change the font to Arial Black and 18 pt, insert a fill-in text box, then save the document.**

e. Exit the Record Macro dialog box, then perform the macro steps as follows:

1. Press CTRL+A to select all the text.
2. Press CTRL+2 to turn on double spacing.
3. Select the Arial Black font.
4. Change the font size to 18 pt.
5. Press the up arrow once.
6. Insert a Fill-in box and click OK.
7. Press ENTER.
8. Save the document.

f. From the Developer tab, stop the macro recording.

g. Type your name at the top of the document, then save and close the document but do not exit Word.

9. Run a macro.

a. Open the file IL_WD_11-7.docx from the location where your Data Files are located, save it as **IL_WD_11_PressReleaseSolar**, then from the Macros dialog box, run the FormatPressRelease macro.

b. Enter **Sun Shine Solar** in the Fill-in text box.

c. Open the Customize the Ribbon and keyboard shortcuts screen in the Word Options dialog box, click Customize, scroll down the list of Categories, select Macros, then select the FormatPressRelease macro in the Macros list box.

d. In the Press new shortcut key text box, enter the keystroke command **ALT+H**, click Assign, then close all open dialog boxes.

e. Open the file **IL_WD_11-8.docx** from the location where you store your Data Files, then save it as **IL_WD_11_PressReleaseWind.**

f. Use the Alt+H macro to format the document, entering **Wind Ways** in the fill-in text box.

Skills Review (continued)

10. Edit a macro in Visual Basic.

a. Open the Macros dialog box, select the FormatPressRelease macro, then click Edit. (*Note*: Two macros are listed—the FormatJournals macro you created in the lessons and the FormatPressRelease macro you just created. In the steps that follow, you make corrections to the FormatPressRelease macro.)

b. Find Selection.Font.Name = "Arial Black", change the font to **Calibri** and keep the quotation marks around Calibri, then change Selection.Font.Size = 18 to **14**.

c. Save the macro, select all the components of the FormatPressRelease macro in the Visual Basic window, copy them, close the Visual Basic window, press CTRL+N to open a new blank Word document, paste the code into the blank document, type **Created by** followed by your name below the last line, save the document as **IL_WD_11_PressReleaseMacroCodes** to the location where you store your files for this book, then close it.

d. Verify that IL_WD_11_PressReleaseWind is the active document, then use the ALT+H keystrokes to run the revised macro. Remember to press Cancel to bypass the Fill-in box.

e. Verify that the font style of the document title is now Calibri and the font size is 14 pt, type your name where indicated at the end of the document, then save the document.

11. Customize Word.

a. Customize the status bar so that Section and Word Count are both selected.

b. In the Language section of the Options dialog box, Add French (Canada) as a proofing language.

c. Remove French (Canada) as a proofing language, then save the document.

12. Sign a document digitally.

a. Delete your name in the current document, then press Enter to position the insertion point where you want to add a signature line.

b. Insert a signature line that includes your name.

c. Save and close the document, then save and close all files.

d. Submit a copy of all the files you created in this module to your instructor, then exit Word.

Independent Challenge 1

One of your duties in the administration department at Riverwalk Medical Clinic in Cambridge, MA, is to write and format the clinic's quarterly news bulletin. You open a draft of the Fall bulletin and set paragraph pagination options, edit pictures, and create and then modify a character style. Finally, you copy a character style from the Spring bulletin to the Fall bulletin and apply it to selected text.

a. Start Word, open the file IL_WD_11-9.docx from the location where you store your Data Files, save it as **IL_WD_11_RiverwalkFallBulletin**, then show formatting marks.

b. Apply the Keep with next option to the heading "Share Your Ideas".

c. Format the text "One of our schedulers will find a time that works best for you." At the end of the "Physical Exams" paragraph on page 1 as hidden.

d. Change the picture on page 1 to the picture **Support_WD_11_Clinic.jpg**.

e. Apply the Texturizer artistic effect to the picture, then set the color saturation at 200% and the color tone at 7200 K.

f. Use the Selection pane to move the picture below the red cross shape, then modify the red cross shape so it uses the Divot 3-D bevel effect.

g. Group the red cross shape and the picture into one object.

h. Select the phrases "Health Hijinks" and "Silent Auction" in the bulleted list, then create a character style called **Event** that uses the following formats: Bold, Italic, and the Blue font color (in the Standard Colors section.)

Independent Challenge 1 (continued)

i. Select "Health Hijinks" and remove italics, then update the Event character style to match the selection.

j. Select the table on page 2, then add Alt text. Enter **Statistics** as the title, then in the description box type **Two-column table showing patient and volunteer statistics from August 1 to September 30.**

k. Save the document, then close it.

l. From a blank Word document, open the Organizer dialog box from the Styles pane. Close the file on the left (the current blank document), then open the file **Support_WD_11_SpringBulletin.docx** from the location where you save your files. This is the source file.

m. Close the file on the right, then open the file **IL_WD_11_RiverwalkFallBulletin.docx**. This is the destination file.

n. Copy the Clinic character style from the Spring Bulletin document on the left to the Fall Bulletin document on the right.

o. Close and save the Riverwalk Fall Bulletin, then close the Organizer dialog box.

p. Open **IL_WD_11_RiverwalkFallBulletin** and use Find and Replace to find every instance of "Riverwalk" and replaced it with **Riverwalk** formatted with the Clinic style.

q. Type your name where shown in the footer on the second page, save the document, then close it. The completed document appears as shown in FIGURE 11-29.

FIGURE 11-29

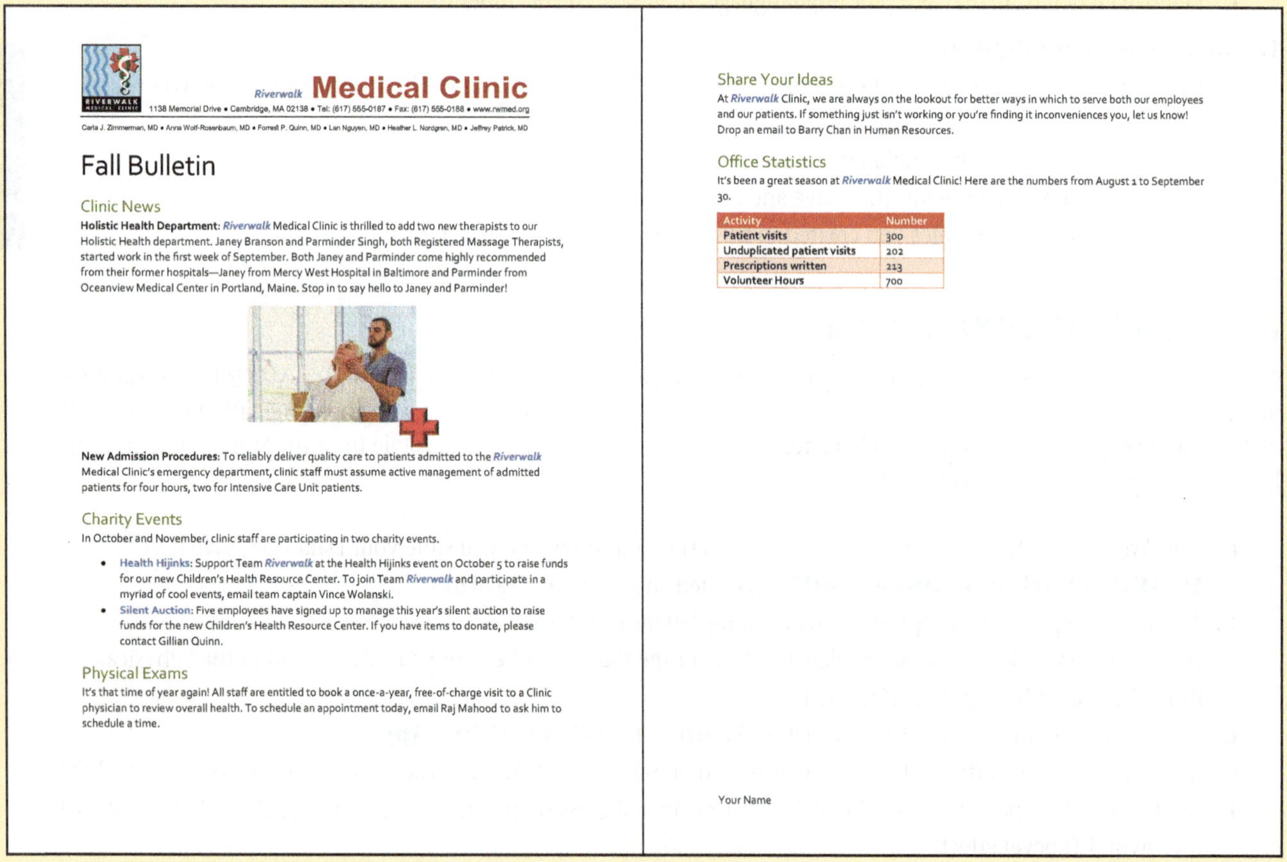
Riverwalk Medical Clinic
1138 Memorial Drive • Cambridge, MA 02138 • Tel: (617) 555-0187 • Fax: (617) 555-0188 • www.rwmed.org
Carla J. Zimmerman, MD • Anna Wolf-Rosenbaum, MD • Forrest P. Quinn, MD • Lan Nguyen, MD • Heather L. Nordgren, MD • Jeffrey Patrick, MD

Fall Bulletin

Clinic News

Holistic Health Department: *Riverwalk* Medical Clinic is thrilled to add two new therapists to our Holistic Health department. Janey Branson and Parminder Singh, both Registered Massage Therapists, started work in the first week of September. Both Janey and Parminder come highly recommended from their former hospitals—Janey from Mercy West Hospital in Baltimore and Parminder from Oceanview Medical Center in Portland, Maine. Stop in to say hello to Janey and Parminder!

New Admission Procedures: To reliably deliver quality care to patients admitted to the *Riverwalk* Medical Clinic's emergency department, clinic staff must assume active management of admitted patients for four hours, two for Intensive Care Unit patients.

Charity Events

In October and November, clinic staff are participating in two charity events.

- Health Hijinks: Support Team *Riverwalk* at the Health Hijinks event on October 5 to raise funds for our new Children's Health Resource Center. To join Team *Riverwalk* and participate in a myriad of cool events, email team captain Vince Wolanski.
- Silent Auction: Five employees have signed up to manage this year's silent auction to raise funds for the new Children's Health Resource Center. If you have items to donate, please contact Gillian Quinn.

Physical Exams

It's that time of year again! All staff are entitled to book a once-a-year, free-of-charge visit to a Clinic physician to review overall health. To schedule an appointment today, email Raj Mahood to ask him to schedule a time.

Share Your Ideas

At *Riverwalk* Clinic, we are always on the lookout for better ways in which to serve both our employees and our patients. If something just isn't working or you're finding it inconveniences you, let us know! Drop an email to Barry Chan in Human Resources.

Office Statistics

It's been a great season at *Riverwalk* Medical Clinic! Here are the numbers from August 1 to September 30.

Activity	Number
Patient visits	300
Unduplicated patient visits	202
Prescriptions written	213
Volunteer Hours	700

Your Name

Africa Studio/Shutterstock.com

Independent Challenge 2

You work for Hilltown Marketing in San Francisco. Over the years, clients have provided testimonials about their experiences with Hilltown Marketing. You create a macro that standardizes the formatting and then you apply it to format two testimonials.

a. Start a new blank document, show the Developer tab if it is not already displayed on the Ribbon, press ENTER three times, then save the blank document as **IL_WD_11_TestimonialMacroSetup**.
b. Open the Record Macro dialog box, then enter **Testimonial** as the macro name.
c. Enter the following description in the Description text box: **Select all the text, change the line spacing to single, change the font to Times New Roman and 12 pt, apply italics, insert a fill-in box, then save the document**.
d. Exit the Record Macro dialog box, then perform the macro steps as follows:
   1. Press CTRL+A to select all the text.
   2. Press CTRL+1 to turn on single spacing.
   3. Select the Times New Roman font.
   4. Change the font size to 12 pt.
   5. Press Ctrl+I to apply italics.
   6. Press the up arrow once.
   7. Insert a Fill-in box and click OK.
   8. Press ENTER.
   9. Save the document.
e. From the Developer tab, stop the macro recording.
f. Type your name at the top of the document, then save and close the document but do not exit Word.
g. Open the file **IL_WD_11-10.docx**, then save it as **IL_WD_11_Testimonial1**.
h. From the Macros dialog box, run the Testimonial macro, entering **Bayside Financing** in the Fill-in text box.
i. Open the Customize the Ribbon and keyboard shortcuts screen in the Word Options dialog box, click Customize, scroll down the list of Categories, select Macros, then select the Testimonials macro in the Macros list box.
j. In the Press new shortcut key box, enter the command ALT+T, click Assign, then close all dialog boxes.
k. Open the file **IL_WD_11-11.docx** from the location where you store your Data Files, then save it as **IL_WD_11_Testimonial2**.
l. Use the Alt+T macro to format the document, entering **Ace Architects** in the fill-in text box.
m. Open the Macros dialog box, select the Testimonial macro, then click Edit.
n. Find Selection.Font.Name = "Times New Roman", change the font to **Arial** and keep the quotation marks around Arial, then change Selection.Font.Size = 12 to **13**.
o. Save the macro, select all the components of the Testimonial macro in the Visual Basic window, copy them, close the Visual Basic window, press CTRL+N to open a new blank Word document, paste the code into the blank document, type **Created by** followed by your name below the last line, save the document as **IL_WD_11_ TestimonialMacroCodes**, then close it.
p. Verify that IL_WD_11_ Testimonial2 is the active document, then use the ALT+T keystrokes to run the revised macro. Remember to press Cancel to bypass the Fill-in box.
q. Verify that the font style of the document title is now Arial and the font size is 13 pt, then type your name where indicated at the end of the document.
r. Customize the status bar so that the language is selected.
s. In the Language section of the Options dialog box, Add English (Canada) as a proofing language.
t. Delete your name in the current document, press Enter then insert a signature line that includes your name. Do not sign the document.
u. Save and close the document, then save and close the Testimonial1 document.
v. Submit a copy of all the files you created for Independent Challenge 2 to your instructor, then exit Word.

Word

Visual Workshop

You work for Gregson Financials in Chicago. Each year, the company awards a trip to the top sales manager. You've been asked to create a poster to distribute around the company to celebrate this year's winner. Open IL_WD_11-12.docx from the location where you store your Data Files, then save it as **IL_WD_11_GregsonFinancialsPoster**. Select Kate Epstein (but not the paragraph mark following), then create a character style called **Winner** that uses these formats: Bold, Italic, 18 pt, and the Light Blue font color. Apply the Winner character style to **Tuscany**. Modify the character style by changing the font size to 14 pt and the color to Red. Format, arrange, and group the three graphic objects so the completed poster appears as shown in **FIGURE 11-30**. You will need to apply the Convex 3-D bevel effect to the sun shape and the Pastels Smooth artistic effect and 8800 K color tone to the oval picture of the Tuscany landscape. Compress all the pictures in the document to 150 ppi. Enter your name where indicated in the footer, save the document, submit a copy to your instructor, then close the document.

FIGURE 11-30

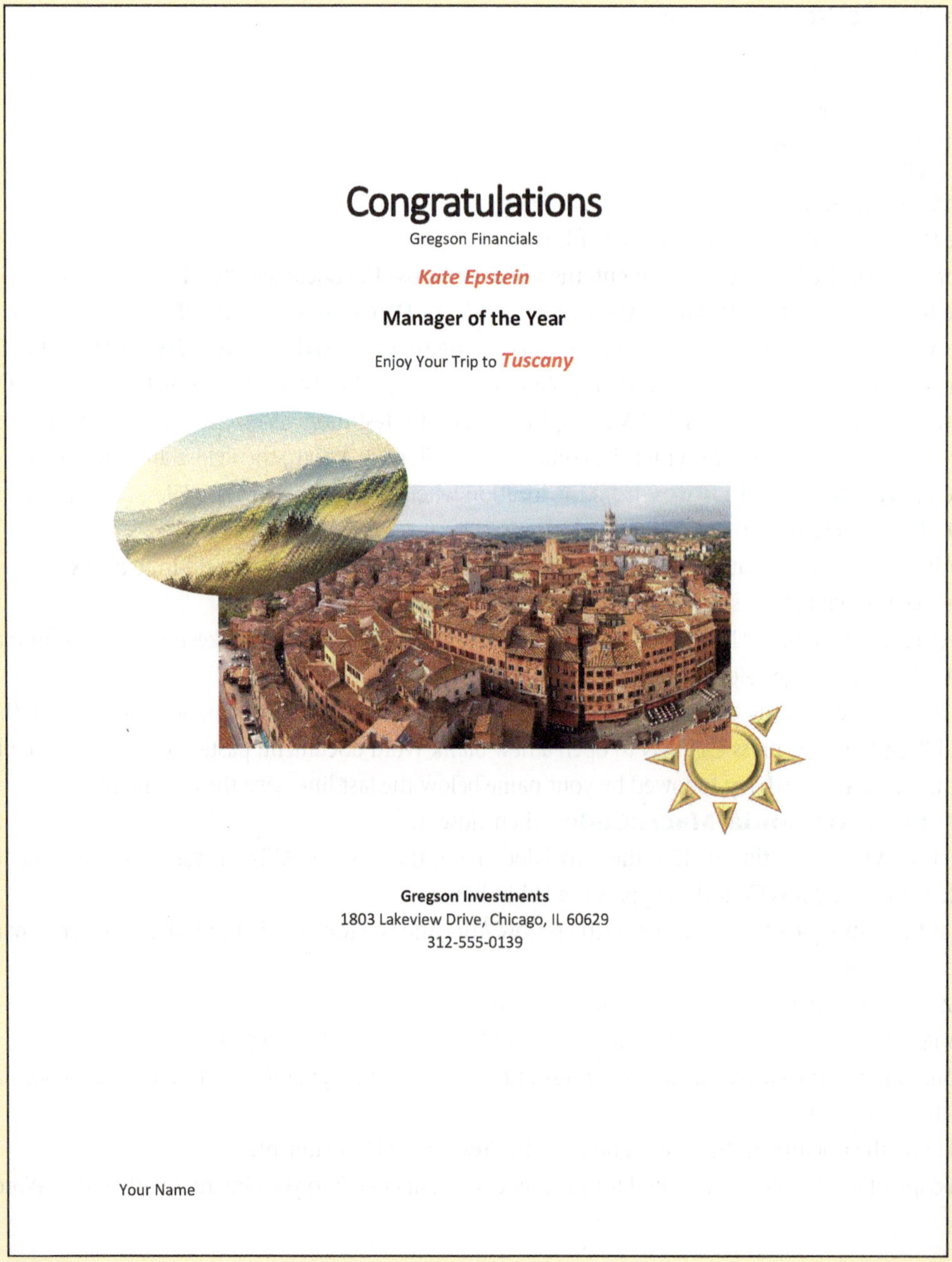
Congratulations

Gregson Financials

Kate Epstein

Manager of the Year

Enjoy Your Trip to ***Tuscany***

Gregson Investments
1803 Lakeview Drive, Chicago, IL 60629
312-555-0139

Your Name

Automating Worksheet Tasks

CASE Cheri McNeil, manager of the Boston office at JCL, is in the process of reviewing the annual revenue generated by each recruiter in the office. She created a worksheet with test data that will act as a form for the collection of data for each recruiter. Cheri asks you to create macros to calculate the annual revenue total and evaluate whether quotas for bonus payments are met.

Module Objectives

After completing this module, you will be able to:

- Plan a macro
- Enable a macro
- Record a macro
- Run a macro
- Edit a macro
- Assign a macro to a button
- Assign a macro to a command button
- Assign a macro to a form control

Files You Will Need

IL_EX_9-1.xlsx
IL_EX_9-2.xlsx
IL_EX_9-3.xlsx
IL_EX_9-4.xlsx
IL_EX_9-5.xlsx

Excel
Module 9

Plan a Macro

Learning Outcomes
- Plan a macro
- Determine the storage location for a macro

A **macro** is a named set of instructions, written in the Visual Basic programming language, that perform tasks automatically in a specified order. You can create macros to automate Excel tasks that you perform frequently. You don't need to know the Visual Basic programming language to create a macro, because instead of writing code you can simply record a series of actions using the macro recorder built into Excel. When recording a macro, the sequence of actions in a macro is important, so you need to plan the macro carefully before you begin recording. **CASE** *You need to create a macro to calculate the total revenue for the Boston office. You work with Cheri to plan the macro.*

DETAILS

To plan a macro, use the following guidelines:

- **Assign the macro a descriptive name**

  The first character of a macro name must be a letter; the remaining characters can be letters, numbers, or underscores. Letters can be uppercase or lowercase. Spaces are not allowed in macro names; use underscores instead. You can press SHIFT+HYPHEN (-) to enter an underscore character. You decide to name the macro AddTotal. See **TABLE 9-1** for a list of macros that could be created to automate other common tasks in JCL spreadsheets.

- **Write out the steps the macro will perform**

  This planning helps eliminate careless errors. After a discussion with Cheri, you write down a description of the new AddTotal macro, as shown in **FIGURE 9-1**.

- **Decide how you will perform the actions you want to record**

  You can use the mouse, the keyboard, or a combination of the two. For the new AddTotal macro, you want to use both the mouse and the keyboard.

- **Practice the steps you want Excel to record, and write them down**

  During your meeting with Cheri, you write down the sequence of actions to include in the macro.

- **Decide where to store the description of the macro and the macro itself**

  Macros can be stored in an active workbook, in a new workbook, or in the **Personal Macro Workbook**, a special workbook that can contain macros that are available to any open workbook; it opens whenever you start Excel to make macros available at any time but is hidden by default. You decide to store the macro in the active workbook.

FIGURE 9-1: Handwritten description of planned macro

Macro to calculate the annual revenue total	
Name:	AddTotal
Description:	Calculates the annual revenue
Steps:	1. Select cell A9 2. Enter Total 3. Click the Enter button 4. Select cell B9 5. Click the AutoSum button 6. Click the Enter button

TABLE 9-1: Possible macros and their descriptive names

description of macro	descriptive name
Enter a frequently used division, such as Technology	TechDiv
Enter a frequently used company name, such as JCL	Company_Name
Print the active worksheet on a single page, in landscape orientation	FitToLand
Add a footer to a worksheet	FooterStamp
Add a total to a worksheet	AddTotal

Excel
Module 9

Enable a Macro

Learning Outcomes
- Create a macro-enabled workbook
- Enable macros by changing a workbook's security level

Because a macro may contain a virus, a destructive type of computer program that can damage your computer files, the default security setting in Excel disables macros from running. Although a workbook containing a macro will open, if macros are disabled they will not function. You can manually change the Excel security setting to allow macros to run if you know a macro came from a trusted source. When saving a workbook with a macro, you need to save it as a macro-enabled workbook with the extension .xlsm. **CASE** *Cheri asks you to change the security level to enable all macros. For your security, as well as that of others who are sharing your computer, you will change the security level back to the default setting after you create and run your macros.*

STEPS

1. **sam Start Excel, open IL_EX_9-1xlsx from the location where you store your Data Files, click the File tab, click Save As, navigate to where you store your Data Files, in the Save As dialog box click the Save as type list arrow, click Excel Macro-Enabled Workbook (*.xlsm), in the File name text box type IL_EX_9_Bonus, then click Save**

   The security settings that enable macros are available on the Developer tab on the ribbon. The Developer tab does not appear by default.

QUICK TIP
If the Developer tab is already displayed on your Ribbon, skip Steps 2 and 3.

2. **Click the File tab on the ribbon, click Options, then click Customize Ribbon in the category list**

   The Customize the Ribbon options open in the Excel Options dialog box, as shown in FIGURE 9-2.

3. **Click the Developer checkbox in the Main Tabs area on the right side of the screen to add a checkmark if necessary, then click OK**

   The Developer tab appears on the Ribbon. You are ready to change the security settings.

QUICK TIP
For increased security, you can click the security setting "Disable all macros with notification" instead. If you are using that setting, you need to click Enable Content to run macros in an .xlsm file.

4. **Click the Developer tab on the ribbon, then click the Macro Security button in the Code group**

   The Trust Center dialog box opens.

5. **Click Macro Settings in the category list if necessary, click the Enable all macros (not recommended; potentially dangerous code can run) option button to select it, as shown in FIGURE 9-3, then click OK**

   The dialog box closes. Macros will remain enabled until you disable them by deselecting the Enable all macros option. As you work with Excel, you should disable macros when you are not working with them.

Adding security to your macro projects

To add security to your projects, you can add a digital signature to the project. A **digital signature** is an electronic attachment not visible in the file that verifies the authenticity of the author or the version of the file by comparing the digital signature to a digital certificate. In Excel, it guarantees your project hasn't been altered since it was signed. Sign macros only after you have tested them and are ready to distribute them. If the code in a digitally signed macro project is changed in any way, its digital signature is removed. To add a digital signature to a Visual Basic project, select the project that you want to sign in the Visual Basic Project Explorer window, click the Tools menu in the Visual Basic Editor, click Digital Signature, click Choose, select the certificate, then click OK twice. If there aren't any certificates available, you will be directed to contact your administrator or insert a smart card. Digital certificates and smart cards, which store digital certificates, can be issued by your administrator. There are also third-party certification authorities that issue certificates that are trusted by Microsoft. When you add a digital signature to a project, the macro project is automatically re-signed whenever it is saved on your computer.

FIGURE 9-2: Excel Options dialog box

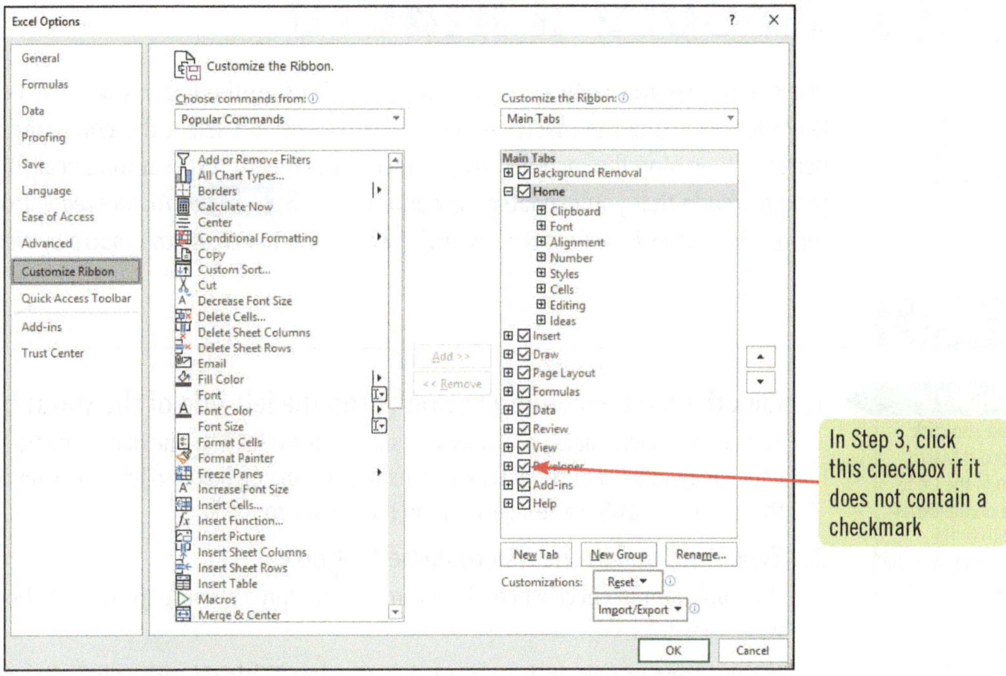

FIGURE 9-3: Trust Center dialog box

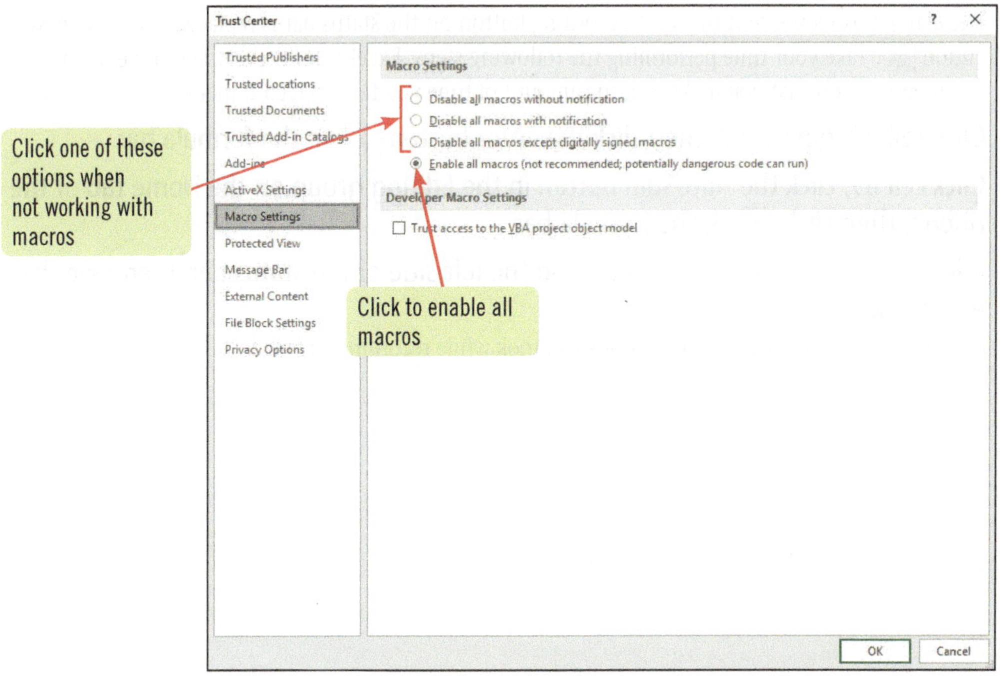

Disabling macros

To prevent viruses from running on your computer, you should disable all macros when you are not working with them. To disable macros, click the Developer tab, then click the Macro Security button in the Code group. Clicking any of the first three options disables macros. The first option disables all macros without notifying you. The second option notifies you when macros are disabled, and the third option allows only digitally signed macros to run.

Record a Macro

Learning Outcomes
- Choose a macro storage location
- Create a macro by recording steps

The easiest way to create a macro is to record it using the Excel Macro Recorder. You turn the Macro Recorder on, name the macro, enter the keystrokes and select the commands you want the macro to perform, then stop the recorder. As you record the macro, Excel automatically translates each action into program code that you can later view and modify. **CASE** *You are ready to create a macro that totals the revenue values in column B of the active worksheet. You create this macro by recording your actions.*

STEPS

QUICK TIP You can also click the Record Macro button in the Code group on the Developer tab or the Macros button in the Macros group of the View tab to record a new macro.

1. **Click the Start Recording button on the left side of the status bar**
   The Record Macro dialog box opens, as shown in FIGURE 9-4. The default name Macro1 is selected. You can either assign this name or enter a new name. This dialog box also lets you assign a shortcut key for running the macro and assign a storage location for the macro.
2. **Type AddTotal in the Macro name text box**
   It is important to check where the macro will be stored because the default choice is the last location that was selected.
3. **If the Store macro in box does not display "This Workbook," click the Store macro in list arrow, then click This Workbook**
4. **Type your name in the Description text box, then click OK**
   The dialog box closes, and the Start Recording button on the status bar is replaced with a Stop Recording button. Take your time performing the following steps. Excel records every keystroke, menu selection, and mouse action that you make, not the amount of time you take to record them.
5. **Click cell A9, type Total, then click the Enter button on the formula bar**
6. **Click cell B9, click the AutoSum button in the Editing group on the Home tab of the ribbon, then click on the formula bar**
7. **Click the Stop Recording button on the left side of the status bar, then save the workbook**
   FIGURE 9-5 shows the result of the actions you took while recording the macro.

QUICK TIP You can also click the Stop Recording button in the Code group on the Developer tab to stop recording a macro.

FIGURE 9-4: Record Macro dialog box

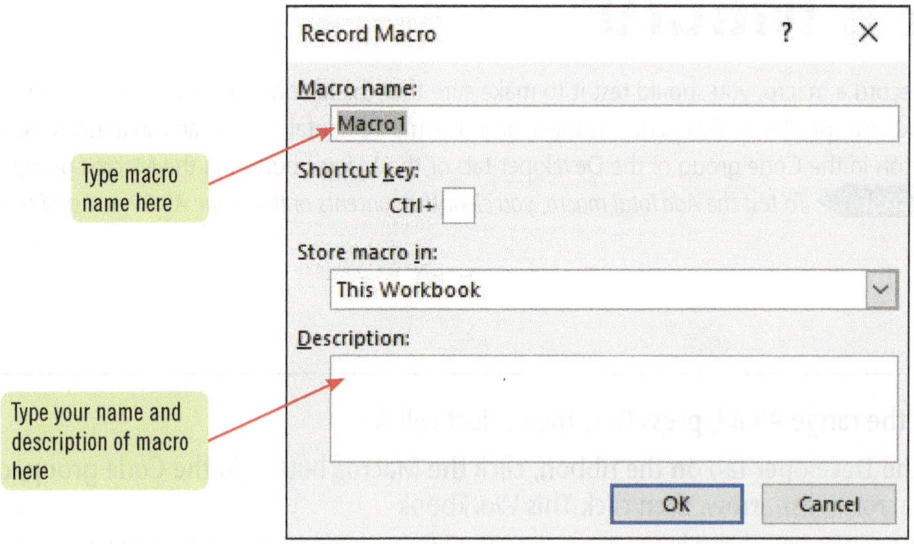

FIGURE 9-5: Worksheet with new data and formula

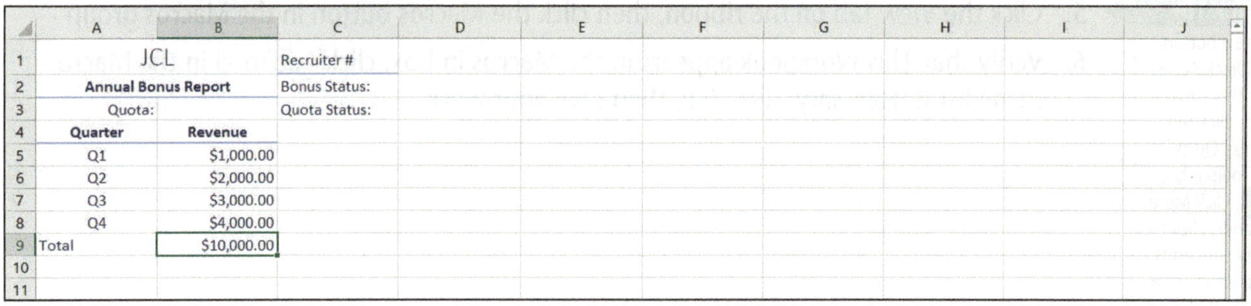

Excel

Excel
Module 9

Run a Macro

Learning Outcomes
- Display selected macros
- Run a macro using the Macro dialog box

Once you record a macro, you should test it to make sure that the actions it performs are correct. To test a macro, you **run** (play) it, which performs the actions the macro contains. You can run a macro using the Macros button in the Code group of the Developer tab or the Macros button in the Macros group of the View tab. **CASE** *To test the AddTotal macro, you clear the contents of the range A9:B9 and add test data.*

STEPS

QUICK TIP
To delete a macro, click the macro name in the Macro dialog box, click Delete, then click Yes to confirm the deletion.

QUICK TIP
To create a button on the Quick Access Toolbar that runs a macro, click the Customize Quick Access Toolbar button, click More Commands, click the Choose commands from list arrow, click Macros, click the desired macro in the list, click Add, then click OK.

1. **Select the range A9:B9, press DEL, then select cell A1**
2. **Click the Developer tab on the ribbon, click the Macros button in the Code group, click the Macros in list arrow, then click This Workbook**
   The Macro dialog box, shown in FIGURE 9-6, displays all the macros contained in the current workbook.
3. **Click AddTotal in the Macro name list if necessary, then click Run**
   The macro quickly plays back the steps you recorded in the previous lesson. When the macro is finished, your screen should look like FIGURE 9-7.
4. **Select the range A9:B9, press DEL, then select cell A1**
   The total label and the total value are deleted to test the macro again.
5. **Click the View tab on the ribbon, then click the Macros button in the Macros group**
6. **Verify that This Workbook appears in the Macros in box, click AddTotal in the Macro name list if necessary, click Run, then save your work**

Running a macro automatically

You can create a macro that automatically performs certain tasks when the workbook in which it is saved opens. This is useful for actions you want to do every time you open a workbook. For example, you may always import data from an external data source into a workbook or format the worksheet data in a certain way. To create a macro that automatically runs when you open the workbook, you need to name the macro Auto_Open and save it in that workbook.

FIGURE 9-6: Macro dialog box

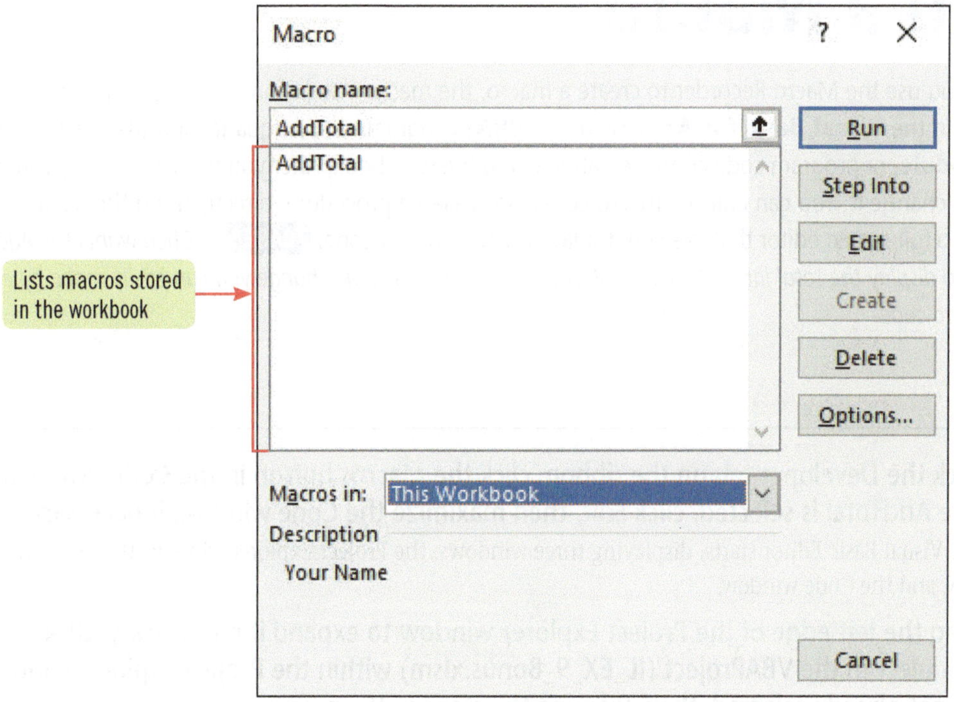

FIGURE 9-7: Result of running AddTotal macro

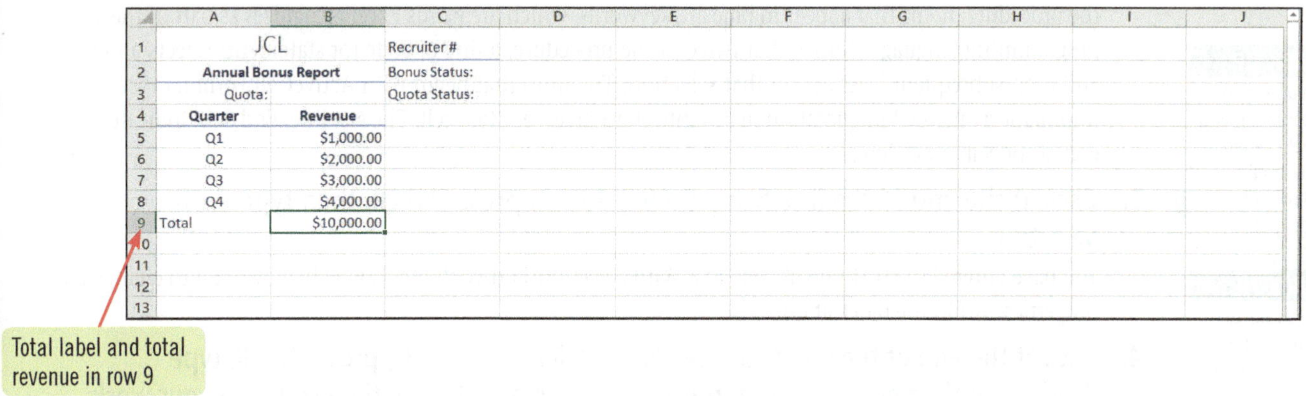

Creating a main procedure

A sequence of VBA statements is called a procedure. For this reason, macros are often referred to as procedures. When you routinely need to run several macros one after another, you can save time by executing them in one procedure. This type of procedure, which contains multiple procedures that run sequentially, is referred to as the **main procedure**. To create a main procedure, you type a **Call statement**, a Visual Basic statement that retrieves a procedure, using the format Call *procedurename*, where *procedurename* is the name of the procedure, or macro, you want to run. For example, Call AddTotal in a main procedure would run the AddTotal macro.

Edit a Macro

Learning Outcomes
- View Visual Basic code
- Edit a macro using VBA

When you use the Macro Recorder to create a macro, the macro instructions, called **program code**, are written in the **Visual Basic for Applications (VBA)** programming language, and the macro is stored as a **module**, or program code container, attached to the workbook. After you record a macro, you might need to change it. You can edit the macro code, also called a procedure, directly using the **Visual Basic Editor**, a full-screen editor that lets you display and edit lines of code. CASE *Cheri wants the AddTotal macro to display the total label aligned right in the cell. This is a small change you can easily make by editing the macro code.*

STEPS

TROUBLE
If the Properties window does not appear in the lower-left portion of your screen, click the Properties Window button on the Visual Basic toolbar, then resize it as shown in the figure if necessary.

QUICK TIP
You can also open the Editor by clicking the Developer tab, then clicking the Visual Basic button in the Code group.

QUICK TIP
Comments are used to document VBA code. To enter a comment, you must type an apostrophe (') before the comment text so the program doesn't interpret the statement as a command. Comments appear in green after you press ENTER.

QUICK TIP
You can return to Excel without closing the module by clicking the View Microsoft Excel button on the Visual Basic Editor toolbar.

1. **Click the Developer tab on the ribbon, click the Macros button in the Code group, make sure AddTotal is selected, click Edit, then maximize the Code window, if necessary**
   The Visual Basic Editor starts, displaying three windows: the Project Explorer window, the Properties window, and the Code window.
2. **Drag the left edge of the Project Explorer window to expand it if necessary, click Module 1 in the VBAProject (IL_EX_9_Bonus.xlsm) within the Project Explorer window if it's not already selected, then examine the steps in the macro**
   Compare your screen to FIGURE 9-8. Excel has translated your keystrokes and commands into macro code. For example, the line Range("A9").Select was generated when you selected cell A9. In the first line of the macro code, the keyword Sub indicates that this is a Sub procedure, a series of Visual Basic statements that perform an action. The code lines in green, beginning with an apostrophe, are comments that help explain the procedure. Items that appear in blue are keywords, which are words Excel recognizes as part of the VBA programming language. Notice that twice in the procedure, a line of code (or statement) selects a range, and then subsequent lines act on that selection. The lines that begin with ActiveCell.Formula insert the information enclosed in quotation marks into the active, selected, cell. The last line, End Sub, indicates the end of the Sub procedure.
3. **Click at the end of the line Range("A9").Select, press ENTER, then type With Selection**
   You have entered the first line of code in a With Selection/End With block, which allows you to change all properties within the block at once.
4. **Click at the end of the line ActiveCell.FormulaR1C1 = "Total", press ENTER, type .HorizontalAlignment = xlRight, press ENTER, type End With, then compare your work with the code shown in FIGURE 9-9**
   You have added a With Selection/End With block to the procedure, so that you only need to refer to the selection once, rather than multiple times.
5. **Click File on the menu bar, then click Close and Return to Microsoft Excel**
   You want to rerun the AddTotal macro to make sure the macro reflects the change you made using the Visual Basic Editor.
6. **Select the range A9:B9, press DEL, then activate cell A1**
7. **Click the Macros button in the Code group on the Developer tab, make sure AddTotal is selected, then click Run**
   The Total label is right-aligned in the cell, as shown in FIGURE 9-10.
8. **Save the workbook**

FIGURE 9-8: Visual Basic Editor

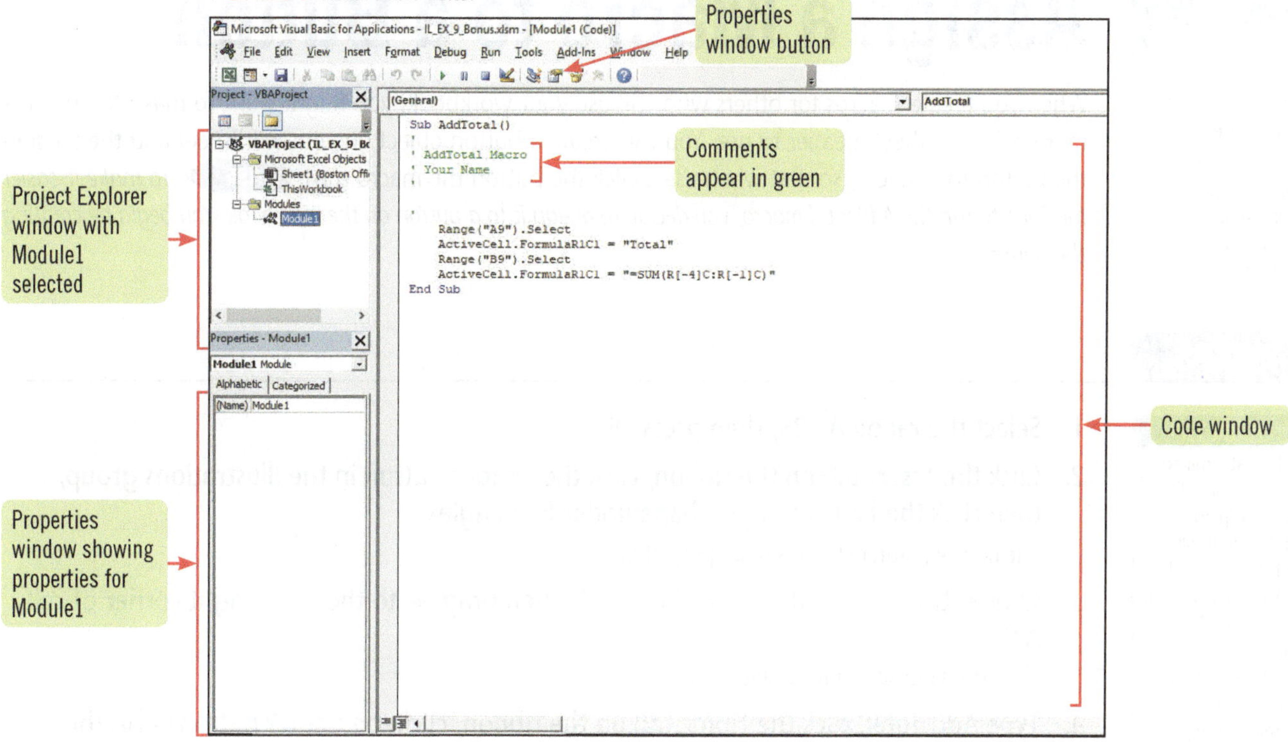

FIGURE 9-9: Edited Visual Basic code

```
Sub AddTotal()
'
' AddTotal Macro
' Your Name
'

'
    Range("A9").Select
    With Selection
    ActiveCell.FormulaR1C1 = "Total"
    .HorizontalAlignment = xlRight
    End With
    Range("B9").Select
    ActiveCell.FormulaR1C1 = "=SUM(R[-4]C:R[-1]C)"
End Sub
```

FIGURE 9-10: Result of running the edited AddTotal macro

Using relative referencing when creating a macro

By default, Excel records absolute cell references in macros, but you can record a macro's actions based on the relative position of the active cell by clicking the Use Relative References button in the Code group prior to recording the action. For example, when you create a macro using the default setting of absolute referencing, bolding the range A1:A3 will always bold that range when the macro is run. However, if you click the Use Relative References button when recording the macro before bolding the range, then running the macro will not necessarily result in bolding the range A1:A3. The range that is bolded will depend on the location of the active cell when the macro is run. If the active cell is F1, then the range F1:F3 will be bolded. Selecting the Use Relative References button highlights the button name, indicating it is active, and it remains active until you click it again to deselect it.

Excel

Excel
Module 9

Assign a Macro to a Button

Learning Outcomes
- Create a button shape in a worksheet
- Assign a macro to a button

When you create macros for others who will use your workbook, you might want to make the macros more visible so they're easier to use. You can create a button object on your worksheet and then assign the button to a macro, so that when users click the button the macro runs. **CASE** *To make it easier for Cheri to run the AddTotal macro, you decide to assign it to a button on the workbook. You begin by creating the button.*

STEPS

QUICK TIP
To format a macro button using 3-D effects, clip art, photographs, fills, and shadows, right-click it, select Format Shape from the shortcut menu, then select the desired options in the Format Shape pane.

QUICK TIP
You can move a shape button by placing the cursor on the shape and dragging it to a new location on the worksheet.

1. **Select the range A9:B9, then press DEL**
2. **Click the Insert tab on the ribbon, click the Shapes button in the Illustrations group, then click the first rectangle shape under Rectangles**
   The mouse pointer changes to a + symbol.
3. **Click at the upper-left corner of cell A10, then drag + to the lower-right corner of cell A11**
   Compare your screen to FIGURE 9-11.
4. **Type Add Total, click the Home tab on the ribbon, click the Center button in the Alignment group, then click the Middle Align button in the Alignment group**
   Now that you have created the button and added a text label, you are ready to assign the macro to it.
5. **Right-click the new button, then on the shortcut menu click Assign Macro**
   The Assign Macro dialog box opens.
6. **Click AddTotal under Macro name, then click OK**
   You have assigned the AddTotal macro to the button.
7. **Click any cell to deselect the button, then click the button**
   The AddTotal macro runs, and the total label and value appear in the range A9:B9, as shown in FIGURE 9-12.
8. **Save the workbook**

FIGURE 9-11: Button shape

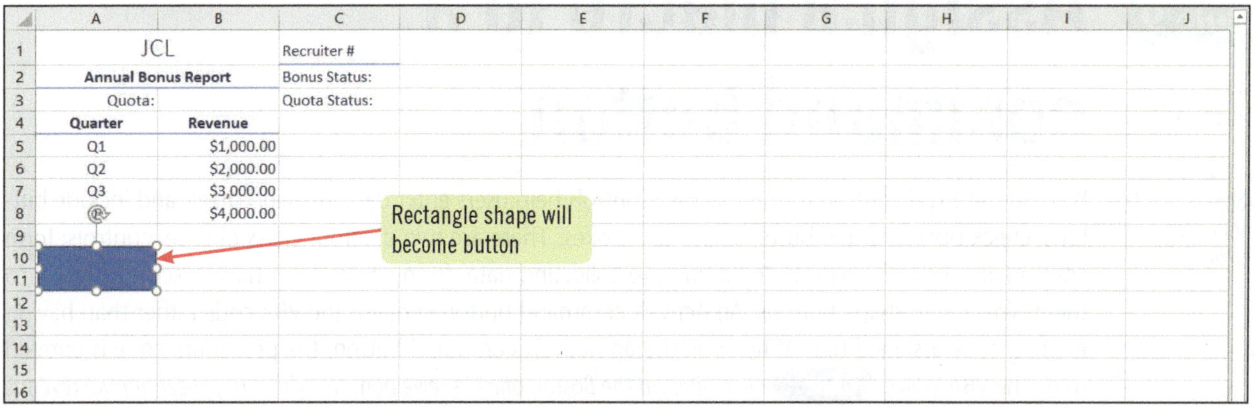

FIGURE 9-12: Result of clicking the macro button

Copying a macro to another workbook

If you would like to use a macro in another macro-enabled workbook, you can copy the module to that workbook using the Visual Basic Editor. To do so, open both the source workbook (the one containing the macro) and destination workbook (the one where you want to use the macro). Open the Visual Basic Editor by clicking the Visual Basic button in the Code group on the Developer tab, then verify that macros are enabled in each workbook. In Project Explorer, drag the module that will be copied from the source workbook to the destination workbook.

Assign a macro to a command button

Learning Outcomes
- Insert a Command Button (ActiveX Control)
- Enter VBA code for a command button

You can use Excel controls to run macros. Controls help users enter data in a worksheet, and include buttons, check boxes, option buttons, and text boxes. There are two different types of Excel controls: form controls and ActiveX controls. In addition to collecting data, form controls can have macros assigned to them, similarly to shape buttons. An ActiveX command button contains the VBA code rather than having existing code assigned to it. When you use an ActiveX command button, the procedure code is entered using the VBA Editor. **CASE** *Recruiters in the Boston office receive bonuses when they meet annual revenue quotas. Cheri asks you to add a button that can be used to determine if a recruiter's annual quota is met.*

STEPS

1. **Click the Developer tab on the ribbon, click the Insert button in the Controls group, then click the Command Button (ActiveX Control) icon**
2. **Click at the upper-left corner of cell A13, then drag + to the lower-right corner of cell A14**
   An ActiveX control named CommandButton1 is displayed on the worksheet. The button name isn't fully displayed because the button isn't large enough. The Design Mode button in the Controls group is selected, indicating you are working in Design Mode, where properties can be changed.
3. **Click the Properties button in the Control group, on the Alphabetic tab in the Properties pane double-click the (Name) box, enter QuotaButton, double-click the Caption box, enter Check Quota, click the BackColor box, click the arrow, scroll if necessary and click Active Title Bar on the System tab, click the Font box, click the ... button, scroll to and click Times New Roman in the Font dialog box, click OK, compare your Properties pane to FIGURE 9-13, then close the Properties pane**
   The name of the command button is used internally to reference it. The caption name is displayed as a label for the button.
4. **Click the View Code button in the Controls group**
   The Visual Basic Editor opens. You will enter the code for the button in the Code window. This button will compare the revenue total in cell B9 with the quota in cell B3. If the total revenue is less than the quota, the text "Missed Quota" will be entered in cell D3; otherwise "Met Quota" will be entered. To specify an action based on certain conditions, you will use an If...Then...Else conditional statement.
5. **Click the General arrow at the top of the Code window, click QuotaButton, then type the procedure code between the Private Sub and End Sub lines exactly as shown in FIGURE 9-14, making sure not to duplicate the Private Sub and End Sub lines**
6. **Click File on the menu bar, click Close and Return to Microsoft Excel, then click the Design Mode button in the Controls group**
   Design Mode is turned off. This mode allows you to change the properties and enter Visual Basic Code for a command button, but for a button to function, it needs to be off.
7. **Click cell B3, type 11000, press ENTER, then click the Check Quota button**
   You need to enter a quota value to test the macro. The text *Missed Quota* is entered in cell D3.
8. **Click cell B3, enter 8000, click the Check Quota button, then save the workbook**
   The new test quota data checks the message entered when the quota is met. The text *Met Quota* is entered in cell D3.

QUICK TIP
If you want a caption on the selected control to wrap to the next line, set the WordWrap property to True.

QUICK TIP
You can add a form control button to a worksheet and assign a macro to it. Click the Developer tab, click the Insert button in the Controls group, then click the Button (Form Control) in the first row. After drawing a button, the Assign Macro dialog box opens where you can select a macro for the button, then click OK.

FIGURE 9-13: Properties pane

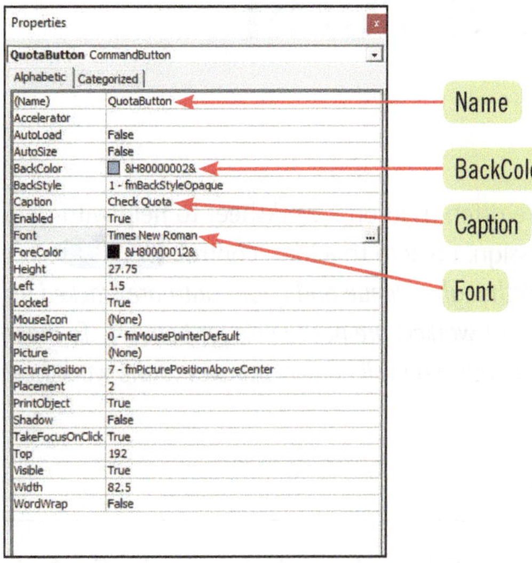

FIGURE 9-14: Code for ActiveX command button

```
Private Sub QuotaButton_Click()

 'If the total revenue is less than B3 then
    'insert "Missed Quota" in cell D3

    If Range("B9") <= Range("B3") Then

        Range("D3").Select
        ActiveCell.Formula = "Missed Quota"

    'otherwise, insert "Met Quota" in cell D3

    Else
        Range("D3").Select
        ActiveCell.Formula = "Met Quota"

    End If

    Range("A1").Select

End Sub
```

Working with ActiveX text boxes

To add an ActiveX text box into a worksheet, click the Developer tab on the ribbon, click the Insert button in the Controls group, then click the Text Box (ActiveX Control) button [ab|] under ActiveX Controls. Click the upper-left corner of the cell where you want to locate the text box, then drag + to draw the desired shape.

To edit the text box's properties, switch to Design Mode if necessary, then click the Properties button in the Controls group. In the LinkedCell box, enter the cell where you want the text box data to be displayed. The Shadow property provides the options True for a shadow and False for no shadow. FIGURE 9-15 shows the properties for a text box with the name Notes in the range A1:D2. Because the LinkedCell in the properties is Quarter1!A9, text entered in the text box will appear on the Quarter1 worksheet in cell A9.

FIGURE 9-15: ActiveX text box properties

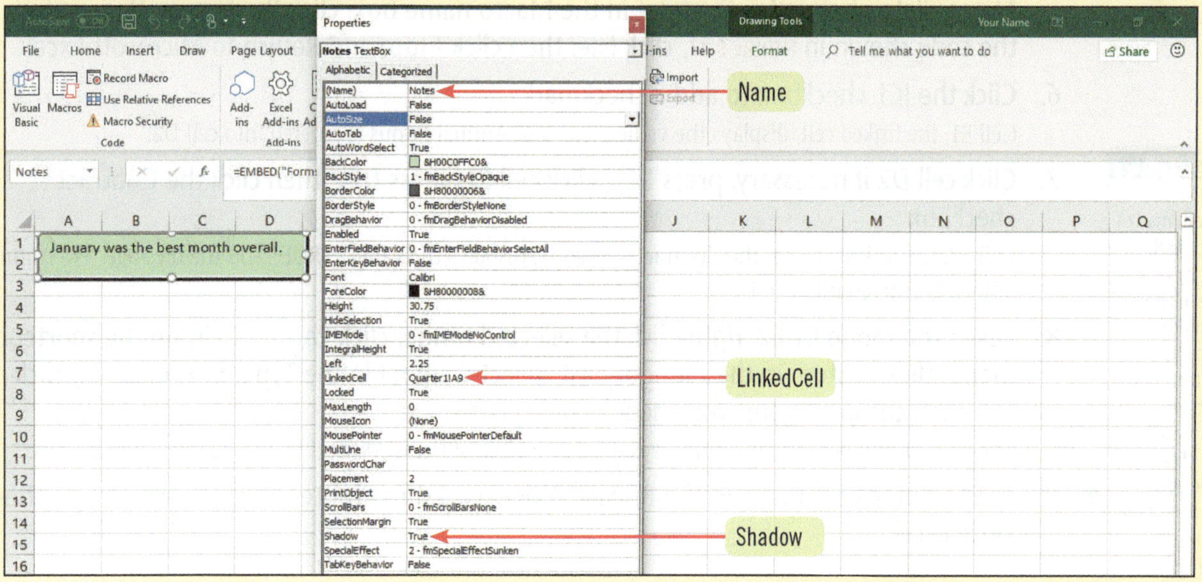

Excel Module 9

Learning Outcomes
- Create a Check Box form control
- Assign a cell link to a Check Box control

Assign a Macro to a Form Control

Form controls such as checkboxes and option buttons are often used on a worksheet to help with data entry. To perform an action based on entered data, you assign a macro to a form control. **CASE** *JCL recruiters who meet their revenue quotas receive bonuses. Although revenue and quota data are tracked for contract workers as a consideration for future contracts, contract workers are not eligible for bonuses. To make it easier for Cheri to determine if a recruiter should receive a bonus, you will add checkboxes to the worksheet form and enter macros for each checkbox.*

STEPS

QUICK TIP
In addition to changing a checkbox caption, you can change the internal name of the checkbox object by right-clicking the checkbox object, then entering the object name in the Name Box.

1. **Click the Developer tab on the ribbon if necessary, click the Insert button in the Controls group, click the Check Box (Form Control) button shape ☑ in the first row, click the upper-left corner of cell A16, drag + to the lower-right corner of that cell, select the text label for the control, then type JCL**
2. **Click the Properties button in the Controls group, in the Format Control dialog box click the Control tab if necessary, enter E1 in the Cell link box, then click OK**
   The cell entered in the Cell link box will display TRUE if the checkbox contains a checkmark.
3. **Right-click the checkbox object, click Assign Macro on the shortcut menu, in the Assign Macro dialog box type JCL in the Macro name box, click New, enter the code shown in FIGURE 9-16, click File, then click Close and Return to Microsoft Excel**
4. **Click any cell outside the checkbox object to deselect it, click the Insert button in the Controls group, click the Check Box (Form Control) button ☑ in the first row, click at the upper-left corner of cell B16, drag + to the lower-right corner of the cell, select the text label for the object, enter Contract, click the Properties button in the Controls group, in the Format Control dialog box enter E2 in the Cell link box, then click OK**
5. **Right-click the checkbox object, click Assign Macro on the shortcut menu, in the Assign Macro dialog box enter Contract in the Macro name box, click the New button, enter the code shown in FIGURE 9-17, click File, then click Close and Return to Microsoft Excel**
6. **Click the JCL checkbox to add a checkmark**
   Cell E1, the linked cell, displays the value TRUE and Annual Bonus is entered into cell D2.
7. **Click cell D2 if necessary, press DEL, click cell E1, press DEL, then click the Contract checkbox**
   Cell E2, the linked cell for the Contract checkbox, displays the value "TRUE" and the message "No Annual Bonus" is entered into cell D2.
8. **Select the range E1:E2, right-click the selected range, click Format Cells on the shortcut menu, click Custom in the Category list, select General in the Type: box, enter ;;;, click OK, then compare your worksheet to FIGURE 9-18**
   The custom number format ;;; improves the appearance of the worksheet by hiding the values in cells.

QUICK TIP
When you finish working with macros you should disable all macros by clicking the Developer tab, clicking the Macro Security button in the Code group, clicking Macro Settings if necessary, clicking the Disable all macros with notification option button to select it, then clicking OK.

9. **sam Enter your name in the Boston Office worksheet footer, save the workbook, then close Excel**

FIGURE 9-16: Code for JCL checkbox

```
Sub JCL()

If Range("E1") = True And Range("D3") = "Met Quota" Then

        Range("D2").Select
        ActiveCell.Formula = "Annual Bonus"

    Else

    If Range("E1") = True And Range("D3") = "Missed Quota" Then

        Range("D2").Select
        ActiveCell.Formula = "No Annual Bonus"

    End If
    End If

End Sub
```

FIGURE 9-17: Code for Contract check box control

```
Sub Contract()

If Range("E2") = True Then

        Range("D2").Select
        ActiveCell.Formula = "No Annual Bonus"


End If

End Sub
```

FIGURE 9-18: Worksheet with checkboxes

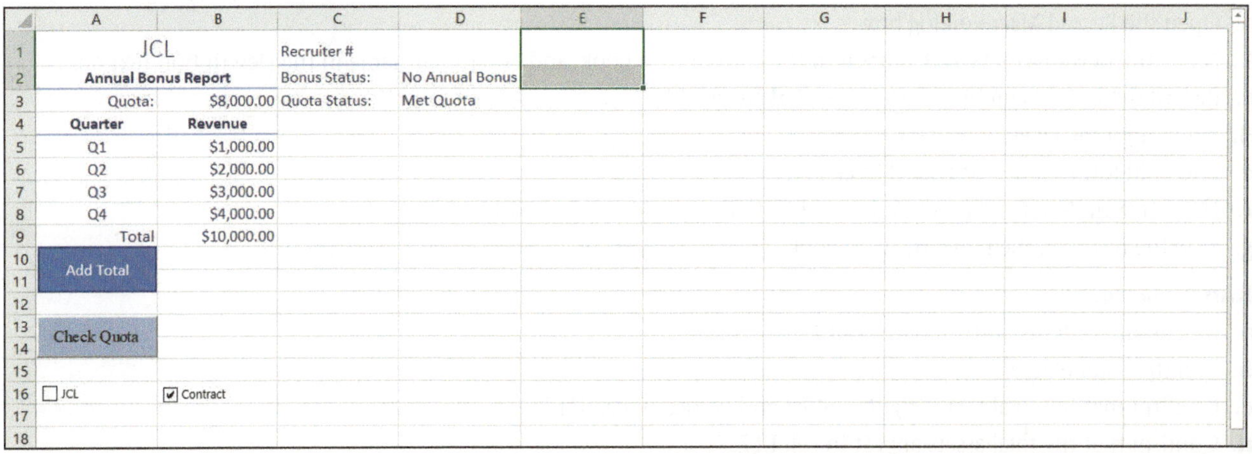

Working with option buttons

You can add option button form controls to a worksheet to allow users to select from a list of available options. To add an option button to a worksheet, click the Developer tab, click the Insert button in the Controls group, then click the Option Button Form Control in the first row and drag + to draw the option button. After adding the desired option buttons, right-click an option button, click Format Control on the shortcut menu, then enter the desired linked cell in the Cell link box in the Format Control dialog box. The clicked option button position will be entered in the linked cell. For example, if you click the second option button, the number *2* will be entered in the linked cell.

You can use an index list (a range to which an Index function refers) with this type of form control to facilitate data entry using option buttons. The index list range consists of all the options, in the order they appear on the worksheet, as option buttons. Then, an Index formula is added to the worksheet with the syntax *Index(range, row)* where *range* equals the list of options corresponding to the option buttons and *row* is the linked cell that holds the number of the clicked option. The result of this Index function is that the range value, at the given row position, is placed in the cell with the Index function. For example, FIGURE 9-19 shows option buttons for the four divisions at JCL. The cell link for the option buttons is B1 and the Index formula in cell D1 references the range named Divisions, which is F1:F4 on the worksheet. The named range can be located on a different worksheet. Clicking the Technical option button places the number *2* (the second option button) in cell B1 (the linked cell), and the index function returns the second entry in the range list.

FIGURE 9-19: Worksheet with option buttons

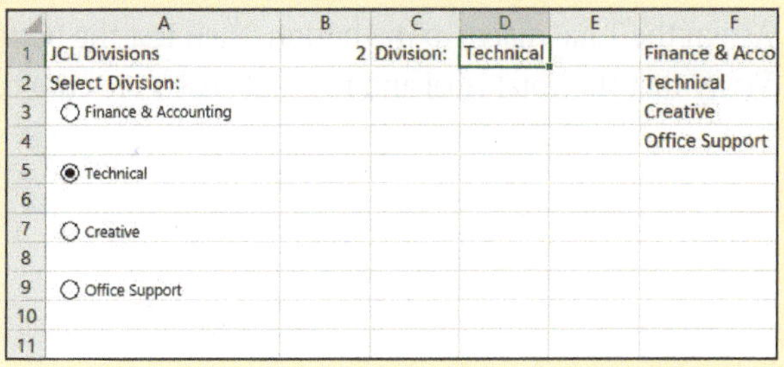

Practice

Skills Review

1. **Plan and enable a macro.**
   a. You need to plan a macro that enters a Total label in cell D17 and a formula in cell E17 that totals the managed assets in the range E3:E16.
   b. Write out the steps the macro will perform, and plan to store the macro in the workbook where you will use it.
   c. Start Excel, open IL_EX_9-2.xlsx from the location where you store your Data Files, then save it as a macro-enabled workbook named **IL_EX_9_Assets**. (*Hint*: The file will have the file extension .xlsm.)
   d. Use the Excel Options feature to display the Developer tab if it does not appear on the Ribbon.
   e. Using the Trust Center dialog box, enable all macros.
2. **Record a macro.**
   a. Open the Record Macro dialog box.
   b. Name the new macro **Total**, store it in the current workbook, and enter your name in the Description text box.
   c. Record the macro, entering the label **Total** in cell D17.
   d. Right-align the label in cell D17.
   e. Add bold formatting to the label in cell D17.
   f. Use AutoSum to enter a function in cell E17 that totals the range E3:E16.
   g. Stop the recorder, then save the workbook.
3. **Run a macro.**
   a. Delete the contents of the range D17:E17.
   b. Run the Total macro.
   c. Confirm that the total text is right-aligned and bolded in cell D17.
   d. Confirm that the total assets appear in cell E17.
   e. Clear the cell entries generated by running the Total macro.
   f. Save the workbook.
4. **Edit a macro.**
   a. Open the Macros dialog box, then open the Total macro for editing.
   b. In the Visual Basic window, change the line of code Selection.Font.Bold = True to **Selection.Font.Bold = False**.
   c. Use the Close and Return to Microsoft Excel command on the File menu to return to Excel.
   d. Test the Total macro, verifying that the Total label is not bold.
   e. Save the workbook.
5. **Assign a macro to a button.**
   a. Clear the cell entries generated by running the Total macro.
   b. Using the first rectangle shape under Rectangles on the Shapes palette, draw a rectangle in cell A17.
   c. Label the button with the text **Total Assets**, then center and middle align the text.
   d. Assign the Total macro to the button, then test the button.
   e. Verify that the Total label and the total assets are entered in the range D17:E17.

Skills Review (continued)

6. **Assign a macro to a command button.**
   a. Add an ActiveX command button control in the range A18:B19.
   b. Add a caption to the button with the text **Target** and change the BackColor property to System Active Title Bar.
   c. Enter the macro code shown in FIGURE 9-20 in the Visual Basic code window. (*Hint*: Remember to use the list arrow at the upper left of the VBA Editor to select the command object.)
   d. Save the macro code and test the Target button. (*Hint*: Remember to deselect the Design Mode button before testing the button.)
   e. Verify that "Met Target" is displayed in cell F2.

FIGURE 9-20

```
Private Sub CommandButton1_Click()

If Range("E17") <= Range("G1") Then

        Range("F2").Select
        ActiveCell.Formula = "Missed Target"

    Else
        Range("F2").Select
        ActiveCell.Formula = "Met Target"

    End If

    Range("A1").Select

End Sub
```

7. **Assign a macro to a form control.**
   a. Add a form control check box in the range A21:B21.
   b. Change the name of the check box to **Jill Hurley**.
   c. Format the check box to enter the cell link of J1.
   d. Assign a new macro to the check box by opening the Visual Basic code window for the object and entering the code shown in FIGURE 9-21.

FIGURE 9-21

```
Sub CheckBox2_Click()

If Range("J1") = True Then

        Range("I1").Select
        ActiveCell.Formula = "Boston Office Manager"


End If

End Sub
```

   e. Save the macro code, close the VBA window, deselect the check box, then select it.
   f. Widen column I to fully display the text in cell I1 and verify that the text "Boston Office Manager" is displayed in that cell. Verify that "True" is displayed in cell J1.
   g. Format the text in cell J1 to hide the value. (*Hint*: Switch to Design Mode to make this change.)
   h. Add your name to the Texas Office footer, then save the workbook.
   i. Disable all macros with notification if you are finished working with macros.
   j. Close the workbook, then close Excel.

Independent Challenge 1

As the office manager of Riverwalk Medical Clinic, you want to develop macros to help work more efficiently with the weekly time sheets. You will modify a worksheet that can be used as a form to collect time sheet data for therapists from the OT and PT departments. You will enter sample data in the form, add macros within the workbook to format the worksheet, calculate the total weekly hours, and determine whether there are overtime hours for the week.

a. Start Excel, open IL_EX_9-3.xlsx from where you store your Data Files, then save it as a macro-enabled workbook called **IL_EX_9_Timesheet**.
b. Check your macro security setting on the Developer tab to be sure that all macros are enabled.
c. Enter the data shown in FIGURE 9-22.

FIGURE 9-22

d. Create a macro named **Format_Total**, enter your name in the macro description, then save it in the current workbook. Record the macro using the following instructions:
   - Add a row to the top of the worksheet.
   - Add the text **Riverwalk Medical Clinic** to the inserted top row and format the text using the Title cell style.
   - Merge and Center the Riverwalk Medical Clinic text over the range A1:D1.
   - In cell B11 enter a function to total the range B5:B10. (*Hint*: Ignore the formula warning that the date isn't included in the summed cells.)
   - End the macro recording.
e. Create a button using the first Rectangle shape tool in the range A12:B13. Label the button **Format & Total**. Center and middle align the button label.
f. Assign the Format_Total macro to the new button.
g. Delete the first row of the worksheet and the total in cell B10, then test the Format_Total macro using the Format & Total button.
h. Insert an ActiveX command button in the range A15:B16. Using the properties panel, change the caption of the button to **Check Overtime**.
i. Enter the ActiveX command button code shown in FIGURE 9-23. (*Hint*: Don't forget to select the Command button in the VBA window by clicking the list arrow at the top of the code window.)

Independent Challenge 1 (continued)

FIGURE 9-23

```
Private Sub CommandButton1_Click()

  If Range("B11") <= "40" Then

      Range("D2").Select
      ActiveCell.Formula = "No Overtime"


    Else
      Range("D2").Select
      ActiveCell.Formula = Range("B11") - "40"

    End If

End Sub
```

j. Click the Check Overtime button to display overtime hours. (*Hint*: Don't forget to deselect Design Mode before using the button.)

k. In cells A18 and B18, create two form control check boxes, the first named **PT** and the second named **OT**. Assign cell E1 as the cell link for the first check box and cell E2 as the cell link for the second check box.

l. Enter the check box code shown in FIGURE 9-24 for the first check box.

m. Enter the check box code for the second check box by copying the code for the first check box and pasting it in the code window for the second check box.

n. Make sure both check boxes aren't checked, exit Design Mode, then check the PT check box. Verify that "PT" is shown in the worksheet header. Delete True from cell E1, then click the OT check box. Verify that "OT" is shown in the worksheet header.

o. Format the range E1:E2 to hide the values.

p. Enter your name in the worksheet footer. Save the file, disable all macros with notification if you are finished working with macros, close the workbook, then close Excel.

FIGURE 9-24

```
Sub CheckBox2_Click()

If Range("E1") = "True" Then


  ActiveWindow.View = xlPageLayoutView
    With ActiveSheet.PageSetup
     .CenterHeader = "PT"
    End With
    Range("A1").Select
    Application.Wait (Now + TimeValue("0:00:02"))
    ActiveWindow.View = xlNormalView

Else

If Range("E2") = "True" Then
ActiveWindow.View = xlPageLayoutView
    With ActiveSheet.PageSetup
     .CenterHeader = "OT"
    End With
    Range("A1").Select
    Application.Wait (Now + TimeValue("0:00:02"))
    ActiveWindow.View = xlNormalView

End If
End If
End Sub
```

Excel

Independent Challenge 2

You are an assistant to the CFO at a national real estate firm. As part of your work, you analyze royalty payments for different offices of the company. The company is planning to expand and offer multiple offices in regions of the country and will begin noting the office's region as documentation on each worksheet. You will create option button form controls to look up the region for an office. You will also create a macro to total royalty payments. (*Note:* Remember to disable all macros when you are finished working with them.)

a. Check your macro security settings to confirm that macros are enabled.

b. Start Excel, open IL_EX_9-4.xlsx from the location where you store your Data Files, then save it as a macro-enabled workbook called **IL_EX_9_Region**.

c. With the Payments sheet active, record a macro with the name **Totals**. Store the macro in this workbook, add your name to the description, and assign the macro a shortcut key combination of CTRL+SHIFT+F (or a different combination if necessary) and store it in the current workbook. (*Hint*: Use the Shortcut key combination in the Record Macro dialog box.)

The macro should do the following:

- Total the residential, commercial, and rental payments in column F.
- Total the Q1, Q2, Q3, Q4, and Total columns in row 6.
- Change the page orientation to landscape.

d. After you finish recording the macro, change the page orientation to Portrait, then delete the totals in the ranges B6:F6 and F3:F5. Test the macro using the shortcut key combination you set in Step B. Verify the macro results are correct.

e. Edit the Format macro to insert an instruction that formats the totals as bold. To do this, add the following code lines before the End Sub line:

Range("F3:F6").Select
Selection.Font.Bold = True
Range("B6:E6").Select
Selection.Font.Bold = True

f. Change the page orientation to Portrait, delete the totals in the range B6:F6 and F3:F5. Test the macro to verify that it runs correctly and that the totals appear in bold format.

g. Create four option button form controls in the range A9:D9. (*Hint*: To insert each button, click the Insert button in the Controls group, then click the Option Button [Form Control].)

h. Label the first button **Boston**, the second button **Chicago**, the third button **Miami**, and the fourth button **Los Angeles.**

i. Align the tops of the buttons. (*Hints*: Right-click one of the buttons, hold CTRL, then right-click each remaining button. With the buttons selected, click the Align button in the Arrange group on the Drawing Tools Format tab, then click Align Top.)

j. Format one of the buttons to enter the cell link of cell I1. (*Hint*: Right-click a button, click Format Control, then enter **I1** in the Cell link box in the Format Control dialog box. The cell link is the same for all option buttons, so you only need to enter it for one button.)

k. Test the cell link by clicking each option button. The first option button should enter 1 in cell I1, the second should enter 2, and the third and fourth should enter 3 and 4, respectively.

l. Activate the Regions sheet, then select the range A1:A4 and verify the range name in the Name box is Region.

Independent Challenge 2 (continued)

m. Activate the Payments sheet, then enter an Index function in cell H2 that looks up the Region range on the Regions sheet using the value in cell I1 for its position. (*Hint*: The Index formula =INDEX(Region,I1) should be entered in cell H2.)

n. Test each option button to verify the correct region appears in cell H2 for each office.

o. Apply a custom format so the value in cell I1 is hidden, click the Boston button, then compare your worksheet to FIGURE 9-25.

FIGURE 9-25

	A	B	C	D	E	F	G	H	I	J	K	L	M	N
1	National Real Estate Franchise Royalty Payments													
2		**Q1**	**Q2**	**Q3**	**Q4**	**Total**	**Region:**	Northeast						
3	**Residential**	$ 7,907,730	$ 6,197,767	$ 6,831,070	$ 7,024,520	**$ 27,961,087**								
4	**Commercial**	$ 7,791,965	$ 5,032,618	$ 5,819,315	$ 6,834,646	**$ 25,478,544**								
5	**Rental**	$ 1,844,925	$ 1,332,499	$ 1,708,599	$ 1,045,821	**$ 5,931,844**								
6	**Total**	**$ 17,544,620**	**$ 12,562,884**	**$ 14,358,984**	**$ 14,904,987**	**$ 59,371,475**								
7														
8														
9	◉ Boston	○ Chicago	○ Miami	○ Los Angeles										
10														
11														
12														
13														
14														
15														
16														

p. Enter your name in the worksheet footer, save the workbook, close the workbook, close Excel, then submit the workbook to your instructor.

Excel

Visual Workshop

Start Excel, open IL_EX_9-5.xlsx from the location where you store your Data Files, then save it as a macro-enabled workbook named **IL_EX_9_Services**. Modify and format the worksheet to match **FIGURE 9-26**. The button named Format & Total runs a macro named Format_Total stored in the workbook that does the following:

- Adds a row at the top of the worksheet
- Inserts a label of MES Commercial Engineering in cell A1, formatted with the Title cell style and merged and centered across columns A through H
- Adds totals in row 9 and column H
- Applies the Accounting format with zero decimal places to the range B3:H9
- Autofits the widths of columns A through H
- Ends with cell A1 as the active cell

Save the workbook, close the workbook, submit the workbook to your instructor, then close Excel. (*Note:* Remember to enable all macros before beginning this visual workshop, and to disable them when you are finished.)

FIGURE 9-26

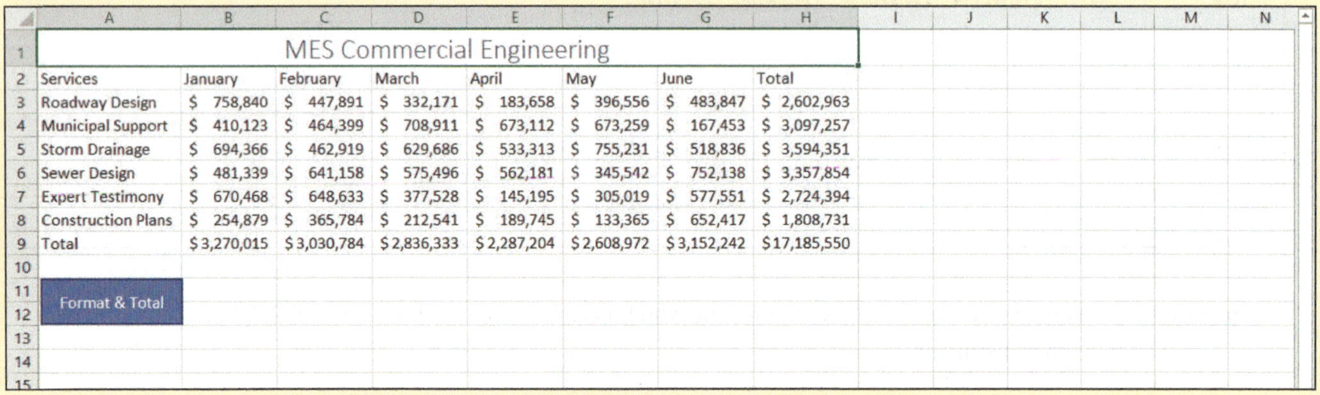

	A	B	C	D	E	F	G	H
1	MES Commercial Engineering							
2	Services	January	February	March	April	May	June	Total
3	Roadway Design	$ 758,840	$ 447,891	$ 332,171	$ 183,658	$ 396,556	$ 483,847	$ 2,602,963
4	Municipal Support	$ 410,123	$ 464,399	$ 708,911	$ 673,112	$ 673,259	$ 167,453	$ 3,097,257
5	Storm Drainage	$ 694,366	$ 462,919	$ 629,686	$ 533,313	$ 755,231	$ 518,836	$ 3,594,351
6	Sewer Design	$ 481,339	$ 641,158	$ 575,496	$ 562,181	$ 345,542	$ 752,138	$ 3,357,854
7	Expert Testimony	$ 670,468	$ 648,633	$ 377,528	$ 145,195	$ 305,019	$ 577,551	$ 2,724,394
8	Construction Plans	$ 254,879	$ 365,784	$ 212,541	$ 189,745	$ 133,365	$ 652,417	$ 1,808,731
9	Total	$3,270,015	$3,030,784	$2,836,333	$2,287,204	$2,608,972	$3,152,242	$17,185,550

Advanced Worksheet Management

CASE Ellie Schwartz, JCL's vice president of Finance, wants to facilitate future tracking of expenses at JCL Talent's U.S. offices. She asks you to use Excel tools and options to help her staff work quickly and efficiently in a customized environment.

Module Objectives

After completing this module, you will be able to:

- Create and apply a template
- Import HTML data
- Create a custom AutoFill list
- Work with themes
- Work with cell comments
- Customize an Excel workbook
- Encrypt a workbook with a password
- Work with Ideas

Files You Will Need

IL_EX_10-1.xlsx
Support_EX_10-2.htm
IL_EX_10-3.xlsx
Support_EX_10-4.htm
IL_EX_10-5.xlsx
Support_EX_10-6.htm
IL_EX_10-7.xlsx
Support_EX_10-8.htm
IL_EX_10-9.xlsx
Support_EX_10-10.htm

Excel Module 10

Create and Apply a Template

Learning Outcomes
- Create a template
- Apply a template

A template is a workbook with an .xltx file extension that contains text, formulas, and formatting that you use repeatedly. When you save a workbook as a template, you can then use it to a create new workbook without having to reenter the repetitive data and formatting. To use a template, you apply it, which means you create a workbook *based on* the template. A workbook based on a template contains the same content, formulas, and formatting contained in the template, but is saved in the .xlsx format. The template file itself remains unchanged. **CASE** *Ellie has a workbook that contains formulas, styles, and labels for tracking this year's expenses at JCL. She asks you to use the workbook to create a template that will allow her to quickly create new workbooks for tracking expenses in future years.*

STEPS

1. **sam Start Excel, then open IL_EX_10-1.xlsx from the location where you store your Data Files**

   The U.S. worksheet contains formulas that analyze this year's expenses for the U.S. offices and is formatted to be easy to read. You can reuse some of this formatting and content in workbooks you create to track future expenses.

2. **Click the File tab on the ribbon, click Save As, click the Save as type list arrow, click Excel Template (*.xltx), click Browse in Backstage view, navigate to where you store your Data Files, type IL_EX_10_Expenses in the File name box, then click Save**

   Excel saves the file as a template, with the .xltx extension.

3. **Select the range C5:F12, press DEL, then click cell A1**

   The data specific to this worksheet is not needed for future worksheets. The reusable information and formatting remain to serve as the basis for future yearly worksheets, as shown in FIGURE 10-1.

4. **Save the template, then close the template**

   The completed template IL_EX_10_Expenses is now available to use in creating new workbooks.

5. **Open File Explorer, navigate to the location where you store your Data Files, then double-click IL_EX_10_Expenses.xltx**

   A new workbook is created and has the default name IL_EX_10_Expenses1, as shown in FIGURE 10-2. The "1" at the end of the name identifies it as a new workbook based on the IL_EX_10_Expenses template, just as "1" at the end of "Book1" identifies a new workbook based on the blank Excel template.

6. **Click cell C5, enter 200, click cell C6, enter 300, select the range C5:C6, then use the fill handle to fill the range C7:C12 with this series**

   You are entering test data to make sure the template contains accurate formulas.

7. **Copy the range C5:C12, paste it into the range D5:F12, then compare your workbook to FIGURE 10-3**

   The totals and percentages appear to be correct.

8. **Close the workbook without saving it**

   Because you created this workbook only to test the template's formulas and formatting, you don't need to save it for future use.

QUICK TIP

The "#DIV/0!" or divide-by-zero error messages in column H are temporary and will no longer appear once you open a document based on the template and enter next year's data.

QUICK TIP

If you want to edit the template itself, open the template (the .xltx file) using the Open dialog box in Excel. After making changes, save the template under the same name in the same location. Your changes are applied only to new documents you create based on the template from this point forward.

FIGURE 10-1: Completed template

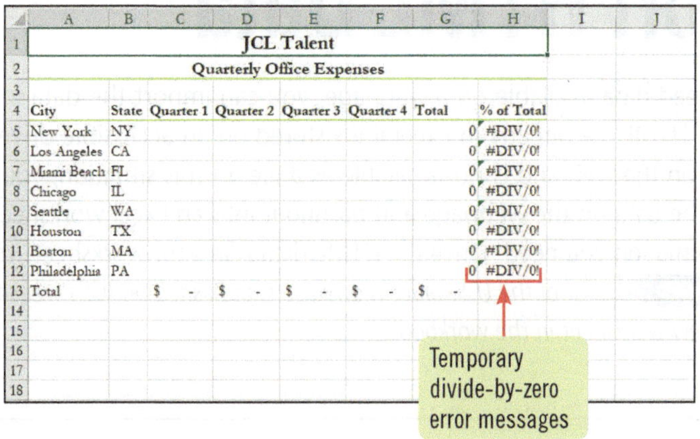

FIGURE 10-2: New workbook based on Expenses template

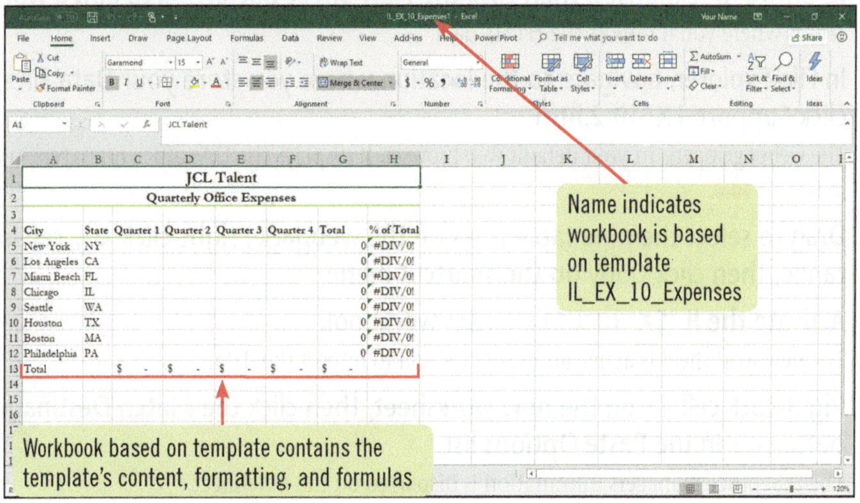

FIGURE 10-3: Test data entered in new workbook

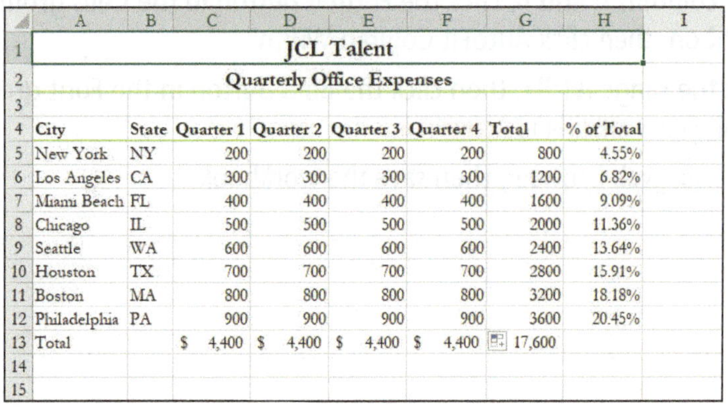

Creating a new workbook using a template

In addition to creating your own templates, you can use one of the many templates Excel offers for common documents such as balance sheets, budgets, or time cards. To create a workbook using an Excel template, click the File tab on the ribbon, then click New on the navigation bar. The New place in Backstage view displays thumbnails of some of the many templates available. The Blank workbook template is selected by default; when you create a new, blank workbook with no content or special formatting, this is the template the workbook is based on. To select a different template, click one of the selections in the New place, view the preview, then click Create.

Excel Module 10

Import HTML Data

Learning Outcome
- Import HTML data into a workbook

When you need data available on a webpage, you can import the data into Excel in a few ways. You can open an HTML file directly in Excel if it's stored on an accessible drive, but often the information is published on the web and is not available as a file. In this situation, you can import the HTML data by copying the data on the webpage and pasting it into an Excel worksheet. This allows you to import only the information you need. Once the HTML data is in your worksheet, you can analyze it using Excel features. **CASE** *A list of the U.S. office managers is published on JCL's website. Ellie asks you to import this data into a new worksheet in the workbook.*

STEPS

1. **Open IL_EX_10-1.xlsx from the location where you store your Data Files, save it as IL_EX_10_USExpenses, then click the New Sheet button to add a worksheet**
   This is where you'll import the HTML data.

QUICK TIP
The webpage formatting may differ on your screen depending on your default web browser.

2. **In File Explorer, navigate to the location where you store your Data Files, then double-click Support_EX_10-2.htm**
   The webpage opens in your default web browser. It displays the U.S. office managers information, as shown in FIGURE 10-4.
3. **Drag to select the nine table rows on the webpage, right-click any cell in the selected range, then click Copy on the shortcut menu**
4. **Activate the IL_EX_10_USExpenses workbook**
   The new worksheet is active and ready for you to import the data.
5. **Right-click cell A1 on the new worksheet, then click the Match Destination Formatting button in the Paste Options list**
   The U.S. office managers information is displayed on the new sheet.
6. **Double-click the Sheet1 sheet tab, type Managers, then press ENTER**
7. **Select columns A and B, click the Format button in the Cells group on the Home tab of the ribbon, then click AutoFit Column Width**
8. **Select the range A1:B1, then click the Bold button in the Font group**
   Compare your worksheet to FIGURE 10-5.
9. **Close your web browser, then save the workbook**

Importing XML data

Excel allows you to import and export XML data, a format often used for storing and exchanging data. To import XML data, click the Developer tab on the ribbon, click the Import button in the XML group, in the Import XML dialog box navigate to the xml file, click Import, then click OK twice. If you wish to specify a schema, or a map that describes the incoming data, before importing it, click the Source button in the XML group, in the XML Source pane click XML Maps, click Add in the XML Maps dialog box, navigate to a schema file in the Select XML source dialog box, click Open, then click OK.

FIGURE 10-4: Webpage listing JCL U.S. office managers

U.S. Managers

Office	Manager
New York	Nyack Afolayan
Los Angeles	Shavonn Rudd
Miami	Rosella Leigh
Chicago	Gary Jaeger
Seattle	Sophie Tan
Houston	Max Gallardo
Boston	Cheri McNeil
Philadelphia	Chris Wang

FIGURE 10-5: Imported and formatted HTML data

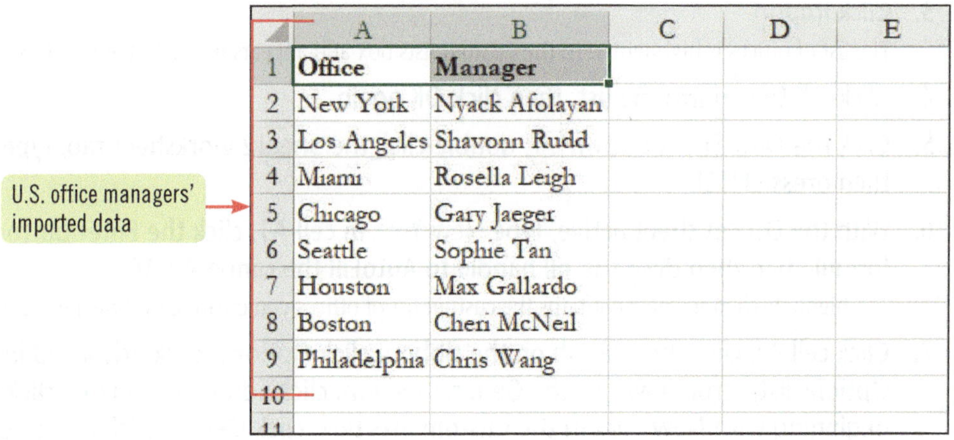

	A	B	C	D	E
1	**Office**	**Manager**			
2	New York	Nyack Afolayan			
3	Los Angeles	Shavonn Rudd			
4	Miami	Rosella Leigh			
5	Chicago	Gary Jaeger			
6	Seattle	Sophie Tan			
7	Houston	Max Gallardo			
8	Boston	Cheri McNeil			
9	Philadelphia	Chris Wang			
10					
11					

Importing HTML files directly into Excel

If you have an Internet connection, you can import data from a webpage online into an Excel worksheet by clicking the Data tab, clicking the From Web button in the Get & Transform group, verifying the Basic option is selected, entering the web address in the URL box of the From Web dialog box, clicking OK, selecting the items you wish to import in the Display Options section of the Navigator dialog box, selecting the Web View or Table view tab, then clicking Load. If you wish to use this method to import html data from a file stored locally on your computer, enter the path to the webpage file in the URL box rather than a web address. If you receive an Unable to Connect error regarding the file path, click Edit, click Browse, navigate to the file, click Import in the Import Data dialog box, click OK, select the data you wish to import and either Web or Table view in the Navigator dialog box, then click Load.

You can also import a locally stored HTML file directly into an Excel workbook by clicking the File tab, clicking Open, clicking Browse, selecting All Files in the Open dialog box, browsing to the HTML file, then clicking Open.

Excel
Module 10

Create a Custom AutoFill List

Learning Outcomes
- Create a custom list
- Use a custom list

Whenever you need to type a list of words regularly, you can save time by creating a custom list. Then you can simply enter the first value in a blank cell and drag the fill handle. Excel AutoFills the range, entering the rest of the information for you. FIGURE 10-6 shows examples of custom lists that are built into Excel.

CASE *JCL's offices are identified by the city where they are located. Ellie often has to enter a list of JCL's U.S. offices in her worksheets. She asks you to create a custom list to save having to manually enter the information each time she needs it.*

STEPS

1. **Click the U.S. sheet, then select the range A5:A12**
2. **Click the File tab on the ribbon, click Options, click the Advanced category, scroll down to the General section, then click Edit Custom Lists**
   The Custom Lists dialog box displays all existing custom lists, including those already built into Excel, as shown in FIGURE 10-7. The Import list from cells text box contains the range you selected before opening the dialog box.
3. **Click Import**
   The list of offices is highlighted in the Custom lists box and appears in the List entries box.
4. **Click OK to confirm the list, then click OK again**
5. **Click the New Sheet button ⊕, double-click the Sheet2 worksheet tab, type Offices, then press ENTER**
6. **With the Offices sheet active, type New York in cell A1, click the Enter button ✓ on the formula bar, then drag the fill handle to AutoFill the range A2:A8**
   The highlighted range now contains the custom list of offices you created, as shown in FIGURE 10-8.
7. **Click cell A1, click the File tab on the ribbon, click Options, click Advanced in the Excel Options list, scroll down to the General section, click Edit Custom Lists, click the list beginning with New York in the Custom lists box, click Delete, click OK to confirm the deletion, then click OK two more times**
   If you share a computer with others, it is best to delete any custom lists you create after you are finished using them.
8. **Save the workbook**

QUICK TIP
You can edit a custom list by selecting it in the Custom lists box, making the change, then clicking OK twice.

QUICK TIP
You can also drag the fill handle to the right to enter a custom list.

FIGURE 10-6: Examples of custom lists

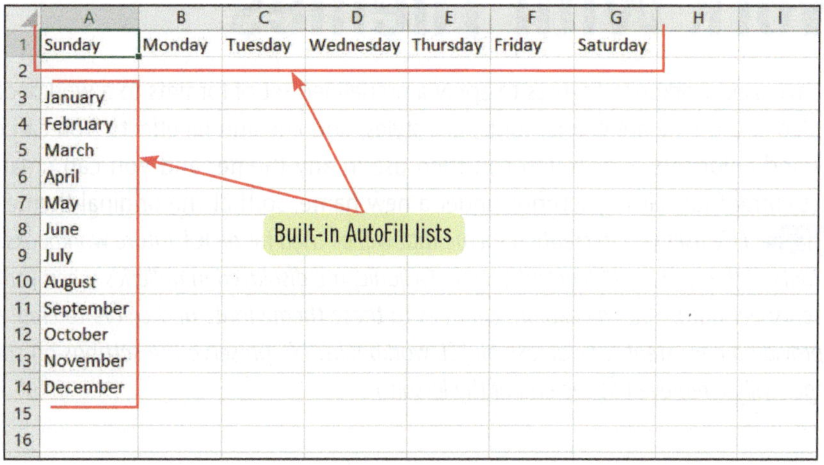

FIGURE 10-7: Custom Lists dialog box

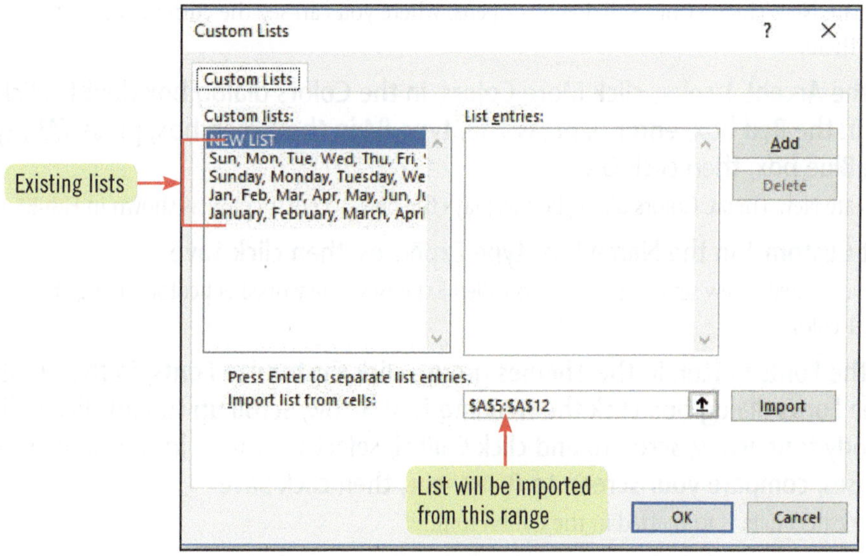

FIGURE 10-8: Custom list of offices

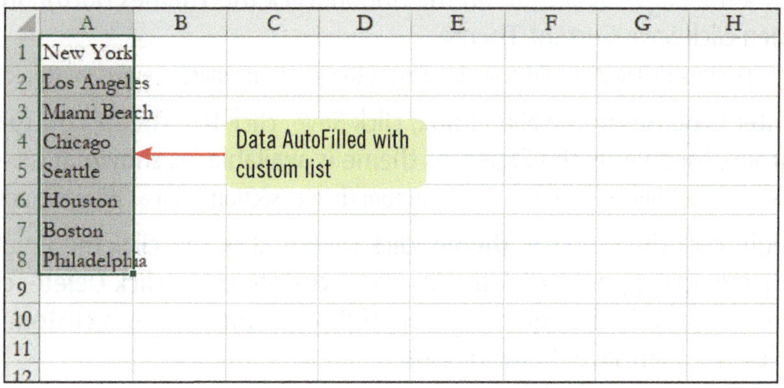

Excel

Excel Module 10

Work with Themes

Learning Outcomes
- Create a custom theme color
- Create custom theme fonts
- Create a custom theme

You have used workbook themes to apply a predefined set of formats to a workbook. Formatting choices included in a theme are colors, fonts, cell styles, and line and fill effects. You can create custom theme fonts and color sets, which you can then use in any theme, and you can create custom themes to reflect current formatting settings under a new name, so that the original theme remains unchanged. **CASE** *Ellie asks you to create a theme that will be used for all JCL future workbooks. The preselected colors and fonts of the workbook's current theme, Organic, are displayed in galleries when you select colors and fonts for worksheet data. You will explore changes to these theme fonts and colors to create a custom theme that will provide a consistent look across all JCL workbooks. (To preserve the settings on shared computers, these changes will be removed at the end of the lesson.)*

STEPS

1. **Click the U.S. sheet tab, click cell A1, click the Page Layout tab on the ribbon, click the Colors button in the Themes group, then click Customize Colors**
   The Create New Theme Colors dialog box opens, where you can see the current colors in this theme and change them.

QUICK TIP
You can change theme effects by clicking the Effect button in the Themes group and selecting an effect from the gallery.

2. **Click the Accent 1 color, click More Colors, in the Colors dialog box double-click the value in the Red box, enter 0, press TAB, type 84 in the Green box, press TAB, type 166 in the Blue box, then click OK**
   The Create New Theme Colors dialog box displays the new Accent 1 color, as shown in FIGURE 10-9.
3. **Select Custom 1 in the Name box, type Expenses, then click Save**
   You have created a new set of theme colors called Expenses. The worksheet colors change to reflect the new Accent 1 color.
4. **Click the Fonts button in the Themes group, click Customize Fonts, in the Create New Theme Fonts dialog box click the Heading font arrow, scroll up to and click Calibri, click the Body font arrow, scroll to and click Calibri, select Custom 1 in the Name box, type Expenses, compare your screen to FIGURE 10-10, then click Save**
   The worksheet data is formatted in the Calibri font.
5. **Select column G, click the Home tab on the ribbon, click the Format button in the Cells group, click AutoFit Column Width, then click cell A1**
   The column fully displays the data in the Calibri font.
6. **Click the Page Layout tab on the ribbon, click the Themes button in the Themes group, then click Save Current Theme**
   The Document Themes folder opens. This is the location where themes are stored for Office files.
7. **Enter Expenses in the Name box, click Save, click the Themes button in the Themes group, then verify the Expenses theme is available, as shown in FIGURE 10-11**
   User-created themes are listed in the Custom themes section, above Office themes.
8. **Right-click the Expenses theme, click Delete, click Yes, click the Colors button in the Themes group, right-click the Expenses custom color, click Delete, click Yes, click the Fonts button in the Themes group, right-click the Expenses custom font, click Delete, click Yes, then save the workbook**
   It is best to remove custom fonts, colors, and themes from Office if you are sharing a computer with other people.

FIGURE 10-9: Create New Theme Colors dialog box

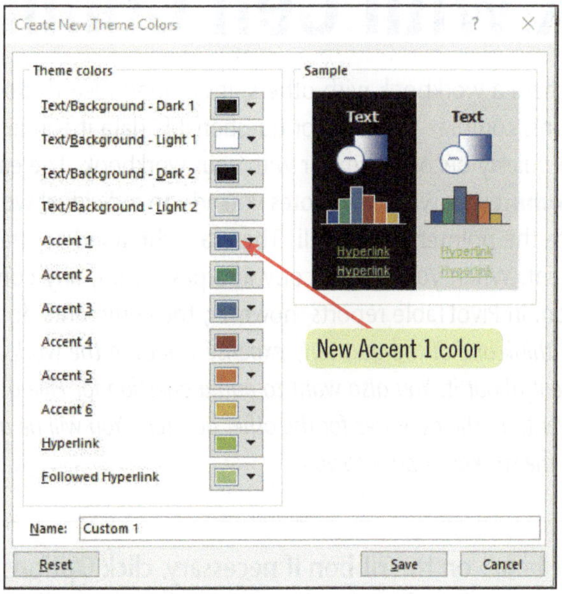

FIGURE 10-10: Create New Theme Fonts dialog box

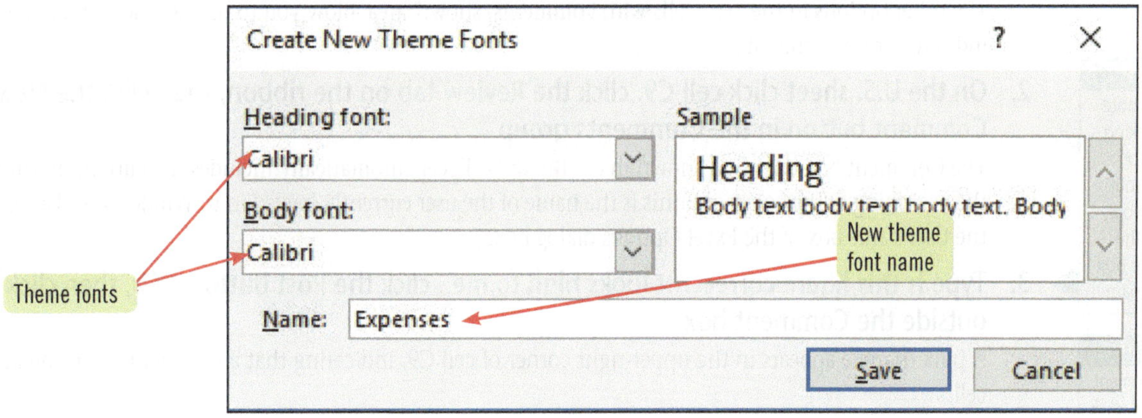

FIGURE 10-11: Workbook themes

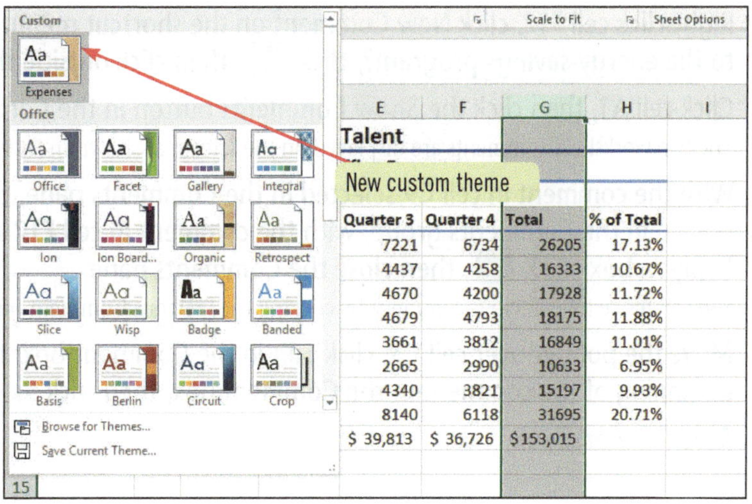

Excel

Excel Module 10

Work with Cell Comments

Learning Outcomes
- Insert a new comment
- Show worksheet comments
- Edit a comment

If you plan to share a workbook with others, it's a good idea to **document**, or make notes about the basic assumptions, complex formulas, or questionable data it contains. By reading your documentation, a coworker can quickly become familiar with your workbook. The easiest way to document a workbook is to use **cell comments**, which are notes you add to individual worksheet cells; the comment appears when you place the pointer over a cell. These are threaded so that you can reply directly below the original comment. When you sort or copy and paste cells, any comments attached to them move to the new location. In PivotTable reports, however, the comments do not move with the worksheet data.

CASE *You think one of the quarterly expense values in the worksheet may be incorrect, so you decide to add a comment about it. You also want to add a question for Ellie about a quarterly expense value that is significantly lower than the expenses for the other quarters. You will be able to see Ellie's reply to the comment when she sends the workbook back to you.*

STEPS

1. **Click the File tab on the ribbon if necessary, click Options, click Advanced in the Excel Options list, scroll to the Display section, click the Indicators only, and comments on hover option button to select it in the For cells with comments, show: section if necessary, then click OK**

   The other options in the "For cells with comments, show:" area allow you to display the comment and its indicator or no comments.

2. **On the U.S. sheet click cell C9, click the Review tab on the ribbon, then click the New Comment button in the Comments group**

   The Comment box opens, as shown in FIGURE 10-12. Excel automatically includes the current username at the beginning of the comment; this is the name of the user currently logged in to Windows, and appears in the User name box of the Excel Options dialog box.

3. **Type Is this figure correct? It looks high to me., click the Post button, then click outside the Comment box**

   A pink triangle appears in the upper-right corner of cell C9, indicating that a comment is attached to the cell.

4. **Place the pointer over cell C9**

   The comment appears next to the cell. When you move the pointer or click outside cell C9, the comment disappears.

5. **Right-click cell F12, click New Comment on the shortcut menu, type Is this decrease due to the energy-savings program?, click , then click outside the Comment box**

6. **Click cell A1, then click the Show Comments button in the Comments group**

   The two worksheet comments are displayed on the screen, as shown in FIGURE 10-13.

7. **With the comment in cell C9 selected in the Comments pane, click the Next Comment button in the Comments group, with the comment in cell F12 selected, type Yes in the Reply ... box, click , then close the Comments pane**

   You can move to a previous comment by clicking the Previous Comment button in the Comments group.

8. **Move the pointer over cell C9, click Edit in the Comment box, type Ellie - at the beginning of the comment in the Comment box, then click Save**

9. **Save the workbook**

QUICK TIP
You can add a note to a cell by clicking the Notes button in the Notes group, clicking New Note, then entering the note text in the box with your username.

QUICK TIP
To delete a comment in a selected cell, click the Delete button in the Comments group. To clear all comments, click the Home tab on the ribbon, click the Find & Select button in the Editing group, click Go To Special, select Comments in the Go To Special dialog box, click OK to close the dialog box, click the Review tab, then click the Delete button in the Comments group.

QUICK TIP
After you save your file, the username for comments may change to Author.

FIGURE 10-12: Comment box

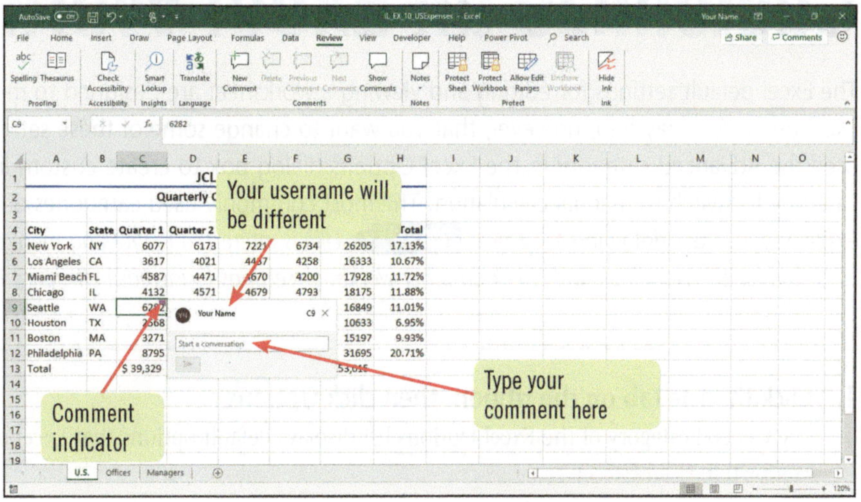

FIGURE 10-13: Comments pane

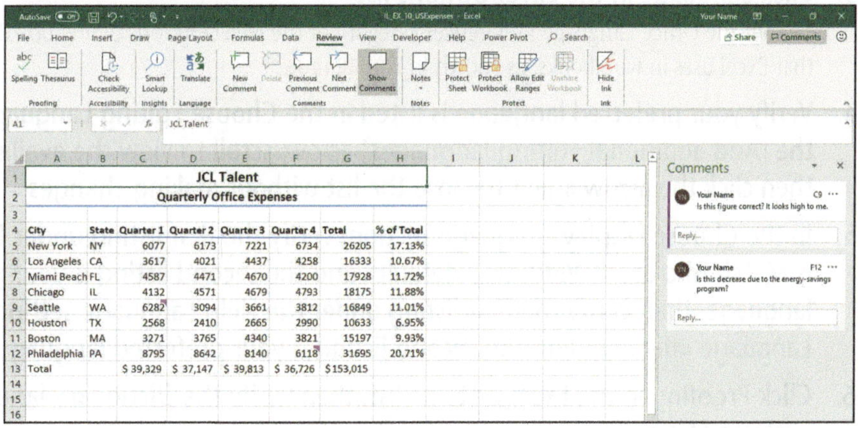

Excel

Sharing Excel workbooks

If you have a subscription to Office 365, you can coauthor a workbook with others to collaboratively add and edit data. When you co-author, you can see the changes made by people with whom you have shared a workbook, and they can see yours. To share your workbook, click the Share button in the upper-right corner of the screen, upload your workbook to a OneDrive account and provide a name for the workbook. The Share pane allows you to enter the email addresses of your coauthors in the Invite people box. You can also select email addresses from your address book. Clicking the Can edit arrow allows you to choose whether the recipients will be able to view or edit the workbook. After entering an optional message, click Share to email a link to the workbook on OneDrive. When a recipient clicks the link, the workbook opens in Excel Online.

You can also use the Share pane to email a copy of a workbook by clicking Send as attachment, then clicking either Send a copy or Send a PDF. You can also click Get a sharing link, then click Create and edit link or Create a view only link to copy the workbook link location on OneDrive to share with others.

When a file is saved to OneDrive, AutoSave is enabled so the workbook is automatically saved as you and other people make changes. When working with a shared workbook, you will see the names of the people with whom you are working in the Share pane.

Excel Module 10

Customize an Excel Workbook

Learning Outcomes
- Work with Excel options
- Customize the Quick Access Toolbar

The Excel default settings for editing and viewing a worksheet are designed to meet the needs of most Excel users. You may find, however, that you want to change some of these settings. You have already used the Advanced category in the Excel Options dialog box to create custom lists and the Formulas category to switch to manual calculation. The most commonly used categories of the Excel Options are explained in more detail in TABLE 10-1. **CASE** *Ellie is interested in working more efficiently. She asks you to customize the workbook and check on other workbook settings to increase efficiency in Excel.*

STEPS

QUICK TIP If you are working on your own computer and don't see your name here, you can edit the contents of the User name box to reflect the correct information; otherwise, leave this setting as is.

QUICK TIP You can change the thesaurus language by clicking the Review tab on the ribbon, clicking the Thesaurus button in the Proofing group, then clicking the arrow for the currently used language in the Thesaurus pane.

QUICK TIP You can also change the dictionary language while spell-checking a worksheet by clicking the Dictionary language arrow in the Spelling dialog box.

1. **Click the File tab on the ribbon, then click Options**
   The General category of the Excel Options list displays default options that Excel uses in new workbooks, as shown in FIGURE 10-14.
2. **In the Personalize your copy of Microsoft Office section, verify that the correct name is displayed in the User name box, then scroll down to view the other settings for the workbook**
3. **Click Language in the Excel Options list**
   The Set the Office Language Preferences category of the Excel Options dialog box displays default options that Excel uses in workbooks, as shown in FIGURE 10-15.
4. **Verify your preferred language is listed in the Choose Editing Languages section, click the [Add additional editing languages] arrow, scroll to view the available languages, then click the arrow again to close the list without making changes**
5. **In the Choose Display Language section, verify the first listing under Display Language is Match Microsoft Windows <default> and the second listing is your preferred language, then verify the first listing under the Help Language setting is Match Display Language <default> and the second listing is your preferred language**
6. **Click Proofing in the Excel Options list, then verify the Dictionary language shows your preferred language**
7. **Click Quick Access Toolbar in the Excel Options list, in the Customize the Quick Access Toolbar section select Email under Popular Commands, click Add, then click OK**
   The Email icon is added to the Quick Access Toolbar.
8. **Click File, click Options, click Quick Access Toolbar in the Excel Options list, click Reset, click Reset only Quick Access Toolbar, click Yes, then click OK**
   If you are working on a shared computer, you should restore the original settings to remove customizations.

Tracking changes in a workbook

You can track modifications to a workbook when you want to show what changes are being made to it from the present point onward. To use this feature, you can add the Track Changes button to the ribbon. To do so, right-click the ribbon, click Customize the Ribbon, right-click Review, click Add New Group, click the Choose Commands from arrow, click Commands Not in the Ribbon, click Track changes (Legacy) in the list of commands, click Add, then click OK. You can use the Highlight Changes command to specify what types of changes to track. Note that this legacy feature is not compatible with newer features in Excel, such as uploading to OneDrive.

FIGURE 10-14: General category of Excel options

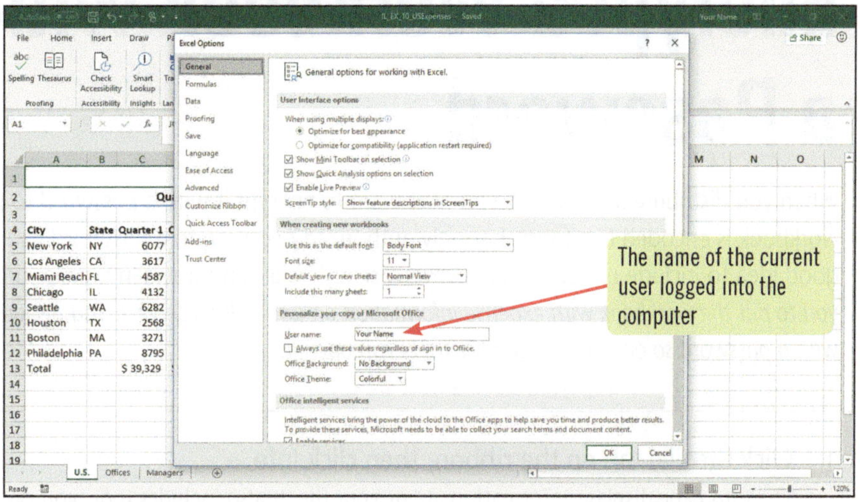

FIGURE 10-15: Language category of Excel Options dialog box

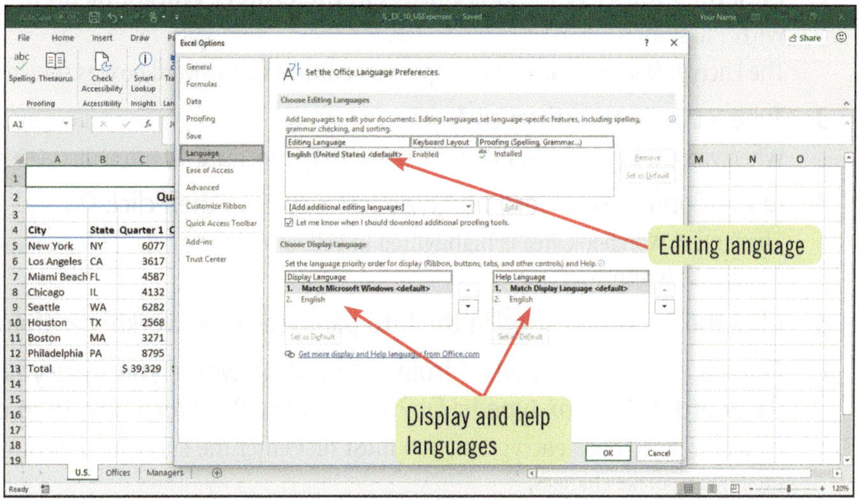

TABLE 10-1: Categories of Excel options you can change

category	allows you to
General	Change the username, customize default settings of new workbooks, enable LinkedIn features, and customize the user interface
Formulas	Control how the worksheet is calculated, how formulas appear, and error-checking settings and rules
Data	Control how data is analyzed and imported
Proofing	Control AutoCorrect and spell-checking options
Save	Select a default format and location for saving files, and customize AutoRecover settings
Language	Control the languages displayed and add additional languages and proofing tools
Ease of Access	Specify options to make Excel more accessible, such as changing the document display font size
Advanced	Set options for pen settings, create custom lists, and customize editing and display options
Customize Ribbon	Add commands, tabs, and groups to the Ribbon
Quick Access Toolbar	Add commands to the Quick Access Toolbar
Add-Ins	Install Excel Add-in programs such as Solver and Analysis ToolPak
Trust Center	Change Trust Center settings to protect your Excel files and your computer

Excel
Module 10

Learning Outcomes
- Use a password to encrypt a workbook
- Delete a password on an encrypted workbook

Encrypt a Workbook with a Password

When you distribute a workbook you may want to encrypt it with a password to protect it. An encrypted workbook is encoded in a form that only authorized people with a password can read. For security, it is a good idea to include uppercase and lowercase letters and numbers in a password. **CASE** *Ellie wants you to put the workbook with expense information on one of JCL's servers. You decide to encrypt the workbook with a password so only authorized JCL users can open it.*

STEPS

1. **Click the File tab on the ribbon, then click Info**

   The Info pane displays information about your file. It also includes tools you can use to check for security issues.

2. **Click the Protect Workbook button in the Protect Workbook area, then click Encrypt with Password**

   The Encrypt Document dialog box opens and displays a Password box, as shown in FIGURE 10-16.

3. **Type JcLQe2021%, then click OK**

   When you enter passwords, the characters you type are masked with bullets (• • •) for security purposes.

4. **In the Confirm password box type JcLQe2021%, then click OK**

   The Protect Workbook area is highlighted in yellow and the message "A password is required to open this workbook" is displayed.

5. **Click the Back button in the Info pane, save the workbook, then close the workbook**

6. **Open IL_EX_10_USExpenses from the location where you store your Data Files, in the Password dialog box type JcLQe2021% in the Password box, then click OK**

   To remove workbook encryption, you must first enter the encryption password, to verify that you are qualified to make changes.

7. **Click the File tab on the ribbon, click Info, click the Protect Workbook button in the Protect Workbook area, then click Encrypt with Password**

   The Encrypt Document dialog is displayed with the masked password, as shown in FIGURE 10-17.

8. **In the Password box select the masked password, press DEL, then click OK**

   The password is removed from the Workbook, and encryption is turned off.

9. **Click , then save the workbook**

FIGURE 10-16: Encrypt Document dialog box

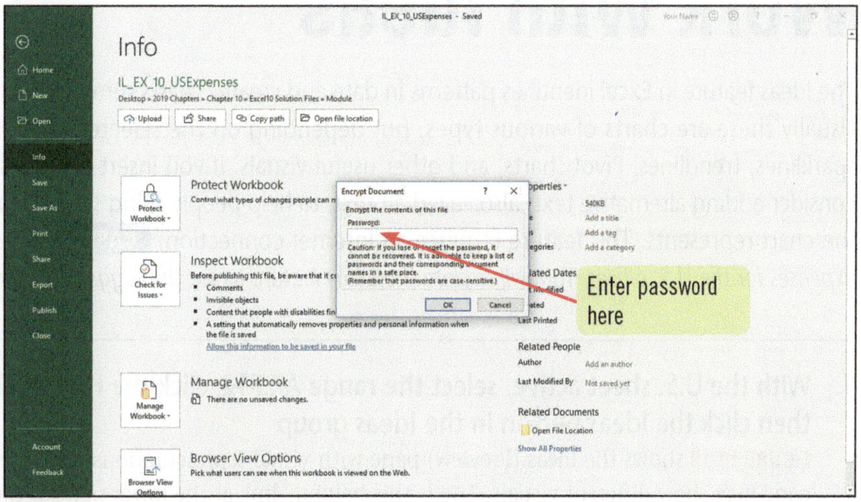

FIGURE 10-17: Masked password

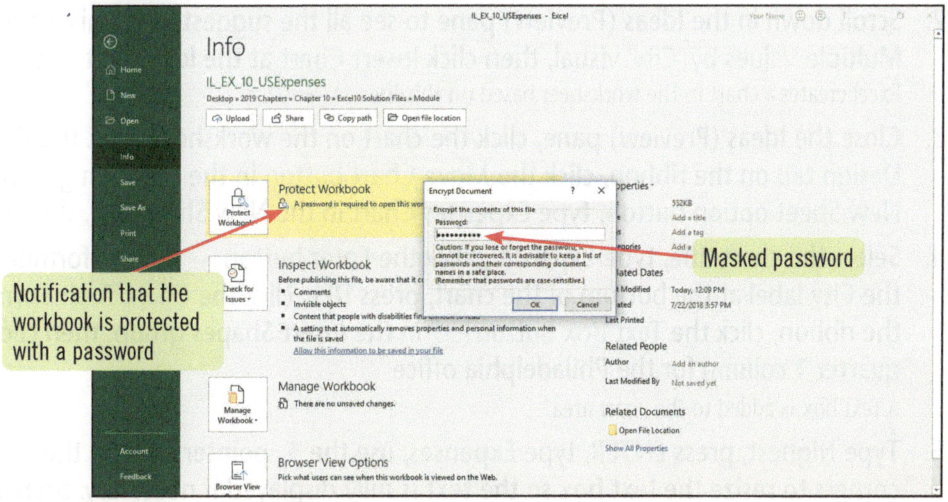

Working with a previous version of an Excel workbook

When you save your Excel files on OneDrive, AutoSave is automatically turned on to save versions of your workbook while you make changes. The older saved versions can be restored if you make errors in newer versions using Version history by clicking the File tab on the ribbon, clicking View and restore previous versions in the Version History area, then clicking the desired version in the Version History pane. FIGURE 10-18 shows two version of a workbook. After your desired version opens, you can click the Restore button above the formula bar to save the file.

FIGURE 10-18: Version History pane

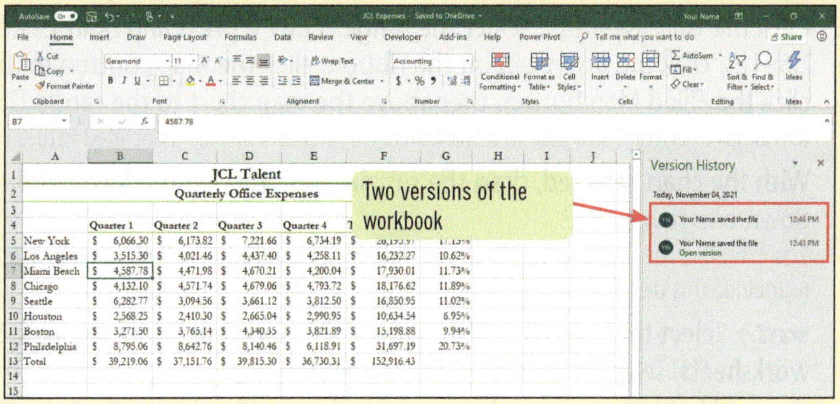

Excel

Work with Ideas

Learning Outcomes
- Create a chart using Ideas
- Add alternative text to a chart

The Ideas feature in Excel identifies patterns in data and creates charts summarizing different data groups. Usually these are charts of various types, but depending on the selected data they may also include sparklines, trendlines, PivotCharts, and other useful visuals. If you insert a suggested chart, you should consider adding alternative text, also called alt text, to help people using screen readers understand what the chart represents. This feature requires an Internet connection. **CASE** *Ellie asks you to chart the expenses for the U.S. offices. You will explore the Ideas feature to see the suggested charts.*

STEPS

TROUBLE
If this is the first time the Ideas feature is used, click Turn on to activate Office Intelligent Services.

1. **With the U.S. sheet active, select the range A4:F12, click the Home tab on the ribbon, then click the Ideas button in the Ideas group**
   FIGURE 10-19 shows the Ideas (Preview) pane with visual representations of the selected data. Your Ideas pane may show different visuals. The Is this helpful? link at the lower right of each visual allows you to provide feedback on each suggestion to improve future suggested visuals.
2. **Scroll down in the Ideas (Preview) pane to see all the suggested visuals, click the Multiple Values by 'City' visual, then click Insert Chart at the lower left of the visual**
   Excel creates a chart in the worksheet based on this Idea.
3. **Close the Ideas (Preview) pane, click the chart on the worksheet, click the Chart Tools Design tab on the ribbon, click the Move Chart button in the Location group, click the New Sheet option button, type Expenses Chart in the New Sheet box, then click OK**
4. **Select the chart title, type Expenses, click the Enter button on the formula bar, select the City label at the bottom of the chart, press DEL, click the Chart Tools Format tab on the ribbon, click the Text Box button in the Insert Shapes group, then click above the quarter 1 column for the Philadelphia office**
   A text box is added to the chart area.
5. **Type Highest, press ENTER, type Expenses, use the pointer to drag the text box corners to resize the text box so the text is fully displayed if necessary, then use the pointer to move the text box above the Philadelphia Quarter 1 column**
   The text box clarifies the information in the column.
6. **Right-click a blank area of the chart, click Edit Alt Text on the shortcut menu, click inside the text box in the Alt Text pane, type Chart showing expenses for U.S. offices by quarter., then close the Alt Text pane**
   The alt text describes the chart to a person with visual impairments. If you have an object that is decorative and not informational, for example a border, you can add a checkmark to the Mark as decorative check box. Because this object is informational, you leave this check box unchecked.
7. **Click the U.S. sheet tab, select the range A5:B11, press and hold CTRL, select the range H5:H11, click the Insert tab on the ribbon, click the Maps button in the Chart group, click the Filled Map button, then move the map chart to the range I2:N15**
   If you have geographical data in a worksheet, map charts display associated values over the region.
8. **With the chart selected, drag the resizing pointer in the lower-right corner of cell B11 down one row to B12**
   You extended the selection to include the Philadelphia location and percentage data, and the chart updated to include this data.
9. **sam Select the map chart title, press DEL, add your name to the footers of all four worksheets, select cell A1, save the workbook, compare your chart to FIGURE 10-20, close the workbook, close Excel, then submit the workbook to your instructor**

QUICK TIP
You can use the Smart Lookup pane to access additional online resources for the currently selected data. Click the Review tab, click the Smart Lookup button in the Insights group, then review the search results for your selected data in the Explore and Define areas.

QUICK TIP
You can add an additional data series to a chart by clicking anywhere in the chart, then dragging the sizing handles to include the new data.

FIGURE 10-19: Ideas (Preview) pane

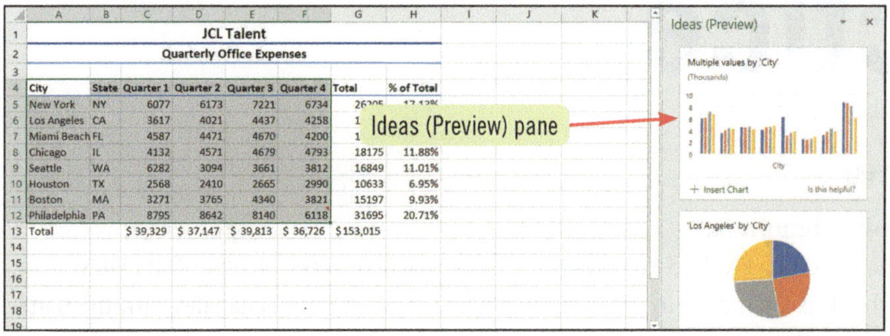

FIGURE 10-20: Map chart

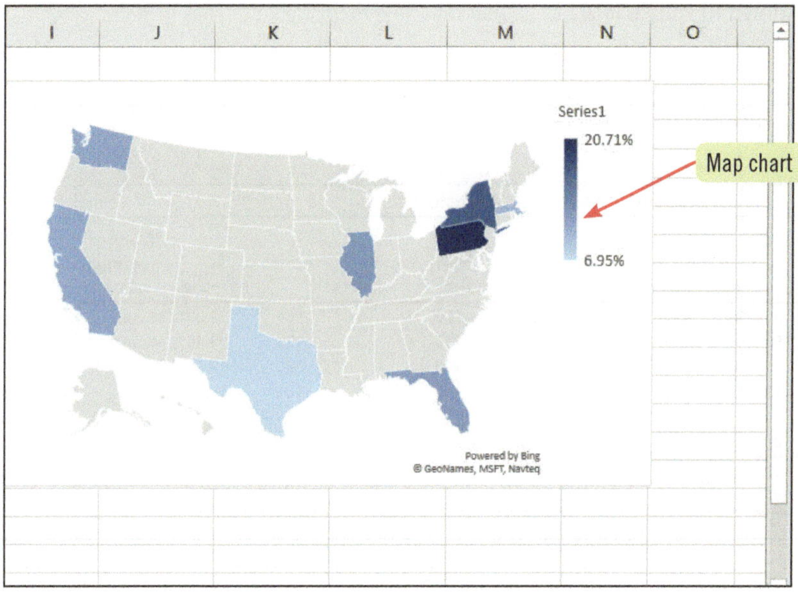

Working with Funnel charts

You can use a funnel chart to show values at different stages of a process. They are most useful when you want to illustrate data values decreasing, so that the resulting chart resembles a funnel. FIGURE 10-21 shows an example of a funnel chart illustrating the number of hours decreasing with each stage in a process.

FIGURE 10-21: Funnel chart

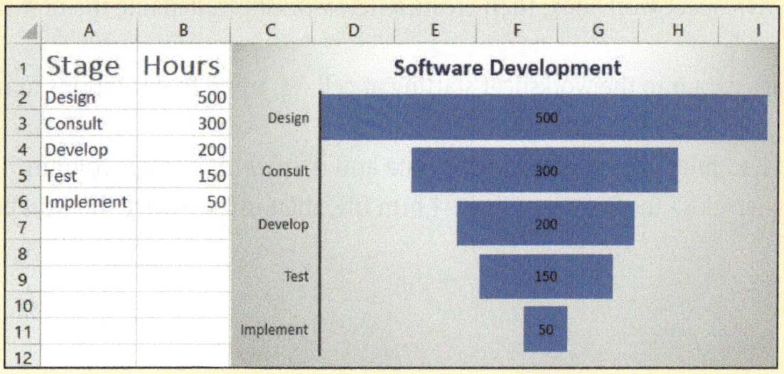

Practice

Skills Review

1. **Create and apply a template.**
   a. Start Excel, then open IL_EX_10-3.xlsx from the location where you store your Data Files.
   b. Save the workbook as a template in the location where you store your Data Files with the name **IL_EX_10_FirstQuarter.xltx**.
   c. Delete the values in ranges B3:D6 and F3:F6. Leave the worksheet formulas intact.
   d. Close the template, then open a new workbook based on the template.
   e. In the new IL_EX_10_FirstQuarter1 workbook, test the template by entering the data in ranges B3:D6 and F3:F6, shown in FIGURE 10-22.

FIGURE 10-22

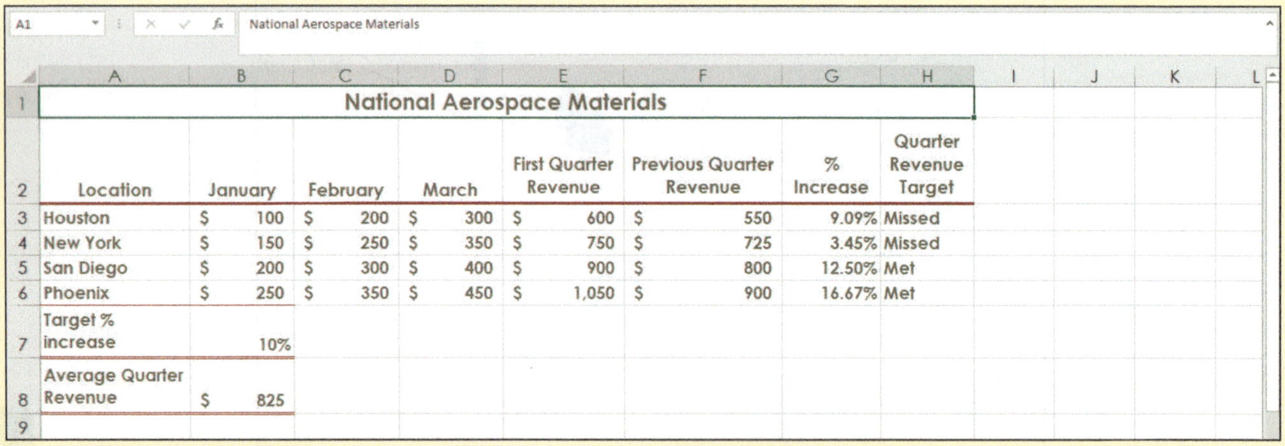

	Location	January	February	March	First Quarter Revenue	Previous Quarter Revenue	% Increase	Quarter Revenue Target
1	National Aerospace Materials							
3	Houston	$ 100	$ 200	$ 300	$ 600	$ 550	9.09%	Missed
4	New York	$ 150	$ 250	$ 350	$ 750	$ 725	3.45%	Missed
5	San Diego	$ 200	$ 300	$ 400	$ 900	$ 800	12.50%	Met
6	Phoenix	$ 250	$ 350	$ 450	$ 1,050	$ 900	16.67%	Met
7	Target % increase	10%						
8	Average Quarter Revenue	$ 825						

   f. After verifying that the formulas and formatting in the workbook appear to work correctly, close the workbook without saving it.

2. **Import HTML data.**
   a. Re-open IL_EX_10-3.xlsx from the location where you store your Data Files, then save the workbook as **IL_EX_10_Aerospace**.
   b. Open File Explorer, navigate to the location where you store your Data Files, then open the webpage Support_EX_10-4.htm in your web browser. Copy the data in the five rows of the webpage table, including the column headings.
   c. Activate the IL_EX_10_Aerospace workbook, then create a new worksheet. Rename the new sheet **Quality Ratings**.
   d. Paste the copied webpage data into the worksheet starting at cell A1, using Paste Options to match the destination formatting.
   e. Autofit columns A and B to fully display the Location data and narrow the Ratings column.
   f. Activate your web browser, close the Support_EX_10-4.htm file, then in Excel save the workbook.

Skills Review (continued)

3. Create a custom AutoFill list.

a. Activate the First Quarter sheet, then select the range A3:A6.

b. Open the Custom Lists dialog box, then import the selected data.

c. Close the dialog box.

d. Add a worksheet to the workbook. Rename the new worksheet **Locations** and move it so it is the last worksheet in the workbook. On the Locations worksheet, enter **Houston** in cell A1.

e. Use the fill handle to enter the custom list through cell A4, then widen column A to fully display the locations.

f. Open the Custom Lists dialog box again, delete the custom list you just created, then save the workbook.

4. Work with themes.

a. Activate the First Quarter sheet and use the Create New Theme Colors dialog box to change the Accent 1 color to a custom color with the RGB values Red: **0**, Green: **138**, and Blue: **135**.

b. Name the new theme color palette **FQ** and save it.

c. Use the Create New Theme Fonts dialog box to change both the heading and body fonts to Calibri. Save the new theme font set as **FQ**.

d. Save the current theme as **FQ**, then compare your worksheet to FIGURE 10-23.

FIGURE 10-23

	A	B	C	D	E	F	G	H
1	National Aerospace Materials							
2	Location	January	February	March	First Quarter Revenue	Previous Quarter Revenue	% Increase	Quarter Revenue Target
3	Houston	$ 59,529	$ 58,017	$ 74,193	$ 191,739	$ 162,571	17.94%	Met
4	New York	$ 68,008	$ 74,471	$ 74,691	$ 217,170	$ 166,545	30.40%	Met
5	San Diego	$ 65,909	$ 72,444	$ 67,841	$ 206,194	$ 179,852	14.65%	Met
6	Phoenix	$ 52,146	$ 56,734	$ 58,770	$ 167,650	$ 176,645	(5.09%)	Missed
7	Target % increase	10%						
8	Average Quarter Revenue	$ 195,688						
9								

e. Verify that the custom FQ color palette is listed in the Theme Colors list, the FQ font set is listed in the Theme Fonts list, and theme is listed the Themes list, then delete each custom setting.

f. Save the workbook.

5. Work with cell comments.

a. Insert a comment in cell E2 that reads **Are these final values?**. (*Hint:* Don't type the period.)

b. Click anywhere outside the Comment box to close it.

c. Insert a comment in cell G4 that reads **Nice Increase!**.

d. Edit the comment in cell E2 to read **Are these final revenue values?**.

e. Add a reply to the comment in cell G4 that reads **Thanks.**.

f. Display all worksheet comments. Hide all worksheet comments.

g. Delete the comment in cell E2.

h. Save the workbook.

Excel

Skills Review (continued)

6. **Customize an Excel workbook.**
   - **a.** Use the General category of the Excel Options dialog box to verify the correct username appears.
   - **b.** Use the Language category of the Excel Options dialog box to verify the editing, display, and help languages are set correctly for your Excel workbook.
   - **c.** Use the Proofing category of the Excel Options dialog box to verify the dictionary language setting is correct for your Excel workbook.
   - **d.** Use the Quick Access Toolbar category of the Excel Options dialog box to add the Open button to the Quick Access Toolbar.
   - **e.** Reset all customizations of the workbook to the defaults.
7. **Encrypt a workbook with a password.**
   - **a.** Encrypt the workbook with the password **FjfmQpin8!**.
   - **b.** Save and close the workbook.
   - **c.** Open the workbook using the password.
   - **d.** Delete the password.
   - **e.** Save the workbook.
8. **Work with Ideas.**
   - **a.** Select the range A2:D6 and use the Ideas feature to see suggested visuals for analyzing the selected data.
   - **b.** Insert the first suggested visual, a chart, from the Ideas (Preview) pane, then close the pane.
   - **c.** Move and resize the chart to fit in the range C7:H18.
   - **d.** Edit the chart title to **Q1 Revenue**.
   - **e.** Add the alternative text: **January, February, and March revenue for Houston, New York, San Diego, and Phoenix**.
   - **f.** Close the Alt Text pane.
   - **g.** Compare your First Quarter worksheet to FIGURE 10-24. Note that your chart may not match the one in FIGURE 10-24 if your Ideas pane displayed a different first visual.

FIGURE 10-24

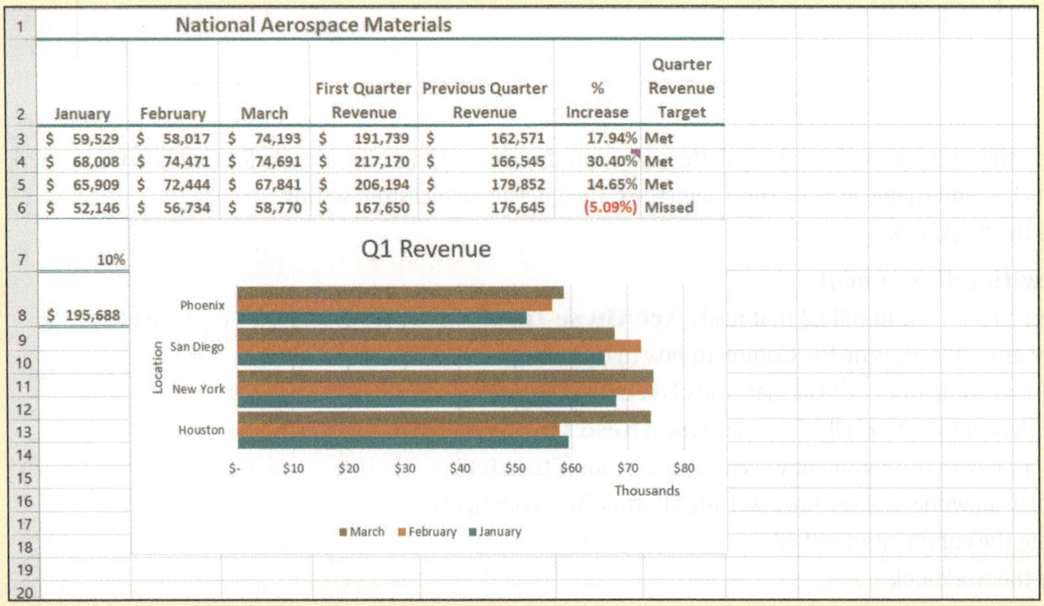

	January	February	March	First Quarter Revenue	Previous Quarter Revenue	% Increase	Quarter Revenue Target
1	National Aerospace Materials						
3	$ 59,529	$ 58,017	$ 74,193	$ 191,739	$ 162,571	17.94%	Met
4	$ 68,008	$ 74,471	$ 74,691	$ 217,170	$ 166,545	30.40%	Met
5	$ 65,909	$ 72,444	$ 67,841	$ 206,194	$ 179,852	14.65%	Met
6	$ 52,146	$ 56,734	$ 58,770	$ 167,650	$ 176,645	(5.09%)	Missed
7	10%						
8	$ 195,688						

- **h.** Group the worksheets, add your name to the center footer section of the sheets, save the workbook, close the workbook, then submit the workbook to your instructor.
- **i.** Close Excel.

Independent Challenge 1

The manager at Riverwalk Medical Clinic has hired you to increase efficiency at an affiliated local imaging facility. You decide to create a template to speed up the facility's monthly billing process, and to use Excel features to make the billing easier to manage each month.

a. Open IL_EX_10-5.xlsx from the location where you store your Data Files.

b. Delete the billing and insurance data in columns B and C, leaving the total formulas. Save the workbook as a template with the name **IL_EX_10_MonthlyBilling.xltx** in the location where you store your Data Files, then close the template.

c. Open a new workbook based on the IL_EX_10_MonthlyBilling template. Enter test data of your choosing for billing and insurance, then check the results to verify the template is calculating the balance correctly. Close the IL_EX_10_MonthlyBilling1 workbook without saving it.

d. Re-open IL_EX_10-5.xlsx from the location where you store your Data Files, then save it as **IL_EX_10_Billing**. Create a new worksheet in the workbook named **NH Locations**. Open the webpage Support_EX_10-6.htm in your web browser from the location where you store your Data Files. Copy the data in the four rows of the webpage table, excluding the column heading. Paste the copied data to the range A1:A4 in the NH Locations worksheet. Match the destination formatting and Autofit column A to fully display the locations. Close the webpage file Support_EX_10-6.htm, then save the workbook.

e. Activate the Jan sheet, then create a custom list based on the locations in the range A3:A9. Test the custom AutoFill list on a new worksheet in the workbook named **Locations**. Position the Locations sheet between the Jan and NH Locations sheets. Use the Custom Lists dialog box to delete the custom list from your computer. Do not delete the list of locations on the Locations sheet.

f. In the Jan sheet, add a comment to cell D5 that reads: **High Balance**.

g. Add a comment to cell A9 that reads: **Is this facility merging with Beverly?**.

h. Use the Next and Previous buttons in the Comments group of the Review tab to move between comments on the worksheet.

i. Edit the comment in cell D5 so it reads **High Balance – any ideas why?**. Show the worksheet comments and compare your Jan worksheet to FIGURE 10-25. Delete the comment in cell A9, then hide the worksheet comments.

FIGURE 10-25

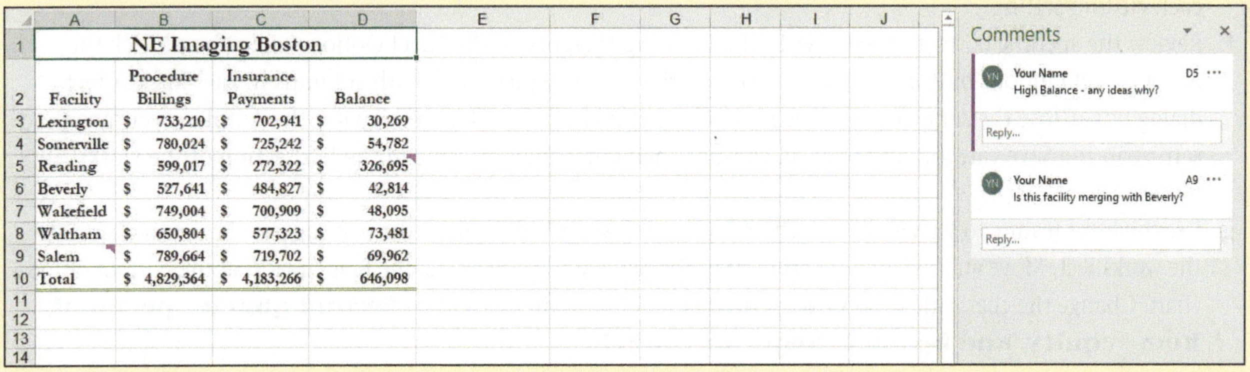

j. Use the Excel Options dialog box to review the user name as well as languages for editing, display, help, and the dictionary.

k. Add the Spelling command to the Quick Access Toolbar. Test the new button, then reset all customizations of the workbook to the defaults.

Excel

Independent Challenge 1 (continued)

l. Encrypt the workbook with the password **BilLne367$**. Test the password by saving the workbook, closing the workbook, and then opening the workbook. Remove encryption from the workbook.

m. Add your name to the center section of all the worksheet footers, then save the workbook.

n. Close the workbook, exit Excel, then submit the workbook to your instructor.

Independent Challenge 2

As the senior loan officer at South Shore Bank, one of your responsibilities is reviewing the quarterly loan portfolios for the four branches. This analysis is completed every quarter, so creating a template will simplify this process. You will also use Excel features to help with this quarterly analysis.

a. Start Excel, then open IL_EX_10-7.xlsx from the location where you store your Data Files.

b. Delete the values in the ranges B4:D7 and F4:F7. Change the label in cell F3 to **Previous Quarter Total**, change the label in cell E3 to **Total for Quarter**, change the label in cell G3 to **Quarter % Increase**, change the label in cell A10 to **Quarter Average**, then change the sheet tab name to **Quarter Report**. Save the workbook as a template with the name **IL_EX_10_QuarterAnalysis** in the location where you store your Data Files, then close the template.

c. Open a new workbook based on the template, verify the template is calculating the formulas correctly by entering test data, then close the IL_EX_10_QuarterAnalysis1 workbook without saving it.

d. Reopen IL_EX_10-7.xlsx from the location where you store your Data Files, then save it as **IL_EX_10_SecondQuarter**. Open the webpage Support_EX_10-8.htm in your browser from the location where you store your Data Files. Copy the data in the four rows of the webpage table, excluding the column heading. Activate the workbook, paste the copied data starting in cell H4 of the worksheet, matching the destination formatting. Delete column H. Enter the label **Survey Positive Rating** in cell H3. Format the new data font in the range H4:H7 as 11 point and bold so that it matches the other worksheet values.

e. Create a new set of theme colors with a custom Accent 1 color with the RGB settings of Red: **128**, Green: **157**, and Blue: **209**. Save the new theme custom colors with the name **QBlue**. Create a new set of theme fonts with both the heading and body fonts of Arial. Save the new theme font set as **QFont**. Widen the worksheet columns as necessary to display all worksheet data in the new font. Save the custom colors and fonts in a custom theme named **QTheme**. Verify the custom color palette, font set, and theme are available, then delete each custom setting.

f. Review the spelling correction settings in the Proofing category of the Excel Options dialog box. Click the AutoCorrect Options button, then review the entries in the Replace and With columns in the AutoCorrect dialog box. Close the AutoCorrect dialog box without making any changes. Review the AutoRecover save time setting in the Save category of the Excel Options then enter the save time in the left section of the worksheet footer.

g. Use the Ideas feature to see visuals that chart data in the range A3:D7. Insert the first suggested column chart into the worksheet. Move and resize the chart to fit in the range C10:G26. Delete the Branch label at the bottom of the chart. Change the chart title to **Second Quarter**. Add the alternative text **Second quarter personal, home equity, and business loans for branches**.

Independent Challenge 2 (continued)

h. Compare your worksheet to **FIGURE 10-26**. Your chart may not match the one in **FIGURE 10-26** if your Ideas pane displayed a different first column chart.

FIGURE 10-26

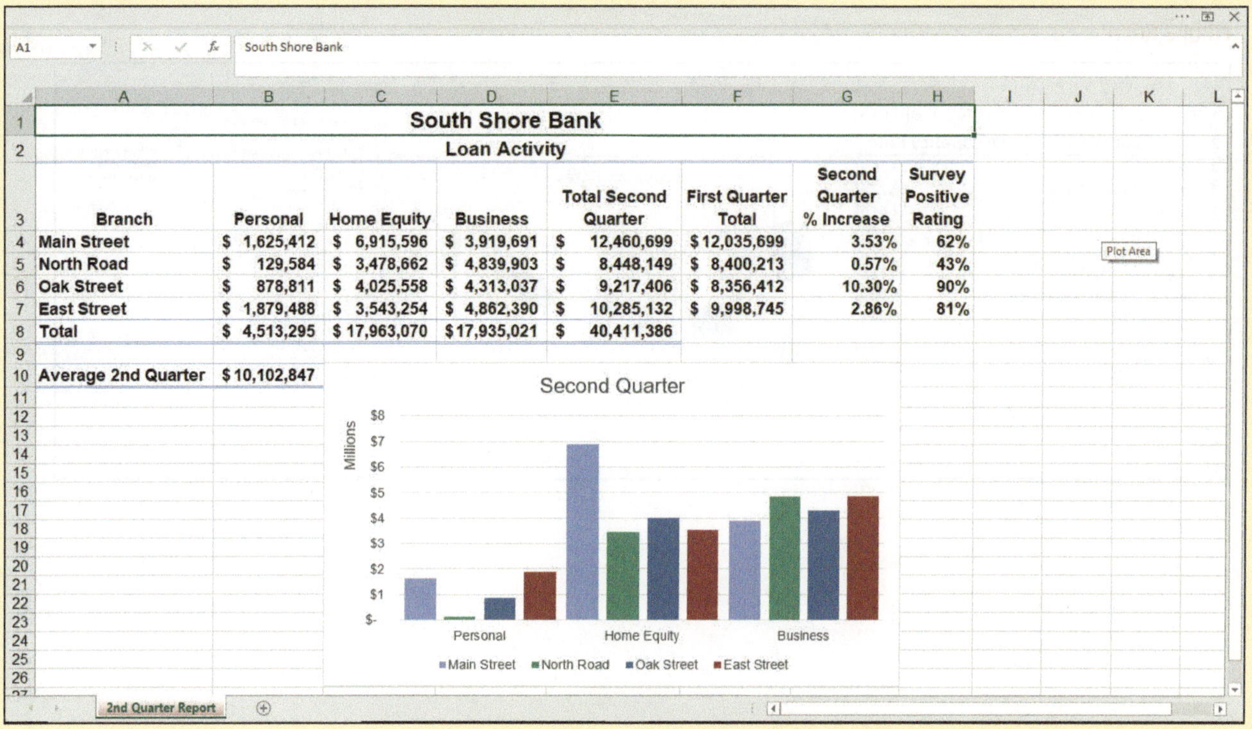

Branch	Personal	Home Equity	Business	Total Second Quarter	First Quarter Total	Second Quarter % Increase	Survey Positive Rating
Main Street	$ 1,625,412	$ 6,915,596	$ 3,919,691	$ 12,460,699	$ 12,035,699	3.53%	62%
North Road	$ 129,584	$ 3,478,662	$ 4,839,903	$ 8,448,149	$ 8,400,213	0.57%	43%
Oak Street	$ 878,811	$ 4,025,558	$ 4,313,037	$ 9,217,406	$ 8,356,412	10.30%	90%
East Street	$ 1,879,488	$ 3,543,254	$ 4,862,390	$ 10,285,132	$ 9,998,745	2.86%	81%
Total	$ 4,513,295	$ 17,963,070	$17,935,021	$ 40,411,386			

i. Add your name to the center section of the worksheet footer, then save the workbook.

j. Close the workbook, close Excel, then submit your workbook to your instructor.

Excel

Visual Workshop

Open IL_EX_10-9.xlsx from the location where you store your Data Files, then save it as **IL_EX_10_Hotels**. Import and add content as necessary so your screen matches **FIGURE 10-27**. (*Hint:* The file Support_EX_10-10.htm contains the data you need to import.) Add your name to the center section of the worksheet footer, then save the workbook. Close the workbook, close Excel, then submit the workbook to your instructor.

FIGURE 10-27

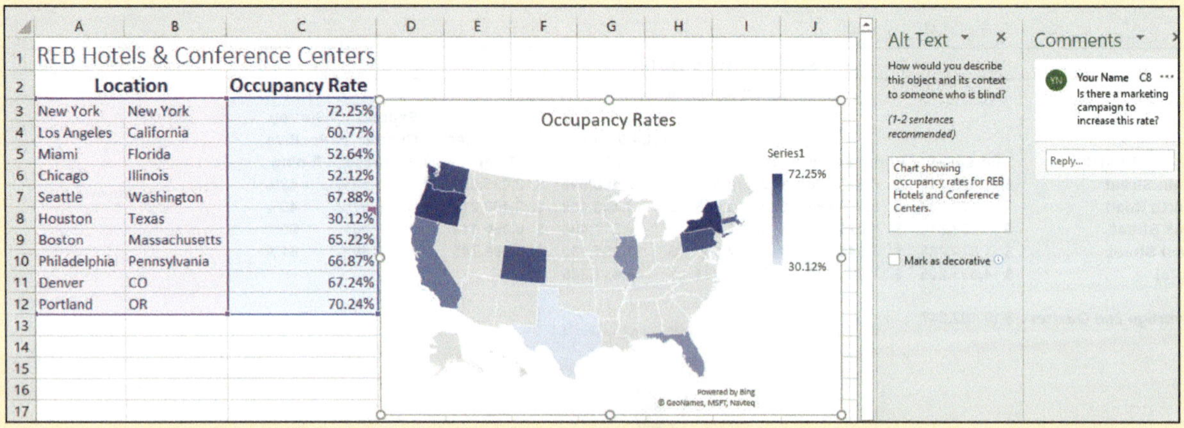

Advanced Formulas and Functions

CASE Ellie Schwartz, JCL's vice president of finance, uses Excel formulas and functions to analyze and consolidate data for the company's regions and divisions. Because management is considering adding a new regional office in the Northeast, Ellie asks you to format and summarize data from the current Northeast offices. You will compare commissions and placements in the Northeast offices and consolidate this data by division and office. Ellie also asks you to estimate the loan costs for the potential new office.

Module Objectives

After completing this module, you will be able to:

- Separate data using Flash Fill
- Format data using text functions
- Sum a data range based on conditions
- Find values based on conditions
- Construct formulas using named ranges
- Consolidate worksheet data
- Audit a worksheet
- Calculate payments with the PMT function

Files You Will Need

IL_EX_11-1.xlsx
IL_EX_11-2.xlsx
IL_EX_11-3.xlsx
IL_EX_11-4.xlsx
IL_EX_11-5.xlsx

Separate Data Using Flash Fill

Learning Outcome
- Separate data into columns

Often, you need to import data into Excel from an outside source, such as another program or the Internet. Sometimes multiple data fields are imported in a single column. You can easily break the fields into separate columns using the Flash Fill feature. CASE *Ellie requested data from the Human Resources Department on recruiters who expressed interest in working at the new office and the divisions in which they specialize, so she can assess future hiring needs. After importing this data into Excel, you notice that the position and division fields were mistakenly combined into one column.*

STEPS

1. **sam Start Excel, open IL_EX_11-1.xlsx from the location where you store your Data Files, then save it as IL_EX_11_NE**
2. **On the Recruiters sheet click cell D2, type Technical, press TAB, in cell E2 type Senior Recruiter, then click the Enter button ✓ in the formula bar**
   You manually separated the data in cell C2 into the adjacent cells, as shown in FIGURE 11-1, by entering the correct data in each cell. Completing this task provides an example for Flash Fill to use to complete the rows below. **Flash Fill** looks for patterns in the data you enter and automatically fills or formats data in remaining cells based on those patterns.
3. **With cell E2 selected click Fill in the Editing group on the ribbon, then click Flash Fill**
   The positions from column C are copied into the range E3:E13.
4. **Select cell D2, click Fill in the Editing group, then click Flash Fill**
   The divisions from Column C are copied into the range D3:D13.
5. **Move the Position label from cell D1 to cell E1, click cell D1, type Division, then press ENTER**
6. **Widen columns D and E to fully display the data, then compare your work to FIGURE 11-2**
7. **Save your work**

FIGURE 11-1: Worksheet with data separated into columns

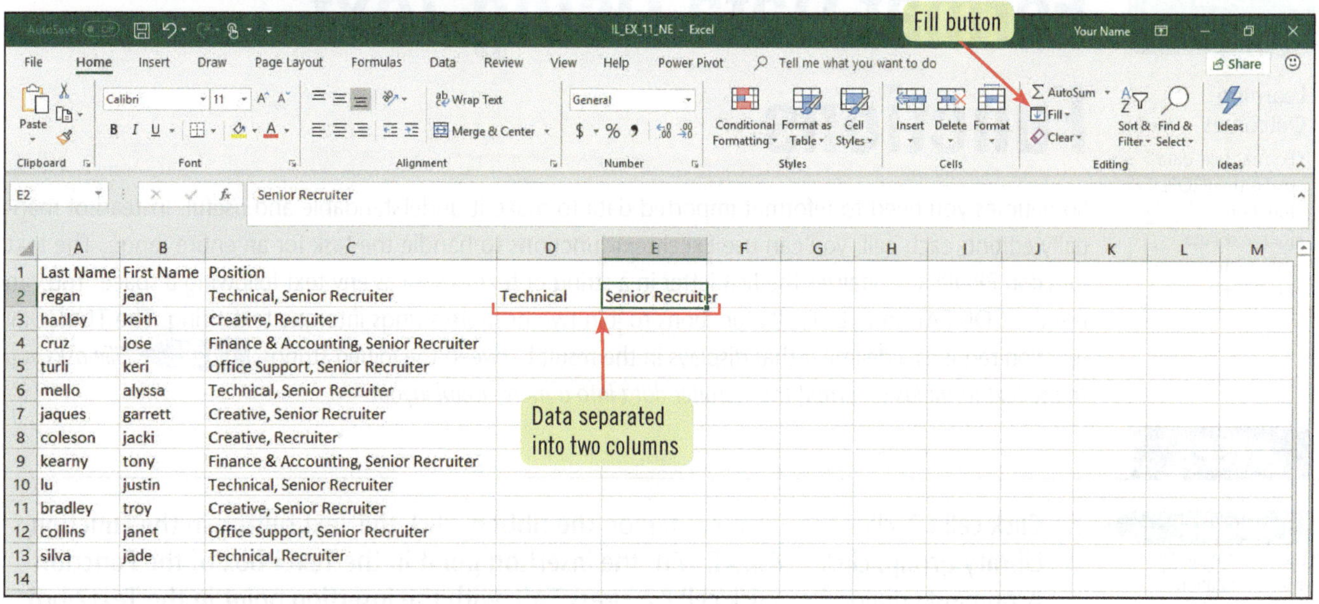

FIGURE 11-2: Worksheet with data formatted in columns

	A	B	C	D	E	F
1	Last Name	First Name	Position	Division	Position	
2	regan	jean	Technical, Senior Recruiter	Technical	Senior Recruiter	
3	hanley	keith	Creative, Recruiter	Creative	Recruiter	
4	cruz	jose	Finance & Accounting, Senior Recruiter	Finance & Accounting	Senior Recruiter	
5	turli	keri	Office Support, Senior Recruiter	Office Support	Senior Recruiter	
6	mello	alyssa	Technical, Senior Recruiter	Technical	Senior Recruiter	
7	jaques	garrett	Creative, Senior Recruiter	Creative	Senior Recruiter	
8	coleson	jacki	Creative, Recruiter	Creative	Recruiter	
9	kearny	tony	Finance & Accounting, Senior Recruiter	Finance & Accounting	Senior Recruiter	
10	lu	justin	Technical, Senior Recruiter	Technical	Senior Recruiter	
11	bradley	troy	Creative, Senior Recruiter	Creative	Senior Recruiter	
12	collins	janet	Office Support, Senior Recruiter	Office Support	Senior Recruiter	
13	silva	jade	Technical, Recruiter	Technical	Recruiter	
14						

Working with Excel series

You can use Excel fill series to generate worksheet data based on linear or growth trends. For example, if you want to review payments for a range of interest rates between 4% and 5%, you can fill a worksheet series with interest rates increasing by a desired amount. To fill the series, enter the starting percentage in a cell, click the Home tab on the ribbon, click the Fill button in the Editing group, click Series, in the Series dialog box select the Rows or Columns options button indicating where the results will be placed, verify the Linear option button is selected in the Type category, in the Step value box enter the increase amount for each subsequent value, in the Stop value box enter the final amount, then click OK. In a situation where you need values to increase by a certain percentage each year, you need to use an exponential growth series, also called a growth trend. To create a growth trend, select the Growth option button in the Type category of the Series dialog box, enter the growth amount in the Step value box, then click OK. For example if you wanted a sales target to increase by 20 percent each year you would enter 1.2 in the Step value box. If the Stop value is blank the values are calculated using the step value as the growth trend.

Excel
Module 11

Learning Outcomes
- Format text data using the PROPER function
- Join text data using a text function

Format Data Using Text Functions

Sometimes you need to reformat imported data to make it understandable and useful. Instead of manually editing each cell, you can use Excel text functions to handle the task for an entire range. The text function PROPER capitalizes the first letter in a string of text as well as any text following a space. You can use the CONCAT and TEXTJOIN functions to join two or more strings into one text string. The TEXTJOIN function requires a delimiter that displays in the result between the joined strings. **CASE** *Ellie asks you to use text formulas to format the recruiter data into a more useful layout.*

STEPS

QUICK TIP
Excel automatically inserts quotation marks to enclose the space.

QUICK TIP
The CONCAT function replaces CONCATENATE from earlier versions of Excel. CONCATENATE remains available in Excel for compatibility purposes.

1. **Click cell F2, click the Formulas tab on the ribbon, click the Text button in the Function Library group, click CONCAT, with the insertion point in the Text1 box of the Function Arguments dialog box click cell B2, press TAB, with the insertion point in the Text2 box press SPACEBAR, press TAB, with the insertion point in the Text3 box click cell A2, then click OK**
2. **Drag the fill handle + to copy the formula in cell F2 into the range F3:F13, then widen column F to fully display the data in the column**
3. **Click cell G2, click the Text button in the Function Library group, click PROPER, with the insertion point in the Text box of the Function Arguments dialog box click cell F2, click OK, then compare your worksheet to FIGURE 11-3**
   The name is copied from cell F2 to cell G2 with the correct uppercase letters for proper names.
4. **Copy the formula in cell G2 into the range G3:G13, then widen column G to fully display the data in the column**
5. **Click cell H2, click the Text button in the Function Library group, click TEXTJOIN, with the insertion point in the Delimiter box of the Function Arguments dialog box press SPACEBAR, press TAB, with the insertion point in the Ignore_empty box press TAB to accept the default, with the insertion point in the Text1 box click cell D2, press TAB, with the insertion point in the Text2 box type Careers, then click OK**
   Like CONCAT, the TEXTJOIN function joins strings of text; however, you enter the delimiter in the Delimiter box of the Function Arguments dialog box rather than in the Text box.
6. **Copy the formula in cell H2 into the range H3:H13, then widen column H to fully display the data in the column**
7. **Select the range G2:H13, click the Home tab, click the Copy button in the Clipboard group, click cell I1, click the Paste button arrow in the Clipboard group, click Values button in the Paste Values category, then press ESC**
8. **Select columns A through H, click the Delete button in the Cells group, then widen column A to fully display the names in the column**
   Compare your worksheet to FIGURE 11-4.
9. **Save your work**

FIGURE 11-3: Names with Proper formatting

	A	B	C	D	E	F	G	H	I
1	Last Name	First Name	Position	Division	Position				
2	regan	jean	Technical, Senior Recruiter	Technical	Senior Recruiter	jean regan	Jean Regan		
3	hanley	keith	Creative, Recruiter	Creative	Recruiter	keith hanley			
4	cruz	jose	Finance & Accounting, Senior Recruiter	Finance & Accounting	Senior Recruiter	jose cruz			
5	turli	keri	Office Support, Senior Recruiter	Office Support	Senior Recruiter	keri turli			
6	mello	alyssa	Technical, Senior Recruiter	Technical	Senior Recruiter	alyssa mello			
7	jaques	garrett	Creative, Senior Recruiter	Creative	Senior Recruiter	garrett jaqu			
8	coleson	jacki	Creative, Recruiter	Creative	Recruiter	jacki coleso.			
9	kearny	tony	Finance & Accounting, Senior Recruiter	Finance & Accounting	Senior Recruiter	tony kearny			
10	lu	justin	Technical, Senior Recruiter	Technical	Senior Recruiter	justin lu			
11	bradley	troy	Creative, Senior Recruiter	Creative	Senior Recruiter	troy bradley			
12	collins	janet	Office Support, Senior Recruiter	Office Support	Senior Recruiter	janet collins			
13	silva	jade	Technical, Recruiter	Technical	Recruiter	jade silva			
14									

Name in Proper format

FIGURE 11-4: Worksheet with data formatted using Text functions

	A	B	C	D	E	F	G	H	I	J	K	L
1	Jean Regan	Technical Careers										
2	Keith Hanley	Creative Careers										
3	Jose Cruz	Finance & Accounting Careers										
4	Keri Turli	Office Support Careers										
5	Alyssa Mello	Technical Careers										
6	Garrett Jaques	Creative Careers										
7	Jacki Coleson	Creative Careers										
8	Tony Kearny	Finance & Accounting Careers										
9	Justin Lu	Technical Careers										
10	Troy Bradley	Creative Careers										
11	Janet Collins	Office Support Careers										
12	Jade Silva	Technical Careers										
13												

Working with other text functions

Other useful text functions include UPPER, LOWER, SUBSTITUTE, LEN, RIGHT, LEFT, and MID. UPPER converts text to all uppercase letters, LOWER converts text to all lowercase letters, SUBSTITUTE replaces text in a text string, and LEN displays the number of characters in a string of text. For example, if cell A1 contains the text string "Today is Wednesday", then =LOWER(A1) would produce "today is wednesday"; =UPPER(A1) would produce "TODAY IS WEDNESDAY"; =SUBSTITUTE(A1, "Wednesday", "Tuesday") would result in "Today is Tuesday"; and =LEN(A1) would result in 18. You can also use functions to display one or more characters at certain locations within a string. Use RIGHT to find the last characters with the syntax =RIGHT(string, # characters), where # is the number of characters you want to display, such as the last 3. Similarly, use LEFT to find the first characters with the syntax =LEFT(string, # characters), or MID to display the middle characters with the syntax =MID(string, starting character, # characters).

Excel

Sum a Data Range Based on Conditions

Learning Outcomes
- Total data using the SUMIF function
- Summarize data using the AVERAGEIF function

You can use Excel functions to sum and average data in a range based on criteria, or conditions, you set. The SUMIF function totals only the cells in a range that meet given criteria. The AVERAGEIF function averages values in a range based on a specified condition. The format for the SUMIF function appears in FIGURE 11-5. **CASE** *Ellie asks you to analyze the Boston office's placement data to provide her with information about each division, including the commission for the technical divisions.*

STEPS

1. **Click the Boston sheet tab, click cell I2, click the Formulas tab on the ribbon, click the Math & Trig button in the Function Library group, scroll down the list of functions, then click SUMIF**

   The Function Arguments dialog box opens.

2. **With the insertion point in the Range box select the range C2:C65, press F4, press TAB, with the insertion point in the Criteria box click cell H2, press TAB, with the insertion point in the Sum_range box select the range E2:E65, press F4, then click OK**

   Your formula, as shown in the formula bar in FIGURE 11-6, asks Excel to search the range C2:C65, and where it finds the value in cell H2, Technical, to add the corresponding amount from column E. The result, the total commission for the technical divisions, appears in cell I2.

3. **Click cell J2, click the More Functions button in the Function Library group, point to Statistical, then click AVERAGEIF**

4. **With the insertion point in the Range box select the range C2:C65, press F4, press TAB, with the insertion point in the Criteria box click cell H2, press TAB, with the insertion point in the Average_range box select the range E2:E65, press F4, then click OK**

   The average commission for the technical division placements, 4736.39, appears in cell J2.

5. **Select the range I2:J2, then drag the fill handle + to fill the range I3:J5**

6. **Click cell I6, click the Math & Trig button in the Function Library group, scroll down the list of functions, then click SUMIFS**

   The SUMIFS function allows you to sum ranges with multiple criteria.

7. **With the insertion point in the Sum_range box select the range E2:E65, press F4, press TAB, with the insertion point in the Criteria_range1 box select the range C2:C65, press F4, press TAB, with the insertion point in the Criteria1 box, type Technical, press TAB, with the insertion point in the Criteria_range2 box select the range D2:D65, press F4, press TAB, with the insertion point in the Criteria2 box type Full-time, then click OK**

   The total commissions for the Technical division's full-time placements, 26397, appears in cell I6.

8. **With cell I6 selected, drag the fill handle + to cell J6, click cell J6, verify that cell I6 is no longer selected, select SUM in the SUMIFS formula displayed in the formula bar, type AVERAGE, then click the Enter button ✓ in the formula bar**

   After copying the formula from cell I6, you edited it to contain the AVERAGEIFS function, which averages ranges with multiple criteria. Cell J2 displays the average commission for the Technical division's full-time placements, as shown in FIGURE 11-7.

9. **Save your work**

FIGURE 11-5: Format of SUMIF function

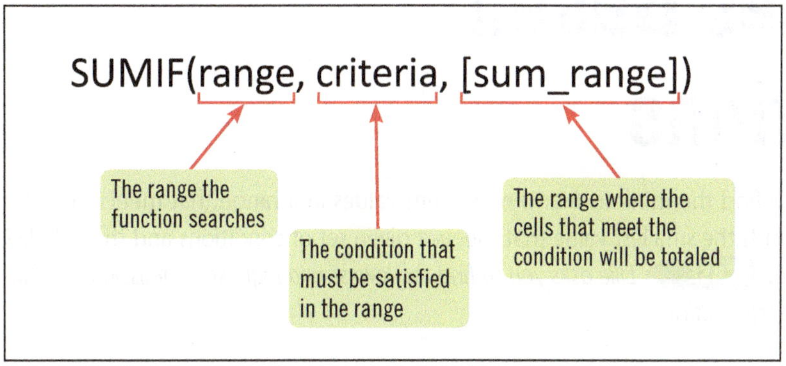

FIGURE 11-6: SUMIF function in the formula bar

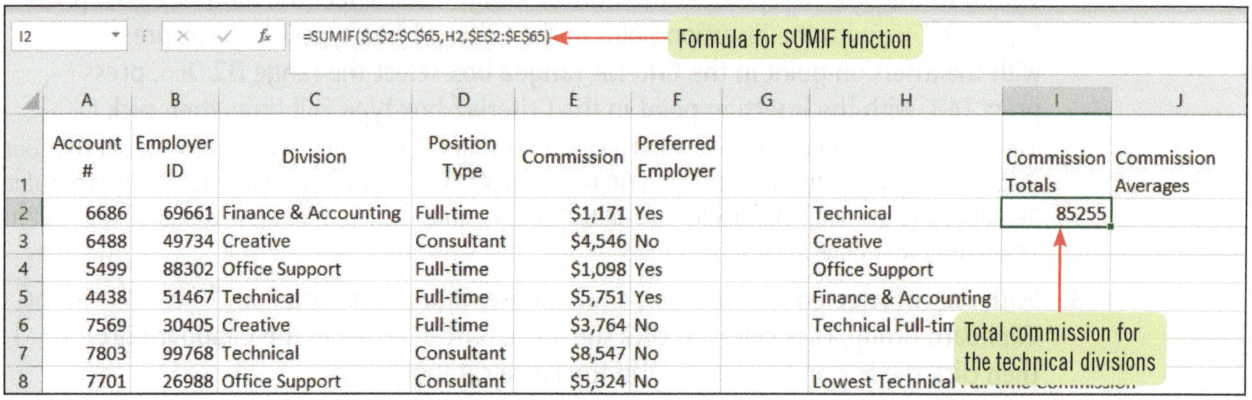

	A	B	C	D	E	F	G	H	I	J
1	Account #	Employer ID	Division	Position Type	Commission	Preferred Employer			Commission Totals	Commission Averages
2	6686	69661	Finance & Accounting	Full-time	$1,171	Yes		Technical	85255	
3	6488	49734	Creative	Consultant	$4,546	No		Creative		
4	5499	88302	Office Support	Full-time	$1,098	Yes		Office Support		
5	4438	51467	Technical	Full-time	$5,751	Yes		Finance & Accounting		
6	7569	30405	Creative	Full-time	$3,764	No		Technical Full-tim		
7	7803	99768	Technical	Consultant	$8,547	No				
8	7701	26988	Office Support	Consultant	$5,324	No		Lowest Technical		

FIGURE 11-7: AVERAGEIFS function

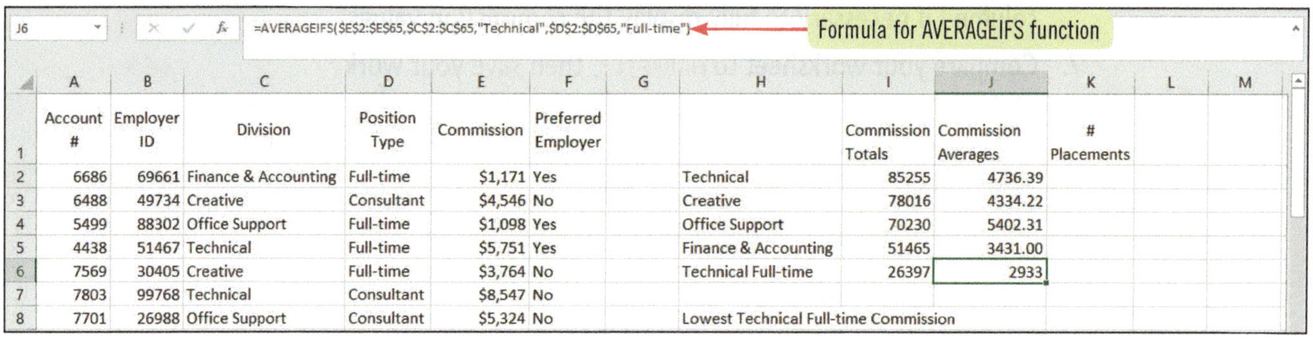

	A	B	C	D	E	F	G	H	I	J	K	L	M
1	Account #	Employer ID	Division	Position Type	Commission	Preferred Employer			Commission Totals	Commission Averages	# Placements		
2	6686	69661	Finance & Accounting	Full-time	$1,171	Yes		Technical	85255	4736.39			
3	6488	49734	Creative	Consultant	$4,546	No		Creative	78016	4334.22			
4	5499	88302	Office Support	Full-time	$1,098	Yes		Office Support	70230	5402.31			
5	4438	51467	Technical	Full-time	$5,751	Yes		Finance & Accounting	51465	3431.00			
6	7569	30405	Creative	Full-time	$3,764	No		Technical Full-time	26397	2933			
7	7803	99768	Technical	Consultant	$8,547	No							
8	7701	26988	Office Support	Consultant	$5,324	No		Lowest Technical Full-time Commission					

Excel Module 11

Find Values Based on Conditions

Learning Outcomes
- Find a minimum value using the MINIFS function
- Find a maximum value using the MAXIFS function

You can use Excel functions to find the minimum and maximum values in a range that meets multiple criteria. The MINIFs function finds the smallest value that meets a given set of conditions and the MAXIFS function finds the largest value. **CASE** *Ellie asks you to find the lowest and highest commissions for full-time technical positions in the Boston office.*

STEPS

1. **Click cell H9, click the Insert Function button in the Function Library group, in the Insert Function dialog box type MINIFS in the Search for a function box, click Go, in the Select a function box verify that MINIFS is selected, then click OK**
2. **With the insertion point in the Min_range box select the range E2:E65, press F4, press TAB, with the insertion point in the Criteria_range1 box select the range C2:C65, press F4, press TAB, with the insertion point in the Criteria1 box type Technical, press TAB, with the insertion point in the Criteria_range2 box select the range D2:D65, press F4, press TAB, with the insertion point in the Criteria2 box type Full-time, then click OK**

   The lowest commission for the technical division's full-time placements, 1311, appears in cell H9. Your formula, as shown in the formula bar in FIGURE 11-8, asks Excel to search the range C2:C65 for the value Technical and the range D2:D65 for the value Full-time, and when both of those conditions are met to return the lowest value in the range E2:E65.
3. **With cell H9 selected click the Home tab on the ribbon, click the Copy button in the Clipboard group, click cell H11, click the Paste button arrow in the Clipboard group, then click the Formulas button in the Paste category**

   The MINIFS formula is pasted in cell H11 and appears in the formula bar.
4. **Press ESC, verify cell H11 is selected, select MIN in the MINIFS formula in the formula bar, type MAX, then click the Enter button in the formula bar**

   The formula is edited to find the maximum value in the commission range for the technical division's full-time placements rather than the minimum, and the result, 9268, appears in cell H11.
5. **Select the range I2:J6, press and hold CTRL, click cell H9, then click cell H11**
6. **Click the Accounting Number Format button in the Number group, then widen column I if necessary to fully display the commission values**
7. **Compare your worksheet to FIGURE 11-9, then save your work**

FIGURE 11-8: MINIFS function

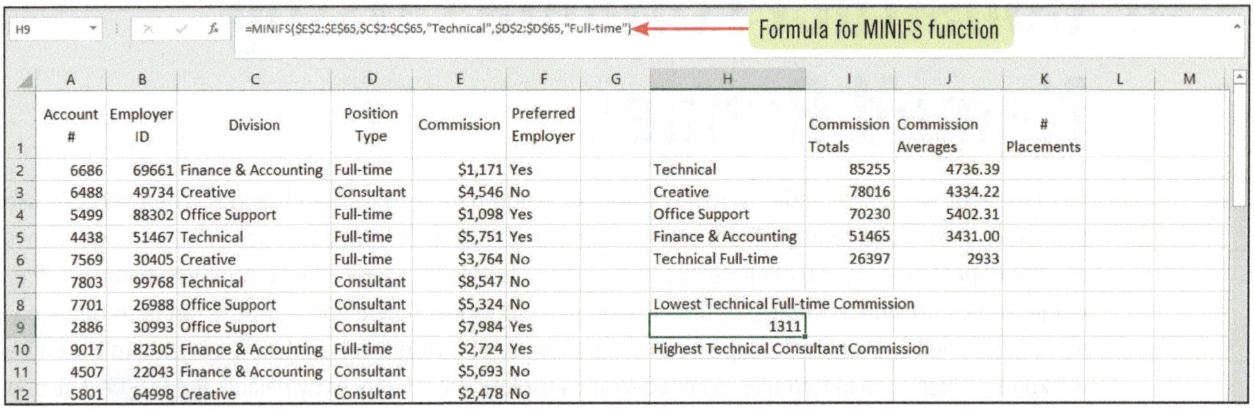

	A	B	C	D	E	F	G	H	I	J	K
1	Account #	Employer ID	Division	Position Type	Commission	Preferred Employer			Commission Totals	Commission Averages	# Placements
2	6686	69661	Finance & Accounting	Full-time	$1,171	Yes		Technical	85255	4736.39	
3	6488	49734	Creative	Consultant	$4,546	No		Creative	78016	4334.22	
4	5499	88302	Office Support	Full-time	$1,098	Yes		Office Support	70230	5402.31	
5	4438	51467	Technical	Full-time	$5,751	Yes		Finance & Accounting	51465	3431.00	
6	7569	30405	Creative	Full-time	$3,764	No		Technical Full-time	26397	2933	
7	7803	99768	Technical	Consultant	$8,547	No					
8	7701	26988	Office Support	Consultant	$5,324	No		Lowest Technical Full-time Commission			
9	2886	30993	Office Support	Consultant	$7,984	Yes		1311			
10	9017	82305	Finance & Accounting	Full-time	$2,724	Yes		Highest Technical Consultant Commission			
11	4507	22043	Finance & Accounting	Consultant	$5,693	No					
12	5801	64998	Creative	Consultant	$2,478	No					

FIGURE 11-9: Formatted commissions

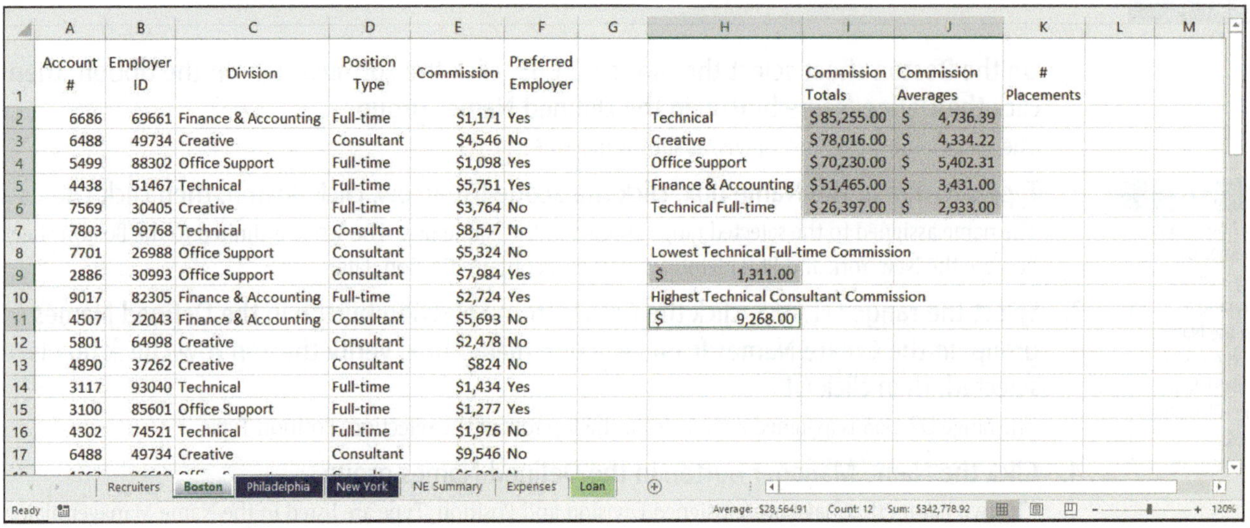

	A	B	C	D	E	F	G	H	I	J	K
1	Account #	Employer ID	Division	Position Type	Commission	Preferred Employer			Commission Totals	Commission Averages	# Placements
2	6686	69661	Finance & Accounting	Full-time	$1,171	Yes		Technical	$ 85,255.00	$ 4,736.39	
3	6488	49734	Creative	Consultant	$4,546	No		Creative	$ 78,016.00	$ 4,334.22	
4	5499	88302	Office Support	Full-time	$1,098	Yes		Office Support	$ 70,230.00	$ 5,402.31	
5	4438	51467	Technical	Full-time	$5,751	Yes		Finance & Accounting	$ 51,465.00	$ 3,431.00	
6	7569	30405	Creative	Full-time	$3,764	No		Technical Full-time	$ 26,397.00	$ 2,933.00	
7	7803	99768	Technical	Consultant	$8,547	No					
8	7701	26988	Office Support	Consultant	$5,324	No		Lowest Technical Full-time Commission			
9	2886	30993	Office Support	Consultant	$7,984	Yes		$ 1,311.00			
10	9017	82305	Finance & Accounting	Full-time	$2,724	Yes		Highest Technical Consultant Commission			
11	4507	22043	Finance & Accounting	Consultant	$5,693	No		$ 9,268.00			
12	5801	64998	Creative	Consultant	$2,478	No					
13	4890	37262	Creative	Consultant	$824	No					
14	3117	93040	Technical	Full-time	$1,434	Yes					
15	3100	85601	Office Support	Full-time	$1,277	Yes					
16	4302	74521	Technical	Full-time	$1,976	No					
17	6488	49734	Creative	Consultant	$9,546	No					

Working with logical functions

IF functions such as MINIFS and MAXIFS are in the logical category in the function library. Other logical functions include IFS and SWITCH. You can use IFS when you are using nested IF functions, to check a condition or conditions and display the value shown for the first true condition. For example, in **FIGURE 11-10**, the IFS function in cell B2 displays the letter grade that corresponds to the numeric grade in cell A2. The SWITCH function looks for a matching value and displays text to switch with it. In the example shown here, the formula in cell C2 is =SWITCH(B2,"A","Excellent","B","Good","C","Fair", "D","Poor","F","Failing"). This function looks at the letter grade in cell B2 and displays the corresponding value.

FIGURE 11-10: Logical functions

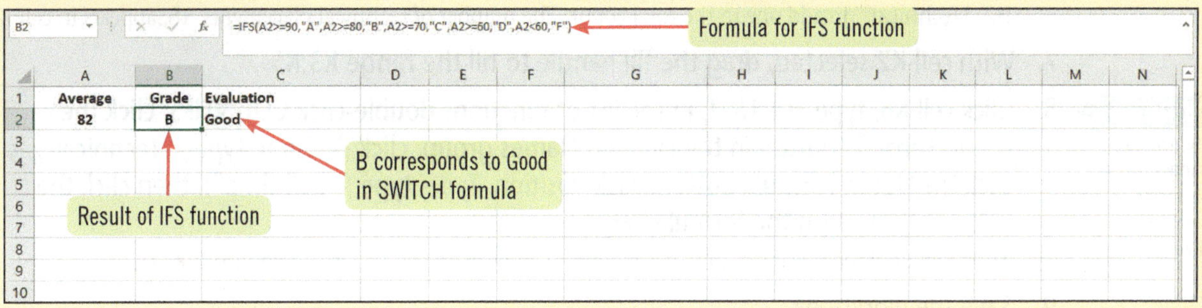

Excel Module 11

Learning Outcomes
- Assign names to cell ranges
- Build formulas using names

Construct Formulas Using Named Ranges

To make your worksheet easier to follow, you can assign names to cells and ranges. Then you can use the names in formulas to make them easier to build and to reduce formula errors. Cell and range names can use uppercase or lowercase letters as well as digits but cannot have spaces. After you name a cell or range, you can define its **scope**, or the location in a worksheet where you want the range to be recognized. When defining a name's scope, you can limit its use to a worksheet or make it available to the entire workbook. When used in formulas, names become absolute cell references by default. CASE *Ellie asks you to calculate the number of placements for each division. You will use range names to construct the formula.*

STEPS

1. **On the Boston sheet select the range C2:C65, click the Formulas tab on the ribbon, then click the Define Name button in the Defined Names group**
   The New Name dialog box opens, as shown in FIGURE 11-11.

2. **Type Division in the Name box, click the Scope list arrow, click Boston, then click OK**
   The name assigned to the selected range appears in the Name Box. The scope is limited to the Boston sheet because the New York and Philadelphia sheets also contain division data.

3. **Select the range D1:D65, click the Create from Selection button in the Defined Names group, in the Create Names from Selection dialog box, verify the Top row check box is selected, then click OK**
   The range D2:D65 is assigned a name from the top row of the selection, Position Type.

4. **Click the Name Manager button in the Defined Names group**
   The two names that have been assigned Division and Position_Type are listed in the Name Manager dialog box, as shown in FIGURE 11-12. Excel added an underscore (_) between *Position* and *Type* because range names cannot contain spaces. The Name Manager can be used to create, delete, and edit names in a workbook.

5. **Click Close, click cell K2, click the More Functions button in the Function Library group, point to Statistical, scroll down the list of functions if necessary, then click COUNTIF**
   Like SUMIF and AVERAGEIF, the COUNTIF function allows you to specify conditions. COUNTIF counts cells based on those specified conditions.

6. **With the insertion point in the Range box type Division, press TAB, with the insertion point in the Criteria box click cell H2, then click OK**
   Your formula asks Excel to search the range named Division, and where it finds the value shown in cell H2, "Technical," to add one to the total count. The number of technical placements, 18, appears in cell K2.

7. **With cell K2 selected, drag the fill handle to fill the range K3:K5**

8. **Click cell K6, type =COUNT, in the list of functions double-click COUNTIFS, click the Use in Formula button in the Defined Names group, click Division, type , "Technical",, click the Use in Formula button, click Position_Type, type , "Full-time"), then click the Enter button ✓ in the formula bar**
   The number of technical full-time placements, 9, appears in cell K6, as shown in FIGURE 11-13.

9. **Save the workbook**

QUICK TIP
You can also create range names by selecting a cell or range, typing a name in the Name Box, then pressing ENTER. By default, its scope will be the workbook.

QUICK TIP
The COUNTBLANK function, which is entered as =COUNTBLANK(range), counts the number of empty cells in a range of cells.

QUICK TIP
You can use named cells and ranges to navigate in a worksheet by selecting a name in the Name box.

FIGURE 11-11: New Name dialog box

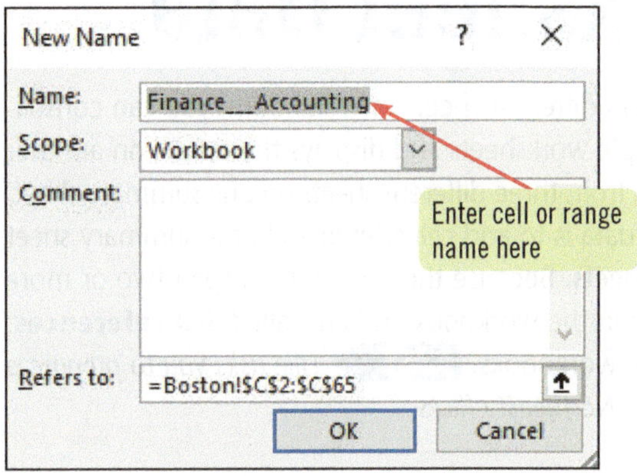

FIGURE 11-12: Name Manager dialog box

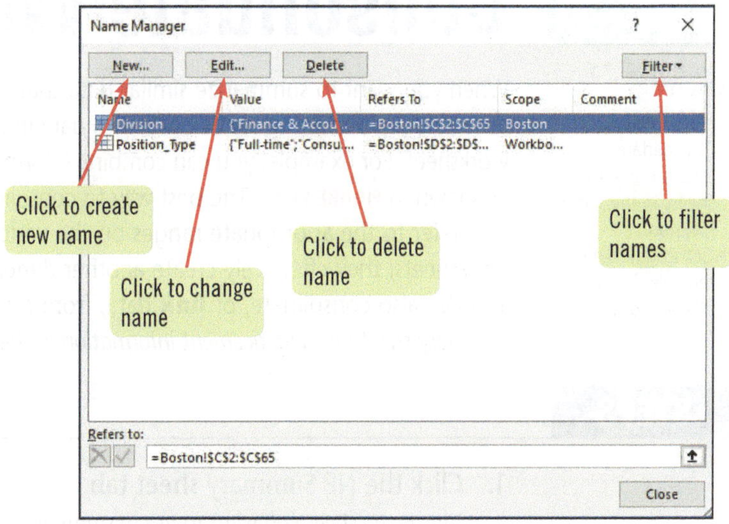

FIGURE 11-13: Worksheet with placement information

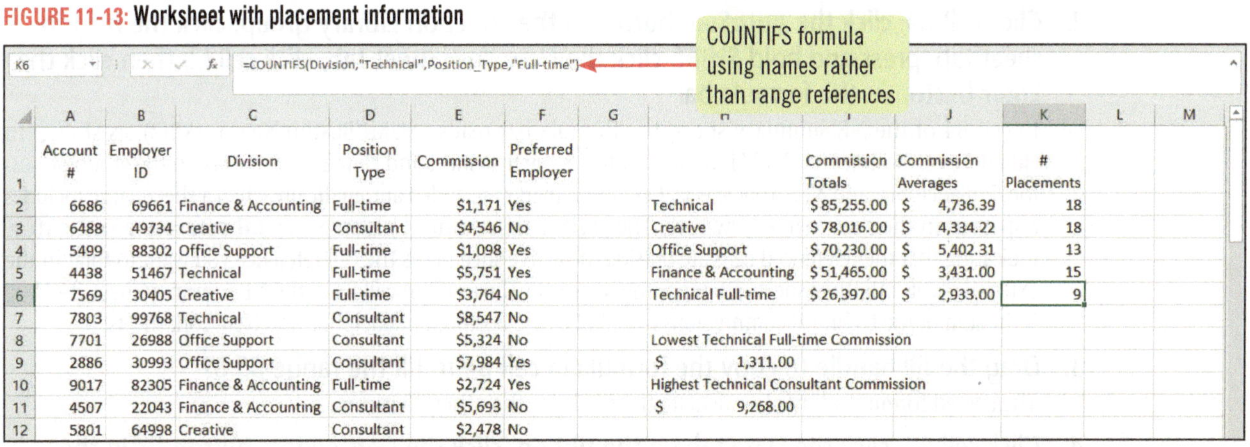

Using formulas to conditionally format data

You can use a formula to format worksheet data by entering it in a conditional formatting rule. To create a conditional formatting rule with a formula, select the cells you want to format, click the Home tab on the ribbon, click the Conditional Formatting button in the Styles group, then click New Rule. In the New Formatting Rule dialog box, click Use a formula to determine which cells to format, enter the formula in the Format values where this formula is true box, click the Format button, choose a format, then click OK. For example, applying the formatting rule shown in FIGURE 11-14 formats the selected range E2:E17 using blue fill.

FIGURE 11-14: Conditional formatting rule with formula

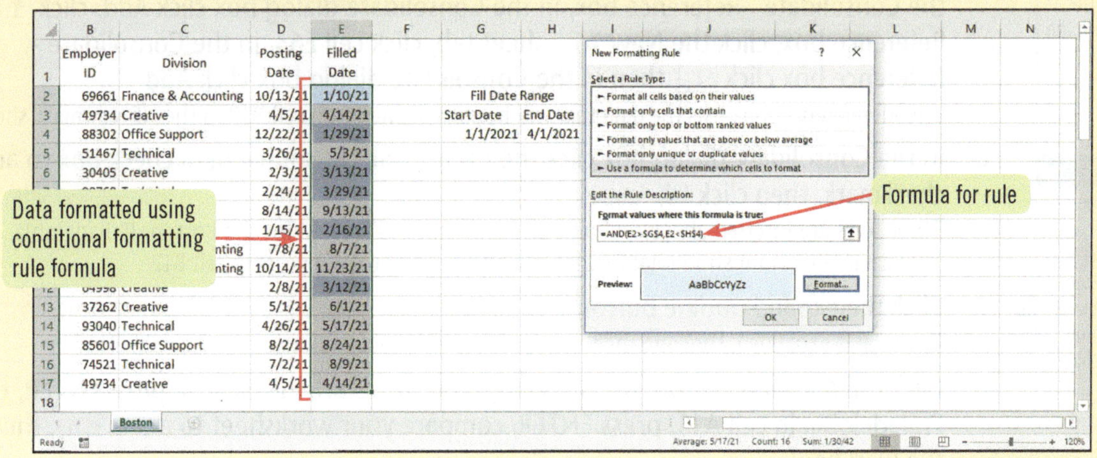

Excel

Consolidate Worksheet Data

Learning Outcomes
- Consolidate data on multiple sheets in the same location
- Consolidate data on multiple sheets in different locations

When you want to summarize similar data that exists in different sheets or workbooks, you can consolidate it. **Consolidating data** combines data in multiple worksheets and displays the results on another worksheet. For example, you can combine information from three different sheets on one summary sheet, as shown in FIGURE 11-15. The best way to consolidate data is to add cell references in the summary sheet that refer to the appropriate ranges on the various sheets. Because these references span two or more worksheets, they effectively create another dimension in the workbook and are called **3-D references**. You can also consolidate, or **link** data, from separate workbooks. CASE *Ellie asks you to prepare a summary sheet for the placement information in the three Northeast offices.*

STEPS

1. **Click the NE Summary sheet tab**

   This is the sheet you want to use to summarize the placement data contained in the other sheets.

2. **Click cell B4, click the AutoSum button in the Function Library group, click the Boston sheet tab, press and hold SHIFT, click the New York sheet tab, click cell I2, then click the Enter button in the formula bar**

   In cell B4 of the NE Summary sheet, the formula bar reads =SUM('Boston:New York'!I2), as shown in FIGURE 11-16. 'Boston:New York' indicates Boston is the first sheet and New York is the last in the group of Boston, Philadelphia, and New York sheets. Quotation marks are added automatically when a sheet name includes a space as in the sheet name New York. The exclamation point (!) is an **external reference indicator**, indicating that the referenced cells are outside the active sheet; I2 is the cell reference you want to total in the external sheets. All three sheets reference the same cell. The result in cell B4 of the NE Summary sheet, 153488, is the sum of the technical commissions in cell I2 of the Boston, Philadelphia, and New York sheets.

3. **Drag the fill handle to copy the formula in cell B4 to fill the range B5:B7**

   The copied formula adjusts to calculate the totals for the other divisions.

4. **Click cell B9, click the Data tab on the ribbon, click the Consolidate button in the Data Tools group, in the Consolidate dialog box verify Sum is selected in the Function box, click the Collapse dialog box button in the Reference box, click the Boston Sheet tab, click cell E66, click the Expand dialog box button in the Consolidate - Reference box, then click Add in the Consolidate dialog box**

   The Consolidate dialog box offers an alternative to using the formula bar to enter external references and consolidates worksheet data located in different ranges of a workbook. The Boston sheet reference to cell E66 is added to the All references box.

QUICK TIP
Entering the formula =SUM(Boston!E66+ Philadelphia!E61+ 'New York'!E63) in cell B12 of the NE Summary worksheet to consolidate the data will result in the same total.

5. **Click in the Reference box, click the Philadelphia sheet tab, click cell E61, click in the Consolidate - Reference box, in the Consolidate dialog box click Add, click in the Reference box, click the New York sheet tab, click cell E63, in the Consolidate - Reference box click , then in the Consolidate dialog box click Add**

   The All references box lists the data that will be consolidated into cell B12 in the NE Summary sheet.

6. **In the Consolidate dialog box click the Create links to source data check box to add a checkmark, then click OK**

   Three rows are inserted above row nine and an outline is created for the Boston, Philadelphia, and New York data. The commission total for all three offices, $510,618, appears in cell B12.

QUICK TIP
You can click the level 2 Outline Symbol button 2 to display the total details and the level 1 Outline Symbol button 1 to hide the details.

7. **Click the expand outline button**

   The total is expanded, showing the totals from the individual offices in the range B9:B11.

8. **Click cell A9, type Boston, press ENTER, type New York in cell A10, press ENTER, type Philadelphia in cell A11, press ENTER, compare your worksheet to FIGURE 11-17, then save the workbook**

FIGURE 11-15: Consolidating data from three worksheets

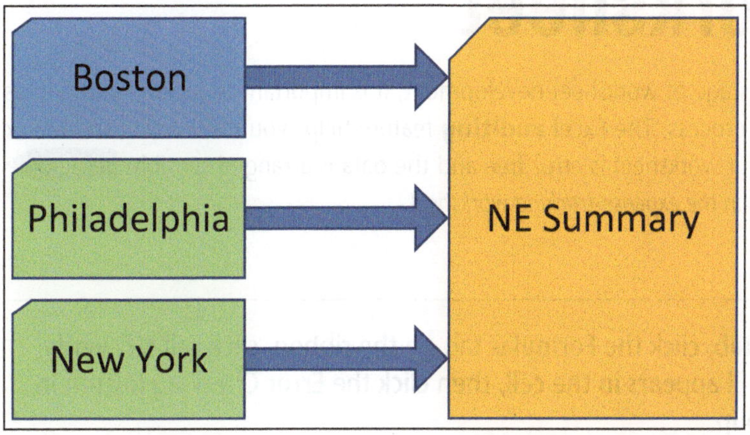

FIGURE 11-16: 3-D reference in formula

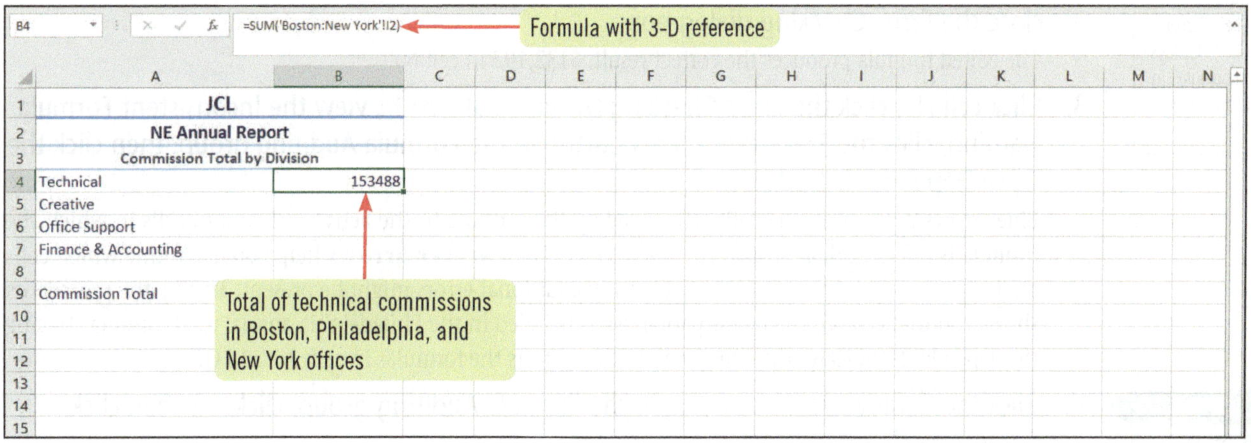

FIGURE 11-17: NE Summary worksheet with totals

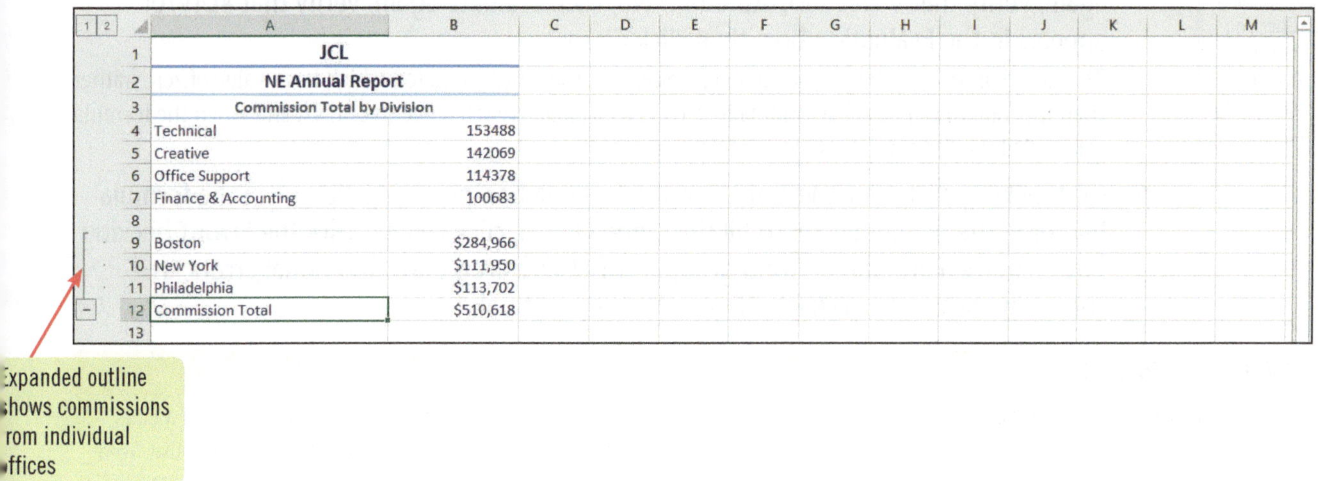

Excel
Module 11

Audit a Worksheet

Learning Outcomes
- Locate formula errors
- Correct formula errors

Because errors can occur at any stage of worksheet development, it is important to include auditing as part of your workbook-building process. The Excel **auditing** feature helps you track errors and check worksheet logic to make sure your worksheet is error free and the data is arranged sensibly. CASE *Ellie asks you to help identify errors in the expense-tracking worksheet.*

STEPS

QUICK TIP
You can use the IFERROR function to display a message that you specify if there is an error in a formula; for example, if editing the formula in cell N7 to =IFERROR(N3+N4+N5+N6, "Error in Formula") displays "Error in Formula" in cell N7 rather than #VALUE!.

1. **Click the Expenses sheet tab, click the Formulas tab on the ribbon, click cell N7, verify the error message #VALUE! appears in the cell, then click the Error Checking button in the Formula Auditing group**
   The Error Checking dialog box opens and alerts you to a data type error. This error is a result of cell N3, which contains text, having been included in the formula, as shown in FIGURE 11-18.
2. **Click Edit in Formula Bar in the Error Checking dialog box, edit the formula in the formula bar to read =N4+N5+N6, click the Enter button in the formula bar, then close the Error Checking dialog box**
   The edited formula produces the correct result, $132,192 in cell N7.
3. **Click cell N5, click the Error Checking Options button, view the Inconsistent Formula warning, click the Trace Precedents button in the Formula Auditing group, then click the Trace Dependents button**
   Blue arrows point from the cells referenced by the formula to the active cell, and to cells in which the formula is referenced, as shown in FIGURE 11-19. These **tracer arrows** help you determine which cells might have caused the error and whether any additional errors might be present. Tracing the precedents shows you that cell B5, the January total, isn't included in the Philadelphia annual total formula. Tracing the dependents indicates that this formula error affects the formulas in cells N7 and O5.

QUICK TIP
You can use the Trace Error tool to highlight the cells used to calculate a formula by clicking the Formulas tab on the Ribbon, clicking the Error Checking button arrow in the Formula Auditing group, then clicking Trace Error.

4. **Click the Remove Arrows button in the Formula Auditing group, click, then click Copy Formula from Above**
   The Philadelphia total changes to $37,898.
5. **Click cell O5, click the Evaluate Formula button in the Formula Auditing group, click Evaluate, verify that 37898 was substituted for N5 in the Evaluation box, click Evaluate again, verify that 0 was substituted for N8, click Evaluate again, verify that #DIV/0! appears in the Evaluation box, then click Close**
   The source of the error lies in the reference to cell N8 in the denominator, which has a value of zero, rather than the total in cell N7. The formula in cell O4 uses a relative reference to cell N7, and when the formula was copied the denominator changed to N8.
6. **Click cell O4, click to the left of N7 in the formula bar, press F4, click in the formula bar, drag the fill handle + to fill the range O5:O6, click cell A1, click the Error Checking button in the Formula Auditing group, verify there aren't any additional errors, as shown in FIGURE 11-20, click OK, then save the workbook**

Watching formulas

As you edit your worksheet, you can watch the effect that cell changes have on selected worksheet formulas. Select the cell or cells that you want to watch, click the Formulas tab on the ribbon, click the Watch Window button in the Formula Auditing group, click Add Watch in the Watch Window, then click Add. The Watch Window lists the workbook name, worksheet name, the cell address you want to watch, the current cell value, and its formula. As cell values that "feed into" the formula change, the resulting formula value in the Watch Window changes. To delete a watch, select the cell information in the Watch Window, click Delete Watch, then close the Watch Window.

FIGURE 11-18: Error Checking dialog box

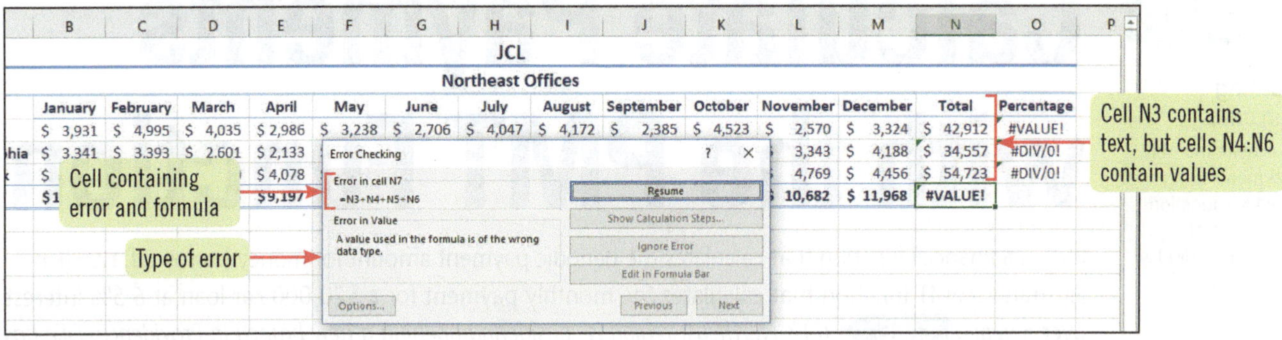

FIGURE 11-19: Worksheet with tracer arrows

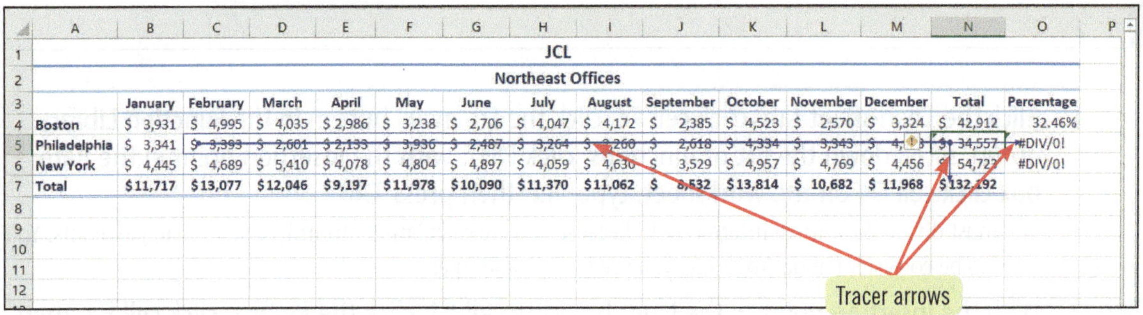

FIGURE 11-20: Final error check results

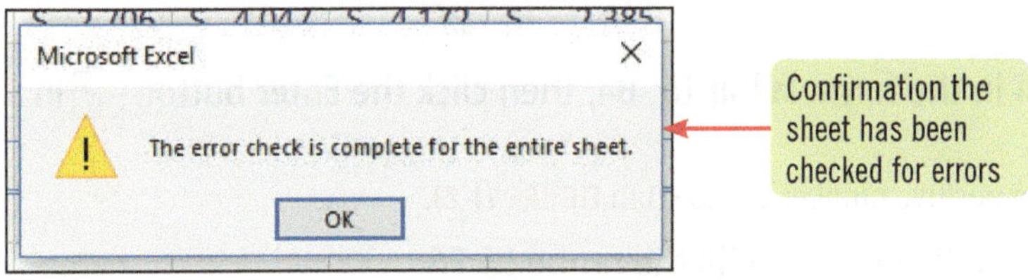

Circling invalid data

If you enter data validation criteria to your worksheet data, you can locate data that doesn't satisfy that criteria by clicking the Data tab on the ribbon, clicking the Data Validation arrow, then clicking Circle Invalid Data. Red circles appear around cells that are not consistent with data validation criteria, as shown in FIGURE 11-21. To clear the circles on the worksheet, click, then click Clear Validation Circles.

FIGURE 11-21: Circled invalid data

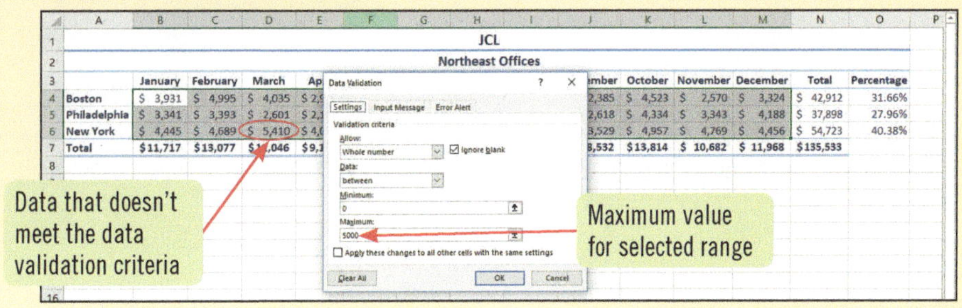

Excel Module 11

Learning Outcomes
- Calculate monthly payments using the PMT function
- Edit the PMT function to display payments as a positive value

Calculate Payments with the PMT Function

PMT is a financial function that calculates the periodic payment amount for money borrowed. FIGURE 11-22 illustrates a PMT function that calculates the monthly payment for a $20,000 car loan at 6.5% interest over 5 years. **CASE** *JCL's Northeast region is considering opening a new branch in Providence. Ellie has obtained loan quotes from a commercial bank, a venture capitalist, and a private lender. She wants you to summarize the loan information.*

STEPS

1. **Click the Loan sheet tab, click cell F4, click the Financial button in the Function Library group, scroll down the list of functions, click PMT, with the insertion point in the Rate box click cell D4 on the worksheet, type /12, then press TAB**

   You must divide the annual interest by 12 because you are calculating monthly, not annual, payments. You need to be consistent about the units you use for rate and nper.

2. **With the insertion point in the Nper box click cell E4, click the Pv box, click cell B4, then click OK**

   The payment of ($5,193.98) in cell F4 appears in red, indicating that it is a negative amount. Excel displays the result of a PMT function as a negative value to reflect the negative cash flow the loan represents to the borrower.

3. **Double-click cell F4, edit B4 in the formula bar to -B4, then click the Enter button ✓ in the formula bar**

   The monthly payment displays a positive number as shown in FIGURE 11-23.

4. **With cell F4 selected, drag the fill handle to fill the range F5:F6**

   A monthly payment of $9,401.29 for the venture capitalist loan appears in cell F5. A monthly payment of $15,019.15 for the private lender loan appears in cell F6.

5. **Click cell G4, type =, click cell E4, type *, click cell F4, press TAB, in cell H4 type =, click cell G4, type –, click cell B4, click ✓, copy cells G4:H4 into the range G5:H6, click cell A1, then compare your worksheet to FIGURE 11-24**

6. **sam Group all the worksheets, add your name to the center section of the grouped footer, ungroup the worksheets, save the workbook, submit the workbook to your instructor, close the workbook, then close Excel**

QUICK TIP

The Fv and Type arguments are optional: Fv is the future value, or the total amount you want to obtain after all payments. If you omit it, Excel assumes you want to pay off the loan completely, so the default Fv is 0. Type indicates when the payments are made; 0 is the end of the period, and 1 is the beginning of the period. The default is the end of the period.

FIGURE 11-22: Example of PMT function for car loan

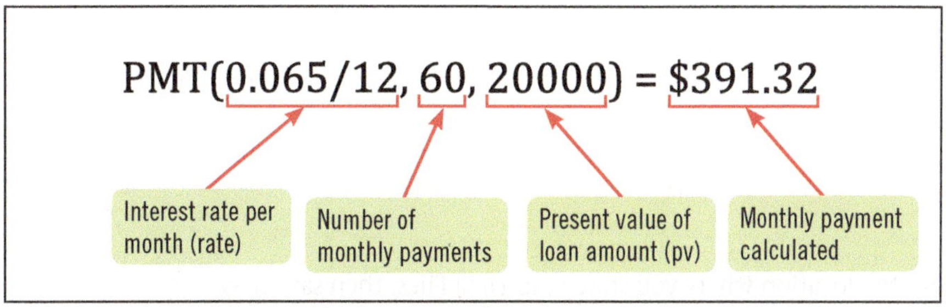

FIGURE 11-23: PMT function calculating monthly loan payment

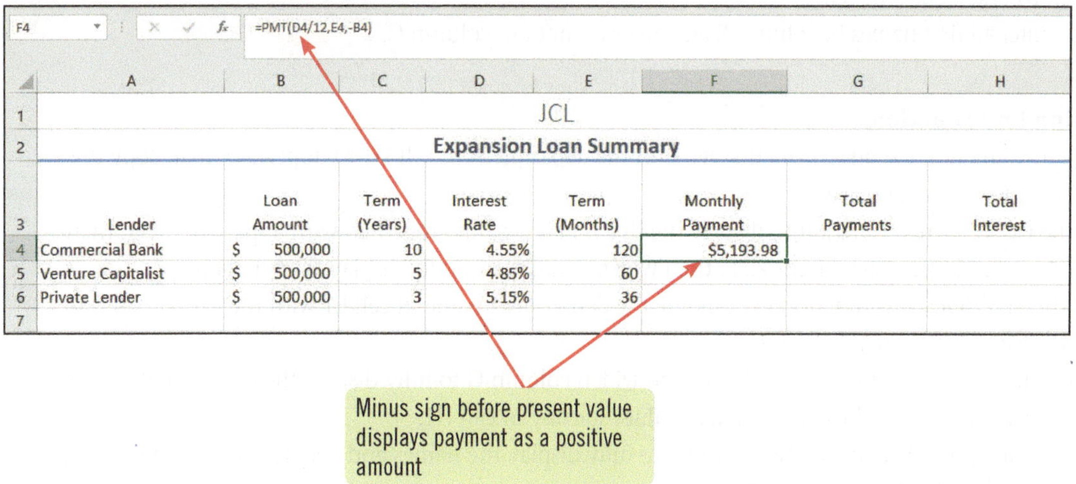

	A	B	C	D	E	F	G	H
1	JCL							
2	Expansion Loan Summary							
3	Lender	Loan Amount	Term (Years)	Interest Rate	Term (Months)	Monthly Payment	Total Payments	Total Interest
4	Commercial Bank	$ 500,000	10	4.55%	120	$5,193.98		
5	Venture Capitalist	$ 500,000	5	4.85%	60			
6	Private Lender	$ 500,000	3	5.15%	36			
7								

FIGURE 11-24: Completed worksheet

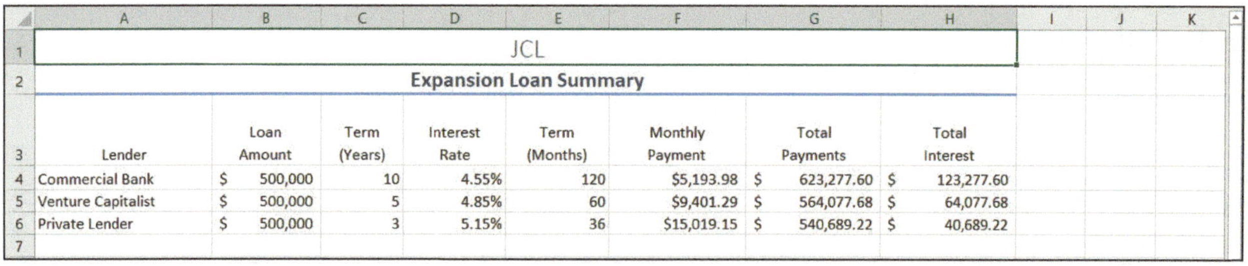

	A	B	C	D	E	F	G	H
1	JCL							
2	Expansion Loan Summary							
3	Lender	Loan Amount	Term (Years)	Interest Rate	Term (Months)	Monthly Payment	Total Payments	Total Interest
4	Commercial Bank	$ 500,000	10	4.55%	120	$5,193.98	$ 623,277.60	$ 123,277.60
5	Venture Capitalist	$ 500,000	5	4.85%	60	$9,401.29	$ 564,077.68	$ 64,077.68
6	Private Lender	$ 500,000	3	5.15%	36	$15,019.15	$ 540,689.22	$ 40,689.22
7								

Working with other financial functions

You can use the FV (Future Value) function to determine the amount of money a given monthly investment will amount to, at a given interest rate, after a given number of payment periods. The syntax is FV(rate,nper,pmt,pv,type), where *rate* is the interest paid by the financial institution, *nper* is the number of periods, and *pmt* is the amount you deposit. For example, suppose you want to invest $1,000 every month for the next 12 months into an account that pays 2% a year, you can enter the function FV(.02/12,12,-1000) and Excel returns the value $12,110.61 as the future value of your investment.

You can use the NPER function to determine the number of payment periods required for a loan or investment. For example, if you want to take out a loan for $20,000 at an interest rate of 6% with payments of $400 monthly, you can enter =NPER(6%/12,400,-20000) and Excel returns the value 57.68. You can use the PV function to find the present value of a loan or an investment. For example, if you have an investment that will pay you an amount of $200 for 10% per month over 30 years, you can enter =PV(10%/12,12*30,200) and Excel returns a value of $22,790.16.

Practice

Skills Review

1. Separate data using Flash Fill.

- **a.** Start Excel, open IL_EX_11-2.xlsx from the location where you store your Data Files, then save it as **IL_EX_11_LegalServices**.
- **b.** On the Managers worksheet, insert two new columns to the left of column B.
- **c.** Enter **Jay** in cell B1 and **Sears** in cell C1.
- **d.** Use Flash Fill to enter all first names in column B and all last names in column C.
- **e.** Save your work.

2. Format data using text functions.

- **a.** In cell E1, use a text function to convert the first letter of the department in cell D1 to uppercase, then copy the formula in cell E1 into the range E2:E8.
- **b.** In cell F1, use the CONCAT text function to display the first and last names together, with a space between them.
- **c.** Copy the formula in cell F1 into the range F2:F8, then widen column F to fully display the full names.
- **d.** In cell G1, use the TEXTJOIN text function to combine the department name in cell E1 with the text **Department**, using a space as a delimiter.
- **e.** Copy the formula in cell G1 into the range G2:G8, then widen column G to fully display the department names.
- **f.** Copy the range F1:G8, then paste the copied data as values starting in cell H1.
- **g.** Delete columns A through G, widen columns A and B to fully display the names and departments, then save your work. Compare your worksheet to FIGURE 11-25.

FIGURE 11-25

	A	B	C	D	E	F	G	H	I	J	K	L	M	N	O
1	Jay Sears	Civil Department													
2	Carol Trull	Land Department													
3	Lucy Knoll	Operations Department													
4	Mia Meng	Land Department													
5	Robert Dally	Civil Department													
6	Carey Degual	Land Department													
7	Jody Wolls	Civil Department													
8	Mary Alworth	Operations Department													
9															
10															

3. Sum a data range based on conditions.

- **a.** Activate the Partners worksheet.
- **b.** In cell B15, use the AVERAGEIF function to average the salaries and bonuses of those with a review of 5.
- **c.** In cell B16, use the SUMIF function to total the salaries of employees with a review of 5.
- **d.** Format cells B15 and B16 with the Accounting Number format using two decimals.
- **e.** Save your work.

4. Find values based on conditions.

- **a.** In cell B20, use the MAXIFS function to find the highest salary of employees with a rating of 5 and professional development hours of 10 or more. Use absolute cell references for the ranges in the formula.
- **b.** In cell B21, use the MINIFS function to find the lowest salary of employees with a rating of 5 and professional development hours of 10 or more. (*Hint:* You can copy the formula in cell B20 and edit it for MINIFS.)
- **c.** Format cells B20 and B21 with the Accounting Number format using two decimals.
- **d.** Save your work.

Skills Review (continued)

5. Construct formulas using named ranges.

a. On the Partners sheet, name the range C3:C11 **Review**, and limit the scope of the name to the Partners worksheet.

b. In cell B17, use the COUNTIF function to count the number of employees with a review of 5 using the named range.

c. Use the Name Manager to add a comment of **Scale of 1 to 5** to the review name. (*Hint:* In the Name Manager dialog box, click the Review name, then click Edit to enter the comment.)

d. Save your work.

e. Compare your worksheet to FIGURE 11-26.

FIGURE 11-26

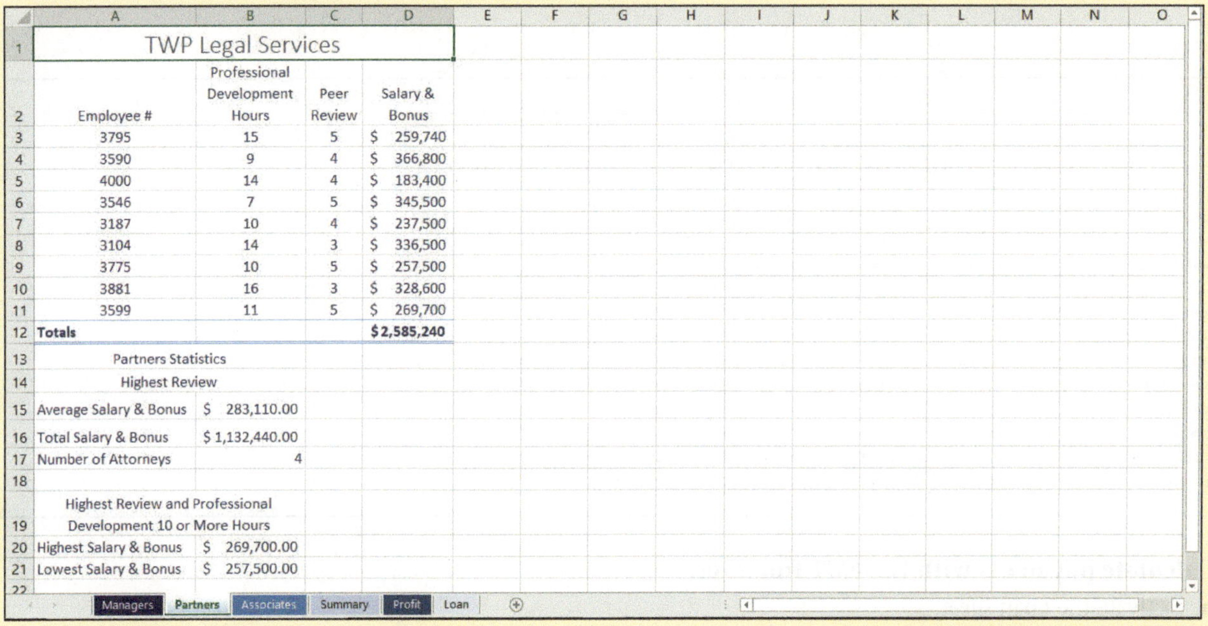

	A	B	C	D
1	TWP Legal Services			
2	Employee #	Professional Development Hours	Peer Review	Salary & Bonus
3	3795	15	5	$ 259,740
4	3590	9	4	$ 366,800
5	4000	14	4	$ 183,400
6	3546	7	5	$ 345,500
7	3187	10	4	$ 237,500
8	3104	14	3	$ 336,500
9	3775	10	5	$ 257,500
10	3881	16	3	$ 328,600
11	3599	11	5	$ 269,700
12	Totals			$2,585,240
13	Partners Statistics			
14	Highest Review			
15	Average Salary & Bonus	$ 283,110.00		
16	Total Salary & Bonus	$ 1,132,440.00		
17	Number of Attorneys	4		
18				
19	Highest Review and Professional Development 10 or More Hours			
20	Highest Salary & Bonus	$ 269,700.00		
21	Lowest Salary & Bonus	$ 257,500.00		

6. Consolidate data using a formula.

a. Activate the Summary sheet.

b. In cell B3, use the AutoSum function to total cell D12 on the Partners and Associates sheets.

c. Format cell B3 with the Accounting Number format with two decimal places.

d. In cell B4, use the Consolidate dialog box to total cell B16 on the Partners sheets and cell G5 on the Associates sheet, creating links to the source data.

e. Expand the outlined data, then enter **Associates** in cell A4 and **Partners** in cell A5.

f. Compare your worksheet to FIGURE 11-27.

FIGURE 11-27

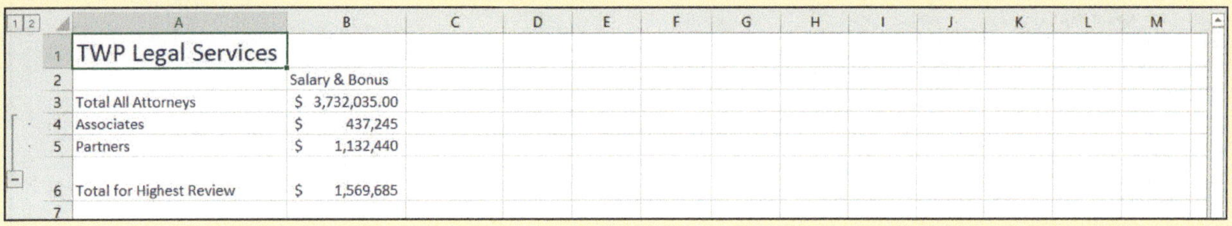

	A	B
1	TWP Legal Services	
2		Salary & Bonus
3	Total All Attorneys	$ 3,732,035.00
4	Associates	$ 437,245
5	Partners	$ 1,132,440
6	Total for Highest Review	$ 1,569,685
7		

7. Audit a worksheet.

a. Activate the Profit worksheet.

b. Select cell B15, then use the Trace Precedents button to find the cells on which that figure is based. Use the Trace Dependents button to find cells that use the value in cell B15. Remove all tracer arrows.

c. Correct the formula in cell B15. (*Hint:* It should subtract Total Expenses from Total Income.)

d. Select cell G5 and use the Error Checking button to review a description of the error. Evaluate the formula in cell G5 to locate the error, then fix the error.

e. Use the Error Checking button to check the worksheet for any other errors. Compare your worksheet to **FIGURE 11-28**, then save the workbook.

FIGURE 11-28

	A	B	C	D	E	F	G
1	TWP Legal Services						
2		Q1	Q2	Q3	Q4	Total	% of Total
3	Income						
4	Civil	$ 1,552,263	$ 1,505,095	$ 2,084,056	$ 1,648,297	$ 6,789,711	47.46%
5	Land	$ 1,514,954	$ 2,414,730	$ 2,063,992	$ 1,524,199	$ 7,517,875	52.54%
6	Total Income	$ 3,067,217	$ 3,919,825	$ 4,148,048	$ 3,172,496	$ 14,307,586	
7							
8	Expenses						
9	Salaries & Bonuses	$ 950,158	$ 928,751	$ 940,582	$ 912,544	$ 3,732,035	95.06%
10	Rent	$ 25,000	$ 25,000	$ 25,000	$ 25,000	$ 100,000	2.55%
11	Advertising	$ 3,900	$ 18,200	$ 18,500	$ 2,300	$ 42,900	1.09%
12	Cleaning	$ 2,100	$ 2,100	$ 2,800	$ 1,900	$ 8,900	0.23%
13	Insurance	$ 10,542	$ 10,542	$ 10,542	$ 10,542	$ 42,168	1.07%
14	Total Expenses	$ 991,700	$ 984,593	$ 997,424	$ 952,286	$ 3,926,003	100.00%
15	Net Profit	$ 2,075,517	$ 2,935,232	$ 3,150,624	$ 2,220,210	$ 10,381,583	
16							

8. Calculate payments with the PMT function.

a. Activate the Loan sheet.

b. In cell B8, determine the monthly payment using the loan information shown. (*Hint:* Use the Function Arguments dialog box to enter the formula **=PMT(B4/12,B5,-B3)**.)

c. In cell B9, enter a formula that multiplies the total number of payments by the monthly payment.

d. In cell B10, enter the formula that subtracts the loan amount from the total payment amount, if necessary format cell B10 as currency, then compare your results to **FIGURE 11-29**.

e. Group the six worksheets, enter your name in the grouped worksheet footer, ungroup the worksheets, save the workbook, then submit your workbook to your instructor.

f. Close the workbook, then close Excel.

FIGURE 11-29

	A	B
1	TWP Legal Services	
2	New Office Loan	
3	Loan Amount	$ 775,000
4	Interest Rate	4.75%
5	Term in Months	48
6		
7		
8	Monthly Payment:	$17,760.07
9	Total Payments:	$852,483.31
10	Total Interest:	$77,483.31
11		
12		
13		
14		

Independent Challenge 1

Tony Sanchez, RM's office manager, uses Excel formulas and functions to analyze insurance reimbursement data for the Northeast imaging facilities. You will help Tony analyze and consolidate imaging data and estimate loan costs for a new imaging center.

a. Start Excel, open IL_EX_11-3.xlsx from the location where you store your Data Files, then save it as **IL_EX_11_Imaging**.

b. On the Technicians sheet, enter **troy silva** in cell B4, enter **boston** in cell C4, then enter **5** in cell D4.

c. Using the data you entered as an example, use FlashFill to enter the names, offices, and years in columns B, C, and D.

d. In cell E4, use the PROPER function to display the name from cell B4 with the correct capitalization for proper names.

e. Use the fill handle to copy the formula in cell E4 to cell F4, then copy the formulas in cells E4:F4 to the range E5:F15.

f. In cell G4, use the TEXTJOIN function to join the text in cell D4 with the text **Years**, using a space as a delimiter.

g. Copy the formula in cell G4 into the range G5:G15. Copy the data in the range E1:G15, then paste the selection as values in the range that begins in cell H1. Delete columns A through G.

h. On the Boston sheet, name the range A4:A22 **Procedure**, and give the name a scope of the workbook. (*Hint:* Select the range A3:A22, then use the top row to create the Procedure name from the selection.)

i. In cell F5, use the COUNTIF function, the named range Procedure, and the value in cell E5 to determine the number of MRI procedures, then copy the formula into the range F6:F8.

j. Assign the name **Insurance_Payment** to the range B4:B22, using the scope of the workbook. In cell G5, use the SUMIF function, the named ranges Procedure and Insurance_Payment, and the value in cell E5 to determine the total insurance payments for MRI procedures, then copy the formula into the range G6:G8.

k. In cell H5, use the AVERAGEIF function, the named ranges Procedure and Insurance_Payment, and the value in cell E5 to determine the average payment for MRI procedures, then copy the formula into the range H6:H8.

l. In cell B4 on the NE Summary sheet, enter a formula that uses 3-D references to total the number of MRI procedures in cell F5 on the Boston and Newton sheets. Copy the formula in cell B4 to cell C4, then copy the formulas in the range B4:C4 to the range B5:C7.

m. In cell F4, use the Consolidate dialog box to total the insurance payments in cell B23 of the Boston sheet and cell B24 of the Newton sheet. Link the total to the source data.

n. Format the value in cell D6 as a percentage with two decimal places. Use error checking to find a description of the error in cell D7. Evaluate the formula in cell D7 to troubleshoot and resolve the error. Use tracer arrows to find cells referenced in the formula, then delete the arrows.

o. Edit the formula in cell D6 so it reads = C6/F6, then copy the formula in cell D6 to the range D7:D9.

p. In cell F4 on the Loan sheet, use the PMT function to calculate the monthly payment using the loan amount in cell B4, the interest rate in cell D4, and the term in cell E4. (*Hint:* Divide the rate by 12 to enter a monthly rate.)

Independent Challenge 1 (continued)

q. Widen column F to fully display the monthly payment, then edit the formula in cell F4 to display the payment as a positive number.

r. In cell G4 enter a formula that calculates the total payments by multiplying the monthly payment by the number of months. In cell H4, enter a formula to calculate the total interest by subtracting the loan amount from the total payments, then widen column H to fully display the total interest.

s. Copy the formulas in the range F4:H4 into the range F5:H6, then compare your worksheet to FIGURE 11-30.

t. Group the worksheets, add your name to the center section of the grouped worksheet footers, ungroup the worksheets, save the workbook, then submit the workbook to your instructor.

u. Close the workbook, then close Excel.

FIGURE 11-30

	A	B	C	D	E	F	G	H	I	J
1	Riverwalk Clinic									
2	Imaging Center Loan Summary									
3	**Lender**	**Loan Amount**	**Term (Years)**	**Interest Rate**	**Term (Months)**	**Monthly Payment**	**Total Payments**	**Total Interest**		
4	Commercial Bank	$400,000	5	5.15%	60	$7,576.01	$454,560.78	$54,560.78		
5	Venture Capitalist	$400,000	3	5.05%	36	$11,997.34	$431,904.26	$31,904.26		
6	Investment Banker	$400,000	2	4.75%	24	$17,503.81	$420,091.34	$20,091.34		
7										
8										
9										
10										

Independent Challenge 2

As an accountant working in RSJ Advertising, you have been asked to analyze revenue in the Texas offices. The firm plans to open a new office in the state and you will examine the options for a loan to finance this expansion.

a. Start Excel, open IL_EX_11-4.xlsx from the location where you store your Data Files, then save it as **IL_EX_11_Revenue**.

b. Name the range containing the company's offices **Office** with a scope of the workbook, name the range containing the revenue data **Revenue** with a scope of the workbook, then name the range containing the type data **Type** with a scope of the workbook.

c. In cell G4, use the SUMIF function and named ranges to calculate the total revenue for print advertising. Use a relative reference to cell F4 for the criteria.

d. In cell H4, use the AVERAGEIF function and named ranges to calculate the average revenue for print advertising. Use a relative reference to cell F4 for the criteria.

e. In cell I4, use the COUNTIF function and a named range to calculate the total number of print ads. Use a relative reference to cell F4 for the criteria.

f. Copy the formulas in G4:I4 into the range G5:I7.

g. In cell G8, use the SUMIFS function and named ranges to calculate the total revenue for Houston broadcast media advertising.

h. In cell H8, use the AVERAGEIFS function and named ranges to calculate the average revenue for Houston broadcast media advertising.

i. In cell I8, use the COUNTIFS function and named ranges to calculate the total number of Houston broadcast media ads.

j. In cell G11, use the MINIFS function and named ranges to calculate the lowest revenue Houston broadcast media ad.

k. In cell G12, use the MAXIFS function and named ranges to calculate the highest revenue Houston broadcast media ad.

l. In cell C3 of the Loan sheet, use the NPER function to find the number of months required to pay off a $500,000 loan with monthly payments of $8000 at an interest rate of 5.15%. (*Hint:* The present value, pv, is in cell A3, the rate needs to be divided by 12 for a monthly rate, and a - needs to be typed before the pv value so the month is displayed as a positive value.)

m. Copy the loan amount in cell A3 into the range A4:A10, then copy the monthly payment in cell D3 into the range D4:D10.

n. Select cell B3, then use FIGURE 11-31 to enter interest rates in the range B4:B10 by increasing the rate by .25% until a rate of 7% is met. (*Hint:* To open the dialog box click the Home tab, click the Fill button in the Editing group, then click Series.)

o. Copy the formula in cell C3 into the range C4:C10.

p. Group the two worksheets, enter your name in the worksheet footer, ungroup the worksheets, save the workbook, then submit it to your instructor.

q. Close the workbook, then close Excel.

FIGURE 11-31

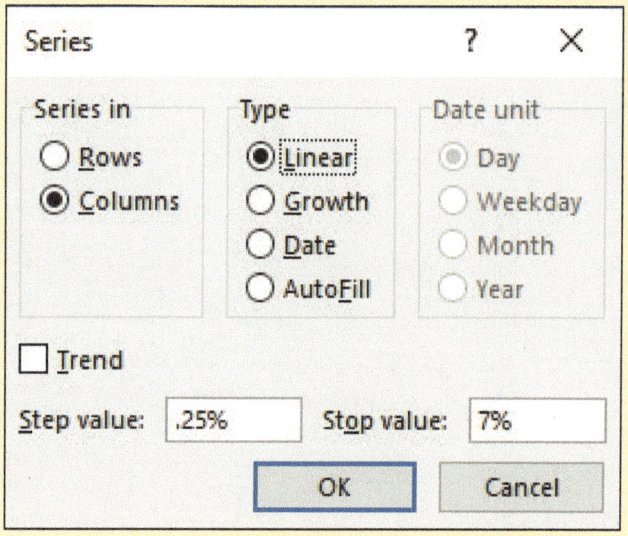

Visual Workshop

Open IL_EX_11-5.xlsx from the location where you store your Data Files, then save it as **IL_EX_11_Enrollment**. Use the data in the Fall, Spring, and Summer worksheets to create summary information on the Annual worksheet shown in FIGURE 11-32. The enrollment data are in the same location on all three worksheets. The number of graduates for each session appears in different locations on the three worksheets. Enter your name in the Annual worksheet footer, save the workbook, submit it to your instructor, then close Excel.

FIGURE 11-32

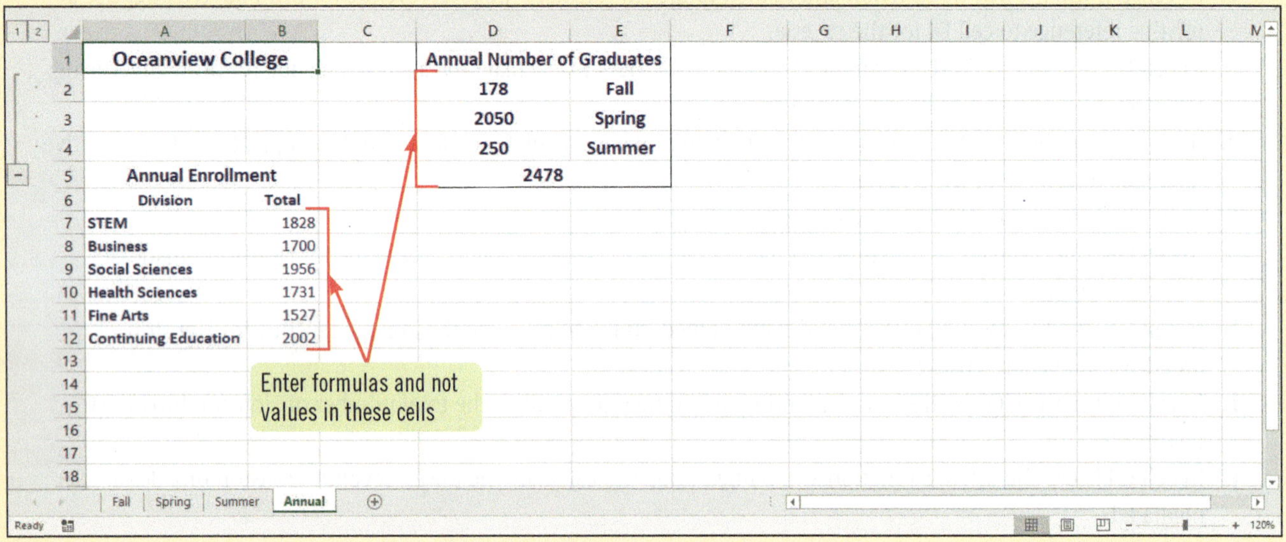

Performing What-If Analysis

CASE Ellie Schwartz, JCL's vice president of finance, uses what-if analysis to analyze regional data and forecast possible outcomes. You will help Ellie using the data analysis tools and add-ins in Excel.

Module Objectives

After completing this module, you will be able to:

- Define what-if analysis
- Track what-if analysis with Scenario Manager
- Generate a scenario summary
- Project figures using a data table
- Use Goal Seek
- Find solutions using Solver
- Manage data using a data model
- Analyze data using Power Pivot

Files You Will Need

IL_EX_12-1.xlsx
IL_EX_12-2.xlsx
IL_EX_12-3.xlsx
IL_EX_12-4.xlsx
IL_EX_12-5.xlsx
IL_EX_12-6.xlsx
IL_EX_12-7.xlsx

Excel
Module 12

Define What-If Analysis

Learning Outcomes
- Develop guidelines for performing what-if analysis
- Define what-if analysis terminology

By performing what-if analysis in a worksheet, you can get immediate answers to questions such as, "What happens to profits if we sell 25 percent more of a certain product?" or, "What happens to monthly payments if interest rates rise or fall?" A worksheet you use to perform what-if analysis is often called a **model** because it acts as the basis for multiple outcomes or sets of results. To perform what-if analysis in a worksheet, you change the value in one or more **input cells** (cells that contain data instead of formulas), then observe the effects on dependent cells. A **dependent cell** usually contains a formula whose resulting value changes depending on the values in the input cells. For more advanced data analysis, you can use Power Pivot, an Excel add-in, to create a Pivot Table from multiple tables to obtain answers to what-if questions. **CASE** *Ellie has received projected revenue, budget, and placement data from the Northeast office managers. She has created a worksheet model to perform an initial what-if analysis, as shown in* **FIGURE 12-1**. *She thinks the Boston revenue projections for the month of January should be higher. You first review the guidelines for performing what-if analysis.*

DETAILS

When performing what-if analysis, use the following guidelines:

- **Understand and state the purpose of the worksheet model**

  Identify what you want to accomplish with the model. What problem are you trying to solve? What questions do you want the model to answer for you? Ellie's worksheet model is designed to total JCL revenue projections for the four offices during the first half of the year and to calculate the percentage of total revenue for each office. It also calculates total revenues and percentages for each month within that period.

- **Determine the data input value(s) that, if changed, affect(s) dependent cell results**

  In what-if analysis, changes in the data input cells produce varying results in the output cells. You will use the model to work with one data input value: the January value for the Boston office, in cell B3.

- **Identify the dependent cell(s) that will contain results**

  The dependent cells usually contain formulas, and the formula results adjust as you enter different values in the input cells. The results of two dependent cell formulas appear in cells H3 (the Total for Boston) and I3 (the Percent of Total Revenue for Boston). Cell B6 (the Total for January) is also a dependent cell, as is cell B7 (the Percent of Total Revenue for January).

- **Formulate questions you want what-if analysis to answer and perform what-if analysis**

  It is important that you know the questions you want your model to answer before performing a what-if analysis. In the JCL model, one of the questions you want to answer is: What January Boston revenue target is required to bring the overall January revenue percentage to 18 percent?

- **Determine when to use advanced what-if analysis**

  If the answers to your what-if questions require data from multiple tables, you can use Power Pivot. Power Pivot enables you to create PivotTables using fields from multiple tables. **FIGURE 12-2** shows a PivotTable created with fields from two tables.

FIGURE 12-1: Worksheet model for a what-if analysis

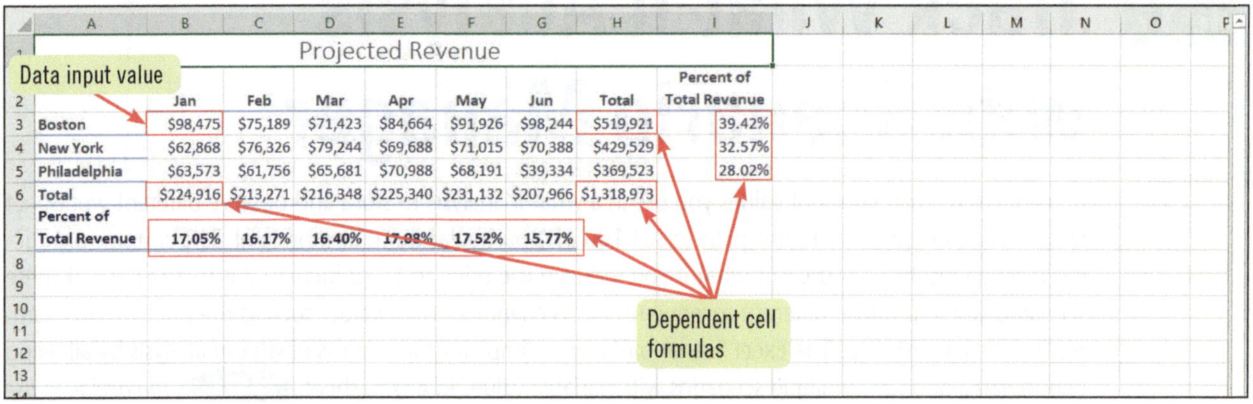

FIGURE 12-2: PivotTable using fields from two tables

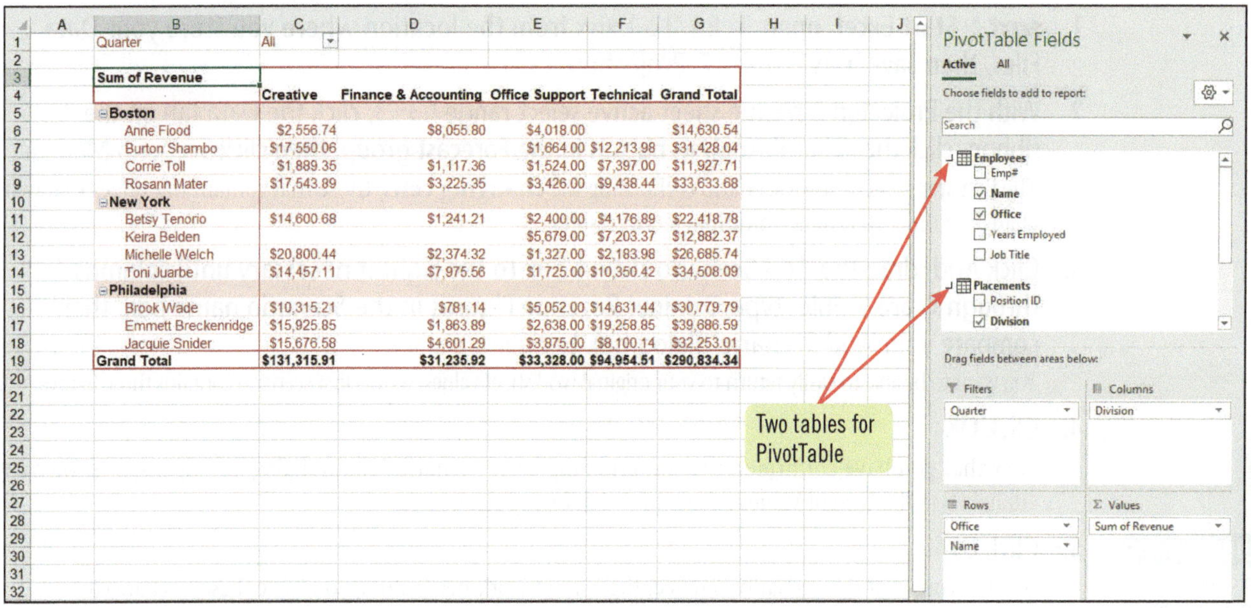

Excel
Module 12

Learning Outcomes
- Create scenarios to analyze Excel data
- Analyze scenarios using Scenario Manager

Track What-If Analysis with Scenario Manager

A **scenario** is a named set of values you use in a what-if analysis to store and observe different worksheet results. For example, you might plan to sell 100 of a particular item, at a price of $5 per item, producing revenue results of $500. But what if you reduced the price to $4 or increased it to $6? Each of these scenarios would produce different revenue results. A changing input value, such as the price in this example, is called a **variable**. The Excel Scenario Manager simplifies the process of what-if analysis by allowing you to name and save multiple scenarios with variable values in a worksheet. CASE *You decide to use Scenario Manager to create scenarios showing how a Boston revenue increase can affect total JCL revenue over the three-month period of February through April.*

STEPS

1. **sam Start Excel, open IL_EX_12-1.xlsx from the location where you store your Data Files, then save it as IL_EX_12_Projection**
2. **With the Projected Revenue sheet active select range C3:E3, click the Data tab on the ribbon, click the What-If Analysis button in the Forecast group, then click Scenario Manager**
   The first step in defining a scenario is choosing the **changing cells**, those that contain the values that will change in order to produce multiple sets of results.
3. **Click Add, drag the Add Scenario dialog box to the right if necessary until columns A through G are visible, type Original Revenue Figures in the Scenario name box, then compare your Add Scenario dialog box to FIGURE 12-3**
   You want to be able to easily return to your original worksheet values, so this first scenario contains those figures.
4. **Click OK**
   Now that you have confirmed the scenario range, the Scenario Values dialog box opens, as shown in FIGURE 12-4. The current values appear in the changing cell boxes.
5. **Click OK**
   Because you want this scenario to reflect the current worksheet values, you leave these unchanged.
6. **Click Add, in the Scenario name box type Increase Feb, Mar, Apr by 4000, verify that the Changing cells box reads C3:E3, click OK, in the Scenario Values dialog box change the value in the C3 box to 79189, change the value in the D3 box to 75423, change the value in the E3 box to 88664, then click Add**
   The second scenario shows the effects of increasing revenue by $4,000 in February, March, and April.
7. **In the Scenario name box type Increase Feb, Mar, Apr by 10000, click OK, in the Scenario Values dialog box change the value in the C3 box to 85189, change the value in the D3 box to 81423, change the value in the E3 box to 94664, then click OK**
   The Scenario Manager dialog box lists the three scenarios, as shown in FIGURE 12-5.
8. **Click the Increase Feb, Mar, Apr by 10000 scenario, click Show, notice that the percent of Boston revenue in cell I3 changes to 40.77%, click the Increase Feb, Mar, Apr by 4000 scenario, click Show, notice that the Boston revenue percent is now 39.96%, click Original Revenue Figures, click Show, then click Close**
9. **Save the workbook**

QUICK TIP
You can delete a scenario by clicking it in the Scenario Manager dialog box, then clicking Delete.

QUICK TIP
To edit a scenario, select it in the Scenario Manager dialog box, click the Edit button, then edit the Scenario.

FIGURE 12-3: Add Scenario dialog box

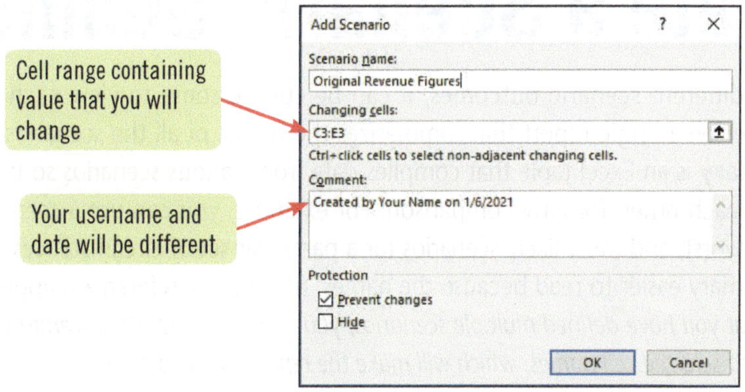

FIGURE 12-4: Scenario Values dialog box

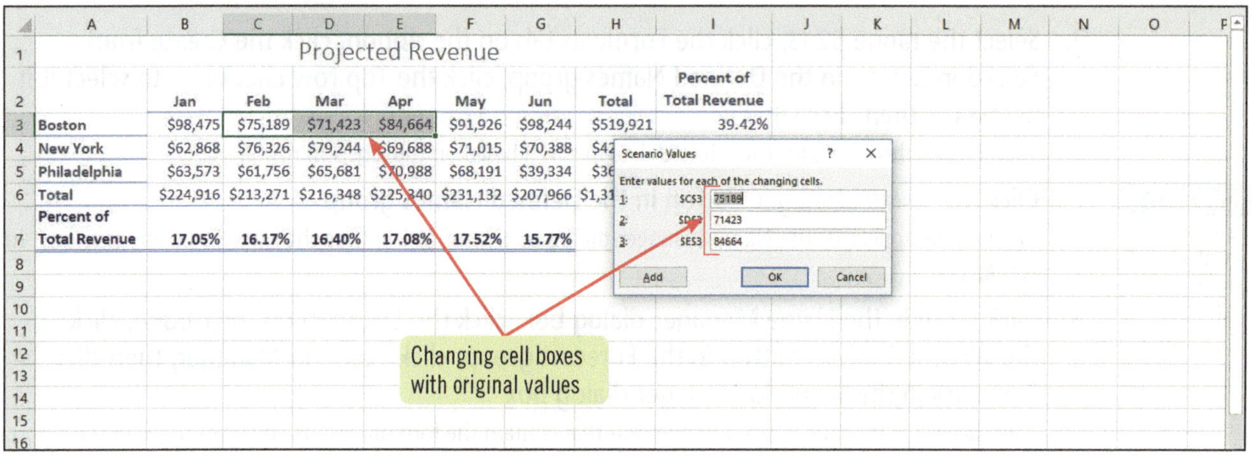

FIGURE 12-5: Scenario Manager dialog box with three scenarios listed

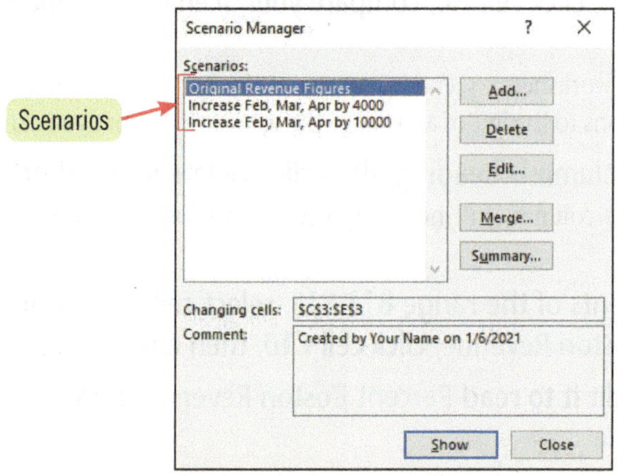

Merging scenarios

Excel stores scenarios on the worksheet of the workbook in which you created them. To apply scenarios from another worksheet or workbook into the current worksheet, click the Merge button in the Scenario Manager dialog box. The Merge Scenarios dialog box opens, letting you select scenarios from other locations. When you click a sheet name in the sheet list, a message under the sheet list tells you how many scenarios exist on that sheet. To merge scenarios from another workbook, such as those sent to you in a workbook from a coworker, open the other workbook file, click the Book list arrow in the Merge Scenarios dialog box, then click the workbook name. When you merge workbook scenarios, it's best if the workbooks have the same structure, so that there is no confusion of cell values.

Excel Module 12

Generate a Scenario Summary

Learning Outcomes
- Display scenarios in a scenario summary report
- Format a scenario summary report

When comparing different scenario outcomes, it can be cumbersome to view each one separately. You might prefer to see a single report that summarizes the results of all the scenarios in a worksheet. A **scenario summary** is an Excel table that compiles data from various scenarios so that you can view the results next to each other, for easy comparison. For example, you can use a scenario summary to compare the best, worst, and most likely scenarios for a particular set of circumstances. Using cell naming makes the summary easier to read because the names, not the cell references, appear in the report.

CASE *Now that you have defined multiple scenarios, you want to generate a scenario summary report. You begin by creating selected cell names, which will make the report easier to read.*

STEPS

1. **Select the range B2:I3, click the Formulas tab on the ribbon, click the Create from Selection button in the Defined Names group, click the Top row check box to select it if necessary, then click OK**

   Excel creates the names for the selected data in row 3 based on the labels in row 2.

> **QUICK TIP**
> You can also click the Name box list arrow on the formula bar to view cell names.

2. **Click the Name Manager button in the Defined Names group**

   Eight labels appear in the Name Manager dialog box, confirming that they were created, as shown in FIGURE 12-6.

3. **Click Close in the Name Manager dialog box, click the Data tab on the ribbon, click the What-If Analysis button in the Forecast group, click Scenario Manager, then click Summary in the Scenario Manager dialog box**

   Excel needs to know the location of the cells that contain the formula results you want to see in the report. You want to see the results for the Boston total and percentage of revenue, and for the total JCL revenue.

> **QUICK TIP**
> To analyze the results of scenarios, you can create a scenario PivotTable report by selecting the Scenario PivotTable report option in the Report type section of the Scenario Summary dialog box.

4. **With the contents of the Result cells box selected click cell H3 on the worksheet, type ,, click cell I3, type ,, click cell H6, compare your Scenario Summary dialog box to FIGURE 12-7, then click OK**

   A summary of the worksheet's scenarios appears on a new sheet named Scenario Summary. The report shows outline buttons to the left of and above the worksheet so that you can hide or show report details.

5. **Right-click the column D heading, then click Delete in the shortcut menu**

   The Current Values column isn't necessary because it shows the same values as the Original Revenue Figures column.

6. **Delete the contents of the range B13:B15, select cell B2, edit it to read Scenario Summary for Boston Revenue, click cell C10, then edit it to read Total Boston Revenue**

> **QUICK TIP**
> The scenario summary is not linked to the worksheet. If you change the values in the worksheet, you must generate a new scenario summary.

7. **Click cell C11, edit it to read Percent Boston Revenue, click cell C12, then edit it to read Total JCL Revenue**

8. **Right-click the column A heading, click Delete in the shortcut menu, right-click the row 1 heading, click Delete in the shortcut menu, change the page orientation to landscape, then save the workbook**

   The scenario summary is now easier to read and understand, as shown in FIGURE 12-8.

FIGURE 12-6: Name Manager dialog box displaying names

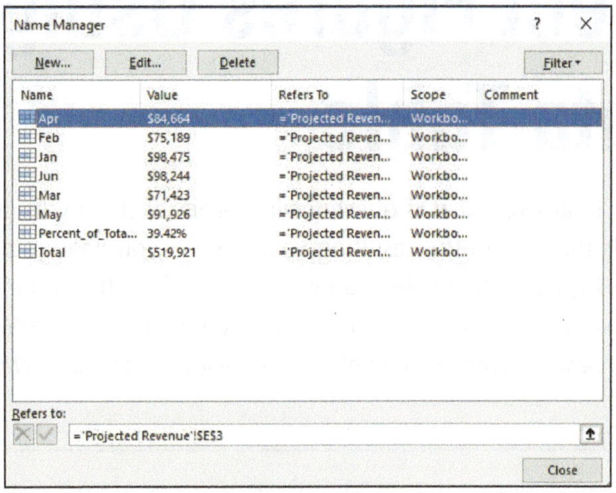

FIGURE 12-7: Scenario Summary dialog box

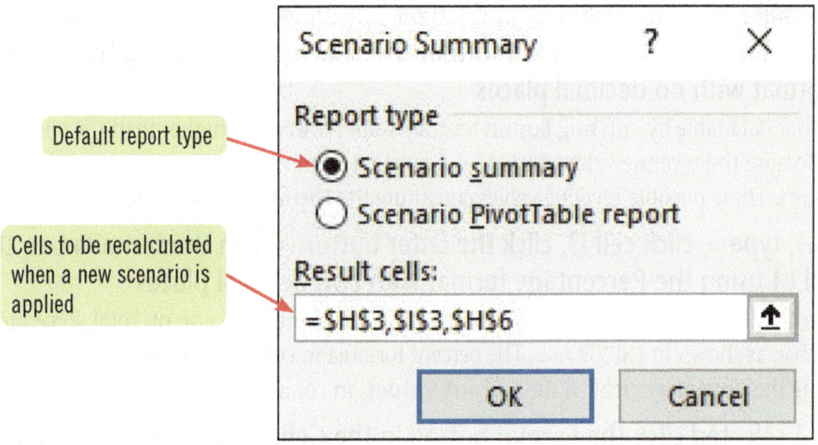

FIGURE 12-8: Completed Scenario Summary report

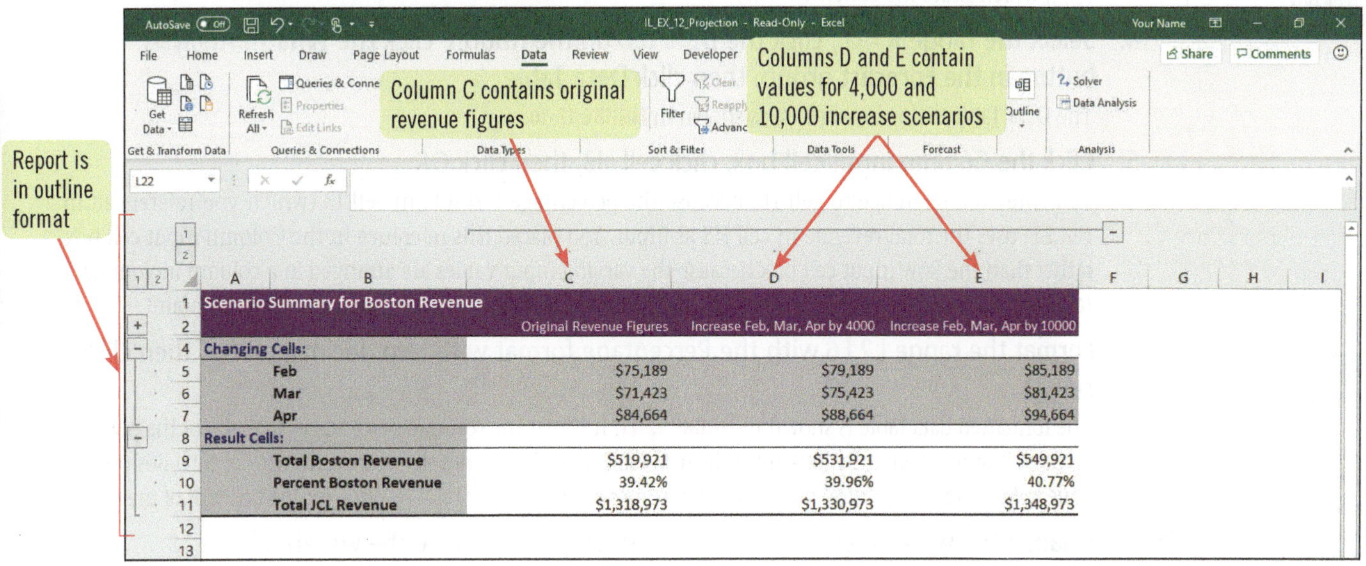

Excel **Module 12**

Learning Outcomes
- Develop a data table structure
- Analyze options using a data table

Project Figures Using a Data Table

Another way to answer what-if questions in a worksheet is by using a data table. A **data table** is a range of cells that shows the resulting values when you change one or more input values in a formula. A **one-input data table** is a range of cells that shows the result of varying one input value. **CASE** *You want to find out how the Boston revenue percentage would change if the Boston total revenue increased. You begin by entering a set of possible values, in $50,000 increments, for the Boston total.*

STEPS

1. **Click the Projected Revenue sheet tab, enter Total Boston Revenue in cell K1, widen column K to fit the label, in cell K2 enter 419921, select the range K2:K6, click the Home tab on the ribbon, click the Fill button in the Editing group, click Series, in the Series dialog box make sure the Columns and Linear option buttons are selected, type 50000 in the Step value box, click OK, then format the selected range using the Accounting number format with no decimal places**

   You set up your data table by entering Boston revenue values lower and higher than the current projection in cell H3. Because the revenue values varied by a constant number, you used a linear series to quickly fill in the amounts. These possible revenue values constitute the **input values** in the data table.

2. **Click cell L1, type =, click cell I3, click the Enter button ✓ on the formula bar, then format cell L1 using the Percentage format with two decimal places**

   The value in cell I3, 39.42%, appears in cell L1, and the cell name =Percent_of_Total_Revenue appears in the formula bar, as shown in FIGURE 12-9. The percent formula in cell I3 will be used to create the data table by calculating the percentages (called the **output values**) in column L.

QUICK TIP
You can create your own custom format by clicking a format that resembles the one you want, then customizing it in the Type box.

3. **With cell L1 selected click the Format button in the Cells group on the Home tab, click Format Cells, click the Number tab in the Format Cells dialog box if necessary, click Custom under Category, select the contents of the Type box, type ;;;, then click OK**

   Because it isn't necessary for users of the data table to see the value in cell L1, although the formula it references will be used in generating the data table, you applied the custom cell format of three semicolons (;;;), which hides the contents.

4. **Select the range K1:L6, click the Data tab on the ribbon, click the What-If Analysis button in the Forecast group, then click Data Table**

   The Data Table dialog box opens, as shown in FIGURE 12-10.

5. **Click the Column input cell box, click cell H3, then click OK**

   You entered a reference to cell H3 because the percentage formula in cell I3 (which you referenced in cell L1) uses the total revenue in cell H3 as input. You placed this reference in the Column input cell box rather than the Row input cell box because the varying input values are arranged in a column in your data table structure. Excel completes the data table by calculating percentages for each revenue amount.

QUICK TIP
You cannot delete individual output values in a data table; you must delete all output values.

6. **Format the range L2:L6 with the Percentage format with two decimal places, then click cell A1**

   The formatted data table is shown in FIGURE 12-11. It shows the revenue percentages for each of the possible levels of Boston revenue. By looking at the data table, Ellie determines that if she can increase total Boston revenue to $619,921, the Boston office will then comprise over 43% of total revenue for the first half of the year.

7. **Change the worksheet orientation to landscape, then save the workbook**

FIGURE 12-9: One-input data table structure

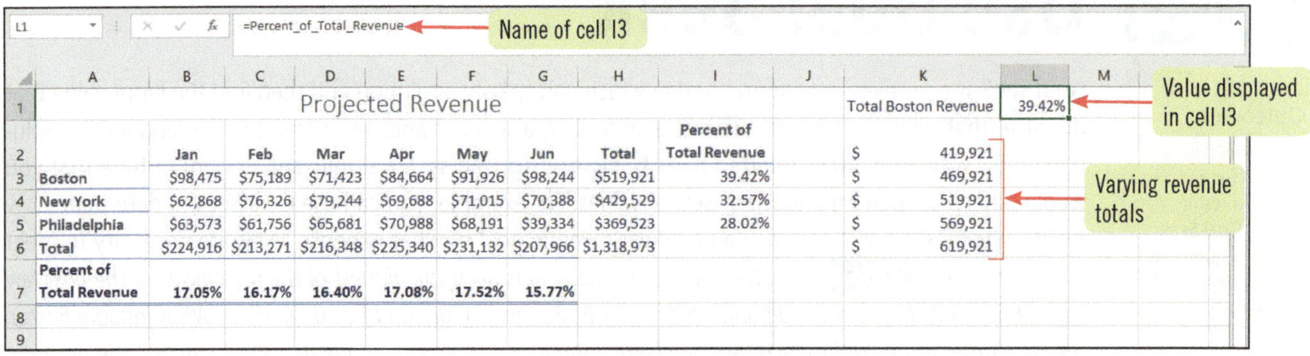

FIGURE 12-10: Data Table dialog box

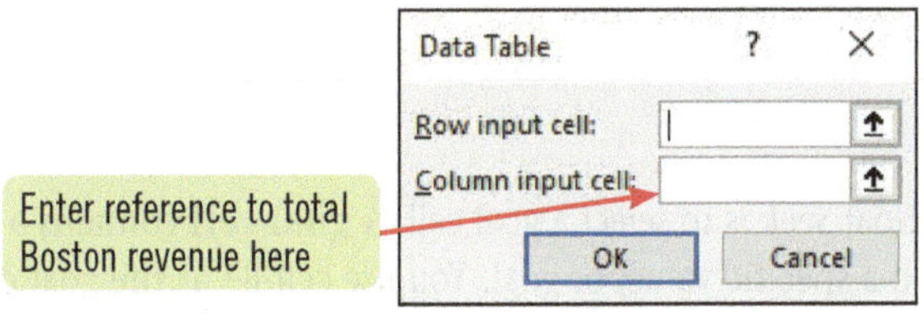

FIGURE 12-11: Completed data table with resulting values

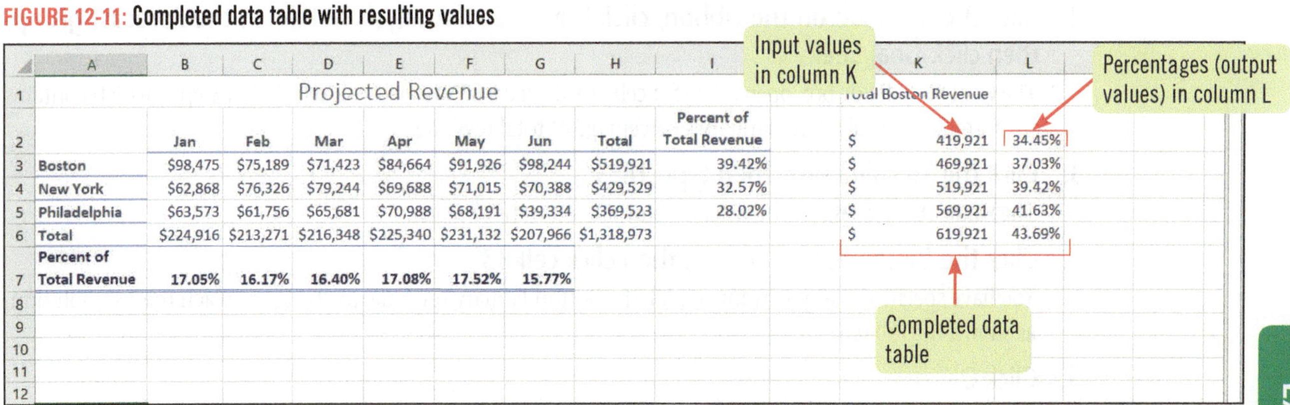

Creating a two-input data table

A **two-input data table** is a table in which you can vary the results in two cells and see the recalculated results. You could, for example, use a two-input data table to calculate your monthly car payment based on both varying interest rates and varying loan terms, as shown in FIGURE 12-12. In a two-input data table, different values of one input cell appear across the top row of the table, while different values of a second input cell are listed down the left column. You create a two-input data table the same way that you create a one-input data table, except you enter both a row and a column input cell. In the example, the two-input data table structure was created by first entering the number of payments in the range B6:D6 and the rates in the range A7:A15. Next, the data table values were created by selecting the range A6:D15, clicking the Data tab, clicking the What-If Analysis button in the Forecast group, then clicking Data Table. In the Data Table dialog box, the row input value is the term in cell B3. The column input value is the interest rate in cell B2. You can check the accuracy of these values by cross-referencing the values in the data table with those in the range B1:B4, where you can see that an interest rate of 3.75% for 60 months has a monthly payment of $302.01.

FIGURE 12-12: Two-input data table

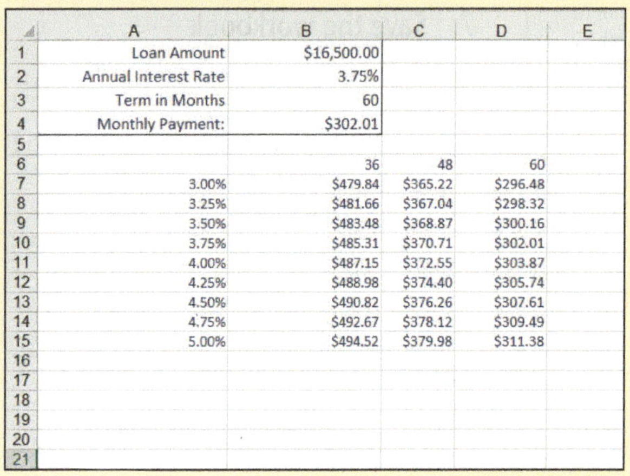

Excel
Module 12

Use Goal Seek

Learning Outcomes
- Determine input values for a desired result using Goal Seek
- Answer questions about data using Goal Seek

Goal seek is a problem-solving method in which you specify a solution and then find the input value that produces that solution. You can think of goal seeking as what-if analysis in reverse. "Backing into" a solution in this way, sometimes referred to as **backsolving**, can save a significant amount of time that you would otherwise spend trying many sets of values. For example, you can use Goal Seek to determine how many units must be sold to reach a particular revenue goal or what expense levels are necessary to meet a budget target. CASE *Boston's January revenue has been the highest of the JCL offices for the past few years. Ellie wants to project additional revenue for Boston in January and has a question: What January Boston revenue target is required to increase the overall January revenue percentage to 18%, assuming the revenues for the other offices don't change?*

STEPS

1. **Click cell B7**

   The first step in using Goal Seek is to select a goal cell. A **goal cell** contains a formula in which you can substitute values to find a specific value, or goal. You use cell B7 as the goal cell because it contains the January percent of total revenue formula.

2. **Click the Data tab on the ribbon, click the What-If Analysis button in the Forecast group, then click Goal Seek**

   The Goal Seek dialog box opens. The Set cell box displays B7, the cell you selected in Step 1, which contains the formula that calculates January's percentage of total revenue.

3. **Click the To value box, then type 18%**

   The value 18% represents the desired solution you want to reach.

4. **Click the By changing cell box, then click cell B3**

   You have specified that you want cell B3, the Boston January revenue, to change to reach the 18% solution, as shown in FIGURE 12-13.

5. **Click OK**

   The Goal Seek Status dialog box opens and displays the message, "Goal Seeking with Cell B7 found a solution." Cell B3 now displays the amount $113,671, the revenue necessary to achieve a January percentage of 18%.

6. **Click OK, then click cell A1**

   Changing the revenue amount in cell B3 changes the other dependent values in the worksheet (B6, H3, I3, and H6), as shown in FIGURE 12-14. The overall revenues increase as a result of increasing the Boston January percentage.

7. **Save the workbook**

QUICK TIP
Before you select another command, you can return the worksheet to its status prior to the Goal Seek by pressing CTRL+Z.

FIGURE 12-13: Completed Goal Seek dialog box

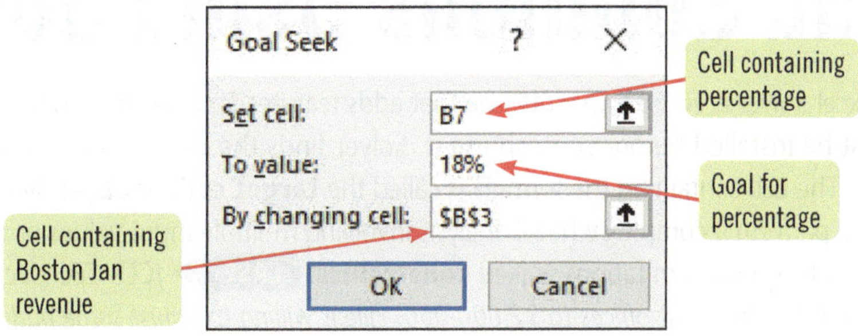

FIGURE 12-14: Worksheet with Goal Seek solution

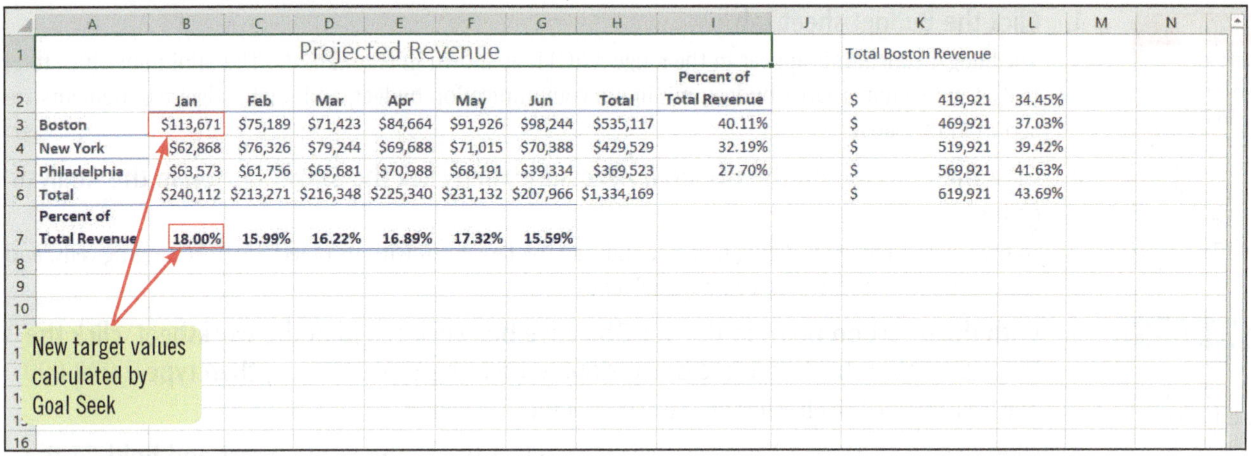

	A	B	C	D	E	F	G	H	I	J	K	L
1	Projected Revenue										Total Boston Revenue	
2		Jan	Feb	Mar	Apr	May	Jun	Total	Percent of Total Revenue	$	419,921	34.45%
3	Boston	$113,671	$75,189	$71,423	$84,664	$91,926	$98,244	$535,117	40.11%	$	469,921	37.03%
4	New York	$62,868	$76,326	$79,244	$69,688	$71,015	$70,388	$429,529	32.19%	$	519,921	39.42%
5	Philadelphia	$63,573	$61,756	$65,681	$70,988	$68,191	$39,334	$369,523	27.70%	$	569,921	41.63%
6	Total	$240,112	$213,271	$216,348	$225,340	$231,132	$207,966	$1,334,169		$	619,921	43.69%
7	Percent of Total Revenue	18.00%	15.99%	16.22%	16.89%	17.32%	15.59%					

Predicting data trends with Forecast Sheet

Forecast Sheet is a tool you can use when you have historical time-based data, to project future data based on past trends. You can forecast the future of your data related to a timeline by selecting the data, clicking the Data tab, then clicking the Forecast Sheet button in the Forecast group. The Create Forecast Worksheet dialog box opens, where you enter your Forecast End date, then click Create. The new chart displays your values along with the forecasted values and related confidence levels. A data table is also added to the worksheet, showing the new projected data for the chart. If your data lacks a valid pattern or seasonality, you can manually set this by expanding the Options area, then choosing the Set Manually option button, lowering the Confidence Interval percentage, or clicking the Fill Missing Points Using list arrow and selecting Zeros. Forecasting sheet functions can also be used to predict future values based on historical data. For example, Forecast.ETS() returns the projected value for a specific future target date. You can also use Forecast.ETS.Confint() and Forecast.ETS.Seasonality() to find confidence intervals and the repetitive pattern length of data.

Excel Module 12

Find Solutions Using Solver

Learning Outcomes
- Add worksheet constraints in Solver
- Use Solver to find the best solution to a problem

The Excel Solver is an **add-in**, software that adds features and commands to Excel or another Office app. It must be installed before you can use it. Solver finds the best solution to a problem that has several inputs. The cell containing the formula is called the **target cell**, or **objective**. Solver is helpful when you need to perform a complex what-if analysis involving multiple input values or when the input values must conform to specific limitations, called **constraints**. CASE *JCL's CEO directed Ellie to limit the budget total for JCL's Northeast offices to $2,000,000. Ellie is willing to adjust some budget items to meet this overall amount, but not others. You use Solver to help her find the best possible allocation.*

STEPS

TROUBLE
If you don't see Solver, click the File tab, click Options, click Add-ins, click Go, then in the Add-ins dialog box click the Solver Add-in check box to select it.

QUICK TIP
If your Solver Parameters dialog box has entries in the By Changing Variable Cells box or in the Subject to the Constraints box, click Reset All, click OK, then continue with Step 3.

QUICK TIP
If your solution needs to be an integer, you can select it in the Add Constraint dialog box.

1. **Click the Budget sheet tab**
   The budget constraints appear in the range A7:C11, as shown in FIGURE 12-15. The minimum office total budget, maximum salaries budget, minimum communication budget, and total budget requirements are shown in this range.
2. **Click the Data tab on the ribbon if necessary, then click the Solver button in the Analysis group**
   In the Solver Parameters dialog box, you indicate the target cell with its objective, the changing cells, and the constraints under which you want Solver to work.
3. **With the insertion point in the Set Objective box click cell I6 in the worksheet, click the Value Of option button if necessary, double-click the Value Of box, then type 2,000,000**
   You have specified an objective of $2,000,000 for the total budget.
4. **Click the By Changing Variable Cells box, select the range B3:B5, press and hold CTRL, then select the range E3:E5**
   You have told Excel which cells to vary to reach the goal of a $2,000,000 total budget.
5. **Click Add, with the insertion point in the Cell Reference box in the Add Constraint dialog box select the range I3:I5 in the worksheet, click the list arrow in the dialog box, click >=, then with the insertion point in the Constraint box click cell C8**
   These settings specify that the values in the range I3:I5, the total office budget amounts, should be greater than or equal to the value in cell C8, the minimum total office budget.
6. **Click Add, with the insertion point in the Cell Reference box select the range E3:E5, verify that <= is selected, click in the Constraint box, then click cell C9**
   You added the constraint that the budgeted salary amounts should be less than or equal to $400,000.
7. **Click Add, with the insertion point in the Cell Reference box select the range B3:B5, click the <= list arrow, click >=, with the insertion point in the Constraint box click cell C10, click OK, then click Solve**
   After you specified a constraint for all communications budgets to be a minimum of $65,000 and ran the Solver, Solver found a solution as indicated in the Solver Results dialog box.
8. **With the Keep Solver Solution option selected, click OK, compare your results to FIGURE 12-16, change the worksheet orientation to landscape, group the worksheets, add your name to the footers of the grouped worksheets, ungroup the worksheets, save and close the workbook, then submit the workbook to your instructor as directed**

FIGURE 12-15: Worksheet with constraints

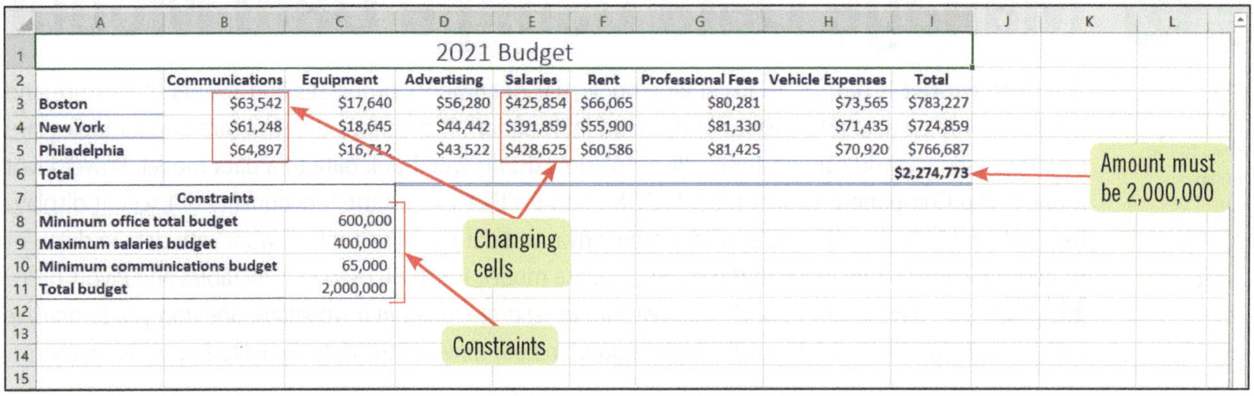

	A	B	C	D	E	F	G	H	I
1	2021 Budget								
2		Communications	Equipment	Advertising	Salaries	Rent	Professional Fees	Vehicle Expenses	Total
3	Boston	$63,542	$17,640	$56,280	$425,854	$66,065	$80,281	$73,565	$783,227
4	New York	$61,248	$18,645	$44,442	$391,859	$55,900	$81,330	$71,435	$724,859
5	Philadelphia	$64,897	$16,712	$43,522	$428,625	$60,586	$81,425	$70,920	$766,687
6	Total								$2,274,773
7	Constraints								
8	Minimum office total budget		600,000						
9	Maximum salaries budget		400,000						
10	Minimum communications budget		65,000						
11	Total budget		2,000,000						

FIGURE 12-16: Solver Solution

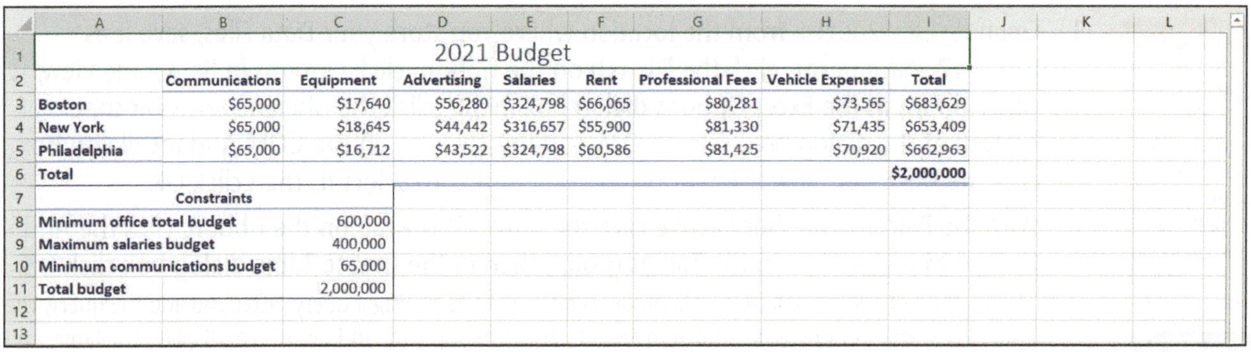

	A	B	C	D	E	F	G	H	I
1	2021 Budget								
2		Communications	Equipment	Advertising	Salaries	Rent	Professional Fees	Vehicle Expenses	Total
3	Boston	$65,000	$17,640	$56,280	$324,798	$66,065	$80,281	$73,565	$683,629
4	New York	$65,000	$18,645	$44,442	$316,657	$55,900	$81,330	$71,435	$653,409
5	Philadelphia	$65,000	$16,712	$43,522	$324,798	$60,586	$81,425	$70,920	$662,963
6	Total								$2,000,000
7	Constraints								
8	Minimum office total budget		600,000						
9	Maximum salaries budget		400,000						
10	Minimum communications budget		65,000						
11	Total budget		2,000,000						

Analyzing data using the Analysis ToolPak

The Analysis ToolPak is an Excel add-in that contains many statistical analysis tools. You can use one of these tools by clicking the Data tab, clicking the Data Analysis button in the Analysis group, selecting the desired analysis tool in the Data Analysis dialog box, clicking OK, entering the input range and other relevant specifications in the data tool's dialog box, then clicking OK. For example, clicking the Descriptive Statistics tool in the Data Analysis dialog box and selecting Summary statistics generates a statistical report including mean, median, mode, minimum, maximum, and sum for an input range you specify on your worksheet.

Creating an Answer Report

After solver finds a solution, you can generate an Answer Report summarizing the target cell information, the adjustable cells, and the constraints by selecting Answer from three types of reports in the Solver Results window, then clicking OK. The report appears as a separate worksheet named Answer Report 1 with three sections. The top section has the target cell information; it compares the original value of the target cell with the final value. The middle section of the report contains information about the adjustable cells. It lists the original and final values for all cells that were changed to reach the target value. The last report section has information about the constraints. Each constraint you added into Solver is listed in the Formula column, along with the cell address and a description of the cell data. The Cell Value column contains the Solver solution values for the cells. The Status column contains information on whether the constraints were binding or not binding in reaching the solution. Binding constraints indicate all of the allocated resource was used or the constraint was pushed to its limit. Nonbinding constraints indicate there was extra resource available after the constraint was met.

Excel
Module 12

Manage Data Using a Data Model

Learning Outcomes
- Add tables to the data model
- Create relationships between tables
- Update Power PivotTables

The **data model** is part of an Excel workbook that documents processes and events to capture and translate complex data into easy-to-understand information. It describes the structure of data tables and how they interact. You can use Power Pivot to add existing workbook data to a data model. Power Pivot is one of the Component Object Model (COM) add-ins that extend the functionality of Excel. It displays the workbook's data model and provides more advanced data analysis tools to work with data in different sources. Once data is included in the workbook data model, it can be used in PivotTables and PivotCharts. **CASE** *Ellie has placement and employee data in separate tables in a workbook. She asks you to analyze the data in both workbooks. You will add the data from both tables to the data model to begin your analysis.*

STEPS

TROUBLE
If a Power Pivot tab isn't displayed on your Ribbon, right-click the Ribbon, click Customize the Ribbon on the shortcut menu, then click the Power Pivot check box under Main Tabs to select it.

QUICK TIP
To open or close the calculation area in the Power Pivot window, click the Calculation Area button in the View group.

QUICK TIP
To add data to a data model that was imported using PowerQuery, click the Query Tools Query tab after loading the data into the workbook, click the Load To button in the Load group, in the Import Data dialog box, click Add this data to the Data Model, then click OK twice.

QUICK TIP
To open the Power Pivot window from the workbook, click the Data tab, then click the Go to the Power Pivot Window button in the Data Tools group.

1. **Open IL_EX_12-2.xlsx from the location where you store your Data Files, save it as IL_EX_12_Placements, click the File tab on the ribbon, click Options in Backstage view, click Add-ins in the Excel Options dialog box menu, click the Manage arrow at the bottom of the dialog box, select COM Add-ins, click Go, in the COM Add-ins dialog box click the Microsoft Power Pivot for Excel check box to select it, then click OK**
2. **With the Placements sheet active click the Power Pivot tab on the ribbon, click the Add to Data Model button in the Tables group, then in the Create Table dialog box click OK**

   This method of adding data to a data model is referred to as adding a query. After you add the query, the Power Pivot window opens, as shown in FIGURE 12-17. The top pane in Power Pivot displays the table, and the bottom pane is the calculation area.
3. **Click the Switch to Workbook button on the Quick Access Toolbar, click the Employees sheet tab, click cell A1, click the Power Pivot tab, click the Add to Data Model button in the Tables group, then click OK**

   The two tables are now part of the data model.
4. **Double-click the Table1 sheet tab in Power Pivot, type Placements, press ENTER, double-click the Table 2 sheet tab, type Employees, then press ENTER**
5. **Click the Design tab on the ribbon, then click the Create Relationship button in the Relationships group, in the Create Relationship dialog box click the first list arrow if necessary and click Employees, select the Emp# field if it is not already highlighted, click the second list arrow and click Placements, click the Recruiter ID field to highlight it, then click OK**

   Creating a relationship between tables allows you to access corresponding data from both tables.
6. **Click the Home tab, then click the Diagram View button in the View group**

   The two tables and their relationship are shown in FIGURE 12-18. This is a one-to-many relationship because each Emp# value can be associated with multiple RecruiterID rows in the Placements table.
7. **Click the Switch to Workbook button on the Quick Access Toolbar, click the Employees sheet tab if necessary, click cell B2, edit the name Anne Chard to Anne Flood, click the Power Pivot tab, click the Manage button in the Data Model group, click the Data View button in the View group, then click the Refresh button**

   The Data Refresh dialog box shows that the data was successfully updated.
8. **Click Close in the Data Refresh dialog box, widen the Name column to fully display the Employees' names, verify that Anne's last name in row 1 is Flood, then save your work**

FIGURE 12-17: PowerPivot window

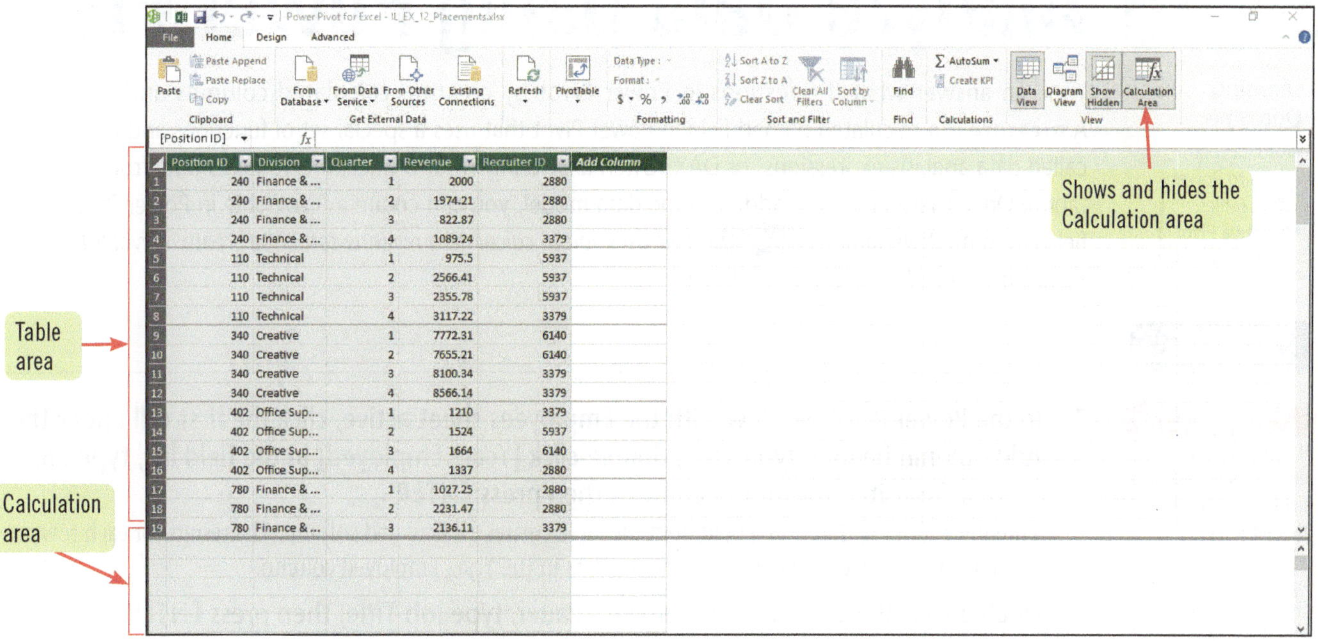

FIGURE 12-18: Diagram of the relationship between tables

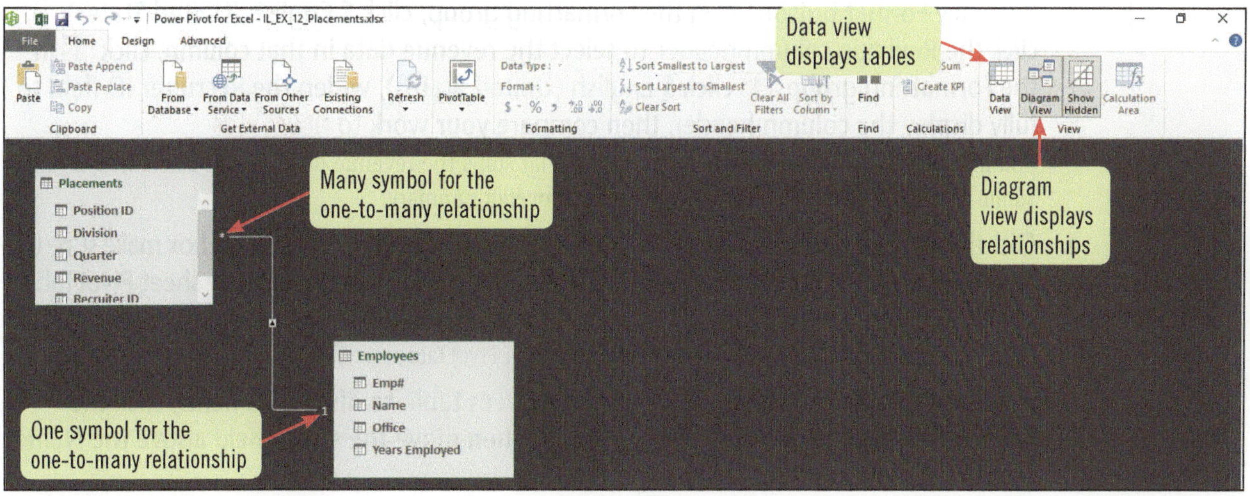

Using Power View to create visualizations

Power View is an Excel COM add-in used to create data visualizations such as charts and tables. You can use Power View to explore data relationships created with Power Pivot. To use Power View, you must first add a button to the ribbon. Right-click the ribbon, click Customize the Ribbon on the shortcut menu, click the Popular Commands list arrow, click Commands Not in the Ribbon, click Power View in the commands list, click the desired tab on the right side of the Excel Options dialog box, click the New Group button, then click Add. When you have table data in a worksheet, clicking the Power View button creates a new report in Power View, which is a single sheet that is added to the workbook. This report displays the table data. You can add a title to the report by clicking the Click here to add a title placeholder and typing the report title. The Power View Fields list allows you to edit the report fields. You can add a chart format visualization by clicking the Design tab if necessary, then clicking the chart type in the Switch Visualization group. To change the visualization type to a card format, click the Table button in the Switch Visualization group, then click Card.

Excel
Module 12

Analyze Data Using Power Pivot

Learning Outcomes
- Add calculations to Power PivotTables
- Create a PivotTable in Power Pivot

You can answer what-if questions in Power Pivot by creating calculated columns and measures. A **measure** is a calculated named field in Power Pivot that uses a special set of functions and commands called data analysis expressions, or DAX. Often answering what-if questions requires data from multiple tables. Once these tables are added to the data model, you can create a PivotTable in Power Pivot using fields from multiple tables. **CASE** *Ellie asks you to calculate a revenue total and create a PivotTable summarizing revenue by office and employee.*

STEPS

TROUBLE

If you receive an error or don't see the field list, make sure that after typing =IF(you type an open bracket ([ ) in the formula. Also, you don't have to type the closing parenthesis ( )) at the end of the formula because Excel adds it for you.

1. **In the Power Pivot window with the Employees sheet active, click the first cell under the Add Column header, type =IF([, double-click [Years Employed] in the field list, type >6, "Senior Recruiter","Junior Recruiter", then press ENTER**

   Entering a formula that uses a field from the table creates a calculated column. The results for each row are filled down the calculated column using the data in the Years Employed column.

2. **Double-click the Calculated Column 1 header, type Job Title, then press ENTER**

3. **Activate the Placements table in the PowerPivot window, click the first cell in the Calculation Area below the Revenue data, click the AutoSum button in the Calculations group, widen the Revenue column to fully display the Sum of Revenue, click the Apply Currency Format button [$] in the Formatting group, click $ English (United States), click the Revenue column header to select the revenue data in that column, click [$] in the Formatting group, [$] click $ English (United States), widen the Recruiter ID field to fully display the column header, then compare your work to FIGURE 12-19**

   You inserted a measure in the calculation area that sums the revenue data. Where calculated columns summarize data in each row, a measure creates an overall summary.

4. **Click the PivotTable button on the Home tab, in the Create PivotTable dialog box make sure the New Worksheet option button is selected, click OK, then rename the new sheet PivotTable**

   The PivotTable Fields pane opens with both tables in the data model. When creating a PivotTable in Power Pivot, you can combine fields from multiple tables in a PivotTable.

5. **In the PivotTable Fields pane click the Employees table to display its fields, click the Name check box, click the Office check box, then move the Office field above the Name field in the Rows area**

   The data from the Name and Office fields are placed in the PivotTable rows.

6. **In the PivotTable Fields pane scroll down, click the Placements table to expand its fields, click the Division check box, move the Division field from the Rows area to the Columns area, click the Quarter check box, move the Quarter field to the Filters area, then click the Revenue check box**

   The PivotTable summarizes data from both tables and can answer questions about revenue from the Placements table related to the JCL offices in the Employee table.

7. **Click the PivotTable Analyze tab on the ribbon, click the Field Headers button in the Show group to deselect it, close the PivotTable Fields pane, change the worksheet orientation to landscape, then compare your PivotTable to FIGURE 12-20**

8. **sam Group the worksheets, add your name to the grouped footers, ungroup the sheets, save the workbook, close the workbook, close Excel, then submit the workbook to your instructor as directed**

FIGURE 12-19: Calculation Area with measure

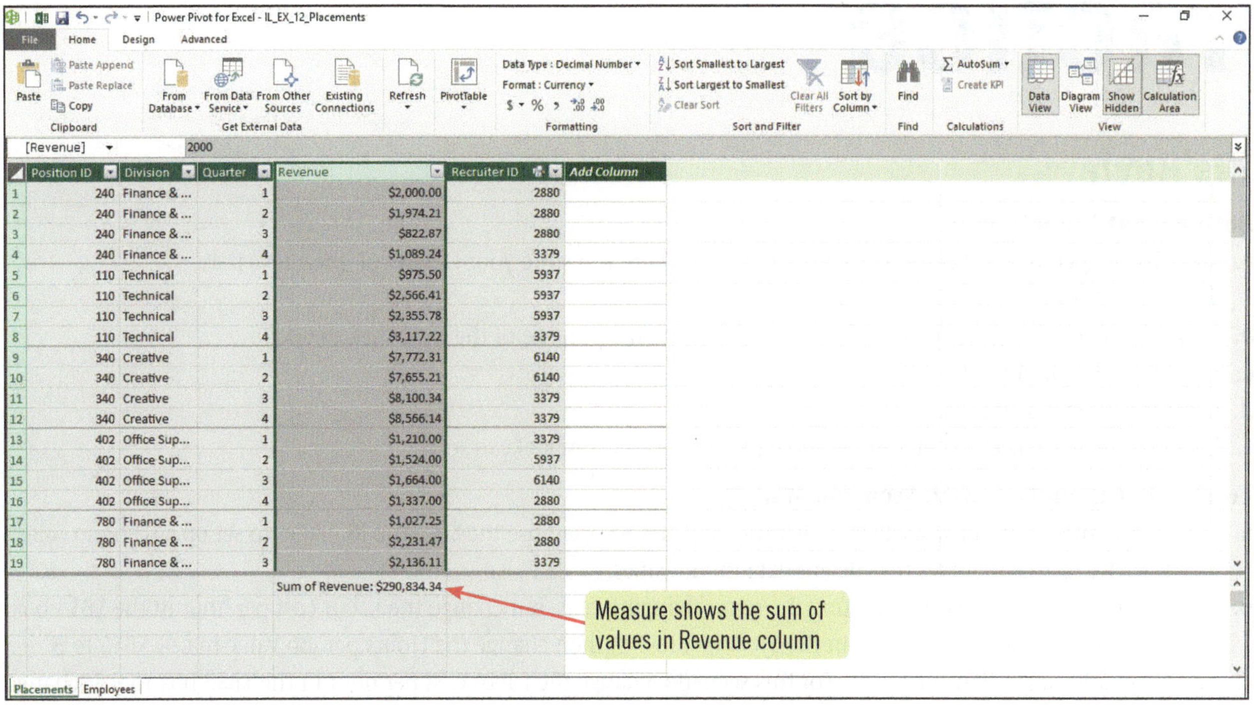

FIGURE 12-20: PivotTable created in Power Pivot

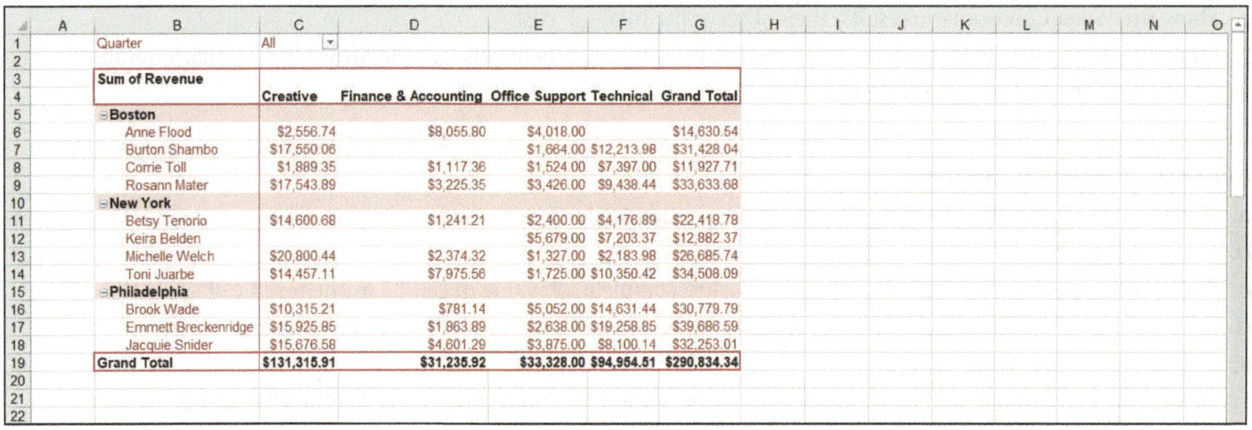

Quarter	All				
Sum of Revenue	**Creative**	**Finance & Accounting**	**Office Support**	**Technical**	**Grand Total**
Boston					
Anne Flood	$2,556.74	$8,055.80	$4,018.00		$14,630.54
Burton Shambo	$17,550.06		$1,664.00	$12,213.98	$31,428.04
Corrie Toll	$1,889.35	$1,117.36	$1,524.00	$7,397.00	$11,927.71
Rosann Mater	$17,543.89	$3,225.35	$3,426.00	$9,438.44	$33,633.68
New York					
Betsy Tenorio	$14,600.68	$1,241.21	$2,400.00	$4,176.89	$22,418.78
Keira Belden			$5,679.00	$7,203.37	$12,882.37
Michelle Welch	$20,800.44	$2,374.32	$1,327.00	$2,183.98	$26,685.74
Toni Juarbe	$14,457.11	$7,975.56	$1,725.00	$10,350.42	$34,508.09
Philadelphia					
Brook Wade	$10,315.21	$781.14	$5,052.00	$14,631.44	$30,779.79
Emmett Breckenridge	$15,925.85	$1,863.89	$2,638.00	$19,258.85	$39,686.59
Jacquie Snider	$15,676.58	$4,601.29	$3,875.00	$8,100.14	$32,253.01
Grand Total	**$131,315.91**	**$31,235.92**	**$33,328.00**	**$94,954.51**	**$290,834.34**

Using the Excel 3D Maps tool

Power Map, also called 3D Maps, is an Excel COM add-in that helps to visualize worksheet data in 3-D formats. To insert a Power Map into a worksheet, click the Insert tab, then click 3D Map in the Tours group. Data should be organized in a table for mapping. The 3D Maps window opens with its own ribbon containing a Home tab, a Tour pane on the left showing Tour 1, an automatically created Tour with a single scene, a Field List showing the fields available to map, and a Layer pane on the right with areas for map locations, height, category, and time. A tour is a list of maps in the 3D Map and each map is a scene. Most often 3D Maps contain several scenes that make up an animation offering different points of focus of the data. You can create a new scene by clicking the New Scene button in the Scene group, then dragging fields from the Field List to the desired areas on the Layer pane. Fields with location data can be dragged to the Location area, fields with values should be placed in the height area, the category area holds fields for different markers, and the time area shows the map changes over time. When you save your workbook, 3D Map tours and scenes are saved.

Practice

Skills Review

1. Define what-if analysis.

- **a.** Start Excel, open IL_EX_12-3.xlsx from the location where you store your Data Files, then save it as **IL_EX_12_Freight**.
- **b.** Examine the Equipment Repair worksheet to determine the purpose of the worksheet model.
- **c.** Locate the data input cells.
- **d.** Locate any dependent cells.
- **e.** Examine the worksheet to determine problems the worksheet model can solve.

2. Track what-if analysis with Scenario Manager.

- **a.** On the Equipment Repair worksheet, select the range B3:B5, then use the Scenario Manager to set up a scenario called **Most Likely** that includes the current data input values.
- **b.** Add a scenario called **Best Case** using the same changing cells, but change the Labor cost per hour in the B3 box to **85**, change the Parts cost per job in the B4 box to **75**, then change the Hours per job value in cell B5 to **3**.
- **c.** Add a scenario called **Worst Case**. For this scenario, change the Labor cost per hour in the B3 box to **95**, change the Parts cost per job in the B4 box to **85**, then change the Hours per job in the B5 box to **4**.
- **d.** If necessary, drag the Scenario Manager dialog box to the right until columns A and B are visible.
- **e.** Show the Worst Case scenario results, then observe the total job cost.
- **f.** Show the Best Case scenario results, then observe the job cost. Finally, display the Most Likely scenario results.
- **g.** Close the Scenario Manager dialog box.
- **h.** Save the workbook.

3. Generate a scenario summary.

- **a.** Create names for the input value cells and the dependent cell using the range selection A3:B7.
- **b.** Verify that the names were created.
- **c.** Create a scenario summary report, using the Cost to complete job value in cell B7 as the result cell.
- **d.** Edit the title of the Summary report in cell B2 to **Scenario Summary for Equipment Repair**.
- **e.** Delete the Current Values column.
- **f.** Delete row 1, column A, and the notes beginning in cell B11. Compare your worksheet to FIGURE 12-21.
- **g.** Add your name in the center section of the Scenario Summary sheet footer, then save the workbook.

FIGURE 12-21

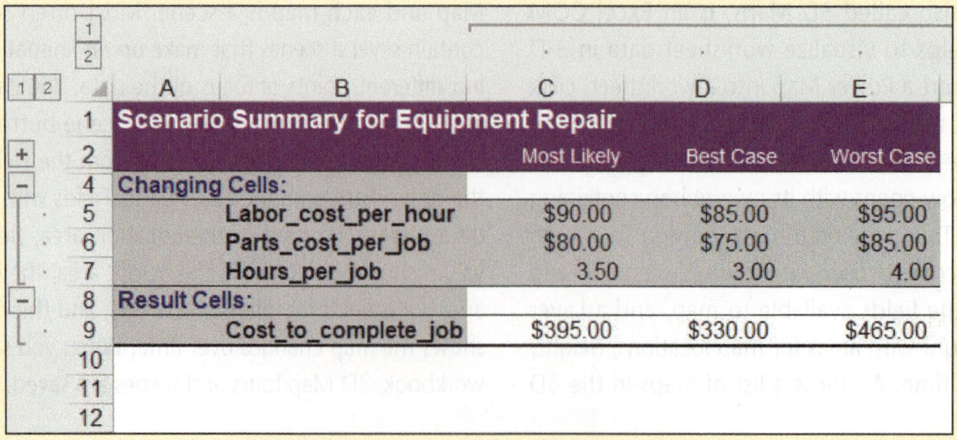

Skills Review (continued)

4. Project figures using a data table.

- **a.** Activate the Equipment Repair sheet.
- **b.** Enter the label **Labor $** in cell D3.
- **c.** Format the label so that it is bold and right-aligned.
- **d.** In cell D4, enter **80**. Select the range D4:D8, then fill the range with values using a linear series in a column with a step value of 5.
- **e.** In cell E3, reference the job cost formula by entering **=B7**.
- **f.** Format the contents of cell E3 as hidden, entering the ;;; Custom formatting type on the Number tab of the Format Cells dialog box.
- **g.** Generate the new job costs based on the varying labor costs. Select the range D3:E8 and create a data table. In the Data Table dialog box, make cell B3 (the labor cost) the column input cell.
- **h.** Format the range D4:E8 as currency with two decimal places.
- **i.** Enter your name in the center section of the worksheet footer, then save the workbook.

5. Use Goal Seek.

- **a.** Click cell B7, then open the Goal Seek dialog box.
- **b.** Assuming the labor rate and hours remain the same, determine what the parts cost per job would have to be so that the cost to complete the job is $350. (*Hint:* Enter a job cost of **350** as the To value, then enter **B4** as the By changing cell.) Write down the parts cost that Goal Seek finds.
- **c.** Click OK, then press CTRL+Z to reset the parts cost to its original value.
- **d.** Enter the parts cost that you found in Step 5b into cell A14, formatted as currency with no decimal places.
- **e.** Assuming the parts cost and hours remain the same, determine the labor cost per hour so that the cost to complete the job is $350. Press CTRL+Z to reset the labor cost to its original value. Enter the labor cost in cell A15.
- **f.** Save the workbook, then compare your worksheet to **FIGURE 12-22**.

FIGURE 12-22

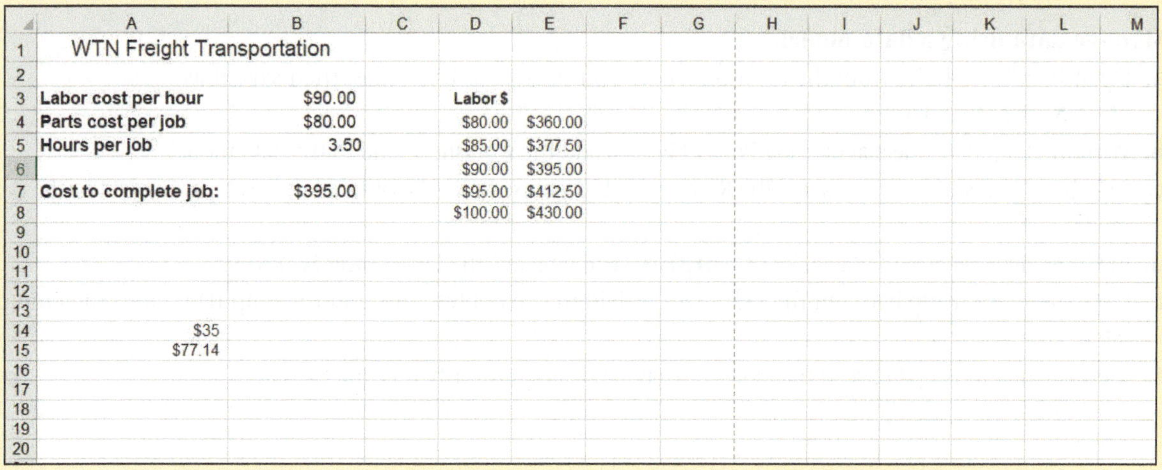

	A	B	C	D	E
1	WTN Freight Transportation				
2					
3	Labor cost per hour	$90.00		Labor $	
4	Parts cost per job	$80.00		$80.00	$360.00
5	Hours per job	3.50		$85.00	$377.50
6				$90.00	$395.00
7	Cost to complete job:	$395.00		$95.00	$412.50
8				$100.00	$430.00
14	$35				
15	$77.14				

Skills Review (continued)

6. Find solutions using Solver.

a. Activate the Transportation Costs sheet, then open the Solver Parameters dialog box.

b. Make B14 (the grand total cost) the objective cell, with a target value of 16,000.

c. Use cells B6:D6 (the number of all scheduled trips) as the changing cells.

d. Specify that cells B6:D6 must be integers. (*Hint:* Select int in the Add Constraint dialog box.)

e. Specify that cells B6:D6 must be greater than or equal to 10.

f. Use Solver to find a solution. Keep the Solver solution, then compare your worksheet to **FIGURE 12-23**.

FIGURE 12-23

	A	B	C	D	E	F	G	H	I	J	K	L	M
1	WTN Freight Transportation												
2													
3		Heavy	Standard	Small									
4	Labor Cost Per Trip	$110.00	$100.00	$95.00									
5	Parts Cost Per Trip	$150.00	$130.00	$100.00									
6	Trips Scheduled	23	33	13									
7													
8	Labor Cost Per Size	$2,483.89	$3,286.00	$1,252.63									
9	Parts Cost Per Size	$3,387.12	$4,271.79	$1,318.56									
10	Total Cost Per Size	$5,871.01	$7,557.79	$2,571.20									
11													
12	Total Labor Cost	$7,022.52											
13	Total Parts Cost	$8,977.48											
14	Grand Total Cost	$16,000.00											
15													
16													
17													
18													
19													
20													

g. Enter your name in the center section of the worksheet footer, save the workbook, close the workbook, then submit the workbook to your instructor as directed.

7. Manage data using a data model.

a. Open IL_EX_12-4.xlsx from the location where you store your Data Files, then save it as **IL_EX_12_Employee**.

b. With the Employee sheet active, use Power Pivot to add the worksheet data to the data model.

c. Switch to Worksheet view, activate the Routes sheet, then use Power Pivot to add the worksheet data to the data model.

d. In Power Pivot, rename the Table1 sheet **Employee**, then name the Table2 sheet **Routes**.

e. Create a relationship between the Employee # field in the Routes table and the Emp ID field in the Employee table.

f. View the relationship between the tables in Diagram View and verify it is one to many.

g. Return to the workbook, activate the Employee sheet, then change the contents of cell B2 to **Concord** and cell D2 to **D. McKay**.

h. Return to the data model in Power Pivot, activate the Employee sheet, then refresh the worksheet data. (*Hint:* To return to the data model in Power Pivot, click the Manage button in the Data Model group.)

8. Analyze data using PowerPivot.

a. Activate the Routes sheet in the Power Pivot window, then add a measure in the calculation area to sum the Trip Cost data. (*Hint:* Click the first cell in the calculation area below the Trip Cost data, then use the AutoSum button in the Calculation group on the Home tab.)

b. Widen the Trip Cost column to fully display the Sum of Trip Cost, then format the value using the $ English (United States) Currency format and no decimal places.

c. Create a PivotTable on a new worksheet named **PivotTable** that adds the Location field from the Employee table to the Rows area, the Manager field from the Employee table to the Rows area, the Employee # field from the Routes table to the Rows area, the Trip Cost field from the Routes table to the Values area, and the Vehicle Size field from the Routes table to the Columns area.

d. Use a tool on the Power Pivot Analyze tab to hide the Field Headers, then compare your PivotTable to FIGURE 12-24.

FIGURE 12-24

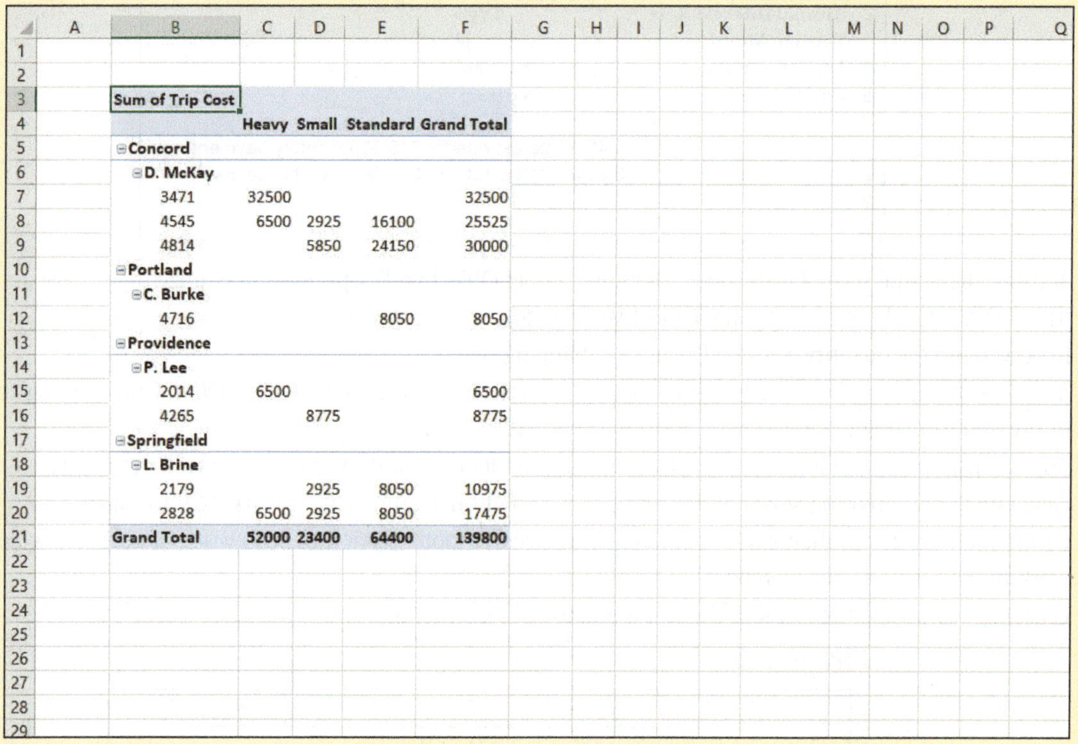

Sum of Trip Cost				
	Heavy	Small	Standard	Grand Total
Concord				
D. McKay				
3471	32500			32500
4545	6500	2925	16100	25525
4814		5850	24150	30000
Portland				
C. Burke				
4716			8050	8050
Providence				
P. Lee				
2014	6500			6500
4265		8775		8775
Springfield				
L. Brine				
2179		2925	8050	10975
2828	6500	2925	8050	17475
Grand Total	52000	23400	64400	139800

e. Close Power Pivot, group the worksheets, add your name to the footer of the worksheets, ungroup the worksheets, save and close the workbook, submit the workbook to your instructor, then close Excel.

Independent Challenge 1

You are assisting Tony Sanchez, the office manager at Riverwalk Medical Clinic, with a disaster recovery plan for the medical records at the clinic. As part of that plan you are looking at two options for storing backup medical records. The first option is to purchase a storage facility, and the second is to use a third-party backup storage company that offers off-site small, medium, and large storage areas. In both cases, you want to keep your monthly payments below $1700. You decide to use Goal Seek to look at various interest rates for purchasing a storage facility and to use Solver to help find the best possible combination of third-party storage areas.

a. Start Excel, open IL_EX_12-5.xlsx from the location where you store your Data Files, then save it as **IL_EX_12_Records**.

b. With the Purchase sheet active, use Goal Seek to find the interest rate that produces a monthly payment of $16,500, and write down the interest rate that Goal Seek finds. Reset the interest rate to its original value, record the interest rate in cell A7, then enter **Interest rate for $16,500 monthly payment** in cell B7.

c. Use Goal Seek to find the interest rate that produces a monthly payment of $16,000. Reset the interest rate to its original value, record the interest rate in cell A8, then enter **Interest rate for $16,000 monthly payment** in cell B8. Compare your worksheet to FIGURE 12-25.

FIGURE 12-25

	A	B	C	D	E
1	Riverwalk Clinic				
2	Annual Interest Rate	5.75%			
3	Term in Months	48			
4	Loan Amount	$ 725,000			
5	Monthly Payment	$16,943.67			
6					
7	4.40%	Interest rate for $16,500 monthly payment			
8	2.85%	Interest rate for $16,000 monthly payment			
9					
10					

d. Activate the Rental sheet. Open Solver, then use the Set Objective To option to maximize the storage amount in cell B12. (*Hint:* Select Max in the Set the Objective To area.)

e. In Solver, use the quantity, cells B6:D6, as the changing cells.

f. Add a constraint to Solver specifying the quantity in cells B6:D6 must be integers. (*Hint:* Choose int as the operator in the Add Constraint dialog box.)

g. Add a constraint specifying that the total monthly payment amount in cell B11 is less than or equal to 17000.

h. Generate a solution using Solver and accept Solver's solution. Compare your worksheet to FIGURE 12-26.

i. Group the worksheets, then enter your name in the center footer section of both worksheets. Preview both worksheets, then save the workbook.

j. Close the workbook, then submit the workbook to your instructor.

FIGURE 12-26

	A	B	C	D
1	Riverwalk Clinic			
2				
3		Large	Medium	Small
4	Rental Fee	$ 4,200	$ 3,000	$ 2,400
5	Capacity (cubic feet)	210	150	100
6	Quantity	3	2	0
7				
8	Monthly Payment	$ 11,604	$ 5,396	$ -
9	Storage Capacity	580	270	0
10				
11	Total Monthly Payment	$ 17,000		
12	Total Storage Capacity	850		
13				

Independent Challenge 2

As a senior financial analyst at North Shore CPA Services, you are researching various options for financing a $250,000 loan for the purchase of a new estate-planning facility. You haven't decided whether to finance the project for three, four, or five years. Each loan term carries a different interest rate. To help with the comparison, you summarize these options using a scenario summary. You will also create a two-input data table to analyze additional interest rates and terms.

- **a.** Start Excel, open IL_EX_12-6.xlsx from the location where you store your Data Files, then save it as **IL_EX_12_Loan**.
- **b.** Create cell names for cells B4:B11 based on the labels in cells A4:A11, using the Create Names from Selection dialog box.
- **c.** Use Scenario Manager to create scenarios that calculate the monthly payment on a $250,000 loan under the three sets of loan possibilities listed below. (*Hint:* Create three scenarios, using cells B5:B6 as the changing cells.)

Scenario Name	Interest Rate	Term
5% 5 Year	.05	60
4.5% 4 Year	.045	48
4% 3 Year	.04	36

- **d.** View each scenario and confirm that it performs as intended, then display the 5% 5 Year scenario.
- **e.** Generate a scenario summary titled **Finance Options**. Use cells B9:B11 as the Result cells.
- **f.** Delete the Current Values column in the report and the notes at the bottom of the report, row 1, and column A. Rename the sheet **Estate Planning Project**.
- **g.** Activate the Loan sheet. Using FIGURE 12-27 as a guide, enter the input values for a two-input data table with varying interest rates for 3-, 4-, and 5-year terms. Use a linear series to enter the interest rates.
- **h.** Reference the monthly payment amount from cell B9 in cell A13, then format the contents of cell A13 so they are hidden.
- **i.** Generate a data table, using cells A13:D22, that shows the effect of varying interest rates and loan terms on the monthly payments. (*Hint:* Use cell B6, Term in Months, as the Row input cell, and cell B5, the Annual Interest Rate, as the Column input cell.)
- **j.** Format the range B14:D22 as currency with two decimal places.
- **k.** Group the two worksheets, then enter your name in the center section of the grouped footer.
- **l.** Save the workbook, close the workbook, submit the workbook to your instructor as directed, then close Excel.

FIGURE 12-27

	A	B	C	D	E
1	North Shore CPA Services				
2	Financing Options				
3					
4	Loan Amount	$250,000.00			
5	Annual Interest Rate	5.00%			
6	Term in Months	60			
7					
8					
9	Monthly Payment:	$4,717.81			
10	Total Payments:	$283,068.50			
11	Total Interest:	$33,068.50			
12					
13		36	48	60	
14	3.00%				
15	3.25%				
16	3.50%				
17	3.75%				
18	4.00%				
19	4.25%				
20	4.50%				
21	4.75%				
22	5.00%				
23					

Visual Workshop

Open the file IL_EX_12-7.xlsx from the location where you store your Data Files, then save it as **IL_EX_12_Orders**. Using the two worksheets, create the data model shown in the Power Pivot window in **FIGURE 12-28**. (*Hint:* When entering the formula to calculate the balance, click each column header to enter the Total and Paid values.) Then, using the data model, create the PivotTable shown in **FIGURE 12-29**. (*Hint:* Create a one-to-many relationship between the ID field in the Customers table and the Cust_ID field in the Orders table, then create the PivotTable.) When you are finished, add your name to the center footer section of the PivotTable sheet, save the workbook, submit the workbook to your instructor as directed, then close Excel.

FIGURE 12-28

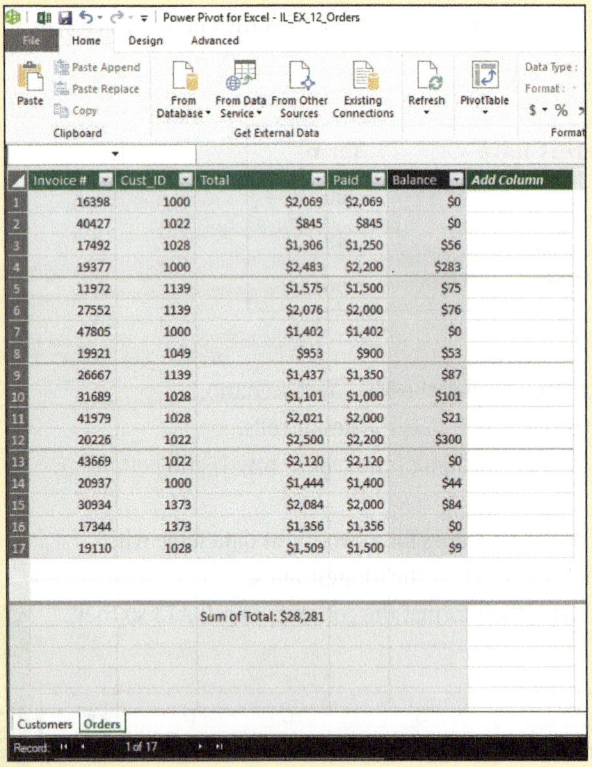

FIGURE 12-29

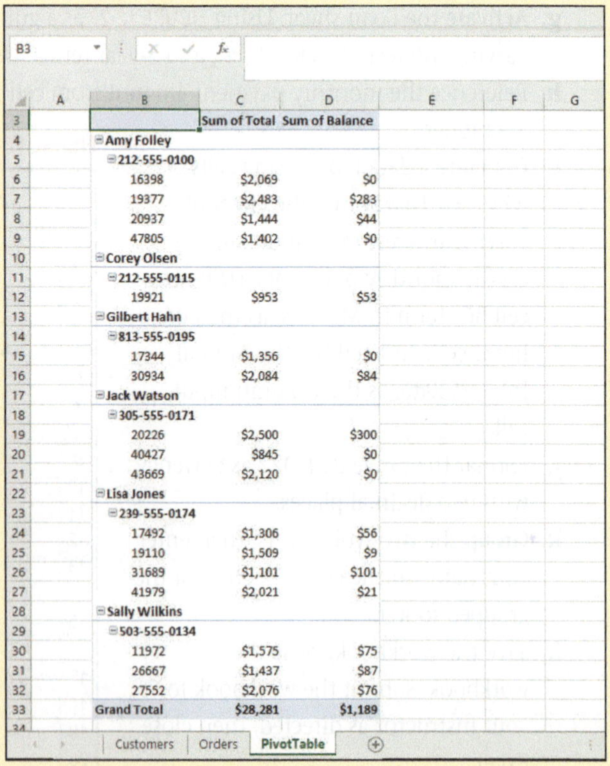

Access **Module 9**

Creating Action Queries

CASE You are working with Lydia Snyder, vice president of operations at JCL Talent, to build a research database to manage industry, company, and job data. In this module, you'll work with action queries to back up and modify data. You will also learn how to modify join properties in a query to answer questions about the relationships between the tables.

Module Objectives

After completing this module, you will be able to:

- Create a Make Table query
- Create an Append query
- Create a Delete query
- Create an Update Query
- Create an outer join
- Apply an outer join
- Create a self join

Files You Will Need

IL_AC_9-1.accdb
IL_AC_9-2.accdb
IL_AC_9-3.accdb
IL_AC_9-4.accdb
IL_AC_9-5.accdb

Create a Make Table Query

Learning Outcomes
- Define action queries
- Create a Make Table query

All the queries you have created prior to this module are Select queries. A **Select query** starts with the SQL keyword **SELECT** to select fields and records that match specific criteria. When you **run** a select query in Access, a datasheet of the selected fields and records is produced. An **action query** not only selects, but also *changes* all the selected data when it is run. Access provides four types of action queries: Make Table, Append, Delete, and Update. See TABLE 9-1 for more information on action queries. A **Make Table query** is a type of action query that creates a new table of data. The location of the new table can be the current database or another Access database. CASE *Lydia Snyder asks you to archive the first month's jobs for the year 2021 that are currently stored in the Jobs table. A Make Table query will handle this request.*

STEPS

1. **sam Start Access, open the IL_AC_9-1.accdb database from the location where you store your Data Files, save it as IL_AC_9_Jobs, enable content if prompted, click the Create tab on the ribbon, click the Query Design button, double-click Jobs in the Show Table dialog box, then click Close**

   All action queries start out as select queries.

2. **Double-click the * (asterisk) at the top of the Jobs field list**

   Adding the asterisk to the query design grid adds all the fields in that table to the grid. Later, if you add new fields to the Jobs table, they are automatically included in this query.

> **QUICK TIP**
> Access automatically adds pound signs (#) around date criteria.

3. **Use ⇕ to resize the field list to see all fields, double-click the FirstPosted field to add it to the second column of the query grid, click the FirstPosted field Criteria cell, type >=1/1/21 and <=1/31/21, click the FirstPosted field Show check box to uncheck it, then use the ✛ resize pointer to widen the FirstPosted column to view the entire Criteria entry, as shown in FIGURE 9-1**

   Before changing this Select query into a Make Table query, it is always a good idea to run the query as a Select query to view the selected data.

> **QUICK TIP**
> For a Select query, the Datasheet View button and the Run button do the same thing: display the selected data in a datasheet.

4. **Click the View button to switch to Datasheet View, click any entry in the FirstPosted field, then click the Descending button in the Sort & Filter group**

   Sorting the records in descending order based on the values in the FirstPosted field allows you to confirm that only records in January of 2021 appear in the datasheet.

5. **Click the View button to return to Design View, click the Make Table button in the Query Type group, type Jan2021 in the Table Name box, then click OK**

   The Make Table query is ready, but action queries do not change data until you click the Run button. All action query icons display an exclamation point to remind you that they change data only when you run them. To prevent running an action query accidentally, use the Datasheet View button to view the selected records for an action query. Use the Run button only when you are ready to run the action.

> **QUICK TIP**
> To quickly copy an entire table, right-click it in the Navigation Pane, then click Copy. Right-click the Navigation Pane, then click Paste.

6. **Click the View button to double-check the records you have selected, click the View button to return to Query Design View, click the Run button to execute the action, click Yes when prompted that you are about to paste 39 rows, save the query with the name MakeJan2021, then close it**

   When you run an action query, Access prompts you with an "Are you sure?" message before actually updating the data. The Undo button cannot undo changes made by action queries.

7. **Double-click the Jan2021 table in the Navigation Pane to view the new table's datasheet, as shown in FIGURE 9-2, then close the Jan2021 table**

FIGURE 9-1: Creating a Make Table query

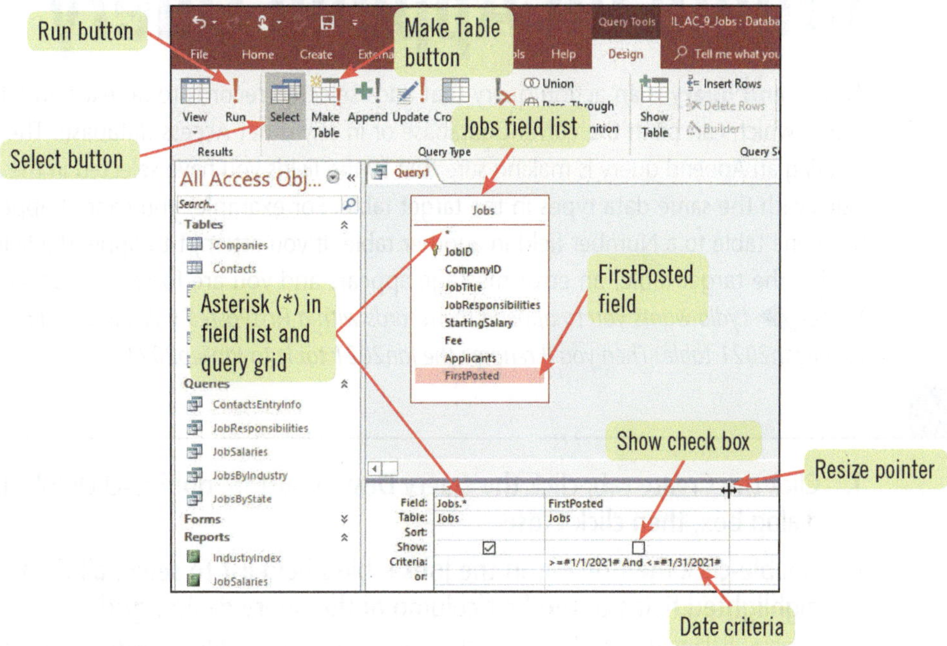

FIGURE 9-2: Jan2021 table datasheet

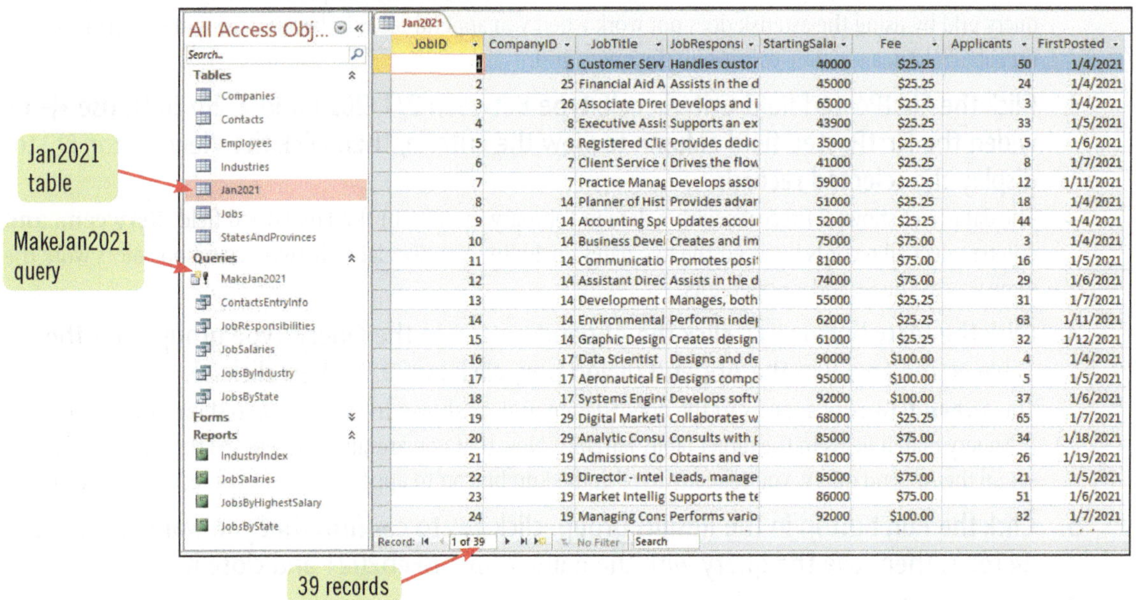

TABLE 9-1: Action queries

action query	query icon	description	example
Make Table		Creates a new table from data in one or more tables	Make a backup copy of employee data in the same or another database
Append		Adds a group of records from one or more tables to the end of another table	Append the records of an employee table from one division of the company to the employee table from another division
Update		Updates the value of a field	Raise prices by 10 percent for selected products in the Products table
Delete		Deletes a group of records from one or more tables	Remove products that are discontinued from a Products table

Access

Access
Module 9

Create an Append Query

Learning Outcome
- Create an Append query

An **Append query** is an action query that adds selected records to an existing table called the **target table**, which can be in the current database or in any other Access database. The most difficult part of creating an Append query is making sure that all the fields you have selected in the Append query match fields with the same data types in the target table. For example, you cannot append a Short Text field from one table to a Number field in another table. If you attempt to append a field to an incompatible field in the target table, an error message appears and you are forced to cancel the append process.

CASE *Lydia wants you to append the records with a FirstPosted value in February 2021 in the Jobs table to the Jan2021 table. Then you'll rename the Jan2021 table to JanFeb2021.*

STEPS

1. **Click the Create tab, click the Query Design button, double-click Jobs in the Show Table dialog box, then click Close**
2. **Double-click the title bar in the Jobs table's field list to select all fields, then drag the highlighted fields to the first column of the query design grid**

   Double-clicking the title bar of the field list selects all the fields, allowing you to quickly add them to the query grid. To successfully append records to a table, you need to identify how each field in the query is connected to an existing field in the target table. Therefore, the technique of adding all the fields to the query grid by using the asterisk does not work when you append records, because using the asterisk doesn't list each field in a separate column in the query grid.
3. **Click the FirstPosted field Criteria cell, type Between 2/1/2021 and 2/28/2021, use ✣ to widen the FirstPosted field column to view the criteria, then click the View button to display the selected records**

   The datasheet shows 24 records with a date in February of 2021 in the FirstPosted field. **Between...and** criteria select all records between the two dates, including the two dates. Between...and operators work the same way as the >= and <= operators.
4. **Click the View button, click the Append button in the Query Type group, click the Table Name arrow in the Append dialog box, click Jan2021, then click OK**

   The **Append To row** appears in the query design grid, as shown in FIGURE 9-3, to show how the fields in the query match fields in the target table, Jan2021. Now that you are sure you selected the right records and set up the Append query, you're ready to click the Run button to append the selected records to the table.
5. **Click the Run button in the Results group, click Yes to confirm that you want to append 24 rows, then save the query with the name AppendFeb2021 and close it**
6. **Double-click the Jan2021 table in the Navigation Pane, click any entry in the FirstPosted field, then click the Descending button in the Sort & Filter group**

   The 24 February records are appended to the Jan2021 table, which previously had 39 records for a new total of 63 records, as shown in FIGURE 9-4.
7. **Save and close the Jan2021 table, right-click the Jan2021 table, click Rename, type JanFeb2021, then press ENTER**

FIGURE 9-3: Creating an Append query

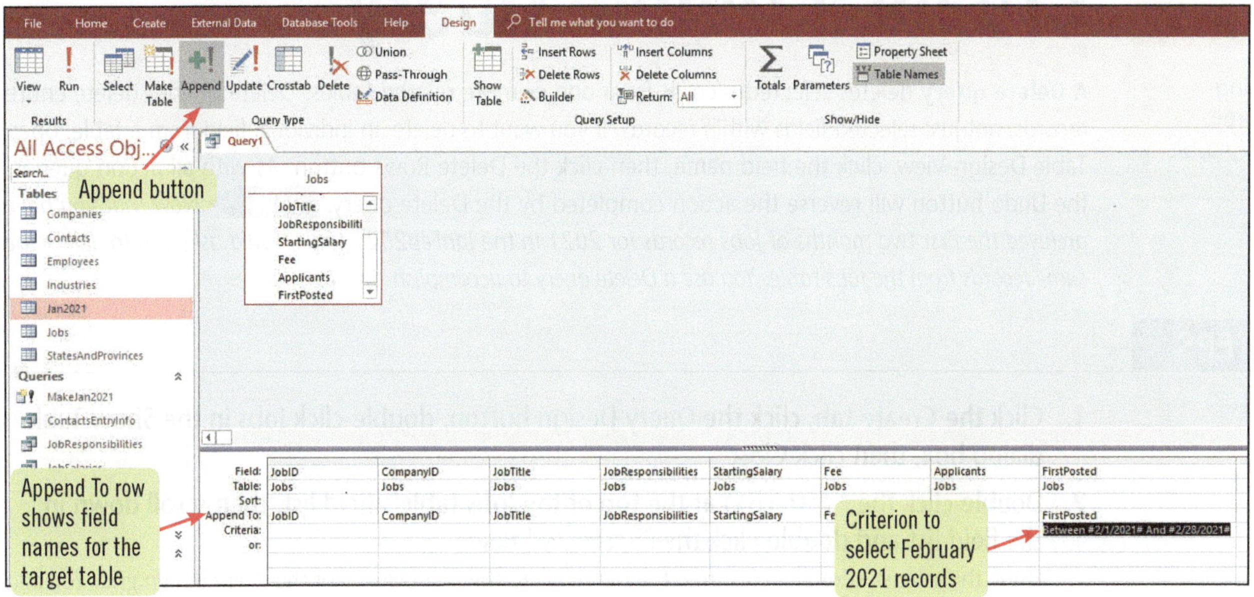

FIGURE 9-4: Jan2021 table with appended records

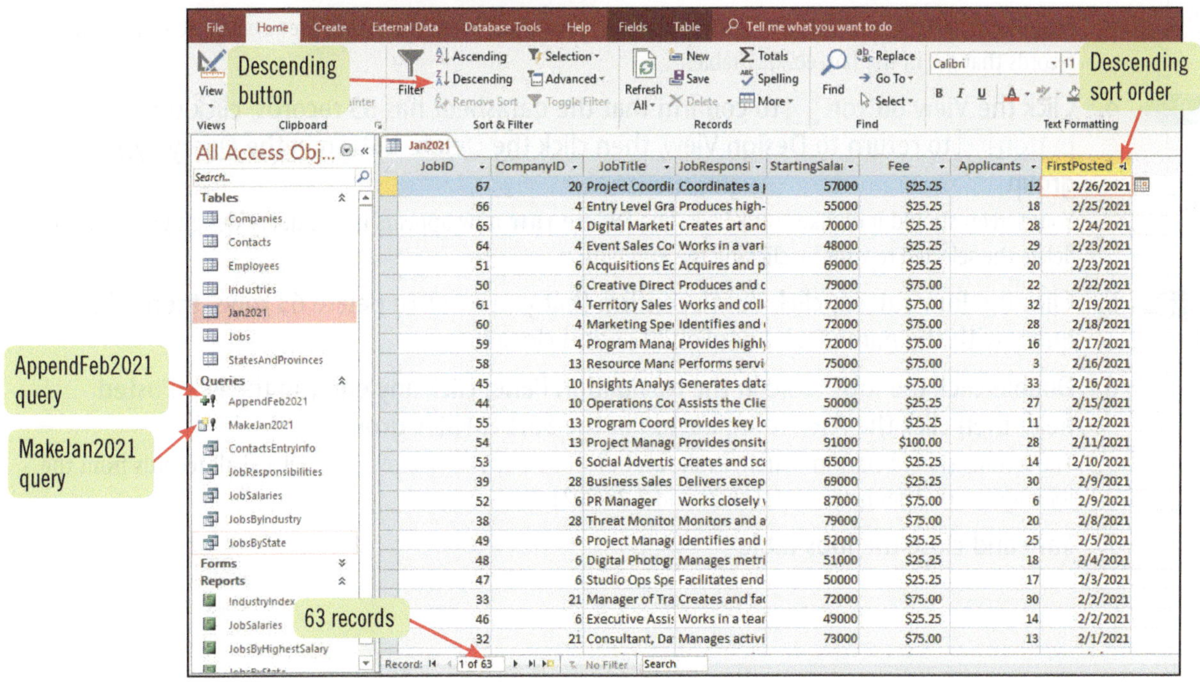

1900 versus 2000 dates

If you type only two digits of a date, Access assumes that the digits 00 through 29 are for the years 2000 through 2029. If you type 30 through 99, Access assumes the years refer to 1930 through 1999. If you want to specify years outside these ranges, you must type all four digits of the year.

Access
Module 9

Create a Delete Query

Learning Outcome
- Create a Delete query

A **Delete query** deletes selected records from one or more related tables. Delete queries delete entire records, not just selected fields within records. If you want to delete an individual field from a table, open Table Design View, click the field name, then click the Delete Rows button. As with all action queries, the Undo button will reverse the action completed by the Delete query. **CASE** *Now that you have archived the first two months of Jobs records for 2021 in the JanFeb2021 table, Lydia asks you to delete the same records from the Jobs table. You use a Delete query to accomplish this task.*

STEPS

QUICK TIP
To delete a row in the query grid, select it using the ➡ pointer (point to the left edge of the row), then press DELETE.

QUICK TIP
The View button is always a safe way to view selected records of all queries.

QUICK TIP
Actions taken by the Run button for any action query cannot be undone.

1. **Click the Create tab, click the Query Design button, double-click Jobs in the Show Table dialog box, then click Close**
2. **Double-click the * (asterisk) at the top of the Jobs table's field list, then scroll down in the field list and double-click the FirstPosted field**

   Using the asterisk adds all fields from the Jobs table to the first column of the query design grid. You add the FirstPosted field to the second column of the query design grid so you can enter limiting criteria for this field.
3. **Click the FirstPosted field Criteria cell, type Between 1/1/21 and 2/28/21, then use ✛ to widen the FirstPosted field column to view the criterion**

   Before you run a Delete query, be sure to check the selected records to make sure you selected the same 63 records that are in the JanFeb2021 table.
4. **Click the View button to confirm that the datasheet has 63 records, click the View button to return to Design View, then click the Delete button in the Query Type group**

   Your screen should look like FIGURE 9-5. The **Delete row** now appears in the query design grid. You can delete the selected records by clicking the Run button.
5. **Click the Run button, click Yes to confirm that you want to delete 63 rows, then save the query with the name DeleteJanFeb2021 and close it**
6. **Double-click the Jobs table in the Navigation Pane, click any entry in the FirstPosted field, then click the Ascending button in the Sort & Filter group**

   The records should start in March, as shown in FIGURE 9-6. The Delete query deleted all records from the Jobs table with dates between 1/1/2021 and 2/28/2021.
7. **Save and close the Jobs table**

FIGURE 9-5: Creating a Delete query

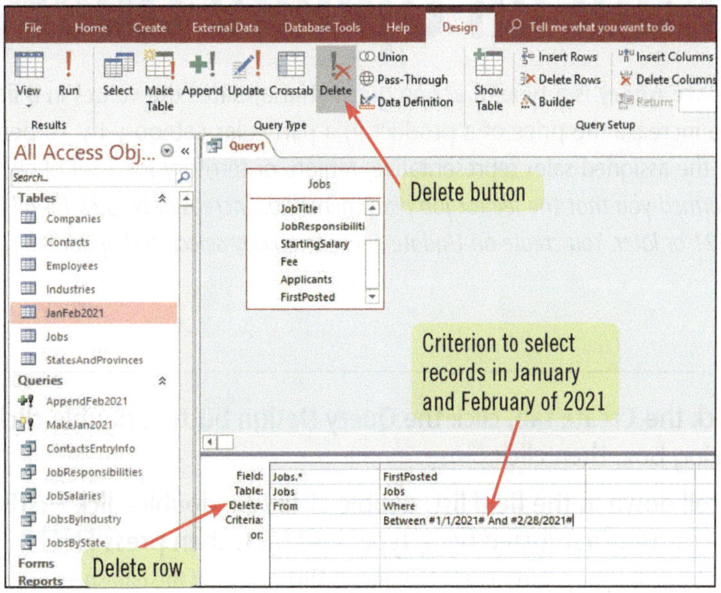

FIGURE 9-6: Final Jobs table

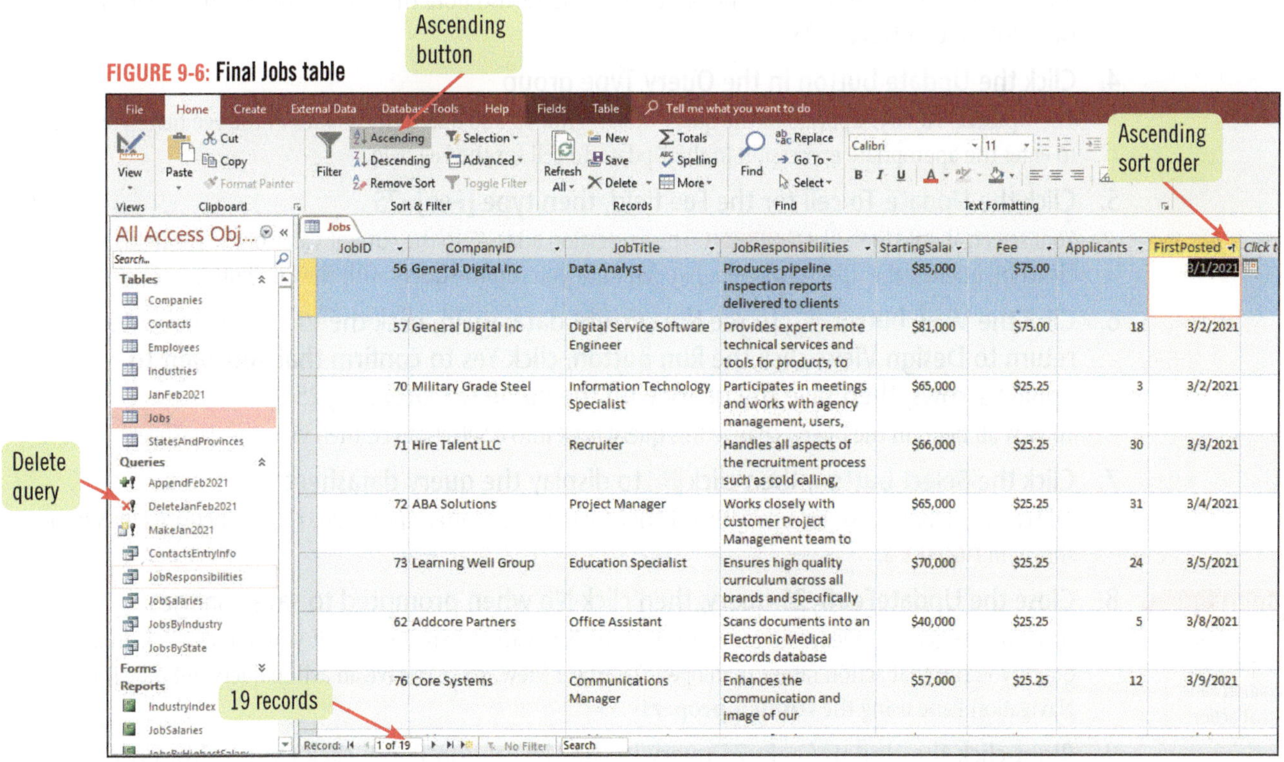

Access
Module 9

Create an Update Query

Learning Outcomes
- Create an Update query
- Hide an object in the Navigation Pane

An **Update query** is a type of action query that updates the values in a field. For example, you might want to increase the price of a product in a particular category by 10 percent. Or you might want to update the assigned sales representative, region, or territory for a set of customers. CASE *Lydia has just informed you that the fee for job placements has increased by $25 for all jobs with a FirstPosted date of 4/1/2021 or later. You create an Update query to quickly select and update this data.*

STEPS

1. **Click the Create tab, click the Query Design button, double-click Jobs in the Show Table dialog box, then click Close**
2. **Scroll down in the field list, double-click Fee, double-click FirstPosted, click the Criteria cell for the FirstPosted field, type >=4/1/21, then press ENTER**
   Every action query starts as a Select query. Always review the datasheet of the Select query before initiating any action that changes data to double-check which records are affected.
3. **Click the View button to display the query datasheet and observe the FirstPosted values and number of records, then click the View button to return to Design View**
   After confirming that you are selecting only records with a FirstPosted value of April 1, 2021, or later, you're ready to change this Select query into an Update query. Also note that the current Fee field value for the two selected records is $25.25.
4. **Click the Update button in the Query Type group**
   The **Update To row** appears in the query design grid. To add $25 to the values in the Fee field, you need to enter the appropriate expression in the Update To cell for the Fee field.
5. **Click the Update To cell for the Fee field, then type [Fee]+25**
   Your screen should look like FIGURE 9-7. The expression adds 25 to the current value of the Fee field. As with all action queries, the update does not happen until you run the query with the Run button.
6. **Click the View button to see the current data again, click the View button to return to Design View, click the Run button, click Yes to confirm that you want to update 2 rows, then save the query with the name UpdateFeeBy25**
   To view all fields in the query, change this query back into a Select query, then view the datasheet.
7. **Click the Select button, then click to display the query datasheet**
   All Fee values for the two records with a FirstPosted date on or after April 1, 2021, have increased by $25, as shown in FIGURE 9-8.
8. **Close the UpdateFeeBy25 query, then click No when prompted to save changes**
   It can be dangerous to leave action queries in the Navigation Pane because if you double-click an action query, you run that action rather than open Datasheet View. You can save an action query but hide it in the Navigation Pane using the **Hidden property**.
9. **Right-click the UpdateFeeBy25 query in the Navigation Pane, click Object Properties, click the Hidden check box, then click OK**

TROUBLE
If you double-click an action query in the Navigation Pane, you run that action.

FIGURE 9-7: Creating an Update query

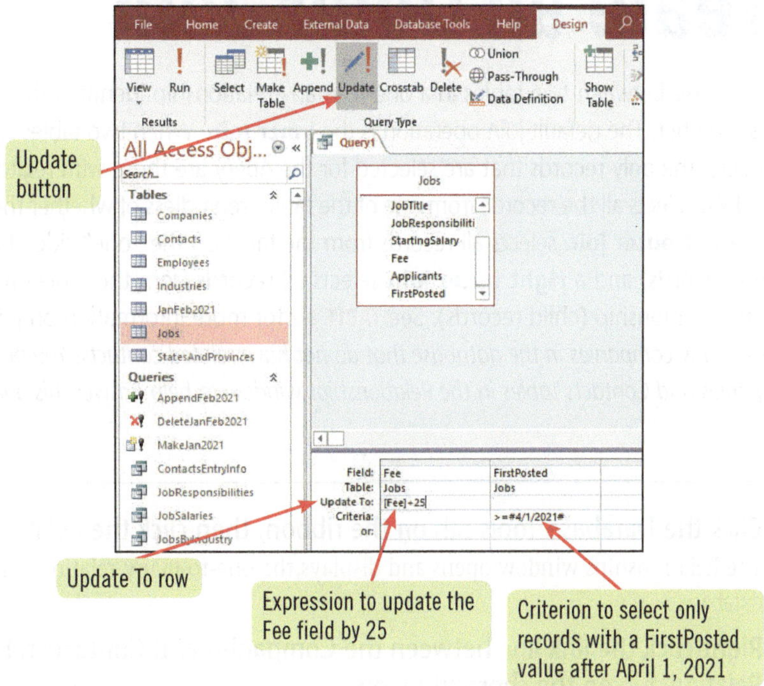

FIGURE 9-8: Viewing updated Fee values

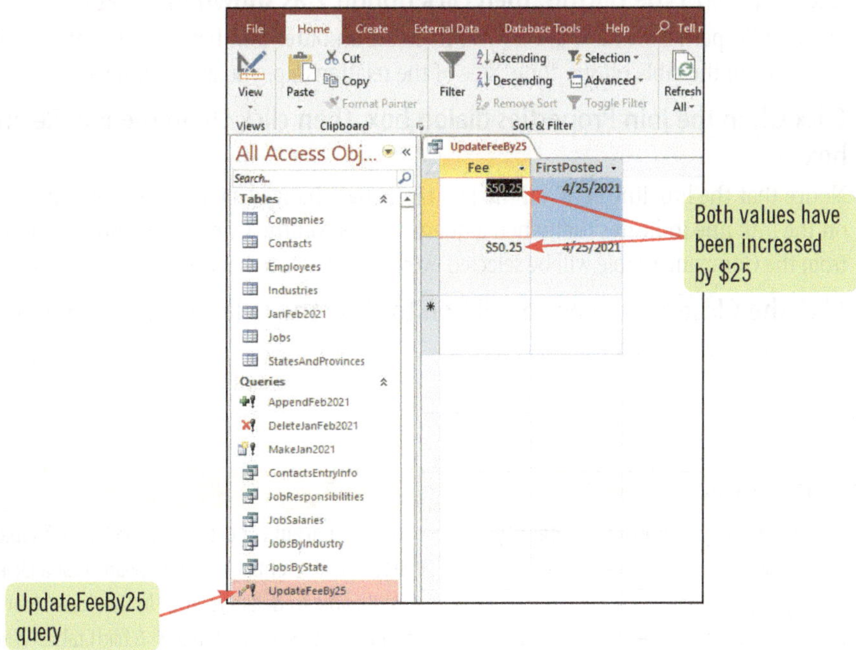

Show hidden objects

To unhide a hidden object, right-click the Navigation Pane title bar, click Navigation Options, then click the Show Hidden Objects check box. The hidden object will appear in the Navigation Pane.

To remove the hidden property, right-click the object, click Object Properties, then uncheck the Hidden attribute check box.

Access
Module 9

Create an Outer Join

Learning Outcomes
- Modify a join in the Relationships window
- Understand join operations

The **join line** between two tables in a one-to-many relationship identifies the common field that links the tables together. The default join operation is the **inner join**. When two tables are related with an inner join in a query, the only records that are selected for the query are those with related records in each table. An **outer join** selects all the records from one of the tables regardless of whether there is a related record in the other. A **left outer join** selects all records from the table on the "one" side of a one-to-many relationship (parent records) and a **right outer join** selects all records from the table on the "many" side of a one-to-many relationship (child records). See TABLE 9-2 for more information on joins. CASE *Lydia asks if there are any companies in the database that do not have related contacts. You build an outer join between the Companies and Contacts tables in the Relationships window to help answer this question.*

STEPS

1. **Click the Database Tools tab on the ribbon, then click the Relationships button**
   The Relationships window opens and displays the one-to-many relationships between the tables in the database.
2. **Right-click the link line between the Companies and Contacts table, then click Edit Relationship on the shortcut menu**
   The Edit Relationships dialog box opens and displays information about the one-to-many relationship between the Companies and Contacts table. The CompanyID field in each table is used as the linking field.
3. **Click the Join Type button, then click option 2 as shown in FIGURE 9-9**
   The Join Properties window allows you to create an outer join between the tables. When you select ALL records from the table on the "one" side of the relationship, you are creating a left outer join.
4. **Click OK in the Join Properties dialog box, then click OK in the Edit Relationships dialog box**
   Notice that the link line between the two tables has changed slightly, as shown in FIGURE 9-10. The arrow on the link line indicates that when a query is based on the Companies and Contacts tables, ALL records from the Companies table will be selected even if they do not have a matching record in the Contacts table.
5. **Click the Close button on the ribbon to close the Relationships window**

Reviewing referential integrity

Recall that you can establish, or enforce, **referential integrity** between two tables when joining tables in the Relationships window. Referential integrity applies a set of rules to the relationship that ensures that no orphaned records are created in the database. A table has an **orphan record** when information in the foreign key field of the "many" table doesn't have a matching entry in the primary key field of the "one" table. The term *orphan* comes from the analogy that the "one" table contains **parent records**, and the "many" table contains **child records**. Referential integrity means that a Delete query would not be able to delete records in the "one" (parent) table that has related records in the "many" (child) table. When a relationship has referential integrity, a "1" symbol appears on the field on the "one" side of the relationship, and an infinity symbol appears on the field on the "many" side of the relationship.

FIGURE 9-9: Modifying join properties in the Relationships window

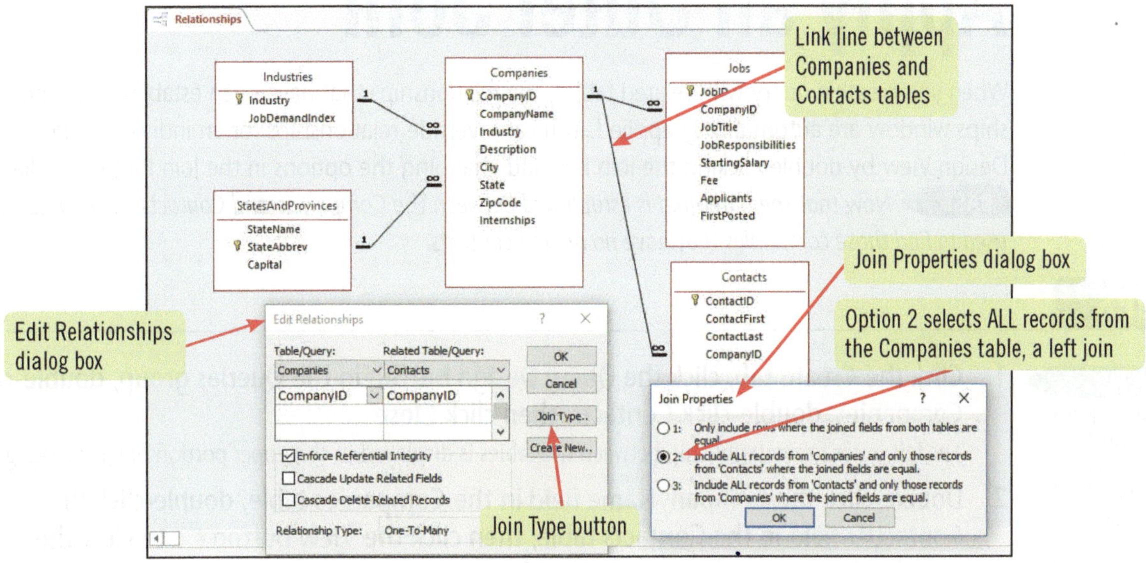

FIGURE 9-10: Relationships window with outer join

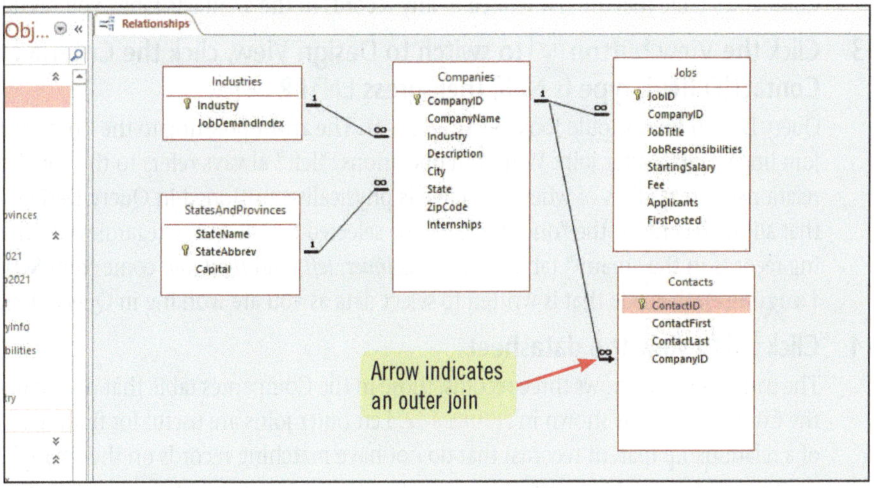

TABLE 9-2: Join operations

join operation	description	example based on a one-to-many relationship between the Customers and Sales tables
inner	Default join; selects records from two related tables in a query that have matching values in the linking field of both tables	Each record from the Customers table must have one or more related records in the Sales table to be selected for the query.
left outer	Selects all the records from the left table (the "one" table in a one-to-many relationship) even if the "one" (parent) table doesn't have matching records in the related "many" (child) table	Select records from the Customers table that have no related records in the Sales table.
right outer	Selects all the records from the right table (the "many" table in a one-to-many relationship) even if the "many" (child) table doesn't have matching records in the related "one" (parent) table	Select orphan records in the Sales table that have no related records in the Customers table. (*Note:* Enforcing referential integrity on a relationship prevents orphan records from being entered into a relational database.)
self	Relates a table to itself	Relate an Employee table to itself using two fields in the same table to identify the relationship between employees and supervisors.

Access
Module 9

Apply an Outer Join

Learning Outcomes
- Use a left outer join
- Use Is Null criteria

When you create a query with related tables, the relationships that have been established in the Relationships window are automatically applied. You can override relationships for an individual query in Query Design View by double-clicking the join line and changing the options in the Join Properties dialog box. **CASE** *Now that the outer join is established between the Companies and Contacts table, a query can be used to find those companies that have no related contacts.*

STEPS

QUICK TIP
Double-click the join line in any query to modify it to be an inner, left, or right join for that query only.

QUICK TIP
Switch to SQL View to view the SQL for any query.

1. **Click the Create tab, click the Query Design button in the Queries group, double-click Companies, double-click Contacts, then click Close**

   The left outer join relationship between the tables is displayed in the upper portion of Query Design View.

2. **Double-click the CompanyName field in the Companies table, double-click the ContactID field in the Contacts table, then click the View button to view the datasheet**

   This query selects 446 records using the left outer join between the tables. To find only those records in the Companies table that are not related to any records in the Contacts table, you need to add criteria.

3. **Click the View button to switch to Design View, click the Criteria cell for the ContactID field, type Is Null, then press ENTER**

   Query Design View should look like FIGURE 9-11. The arrow pointing to the Contacts table indicates that the join line is a left outer join. With join operations, "left" always refers to the "one" table of a one-to-many relationship regardless of where the table is physically positioned in Query Design View. A left join means that all the records in the "one" table will be selected for the query regardless of whether they have matching records in the "many" table. The terms *inner*, *left*, and *right join* come from **SQL (Structured Query Language)**, the code that is written to select data as you are working in Query Design View.

4. **Click to view the datasheet**

   The datasheet now shows three records, those in the Companies table that do not have matching records in the Contacts table, as shown in FIGURE 9-12. Left outer joins are useful for finding records on the "one" side of a relationship (parent records) that do not have matching records on the "many" side (child records).

   When referential integrity is enforced on a relationship before data is entered, you cannot create new records on the "many" side of a relationship that do not have matching records on the "one" side. Although a right outer join helps you find orphan records in a poorly designed database, it would not be very useful in the JCL jobs database because referential integrity was applied on all relationships before any records were entered.

5. **Close the query and save it with the name CompaniesWithoutContacts**

FIGURE 9-11: Using Is Null criteria

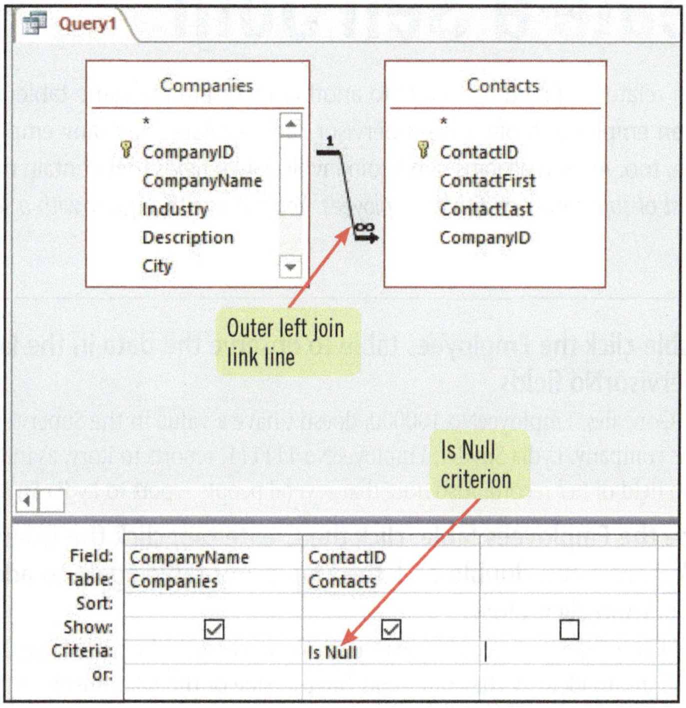

FIGURE 9-12: Companies without contacts

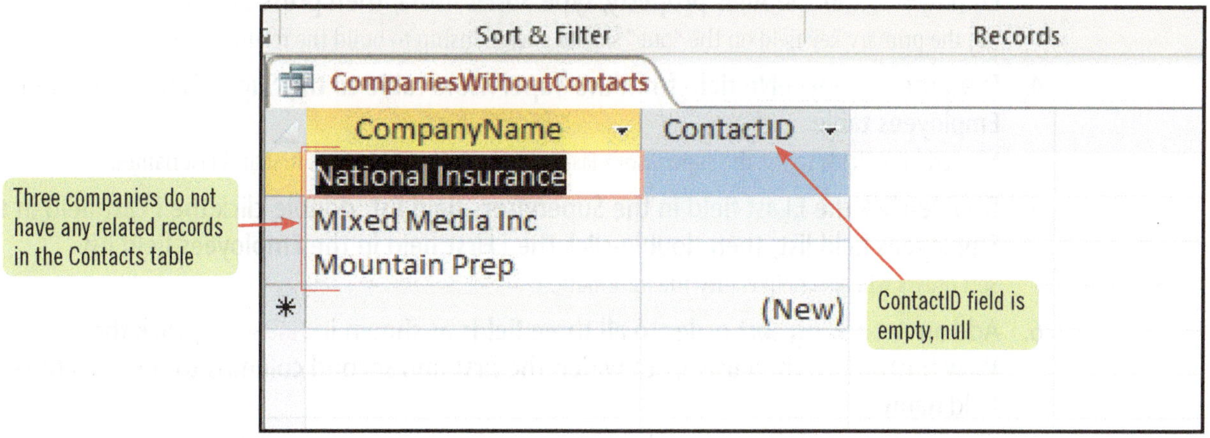

Null versus zero-length string values

The term **null** describes a field value that does not exist because it has never been entered. In a datasheet, null values look the same as a zero-length string value but have a different purpose. A **zero-length string** value is a deliberate entry that contains no characters. You enter a zero-length string by typing two quotation marks ("") with no space between them. A null value, on the other hand, indicates unknown data. By using null and zero-length string values appropriately, you can later query for the records that match one or the other condition. To query for zero-length string values, enter two quotation marks ("") as the criterion. To query for null values, use **Is Null** as the criterion. To query for any value other than a null value, use **Is Not Null** as the criterion.

Access

Access
Module 9

Create a Self Join

Learning Outcome
• Create a self join

A self join relates a record of a table to another record in the same table. A classic example of a self join involves an employee table. One supervisor can be related to many employees, yet the supervisor is an employee, too. As with all joins, a self join involves two fields that contain matching data. **CASE** *Lydia needs a list of supervisors and their employees. You will create a query with a self join to satisfy this request.*

STEPS

1. **Double-click the Employees table to observe the data in the EmployeeNo and SupervisorNo fields**
   Rory Gonzales, EmployeeNo 100000, doesn't have a value in the SupervisorNo field because he's the CEO of the company. Lydia Snyder, EmployeeNo 111111, reports to Rory, as indicated by 100000 in the SupervisorNo field of her record. Also note that several people report to Lydia Snyder.

2. **Close the Employees table, click the Create tab, click the Query Design button, double-click Employees, double-click the Employees table again to add it to Query Design View twice, then click Close**
   A self join relates one record of a table to many others in the same table. Before making the join, however, it's helpful to identify the "one" and "many" side of the relationship. In this case, one supervisor can be related to many employees.

3. **Right-click the Employees_1 field list, click Properties on the shortcut menu, select Employees_1 in the Alias property, type Supervisors, then press ENTER**
   Use the primary key field on the "one" side of a relationship to build the relationship.

4. **Drag the EmployeeNo field from the Supervisors table to the SupervisorNo field in the Employees table**
   Now add the fields to list the supervisor's last name and the employee's first and last names.

5. **Double-click the ELast field in the Supervisors field list, double-click the ELast field in the Employees field list, then double-click the EFirst field in the Employees field list**
   Sort orders will also help clarify the information.

6. **Add an Ascending sort order to all three fields as shown in FIGURE 9-13, click the Datasheet View button, then use ✚ to widen the first and second columns to see the entire field name**
   The datasheet lists the supervisor's last name in the first column and the employee's last and first names, as shown in FIGURE 9-14. Given you selected the ELast field twice, it is further qualified with the table name prefix. Also note that Lydia Snyder is listed as an employee once, reporting to Gonzalez, but that her last name is listed many times because many employees report to her.

7. **Close the query and save it with the name SupervisorList**

8. **sam Open the Employees table, add your name as a new record with the EmployeeNo value of 727272 and a SupervisorNo value of 100000, close the Employees table, compact and close the IL_AC_9_Jobs.accdb database, then close Access**

FIGURE 9-13: Creating a self join

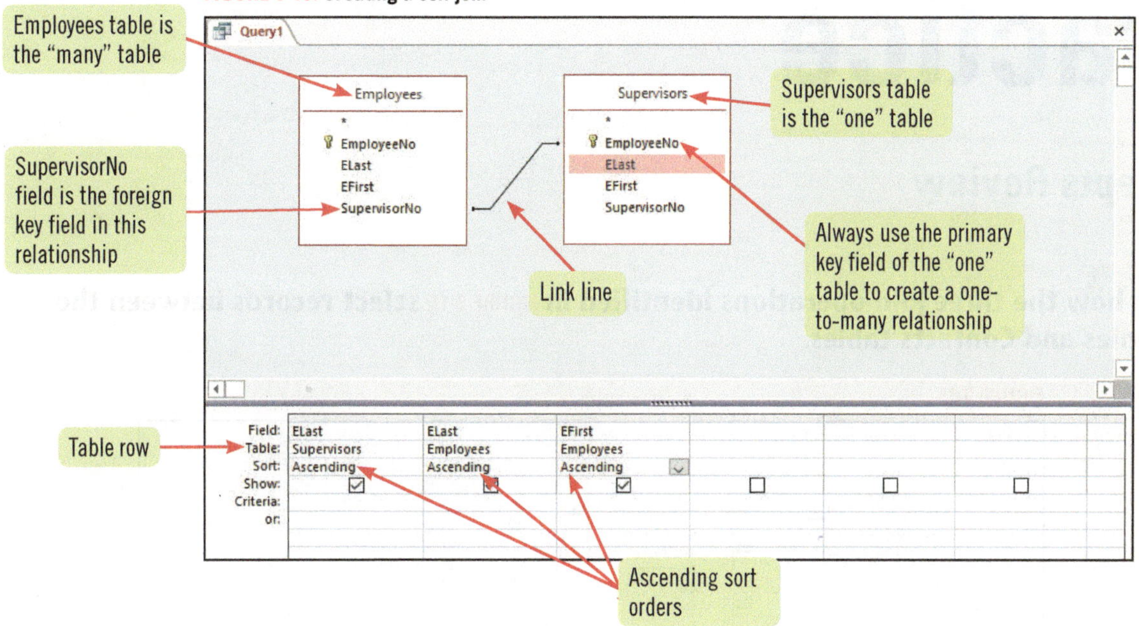

FIGURE 9-14: Datasheet for SupervisorList query

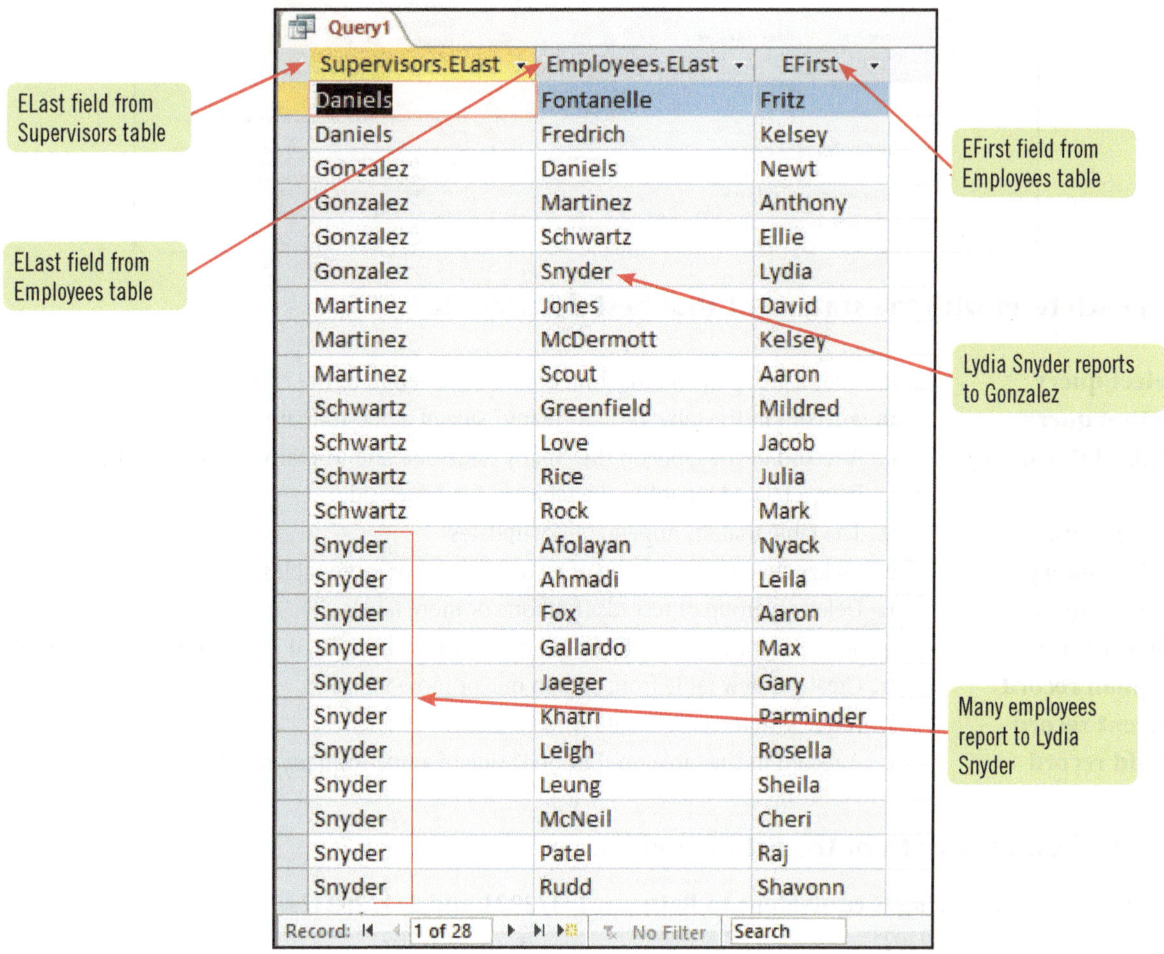

Supervisors.ELast	Employees.ELast	EFirst
Daniels	Fontanelle	Fritz
Daniels	Fredrich	Kelsey
Gonzalez	Daniels	Newt
Gonzalez	Martinez	Anthony
Gonzalez	Schwartz	Ellie
Gonzalez	Snyder	Lydia
Martinez	Jones	David
Martinez	McDermott	Kelsey
Martinez	Scout	Aaron
Schwartz	Greenfield	Mildred
Schwartz	Love	Jacob
Schwartz	Rice	Julia
Schwartz	Rock	Mark
Snyder	Afolayan	Nyack
Snyder	Ahmadi	Leila
Snyder	Fox	Aaron
Snyder	Gallardo	Max
Snyder	Jaeger	Gary
Snyder	Khatri	Parminder
Snyder	Leigh	Rosella
Snyder	Leung	Sheila
Snyder	McNeil	Cheri
Snyder	Patel	Raj
Snyder	Rudd	Shavonn

Access

Practice

Concepts Review

Explain how the three join operations identified in FIGURE 9-15 select records between the Companies and Contacts tables.

FIGURE 9-15

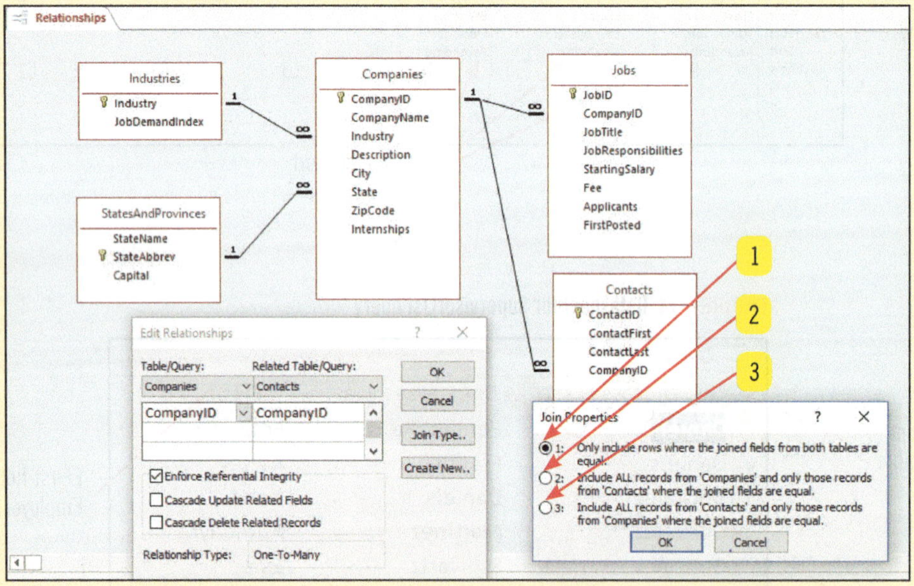

Match each term with the statement that best describes it.

4. Select query	**a.** Adds a group of records from one or more tables to the end of another table
5. Action query	**b.** A record in the table on the "many" side of a one-to-many relationship
6. Make Table query	**c.** A record in the table on the "many" side of a one-to-many relationship that does not have a related record in the table on the "one" side
7. Append query	**d.** The table that an Append query updates
8. Delete query	**e.** Makes changes to a group of records in one or more tables
9. Update query	**f.** Deletes a group of records from one or more tables
10. Target table	**g.** Selects records and fields from one or more tables and displays them in a datasheet
11. Orphan record	**h.** Creates a new table from data in one or more tables
12. Parent record	**i.** A query that changes data when it is run
13. Child record	**j.** A record in the table on the "one" side of a one-to-many relationship

Select the best answer from the list of choices.

14. Which of the following is equivalent to Between 1/1/2021 and 2/1/2021?

a. > 1/1/2021 and < 2/1/2021
b. >= 1/1/2021 and <= 2/1/2021
c. >= 1/1/2021
d. <= 2/1/2021

15. What happens when you double-click an action query in the Navigation Pane?

a. You open its datasheet.
b. You open it in Design View.
c. You run the query.
d. You rename the query.

16. In Query Design View, which button do you click to initiate the process that an action query takes?

a. Datasheet View
b. Design View
c. Update
d. Run

17. If you want to find records in the table on the "one" side of a one-to-many relationship that do not have related records in the "many" side, which join do you use?

a. Inner
b. Left outer
c. Right outer
d. Self

18. If you want to select records in the table on the "many" side of a one-to-many relationship that do not have related records in the "one" side, which join do you use?

a. Inner
b. Left outer
c. Right outer
d. Self

19. If you want to select records that have related records in both the "one" and "many" sides of a one-to-many relationship, which join do you use?

a. Inner
b. Left outer
c. Right outer
d. Self

20. If you want to select records that have no value in a field, which criterion do you use?

a. Is Null
b. Is Not Null
c. "" (two quotation marks)
d. " " (two quotation marks with a space between them)

Skills Review

1. Create a Make Table query.

a. Start Access, open the IL_AC_9-2.accdb database from the location where you store your Data Files, then save it as **IL_AC_9_SupportDesk**. Enable content if prompted.
b. Create a new query in Query Design View based on the Calls table.
c. Select all fields from the Calls table using the asterisk (*), then add the CallDate field a second time and add criteria to select only those calls in April of 2021. (*Hint*: There are several ways to select all the records in a single month, but using the asterisk as a wildcard, as in **4/*/2021**, is one of the shortest.)
d. Uncheck the Show check box for the CallDate field, then display the datasheet to make sure you've selected the correct records. The datasheet should have eight records.
e. Return to Design View and change the query into a Make Table query using the name **April2021** for the new table, then run the query.
f. Save the query with the name **MakeApril2021**, then close it.
g. Open the April2021 table to make sure that it has eight records with a CallDate value in April of 2021, then close it.

2. Create an Append query.

a. Create a new query in Query Design View based on the Calls table. Add all the fields to the query grid *except* for the CallID field.
b. Add criteria to the CallDate field to select only those records from May of 2021, then display the datasheet. It should have seven records.

Access

Skills Review (continued)

c. Return to Design View and change the query into an Append query to append the records to the April2021 table.

d. Run the query to append the seven records, save it with the name **AppendMay2021**, then close the query.

e. Open the April2021 table to make sure it now has 15 records, close it, then rename it to be **AprilMay2021**.

3. **Create a Delete query.**

a. Create a new query in Query Design View based on the Cases table.

b. Select all fields from the Cases table using the asterisk (*), then add the ResolvedDate field a second time. Add criteria to select only those records where the ResolvedDate field has a value using the criterion of **Is Not Null**.

c. Uncheck the Show check box for the ResolvedDate field, then display the datasheet to make sure you've selected the correct records. The datasheet should have six records.

d. Return to Design View and change the query into a Delete query.

e. Run the query to delete six records, save it with the name **DeleteResolvedCases**, then close it.

4. **Create an Update query.**

a. Start a new query in Query Design View with the Employees table.

b. Add the Department field and the Salary field to the query grid.

c. Add criteria to select all employees in the **Production** department, then sort the records in descending order on the Salary field.

d. Display the datasheet and note that six records are selected with Salary field values ranging from $55,000 to $52,000.

e. Return to Design View and change the query into an Update query.

f. Add the expression **[Salary]*1.1** to the Update To cell of the Salary field to represent a 10% increase.

g. Run the query to update the six records, then view the datasheet to view the updated values that should now range from $60,500 to $57,200.

h. Save the query with the name **UpdateProductionSalaries**, then close it.

i. Hide the UpdateProductionSalaries query in the Navigation Pane.

5. **Create an outer join.**

a. Open the Relationships window, then double-click the join line between the Employees and Cases table.

b. Click the Join Type button and select option 2 to include ALL records from the Employees table even if there are no related records in the Cases table.

c. Save and close the Relationships window.

6. **Use an outer join.**

a. Create a new query in Query Design View using the Employees and Cases tables.

b. Select the FirstName and LastName fields from the Employees table and the CaseID field from the Cases table.

c. Add **Is Null** criteria to the CaseID field, then display the datasheet, which should show 12 records.

d. Save the query with the name **EmployeesWithoutCases**, then close it.

7. **Create a self join.**

a. Start a new query in Query Design View and add the Employees table twice.

b. Change the Alias property of the Employees_1 table to **Managers**.

c. Link the tables by dragging the EmployeeID field from the Managers table to the ManagerID field in the Employees table.

d. Add the LastName field from the Managers table, and the Department, LastName, and FirstName fields from the Employees table in that order to the grid.

e. Add an ascending sort order to the Department, LastName, and FirstName fields from the Employees table, then view the datasheet and widen all columns to view the field names, as shown in FIGURE 9-16.

Skills Review (continued)

FIGURE 9-16

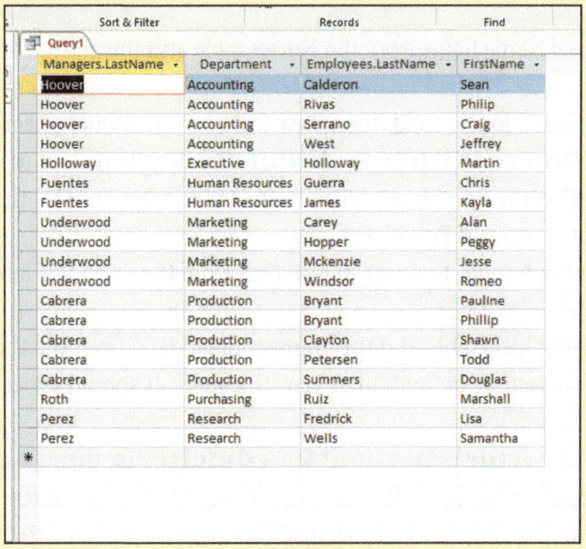

Managers.LastName	Department	Employees.LastName	FirstName
Hoover	Accounting	Calderon	Sean
Hoover	Accounting	Rivas	Philip
Hoover	Accounting	Serrano	Craig
Hoover	Accounting	West	Jeffrey
Holloway	Executive	Holloway	Martin
Fuentes	Human Resources	Guerra	Chris
Fuentes	Human Resources	James	Kayla
Underwood	Marketing	Carey	Alan
Underwood	Marketing	Hopper	Peggy
Underwood	Marketing	Mckenzie	Jesse
Underwood	Marketing	Windsor	Romeo
Cabrera	Production	Bryant	Pauline
Cabrera	Production	Bryant	Phillip
Cabrera	Production	Clayton	Shawn
Cabrera	Production	Petersen	Todd
Cabrera	Production	Summers	Douglas
Roth	Purchasing	Ruiz	Marshall
Perez	Research	Fredrick	Lisa
Perez	Research	Wells	Samantha

f. Save the query with the name **ManagerList**, then close it.

g. Add your name as a new record to the Employees table with reasonable Salary and Dependents values, **Information Systems** as the Department, and **3** for the ManagerID value, then close the Employees table.

h. Compact and close the IL_AC_9_ SupportDesk.accdb database, then close Access.

Independent Challenge 1

As the manager of Riverwalk, a multispecialty health clinic, you have created a database to manage nurse and doctor schedules to efficiently handle patient visits. In this exercise, you will create left outer joins to query for nurses and providers who have not been assigned to the schedule.

a. Start Access, open the IL_AC_9-3.accdb database from the location where you store your Data Files, then save it as **IL_AC_9_Riverwalk**. Enable content if prompted.

b. Open the Relationships window and change the relationship between the Nurses and ScheduleItems tables to be a left outer join that includes ALL records from the Nurses table even if there are no related records in the ScheduleItems table, as shown in FIGURE 9-17.

FIGURE 9-17

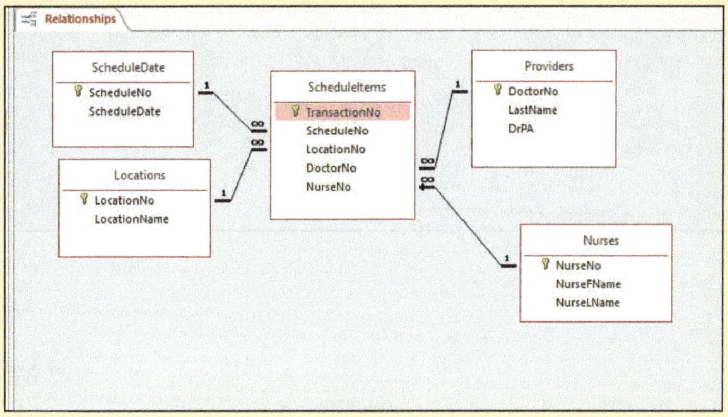

Access

Independent Challenge 1 (continued)

c. Save and close the Relationships window, then start a new query in Query Design view using the Nurses and ScheduleItems tables.

d. Add the NurseFName and NurseLName fields from the Nurses table and the TransactionNo field from the ScheduleItems table.

e. Add **Is Null** criteria to the TransactionNo field, then view the query. It should select one record.

f. Save the query with the name **NursesWithoutScheduleItems**, then close it.

g. Add your name as a new record in the Providers table with the DrPA value of **MD**, then start a new query in Query Design View using the ScheduleItems and Providers tables.

h. Modify the join line to be a left outer join to select ALL records from the Providers table even if there are no related records in the ScheduleItems table.

i. Select the LastName from the Providers table and the TransactionNo field from the ScheduleItems table.

j. Add **Is Null** criteria to the TransactionNo field, then view the query. It should select two records, one of which contains your last name.

k. Save the query with the name **ProvidersWithoutScheduleItems**, then close it.

l. Consider the difference between specifying a left outer join between two tables in the Relationships window versus specifying a left outer join between tables in Query Design View, and be prepared to discuss the difference in class.

m. Compact and close the IL_AC_9_Riverwalk.accdb database, then close Access.

Independent Challenge 2

You are working for a city to coordinate a series of community-wide preparedness activities. You have created a database to track the activities and volunteers who are attending the activities. In this exercise, you will create a left outer join to identify those activities that have been planned but for which no volunteer attendance has been recorded.

a. Start Access, open the IL_AC_9-4.accdb database from the location where you store your Data Files, then save it as **IL_AC_9_Volunteers**. Enable content if prompted.

b. In the Relationships window, modify the relationship between the Activities table and the Attendance table to be a left outer join to include ALL records in the Activities table even if there are no related records in the Attendance table, as shown in FIGURE 9-18.

FIGURE 9-18

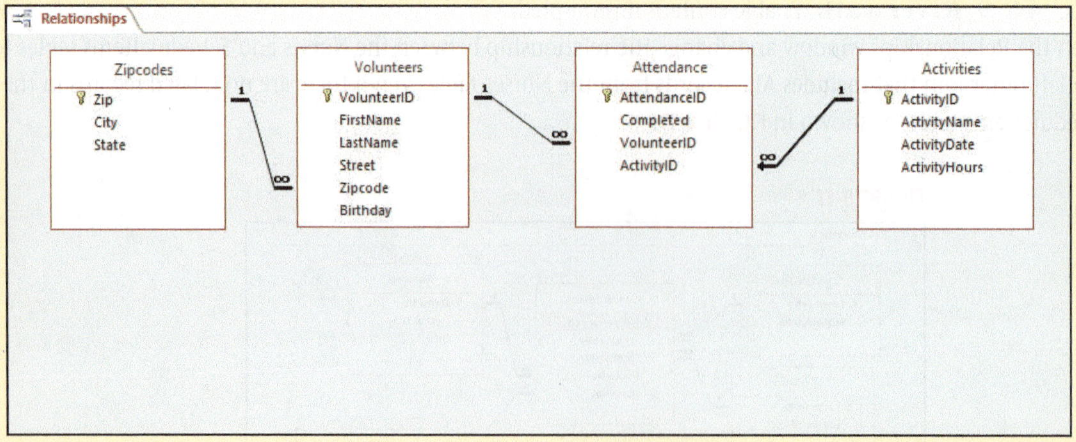

Independent Challenge 2 (continued)

c. In the Edit Relationships dialog box of the relationship between the Activities and Attendance tables, consider the Cascade Update Related Fields and Cascade Delete Related Records options on the one-to-many relationship, as compared to the Update and Delete action queries. Be prepared to discuss how these features are similar and different in class.
d. Save and close the Relationships window.
e. Start a new query in Query Design View with the Attendance and Activities tables.
f. Add the AttendanceID field from the Attendance table and the ActivityName field from the Activities table.
g. Add **Is Null** criteria to the AttendanceID field, then display the datasheet. It should have 15 records.
h. Save the query with the name **ActivitiesWithoutAttendance**, then close it.
i. Add your name as a new record to the Volunteers table. Use realistic but fictitious data for the other fields of the record and use **66210** for the Zipcode.
j. Compact and close the IL_AC_9_Volunteers.accdb database, then exit Access 2019.

Visual Workshop

Start Access, open the IL_AC_9-5.accdb database from the location where you store your Data Files, then save it as **IL_AC_9_CollegeCourses**. Enable content if prompted. Add your name as a new record to the Students table using a StudentID of **777** and fictitious but realistic data for the rest of the record. Close the Students table. Create a new query in Query Design View using the Students and Enrollments table. Create a left outer join on the join line to select ALL students even if there are no related records in the Enrollments table. Select all the fields from the Students table and the EnrollmentID field from the Enrollments table. Use **Is Null** criteria in the EnrollmentID field, save the query with the name **StudentsWithoutEnrollments**, display it in Datasheet View, then widen all columns to show all data, as shown in FIGURE 9-19. Close the StudentsWithoutEnrollments query, compact and close the IL_AC_9_CollegeCourses.accdb database, then close Access 2019.

FIGURE 9-19

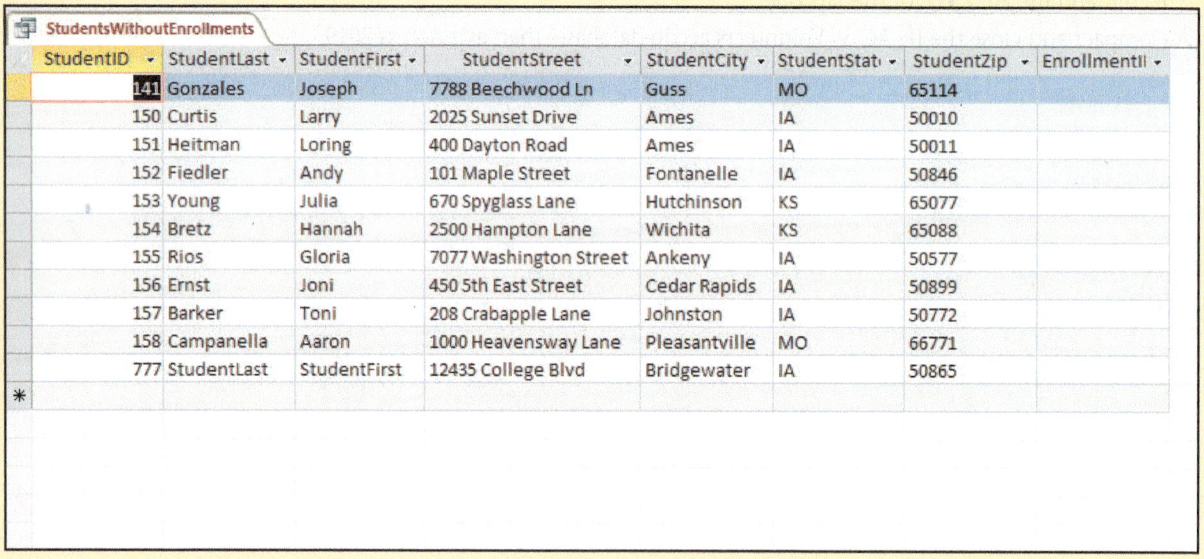
StudentsWithoutEnrollments

StudentID	StudentLast	StudentFirst	StudentStreet	StudentCity	StudentStat	StudentZip	EnrollmentI
141	Gonzales	Joseph	7788 Beechwood Ln	Guss	MO	65114	
150	Curtis	Larry	2025 Sunset Drive	Ames	IA	50010	
151	Heitman	Loring	400 Dayton Road	Ames	IA	50011	
152	Fiedler	Andy	101 Maple Street	Fontanelle	IA	50846	
153	Young	Julia	670 Spyglass Lane	Hutchinson	KS	65077	
154	Bretz	Hannah	2500 Hampton Lane	Wichita	KS	65088	
155	Rios	Gloria	7077 Washington Street	Ankeny	IA	50577	
156	Ernst	Joni	450 5th East Street	Cedar Rapids	IA	50899	
157	Barker	Toni	208 Crabapple Lane	Johnston	IA	50772	
158	Campanella	Aaron	1000 Heavensway Lane	Pleasantville	MO	66771	
777	StudentLast	StudentFirst	12435 College Blvd	Bridgewater	IA	50865	

Access **Module 10**

Creating Macros

CASE You are working with Lydia Snyder, vice president of operations at JCL Talent, to build a research database to manage industry, company, and job data. In this module, you'll create and modify macros that make the database application easier to use and automate repetitive tasks.

Module Objectives

After completing this module, you will be able to:

- Understand macros
- Create a macro
- Modify actions and arguments
- Assign a macro to a command button
- Use Macro If statements
- Use the Macro Else clause
- Create a data macro
- Troubleshoot macros

Files You Will Need

IL_AC_10-1.accdb
IL_AC_10-2.accdb
IL_AC_10-3.accdb
IL_AC_10-4.accdb
IL_AC_10-5.accdb

Access
Module 10

Understand Macros

Learning Outcomes
- Describe the benefits of macros
- Define macro terminology
- Describe Macro Design View components

A **macro** is a database object that stores actions to complete Access tasks. Repetitive Access tasks, such as printing several reports or opening and maximizing a form, are good candidates for a macro. Automating routine tasks by using macros builds efficiency, accuracy, and flexibility into your database. CASE *Lydia Snyder encourages you to study the major benefits of using macros, macro terminology, and the components of Macro Design View before building your first macro.*

DETAILS

The major benefits of using macros include the following:

- Saving time by automating routine tasks
- Increasing accuracy by ensuring that tasks are executed consistently
- Improving the functionality and ease of use of forms by using macros connected to command buttons
- Ensuring data accuracy in forms by using macros to respond to data entry errors
- Automating data transfers such as collecting data from Excel
- Helping users by responding to their interactions within a form

Macro terminology:

- A **macro** is an Access object that stores a series of actions to perform one or more tasks.
- **Macro Design View** is the window in which you create a macro. FIGURE 10-1 shows Macro Design View with an OpenForm action. See TABLE 10-1 for a description of the Macro Design View components.
- Each task that you want the macro to perform is called an **action**. A macro may contain one or more actions.
- **Arguments** are properties of an action that provide additional information on how the action should execute.
- A **conditional expression** is an expression resulting in either a true or a false answer that determines whether a macro action will execute. Conditional expressions are used in **If statements**.
- An **event** is something that happens to a form, window, toolbar, or control—such as the click of a command button or an entry in a field—that can be used to initiate the execution of a macro.
- A **submacro** is a collection of actions within a macro object that allows you to name and create multiple, separate macros within a single macro object. Submacros are referenced in macro lists using a Macroname.Submacroname syntax.

FIGURE 10-1: Macro Design View with OpenForm action

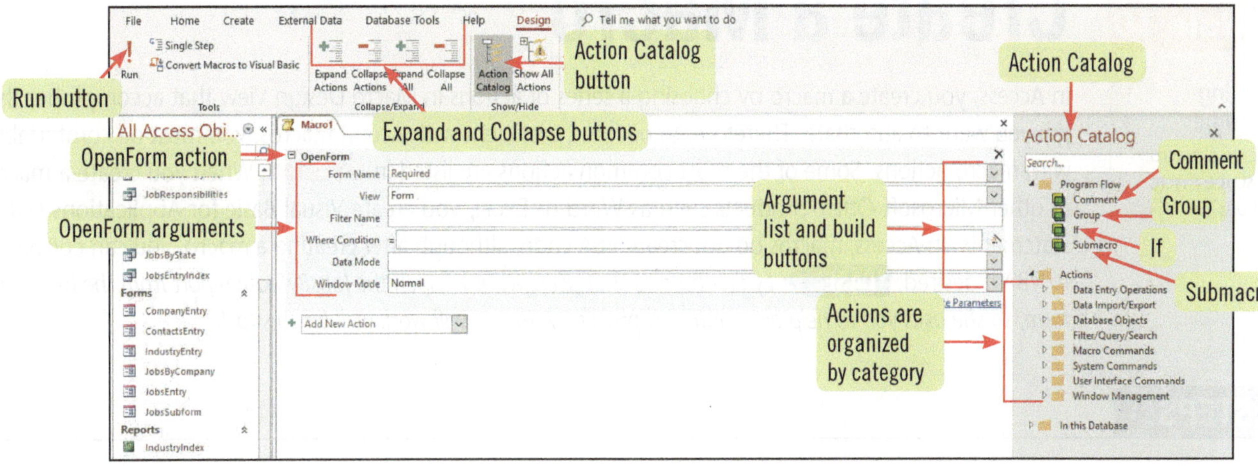

TABLE 10-1: Macro Design View components

component	description
Action Catalog	Lists all available macro actions organized by category. Use the Search box to narrow the number of macro actions to a particular subject.
Program Flow	Contains useful tools to comment and organize your code, including Comment, Group, If, and Submacro.
Comment	Provides a way to document the macro with explanatory text.
Group	Allows for actions and program flow to be grouped in a named, collapsible block that is not executed.
If	Provides a way to add a conditional expression that is evaluated as either true or false to a macro. If true, the macro action is executed. If false, the macro action is skipped. If statements in Access 2019 may contain Else If and Else clauses.
Submacro	Allows for a named collection of macro actions that are executed using the RunMacro or OnError macro actions.
Arguments	Lists required and optional arguments for the selected action.
Run button	Runs the selected macro.
Expand and Collapse buttons	Allows you to expand or collapse the macro actions to show or hide their arguments.

Access

Create a Macro

Learning Outcomes
- Create a macro
- Describe macro actions

In Access, you create a macro by choosing a series of actions in Macro Design View that accomplishes the job you want to automate. Therefore, to become proficient with Access macros, you must be comfortable with macro actions. Some of the most common actions are listed in TABLE 10-2. When you create a macro in other Microsoft Office products such as Word or Excel, you create Visual Basic for Applications (VBA) statements. In Access, macros do not create VBA code, although after creating a macro, you can convert it to VBA if desired. CASE *Lydia observes that users want to open the JobsByState report from the JobsEntry form, so she asks you to help automate this process. A macro will work well for this task.*

STEPS

TROUBLE
If you do not enable content, your macros will not run.

TROUBLE
If you choose the wrong macro action, click the Delete button in the upper-right corner of the macro action block and try again.

QUICK TIP
Hover over any macro action or argument to see a ScreenTip of information about that item.

QUICK TIP
To print a macro from Macro Design View, click the File tab, click Print, click the Print button, then click OK.

1. **sam Start Access, open the IL_AC_10-1.accdb database from the location where you store your Data Files, save it as IL_AC_10_Jobs, enable content if prompted, click the Create tab, then click the Macro button**

   Macro Design View opens, ready for you to choose your first action.

2. **Click the Action list arrow, then scroll and click OpenReport**

   The OpenReport action is now the first action in the macro, and the arguments that further define the OpenReport action appear in the action block. The **action block** organizes all the arguments for a current action and is visually highlighted with a rectangle and gray background. You can expand or collapse the action block to view or hide details by clicking the Collapse/Expand button to the left of the action name or the Expand and Collapse buttons on the Design tab in Macro Design View.

   The **OpenReport action** has three required arguments: Report Name, View, and Window Mode. View and Window Mode have default values. If you start working with the OpenReport action's arguments but do not select a Report Name, the word *Required* is shown, indicating that you must select a choice for that argument. The Filter Name and Where Condition arguments are optional as indicated by their blank boxes.

3. **Click the Report Name argument list arrow, then click JobsByState**

   All the report objects in the current database appear in the Report Name argument list, making it easy to choose the report you want.

4. **Click the View argument list arrow, then click Report if it is not already selected**

   Your screen should look like FIGURE 10-2. Macros can contain one or many actions. In this case, the macro has only one action.

5. **Click the Save button on the Quick Access toolbar, type OpenJobsByStateReport in the Macro Name text box, click OK, right-click the OpenJobsByStateReport macro tab, then click Close**

   The Navigation Pane lists the OpenJobsByStateReport object in the Macros group.

6. **Double-click the OpenJobsByStateReport macro in the Navigation Pane to run the macro**

   The JobsByState report opens in Report View.

7. **Close the JobsByState report**

FIGURE 10-2: Macro Design View with OpenReport action

TABLE 10-2: Common macro actions

subject area	macro action	description
Data Entry Operations	DeleteRecord	Deletes the current record
	SaveRecord	Saves the current record
Data Import/Export	EMailDatabaseObject	Sends the specified database object through Outlook with specified email settings
	ImportExportSpreadsheet*	Imports or exports the spreadsheet you specify
	ImportExportText*	Imports or exports the text file you specify
Database Objects	GoToControl	Moves the focus (where you are currently typing or clicking) to a specific field or control
	GoToRecord	Makes a specified record the current record
	OpenForm	Opens a form in Form View, Design View, Print Preview, or Datasheet View
	OpenReport	Opens a report in Report View, Design View, or Print Preview, or prints the report
	OpenTable	Opens a table in Datasheet View, Design View, or Print Preview
	SetValue*	Sets the value of a field, control, or property
Filter/Query/Search	ApplyFilter	Restricts the number of records that appear in the resulting form or report by applying limiting criteria
	FindRecord	Finds the first record that meets the criteria
	OpenQuery	Opens a select or crosstab query; runs an action query
Macro Commands	RunCode	Runs a Visual Basic function (a series of programming statements that does a calculation or comparison and returns a value)
	RunMacro	Runs a macro or attaches a macro to a custom menu command
	StopMacro	Stops the currently running macro
System Commands	Beep	Sounds a beep tone through the computer's speaker
	PrintOut*	Prints the active object, such as a datasheet, report, form, or module
	SendKeys*	Sends keystrokes directly to Microsoft Access or to an active Windows application
User Interface Commands	MessageBox	Displays a message box containing a warning or an informational message
	ShowToolbar*	Displays or hides a given toolbar
Window Management	CloseWindow	Closes a window
	MaximizeWindow	Enlarges the active window to fill the Access window

*You must click the Show All Actions button on the ribbon for these actions to appear.

Modify Actions and Arguments

Learning Outcomes
- Modify macro actions
- Modify macro arguments

Macros can contain as many actions as necessary to complete the process that you want to automate. Each action is evaluated in the order in which it appears in Macro Design View, starting at the top. Whereas some macro actions open, close, preview, or export data or objects, others are used only to make the database easier to use. **MessageBox** is a useful macro action because it displays an informational message to the user. CASE *Lydia asks if you can display a descriptive message when the JobsByState report opens to explain how the data is sorted. The MessageBox macro action will handle this request.*

STEPS

1. **Right-click the OpenJobsByStateReport macro in the Navigation Pane, then click Design View on the shortcut menu**
   The OpenJobsByStateReport macro opens in Macro Design View.
2. **Click the Add New Action list arrow, scroll, then click MessageBox**
   Each action has its own arguments that further clarify what the action does.
3. **Click the Message argument box in the action block, then type sorted by state, city, company, and starting salary**
   The Message argument determines what text appears in the message box. By default, the Beep argument is set to "Yes" and the Type argument is set to "None."
4. **Click the Type argument list arrow in the action block, then click Information**
   The Type argument determines which icon appears in the dialog box the MessageBox action creates.
5. **Click the Title argument box in the action block, then type Sort information...**
   Your screen should look like FIGURE 10-3. The Title argument specifies what text is displayed in the title bar of the resulting dialog box. If you leave the Title argument blank, the title bar of the resulting dialog box displays "Microsoft Access."
6. **Save the macro, then click the Run button in the Tools group**
   If your speakers are turned on, you should hear a beep, then the message box appears, as shown in FIGURE 10-4.
7. **Click OK in the dialog box, close the JobsByState report, then save and close Macro Design View**

FIGURE 10-3: Adding the MessageBox action

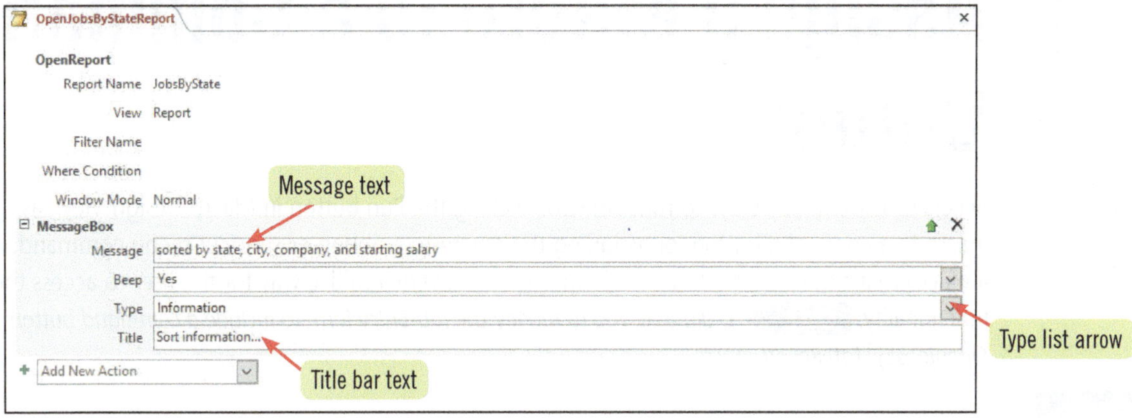

FIGURE 10-4: Dialog box created by MessageBox action

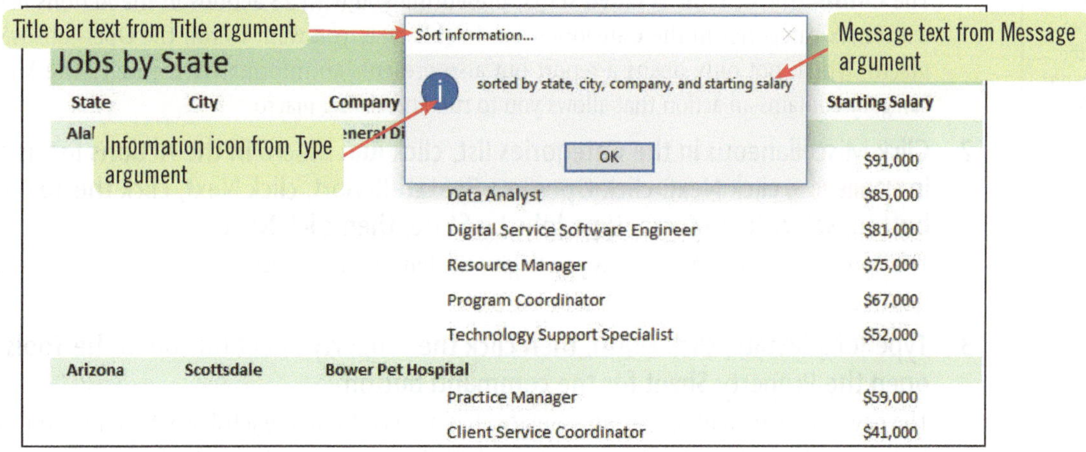

Access

Assigning a macro to a key combination

You can assign a key combination such as SHIFT+CTRL+L to a macro by creating a macro with the name **AutoKeys**. Enter the key combination for the submacro action's name. Use + for SHIFT, % for ALT, and ^ for CTRL. Enclose special keys such as F3 in {curly braces}. For example, to assign a macro to SHIFT+CTRL+L, use +^L as the submacro name. To assign a macro to SHIFT+F3, use +{F3} as the submacro name. Any key combination assignments you make in the AutoKeys macro override those that Access has already specified. Therefore, check the Keyboard Shortcuts information in the Microsoft Access Help system to make sure that the AutoKeys assignment you are creating doesn't override an existing Access quick keystroke that may be used for another purpose.

Learning Outcomes
- Connect a command button to a macro
- Describe trusted folders and files

Assign a Macro to a Command Button

Access provides many ways to run a macro: clicking the Run button in Macro Design View, assigning the macro to a command button, or assigning the macro to a ribbon or shortcut menu command. Assigning a macro to a command button on a form provides a very intuitive way for the user to access the macro's functionality. **CASE** *Lydia asks you to modify the JobsEntry form to include a command button to run the OpenJobsByStateReport macro.*

STEPS

QUICK TIP
Be sure the Use Control Wizards button is selected. To find it, click the More button in the Controls group on the Design tab.

1. **Right-click the JobsEntry form in the Navigation Pane, click Design View, use ✛ to expand the Form Footer about 0.5", click Button in the Controls group, then click at about the 1" mark on the horizontal ruler in the Form Footer section**

   The **Command Button Wizard** starts, presenting you with 28 actions in the Actions list organized within six categories in the Categories list. In this case, you want to run the OpenJobsByStateReport macro, which not only opens a report but also presents an informative message. The Miscellaneous category contains an action that allows you to run an existing macro.

2. **Click Miscellaneous in the Categories list, click Run Macro in the Actions list as shown in FIGURE 10-5, click Next, click OpenJobsByStateReport, click Next, click the Text option button, select Run Macro, type Jobs by State, then click Next**

   The Command Button Wizard asks you to give the button a meaningful name. Macro names may not have spaces.

3. **Type JobsByState, click Finish, then click the Property Sheet button in the Tools group to open the Property Sheet for the command button**

   The new command button that runs a macro has been added to the JobsEntry form in Form Design View. You work with the Property Sheet to examine how the macro was attached to the command button.

4. **Click the Event tab in the Property Sheet, then note that the On Click property contains [Embedded Macro]**

   The OpenJobsByStateReport macro was attached to the **On Click property** of this command button. In other words, the macro runs when the user clicks the command button. To make sure that the new command button works as intended, you view the form in Form View and test the command button.

5. **Close the Property Sheet, click the View button to switch to Form View, click the Jobs by State command button in the Form Footer section, click OK in the message box, then close the JobsByState report**

   The JobsEntry form with the new command button should look like FIGURE 10-6. It's common to put command buttons in the Form Footer so that users have a consistent location to find them.

6. **Save and close the JobsEntry form**

FIGURE 10-5: Adding a command button to run a macro

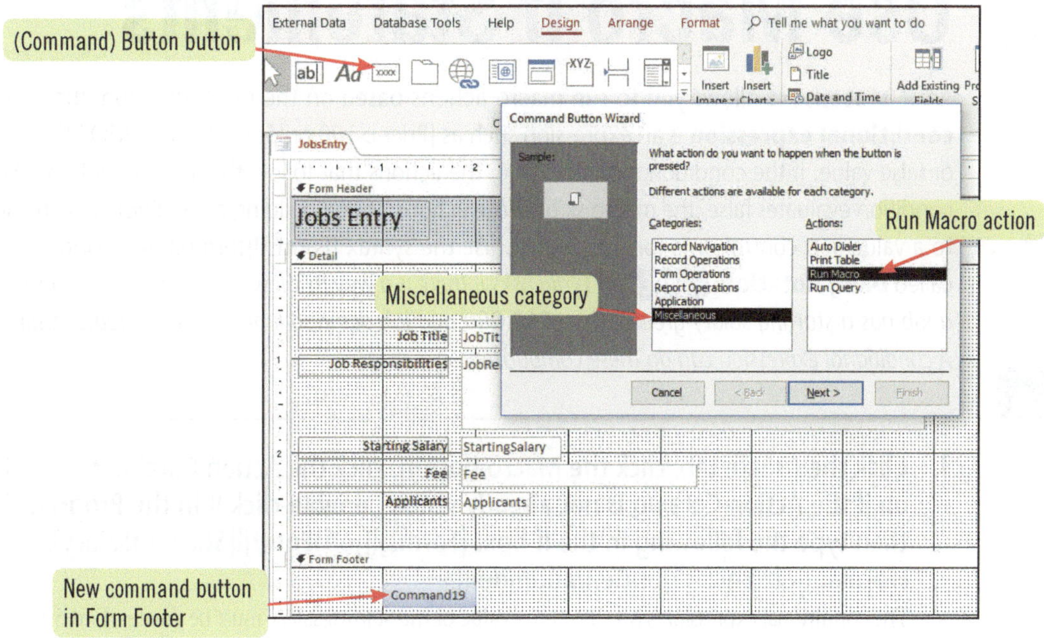

FIGURE 10-6: JobsEntry form with new command button

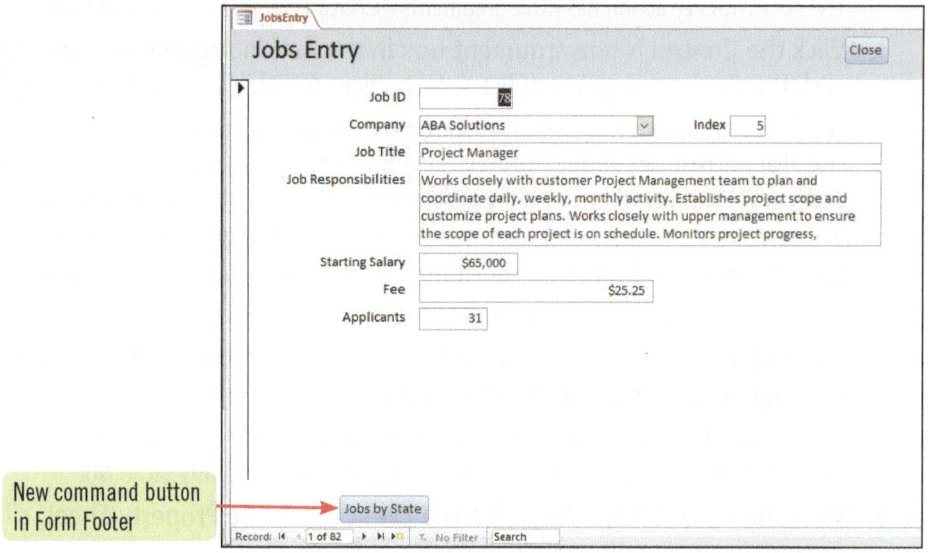

Using a trusted database and setting up a trusted folder

A **trusted database** allows you to run macros and Visual Basic for Applications code (VBA). By default, a database is not trusted. To trust a database, click the Enable Content button on the Security Warning bar each time you open a database. To permanently trust a database, store the database in a **trusted folder**. To create a trusted folder, open the Options dialog box from the File tab, click the Trust Center, click the Trust Center Settings button, click the Trusted Locations option, click the Add new location button, then browse to and choose the folder you want to trust.

Use Macro If Statements

Learning Outcomes
- Apply If statements to macros
- Enter conditional expressions
- Attach macros to form events

An **If statement** allows you to run macro actions based on the result of a conditional expression. A **conditional expression** is an expression such as [Price]>100 or [StateName]="MO" that results in a true or false value. If the condition evaluates true, the actions that follow the If statement are executed. If the condition evaluates false, the macro skips those actions. When building a conditional expression that refers to a value in a control on a form or report, use the syntax [Forms]![formname]![controlname], which is called **bang notation**. CASE *Lydia asks if there is a way to show a message on the JobsEntry form when a job has a starting salary greater than $50,000 and job demand index value of greater than or equal to 4. A conditional expression can do these comparisons.*

STEPS

1. **Click the Create tab, click the Macro button, click the Action Catalog button to toggle it on if the Action Catalog is not already visible, double-click If in the Program Flow area, then type the following in the If box: [Forms]![JobsEntry]![StartingSalary]>50000 And [Forms]![JobsEntry]![JobDemandIndex]>=4**

   The conditional expression says, "Both the value of the StartingSalary must be greater than 50,000 and the value of the JobDemandIndex must be greater than or equal to 4 to evaluate as true. Otherwise, evaluate false." Given the expression is built with the **And operator**, both parts must be true for any actions nested within the If statement to run. Using the **Or operator** would mean that only one part of the expression would have to be true.

> **TROUBLE**
> Be sure to click the Add New Action list arrow in the If block.

2. **Click the Add New Action list arrow in the If block, then scroll and click SetProperty**

   The **SetProperty** action has three arguments—Control Name, Property, and Value.

3. **Click the Control Name argument box in the Action Arguments pane, type HighLabel, click the Property argument list arrow, click Visible, click the Value box, then type True**

   Your screen should look like FIGURE 10-7. The **Control Name** argument must match the **Name property** of the label that will be modified. The **Property argument** determines what property is being modified. The **Value argument** determines the value of the **Visible property** of the label. For properties such as the Visible property that have only two choices in the Property Sheet, Yes or No, you enter a value of False for No and True for Yes.

4. **Save the macro with the name HighMessage, then close Macro Design View**

   Test the macro using the JobsEntry form.

5. **Right-click the JobsEntry form, click Design View, then click the Property Sheet button to toggle it on if it is not already visible**

   A label with HighLabel as its Name property is already positioned in the Form Header section. Its Visible property (found on the Format tab of the Property Sheet) is currently set to No.

> **QUICK TIP**
> Submacros are referenced in the list of macros using Macroname. Submacroname syntax.

6. **With the form still selected, click the Event tab in the Property Sheet, click the On Current list arrow, then click HighMessage**

   An **event** is a specific activity that occurs within the database, such as clicking a command button, moving from record to record, editing data, or opening or closing a form. The **On Current** event of the form occurs when focus moves from one record to another. By attaching the HighMessage macro to the form's On Current event, the macro will run every time you move to a new record in the form.

7. **Save the form, switch to Form View, then navigate to the second record**

   The macro runs twice, for the first record where the starting salary value of $45,000 evaluates false, and also for the second record where the starting salary of $65,000 and job demand index value of 4 evaluate true, which displays the High Wage / High Demand! label as shown in FIGURE 10-8.

8. **Navigate through five more records, observing the label, Index value, and Starting Salary value**

   You need to modify the macro so that the label's Visible property is set back to False when the Index value is less than 4 or the Starting Salary value is less than or equal to $50,000. You complete that task in the next lesson.

FIGURE 10-7: Using an If statement to set a control's Visible property

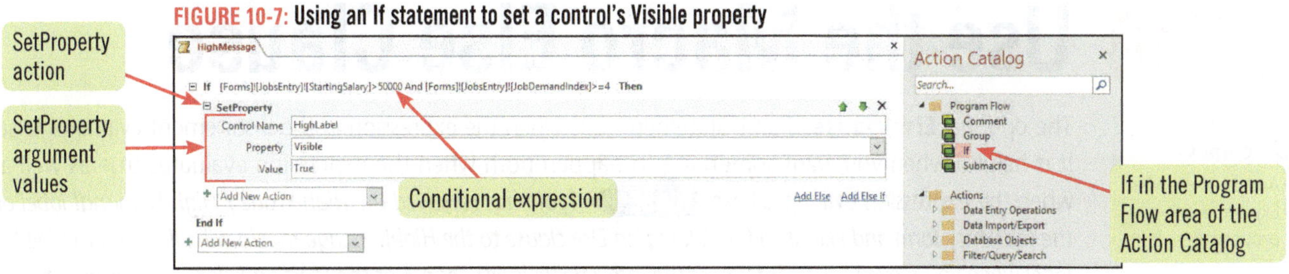

FIGURE 10-8: Running the HighMessage macro

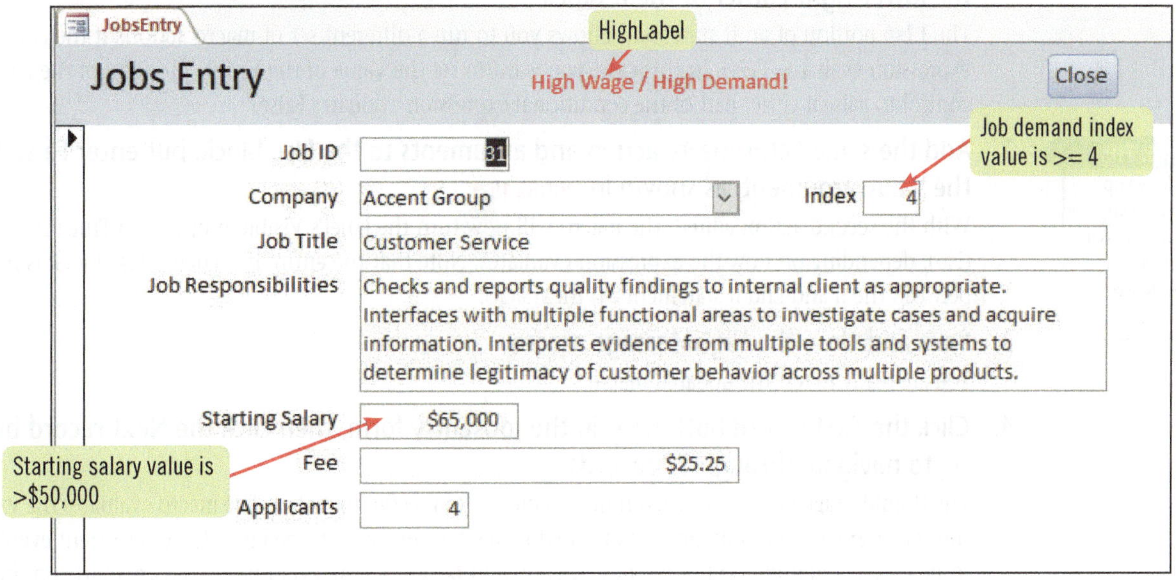

Access

Access
Module 10

Use the Macro Else Clause

Learning Outcomes
- Add an Else clause
- Explore event properties

The optional **Else clause** of an If statement runs when the expression in the If statement evaluates false. It is helpful when you want something to happen both when the expression evaluates true as well as when the expression evaluates false. CASE *Lydia has reviewed the High Wage / High Demand! label on the JobsEntry form and likes it so far. Adding an Else clause to the HighMessage macro will allow you to hide the label when you move to a record where the Index value is less than 4 or the Starting Salary value is less than or equal to $50,000.*

STEPS

1. **Right-click the HighMessage macro in the Navigation Pane, click Design View on the shortcut menu, click anywhere in the If block to activate it, then click the Add Else link in the lower-right corner of the If block**

   The **Else** portion of an If statement allows you to run a different set of macro actions if the conditional expression evaluates False. In this case, you want to set the Value of the Visible property of the HighLabel control to False if either part of the conditional expression evaluates False.

QUICK TIP
Use the Move up and Move down buttons as necessary to move macro actions in Macro Design View.

2. **Add the same SetProperty action and arguments to the Else block, but enter False for the Value argument, as shown in FIGURE 10-9**

   With the second action edited, the macro will now turn the label's Visible property to True (Yes) or False (No), depending on how the expression evaluates. Note that the entire If – Then – Else block is included between the If and End If statements in the macro.

3. **Save and close the HighMessage macro**

   You are ready to test the updated macro.

4. **Click the First record button in the JobsEntry form, then click the Next record button to navigate through 17 records**

   The HighMessage macro runs each time you move from record to record. The macro evaluates the values in the StartingSalary and JobDemandIndex text boxes because you attached it to the On Current event of the form. Other common event properties are shown in TABLE 10-3. All event properties are found on the Event tab of the Property Sheet for the selected object or control.

5. **Save and close the JobsEntry form**

FIGURE 10-9: Adding an Else portion to an If block

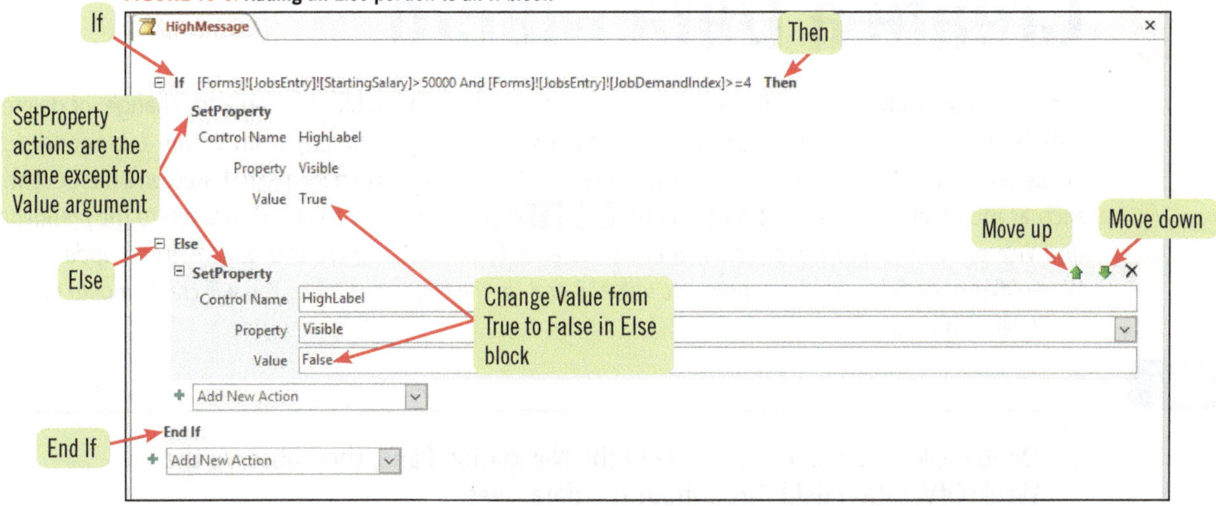

TABLE 10-3: Common event properties

item	event property	runs...
Form	On Current	when the focus moves from record to record
Form, report	On Load	when a form or report is initially loaded
Form, report, control	On Click	when a form, report, or control is clicked
Form, bound control	Before Update	before a record (form) or field is updated
Form, bound control	After Update	after a record (form) or field value is updated
Form, bound control	On Dirty	when the contents of the specified control change
Form, bound control	On Got Focus	when a form or control gets the focus
Form, report	On Close	when the form or report closes

Access

Create a Data Macro

Learning Outcomes
- Describe the use of data macros
- Create a data macro

A **data macro** allows you to embed macro capabilities directly in a table that can add, change, or delete data based on conditions you specify. Data macros are managed directly from within tables and do not appear in the Macros group in the Navigation Pane. You typically run a data macro based on a table event, such as modifying data or deleting a record. **CASE** *JCL grants four weeks of vacation to the president and vice presidents and three weeks to everyone else. Lydia asks if there is a quick way to update the WeeksOfVacation field with the appropriate value, 3 or 4, in the Employees table. You will create a data macro to address this need.*

STEPS

1. **Double-click the Employees table in the Navigation Pane, then observe the WeeksOfVacation field throughout the datasheet**

   Currently, the WeeksOfVacation field is empty for each employee. Note that Lydia (as well as the other vice presidents of the company) reports to SupervisorNo 100000, who is Rory Gonzales, the CEO of JCL.

2. **Right-click the Employees table tab, click Design View on the shortcut menu, click the Create Data Macros button in the Field, Record & Table Events group, click After Insert, then click the Action Catalog button in the Show/Hide group if it is not already open**

   In this case, you chose the After Insert event, which runs after a new record is entered. See TABLE 10-4 for more information on table events. Creating a data macro is very similar to creating a regular macro. You add the logic and macro actions needed to complete the task at hand.

QUICK TIP
You can also drag a block or action from the Action Catalog to Macro Design View.

3. **Double-click the ForEachRecord data block in the Action Catalog, click the For Each Record In list arrow, click Employees in the list, click the Where Condition text box, type [SupervisorNo]<>"100000", double-click the EditRecord data block in the Action Catalog, double-click the SetField data action in the Action Catalog, click the Name box in the SetField block, type WeeksOfVacation, click the Value box in the SetField block, then type 3, as shown in FIGURE 10-10**

   The <> symbols mean "is not equal to" so all employees who do not directly report to Rory Gonzales, EmployeeNo 100000, should be assigned three weeks of vacation. The EmployeeNo field is defined with a Short Text, not a Number data type, so "quotation marks" are used to surround the field value of "100000". Test the new data macro by adding a new record.

TROUBLE
Be sure to tab to a new record to trigger the data macro attached to the After Insert event of the table.

4. **Click the Save button, click the Close button on the ribbon, click the View button to display the datasheet, click Yes to save the table, click the New button in the Records group, enter a new record as shown in FIGURE 10-11 with your name, then press TAB to move to a new record**

   The macro is triggered by the After Insert event of the table, and the WeeksOfVacation field is automatically updated to 3 for the new record and all other records with a SupervisorNo not equal to "100000", as shown in FIGURE 10-11.

5. **Right-click the Employees table tab, then click Close on the shortcut menu**

   New or edited data is automatically saved when you move from record to record or close a database object.

FIGURE 10-10: Creating a data macro

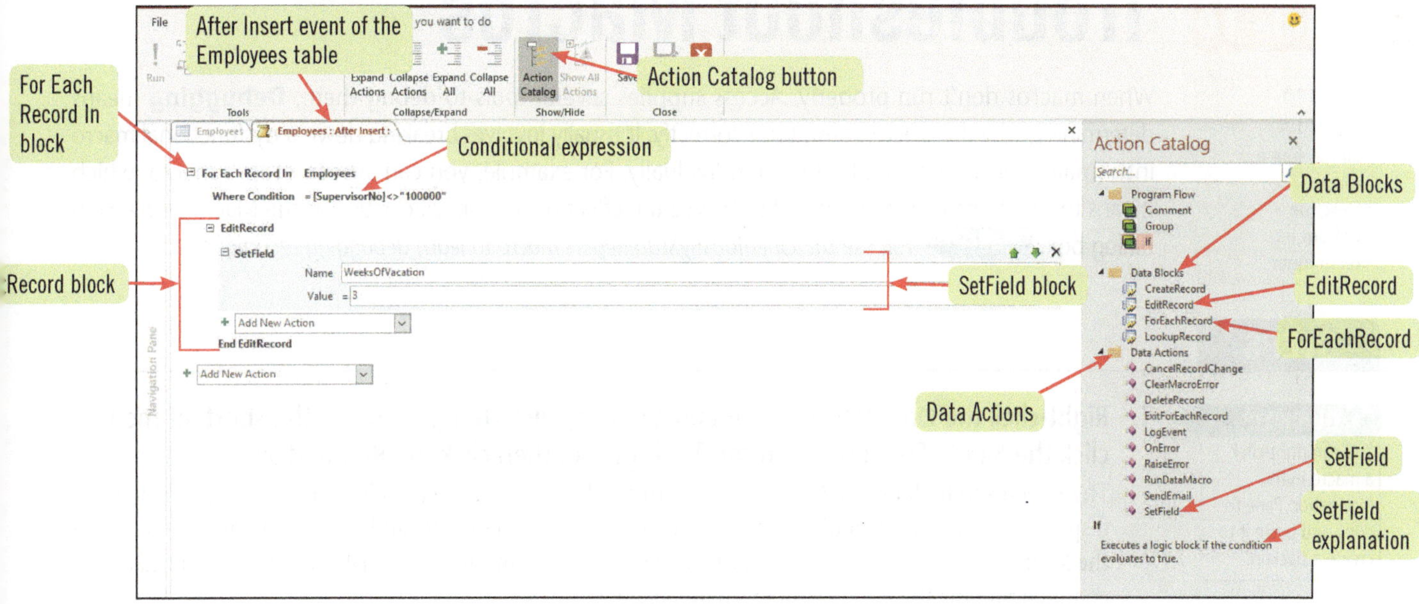

FIGURE 10-11: Running a data macro

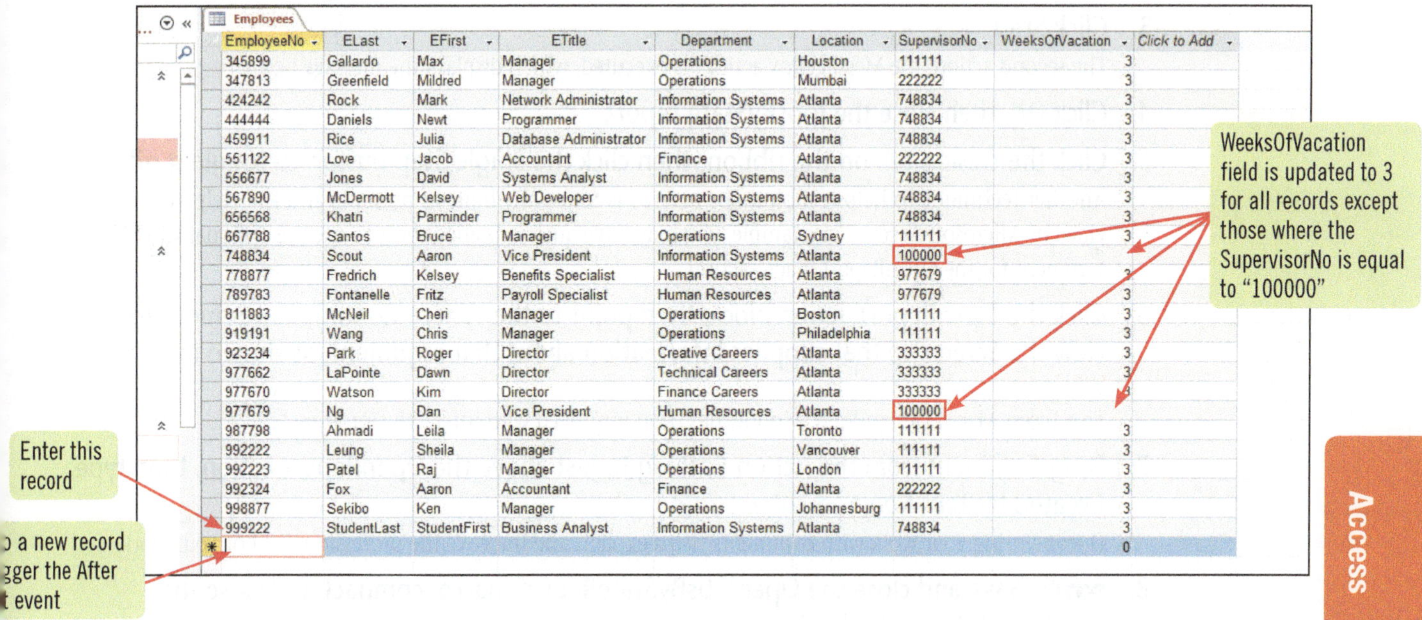

TABLE 10-4: Table events

table event	runs...
After Insert	after a new record has been inserted into the table
After Update	after an existing record has been changed
After Delete	after an existing record has been deleted
Before Delete	before a record is deleted, to help the user validate or cancel the deletion
Before Change	before a record is changed, to help the user validate or cancel the edits

Access

Access
Module 10

Troubleshoot Macros

Learning Outcomes
- Single step a macro
- Describe debugging techniques

When macros don't run properly, Access supplies several tools to debug them. **Debugging** means determining why the macro doesn't run correctly. It usually involves breaking down a dysfunctional macro into smaller pieces that can be tested individually. For example, you can **single step** a macro, which means to run it one action at a time to observe the effect of each specific action in the Macro Single Step dialog box. CASE *You use the OpenJobsByStateReport macro to learn debugging techniques.*

STEPS

QUICK TIP
You can right-click a macro in the Navigation Pane to copy and paste it to create a backup.

1. **Right-click the OpenJobsByStateReport macro, click Design View on the shortcut menu, click the Single Step button in the Tools group, then click the Run button**
   The screen should look like FIGURE 10-12, with the Macro Single Step dialog box open. This dialog box displays information, including the macro's name, the action's name, and the action's arguments. From the Macro Single Step dialog box, you can step into the next macro action, halt execution of the macro, or continue running the macro without single stepping.
2. **Click Step in the Macro Single Step dialog box**
   Stepping into the second action lets the first action run and pauses the macro at the second action. The Macro Single Step dialog box now displays information about the second action.
3. **Click Step**
   The second action, the MessageBox action, is executed, which displays the message box.
4. **Click OK, then close the JobsByState report**
5. **Click the Design tab on the ribbon, then click the Single Step button to toggle it off**
   Another technique to help troubleshoot macros is to use the built-in prompts and the Help system provided by Microsoft Access. For example, you may have questions about how to use the optional Filter Name argument for the OpenReport macro action.
6. **Click the OpenReport action block, then point to the Where Condition argument to view the ScreenTip that supplies information about that argument, as shown in FIGURE 10-13**
   The Access Macro Design View window has been improved with interactive prompts.
7. **Drag Comment from the Action Catalog to just above the OpenReport action, then type Created by *Your Name* on *current date***
   Documenting your work with comments helps explain and improve the professionalism of your work.
8. **sam Save and close the OpenJobsByStateReport macro, compact and close the IL_AC_10_Jobs.accdb database, then close Access**

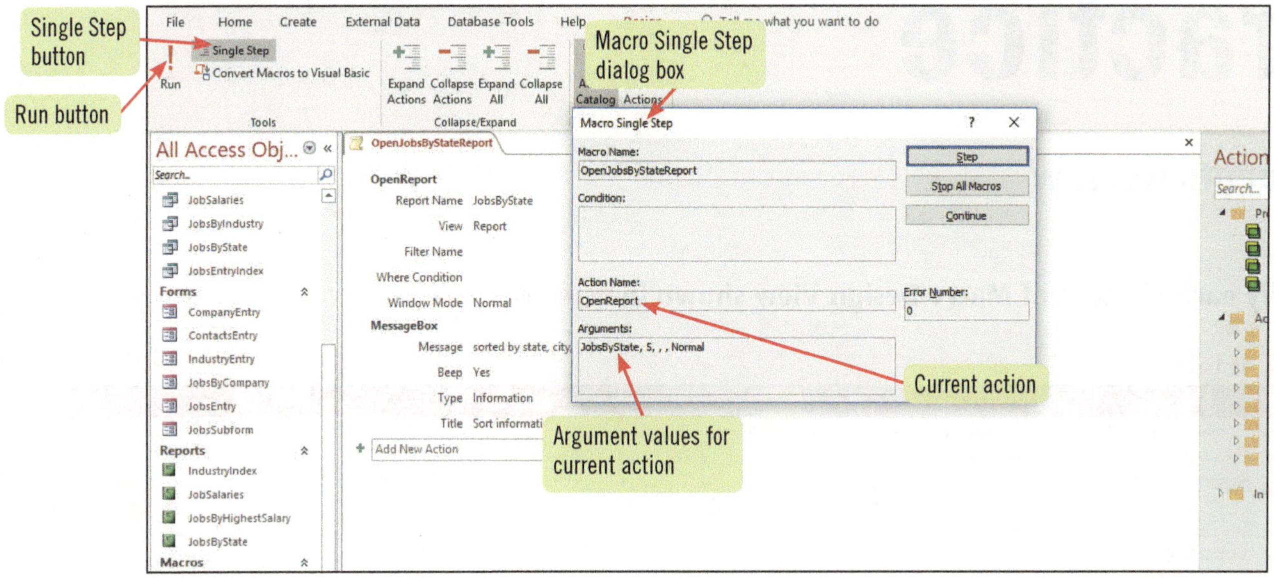

FIGURE 10-12: Single stepping through a macro

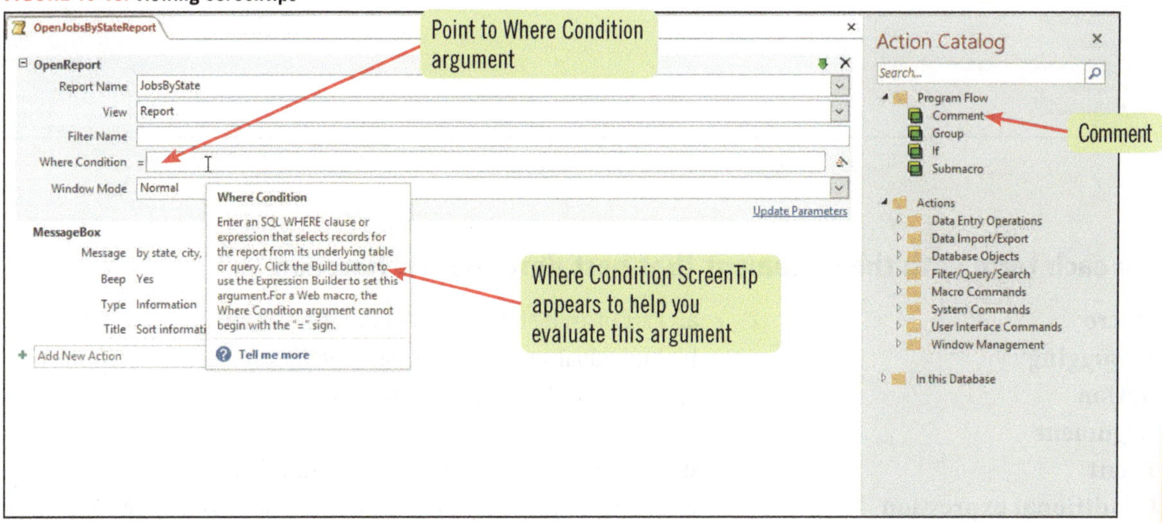

FIGURE 10-13: Viewing ScreenTips

Access

Practice

Concepts Review

Identify each element of Macro Design View shown in FIGURE 10-14.

FIGURE 10-14

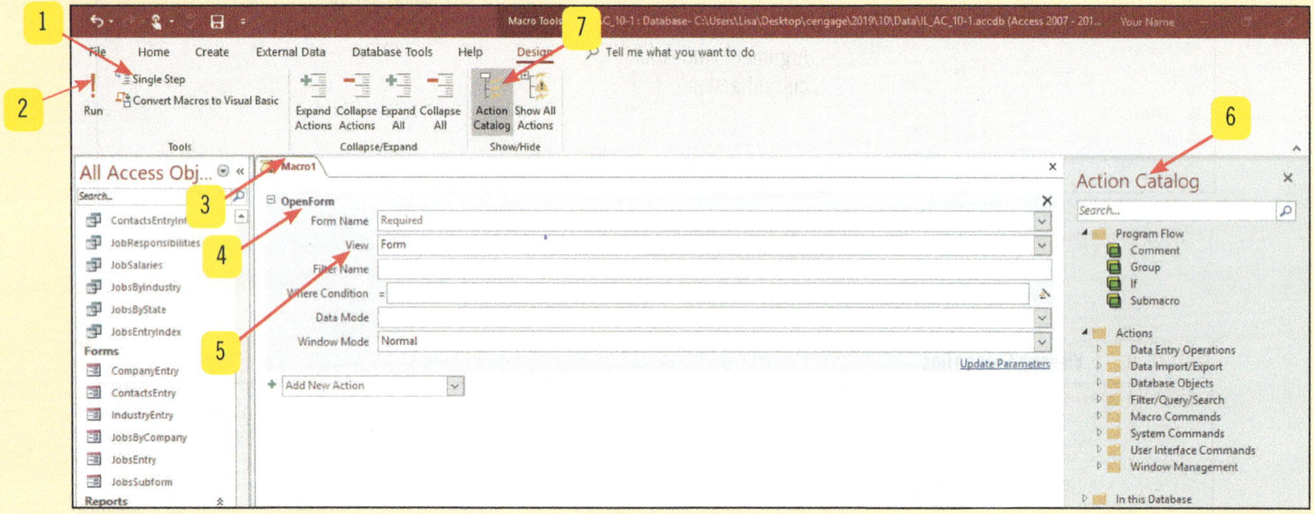

Match each term with the statement that best describes its function.

8. Macro
9. Debugging
10. Action
11. Argument
12. Event
13. Conditional expression

a. Part of an If statement that evaluates as either true or false
b. Individual step that you want the Access macro to perform
c. Provides additional information to define how an Access action will perform
d. Determines why a macro doesn't run properly
e. Access object that stores one or more actions that perform one or more tasks
f. Specific action that occurs within the database, such as clicking a button or opening a form

Select the best answer from the list of choices.

14. Which of the following is *not* a major benefit of using a macro?

a. To save time by automating routine tasks
b. To ensure consistency in executing routine or complex tasks
c. To redesign the relationships among the tables of the database
d. To make the database more flexible or easy to use

15. Which of the following best describes the process of creating an Access macro?

a. Open Macro Design View and add actions, arguments, and If statements to accomplish the desired task.
b. Use the single step recorder to record clicks and keystrokes as you complete a task.
c. Use the Macro Wizard to determine which tasks are done most frequently.
d. Use the macro recorder to record clicks and keystrokes as you complete a task.

16. Which of the following would *not* be a way to run a macro?

a. Double-click a macro action within the Macro Design View window.
b. Assign the macro to an event of a control on a form.
c. Assign the macro to a command button on a form.
d. Click the Run Macro button on the Database Tools tab.

17. Which of the following is *not* a reason to run a macro in single step mode?

a. You want to change the arguments of a macro while it runs.
b. You want to run only a few of the actions of a macro.
c. You want to observe the effect of each macro action individually.
d. You want to debug a macro that isn't working properly.

18. Which of the following is *not* true of conditional expressions in If statements in macros?

a. Conditional expressions give the macro more power and flexibility.
b. Macro If statements provide for Else and Else If clauses.
c. More macro actions are available when you are also using conditional expressions.
d. Conditional expressions allow you to skip over actions when the expression evaluates as false.

19. Which example illustrates the proper syntax to refer to a specific control on a form?

a. (Forms) ! (formname) ! (controlname)
b. {Forms} ! {formname} ! (controlname)
c. [Forms] ! [formname] ! [controlname]
d. Forms ! formname. controlname

20. Which event is executed every time you move from record to record in a form?

a. New Record
b. On Current
c. On Move
d. Next Record

Skills Review

1. Understand macros.

a. Start Access, open the IL_AC_10-2.accdb database from the location where you store your Data Files, then save it as **IL_AC_10_SupportDesk**. Enable content if prompted.
b. Open the ViewReports macro in Macro Design View, then record your answers to the following questions:
- How many macro actions are in the macro?
- What arguments does the first action contain?
- What values were chosen for the arguments of the first macro action?

c. Close Macro Design View for the ViewReports macro.

2. Create a macro.

a. Start a new macro in Macro Design View.
b. Add the OpenQuery action.
c. Select EmployeesByDepartment as the value for the Query Name argument.
d. Select Datasheet for the View argument.
e. Select Edit for the Data Mode argument.
f. Save the macro using **ViewEmployees** as the name.
g. Run the macro to make sure it works, close the EmployeesByDepartment query, then close the ViewEmployees macro.

Skills Review (continued)

3. Modify actions and arguments.

a. Open the ViewEmployees macro in Macro Design View.

b. Add a MessageBox action as the second action of the query.

c. Type **Sorted by last name within department** for the Message argument.

d. Select No for the Beep argument.

e. Select Information for the Type argument.

f. Type **Employee list information** for the Title argument.

g. Save the macro, then run it to make sure the MessageBox action works as intended.

h. Click OK in the dialog box created by the MessageBox action, close the EmployeesByDepartment query, then save and close the ViewEmployees macro.

i. Open the ViewReports macro object in Design View.

j. Modify the View argument for the OpenReport action for the EmployeeMasterList report from Report to **Print Preview**.

k. Save and close the ViewReports macro.

4. Assign a macro to a command button.

a. In Design View of the EmployeesByDepartment form, expand the height of the Form Footer section to be about 0.5" tall.

b. Use the Command Button Wizard to add a new command button to the Form Footer section at about the 0.5" mark on the horizontal ruler. The new button should run the ViewEmployees macro.

c. The text on the button should read **View Employees by Department**.

d. The meaningful name for the button should be **ViewEmployees**.

e. Save the form, then test the command button in Form View.

f. Click OK in the message box, then close the EmployeesByDepartment query.

g. Save and close the EmployeesByDepartment form.

5. Use Macro If Statements.

a. Start a new macro in Macro Design View, then open the Action Catalog window if it is not already open.

b. Double-click If in the Action Catalog pane to add an If block to the macro.

c. Enter the following condition in the If box that tests whether the Salary value in the EmployeeMaster form is greater than or equal to $70,000: **[Forms]![EmployeeMaster]![Salary]>=70000**

d. Add the SetProperty action to the If block.

e. Type **BenefitLabel** in the Control Name box for the SetProperty action.

f. Select Visible for the Property argument for the SetProperty action.

g. Enter **True** for the Value argument, and save the macro with the name **BenefitMessage**.

6. Use the Macro Else clause.

a. With the BenefitMessage macro still open in Design View, click the Add Else link in the lower-right corner of the If block.

b. Enter the same SetProperty action from the If statement under the Else clause with the same values for the Control Name and Property arguments, but modify the Value property from True to **False**.

c. Save the macro and compare it with FIGURE 10-15 to make any necessary adjustments.

FIGURE 10-15

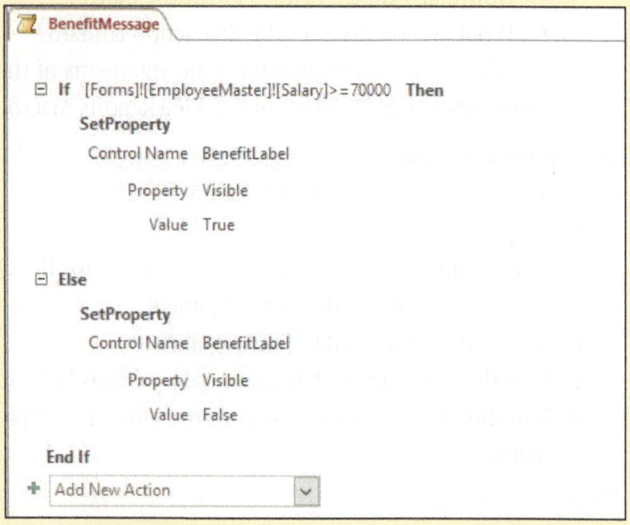

Skills Review (continued)

d. Add a comment to the top of the macro with your name and today's date, then close and save Macro Design View.

e. Open the EmployeeMaster form in Design View then attach the BenefitMessage macro to the On Current event property of the form.

f. Save the form and open it in Form View. Navigate through several records to test whether the label appears based on the value in the Salary text box. The label should only appear when the Salary value is greater than or equal to $70,000.

g. Close the EmployeeMaster form.

7. Create a data macro.

a. Open the Cases table in Table Design View.

b. Add a field named **DaysToResolve** with a Number data type and the following Description: **The number of days between the OpenedDate and the ResolvedDate**.

c. Delete 0 in the Default Value property of the new DaysToResolve field so that new records will not automatically have the value of 0 in this field, save the Cases table, then switch to Datasheet View to note that the DaysToResolve field is blank for every record.

d. Switch back to Table Design View, then create a data macro based on the Before Change event.

e. Insert an If block, then specify **IsNull([ResolvedDate])** for the expression, which will test to see if the ResolvedDate field has an entry. If the ResolvedDate field is empty (null), the expression will evaluate true. If the ResolvedDate field contains a value, the expression will evaluate false.

f. Click the Add Else link. Add a SetField data action and set the Name argument to **DaysToResolve** and the Value to **[ResolvedDate]-[OpenedDate]** to calculate the number of days between these dates, as shown in FIGURE 10-16.

g. Save and close the data macro, save the Cases table, switch to Datasheet View, then test the new data macro by entering a ResolvedDate value of **4/2/2021** in the first record (CaseID 1) and **4/3/2021** in the second record (CaseID 2).

h. Close the Cases table.

FIGURE 10-16

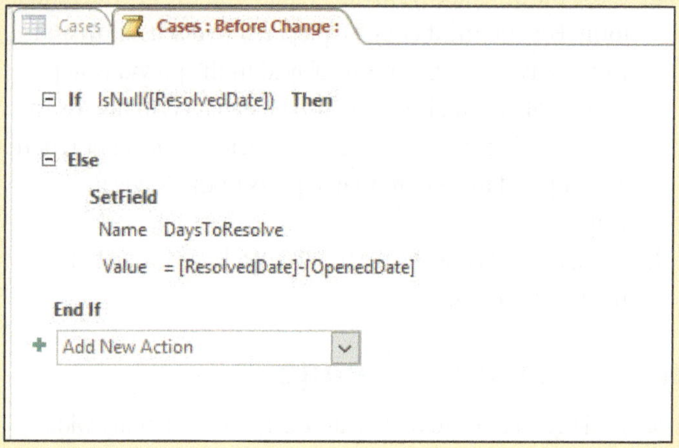

8. Troubleshoot macros.

a. Open the ViewReports macro in Macro Design View.

b. Click the Single Step button, then click the Run button.

c. Click Step three times to step through the three actions of the macro, then close all three reports.

d. Return to Macro Design View of the ViewReports macro then click the Single Step button on the Design tab to toggle off this feature.

e. Add a comment to the top of the macro with your name and today's date, then save and close the ViewReports macro.

f. Compact and close the IL_AC_10_SupportDesk.accdb database, then close Access 2019.

Independent Challenge 1

As the manager of Riverwalk, a multispecialty health clinic, you have created a database to manage nurse and doctor schedules to efficiently handle patient visits. In this exercise, you will create macros to help automate the application.

Independent Challenge 1 (continued)

a. Start Access, open the IL_AC_10-3.accdb database from the location where you store your Data Files, then save it as **IL_AC_10_Riverwalk**. Enable content if prompted.

b. Open the ProviderEntry form in Form Design View, then expand the Form Footer to be about 0.5" in height.

c. Add a command button to the Form Footer section at about the 1" mark on the horizontal ruler. Use the Command Button Wizard, and select the Preview Report action from the Report Operations category.

d. Select the ScheduleByProvider report.

e. Use the text **Preview Schedule Report** on the command button and the meaningful name of **ScheduleReport**.

f. Select the command button and open the Property Sheet. Note that the On Click property on the Event tab of the Property Sheet shows that an [Embedded Macro] is attached to that event. Click the Build button for the On Click property to open Macro Design View for the embedded macro.

g. Modify the View property from Print Preview to Report.

h. Add a MessageBox action with the argument values shown in FIGURE 10-17.

i. Save and close the embedded macro, then save the ProviderEntry form and display it in Form View.

j. Click the Preview Schedule Report button, enter **12/1/21** in the Enter Parameter Prompt dialog box, then click OK in the Report Information dialog box to display the ScheduleByProvider report.

k. Close the ScheduleByProvider report and the ProviderEntry form. For your next class, be prepared to discuss how and why the two dialog boxes displayed in the previous step were created and displayed. Also be prepared to discuss the difference between an embedded macro in a form or report as compared to a macro that appears in the Navigation Pane.

l. Compact and close the IL_AC_Riverwalk.accdb database, then close Access.

FIGURE 10-17

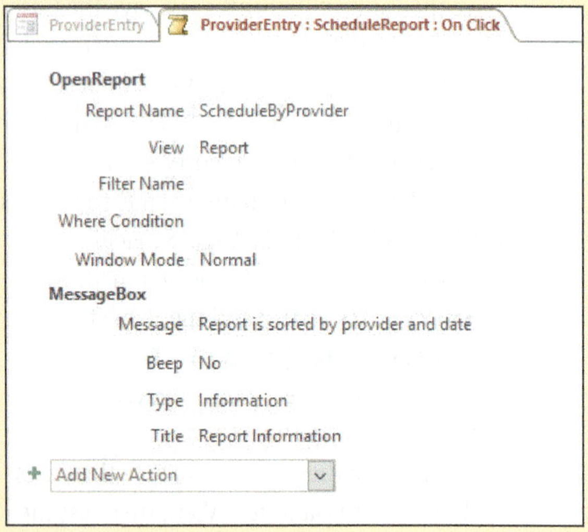

Independent Challenge 2

You are working for a city to coordinate a series of community-wide preparedness activities. You have created a database to track the activities and volunteers who are attending the activities. In this exercise, you will create macros to help automate the application.

a. Start Access, open the IL_AC_10-4.accdb database from the location where you store your Data Files, then save it as **IL_AC_10_Volunteers**. Enable content if prompted.

b. Open the Volunteers table in Design View and add a new field named **Team** with a Short Text data type.

c. Add a data macro on the After Insert event to the table that determines which value to automatically insert into the Team field based on the value in the Birthday field, as shown in FIGURE 10-18.
The expression **[Birthday]<(Date()-60*365.25)** determines if the person has an age greater than 60. If so, the Team value will be Gold. Date() returns the number of days

FIGURE 10-18

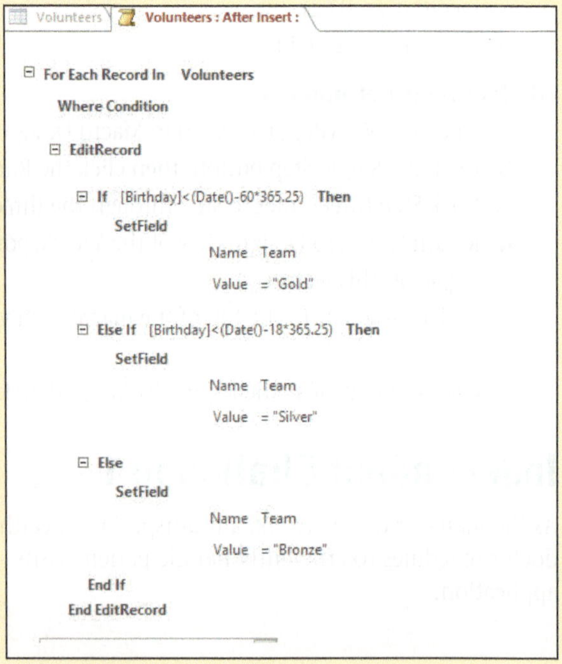

between 1/1/1900 and today (around 44,000). The expression 60*365.25 returns a value that represents the number of days in 60 years (21,915). The complete expression Date()-60*365.25 returns the difference between those two values. If the [Birthday] value (the number of days between 1/1/1900 and the Birthday) is less than the difference, the person is older than 60 years old.

The Else If clause only runs when the If clause evaluates false.

The expression **[Birthday]<(Date()-18*365.25)** determines if the person is older than 18. If so, the Team value will be Silver.

The Else clause only runs when both the If and the Else If clauses evaluate false. Birthdays that do not evaluate true for ages greater than 60 or greater than 18 are minors and are assigned a Team value of Bronze.

d. Save the data macro then switch to Datasheet View of the Volunteers table. Add your name, the school's street address, the Zipcode of **66215**, and today's date for the Birthday value, then press TAB to add a new record. All Team values should automatically update.

e. Sort the records in descending order based on the Birthday field (which should put your record on top), then scroll through the records to observe when the Team value changes from Bronze (under 18) to Silver (18 to 59 years old) and Silver to Gold (60 and over).

f. Save and close the Volunteers table.

g. Compact and close the IL_AC_10_Volunteers.accdb database, then close Access.

Visual Workshop

Start Access, open the IL_AC_10-5.accdb database from the location where you store your Data Files, then save it as **IL_AC_10_CollegeCourses**. Enable content if prompted. Develop a new macro called **GradeFilters** with the four submacros, actions, and argument values shown in FIGURE 10-19. Add a comment with your name and the current date to the top of the GradeFilters macro, then save and close the GradeFilters macro. Open the StudentGradeListing report in Design View and attach these submacros to the On Click event of their associated command buttons:

- **GradeFilters.GradeAorB** to the command button with the caption of A and B
- **GradeFilters.GradeC** to the command button with the caption of C
- **GradeFilters.GradeDorF** to the command button with the caption of D and F
- **GradeFilters.GradeAll** to the command button with the caption of All

Save the StudentGradeListing report and display it in Report View. Test the command buttons, close the report, compact and close the IL_AC_10_CollegeCourses.accdb database, then close Access.

FIGURE 10-19

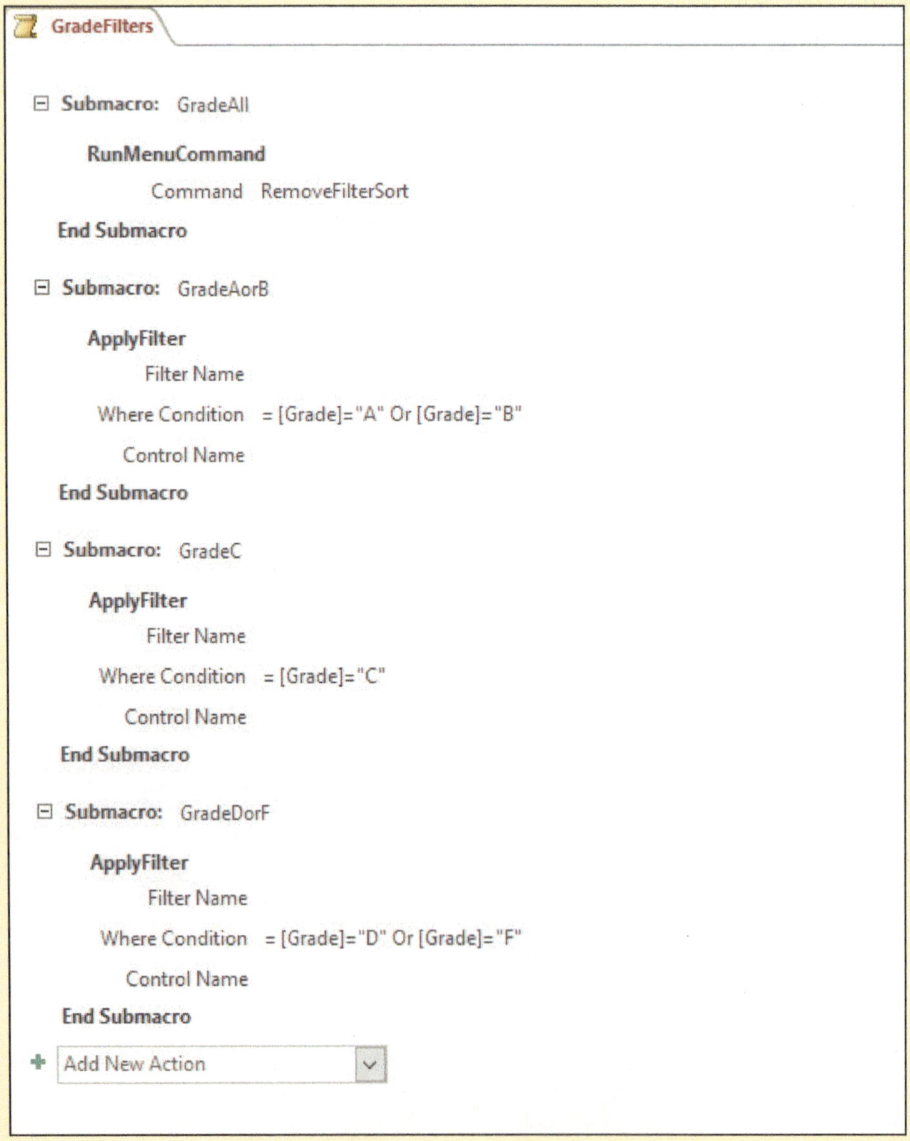

Creating Modules and VBA

CASE You are working with Lydia Snyder, vice president of operations at JCL Talent, to build a research database to manage industry, company, and job data. In this module, you create and modify modules and VBA to make the database application easier to use and to extend its capabilities.

Module Objectives

After completing this module, you will be able to:

- Understand modules and VBA
- Compare macros and modules
- Create functions
- Use VBA If statements
- Document procedures
- Build class modules
- Modify procedures
- Troubleshoot VBA

Files You Will Need

IL_AC_11-1.accdb
IL_AC_11-2.accdb
IL_AC_11-3.accdb
IL_AC_11-4.accdb
IL_AC_11-5.accdb

Access Module 11

Understand Modules and VBA

Learning Outcomes
- Define VBA terms
- Describe Visual Basic Editor components

Access is a robust relational database program for small applications. Access also provides user-friendly tools, such as wizards and Design Views, to help users quickly create reports and forms that previously took programmers many hours to build. You may, however, want to automate a task or create a new function that goes beyond the capabilities of the built-in Access features. Within each program of the Microsoft Office suite, a programming language called **Visual Basic for Applications (VBA)** is provided to help you extend the program's capabilities. In Access, VBA is stored within modules. A **module** is an Access object that stores Visual Basic for Applications (VBA) programming code. VBA is written in the **Visual Basic Editor (VBE)**, shown in FIGURE 11-1. The components and text colors of the VBE are described in TABLE 11-1. An Access database has two kinds of modules. **Standard modules** contain global code that can be executed from anywhere in the database. Standard modules are displayed as module objects in the Navigation Pane. **Class modules** are stored within a form or report object for use within that individual form or report. **CASE** *You ask some questions about VBA.*

DETAILS

The following questions and answers introduce the basics of Access modules:

- **What does a module contain?**

  A module contains VBA programming code organized in procedures. **Standard modules** are stored in the Navigation Pane and contain procedures available to all other objects. **Class modules** are stored in an individual form or report.

- **What is a procedure?**

  A **procedure** performs an operation or calculates an answer with one or several lines of code, each of which is called a **statement**. VBA has two types of procedures: functions and subs. **Declaration statements** precede procedure statements and help set rules for how the statements in the module are processed.

- **What is a function?**

  A **function** is a procedure that returns a value. Access supplies many **built-in functions**, such as Sum, Count, Pmt, and Now, that can be used in an expression in a query, form, or report to calculate and return a value. You might want to create a custom function, however, to calculate answers using formulas unique to your business.

- **What is a sub?**

  A **sub** (also called **sub procedure**) performs a series of VBA statements to manipulate data, controls, and objects. Subs are generally executed when an event occurs, such as when a command button is clicked or a form is opened.

- **What are arguments?**

  Arguments are constants, variables, or expressions passed to a procedure that the procedure needs to execute. For example, the full syntax for the Sum function is Sum(*expr*), where *expr* represents the argument for the Sum function, typically the field that is being summed. In VBA, arguments are declared in the first line of the procedure immediately after a procedure's name and are enclosed in parentheses. Multiple arguments are separated by commas.

- **What is an object?**

  In VBA, an **object** is any item that can be used or manipulated, including the traditional Access objects (table, query, form, report, macro, and module), as well as form controls and sections, existing procedures, and built-in VBA objects that provide functionality to your code.

- **What is a method?**

  A **method** is an action that an object can perform. Procedures are often written to invoke methods in response to user actions. For example, you could invoke the GoToControl method to move the focus to a specific control on a form in response to the user clicking a command button.

FIGURE 11-1: Visual Basic Editor (VBE) window for a standard module

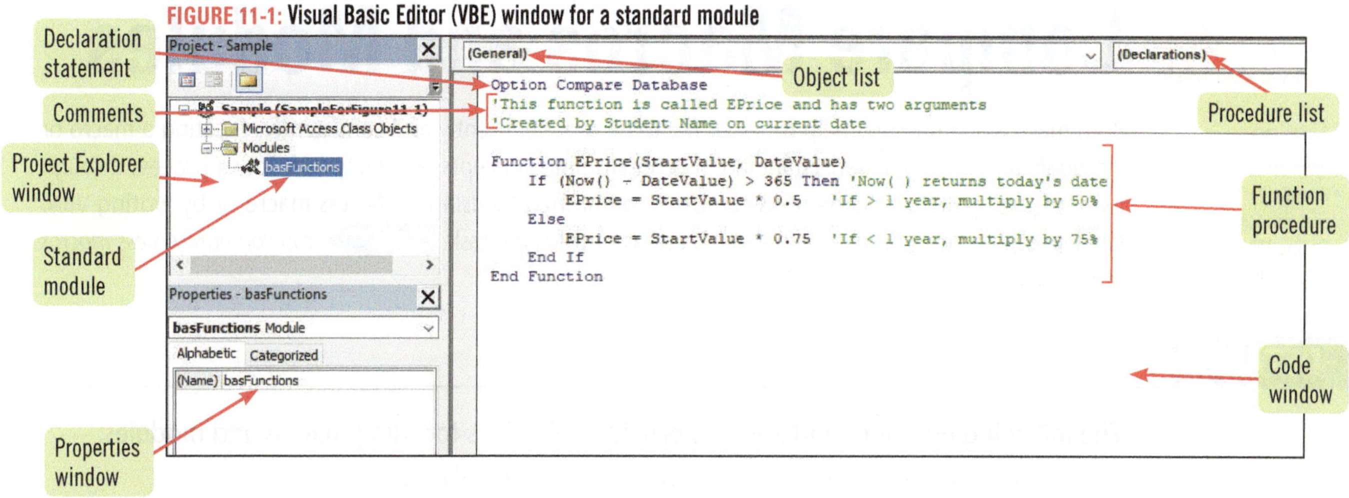

TABLE 11-1: Components and text colors for the Visual Basic Editor window

component or color	description
Visual Basic Editor (VBE)	Comprises the entire Microsoft Visual Basic program window that contains smaller windows, including the Code window and Project Explorer window
Code window	Contains the VBA for the project selected in the Project Explorer window
Project Explorer window	Displays a hierarchical list of the projects in the database; a project can be a module object or a form or report object that contains a class module
Declaration statements	Includes statements that apply to every procedure in the module, such as declarations for variables, constants, user-defined data types, and external procedures in a dynamic-link library
Object list	In a class module, lists the objects associated with the current form or report
Procedure list	In a standard module, lists the procedures in the module; in a class module, lists events (such as Click or Dblclick)
Blue	Indicates a VBA keyword; blue words are reserved by VBA and are already assigned specific meanings
Black	Indicates normal text; black text is the unique VBA code created by the developer
Red	Indicates syntax error; a red statement indicates that it will not execute correctly because of a syntax error (perhaps a missing parenthesis or a keyword spelling error)
Green	Indicates comment text; any text after an apostrophe is considered a comment, and is therefore ignored in the execution of the procedure

Converting macros to VBA

You can convert a form or report's embedded macros to VBA by opening the form or report in Design View, then clicking the Convert Form's (Report's) Macros to Visual Basic button in the Tools group. The VBA is inserted as a class module within the form or report and can be viewed by clicking the View Code button in the Tools group in Form or Report Design View.

You can also convert global macros found in the Navigation Pane to VBA by opening the macro in Macro Design View, and then clicking the Convert Macros to Visual Basic button in the Tools group. The VBA is stored in a standard module located in the Navigation Pane and identified with a name that starts with "Converted Macro."

Access
Module 11

Compare Macros and Modules

Learning Outcomes
- Contrast macros and modules
- Define VBA keywords

Both macros and modules help run your database more efficiently and consistently. Creating a macro or a module requires some understanding of programming concepts, an ability to follow a process through its steps, and patience. Some tasks can be accomplished by using an Access macro or by writing VBA. Guidelines can help you determine which tool is best for the task. **CASE** *You compare Access macros and modules by asking more questions.*

DETAILS

The following questions and answers provide guidelines for using macros and modules:

- ## For what types of tasks are macros best suited?

  Macros are an easy way to handle common, repetitive, and simple tasks such as opening and closing forms and reports, applying filters, and printing reports.

- ## Which is easier to create, a macro or a module, and why?

  Macros are generally easier to create because Macro Design View is more structured than the VBE. The hardest part of creating a macro is choosing the correct macro action. But once the action is selected, the arguments associated with that macro action are displayed, eliminating the need to learn any special programming syntax. To create a module, however, you must know a robust programming language, VBA, as well as the correct **syntax** (rules) for each VBA statement. In a nutshell, macros are simpler to create, but VBA is more powerful.

- ## When must I use a macro?

  You must use macros to make global, shortcut key assignments. **AutoExec** is a special macro name that automatically executes when the database first opens.

- ## When must I use a module?

  1. You must use modules to create unique functions. For instance, you might want to create a function called Commission that calculates the appropriate commission using your company's unique commission formula.
  2. Access error messages can be confusing to the user. However, by using VBA procedures, you can detect the error when it occurs and display your own message.
  3. Although Access macros have recently been enhanced to include more powerful If-Then logic, VBA is still more robust in the area of programming flow statements with tools such as nested If statements, Case statements, and multiple looping structures. Some of the most common VBA keywords, including If...Then, are shown in **TABLE 11-2**. VBA keywords appear in blue in the VBE code window.
  4. VBA code may declare **variables**, which store data that can be used, modified, or displayed during the execution of the procedure.
  5. VBA may be used in conjunction with **SQL (Structured Query Language)** to select, update, append, and delete data.

  Like macros, modules can be accessed through the Navigation Pane or embedded directly within a form or report. When embedded in a form or report object, the module is called a **class module**, like the one shown in **FIGURE 11-2**. If you develop forms and reports in one database and copy them to another, the class modules automatically travel with the object that stores it. Use class modules for code that is unique to that form or report. Use standard modules (also called **global modules**) to store code that will be reused in many places in the database application.

FIGURE 11-2: Visual Basic Editor window for a class module

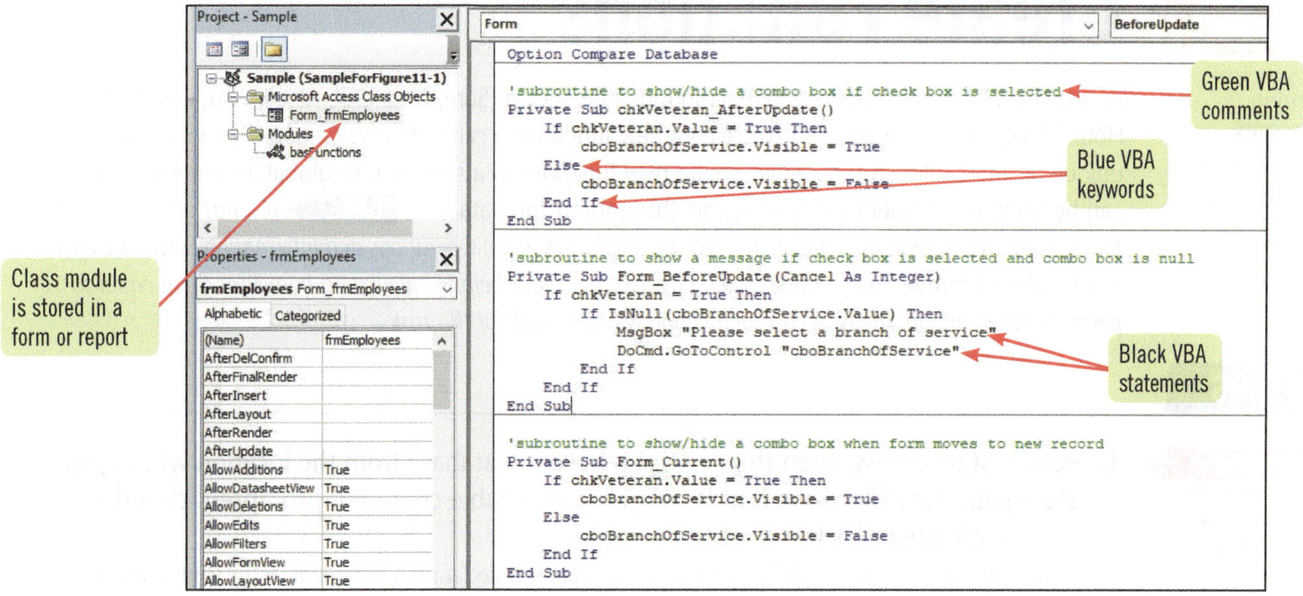

TABLE 11-2: Common VBA keywords

statement	explanation
Function	Declares the name and arguments that create a new function procedure
End Function	When defining a new function, the End Function statement is required as the last statement to mark the end of the VBA code that defines the function
Sub	Declares the name for a new Sub procedure; Private Sub indicates that the Sub is accessible only to other procedures in the module where it is declared
End Sub	When defining a new sub, the End Sub statement is required as the last statement to mark the end of the VBA code that defines the sub
If...Then	Executes code (the code follows the Then statement) when the value of an expression is true (the expression follows the If statement)
End If	When creating an If...Then...Else clause, the End If statement is required as the last statement
Const	Declares the name and value of a constant, an item that retains a constant value throughout the execution of the code
Option Compare Database	A declaration statement that determines the way string values (text) will be sorted
Option Explicit	A declaration statement that specifies that you must explicitly declare all variables used in all procedures; if you attempt to use an undeclared variable name, an error occurs at compile time, the period during which source code is translated to executable code
Dim	Declares a variable, a named storage location that contains data that can be modified during program execution
On Error GoTo	Upon an error in the execution of a procedure, specifies the location (the statement) where the procedure should continue
Select Case	Executes one of several groups of statements called a Case depending on the value of an expression; using the Select Case statement is an alternative to using ElseIf in If...Then...Else statements when comparing one expression with several different values
End Select	When defining a new Select Case group of statements, the End Select statement is required as the last statement to mark the end of the VBA code

Access

Create Functions

Learning Outcomes
- Create a custom function
- Use a custom function

Access and VBA supply hundreds of built-in functions such as Sum, Count, Iif, IsNull, First, Last, Date, and Hour. However, you might want to create a new function to calculate a value based on your company's unique business rules. You generally create new functions in a standard, or global, module so that they can be used in any query, form, or report throughout the database. **CASE** *JCL has gone through a major computer systems upgrade. To reward the employees in the Operations and Information Systems Departments for their extraordinary efforts, Lydia has asked for your help to calculate a bonus for them equal to 10 percent of their annual salary. A custom function will work well for this task.*

STEPS

TROUBLE
If you do not enable content, your VBA code will not run.

QUICK TIP
The Option Explicit statement appears if the Require Variable Declaration option is checked in the VBA Options dialog box. To view the default settings, click Tools on the VBA menu bar, then click Options.

1. **sam Start Access, open the IL_AC_11-1.accdb database from the location where you store your Data Files, save it as IL_AC_11_Jobs, enable content if prompted, click the Create tab, then click the Module button**
   Access automatically inserts the Option Compare Database declaration statement in the Code window. You will create the custom function to calculate employee bonuses one step at a time.
2. **Type function Bonus(Salary), then press ENTER**
   This statement creates a new function named Bonus, which uses one argument, Salary. The VBE automatically capitalized Function and added the **End Function** statement, a required statement to mark the end of the function. VBA keywords are blue.
3. **Press TAB, type Bonus = Salary * 0.1, then press ENTER**
   Your screen should look like FIGURE 11-3. The Bonus = statement explains how the Bonus function will calculate a value and what value it will return. The function will multiply the Salary by 0.1 and return the result.
   It is not necessary to indent statements, but indenting code between matching Function/End Function, Sub/End Sub, or If/End If statements enhances the program's readability. When you press ENTER at the end of a VBA statement, the VBE automatically adds spaces as appropriate to enhance the readability of the statement.
4. **Click the Save button on the Standard toolbar, type basFunctions in the Save As dialog box, click OK, then click the upper Close button in the upper-right corner of the VBE window to close the Visual Basic Editor**
   It is common for VBA programmers to use three-character prefixes to name objects and controls. This makes it easier to identify that object or control in expressions and modules. The prefix **bas** is short for (Visual) Basic and applies to standard (global) modules. Naming conventions for other objects and controls are listed in TABLE 11-3 and are used throughout the IL_AC_11_Jobs.accdb database. You can use the new function, Bonus, in a query, form, or report.
5. **Click the Create tab, click the Query Design button, double-click tblEmployees, then click Close in the Show Table dialog box**
   You use the new Bonus function in the query to calculate the 10 percent bonus.

QUICK TIP
Field names used in expressions are not case sensitive, but they must exactly match the spelling of the field name as defined in Table Design View.

6. **Double-click EFirst, double-click ELast, double-click Department, double-click AnnualSalary, click the blank Field cell to the right of the AnnualSalary field, type BonusPay:Bonus([AnnualSalary]), then click the View button as shown in FIGURE 11-4**
   You created a new field called BonusPay that uses the custom Bonus function that calculates and returns 10 percent of the AnnualSalary.
7. **Save the query with the name qryBonus, then close it**

FIGURE 11-3: Creating the Bonus function

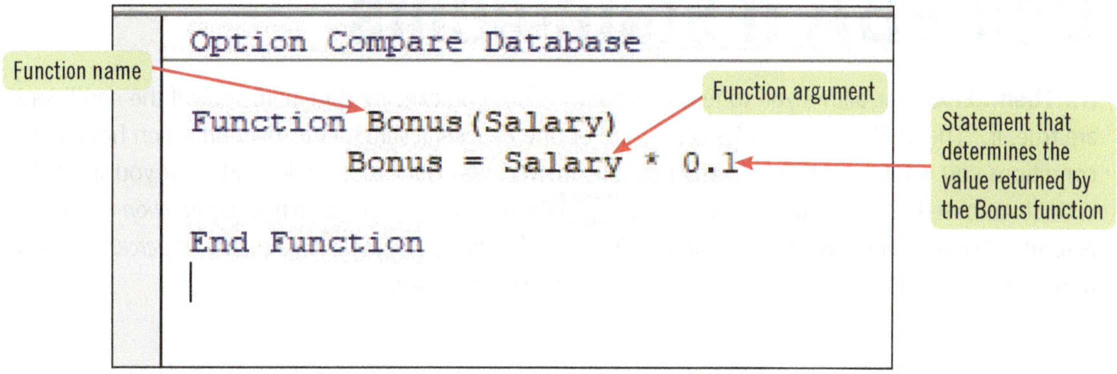

FIGURE 11-4: Using the Bonus function in a query

qryBonus

EFirst	ELast	Department	AnnualSalary	BonusPay
Rory	Gonzalez	Executive	$340,000.00	34000
Lydia	Snyder	Operations	$175,000.00	17500
Ellie	Schwartz	Finance	$155,000.00	15500
Nyack	Afolayan	Operations	$89,000.00	8900
Shavonn	Rudd	Operations	$90,000.00	9000
Rosella	Leigh	Operations	$88,000.00	8800
Anthony	Martinez	Sales and Marketing	$165,000.00	16500
Gary	Jaeger	Operations	$91,500.00	9150
Sophie	Tan	Operations	$90,000.00	9000
Max	Gallardo	Operations	$91,000.00	9100
Mildred	Greenfield	Operations	$87,000.00	8700
Mark	Rock	Information Systems	$81,000.00	8100
Newt	Daniels	Information Systems	$75,000.00	7500
Julia	Rice	Information Systems	$76,000.00	7600
Jacob	Love	Finance	$73,000.00	7300
David	Jones	Information Systems	$70,500.00	7050
Kelsey	McDermott	Information Systems	$65,000.00	6500

Calculated field, BonusPay, uses Bonus custom function to multiply the AnnualSalary by 0.1

TABLE 11-3: Common three-character prefix naming conventions

object or control	prefix	example
Table	tbl	tblProducts
Query	qry	qrySalesByRegion
Form	frm	frmProducts
Report	rpt	rptSalesByCategory
Macro	mcr	mcrCloseInventory
Module	bas	basRetirement
Label	lbl	lblFullName
Text Box	txt	txtLastName
Combo box	cbo	cboStates
Command button	cmd	cmdPrint

Access Module 11

Use VBA If statements

Learning Outcomes
- Use VBA If...Then...Else logic
- Use the Zoom feature

If...Then...Else logic allows you to test logical conditions and execute statements only if the conditions are true. If...Then...Else code can be composed of one or several statements, depending on how many conditions you want to test, how many possible answers you want to provide, and what you want the code to do based on the results of the tests. CASE *At this point, the custom Bonus function returns 10 percent of the annual salary for all employees. You add If...Then...Else logic to calculate 10 percent for only those employees in the Information Systems and Operations departments.*

STEPS

1. **Right-click the basFunctions module in the Navigation Pane, then click Design View**
   To determine the employee's department, the Bonus function needs another piece of information; it needs another argument.
2. **Click just before the right parenthesis in the Function statement, type , (a comma), type Dept, then press ↓**
   Now that you established another argument named Dept, you can work with the argument in the definition of the function.
3. **Click to the right of the right parenthesis in the Function statement, press ENTER, press TAB, then type If (Dept = "Information Systems") Then**
   The expression compares the Dept argument to the string "Information Systems". If true, Bonus is calculated as Salary * 0.1.
4. **Indent and type the rest of the statements exactly as shown in FIGURE 11-5**
   The **ElseIf** statement is executed when the first If expression evaluates to false. In this case, it multiplies Salary by 0.1 if Dept is equal to "Operations." You can add as many ElseIf clauses to the statement as desired.
   The **Else** statement is executed when all If and ElseIf statements evaluate to false. In this case, the Else statement will execute if Dept is equal to anything other than "Information Systems" or "Operations."
   The **End If** statement is needed to mark the end of the If...Then...Else block of code.
5. **Click the Save button on the Standard toolbar, close the Visual Basic window, right-click the qryBonus query, then click Design View**
   You need to modify the calculated BonusPay field to include a value for each argument in the modified Bonus function.
6. **Right-click the BonusPay field in the query design grid, click Zoom on the shortcut menu, click between the right square bracket and right parenthesis, then type ,[Department]**
   Your Zoom dialog box should look like FIGURE 11-6. Both of the arguments used to define Bonus function in the VBA code are replaced with actual field names that contain the data for the argument. Commas separate multiple arguments in the function.
7. **Click OK in the Zoom dialog box, then click the View button as shown in FIGURE 11-7**
   The Bonus function now calculates one of two different results for the BonusPay field, depending on the value in the Department field.
8. **Save then close the qryBonus query**

QUICK TIP
Indentation doesn't affect the way the function works, but it does make the code easier to read.

TROUBLE
If a compile or syntax error appears, open the VBE window, compare your function with FIGURE 11-5, then correct any errors.

FIGURE 11-5: If...Then...ElseIf...Then...Else

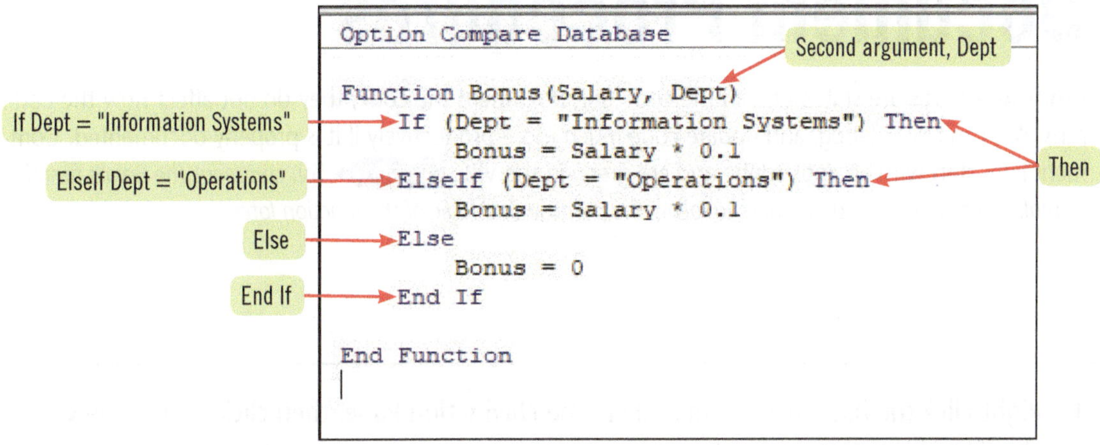

FIGURE 11-6: Using the Zoom dialog box for long expressions

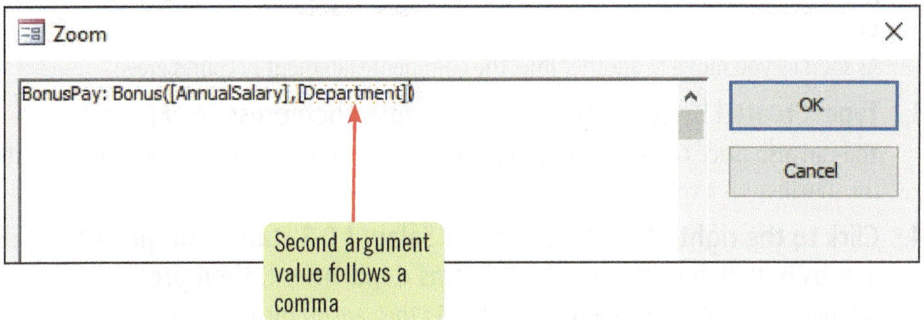

FIGURE 11-7: BonusPay field calculates 10% of AnnualSalary based on Department value

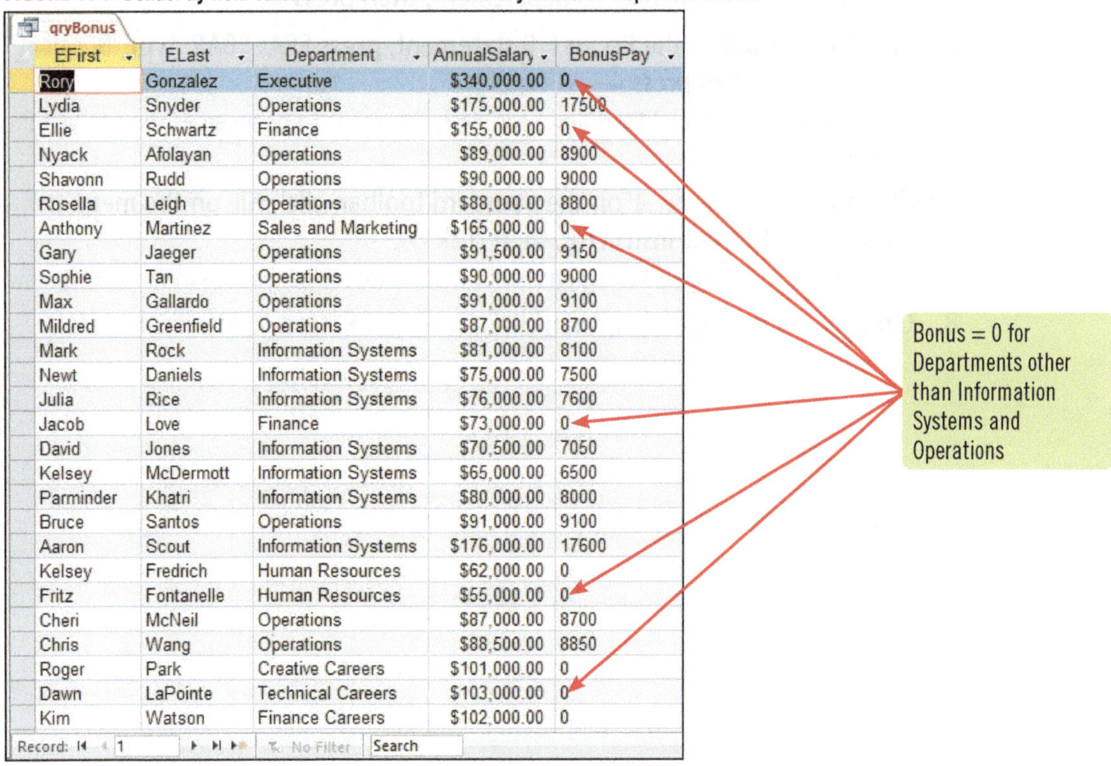

EFirst	ELast	Department	AnnualSalary	BonusPay
Rory	Gonzalez	Executive	$340,000.00	0
Lydia	Snyder	Operations	$175,000.00	17500
Ellie	Schwartz	Finance	$155,000.00	0
Nyack	Afolayan	Operations	$89,000.00	8900
Shavonn	Rudd	Operations	$90,000.00	9000
Rosella	Leigh	Operations	$88,000.00	8800
Anthony	Martinez	Sales and Marketing	$165,000.00	0
Gary	Jaeger	Operations	$91,500.00	9150
Sophie	Tan	Operations	$90,000.00	9000
Max	Gallardo	Operations	$91,000.00	9100
Mildred	Greenfield	Operations	$87,000.00	8700
Mark	Rock	Information Systems	$81,000.00	8100
Newt	Daniels	Information Systems	$75,000.00	7500
Julia	Rice	Information Systems	$76,000.00	7600
Jacob	Love	Finance	$73,000.00	0
David	Jones	Information Systems	$70,500.00	7050
Kelsey	McDermott	Information Systems	$65,000.00	6500
Parminder	Khatri	Information Systems	$80,000.00	8000
Bruce	Santos	Operations	$91,000.00	9100
Aaron	Scout	Information Systems	$176,000.00	17600
Kelsey	Fredrich	Human Resources	$62,000.00	0
Fritz	Fontanelle	Human Resources	$55,000.00	0
Cheri	McNeil	Operations	$87,000.00	8700
Chris	Wang	Operations	$88,500.00	8850
Roger	Park	Creative Careers	$101,000.00	0
Dawn	LaPointe	Technical Careers	$103,000.00	0
Kim	Watson	Finance Careers	$102,000.00	0

Access

Document Procedures

Learning Outcomes
- Add VBA comments
- Use the VBE toolbar

Comment lines are statements in the code that document the code; they do not affect how the code runs. You can read, debug, and update code much more productively if it is properly documented. Comment lines start with an apostrophe and are green in the VBE. **CASE** *You comment the Bonus function to make it easier for you and others to follow the purpose and logic of the function later.*

STEPS

QUICK TIP
You can also create comments by starting the statement with the **rem** statement (short for remark).

TROUBLE
Be sure to use an ' (apostrophe) and not a " (quotation mark) to begin the comment line.

1. **Right-click the basFunctions module in the Navigation Pane, then click Design View**
   The VBE window for the basFunctions module opens.
2. **Click the blank line between the Option Compare Database and Function statements, press ENTER, type 'This function is called Bonus and has two arguments, then press ENTER**
   As soon as you move to another line, the comment statement becomes green.
3. **Type 'Created by *your name* on *current date*, then press ENTER**
   You can also place comments at the end of a line by entering an apostrophe to mark that the next part of the statement is a comment.
4. **Click to the right of the first Bonus = Salary * 0.1 statement, press SPACEBAR, type 'Bonus is 10% for Information Systems department, then press ↓**
   All comments are green, regardless of whether they are on their own line or at the end of an existing line.
5. **Click to the right of the second Bonus = Salary * 0.1 statement, press SPACEBAR, type 'Bonus is 10% for Operations department, then press ↓**
6. **Click to the right of the Bonus = 0 statement, press SPACEBAR, type 'Bonus is 0 for other departments, then press ↓**
   Your screen should look like **FIGURE 11-8**. Each comment turns green as soon as you move to a new statement.
7. **Click the Save button on the Standard toolbar, click File on the menu bar, click Print if requested by your instructor, then click OK**
   TABLE 11-4 provides more information about the Standard toolbar buttons in the VBE window.
8. **Click File on the menu bar, then click Close and Return to Microsoft Access**

FIGURE 11-8: Adding comments to a module

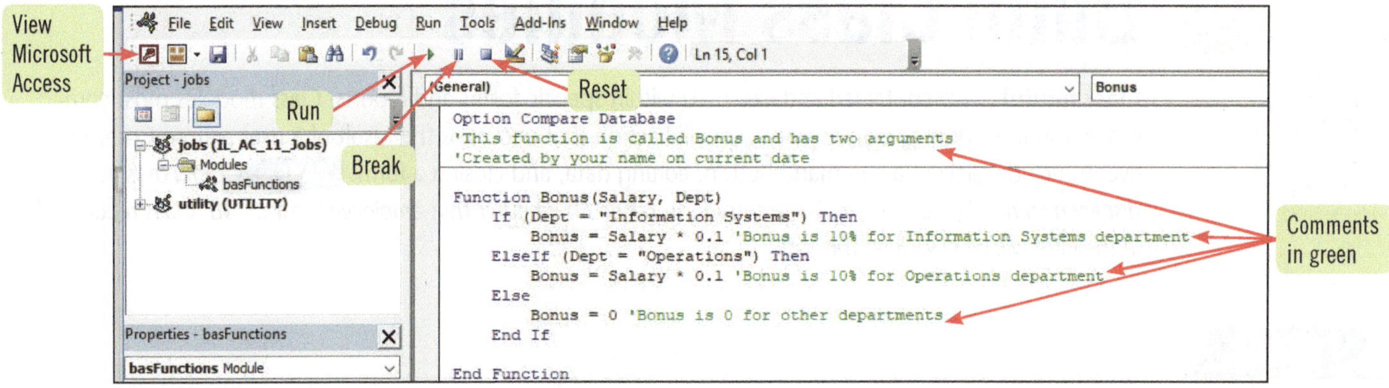

TABLE 11-4: Standard toolbar buttons in the Visual Basic window

button name	button	description
View Microsoft Access		Switches from the active Visual Basic window to the Access window
Insert Module		Opens a new module or class module Code window, or inserts a new procedure in the current Code window
Run Sub/UserForm		Runs the current procedure if the insertion point is in a procedure, or runs the UserForm if it is active
Break		Stops the execution of a program while it's running and switches to Break mode, which is the temporary suspension of program execution in which you can examine, debug, reset, step through, or continue program execution
Reset		Resets the procedure
Project Explorer		Displays the Project Explorer, which provides a hierarchical list of the currently open projects (set of modules) and their contents
Object Browser		Displays the Object Browser, which lists the defined modules and procedures as well as available methods, properties, events, constants, and other items that you can use in the code

Using comments for debugging

You can use comments to "comment out" or temporarily hide statements that you want to leave in your module but do not want to execute. "Commenting out" statements that do not work (versus editing the same broken statement(s) over and over) keeps a trail of every line of code that you have written. This process makes development, debugging, and sharing your thought processes with other developers much more productive. When the code is working as intended, extra lines that have been "commented out" that are no longer needed for the testing or debugging process can be deleted.

Build Class Modules

Learning Outcome
- Build event handlers

Class modules are contained and executed within specific forms and reports. Class modules most commonly run in response to an **event**, a specific action that occurs as the result of a user action. Common events include clicking a command button, editing data, and closing a form. CASE *Lydia asks you to display a combo box on an employee entry form based on whether that employee is a veteran. Class modules in the form will work well for this task.*

STEPS

TROUBLE
If the first line of your procedure is not Private Sub chkVeteran_AfterUpdate( ), delete the stub, close the VBE, and repeat Step 2.

QUICK TIP
Write your VBA code in lowercase. The VBE will automatically correct the case.

QUICK TIP
The **On Current** event of the form is triggered when you navigate through records.

TROUBLE
If the Code window appears with a yellow line, it means the code cannot be run successfully. Click the Reset button on the Standard toolbar, then compare your VBA with FIGURE 11-10.

1. **Double-click the frmEmployeeEntry form in the Navigation Pane to open it in Form View, then click the Branch of Service combo box arrow to review the choices**
   A choice in the Branch of Service combo box only makes sense if an employee is a veteran. You'll use a class module to set the Visible property for the Branch of Service combo box to True if the Veteran check box is checked and False if the Veteran check box is not checked.
2. **Right-click the frmEmployeeEntry tab, click Design View, double-click the Veteran check box to open its Property Sheet, click the Event tab in the Property Sheet, click the After Update property, click the Build button, click Code Builder, then click OK**
   The class module for the frmEmployeesEntry form opens. Because you opened the VBE window from a specific event of a control on the form, the **stub**, the first and last lines of the sub procedure, was automatically created. The procedure's name, chkVeteran_AfterUpdate, contains the **Name property** of the control, and the name of the event that triggers this procedure. A procedure triggered by an event is often called an **event handler**.
3. **Enter the statements shown in FIGURE 11-9**
   The If structure makes the cboBranchOfService control visible or not visible based on whether the chkVeteran control is checked (true) or unchecked (false).
4. **Save the changes and close the VBE window, click the View button, click the Veteran check box for the first record several times, then navigate through several records**
   Clicking the Veteran check box triggers the procedure that responds to the After Update event. However, you need the procedure to run every time you move from record to record, not just when the Veteran check box is clicked.
5. **Right-click the frmEmployeeEntry tab, click Design View, click the Form Selector button, click the Event tab in the Property Sheet, click the On Current event property, click the Build button, click Code Builder, click OK, then copy or retype the If structure from the chkVeteran_AfterUpdate sub to the Form_Current sub, as shown in FIGURE 11-10**
   You have now created a second event handler in this class module. The cboBranchOfService combo box will be visible based on updating the chkVeteran check box or by moving from record to record. To test the new sub procedure, switch to Form View.
6. **Save the changes and close the VBE window, click to switch to Form View, then navigate through several records to test the new procedure**
   Now, as you move from record to record, the Branch of Service combo box should be visible for those employees with the Veteran check box selected and not visible if the Veteran check box is not selected.
7. **Return to the first record for Rory Gonzalez, click the Veteran check box (if it is not already selected), click the Branch of Service combo box arrow, click Army as shown in FIGURE 11-11, then save and close frmEmployeeEntry**

FIGURE 11-9: Creating an event handler procedure

chk prefix identifies a check box

cbo prefix identifies a combo box

```
Option Compare Database

Private Sub chkVeteran_AfterUpdate()
    If chkVeteran.Value = True Then
        cboBranchOfService.Visible = True
    Else
        cboBranchOfService.Visible = False
    End If
End Sub
```

FIGURE 11-10: Copying the If structure to a new event handler procedure

Copy If structure from chkVeteran_ AfterUpdate sub to Form_Current sub

```
Option Compare Database

Private Sub chkVeteran_AfterUpdate()
    If chkVeteran.Value = True Then
        cboBranchOfService.Visible = True
    Else
        cboBranchOfService.Visible = False
    End If
End Sub

Private Sub Form_Current()
    If chkVeteran.Value = True Then
        cboBranchOfService.Visible = True
    Else
        cboBranchOfService.Visible = False
    End If
End Sub
```

FIGURE 11-11: Branch of Service combo box is visible when Veteran box is checked

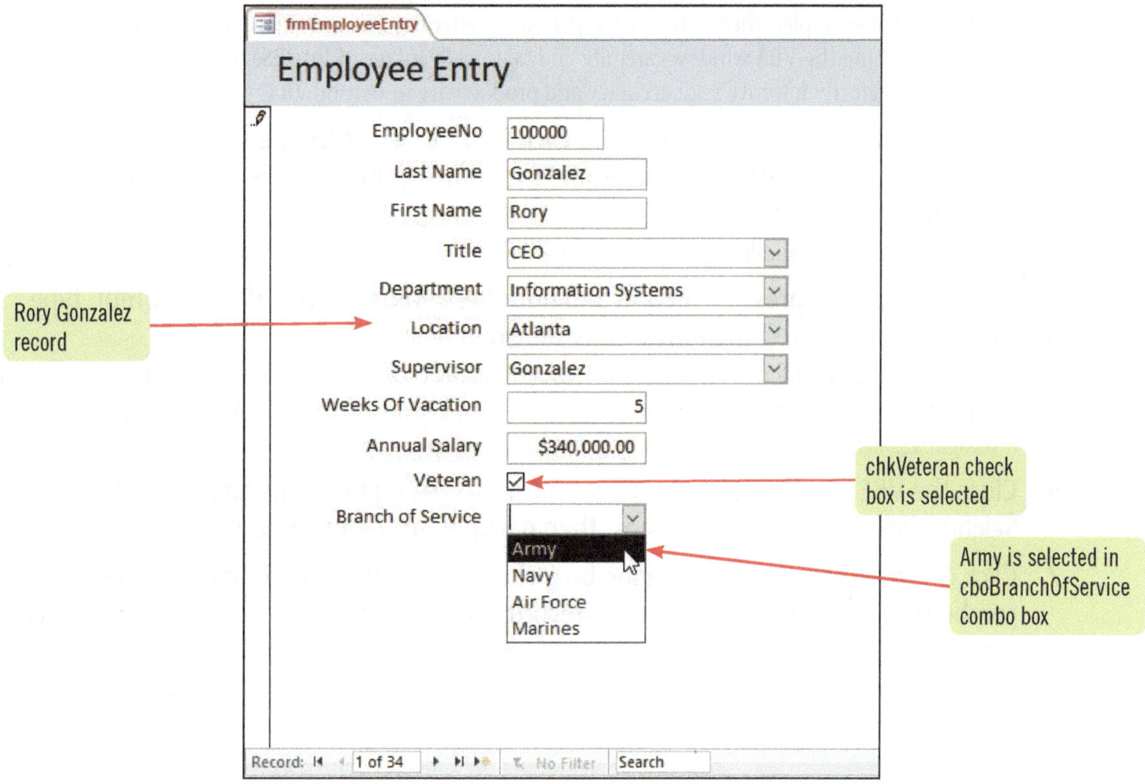

Modify Procedures

Learning Outcomes
- Attach procedures to events
- Use IntelliSense technology

Sub procedures can be triggered on any event in the Property Sheet such as **On Got Focus** (when the control gets the focus), **After Update** (after a field is updated), or **On Dbl Click** (when the control is double-clicked). Not all controls have the same set of event properties. For example, a text box control has both a Before Update and After Update event property, but neither of these events are available for a label or command button because those controls are not used to update data. CASE *Lydia asks if there is a way to require a choice in the Branch of Service combo box when the Veteran check box is checked. You modify the VBA in the form to handle this request.*

STEPS

QUICK TIP
If you select the Always use event procedures check box in the Object Designers section of the Access Options dialog box, you bypass the Choose Builder dialog box and go directly to the VBE.

1. **Right-click the frmEmployeeEntry form, click Design View, click the Before Update property in the Property Sheet, click the Build button [...], click Code Builder, click OK, then enter the code shown in FIGURE 11-12 into the Form_BeforeUpdate stub**
   Test the procedure.
2. **Close the VBE window, click the View button to switch to Form View, click the Last record button to navigate to the Ken Sekibo record, click the Veteran check box to select it, then navigate to the previous record**
   Because the chkVeteran control is selected but the cboBranchOfService combo box is null, the MsgBox statement produces the message shown in FIGURE 11-13.
3. **Click OK, navigate back to the last record, then click the Veteran check box to uncheck it**
   The code produces the correct message, but you want the code to place the focus in the cboBranchOfService combo box to force the user to choose a branch of service when this condition occurs.

   DoCmd is a VBA object that supports many methods to run common Access commands, such as closing windows, opening forms, previewing reports, navigating records, setting focus, and setting the value of controls. As you write a VBA statement, visual aids that are part of **IntelliSense technology** help you complete it. For example, when you type the period (.) after the DoCmd object, a list of available methods appears. Watching the VBA window carefully and taking advantage of IntelliSense clues as you complete a statement can greatly improve your accuracy and productivity in writing VBA.
4. **Right-click the frmEmployeeEntry tab, click Design View, click the View Code button in the Tools group, click after the MsgBox statement, press ENTER, then type docmd. (including the period)**
   Your sub procedure should look like FIGURE 11-14.
5. **Type gotocontrol, press SPACEBAR and note the additional IntelliSense prompt, type "cboBranchOfService", then press ↓ as shown in FIGURE 11-15**
   IntelliSense helps you fill out each statement, indicating the order of arguments needed. The current argument is listed in bold. Optional arguments are listed in [square brackets]. The VBE also capitalizes the VBA it recognizes, such as DoCmd.GoToControl. Test the new procedure.
6. **Close the VBE window, click the View button, navigate to the last record for Ken Sekibo, click the Veteran check box, then navigate to the previous record**
7. **Click OK to respond to the message box, choose Navy from the Branch of Service combo box, navigate to the previous record, then save and close the frmEmployeesEntry form**
   With modest programming skills, you can create sub procedures that help users work more efficiently and effectively in forms.

FIGURE 11-12: Form_BeforeUpdate sub

```
Private Sub Form_BeforeUpdate(Cancel As Integer)
    If chkVeteran.Value = True Then
        If IsNull(cboBranchOfService.Value) Then
            MsgBox "Please select a branch of service"
        End If
    End If
End Sub
```

Form_BeforeUpdate sub

FIGURE 11-13: Message produced by MsgBox statement

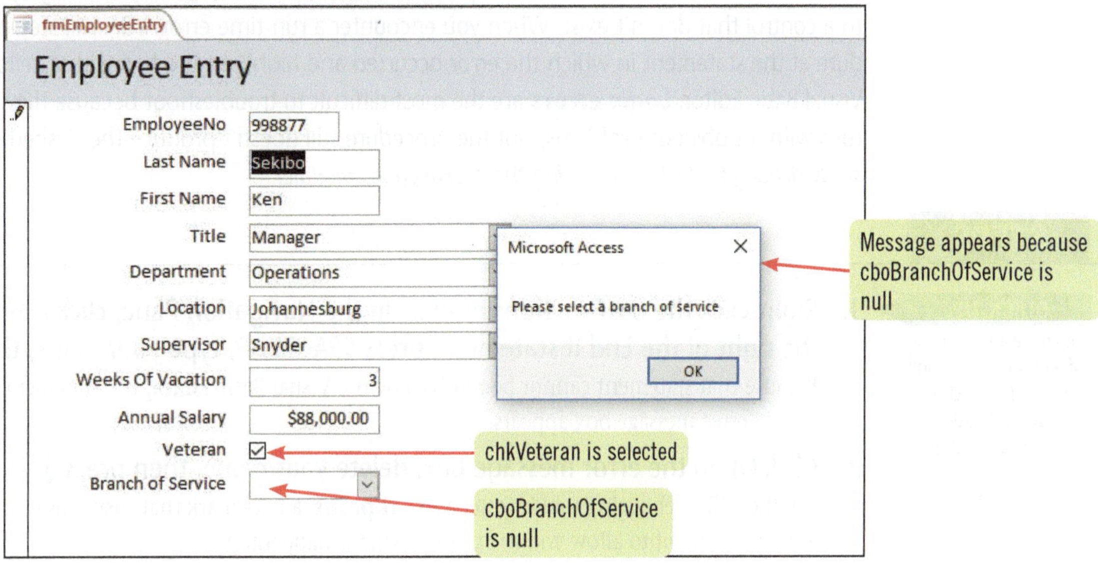

FIGURE 11-14: IntelliSense technology prompts

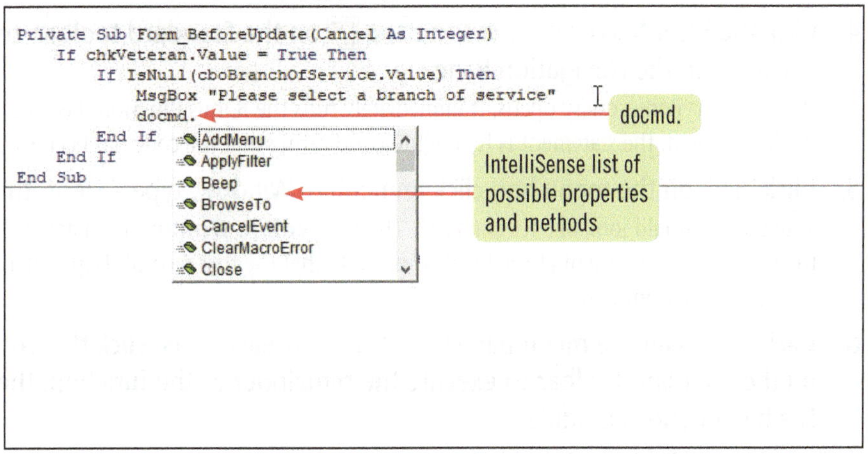

FIGURE 11-15: New DoCmd statement

```
Private Sub Form_BeforeUpdate(Cancel As Integer)
    If chkVeteran.Value = True Then
        If IsNull(cboBranchOfService.Value) Then
            MsgBox "Please select a branch of service"
            DoCmd.GoToControl "cboBranchOfService"
        End If
    End If
End Sub
```

New DoCmd statement

Access

Troubleshoot VBA

Learning Outcomes
- Set breakpoints
- Use the Immediate window

Access provides several techniques to help you **debug** (find and resolve) different types of VBA errors. A **syntax error** occurs immediately as you are writing a VBA statement that cannot be read by the Visual Basic Editor. This is the easiest type of error to identify because your code turns red when the syntax error occurs. **Compile-time errors** occur as a result of incorrectly constructed code and are detected as soon as you run your code or select the Compile option on the Debug menu. For example, you may have forgotten to insert an End If statement to finish an If structure. **Run-time errors** occur as incorrectly constructed code runs and include attempting an illegal operation such as dividing by zero or moving focus to a control that doesn't exist. When you encounter a run-time error, VBA will stop executing your procedure at the statement in which the error occurred and highlight the line with a yellow background in the Visual Basic Editor. **Logic errors** are the most difficult to troubleshoot because they occur when the code runs without obvious problems, but the procedure still doesn't produce the desired result. **CASE** *You study debugging techniques using the basFunctions module.*

STEPS

QUICK TIP
To create a backup of a module, you can right-click a module to copy and paste it just like any other object.

QUICK TIP
Click the gray bar to the left of a statement to toggle a breakpoint on and off.

QUICK TIP
Pointing to an argument in the Code window displays a ScreenTip with the argument's current value.

1. **Right-click the basFunctions module in the Navigation Pane, click Design View, click to the right of the End If statement, press SPACEBAR, type your name, then press ↓**
   Because that statement cannot be resolved by the Visual Basic Editor, the statement immediately turns red and an error message box appears.
2. **Click OK in the error message box, delete your name, then press ↓**
   Another VBA debugging tool is to set a **breakpoint**, a bookmark that suspends execution of the procedure at that statement to allow you to examine what is happening.
3. **Click the If statement line, click Debug on the menu bar, then click Toggle Breakpoint**
   Your screen should look like FIGURE 11-16.
4. **Click the View Microsoft Access button on the Standard toolbar, then double-click qryBonus in the Navigation Pane**
   When the qryBonus query opens, it immediately runs the Bonus function. Because you set a breakpoint at the If statement, the statement is highlighted, indicating that the code has been suspended at that point.
5. **Click View on the menu bar, click Immediate Window, type ? Dept, then press ENTER**
   Your screen should look like FIGURE 11-17. The **Immediate window** is an area where you can determine the value of any argument at the breakpoint. Note that the first record's Department value is Executive for the CEO, Rory Gonzales.
6. **Click Debug on the menu bar, click Clear All Breakpoints, click the Continue button on the Standard toolbar to execute the remainder of the function, then save and close the basFunctions module**
   You return to qryBonus in Datasheet View.
7. **sam ↑ Close the qryBonus datasheet, compact and close the IL_AC_11_Jobs.accdb database, then close Access**

FIGURE 11-16: Setting a breakpoint

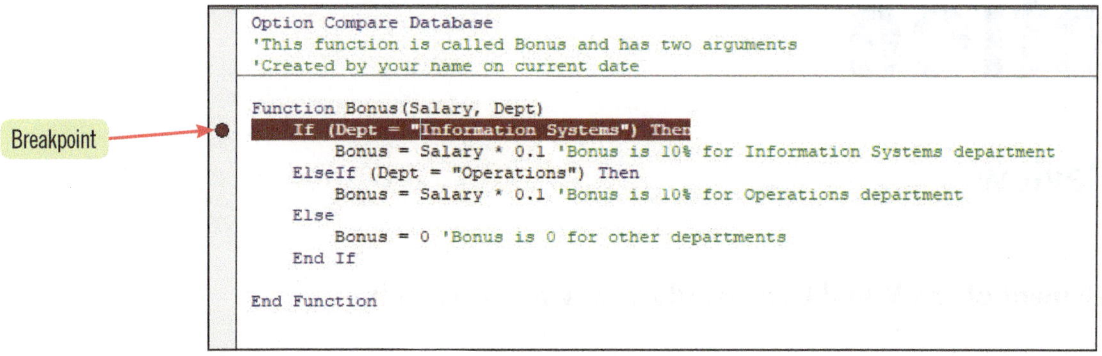

FIGURE 11-17: Stopping execution at a breakpoint

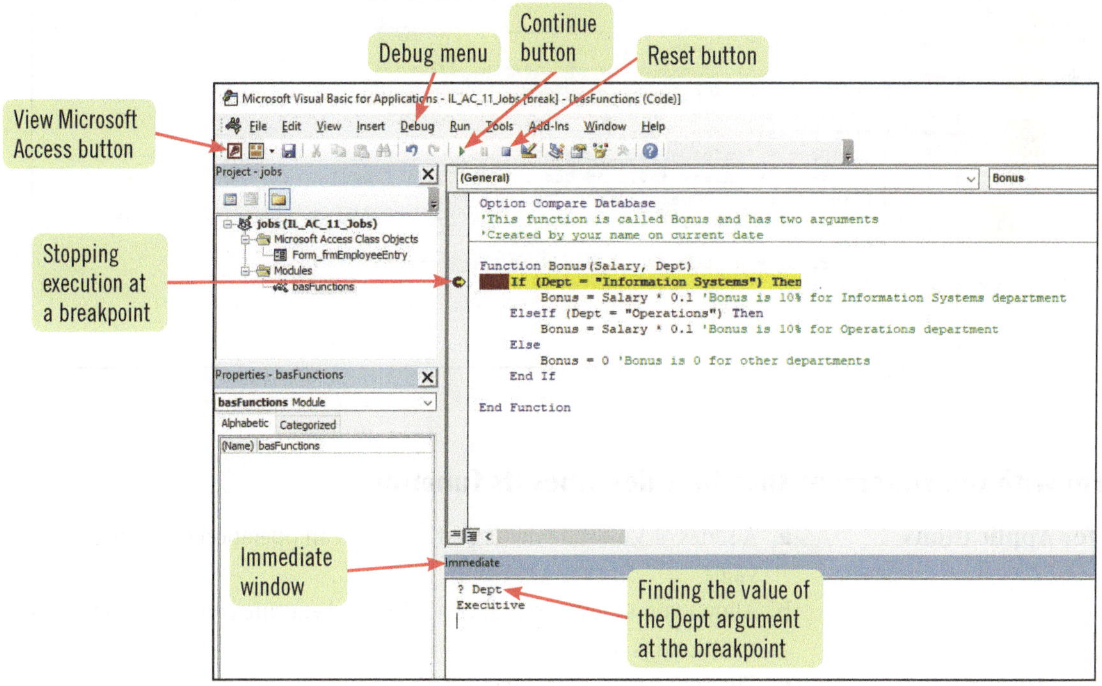

Access

Debugging

Debugging is the process of finding and resolving bugs or problems in code. The term is generally attributed to Grace Hopper, a computer pioneer. Wikipedia (https://en.wikipedia.org/wiki/Debugging) states that while Grace was working at Harvard University in the 1940s, a moth was found in a relay component of the computer, which impeded operations. After the moth was removed, Grace remarked that they were "debugging" the system.

Practice

Concepts Review

Identify each element of the Visual Basic window shown in FIGURE 11-18.

FIGURE 11-18

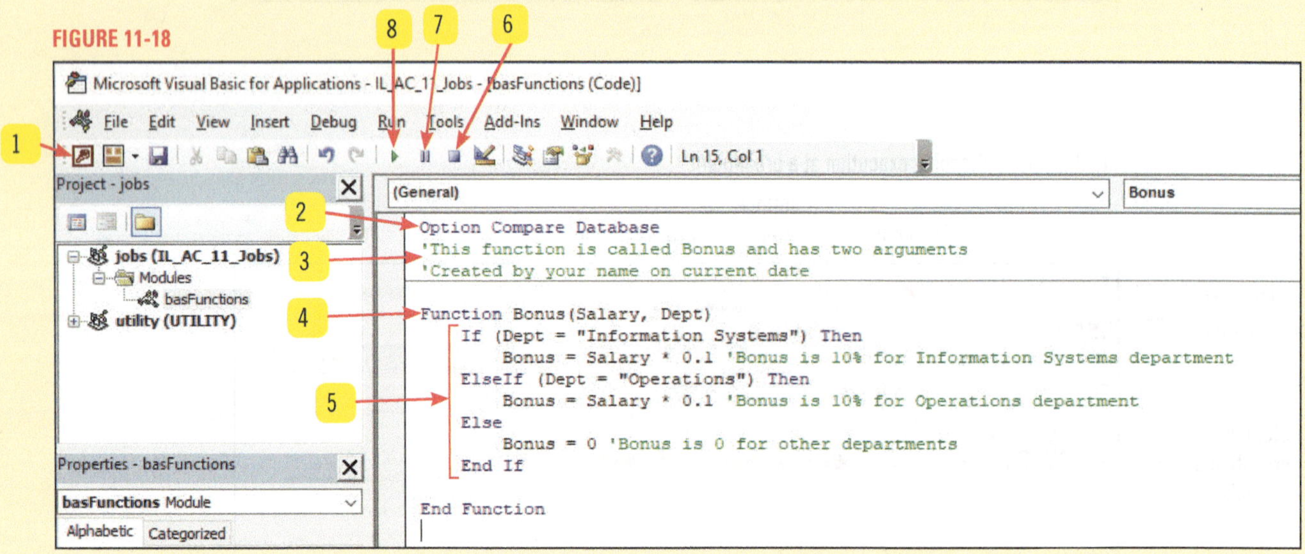

Match each term with the statement that best describes its function.

9. **Visual Basic for Applications (VBA)**
10. **Module**
11. **Debugging**
12. **If...Then...Else statement**
13. **Procedure**
14. **Class modules**
15. **Breakpoint**
16. **Arguments**
17. **Function**

a. A series of VBA statements that performs an operation or calculates a value
b. Allows you to test a logical condition and execute commands only if the condition is true
c. The programming language used in Access modules
d. A line of code that automatically suspends execution of the procedure
e. A process to find and resolve programming errors
f. A procedure that returns a value
g. Constants, variables, or expressions passed to a procedure to further define how it should execute
h. Stored as part of the form or report object in which they are created
i. The Access object where global VBA code is stored

18. The term *debugging* is attributed to which computer science pioneer?

a. Tim Berners-Lee
b. Grace Hopper
c. Bill Gates
d. Ida Lovelace

19. **Which character is used to indicate a comment in VBA?**
   - **a.** quotation mark (")
   - **b.** forward slash (/)
   - **c.** exclamation point (!)
   - **d.** apostrophe (')

20. **Which of the following is a run-time error?**
   - **a.** Dividing by zero
   - **b.** Mistyping the word *function*
   - **c.** Forgetting an End If statement
   - **d.** Using too many comments

Skills Review

1. **Understand modules and VBA.**
   - **a.** Start Access, open the IL_AC_11-2.accdb database from the location where you store your Data Files, then save it as **IL_AC_11_SupportDesk**. Enable content if prompted.
   - **b.** Open the VBE window for the basFunctions module.
   - **c.** Record your answers to the following questions about this module:
     - What is the name of the function?
     - What are the names of the arguments of the function?
     - What is the purpose of the End Function statement?
     - Why are the End Function statements in blue?
     - Why are some of the lines indented?
     - What is the purpose of the Dim keyword?

2. **Compare macros and modules.**
   - **a.** If not already opened, open the VBE window for the basFunctions module.
   - **b.** Record your answers to the following questions on a sheet of paper:
     - Why was a module rather than a macro used to create these procedures?
     - Why is VBA generally more difficult to create than a macro?
     - Identify each of the VBA keywords or keyword phrases, and explain the purpose for each.

3. **Create functions.**
   - **a.** If not already opened, open the VBE window for the basFunctions module.
   - **b.** Create a function called **TuitionReimbursement** below the End Function statement of the RetireYears function by typing the VBA statements shown in FIGURE 11-19. The company has a tuition reimbursement policy that assists employees with college tuition if they make less than $50,000 per year and have more than one dependent. This function will help identify qualifying employees.
   - **c.** Save the basFunctions module, then close the VBE window.
   - **d.** Use Query Design View to create a new query using the FirstName, LastName, Salary, and Dependents fields from the tblEmployees table.
   - **e.** Create a calculated field named **Tuition** in the next available column by carefully typing the expression as follows: **Tuition: TuitionReimbursement ([Salary],[Dependents])** (*Hint*: Use the Zoom dialog box to more easily enter long expressions.)

FIGURE 11-19

```
Function TuitionReimbursement(SalaryValue, DependentsValue)

        TuitionReimbursement = "Qualified"

        TuitionReimbursement = "Not Qualified"

End Function
```

Access

Skills Review (continued)

f. Create a second calculated field named **RetirementCalc** in the next available column by carefully typing the expression as follows: **RetirementCalc: RetireYears([Birthday],[StartDate])** (*Hint*: Use the Zoom dialog box to enter long expressions.)

g. View the datasheet, then widen the RetirementCalc column to view the entire field name. At this point the RetirementCalc calculation should work correctly, but the Tuition field should calculate to "Not Qualified" for all employees, which is not correct. Save the query as **qryEmployeeData**, then close it.

4. Use VBA If statements.

a. Open the VBE window for the basFunctions module, then modify the TuitionReimbursement function to add the If structure shown in FIGURE 11-20. The If structure tests to see if the SalaryValue is less than $50,000 and if the DependentsValue is greater than 1.

b. Save the basFunctions module, then close the VBE window.

c. Open the qryEmployeeData datasheet, then change the Dependents field value for Eugene Fuentes to **2**. His Tuition field should change from Not Qualified to Qualified.

d. Close the datasheet.

FIGURE 11-20

```
Function TuitionReimbursement(SalaryValue, DependentsValue)
    If SalaryValue < 50000 And DependentsValue > 1 Then
        TuitionReimbursement = "Qualified"
    Else
        TuitionReimbursement = "Not Qualified"
    End If
End Function
```

5. Document procedures.

a. Open the VBE window for the basFunctions module, then add the comments to the top of the module, to the RetireYears function, and to the TuitionReimbursement function, as shown in FIGURE 11-21. Be sure to insert your actual name and today's date.

FIGURE 11-21

```
Option Compare Database

'Created by your name on the current date
'Function RetireYears adds an employees age to the years of employment

Function RetireYears(BirthDate, HireDate)
    Dim YearsOld
     YearsOld = Int((Date - BirthDate) / 365.25)      'calculates an employees age
    Dim YearsWorked
        YearsWorked = Int((Date - HireDate) / 365.25) 'calculates full years of employment
    RetireYears = YearsOld + YearsWorked              'adds years of age to years of employment
End Function

'Function TuitionReimbursement determines if an employee is eligible for tuition benefit
Function TuitionReimbursement(SalaryValue, DependentsValue)
    If SalaryValue < 50000 And DependentsValue > 1 Then 'salary must be < $50,000 and dependents must be > 1
        TuitionReimbursement = "Qualified"
    Else
        TuitionReimbursement = "Not Qualified"
    End If
End Function
```

b. Save the changes to the basFunctions module, print the module if requested by your instructor, then close the VBE window.

6. Build class modules.

a. Open frmEmployeeMaster in Form View, then move through several records to observe the data.

b. Switch to Design View, and add a new text box control below the StartDate text box. Change the Name property of the text box to **txtRetirementCalc**, the Control Source property of the text box to **=RetireYears([txtBirthday],[txtStartDate])**, and the Tab Stop property to **No**.

c. Change the Caption property of the label to **Retirement Calculation**.

d. Below the new txtRetirementCalc text box, add another label control. Type **Eligible for Tuition Reimbursement!** in the label control. Change the Name property to **lblTuition** and the Visible property to **No**. Save the form, view it in Form View, and move through several records. At this point the txtRetirementCalc text box shows a number that is the person's age plus their years of service at the company, but the tuition reimbursement label is not visible for any record.

Skills Review (continued)

e. Switch to Form Design View, then format the new labels and txtRetirementCalc text box with a dark black font color. Resize the labels to display all of their text. Modify the After Update event of the form with a VBA procedure, as shown in FIGURE 11-22.

f. Save and close the Visual Basic Editor. Save the form, switch to Form View, and enter a new record as shown in FIGURE 11-23 to make sure the message appears. The Retirement Calculation varies based on the current date.

g. Click OK in the dialog box, enter **2** in the txtDependents text box, then save and close the form.

7. Modify procedures.

a. Open the frmEmployeeMaster form in Design View, then click the Build button on the After Update event of the form to return to the same procedure in the VBE.

b. Modify the subprocedure to include another If... Then...Else block of code, as shown in FIGURE 11-24.

c. Copy the If...Then...Else structure that tests for the salary and dependents values from the Form_AfterUpdate sub procedure to the Form_Current procedure.

d. Save then close the VBE window. Save the frmEmployeeMaster form, then switch to Form View.

e. Navigate to the last record with your name, then edit the record to test for salary values of **$50,000** and **$49,000**, then dependent values of **null**, **1**, and finally **2** dependents.

f. After testing your code, save, then close the frmEmployeeMaster form.

8. Troubleshoot VBA.

a. Open the VBE window for the basFunctions module.

b. Click anywhere in the following statement in the TuitionReimbursement function:
If SalaryValue < 50000 And DependentsValue > 1 Then

c. Click Debug on the menu bar, then click Toggle Breakpoint to set a breakpoint at this statement.

d. Save the changes, then close the VBE window and return to Microsoft Access.

e. Open the qryEmployeeData query datasheet. This action attempts to use the TuitionReimbursement function to calculate the value for the Tuition field, which stops and highlights the statement in the VBE window where you set a breakpoint.

f. Click View on the menu bar, click Immediate Window (if not already visible), delete any previous entries in the Immediate window, type **?SalaryValue**, then press ENTER. At this point in the execution of the VBA, the SalaryValue should be 55000, the value you entered for the first record.

g. Type **?DependentsValue**, then press ENTER. At this point in the execution of the VBA code, the DependentsValue should be 3, the value for the first record. (*Hint*: You can resize the Immediate window by dragging the top edge.)

h. Click Debug on the menu bar, click Clear All Breakpoints, then click the Continue button on the Standard toolbar. Close the VBE window and close the qryEmployeeData object.

i. Compact and repair, then close the IL_AC_11_SupportDesk.accdb database and close Access 2019.

FIGURE 11-22

```
Private Sub Form_AfterUpdate()
 If IsNull(txtDependents) Then
    MsgBox ("Please enter # of dependents")
    DoCmd.GoToControl "txtDependents"
 End If
End Sub
```

FIGURE 11-23

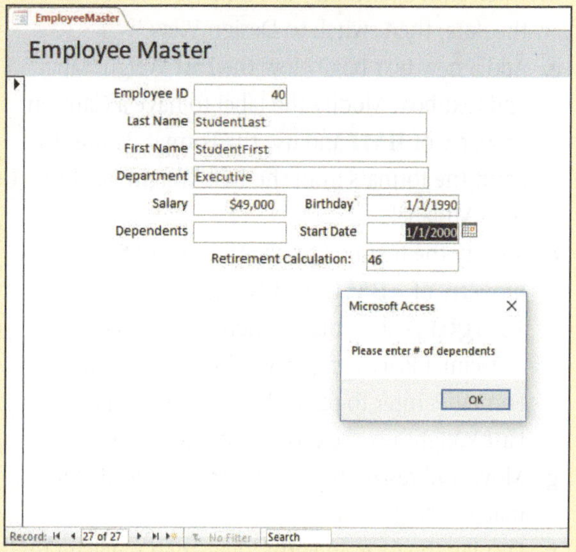

FIGURE 11-24

```
Private Sub Form_AfterUpdate()
 If IsNull(txtDependents) Then
    MsgBox ("Please enter # of dependents")
    DoCmd.GoToControl "txtDependents"
 End If
 If txtSalary.Value < 50000 And txtDependents.Value > 1 Then
    lblTuition.Visible = True
 Else
    lblTuition.Visible = False
 End If
End Sub
```

Access

Independent Challenge 1

As the manager of Riverwalk, a multispecialty health clinic, you have created a database to manage patient outcomes. In this exercise, you will create a custom function and use it on a form to help calculate body mass index.

a. Start Access, open the IL_AC_11-3.accdb database from the location where you store your Data Files, then save it as **IL_AC_11_Riverwalk**. Enable content if prompted.

b. Create a new standard module with the VBA and comments shown in FIGURE 11-25.

c. Save the module with the name **basFunctions**, then close the VBE window.

d. Open frmPatientEntry in Form View to review the data, then switch to Design View.

e. Add a new text box below the Last Weight label and text box. Modify the label to have a Caption property of **BMI** and use the Format Painter to paint the formats from the Last Weight label to the BMI label.

f. Modify the text box to have a Control Source property of **=BMI([txtHeight],[txtWeight])**, a Format property of Standard, and a Decimal Places property value of **1**. Use the Format Painter to paint the formats from the Last Weight text box to the BMI text box.

g. Move and resize the new controls as needed to match FIGURE 11-26.

h. Display the form in Form View, then navigate to the second record, as shown in FIGURE 11-26.

i. Compact and close the IL_AC_Riverwalk.accdb database, then close Access.

FIGURE 11-25

```
'Student name - current date
'Calculate BMI (Body Mass Index)
'A healthy BMI is 21-24.

Function BMI(HeightValue, WeightValue)
    If HeightValue = 0 Then
        BMI = 0
    Else
        BMI = (WeightValue * 0.4536) / (HeightValue * 0.0254) ^ 2
    End If

End Function
```

FIGURE 11-26

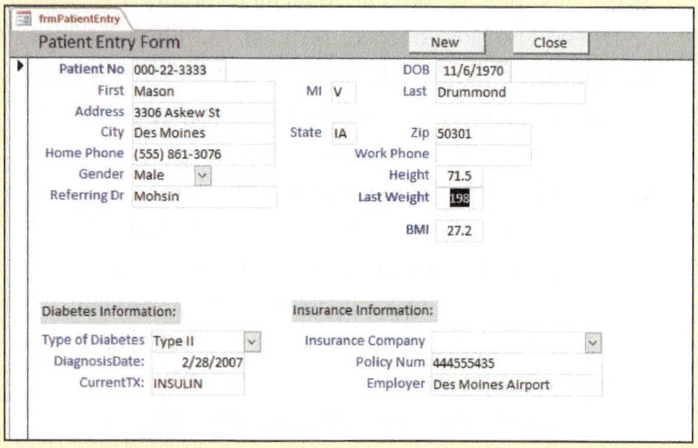

Independent Challenge 2

You are working for a city to coordinate a series of community-wide preparedness activities. You have created a database to track the activities and volunteers who are attending the activities. In this exercise, you will create a class module to help identify a requirement for minor volunteers.

a. Start Access, open the IL_AC_11-4.accdb database from the location where you store your Data Files, then save it as **IL_AC_11_Volunteers**. Enable content if prompted.

b. Open the frmVolunteerEntry form in Form View, click in the Birthday text box, click the Descending button to sort the records in descending order by Birthday, then navigate through several records. Some of the volunteers are under 18 years old, and you want the form to display a message when the volunteer is under 18 years old.

c. Switch to Form Design View, click the Birthday text box, open the Property Sheet for the Birthday text box, click the Build button for the After Update event, click the Code Builder option, then enter the code for the procedure shown in FIGURE 11-27 as well as the comments above it.

d. Create a Form_Current() sub procedure and copy the statements from Birthday_AfterUpdate() to the Form_Current() so that the statements also run when you move from record to record.

e. Save the VBA code, close the VBE, then open the form in Form View to test the class procedures. You should be prompted with the message for the first record. Make sure the records are still sorted in descending order on the Birthday field.

f. Click OK, then modify the Birthday value for the first record (Volunteer ID 35 Taney Wilson) to be **1/1/99**. You should not be prompted with a message after entering that date.

g. Move to the second record (Volunteer ID 26 Sally Olingback) and test it with the Birthday value of **1/1/99** (no prompt) and then **11/1/08** (prompt).

h. Compact and close the IL_AC_11_Volunteers.accdb database, then close Access.

FIGURE 11-27

```
'Created by your name on current date
'Date represents today's date
'Birthday represents the value in the Birthday text box
'Date - Birthday gives the days between the two dates
'(Date - Birthday) / 365.25 produces the number of years between the two dates
'Int() produces the integer portion of the date

Private Sub Birthday_AfterUpdate()
  If Int((Date - Birthday) / 365.25) < 18 Then
       MsgBox ("Volunteer must be accompanied by adult.")
  End If
End Sub
```

Visual Workshop

Start Access, open the IL_AC_11-5.accdb database from the location where you store your Data Files, then save it as **IL_AC_11_CollegeCourses**. Enable content if prompted. Use FIGURE 11-28 to develop a new function named **Points** in a standard module named **basFunctions**. Include *your* name and the current date as a comment.

Modify the qryEnrollmentAndGrades query by adding two calculated fields after the Grade field. The first calculated field is named **PointsPerClass** and uses the new Points function as follows to determine the points per class based on the grade earned in that class:

PointsPerClass: Points([Grade])

The second calculated field is named QPPC (short for quality points per class), which is determined by the credits for the class multiplied by the points earned per class:

QPPC: [Credits]*[PointsPerClass]

FIGURE 11-28

```
Option Compare Database
Option Explicit

'Created by your name on current date

Function Points(grade)
    If grade = "A" Then
        Points = 4
    ElseIf grade = "B" Then
        Points = 3
    ElseIf grade = "C" Then
        Points = 2
    ElseIf grade = "D" Then
        Points = 1
    Else
        Points = 0
    End If
End Function
```

Save and view the qryEnrollmentAndGrades query in Datasheet view to make sure that the PointsPerClass and QPPC calculated fields are calculating successfully. A 4-credit class with a grade of B should result in 3 PointsPerClass and 12 QPPC.

Open frmStudents in Design View and make these property modifications on the Control Source property of these text boxes. The text boxes are identified by their Name property and location:

txtQPPC in the Detail section of the subform: **QPPC**

txtSumQPPC in the Form Footer section of the subform: **=Sum([QPPC])**

txtSumCredits in the Form Footer section of the subform: **=Sum([Credits])**

txtGPA in the Detail section of the main form: **=[frmEnrollmentsSubform].[Form]![txtSumQPPC]/[frmEnrollmentsSubform].[Form]![txtSumCredits]**

This expression divides the value in the txtSumQPPC text box in the frmEnrollmentsSubform's Form Footer section and divides it by the value in the txtSumCredits text box. Save the frmStudents form and display it in Form View, as shown in FIGURE 11-29. Navigate through several records to make sure all calculations are displayed correctly. Save and close frmStudents, compact and close the IL_AC_11_CollegeCourses.accdb database, then close Access.

FIGURE 11-29

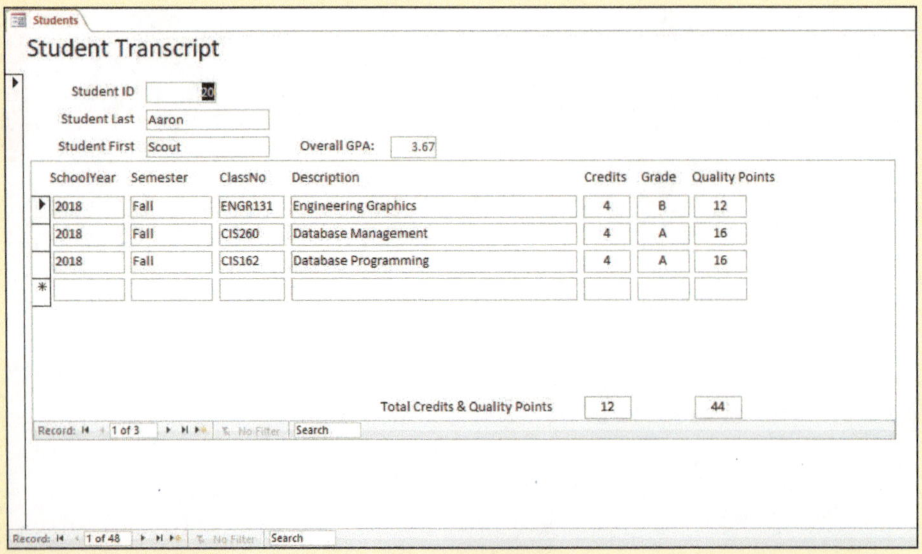

Access **Module 12**

Completing the Application

CASE You are working with Lydia Snyder, vice president of operations at JCL Talent, to build a research database to manage industry, company, and job data. In this module, you'll create a navigation form. You also work with several administrative issues, such as setting passwords, changing startup options, and analyzing database performance to protect, improve, and enhance the database.

Module Objectives

After completing this module, you will be able to:

- Create a navigation form
- Set startup options
- Analyze database performance
- Secure a database
- Split a database
- Document a database

Files You Will Need

IL_AC_12-1.accdb
IL_AC_12-2.accdb
IL_AC_12-3.accdb
IL_AC_12-4.accdb
IL_AC_12-5.accdb

Create a Navigation Form

Learning Outcomes
- Create a navigation form
- Add and edit navigation buttons

A **navigation form** is a special Access form that includes a **navigation control**, a special type of control that contains **navigation button controls** that allow a user to easily switch between the various forms and reports in your database. CASE *Lydia asks you to create an interface to make it easy to access the forms and reports in the JCL jobs database. A navigation form will work well for this purpose.*

STEPS

1. **sam Start Access, open the IL_AC_12-1.accdb database from the location where you store your Data Files, save it as IL_AC_12_Jobs, enable content if prompted, click the Create tab, click the Navigation button in the Forms group, click the Vertical Tabs, Left option, then close the Field List window if it opens**

   The new navigation form opens in Layout View. Vertical Tabs, Left is a **navigation system style** that determines how the navigation buttons are displayed in the navigation control on the form. Other navigation system styles include additional vertical and horizontal arrangements for the tabs.

2. **Drag the frmEmployeeEntry form from the Navigation Pane to the first navigation button, which displays [Add New]**

   The frmEmployeeEntry form is added as the first navigation button, as shown in FIGURE 12-1, and a new navigation button with [Add New] is automatically created as well. The second and third navigation buttons will contain reports.

3. **Drag the rptJobSalaries report from the Navigation Pane to the second navigation button, which displays [Add New], then drag the rptJobsByState report to the third navigation button, which also displays [Add New]**

   With the objects in place, you can rename the navigation buttons to be less technical.

4. **Double-click the frmEmployeeEntry navigation button, edit it to read Employees, double-click the rptJobSalaries navigation button, edit it to read Salaries, double-click the rptJobsByState navigation button, then edit it to read Jobs by State**

   You can reorder the navigation buttons by dragging them to their new location.

5. **Drag the Jobs by State navigation button up between the Employees and Salaries navigation buttons, then click the Form View button to display the form, as shown in FIGURE 12-2**

   Test, save, and close the new navigation form.

6. **Click the Employees navigation button in the form, click the Jobs by State navigation button, click the Salaries navigation button, click the Save button on the Quick Access Toolbar, type frmNavigation, click OK, then close frmNavigation**

QUICK TIP
In the Navigation Pane, click the object expand and collapse buttons to display or hide objects. Click the Shutter Bar Open/Close button « to open or close the entire pane.

QUICK TIP
You can also modify the text on a navigation button in Form Design View by modifying the navigation button's Caption property.

TROUBLE
Click the Jobs by State navigation button if it is not already selected.

FIGURE 12-1: Creating a navigation form

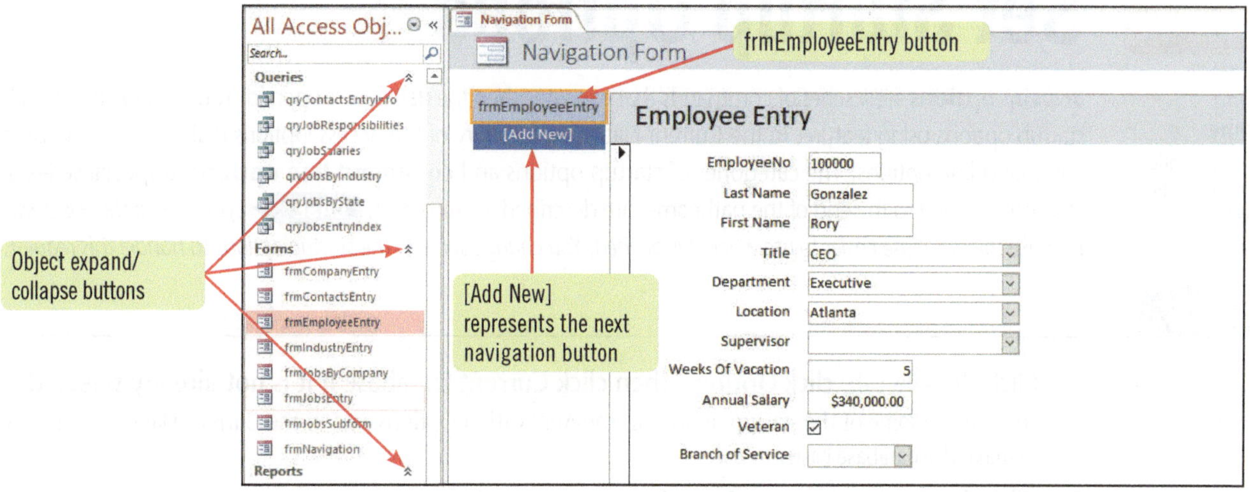

FIGURE 12-2: Navigation form in Form View

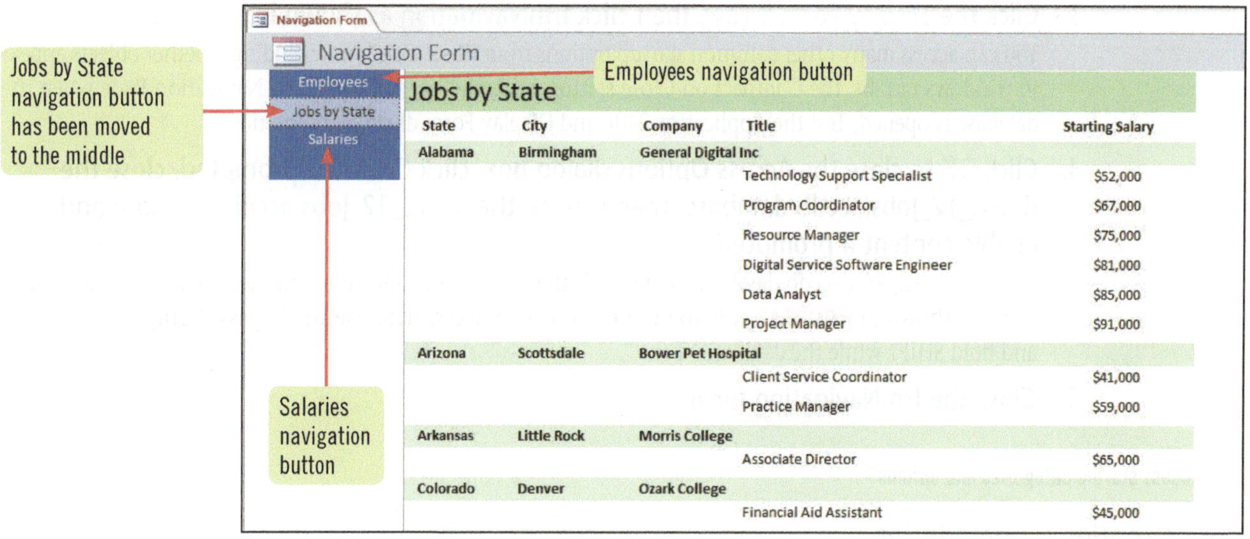

Setting Navigation Pane options

You can change the way the Navigation Pane appears by clicking the title bar of the Navigation Pane and choosing a different way to organize the objects (e.g., by Object Type, Created Date, or Custom Groups) in the upper portion of the menu. The lower portion of the menu lets you display only one object type (e.g., Tables, Queries, Forms, Reports, or All Access Objects). Right-click the Navigation Pane for more options on the shortcut menu, including Navigation Options, which allows you to create custom groups within the Navigation Pane.

Access

Access
Module 12

Set Startup Options

Learning Outcomes
- Set the Application Title startup option
- Set the Display Form startup option

Startup options are a series of commands that execute when the database is opened. You manage the default startup options using features in the Current Database category of the Access Options dialog box or by using command-line options. The categories of startup options and **command-line options**, a special series of characters added to the end of the pathname, are described in TABLE 12-1. CASE *Lydia asks if there is a way to make the database easier to use when it is opened. You change some of the startup options to handle this request.*

STEPS

1. **Click the File tab, click Options, then click Current Database if it is not already selected**
   You can use some of the startup options in the Application Options area of the Current Database category to make the database easier to use.
2. **Click the Application Title box, then type JCL Talent**
   When filled in, the **Application Title** property value appears in the title bar instead of the database filename.
3. **Click the Display Form arrow, then click frmNavigation as shown in FIGURE 12-3**
   You can access many other common startup options from this dialog box, including whether objects appear in windows or tabs, the Compact on Close setting, and whether to display the Navigation Pane when the database is opened. Test the Application Title and Display Form database properties.
4. **Click OK to close the Access Options dialog box, click OK when prompted, close the IL_AC_12_Jobs.accdb database, then reopen the IL_AC_12_Jobs.accdb database and enable content if prompted**
   The IL_AC_12_Jobs.accdb database opens with the new application title, followed by the frmNavigation form, as shown in FIGURE 12-4. If you want to open an Access database and bypass startup options, press and hold SHIFT while the database opens.
5. **Close the frmNavigation form**

TABLE 12-1: Access startup categories and options

category or option	description
General	Sets default interface, file format, default database folder, and username options
Current Database	Provides for application changes, such as whether the windows are overlapping or tabbed, the database compacts on close, and Layout View is enabled; also provides Navigation Pane, ribbon, toolbar, and AutoCorrect options
Datasheet	Determines the default gridlines, cell effects, and fonts of datasheets
Object Designers	Determines default Design View settings for tables, queries, forms, and reports; also provides default error-checking options
Proofing	Sets AutoCorrect and Spelling options
Language	Sets Editing, Display, and Help languages
Client Settings	Sets defaults for cursor action when editing display elements, printing margins, date formatting, and advanced record management options
Customize Ribbon	Provides an easy-to-use interface to modify the buttons and tabs on the ribbon
Quick Access Toolbar	Provides an easy-to-use interface to modify the buttons on the Quick Access Toolbar
Add-ins	Provides a way to manage add-ins, software that works with Access to add or enhance functionality
Trust Center	Provides a way to manage trusted publishers, trusted locations, trusted documents, macro settings, and other privacy and security settings
/excl	Command-line option that opens the database for exclusive access, as in C:\Documents\JCL.accdb /excl
/ro	Command-line option that opens the database for read-only access, as in C:\Documents\JCL.accdb /ro

FIGURE 12-3: Setting startup options

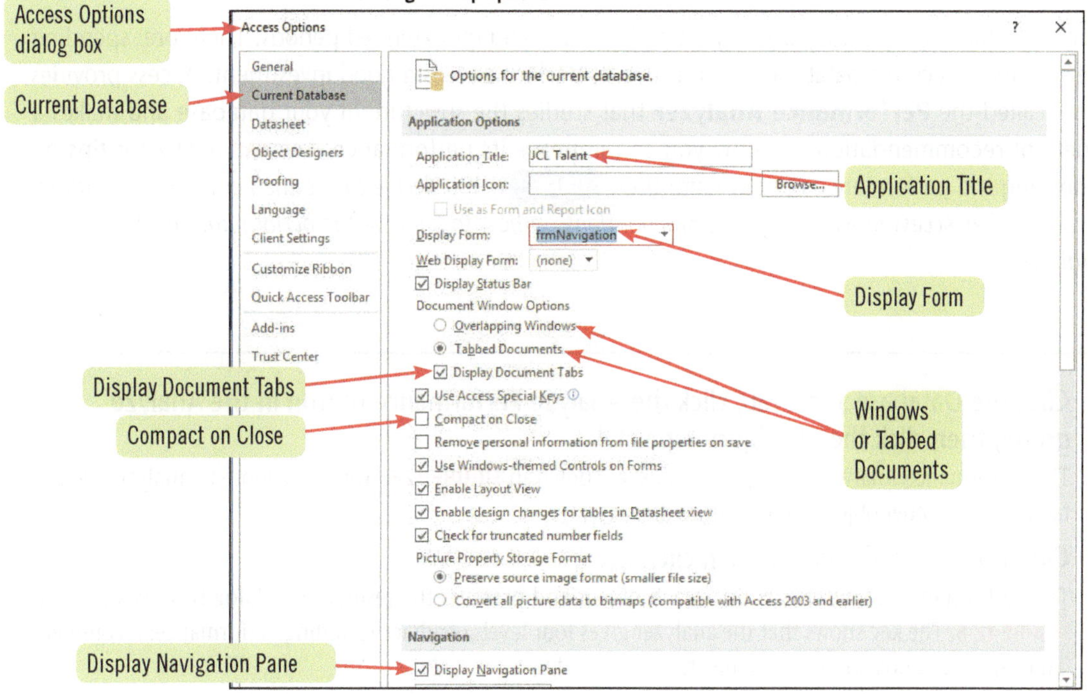

FIGURE 12-4: Display Form and Application Title startup options are in effect

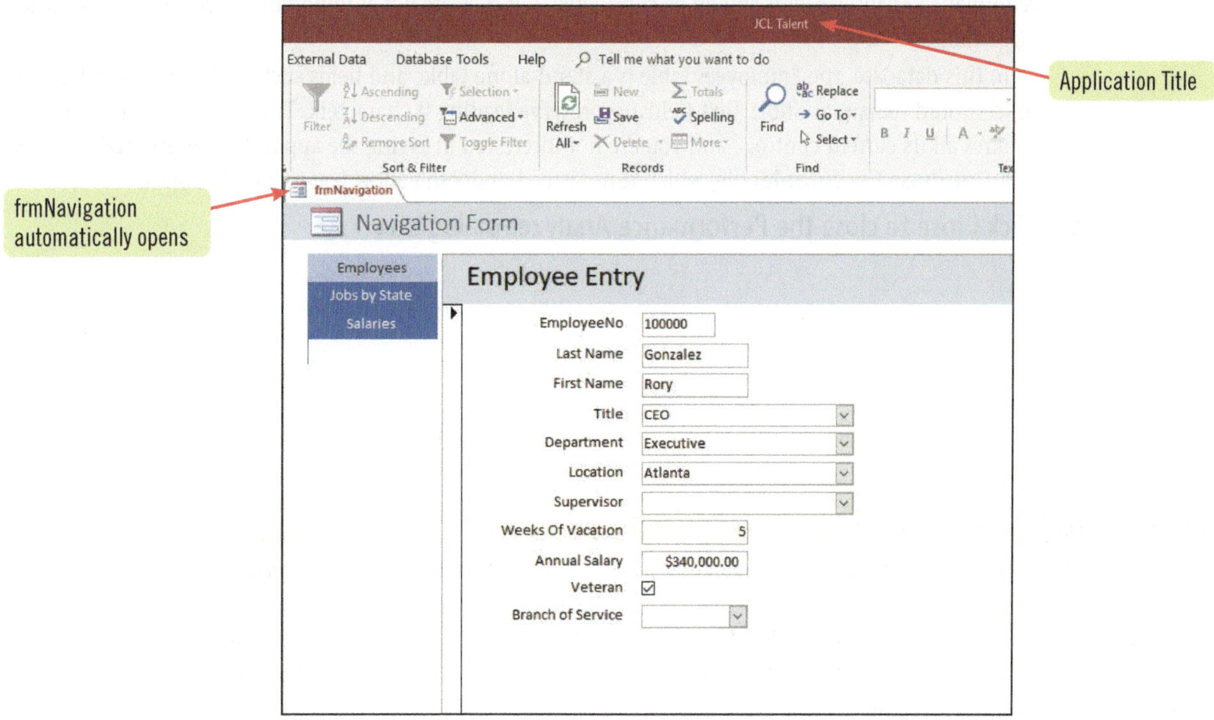

Access
Module 12

Analyze Database Performance

Learning Outcomes
- Use the Performance Analyzer
- Describe performance tips

Access databases are typically used by multiple people and for extended periods. Therefore, spending a few hours to secure a database and improve its performance is a good investment. Access provides a tool called the **Performance Analyzer** that studies the structure of your database and makes a variety of recommendations on how you can improve its performance. See TABLE 12-2 for tips on optimizing the performance of your computer. CASE *You decide to use the Performance Analyzer to see whether Access provides any recommendations on how to improve the performance of the JCL jobs database.*

STEPS

1. **Click the Database Tools tab, click the Analyze Performance button in the Analyze group, then click the All Object Types tab**

   The Performance Analyzer dialog box opens, as shown in FIGURE 12-5. You can choose to analyze selected tables, forms, other objects, or the entire database.

2. **Click the Select All button, then click OK**

   The Performance Analyzer examines each object and presents the results in a dialog box, as shown in FIGURE 12-6. The key shows that the analyzer gives four levels of advice regarding performance: recommendations, suggestions, ideas, and items that were fixed.

3. **Click each line in the Analysis Results area, then read each description in the Analysis Notes area**

   The lightbulb icon next to an item indicates that this is an idea. The Analysis Notes section of the Performance Analyzer dialog box gives you additional information regarding the specific item. All the Performance Analyzer's ideas should be considered, but they are not as important as recommendations and suggestions.

   In this database, the Employees table is a stand-alone table, and fields such as ZipCode and EmployeeNo should remain as Short Text fields to preserve leading 0 characters. The frmEmployeeEntry form requires all its current controls, and you are not interested in saving the application as an **MDE (Microsoft Database Executable)** file, which runs faster, but doesn't allow you to modify objects.

4. **Click Close to close the Performance Analyzer dialog box**

Viewing object dependencies

Click any object in the Navigation Pane, click the Database Tools tab, then click the Object Dependencies button in the Relationships group to view object dependencies. **Object dependencies** appear in the Object Dependencies pane and display "Objects that depend on me" (the selected object). For example, before deleting a query, you might want to select it to view its object dependencies to determine if any other queries, forms, or reports depend on that query. The Object Dependencies pane also allows you to view "Objects that I depend on." For a selected query, this option would show you what tables or queries are used in the upper pane of Query Design View.

FIGURE 12-5: Performance Analyzer dialog box

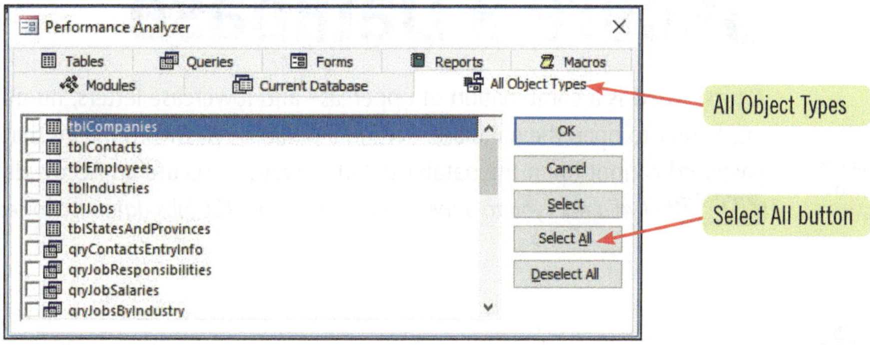

FIGURE 12-6: Performance Analyzer results

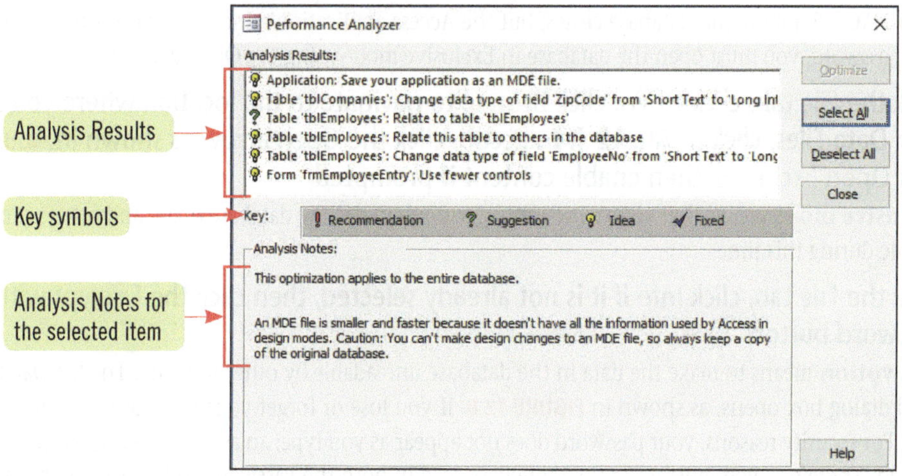

TABLE 12-2: Tips for optimizing performance

degree of difficulty	tip
Easy	Close all applications that you don't currently need
Easy	Eliminate unneeded memory-resident programs, such as complex screen savers, email alert programs, and unneeded virus checkers
Easy	If you are the only person using a database, open it in Exclusive mode
Easy	Use the Compact on Close feature
Moderate	Add more memory to your computer
Moderate	If others don't need to share the database, load it on your local hard drive instead of the network's file server (but be sure to back up local drives regularly, too)
Moderate	Split the database so that the data is stored on the file server but other database objects are stored on your local (faster) hard drive
Moderate to difficult	Move the database to an uncompressed drive
Moderate to difficult	Run Performance Analyzer on a regular basis, examining and appropriately acting on each recommendation, suggestion, and idea
Moderate to difficult	Make sure that all PCs are running the latest versions of Windows and Access
Essential	Make sure your database is normalized correctly and that appropriate one-to-many relationships are established in the Relationships window

Secure a Database

Learning Outcomes
- Open the database in Exclusive mode
- Set a password and encryption

A **password** is a combination of uppercase and lowercase letters, numbers, and symbols that the user must enter to open the database. Setting a database password means that anyone who doesn't know the password cannot open the database. Other ways to secure an Access database are listed in TABLE 12-3.

CASE *Lydia asks you to apply a password to the JCL jobs database to secure its data.*

STEPS

1. **Click the File tab, then click Close**

   The IL_AC_12_Jobs.accdb database closes, but the Access application window remains open. To set a database password, you must open the database in Exclusive mode using the Open dialog box.

2. **Click the File tab, click Open, click Browse to navigate to the location where you store your Data Files, click IL_AC_12_Jobs.accdb, click the Open arrow as shown in FIGURE 12-7, click Open Exclusive, then enable content if prompted**

   Exclusive mode means that you are the only person who has the database open, and others cannot open the file during this time.

3. **Click the File tab, click Info if it is not already selected, then click the Encrypt with Password button**

   Encryption means to make the data in the database unreadable by other software. The Set Database Password dialog box opens, as shown in FIGURE 12-8. If you lose or forget your password, it cannot be recovered. For security reasons, your password does not appear as you type; an asterisk appears for each keystroke instead. Therefore, you must enter the same password in both the Password and Verify text boxes to make sure you haven't made a typing error.

4. **Type GoJCL!22 in the Password box, press TAB, type GoJCL!22 in the Verify box, click OK, then click OK if prompted about row level locking**

   Passwords should be easy to remember but not easy to guess. **Strong passwords** are longer than eight characters and use the entire keyboard, including uppercase and lowercase letters, numbers, and symbols.

5. **Close, then reopen the IL_AC_12_Jobs.accdb database**

   The Password Required dialog box opens.

6. **Type GoJCL!22, then click OK**

   The IL_AC_12_Jobs.accdb database opens, giving you full access to all the objects. To remove a password, you must exclusively open a database, just as you did when you set the database password.

7. **Click the File tab, click Close, click the File tab, click Open, click Browse to navigate to the location where you store your Data Files, single-click IL_AC_12_Jobs.accdb, click the Open arrow, click Open Exclusive, type GoJCL!22 in the Password Required dialog box, then click OK**

8. **Click the File tab, click Info, click the Decrypt Database button, type GoJCL!22, click OK, then close the IL_AC_12_Jobs.accdb database and exit Access**

TROUBLE
You cannot use the Recent list to open a database in Exclusive mode.

QUICK TIP
Passwords are case sensitive, so, GoJCL! and gojcl! are different passwords.

TROUBLE
You must browse for the file to open it exclusively.

FIGURE 12-7: Opening a database in Exclusive mode

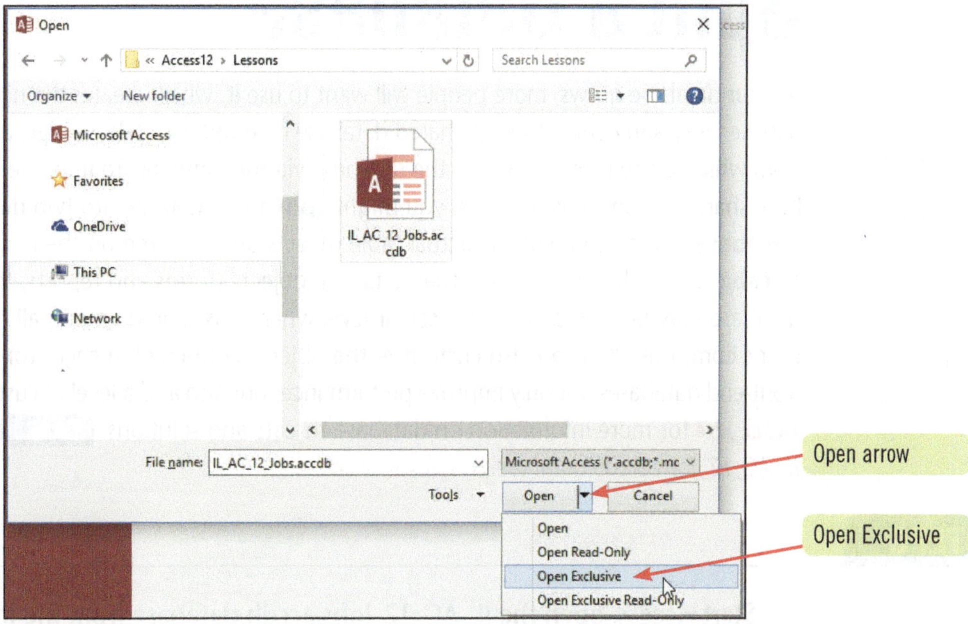

FIGURE 12-8: Set Database Password dialog box

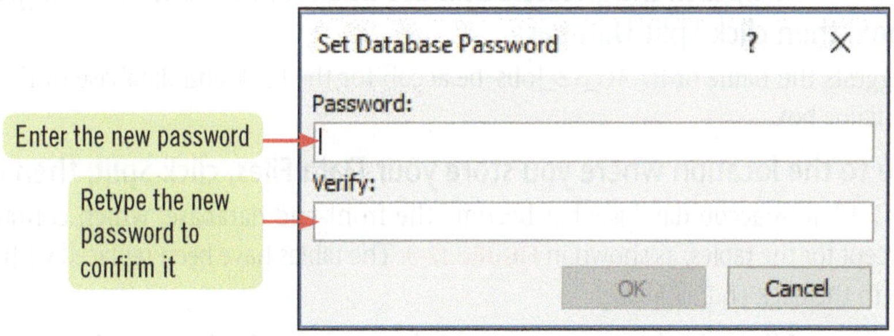

TABLE 12-3: Methods to secure an Access database

method	description
Password	Restricts access to the database to only those who know the password
Encryption	Makes the data indecipherable to other programs when sent across a network
Startup options	Hides or disables certain functions when the database is opened
Show/hide objects	Shows or hides objects in the Navigation Pane; a simple way to prevent users from unintentionally deleting objects is to hide them in the Navigation Pane by checking the Hidden property in the object's Property Sheet
Split a database	Separates the back-end data and the front-end objects (such as forms and reports) into two databases that work together; splitting a database allows you to give each user access to only those objects they need

Trusting a database to automatically enable content

Trusting a database means to identify the database file as one that is safe to open. Trusted databases automatically enable all content, including all macros and VBA, and, therefore, do not present the Enable Content message when they are opened. To trust a database, click the File tab, click Options, click Trust Center on the left, click the Trust Center Settings button, then use the Trusted Documents or Trusted Locations options to either trust an individual database file or an entire folder. To trust the folder, click Trusted Locations, click Add new location, click Browse to locate the folder to trust, select the desired folder, click the Subfolders of this location are also trusted check box to also trust subfolders, and then click OK to move through the dialog boxes and complete the process.

Access

Split a Database

Learning Outcomes
- Split a database
- Use the Linked Table Manager

As your database grows, more people will want to use it, which creates the need for higher levels of database security and connectivity. A shared database is stored on a **file server**, a centrally located computer from which every user can access the database via the network. To improve the performance of a database shared among several users, you might **split** the database into two database files: the **back-end database**, which contains the actual table objects and is stored on the file server, and the **front-end database**, which contains the other database objects (forms and reports, for example). The front-end database may be stored at the file server level where it is shared among all the users or placed on each user's computer. You can also customize the objects contained in each front-end database. Therefore, front-end databases not only improve performance, but also add a level of customization and security. See TABLE 12-4 for more information on database threats and solutions. **CASE** *Lydia asks you to split the IL_AC_12_Jobs.accdb database.*

STEPS

1. **Start Access, open the IL_AC_12_Jobs.accdb database from the location where you store your Data Files, enable content if prompted, close the frmNavigation form, click the Database Tools tab, click the Access Database button in the Move Data group, read the dialog box, then click Split Database**

   Access suggests the name of IL_AC_12_Jobs_be.accdb for the back-end database in the Create Back-end Database dialog box.

2. **Navigate to the location where you store your Data Files, click Split, then click OK**

   The IL_AC_12_Jobs.accdb database has become the front-end database, which contains all the Access objects except for the tables, as shown in FIGURE 12-9. The tables have been replaced with links to the physical tables in the back-end database.

TROUBLE
The path to your back-end database will be different.

3. **Point to several linked table icons to read the path to the back-end database, right-click any of the linked table icons, click Linked Table Manager, then click the Expand button [+] to the left of Access, as shown in FIGURE 12-10**

   The Linked Table Manager dialog box allows you to select and manually update tables. This is useful if the path to the back-end database changes and you need to reconnect the front-end and back-end database.

4. **sam ↑ Click Close**

   To the front-end database, a linked table functions the same as a regular table even though the data is physically stored elsewhere. To modify the structure of a linked table, you need to open the database where the table is physically stored.

   In addition to tables in another Access database, Access can link to data in several different file formats, including Excel, dBASE, SharePoint lists, HTML, and any data that can be reached with an **ODBC (Open Database Connectivity)** connection. Use the External Data tab on the ribbon along with the New Data Source button to create an individual link to an external data source.

FIGURE 12-9: Front-end database with linked tables

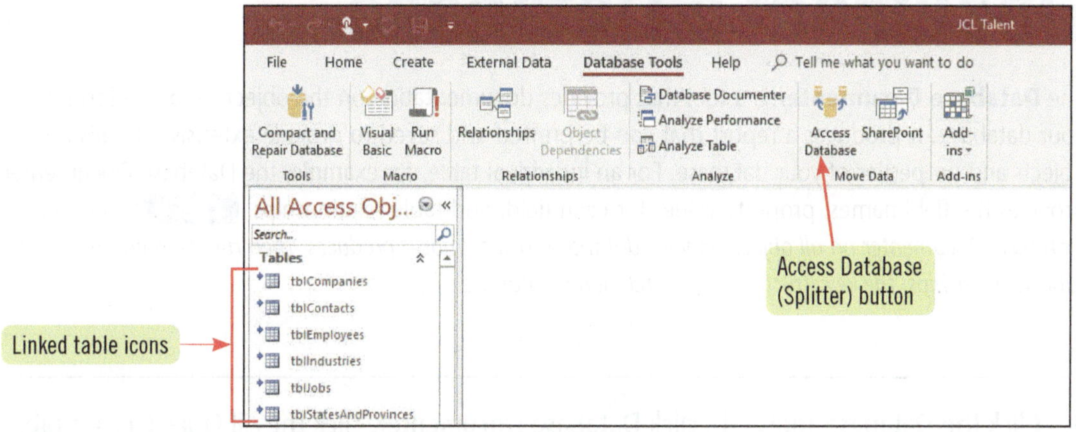

FIGURE 12-10: Linked Table Manager

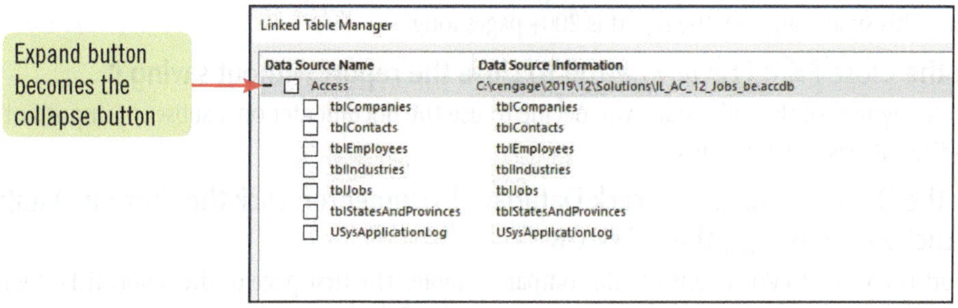

TABLE 12-4: Database threats and solutions

incident	what can happen	appropriate actions
Virus	Viruses can cause a wide range of harm, from profane messages to corrupted files	Install virus-checking software
Power outage	Power problems such as **brownouts** (dips in power), and **spikes** (surges in power) can damage the hardware	Purchase a **UPS (uninterruptible power supply)** and **surge protectors** (power strip with surge protection)
Theft or intentional damage	Computer thieves or other scoundrels steal or vandalize computer equipment	Physically secure the file server in a locked room, back up data in an off-site location on a daily basis, and set database passwords

Access

Document a Database

Learning Outcomes
- Use the Database Documenter
- Study one-to-many relationships

The **Database Documenter** is a tool that provides documentation on the objects and relationships in your database. It produces a report that can be printed and saved to provide extensive details on the objects and properties of your database. For an individual table, for example, the Database Documenter provides the field names, property values for each field, and table relationships. CASE *You run the Database Documenter on all objects in your database to see what it produces, then run it again on only the table relationships, the key structure of your relational database.*

STEPS

1. **Click the Database Tools tab, click Database Documenter, click the All Object Types tab, click the Select All button as shown in FIGURE 12-11, then click OK**
   The Database Documenter tool analyzes the selected objects and prepares a report starting with the properties of tblCompanies, the fields in tblCompanies, each of the properties of each of the fields, and so on. Even for this small database, the report is 200+ pages long.
2. **Click the Close Print Preview button to close the report without saving it**
   Given the length of the full report, you decide to use the documenter on a subset of important information—the database relationships.
3. **Click the Database Tools tab, click Database Documenter, click the Current Database tab, click Relationships, then click OK**
   A report is created to document the tblCompanies table. The first page of the report lists the properties of the table as a whole, then the report starts listing the Columns (fields) of the report and the properties of each.
4. **Click the report to zoom in to view the table relationships, as shown in FIGURE 12-12**
   The first page of the report shows you the one-to-many relationships in the database starting with these three:
   tblCompanies has a one-to-many relationship with tblContacts.
   tblCompanies has a one-to-many relationship with tblJobs.
   tblIndustries has a one-to-many relationship with tblCompanies.
5. **Click the Close Print Preview button**
   You can print reports from the Database Documenter, but they close without allowing you to save them. You can easily re-create them using the Database Documenter tool as needed.
6. **Compact and close the IL_AC_12_Jobs.accdb database, then exit Access**

FIGURE 12-11: Documenter dialog box

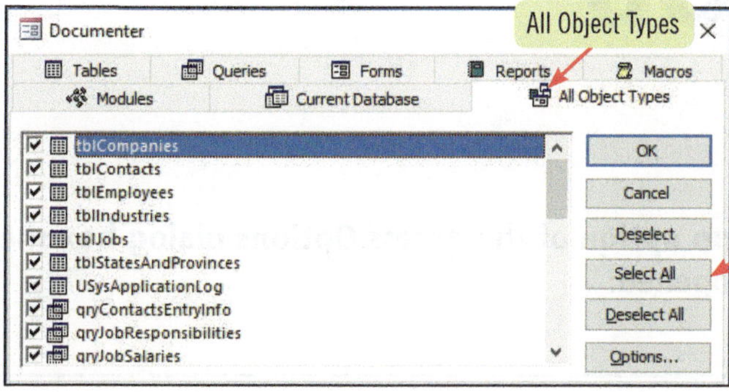

FIGURE 12-12: Database Documenter report of database relationships

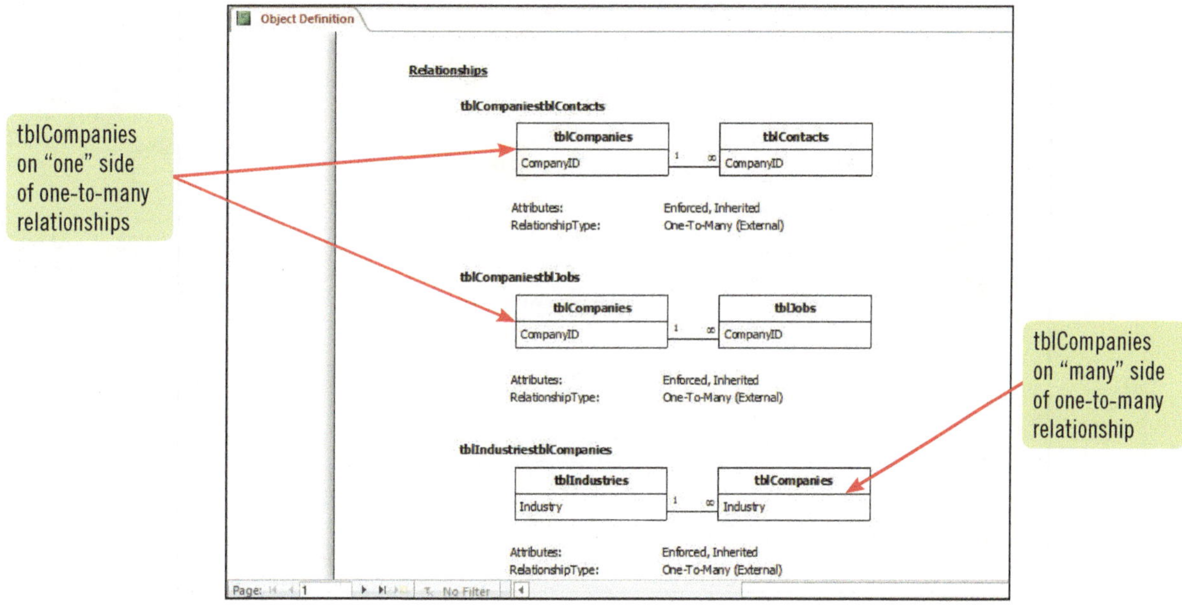

Access

Practice

Concepts Review

Describe how each startup option of the Access Options dialog box shown in FIGURE 12-13 affects the database when it is opened.

FIGURE 12-13

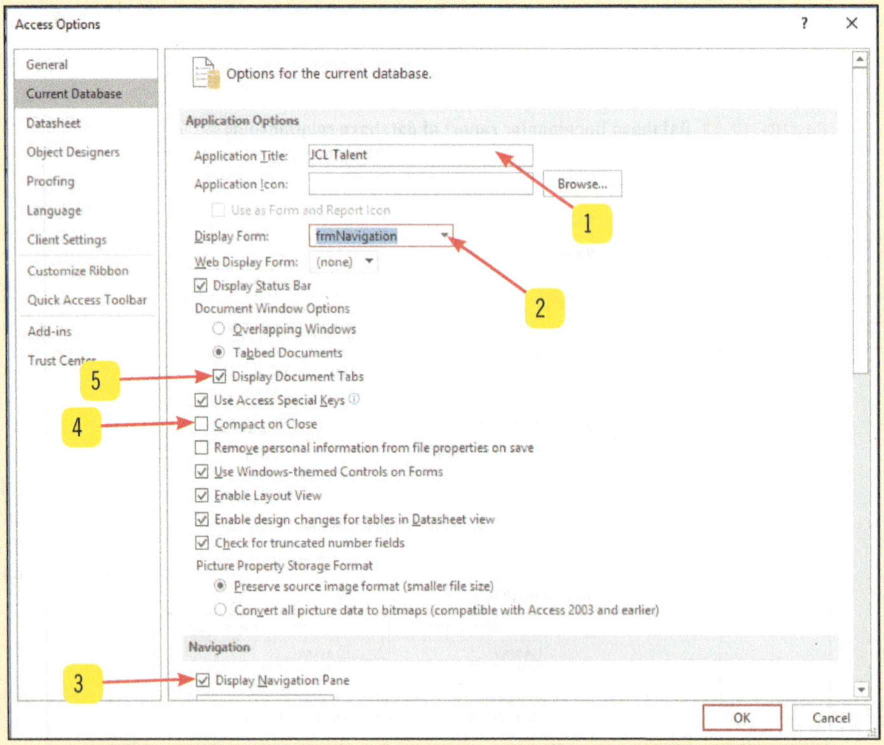

Match each term with the statement that best describes its function.

6. Database Documenter	**a.** Means that no other users can have access to the database file while it's open
7. Exclusive mode	**b.** Scrambles data so that it is indecipherable when opened by another program
8. Performance Analyzer	**c.** Studies the structure and size of your database and makes a variety of recommendations on how you may be able to improve its speed
9. Navigation form	**d.** Contains database tables
10. Back-end database	**e.** Provides an easy-to-use database interface
11. Encrypting	**f.** Provides a report on the selected objects and relationships in your database Select the best answer from the list of choices.

Select the best answer from the list of choices.

12. Which of the following is *not* true about the reports created by the Database Documenter?

a. They may be saved in the database.
b. They may be printed.
c. They document table relationships.
d. They document field property values.

13. Which is *not* a strong password?

a. 1234$College=6789
b. 5Matthew14?
c. Lip44Balm*!
d. password

14. Which character precedes a command-line option?

a. !
b. @
c. ^
d. /

15. The Application Title and Display Form startup options are found in which category in the Access Options dialog box?

a. General
b. Current Database
c. Object Designers
d. Proofing

16. Compacting and repairing a database does *not* help with which issue?

a. Identifying unused database objects
b. Preventing data integrity problems
c. Eliminating wasted space
d. Making the database as small as possible

17. How does the object dependencies feature help the database developer?

a. It identifies performance issues based on object dependencies.
b. It identifies naming convention issues between objects in the database.
c. It deletes unused objects.
d. It helps prevent the developer from deleting a query used by another object.

18. Which of the following is *not* a reason to create a backup?

a. Protect against theft
b. Minimize damage caused by an incident that corrupts data
c. Improve performance of the database
d. Safeguard information should a natural disaster destroy the database

19. Why might you split a database?

a. To make access to the database more secure
b. To improve performance
c. To customize the front-end databases
d. All of the above

20. What controls are automatically created on a navigation form?

a. Navigation control and navigation buttons
b. Navigation control and hyperlinks
c. Navigation buttons and command buttons
d. Navigation buttons and page breaks

Skills Review

1. Create a navigation form.

a. Start Access, open the IL_AC_12-2.accdb database from the location where you store your Data Files, then save it as **IL_AC_12_SupportDesk**. Enable content if prompted.

b. Create a navigation form using the Horizontal Tabs style.

c. Close the Field List if it opens.

d. Add the frmEmployeeMaster form, the rptCallLog report, the rptCaseInfo report, and the rptEmployeeMasterList report as navigation buttons.

e. Rename the navigation buttons to **Employee Entry**, **Call Log**, **Case Info**, and **Employee List**.

f. Display the form in Form View, then test each navigation button.

g. Save the form with the name **frmNavigation** as shown in FIGURE 12-14, then close it.

FIGURE 12-14

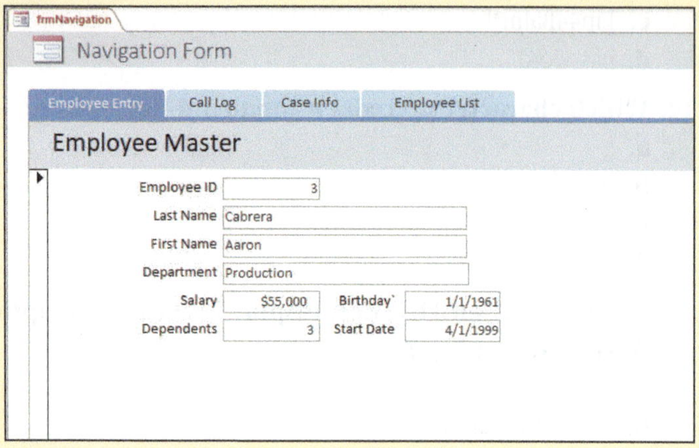

2. Set startup options.

a. Open the Access Options dialog box to the Current Database category.

b. Type **Technical Support Center** in the Application Title box, click the Display Form arrow, click the frmNavigation form, then apply the changes.

c. Close the IL_AC_12_SupportDesk.accdb database, then reopen it to check the startup options. Notice the change in the Access title bar.

d. Close the frmNavigation form that automatically opened when you opened the database.

3. Analyze database performance.

a. On the Database Tools tab, click the Analyze Performance button.

b. On the All Object Types tab, select all objects, then click OK.

c. Read each of the ideas and descriptions, then close the Performance Analyzer.

d. Open the frmEmployeeMaster form in Design View, then click the View Code button. This form contains an empty module. According to the Performance Analyzer suggestions from the previous step, removing an empty module can improve performance.

e. Close the code window, then open the Property Sheet for the form. On the Other tab, change the Has Module property from Yes to **No**, then click Yes when prompted if you are sure.

f. Save and close the frmEmployeeMaster form, then close Access.

4. Secure a database.

a. Start Access and open the IL_AC_12_SupportDesk.accdb database in Exclusive mode. (*Hint*: Remember that you must browse for a database from within Access to open it in Exclusive mode.)

b. Encrypt the database and set the password to **HelpIs#1**. (*Hint*: Check to make sure the Caps Lock key is not selected because passwords are case sensitive.) Click OK if prompted about row level locking.

c. Close the IL_AC_12_SupportDesk.accdb database, but leave Access open.

d. Reopen the IL_AC_12_SupportDesk.accdb database to test the password. Close the IL_AC_12_SupportDesk.accdb database.

e. Reopen the IL_AC_12_SupportDesk.accdb database in Exclusive mode. Type **HelpIs#1** as the password.

f. Unset the password and decrypt the database.

g. Close the frmNavigation form, then close Access.

Skills Review (continued)

5. Split a database.

- **a.** Start Access, open the IL_AC_12_SupportDesk.accdb database from the location where you store your Data Files, then enable content if prompted.
- **b.** Close the frmNavigation form.
- **c.** On the Database Tools tab, click the Access Database button and split the database.
- **d.** Name the back-end database with the default name **IL_AC_12_SupportDesk_be** and save it in the location where you store your Data Files.
- **e.** Point to the linked table icons to observe the path to the back-end database.

6. Document a database.

- **a.** Use the Database Documenter tool to document the relationships in the database.
- **b.** Print the one-page report, then close it.
- **c.** Compact and repair then close the IL_AC_12_ SupportDesk.accdb database and close Access 2019.

Independent Challenge 1

As the manager of Riverwalk, a multispecialty health clinic, you have created a database to manage patient outcomes. In this exercise, you will use the Performance Analyzer to improve the performance of the database.

- **a.** Start Access, open the IL_AC_12-3.accdb database from the location where you store your Data Files, and save it as **IL_AC_12_Riverwalk**. Enable content if prompted.
- **b.** On the Database Tools tab, click the Analyze Performance button.
- **c.** On the All Object Types tab, select all objects, then click OK.
- **d.** Read each of the ideas and descriptions, then close the Performance Analyzer.
- **e.** Open the frmPatientEntry form in Design View, then click the View Code button. This form contains a module with one declaration statement and one comment but without any procedures.
- **f.** Close the code window, then open the Property Sheet for the form. On the Other tab, change the Has Module property from Yes to **No**, then click Yes when prompted if you are sure.
- **g.** Save and close the frmPatientEntry form.
- **h.** Run the Performance Analyzer on all objects in the database again.
- **i.** Four of the suggestions are to change fields that have a Data Type of Short Text to a Number field with a Field Size of Long or Double Integer, as shown in FIGURE 12-15. Be prepared to discuss in class why those ideas should not be implemented in this database.
- **j.** Compact and close the IL_AC_12_Riverwalk.accdb database, then close Access.

FIGURE 12-15

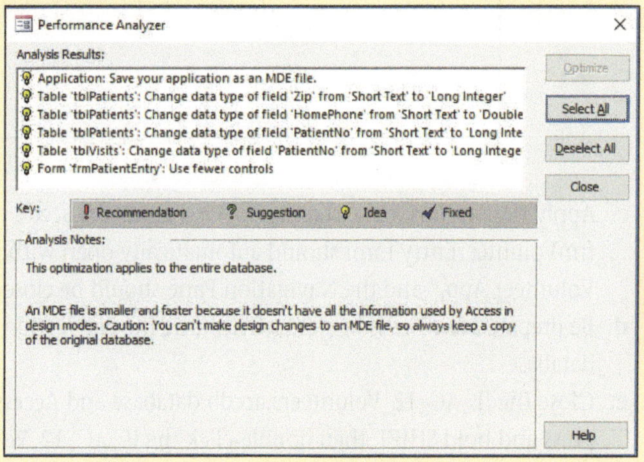

Independent Challenge 2

You are working for a city to coordinate a series of community-wide preparedness activities. You have created a database to track the activities and volunteers who are attending the activities. In this exercise, you will experiment with startup options and how to override them as the database developer.

a. Start Access, open the IL_AC_12-4.accdb database from the location where you store your Data Files, then save it as **IL_AC_12_Volunteers**. Enable content if prompted.

b. Click File on the ribbon, click Options, then click the Current Database category. Make the changes to startup options shown in **FIGURE 12-16** and listed below:

Application Title: **Community Volunteer App**

Display Form: frmVolunteerEntry

Display Document Tabs: No

Compact on Close: Yes

Display Navigation Pane: No

FIGURE 12-16

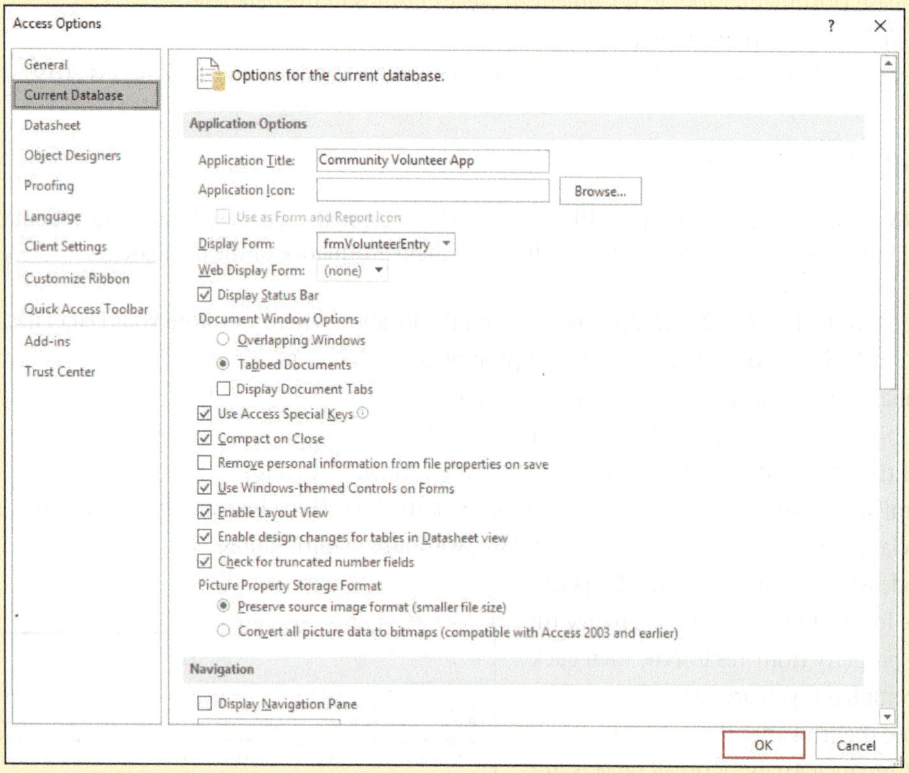

c. Apply the options, close the IL_AC_12_Volunteers.accdb database, then reopen it to observe the changes. The frmVolunteerEntry form should automatically open without a tab, the title bar should display "Community Volunteer App," and the Navigation Pane should be closed.

d. Be prepared to discuss in class why hiding the Navigation Pane and not displaying object tabs can help secure a database.

e. Close the IL_AC_12_Volunteers.accdb database and Access, navigate to the folder where you store your Data Files, press and hold SHIFT, then double-click the IL_AC_12_Volunteers.accdb database to open it. Be sure to not release SHIFT until the database is opened. Pressing SHIFT while opening an Access database file bypasses the startup options.

f. Compact and close the IL_AC_12_Volunteers.accdb database, then close Access.

Visual Workshop

Start Access, open the IL_AC_12-5.accdb database from the location where you store your Data Files, then save it as **IL_AC_12_CollegeCourses**. Create a navigation form as shown in FIGURE 12-17 using the Horizontal Tabs navigation style. Add the frmDepartments, frmProfessors, frmClasses, and frmStudentTranscript forms and modify the navigation button text as shown. Save the navigation form with the name **frmNavigation** and set frmNavigation to be the Display Form when the database opens. Close and reopen the database to make sure the startup option has been applied correctly, then close Access.

FIGURE 12-17

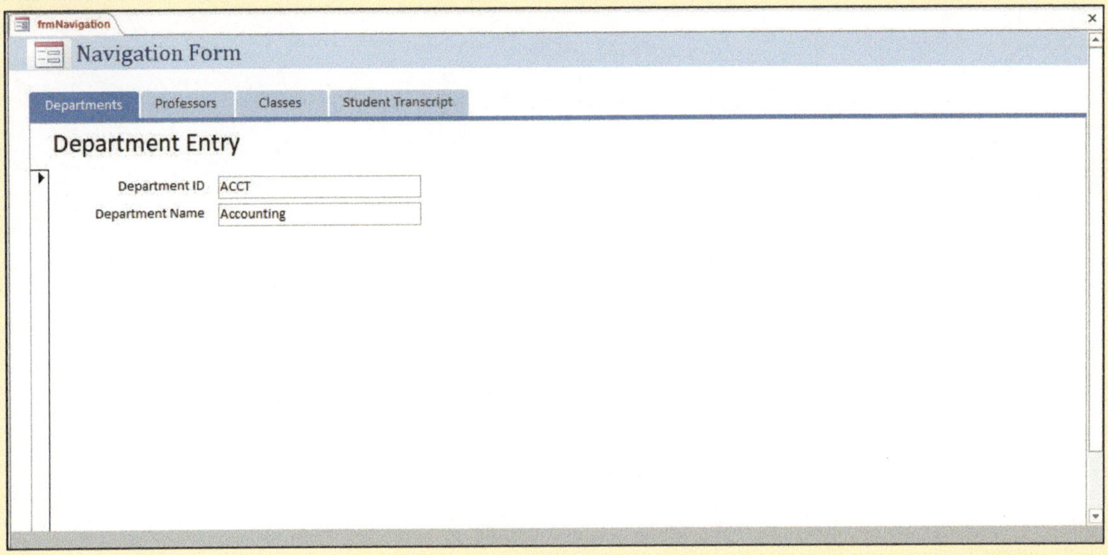

Access

Delivering Presentations

CASE Before you complete your presentation, you work with PowerPoint views and customize Handout and Notes masters. You will then create a custom slide show, change slide show options, prepare the presentation for distribution, and then make it possible for others to view on the Internet. You end your day by creating a photo album of a recent trip to the state capital in Austin, Texas.

Module Objectives

After completing this module, you will be able to:

- Work with presentation views
- Customize Handout and Notes masters
- Set up a slide show
- Create a custom show
- Prepare a presentation for distribution
- Deliver a presentation online
- Create a photo album

Files You Will Need

IL_PPT_8-1.pptx
Support_PPT_8_Austin1.jpg
Support_PPT_8_Austin2.jpg
Support_PPT_8_Austin3.jpg
Support_PPT_8_Austin4.jpg
IL_PPT_8-2.pptx
Support_PPT_8_Pic1.jpg
Support_PPT_8_Pic2.jpg
Support_PPT_8_Pic3.jpg
Support_PPT_8_Pic4.jpg
IL_PPT_8-3.pptx
Support_PPT_8_ICPic1.jpg
Support_PPT_8_ICPic2.jpg
Support_PPT_8_ICPic3.jpg
Support_PPT_8_ICPic4.jpg

Work with Presentation Views

Learning Outcomes
- Use PowerPoint views
- Use Presenter view
- Use Notes Page view
- Create a PowerPoint Show

PowerPoint has five primary views: Slide view, Slide Sorter view, Outline view, Slide Show view, and Notes Page view. Each of these views is designed for a specific purpose and provides you with a variety of tools to easily and quickly develop and present a presentation. There is also Presenter view, which you can access only while in Slide Show view and is designed to help a presenter give a presentation using two monitors. Presenter view along with Notes Page view and the features in these views are important to understand before you attempt to give a presentation to an audience. **CASE** *In this lesson, you examine Notes Page view and Presenter view and then you insert a symbol and change the slide orientation.*

STEPS

QUICK TIP
To change the slide orientation, click the Design tab, then click the Slide Size button in the Customize group. Click Custom Slide Size, then click the landscape or portrait option buttons for slides.

1. **sam Start PowerPoint, open the presentation IL_PPT 8-1.pptx from the location where you store your Data Files, then save the presentation as IL_PPT_8_JCL**
2. **Click the View tab on the Ribbon, then click the Notes Page button in the Presentation Views group**
   Notes Page view appears, showing a reduced image of the current slide above a large text placeholder. You can enter text in this placeholder, which as the presenter you can see during a slide show.
3. **Click in the text placeholder, type Be sure to introduce guest speaker, click the Normal button on the status bar, then click the Notes button on the status bar**
   The text you typed appears in the Notes pane, as shown in FIGURE 8-1.
4. **Click the Insert tab on the Ribbon, click after the word Talent in the subtitle text object, click the Symbol button in the Symbols group, then scroll to the seventh row from the top of the dialog box to view the Registered symbol**
   The Symbol dialog box opens with the Normal font selected. You want to select the registered symbol, which is the letter "R" inside a circle.
5. **Click the Registered Sign symbol, click Insert, then click Close**
   The Registered symbol appears after the word "Talent" on Slide 1.
6. **Click the Slide Show view button on the status bar, click the More slide show options button on the Slide Show menu, then click Show Presenter View**
   Presenter view opens.
7. **Click the See all slides button, click the Slide 5 thumbnail, click, then click the Slide 8 thumbnail**
8. **Click the Zoom into the slide button, click the chart, compare your screen to FIGURE 8-2, click, then press ESC**
   You can zoom in on any part of the slide in Presenter view.
9. **Save the presentation, click the File tab on the Ribbon, click Save As, click the PowerPoint Presentation arrow, click PowerPoint Show (*.ppsx), then click the Save button**
   Your presentation is saved as a PowerPoint Show, which is a special file format that automatically starts your presentation in Slide Show view when opened.
10. **Click the File tab, click Close to close the PowerPoint Show presentation, then open the presentation IL_PPT_8_JCL.pptx from the location where you store your Data Files**

FIGURE 8-1: Text entered in the Notes pane

Rawpixel.com/Shutterstock.com

FIGURE 8-2: Zoomed-in slide in Presenter view

Asier Romero/Shutterstock.com

Recording a narration on a slide

If you have a microphone, you can record a voice narration and then play it during a slide show. To record a narration, click the Insert tab on the Ribbon, click the Audio button in the Media group, then click Record Audio. The Record Sound dialog box opens. To start recording, click the Record button in the dialog box, then click the Stop button when you are finished. A sound icon appears on the slide. Narration recordings and other sounds are embedded in the presentation and will increase the PowerPoint file size. You can preview a narration in Normal view by pointing to the sound icon on the slide, then clicking the Play/Pause button in the audio control bar.

PowerPoint **Module 8**

Customize Handout and Notes Masters

Learning Outcomes
- Modify the handout master
- Change page orientation

It is often helpful to provide your audience with supplemental materials of the presentation. Creating handouts for your audience provides them a way to follow along and take notes during your presentation. As the presenter, creating notes pages that you can refer to while giving the presentation can be useful, especially when your presentation is complex or detailed. Before you create handouts or notes pages, you might want to customize them to fit your specific needs. **CASE** *You plan to create supplemental materials to hand out when you give the presentation. You customize the Handout master by changing the slides per page and the background style. Then you modify the Notes master by changing the page setup and the notes page orientation.*

STEPS

1. **Click the Slide 1 thumbnail in the Slides tab, click the View tab on the Ribbon, then click the Handout Master button in the Master Views group**
   The Handout Master view opens. The master has six large empty placeholders that represent where the slides will appear on the printed handouts. The four smaller placeholders in each corner of the page are the header, footer, date, and page number placeholders. The date placeholder displays today's date.
2. **Click the Background Styles button in the Background group, then click Style 10**
   When you print handouts on a color printer, they will have a gradient gray background.
3. **Click the Slides Per Page button in the Page Setup group, then click 3 Slides on the menu**
   Three slide placeholders appear on the handout, as shown in FIGURE 8-3.
4. **Click the Header placeholder, drag the Zoom Slider on the status bar to 100%, type JCL Talent, press PAGE DOWN, click the Footer placeholder, then type your name**
   Now your handouts are ready to print when you need them.
5. **Click the Fit slide to current window button on the status bar, then click the Close Master View button in the Close group**
   Your presentation is in Normal view, so you don't see the changes you made to the Handout master.
6. **Click the View tab on the Ribbon, then click the Notes Master button in the Master Views group**
   Notes Master view opens. It has four corner placeholders—one each for the header, footer, date, and page number—a large notes text box placeholder, and a large slide master image placeholder.
7. **Click the Notes Page Orientation button in the Page Setup group, click Landscape, click the Footer placeholder, type JCL Talent, then click a blank area of the slide master**
   The page orientation changes to landscape. Notice that all the text placeholders are now resized to fill the width of the page. Compare your screen to FIGURE 8-4.
8. **Click the Close Master View button in the Close group, click the File tab on the Ribbon, click Print, click Full Page Slides, click 9 Slides Horizontal, click Print, then save your work**
   The presentation prints nine slides per page. The presentation has nine slides, so one page was all that was needed to print this presentation.

QUICK TIP
To save one or more slides as a picture, click the File tab on the Ribbon, click Save As, click the arrow next to the Save button, click a picture format (such as .jpg or .tif), click the Save button, then choose which slides to export.

QUICK TIP
To create custom theme fonts, click the View tab, click the Slide Master button, click the Fonts button, then click Customize Fonts.

FIGURE 8-3: Handout Master view

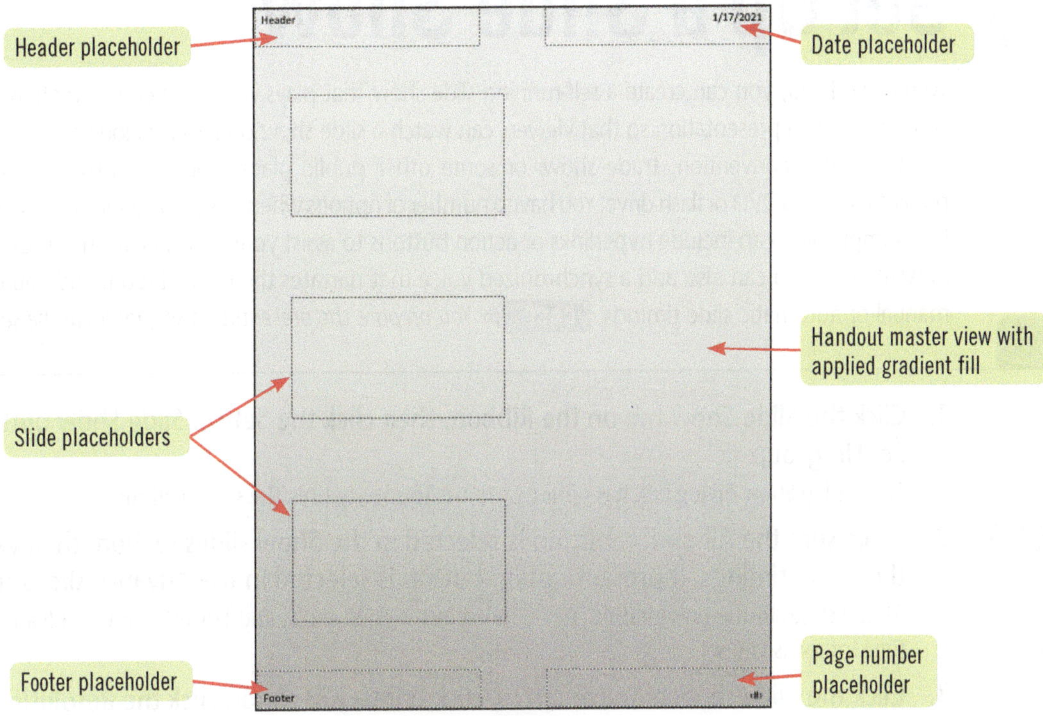

FIGURE 8-4: Notes Master view in landscape orientation

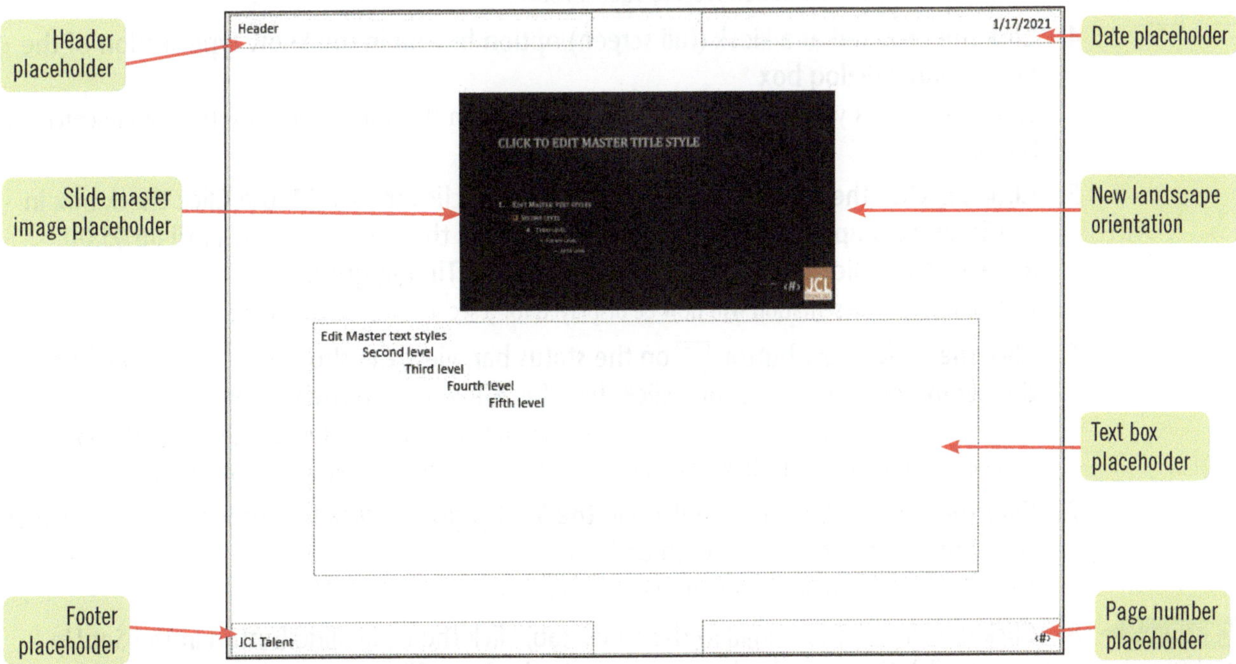

Creating handouts in Microsoft Word

Sometimes it's helpful to use a word processing program like Microsoft Word to create detailed handouts or notes pages. You might also want to create a Word document based on the outline of your presentation. To send your presentation to Word, click the File tab on the Ribbon, click Export, click Create Handouts, then click the Create Handouts button. The Send to Microsoft Word dialog box opens and provides you with five document layout options. Two layouts include notes entered in the Notes pane. Select a layout, then click OK. Word opens and a new document opens with your inserted presentation, using the layout you selected. To send just the text of your presentation to Word, click the Outline only page layout. To link the slides to your Word document, which will reduce the file size of the handout, click the Paste link option button.

PowerPoint Module 8

Set Up a Slide Show

Learning Outcomes
- Automate a slide show
- Hide a slide

With PowerPoint, you can create a self-running slide show that plays without user intervention. For example, you can set up a presentation so that viewers can watch a slide show on a stand-alone computer, in a booth or **kiosk**, at a convention, trade show, or some other public place. You can also create a self-running presentation on a DVD or flash drive. You have a number of options when designing a self-running presentation; for example, you can include hyperlinks or action buttons to assist your audience as they move through the presentation. You can also add a synchronized voice that narrates the presentation, and you can set either manual or automatic slide timings. CASE *You prepare the presentation so that it can be self-running.*

STEPS

1. **Click the Slide Show tab on the Ribbon, then click the Set Up Slide Show button in the Set Up group**
   The Set Up Show dialog box has options you use to specify how the show will run.
2. **Make sure the All option button is selected in the Show slides section, then verify that the Using timings, if present option button is selected in the Advance slides section**
   All the slides in the presentation are included in the slide show, and PowerPoint will advance the slides at time intervals you set.
3. **Click the Slide show monitor arrow, click Primary Monitor, click the Resolution arrow, then click the resolution closest to 1360 x 768**
   The primary monitor resolution is set to 1360 x 768.
4. **Click the Browsed at a kiosk (full screen) option button in the Show type section of the Set Up Show dialog box**
   This option allows you to have a self-running presentation that can be viewed without a presenter. See FIGURE 8-5.
5. **Click OK, click the Transitions tab on the Ribbon, click the On Mouse Click check box in the Timing group to remove the check mark, click the After up arrow until 00:05.00 appears, then click the Apply To All button in the Timing group**
   Each slide in the presentation will now be displayed for 5 seconds before advancing.
6. **Click the Slide Show button on the status bar, view the show, let it start over from the beginning, press ESC, then click the Slide Show tab on the Ribbon**
   PowerPoint advances the slides automatically at 5-second intervals. After the last slide, the slide show starts over because the kiosk slide show option loops the presentation until someone presses ESC.
7. **Click the Set Up Slide Show button in the Set Up group, click the Presented by a speaker (full screen) option button, then click OK**
   The slide show options are back to their default settings.
8. **Click the Slide 1 thumbnail in the Slides tab, click the Hide Slide button in the Set Up group, click the From Beginning button in the Start Slide Show group, watch Slide 2 appear, then press ESC**
   The slide show begins with Slide 2. Notice the Slide 1 thumbnail in the Slides tab is dimmed and has a backslash through its number indicating it is hidden, as shown in FIGURE 8-6.
9. **Right-click the Slide 1 thumbnail in the Slides tab, click Hide Slide in the shortcut menu, then save your changes**
   Slide 1 is no longer hidden.

QUICK TIP
You must use automatic timings, navigation hyperlinks, or action buttons when you use the kiosk option; otherwise, you will not be able to progress through the slides.

QUICK TIP
To view a hidden slide while in Slide Show view, click the See all slides button on the Slide Show toolbar, then click the hidden slide.

FIGURE 8-5: Set Up Show dialog box

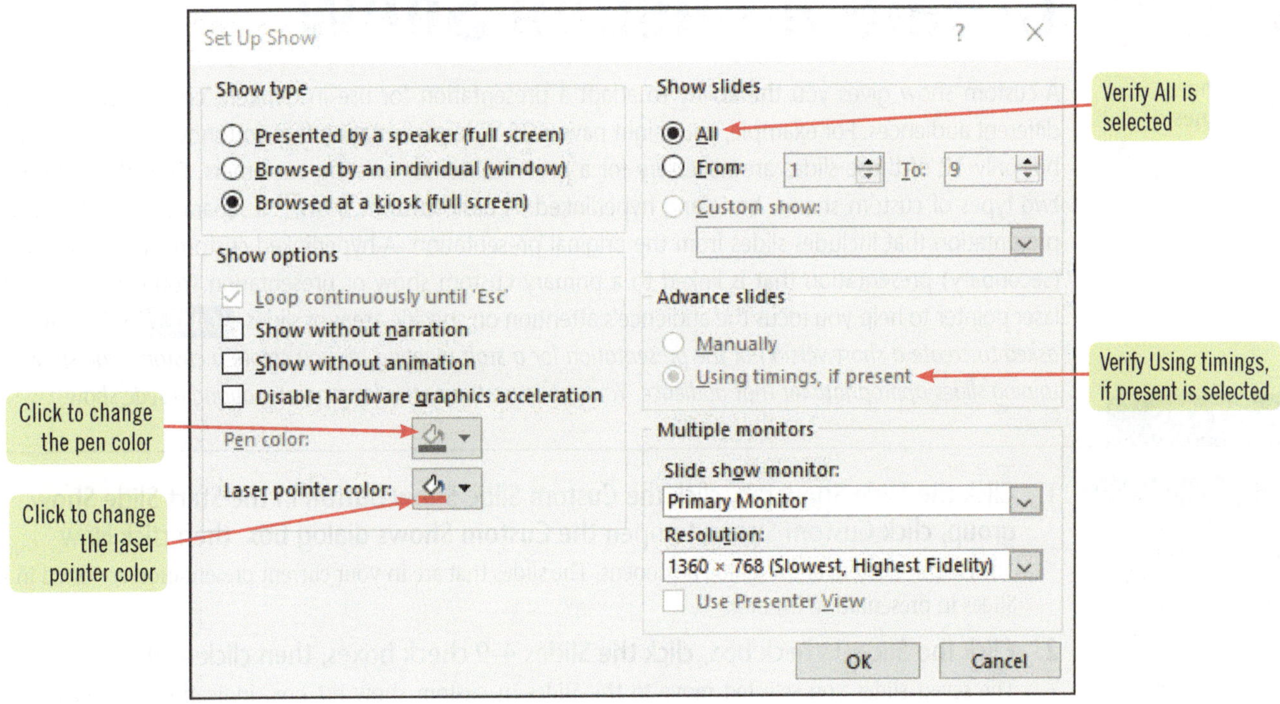

FIGURE 8-6: Slide 1 is a hidden slide

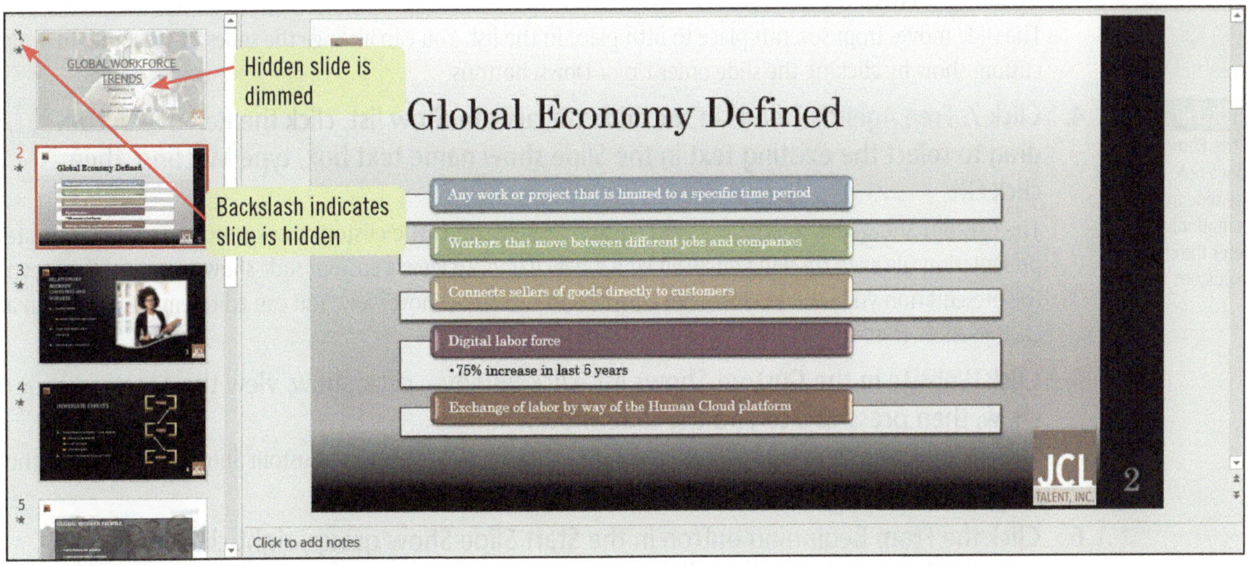

Installing and managing Office Add-ins

Office add-ins are applications you can download to PowerPoint and your other Office programs for free (or for a small fee) from the Microsoft Office Store on the Internet. Typical add-ins available to download to PowerPoint include navigation and mapping add-ins, dictionary and word usage add-ins, and news and social media add-ins. To install an add-in, click the Get Add-ins button in the Add-ins group on the Insert tab, then search through the add-in categories and add it to PowerPoint. To manage or uninstall an add-in, click the My Add-ins arrow, click Manage Other Add-ins, click Go at the bottom of the PowerPoint Options dialog box, then add or uninstall add-ins.

PowerPoint Module 8

Create a Custom Show

Learning Outcomes
- Create and modify a custom slide show
- Use the laser pointer

A custom show gives you the ability to adapt a presentation for use in different circumstances or with different audiences. For example, you might have a 25-slide presentation that you show to new customers, but only 12 of those slides are necessary for a presentation for existing customers. PowerPoint provides two types of custom shows: basic and hyperlinked. A basic custom show is a separate presentation or a presentation that includes slides from the original presentation. A hyperlinked custom show is a separate (secondary) presentation that is linked to a primary custom show or presentation. You can also use the laser pointer to help you focus the audience's attention on specific areas of slides. **CASE** *You have been asked to create a short version of the presentation for a staff meeting, so you create a custom slide show containing slides appropriate for that audience. You also learn to use the laser pointer during a slide show.*

STEPS

QUICK TIP
To print a custom show, click the File tab, click Print, click Print All Slides under Settings, then click the name of the custom show under Custom Shows.

1. **Click the Slide Show tab, click the Custom Slide Show button in the Start Slide Show group, click Custom Shows to open the Custom Shows dialog box, then click New**
   The Define Custom Show dialog box opens. The slides that are in your current presentation are listed in the Slides in presentation list box.
2. **Click the Slide 1 check box, click the Slides 4–9 check boxes, then click Add**
   The seven slides you selected move to the Slides in custom show list box, indicating that they will be included in the custom show. See FIGURE 8-7.
3. **Click 7. Skills and Work-Life in the Slides in custom show list, then click the slide order Up button twice**
   The slide moves from seventh place to fifth place in the list. You can arrange the slides in any order in your custom show by clicking the slide order Up or Down buttons.

QUICK TIP
Clicking the Remove button does not delete the slide from the presentation; it only deletes the slide from the custom show.

4. **Click 7. Free Agency Trends in the Slides in custom show list, click the Remove button, drag to select the existing text in the Slide show name text box, type Meeting, then click OK**
   The Custom Shows dialog box lists your custom presentation. The custom show is not saved as a separate presentation file even though you assigned it a new name. To view a custom slide show, you must first open the presentation you used to create the custom show in Slide Show view. You can edit, remove, and open a custom show from the Custom Shows dialog box.
5. **Click Website in the Custom Shows list, click Remove, click Show, view the Meeting slide show, then press ESC to end the slide show**
   The slides in the custom show appear in the order you set in the Define Custom Show dialog box. At the end of the slide show, you return to the presentation in Normal view.
6. **Click the From Beginning button in the Start Slide Show group, right-click the screen, point to Custom Show, then click Meeting**
   The Meeting custom show appears in Slide Show view.

QUICK TIP
To change the color of the laser pointer, click the Slide Show tab, click the Set Up Slide Show button, then click the Laser pointer color button.

7. **When Slide 4 appears, press and hold CTRL, press and hold the left mouse button, move the laser pointer around the slide as shown in FIGURE 8-8, release CTRL, then release the left mouse button**
   Automatic slide timings are set so your slide show can advance to the next slide even though you use the laser pointer. You can use the laser pointer in any presentation on any slide during a slide show.
8. **Press ESC at any point to end the slide show, then save your changes**

FIGURE 8-7: Define Custom Show dialog box

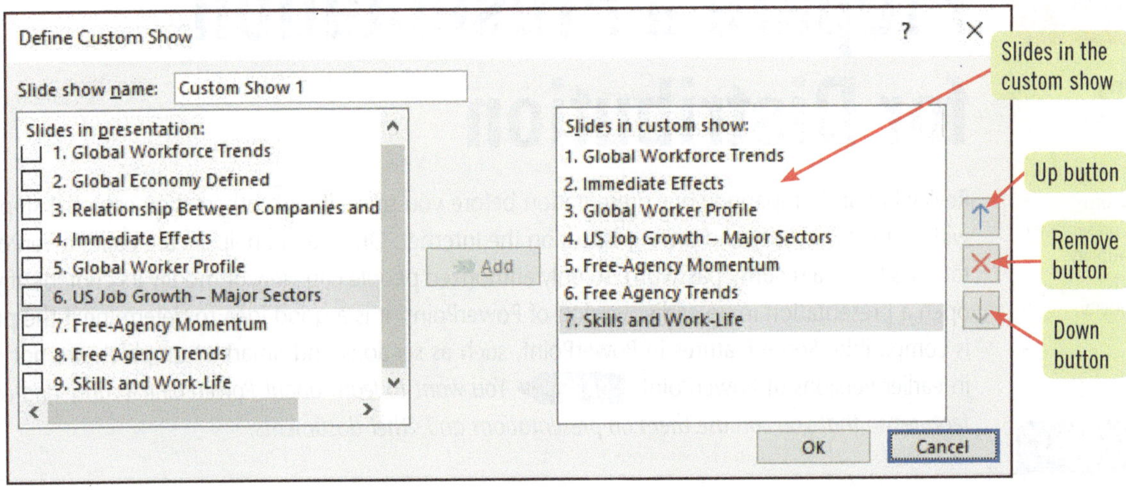

FIGURE 8-8: First slide of custom slide show with laser pointer

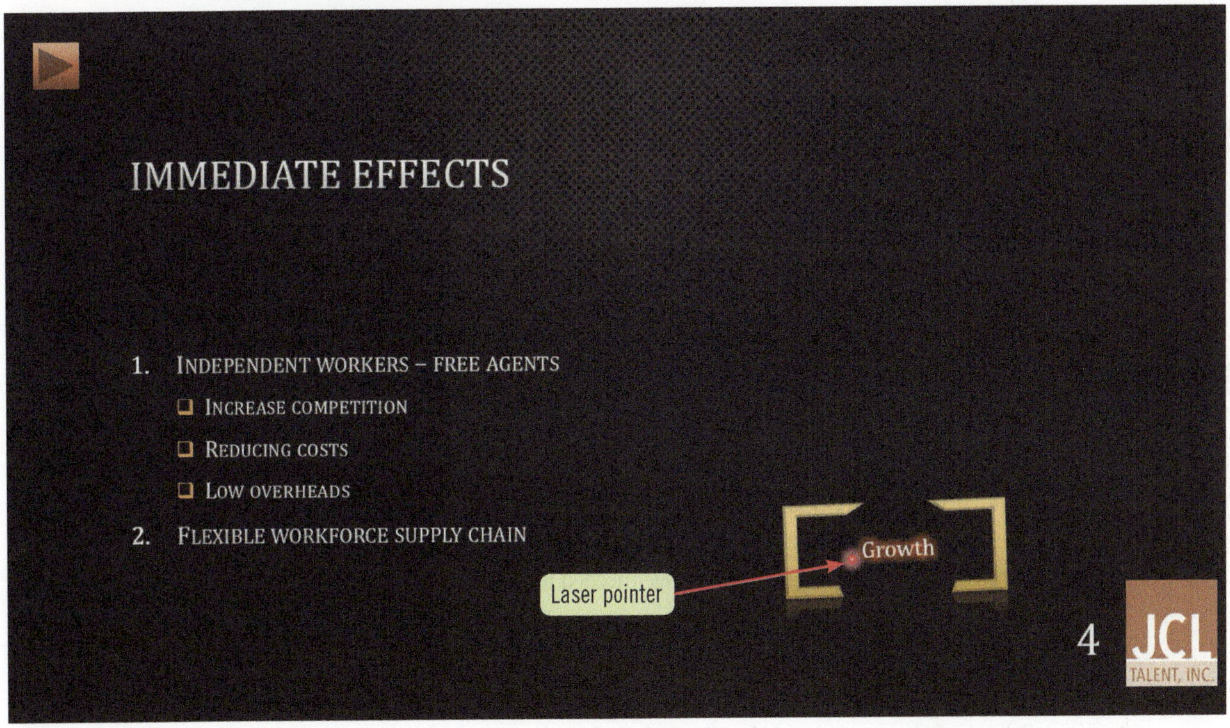

Linking to a custom slide show

You can use action buttons to switch from the "parent" show to the custom show. Click the Shapes button in the Drawing group on the Home tab, then click an action button. Draw an action button on the slide. Click the Hyperlink to arrow, click Custom Show, click the custom show you want to link, then click OK.

Now when you run a slide show you can click the action button you created to run the custom show. You can also create an interactive table of contents using custom shows. Create your table of contents entries on a slide, then hyperlink each entry to the section it refers to using a custom show for each section.

Learning Outcomes
- Protect a presentation with a password
- Check presentation compatibility
- Check for accessibility

Prepare a Presentation for Distribution

Reviewing and preparing your presentation before you share it with others is an essential step, especially with so many security and privacy issues on the Internet. One way to help secure your PowerPoint presentation is to set a security password, so only authorized people can view or modify its content. If you plan to open a presentation in an earlier version of PowerPoint, it is a good idea to determine if the presentation is compatible. Some features in PowerPoint, such as sections and SmartArt graphics, are not compatible in earlier versions of PowerPoint. **CASE** *You want to learn about PowerPoint security and compatibility features so that you can use them on presentations and other documents.*

STEPS

1. **Click the Slide 1 thumbnail in the Slides tab, click the File tab on the Ribbon, click the Protect Presentation button, then click Encrypt with Password on the menu**
   The Encrypt Document dialog box opens.
2. **Type 123abc**
   As you type, solid black symbols appear in the text box, as shown in FIGURE 8-9, which hides the password and makes it unreadable. This protects the confidentiality of your password if anyone happens to be looking at your screen while you type.
3. **Click OK to open the Confirm Password dialog box, type 123abc, then click OK**
   A password is now required to open this presentation. Once the presentation is closed, this password must be entered in the Password dialog box to open it. The presentation is now password protected.
4. **Click Close, click Save to save changes, click the File tab, then click IL_PPT_8_JCL.pptx in the Presentations list**
   The Password dialog box opens.
5. **Type 123abc, then click OK to open the presentation**
   The presentation opens. Be aware that if you don't remember your password, there is no way to open or view the presentation.
6. **Click the File tab on the Ribbon, click the Protect Presentation button, click Encrypt with Password, select the password, press DELETE, click OK, then click Save**
   The password is removed and is no longer needed to open the presentation.
7. **Click the File tab on the Ribbon, click the Check for Issues button, then click Check Compatibility**
   The Compatibility Checker analyzes the presentation, and the Microsoft PowerPoint Compatibility Checker dialog box opens, as shown in FIGURE 8-10. Each item in the dialog box represents a feature that is not supported in earlier versions of PowerPoint.
8. **Click the down scroll arrow, read all the items in the dialog box, click OK, click the File tab, click the Check for Issues button, then click Check Accessibility**
   The Check Accessibility feature analyzes the presentation for content that people with disabilities might find hard to read, as shown in FIGURE 8-11.
9. **Read the items in the Accessibility Checker pane, close the Accessibility Checker pane, then save your work**

TROUBLE
If you mistype the password in the Confirm Password dialog box, an alert dialog box opens.

QUICK TIP
To set other password options, open the Save As dialog box, click Tools, then click General Options.

QUICK TIP
If a Make your documents more accessible tip box opens, click Got it.

FIGURE 8-9: Encrypt Document dialog box

FIGURE 8-10: Compatibility Checker dialog box

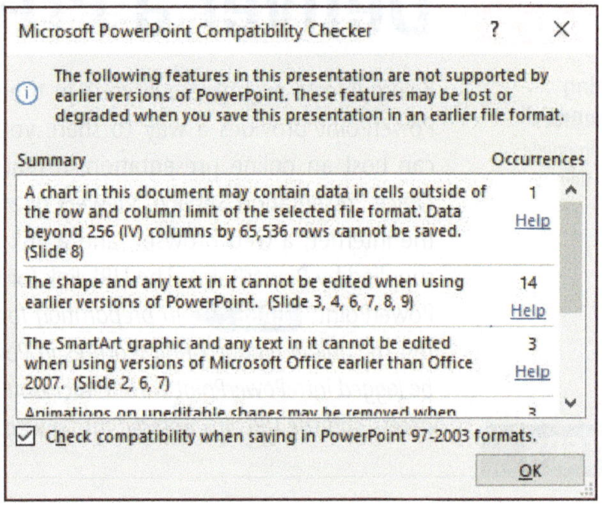

FIGURE 8-11: Accessibility Checker pane open

Rawpixel.com/Shutterstock.com

Digitally signing a presentation

What is a digital signature, and why would you want to use one in PowerPoint? A digital signature is similar to a handwritten signature in that it authenticates your document; however, a digital signature, unlike a handwritten signature, is created using computer cryptography and is not visible within the presentation itself. There are three primary reasons you would add a digital signature to a presentation: one, to authenticate the signer of the document; two, to ensure that the content of the presentation has not been changed since it was signed; and three, to assure the reader of the origin of the signed document. To add a digital signature, click the File tab on the Ribbon, click the Protect Presentation button, click Add a Digital Signature, then follow the instructions in the dialog boxes.

PowerPoint
Module 8

Deliver a Presentation Online

Learning Outcome
- Give an online presentation

Being able to assemble everyone in the same room for a presentation can be difficult, which is why PowerPoint provides a way to share your presentation with remote viewers. Using PowerPoint, you can host an online presentation in real time over the Internet to viewers using the Microsoft free Office Presentation Service. Viewers of an online presentation need to have a computer connected to the Internet, a web browser, and a link to an Internet address, called a **URL**, which is automatically supplied by PowerPoint. The URL link for your online broadcast can be emailed to viewers directly from PowerPoint. CASE *In preparation for hosting an online presentation to others in your company, you test the online broadcasting features in PowerPoint. (NOTE: To complete this lesson as a host, you need to be logged into PowerPoint with a Microsoft account and have Internet access. As a viewer, you need Internet access and the URL link entered into a web browser.)*

STEPS

1. **Click the Slide 1 thumbnail in the Slides tab, click the Slide Show tab on the Ribbon, then click the Present Online button in the Start Slide Show group**
   Read the information on the screen. If you don't have a Microsoft account, you need to acquire one from the Microsoft website before you proceed.

TROUBLE
If you get a service error message, try to connect again. See your instructor or technical support person for additional help.

2. **Click Connect**
   The Present Online dialog box opens, and PowerPoint connects to the Office Presentation Service online. Once connected, PowerPoint prepares your presentation to be viewed online, which may take a short time. The Present Online dialog box eventually displays a URL link, as shown in FIGURE 8-12.
3. **If approved by your instructor, click the Send in Email link to open a new Outlook message window, type an email address in the To text box, then click Send**
   The Microsoft Outlook window opens with the URL link in the message box and is then sent to the person you want to view the online presentation. Anyone to whom you provide the URL link can enter the link into their web browser and watch the broadcast.
4. **Click the START PRESENTATION button**
   The first slide of the presentation opens in Slide Show view. Make sure viewers can see the presentation in their web browser.

QUICK TIP
Until you end the broadcast or close the presentation, you are continuously broadcasting the presentation.

5. **Press SPACEBAR, wait for your viewers to see the slide, press SPACEBAR, wait for your viewers to see the slide, end the slide show, then click the Present Online tab on the Ribbon**
   Each slide in the presentation is viewed by you and your online viewers. The Present Online tab opens, as shown in FIGURE 8-13. Use this tab to start the slide show from different slides, share meeting notes using OneNote, invite others to view the broadcast, and end the broadcast.
6. **When you are finished broadcasting click the End Online Presentation button in the Present Online group**
   A message box opens asking if you want to end the online presentation.
7. **Click End Online Presentation, close the presentation, but do not close PowerPoint**
   The online presentation stops, and the presentation closes.

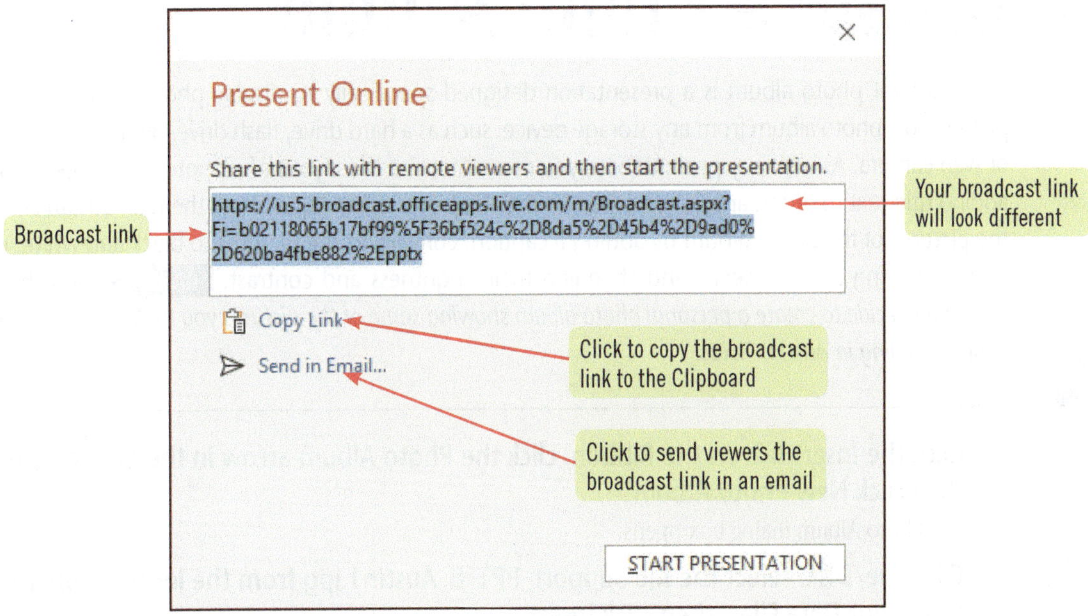

FIGURE 8-12: Present Online dialog box

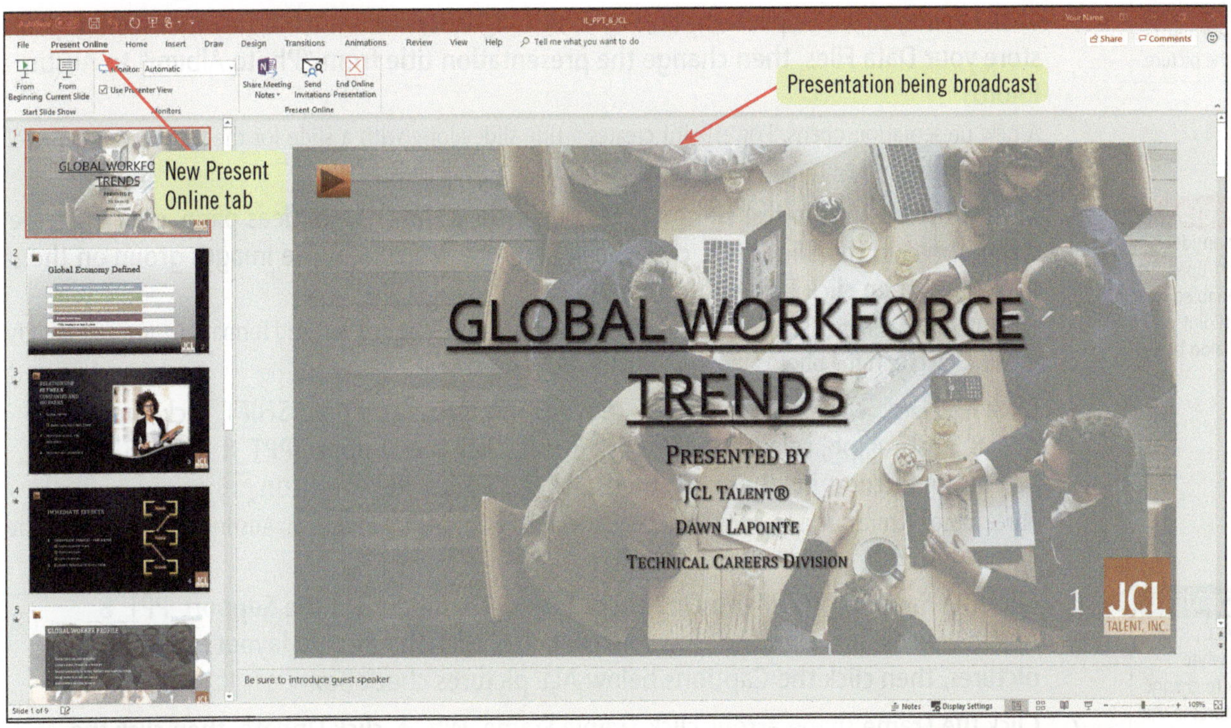

FIGURE 8-13: Online presentation broadcast

Rawpixel.com/Shutterstock.com

Coauthoring a presentation

By using collaboration software, such as SharePoint Online or saving a presentation to a OneDrive location, you have the ability to work with others on a presentation over the Internet at the same time. To set up a presentation to be coauthored with you as the original author, click the File tab, click Share, click Share with People, click Save To Cloud, then click your OneDrive location. Choose a shared location or server to store a primary copy of your presentation, then click the Save button. Open the presentation and begin working, and if someone else is working on the presentation, you will see a Co-authoring icon in the status bar. All changes made to the presentation are recorded, including who is working on the presentation and where in the presentation they are working. When updates to a presentation are available, an Updates Available button appears in the status bar. To use this feature, all authors must have PowerPoint 2010 or later installed on their computers.

PowerPoint
Module 8

Create a Photo Album

Learning Outcomes
- Create a photo album
- Customize a photo album

A PowerPoint photo album is a presentation designed specifically to display photographs. You can add pictures to a photo album from any storage device, such as a hard drive, flash drive, digital camera, scanner, or web camera. As with any presentation, you can customize the layout of a photo album presentation by adding title text to slides, applying frames around the pictures, and applying a theme. You can also format the pictures of the photo album by adding a caption, converting the pictures to black and white, rotating them, applying artistic effects, and changing their brightness and contrast. **CASE** *On a break from work, you decide to create a personal photo album showing some of the pictures you took on a trip to the state capitol building in Austin, Texas.*

STEPS

1. **Click the Insert tab on the Ribbon, click the Photo Album arrow in the Images group, then click New Photo Album**
   The Photo Album dialog box opens.

2. **Click File/Disk, select the file Support_PPT_8_Austin1.jpg from the location where you store your Data Files, then click Insert**
   The picture appears in the Preview box and is listed in the Pictures in album list, as shown in FIGURE 8-14.

QUICK TIP
In the Photo Album dialog box, click a picture check box, then click New Text Box to create a text box after the picture.

3. **Click Create, save the presentation as IL_PPT_8_AustinAlbum to the location where you store your Data Files, then change the presentation title from "Photo Album" to Austin Photos**
   A new presentation opens. PowerPoint creates a title slide along with a slide for the picture you inserted. The computer user name appears in the subtitle text box by default.

4. **Review the options in the Design Ideas pane, close the Design Ideas pane, click the Slide 2 thumbnail in the Slides tab, click the Photo Album arrow in the Images group on the Insert tab, then click Edit Photo Album**
   The Edit Photo Album dialog box opens. You can use this dialog box to add and format pictures and modify the slide layout in the photo album presentation.

TROUBLE
If the Design Ideas pane didn't open, it was not enabled in the PowerPoint options dialog box.

5. **Click File/Disk, click Support_PPT_8_Austin2.jpg, press and hold SHIFT, click Support_PPT_8_Austin4.jpg, release SHIFT, click Insert, click the Support_PPT_8_Austin3 check box in the Pictures in album list, then click the Rotate Right button**
   Three more pictures are added to the presentation, and picture Support_PPT_8_Austin3.jpg is rotated to the right 90 degrees.

6. **Click the Support_PPT_8_Austin2 check box, click to deselect the Support_PPT_8_Austin3 check box, click the Down arrow twice, click the Picture layout arrow, click 2 pictures, then click the Captions below ALL pictures check box**

QUICK TIP
Click the ALL pictures black and white check box to change all the pictures in the photo album to black and white.

7. **Click the Frame shape arrow, click Simple Frame, White, click Update, then click the Slide 2 thumbnail in the Slides tab**
   Two pictures with a caption below each picture (currently the picture file name) appear on each slide, and each picture is formatted with a soft edge.

8. **Click the Slide Sorter view button, then drag the Zoom Slider on the status bar until your screen looks similar to FIGURE 8-15**

9. **sam Save your changes, submit your presentation to your instructor, close the presentation, then close PowerPoint**

FIGURE 8-14: Photo Album dialog box

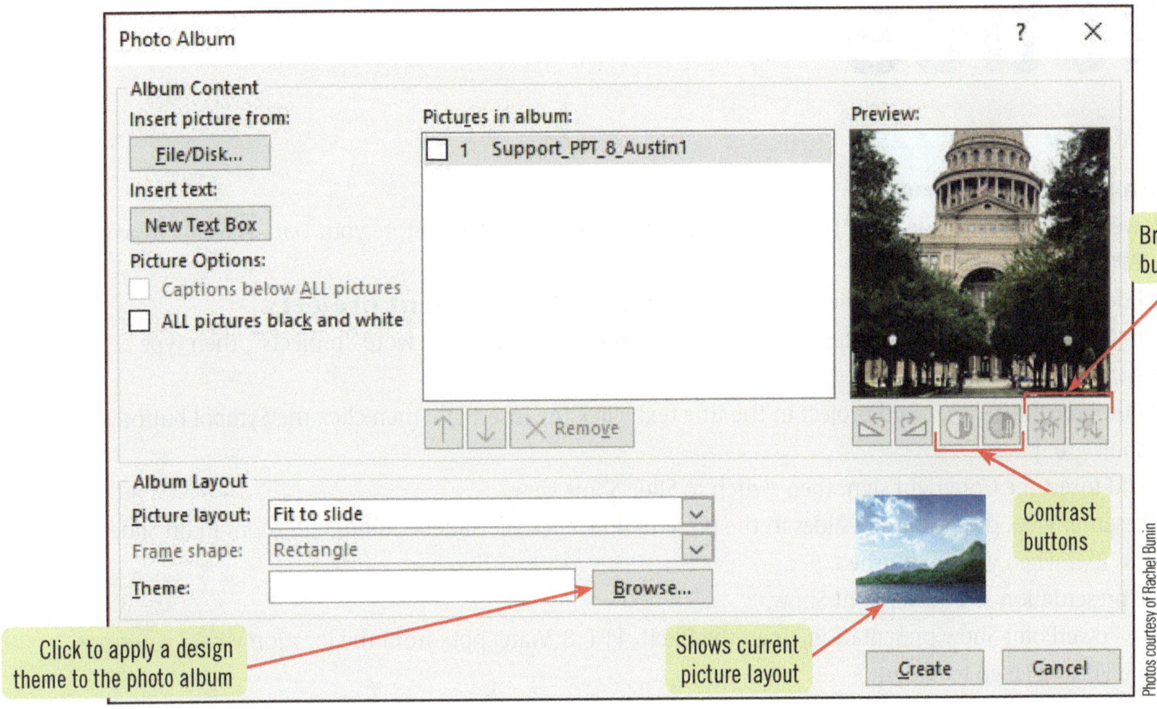

FIGURE 8-15: Completed photo album

Working with macros

A macro is a recording of an action or a set of actions that you use to automate tasks. The contents of a macro consist of a series of command codes that you create in the Visual Basic for Applications programming language using Microsoft Visual Basic. You can use macros to automate almost any action that you perform repeatedly when creating presentations, which saves you time. Any presentation with the .pptm file extension is saved with a macro. To use a macro in PowerPoint, click the View tab, click the Macros button in the Macros group, name the macro, then click Create to open the Microsoft Visual Basic for Applications window and create your macro.

Practice

Skills Review

1. **Work with presentation views.**
   a. Start PowerPoint, open the file IL_PPT_8-2.pptx from the location where you store your Data Files, then save it as **IL_PPT_8_Water**.
   b. Go to Slide 4, switch to Notes Page view, then type **Refer to development projects**.
   c. Switch to Normal view, click the Notes button in the status bar, click after the word "projects", then type **in Uganda**.
   d. Go to Slide 1, click after the word project in the title text, click the Insert tab, then click the Symbol button in the Symbols group.
   e. Locate and insert the Copyright sign, then switch to Slide Show view.
   f. Open Presenter view, display all the slides in the presentation, click the Slide 7 thumbnail, zoom in on Slide 7, then press ESC when you are finished.
   g. Save the presentation as a PowerPoint Show.
   h. Close the PowerPoint Show presentation, open the file IL_PPT_8_Water.pptx from the location where you store your Data Files, then go to Slide 1.

2. **Customize Handout and Notes masters.**
   a. Switch to Handout Master view, then change the slides per page to 3 slides.
   b. Change the handout orientation to Landscape, then type **Uganda** in the header text placeholder.
   c. Switch to Notes Master view, change the background style to Style 10, type **Uganda** in the header text placeholder, Close Notes Master view, then save your work.
   d. Print handouts 3 per page.

3. **Set up a slide show.**
   a. Click the Slide Show tab, click the Set Up Slide Show button, verify automatic slide timings is selected, set up a slide show so that it will be browsed at a kiosk, change the monitor resolution to Automatic, close the Set Up Show dialog box, then click the Transitions tab.
   b. Remove the check mark from the On Mouse Click check box, set a slide timing of 3 seconds to all the slides, run the slide show all the way through to Slide 1, then end the slide show.
   c. Change the slide show options to be presented by a speaker, then change the slide timings to manual in the Set Up Show dialog box.
   d. Manually run through the slide show from Slide 1. Move forward and backward through the presentation, then press ESC when you are finished.
   e. When you have finished viewing the slide show, reset the slide timings to automatic, then save your work.

4. **Create a custom show.**
   a. Open the Custom Shows dialog box, remove Custom Show 1, then create a custom show called **Development** that includes Slides 1, 4, 5, and 6.
   b. View the show from within the Custom Shows dialog box, then press ESC to end the slide show.
   c. Go to Slide 1, then save your work.

5. **Prepare a presentation for distribution.**
   a. Click the File tab, click Protect Presentation, then click Encrypt with Password.
   b. Type **123abc**, then type the same password in the Confirm Password dialog box.
   c. Close the presentation, save your changes, open the presentation, then type **123abc** in the Password dialog box.

Skills Review (continued)

d. Open the Encrypt Document dialog box again, then delete the password.
e. Click the File tab, click Check for Issues, click Check Compatibility, read the results, then close the dialog box.
f. Click the File tab, click Check for Issues, click Check Accessibility, then read the information.
g. If the Keep accessibility checker running while I work check box is selected, click the check box to remove the check mark, close the Accessibility Checker pane, then save your work.

6 Deliver a presentation online.

a. Click the Slide Show tab, click Present Online button, then click Connect.
b. Send invitations to people you want to view the broadcast using the Send in Email link in the Present Online dialog box.
c. Start the online presentation, then move through each slide in the presentation.
d. When you are finished broadcasting, end the online presentation, save your work, close the presentation, then submit the presentation to your instructor. The completed presentation is shown in FIGURE 8-16.

FIGURE 8-16

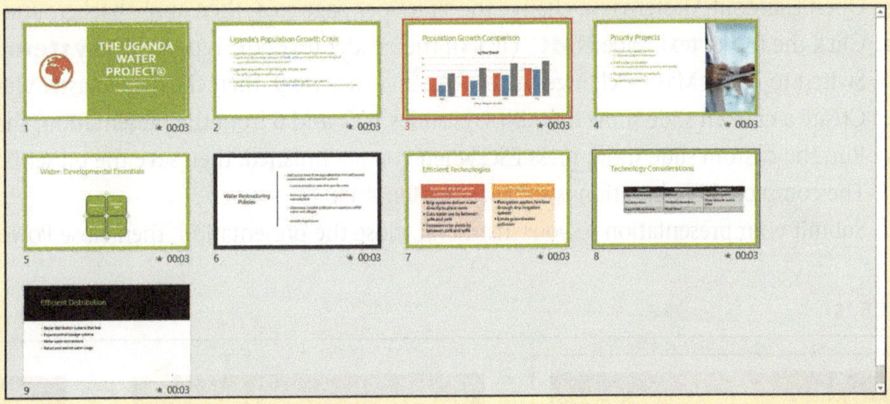

Guschenkova/Shutterstock.com

7. Create a photo album.

a. Create a new photo album presentation, navigate to the location where you store your Data Files, then insert the files Support_PPT_8_Pic1.jpg, Support_PPT_8_Pic2.jpg, Support_PPT_8_Pic3.jpg, and Support_PPT_8_Pic4.jpg.
b. Rotate picture Support_PPT_8_Pic1.jpg to the right, move the picture so that it is third in the list, create the photo album, then save it as **IL_PPT_8_Album** to the location where you store your Data Files.
c. Change the title on the title slide to **Best Things in Life**, then type your name in the subtitle text box.
d. Open the Edit Photo Album dialog box, change the picture layout to 1 picture, then change the frame shape to Soft Edge Rectangle.
e. Save your changes, submit your presentation to your instructor, close the presentation, then close PowerPoint. The completed photo album is shown in FIGURE 8-17.

FIGURE 8-17

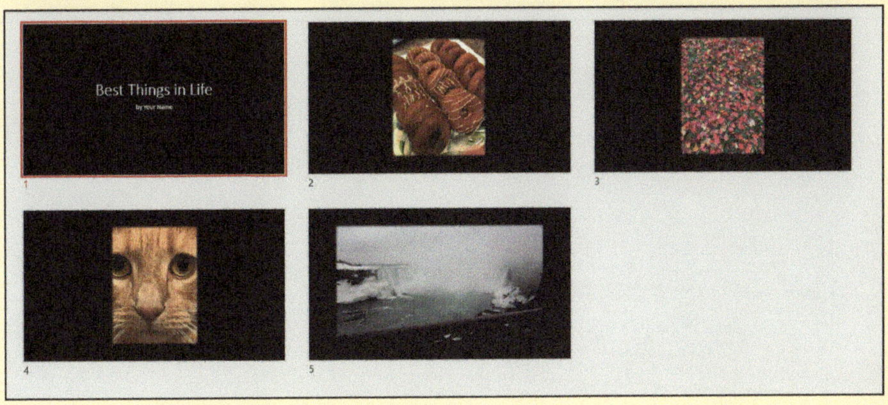

Photos courtesy of Rachel Bunin

PowerPoint

Independent Challenge 1

Riverwalk Medical Clinic (RMC) is a large medical facility in Cambridge, Massachusetts. You have been working on an EMS system presentation for the clinic, and you have just a couple things left to do before you are finished. In this challenge, you customize handouts and notes pages, create a custom show, and prepare the presentation for distribution.

a. Start PowerPoint, open the presentation IL_PPT_8-3.pptx from the location where you store your Data Files, then save it as **IL_PPT_8_RMC.pptx**.

b. Switch to Notes Page view, type **Start online feed**, switch to Normal view, then switch to Slide Show view.

c. Open Presenter view, display all slides, go to Slide 3, use the zoom feature, then press ESC when you are finished.

d. Go to Slide 3, click after the word "curriculum", open the Symbol dialog box, then insert the Section Sign symbol located on the same row as the copyright symbol.

e. Use the Compatibility Checker on the presentation and review the results.

f. Use the Accessibility Checker on the presentation, then review the results.

g. Open Handout Master view, change the slides per page to 4, then apply background Style 5.

h. Click the footer text, type **RMC**, click in the header text box, type **EMS System**, then close the master view.

i. Switch to Notes Master, change the background to Style 9, then close the master view.

j. Create a custom slide show that displays slides 1, 5, and 6 from the presentation, then save it as **EMS**.

k. Run the custom slide show, press ESC when you are finished, then save the presentation as a PowerPoint Show. The completed presentation is shown in FIGURE 8-18.

l. Submit your presentation to your instructor, close the presentation, then close PowerPoint.

FIGURE 8-18

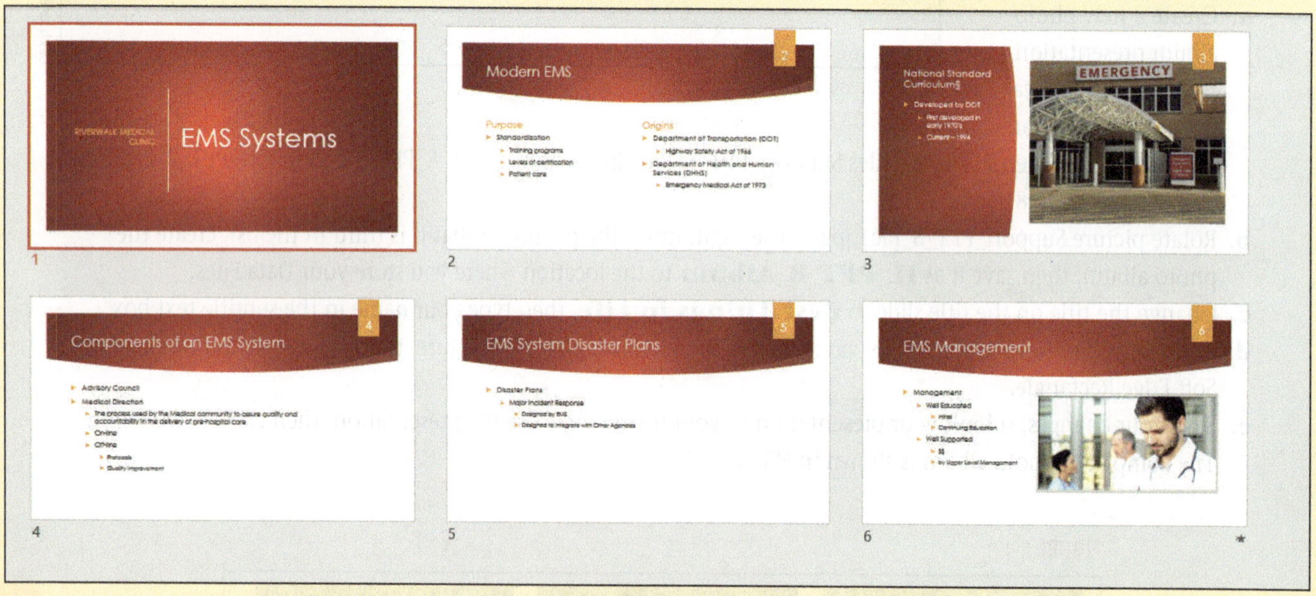

dcwcreations/Shutterstock.com; wavebreakmedia/Shutterstock.com

Independent Challenge 2

You have just been given an assignment in your Cultural Geography class to create a photo album that shows aspects of your living environment. Include photos of buildings, landscapes, means of travel, anything you think is relevant to your life. You are encouraged to use your own pictures for this assignment or you can use the pictures provided.

a. Start PowerPoint, create a photo album presentation, insert your pictures, then save the presentation as **IL_PPT_8_Geography** to the location where you store your Data Files. If you don't have your own pictures, then locate the following pictures where you store your Data Files: Support_PPT_8_ICPic1.jpg, Support_PPT_8_ICPic2.jpg, Support_PPT_8_ICPic3.jpg, and Support_PPT_8_ICPic4.jpg.

b. Enter a title in the title text placeholder, add your name to the subtitle text placeholder, then apply a design.

c. Use the Edit Photo Album dialog box to format the pictures as needed. An example of a photo album is shown in FIGURE 8-19.

d. Check the spelling of the presentation, save your changes, then broadcast this presentation to two friends using the Present Online feature.

e. Print handouts 2 slides per page, then save the presentation as a PowerPoint Show.

f. Submit your presentation and your handouts to your instructor. Close the presentation, then close PowerPoint.

FIGURE 8-19

Photos courtesy of Rachel Bunin

PowerPoint

Visual Workshop

Use an instructor-approved topic for your presentation and the following task list to help you complete this Visual Workshop:

- Create a new presentation, save the presentation as **IL_PPT_8_FinalProject** to the location where you store your Data Files, then enter and format slide text.
- Create and format new slides, create slide sections, then create Zoom links.
- Apply a design theme, then modify the design theme by changing its variation.
- Format a slide background, then use the Design Ideas pane to customize a slide.
- Insert and format at least one picture, video, and audio.
- Use the Remove Background feature to remove part or all of a picture background.
- Insert, format, and merge shapes, then insert and format a SmartArt graphic.
- Insert and format a table and a chart, then apply animations, transitions, and timings to objects and slides.
- Insert, modify, and animate a 3-D model.
- Modify slide, handout and notes masters, then create a custom show.
- Insert action buttons or hyperlinks, then send to a class member for revision changes and comments.
- Merge the reviewed presentation with your original presentation; make necessary changes and keep comments. Check the presentation for accessibility, making any suggested changes that might make the presentation more accessible.
- Deliver the presentation online to members of your class.

Add your name as a footer on the slide, save the presentation, submit the presentation to your instructor, close the presentation, then close PowerPoint. FIGURE 8-20 shows an example of a presentation you can create.

FIGURE 8-20

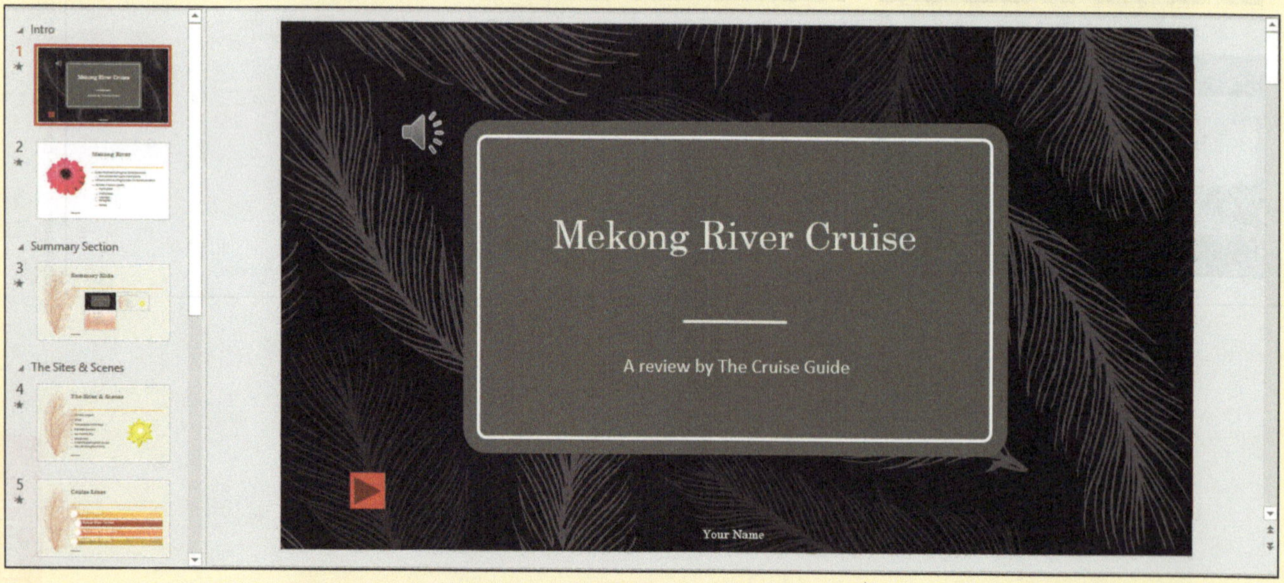

Index

A

B

C

D

E

F

G

H

I

J

K

L

M

N

O

P

Q

R

S

T

92345678908257882556